The
METHODIST
EXPERIENCE IN
AMERICA

VOLUME II

THE METHODIST EXPERIENCE IN AMERICA

A SOURCEBOOK

Volume II

Russell E. Richey

Kenneth E. Rowe

Jean Miller Schmidt

ABINGDON PRESS
NASHVILLE

THE METHODIST EXPERIENCE IN AMERICA VOLUME II
SOURCEBOOK

Copyright © 2000 by Abingdon Press

This book is printed on acid-free, recycled, elemental-chlorine–free paper.

Library of Congress Cataloging-in-Publication Data

The Methodist experience in America / Russell E. Richey, Kenneth E. Rowe, Jean Miller Schmidt, [editors].
    p. cm.
   Contents:—v. 2. Sourcebook.
   ISBN 0-687-24673-3 (alk. paper)
   1. Methodist Church—United States—History. 2. United States—Church history. I.
Richey, Russell E. II. Rowe, Kenneth E. III. Schmidt, Jean Miller.

BX8235 .M43 2000
287'.6'09—dc21

00-042023

00 01 02 03 04 05 06 07 08 09—10 9 8 7 6 5 4 3 2 1

MANUFACTURED IN THE UNITED STATES OF AMERICA

ACKNOWLEDGMENTS

The editors gratefully acknowledge and express appreciation for the conferral of rights to print or reprint selections or excerpts as follows:

- to The United Methodist Publishing House (Abingdon) for the many items that derive from its books and serials;
- to other United Methodist general and conference boards, agencies, and councils, including the Council of Bishops and Judicial Council, for the selections that are taken from their serials, publications, and papers, or from those of their predecessor organizations;
- to the General Commission on Christian Unity and Interreligious Concerns, The Methodist Church, for permission to use *In Search of Unity: A Conversation with Recommendations for the Unity of The United Methodist Church,* 1998;
- to the General Commission on Archives and History, and Drew University for the several selections from United Methodist or Drew Archives;
- to Bridwell Library, Southern Methodist University, Dallas, Texas, for letters for the Mouzon Collection, 1922;
- to United Methodist News Service for documents derived from UMNS releases, including items downloaded from the UMNS Web site;
- to Metodistas Asociados Representando la Causa de los Hispano-Americanos (MARCHA) for selections from documents;
- to United Methodist Reporter for "Bishop Muzorewa Cites Missionary 'Mistakes' Made in Africa by West." Reprinted by permission of the United Methodist Reporter, Dallas, Texas, 1975;
- to Kentucky Annual Conference of The United Methodist Church for the excerpt from Charles F. Golden's "Memorial Presented to the Lexington Annual Conference" *Lexington Conference Journal,* 1951;
- to the Center for the Evangelical United Brethren Heritage at the United Theological Seminary for excerpts from George Miller's translation of *The Life of Jacob Albright* (the full text in both German and English, with Introduction, is to be found at http://www.united.edu/eubcenter);
- to the *Mississippi Methodist Advocate* for permission to use the excerpt from "Born

of Conviction," 1963;

- to the Native American International Caucus of The United Methodist Church for permission to reprint from *The Sacred Circle of Life: A Native American Vision,* 1988;
- to Bishop Othal H. Lakey for the use of excerpts from *The History of the CME Church* (CME Publishing House, 1996);
- to William Warren Sweet, ed., and the University of Chicago Press, for the use of excerpts from *Religion on the American Frontier: The Methodists;*
- to Jimmy Creech for his letter "Response to the Judicial Charge," 1998;
- to Scarecrow Press for excerpts from J. Steven O'Malley translation of William Otterbein's *Die Heilbringende Menschwerdung und der Herrliche Sieg Jeru Christi ueber den Teufel und Tod;*
- to the Christian Century Foundation for "Women of Passaic," by Winifred Chappell. Copyright © 1926 Christian Century Foundation. Reprinted, by permission, from the May 6, 1926, issue of *The Christian Century;*
- to The Confessing Movement Within The United Methodist Church for documents.

This volume, part of a two-volume set entitled *The Methodist Experience in America*, contains documents pertaining to the movements constitutive of American United Methodism. We identify individual documents by date, primary agent, and central theme or important action. We include here also charts, graphs, time lines, and graphics which pertain to many points in time. Another set of documents—the historical prefaces to the several American Methodist movements, which provide the "official" version of each denomination's beginning—will be found in our *Narrative* volume.

Beginnings do seem to us important. A beginning date for the Methodist movements, and appropriate starting place for their history have been much debated. Does one start with the formative experiences in the Susanna and Samuel Wesley home? or with John and Charles Wesley in Georgia in the 1730s? or with John's Aldersgate experience? or with George Whitefield's American tours? or with competitive "spontaneous" beginnings in the 1760s through Robert Strawbridge in Maryland and through Barbara Heck, Philip Embury, and Thomas Webb in New York? or with the roots of the several evangelical movements in Pietism? Cases for starting the narrative in each of the above, and indeed in other, beginning points have been made. We elect to start by accenting the rootage of the movements that constitute United Methodism in Pietism—the transatlantic religion of the heart, which affected a variety of religious traditions and found its way into American Methodism through the Wesleys and British evangelicalism, continental (including Moravian) Pietism, late Puritanism, and American revivalism. Hence we begin with a sermon by William Otterbein in 1760 that enunciates long shared evangelical or Pietist doctrines and practices. We end with efforts in 1998 to identify and reclaim those shared doctrines and practices as a resource for healing within the denomination.

The volume has been constructed to be used with our narrative. There the interpretation of individual documents, discussions of context, details about events and individuals, and treatment of the larger developments can be found. For that reason we have kept the apparatus here to a minimum—a defining date, a descriptive title, and our source for the document. Identifications or explanations, where absolutely necessary, we lodge in brackets in the text. We have made silent corrections where changed linguistic usages, typesetting mistakes, and similar errors would frustrate the modern reader. Otherwise, we preserve the spelling and phrasing of the originals, sometimes with *[sic]* added to stimulate the imagination of the user.

We organize the documents on a strictly chronological basis, by the date of the significant action in the excerpt, believing that such ordering will serve both those who teach or pursue issues organically and those who opt for topical or thematic approaches. Instructors who organize the course or subsections thereof around issues, problems, or themes should consult the Document Index for our suggested groupings of documents on selected topics. We would note especially the number of items pertaining to women and to African Americans, and the value the volume might have in courses on those concerns.

In the future we anticipate making these documents and twice as many in addition, most already typed or scanned, available in electronic or CD-ROM form so as to permit teachers to make their own selections for classroom use. Among the documents projected for inclusion in the electronic or CD form are many of a theological or doctrinal nature. We have omitted those from this collection intentionally, mindful of Thomas Langford's revision of *Practical Divinity* and its companion *Wesleyan Theology: A Sourcebook,* the latter now being titled *Practical Divinity: Readings in Wesleyan Theology.* Standard items of Methodist theology and doctrine, which we do intend to include in the electronic or CD version, we presume that students of American Methodism will have access to in the Langford volumes. We also assume knowledge of and access to the basic works of John and Charles Wesley. Two other works which we expect to be "at hand" are our *Perspectives on American Methodism: Interpretive Essays,* which we originally envisioned as the third part of a *Methodist Experience in America* trilogy, and Rowe's *United Methodist Studies: Basic Bibliographies,* the fourth edition of which appeared in 1998.

With regard to both this collection and the narrative, we have settled on a focus on United Methodism and its predecessor movements, with primary attention to its United States expression. Some of American Methodism's global interests we represent by letters, reports, or journals, but even those were originally aimed at the North American reader. Neither the fullness of Methodism's missionary endeavor nor the vitality of United Methodism's present global character are adequately represented here. Documents in the many languages of the global church—Korean, Portuguese, Russian, Spanish, German, Shona, Swedish, and so forth—and English renderings thereof we have left for another laborer to assemble. We have largely limited this collection to the United States; we have also limited it to United Methodism. Developments that resulted in the formation of the African Methodist Episcopal Church or the Wesleyan Methodists or the Free Methodists we have followed only up to the point of the fracturing of the denomination, and thereafter we remain with the movement that continues in United Methodism. We remain painfully aware that this collection cannot represent the entire United Methodist experience or the wider family that gathers as the World

Methodist Council. The documents do, we hope, attend to the various parties and groups within American United Methodism, particularly the ethnic groups and caucuses through which much of the vitality of contemporary United Methodism comes to expression.

The three of us have incurred many debts over the long process that has led to this volume. We acknowledge particularly the support given each of us by our deans and schools, by The United Methodist Publishing House, and by the General Board of Higher Education and Ministry (we thank Robert Kohler in particular for financial support). We have exhausted a number of typists who have suffered with manuscripts, old newsprint, fuzzy photocopies, and garbled guidelines. We praise especially the work of Melisa LaVergne, Cynthia T. LaMaster, Clare J. Sulgit, and Mary Stringham. We thank also, and Richey in particular thanks, the Lilly Endowment for support rendered through the United Methodism and American Culture project. One person, now deceased, whose efforts should be acknowledged is Frederick Norwood. His *Sourcebook of American Methodism* and the relation of that to his *Story of American Methodism* provided important models for our work. While we diverge from him at a variety of points, we nevertheless build on his selections. Those who have taught using Norwood's *Sourcebook* will, we trust, find this a comparable resource.

Jean Miller Schmidt, *Iliff School of Theology*
Kenneth E. Rowe, *Drew Theological School*
Russell E. Richey, *Duke Divinity School*

THE DOCUMENTS

MEA I: 1760–1815

1760

1770

1780

MEA II: 1816–65

1816   Daniel Coker celebrates liberation of Bethel Church, Philadelphia, from control of white conference

1820

1821a   African American Methodists in New York search for ordination and organization

1821b   William Stockton proposes lay representation in the governing conferences

1822   Peter Cartwright presides at quarterly meeting in Kentucky

1824   New York City church tries and expels Parmelia Olmstead and John Hoare for breach of discipline

1827a   Mississippi Conference addresses spiritual and temporal concerns in pastoral letter

1827b   Reformers petition General Conference to admit lay members to conferences

1828   General Conference majority denounces Reform movement

1829   Cherokee converts in North Carolina hold camp meeting

1830

1830a   Sally Thompson tried and expelled for preaching

1830b   Missionaries among Cherokees in Georgia protest removal

1832a   African American members in Philadelphia favor appointment of black preachers

1832b   Henry Bascom promotes goals and raises funds for the American Colonization Society

1833   William Capers publishes special catechism for use in slave missions

1834   Abolitionist clergy in New England urge immediate end to slavery

1836   South Carolina Conference upholds slavery and promotes plantation missions

1838   Preacher's wife, Mary Orne Tucker, details hardships of circuit life in Massachusetts

1839   George Cookman celebrates achievements at centennial

1840

1841a   Editor Thomas Bond ponders growing practice of station versus circuit appointments

1841b   *Ladies' Repository* celebrates pious life and happy death of Caroline Pilcher

1842a   Chippewa convert Peter Marksman narrates his conversion and call to preach

1842b   Abolitionist clergy issue public letter of withdrawal

1920

1930

MEA V: 1940–67

1940

1950

1950	Seminary dean Walter Muelder protests High's "Pink Fringe" magazine article
1951	Black conference petitions General Conference to establish policy and practice of racial inclusiveness
1952	Woman's Division issues charter of racial policies
1953	Bishop Oxnam publicly protests McCarthy committee charges
1954	Editor of black church paper, Prince Taylor, and Council of Bishops assess landmark Supreme Court decision on school desegregation
1955	EUB church women deplore segregation
1956	Maud Keister Jensen remembers honor of being first woman granted full clergy rights

1960

1963a	Mississippi pastors speak out against racial discrimination
1963b	Liberia Conference requests autonomy from American church
1966a	Charles Keysor speaks up for "orthodoxy," launches Good News movement
1966b	EUB Bishop Washburn answers questions on church union with the Methodists
1967	Editor of campus ministry magazine, B. J. Stiles, challenges the conscience of America on the war in Vietnam

MEA VI: 1968–98

1968a	Black church leaders reject tokenism and form Black Methodists for Church Renewal
1968b	Professor Albert Outler details "unfinished business" in sermon to uniting conference
1969	Mission executive Tracey Jones looks to the future

1970

1970	Hispanic caucus appeals to General Conference
1972a	Student movement magazine "comes out" in favor of gay and lesbian rights
1972b	General Conference laments tragedy of Vietnam War
1972c	Seminary professor James White introduces revised rite for holy communion
1972d	Thelma Stevens chronicles formation of The United Methodist Women's Caucus
1973	Black women in triple jeopardy, asserts Theressa Hoover
1975	Bishop Muzorewa cites missionary mistakes made in Africa

| 1976 | Thomas Roughface speaks for Native Americans at General Conference |
| 1978 | Hispanic women want no melting pot |

1980

1985	Hispanic caucus issues "Vision for Century III"
1986a	Hymnal revision committee promises politically correct hymnal
1986b	Bishops issue pastoral letter on the nuclear crisis and a just peace
1988a	Native American caucus issues vision document
1988b	Bishops issue pastoral statement on ministry to undocumented persons

1990

1990	Conservatives issue right-to-life declaration on abortion
1992	Study committee splits on homosexuality issue
1994a	Women church leaders issue reply to "Re-imagining" conference critics
1994b	Conservatives call forth "Confessing Movement"
1996a	Korean American caucus favors formation of separate Korean Missionary Conference
1996b	First Lady Hillary Clinton confesses indebtedness to Methodism
1998a	Nebraska pastor Jimmy Creech defends "holy unions" of same-sex couples
1998b	Bishops issue pastoral statement on "holy unions" and homosexuality
1998c	Judicial Council determines disciplinary prohibition against homosexual unions enforceable
1998d	Diversity Dialogue Team develops recommendations for the unity of the church

U. S. FAMILY TREE

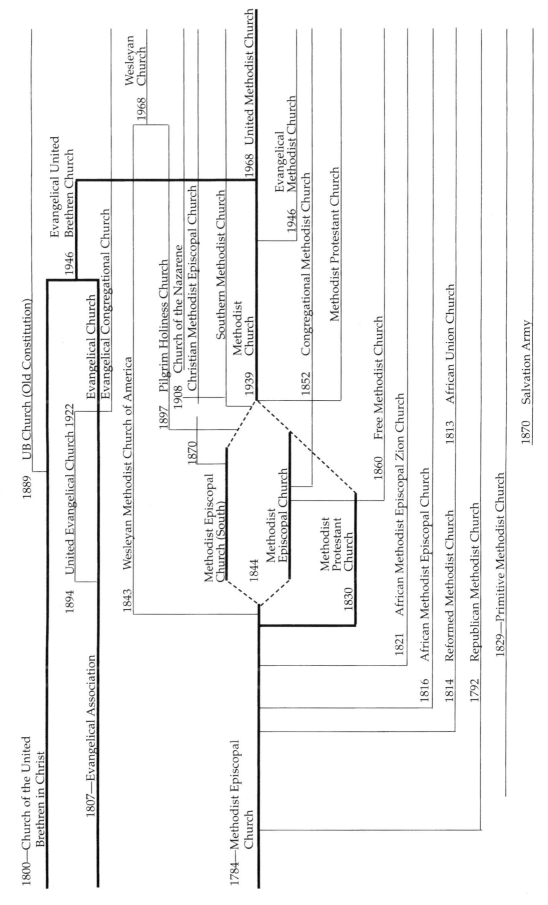

UNITED METHODIST
LAY MEMBERSHIP AS COMPARED TO
UNITED STATES POPULATION CENSUS

UNITED METHODIST LAY MEMBERSHIP					UNITED STATES POPULATION		
EUB	METHODIST	TOTAL	%CHANGE	YEAR	NUMBER	%CHANGE	%UMC
-	57,858	57,858	-	1790	3,929,214	-	1.5
-	65,181	65,181	12.7	1800	5,308,483	35.1	1.2
528	174,560	175,088	168.6	1810	7,239,881	36.4	2.4
10,992	257,736	268,728	53.5	1820	9,638,453	33.1	2.8
23,245	478,053	501,298	86.5	1830	12,866,020	33.5	3.9
38,992	855,761	894,753	78.5	1840	17,069,453	32.7	5.2
61,175	1,185,902	1,247,077	39.4	1850	23,191,876	35.9	5.4
141,841	1,661,086	1,802,927	44.6	1860	31,443,321	35.6	5.7
190,034	1,821,908	2,011,942	11.6	1870	38,558,371	22.6	5.2
270,032	2,693,691	2,963,723	47.3	1880	50,189,209	30.2	5.9
346,751	3,441,675	3,788,426	27.8	1890	62,979,766	25.5	6.0
423,699	4,226,327	4,650,026	22.7	1900	76,212,168	21.0	6.1
498,551	5,073,200	5,571,751	19.8	1910	92,228,496	21.0	6.0
608,519	6,140,318	6,748,837	21.1	1920	106,021,537	15.0	6.4
667,294	7,319,125	7,986,419	18.3	1930	123,202,624	16.2	6.5
663,817	7,682,187	8,346,004	4.5	1940	132,164,569	7.3	6.3
801,105	8,935,647	9,736,752	16.7	1950	151,325,798	14.5	6.4
763,380	9,884,484	10,647,864	9.4	1960	179,323,175	18.5	5.9
-	-	10,671,774	0.2	1970	203,211,926	13.3	5.3
-	-	9,519,407	-10.8	1980	226,505,000	11.5	4.2
-	-	8,853,455	-7.0	1990	248,709,873	9.8	3.6
-	-	-	-	2000	-	-	-

FIRST METHODIST EPISCOPAL CHURCH BRYDEN ROAD, CORNER EIGHTEENTH STREET COLUMBUS, OHIO

FIRST BUILDING: "ZION CHURCH"
BUILT **1814.**   TORN DOWN **1825.**

SECOND BUILDING: "ZION CHURCH"
BUILT **1826.**   TORN DOWN **1852.**

THIRD BUILDING:
"TOWN STREET CHURCH"
BUILT **1853.**   SOLD **1890.**

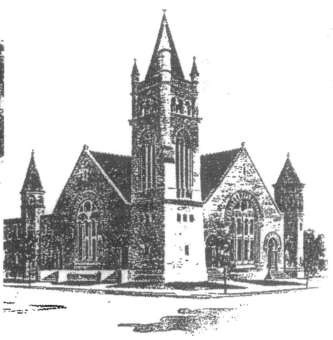

1890 - 1900

PLAN OF APPOINTMENTS FOR THE CINCINNATI STATION, FROM 6TH OF OCTOBER, 1833, TO 17TH OF AUGUST, 1834.

The table lists, for each church (Wesley Chap., Brick Church, McKendree, Asbury, African, Wesley, Brick) and each service hour (11, 3, N), the numbered preacher appointed on each day of the month across the months October through August. Letters B. (Baptism) and S. (Sacrament) appear within the grid.

REFERENCES.

1 James B. Finley.
2. John Collins.
3. Joseph Mc. D. Trimble.
4. Joseph Mc. D. Mathews.
5. Thomas F. Sargeant.
6 Charles Holliday.
7 John F. Wright.
8 Oliver M. Spencer.
9 William C. Morrison.
10 I. P. Vanhagen.
11 Robert Richardson.
12 David Hand.
13 Thomas Biggs.
14 John Cathel.
15 William B. Ross.

N. Night.
B. Baptism.
S. Sacrament.

Preacher's Office on Fifth Street, next door East of Broadway. Office hours from 9 A.M. until 12, all days except Sabbath.

P. S. If any of the Preachers are sick, or to be absent they are requested to procure substitutes, or let it be known to the Preacher in charge.

METHODIST PROTESTANT CHURCH
1829 – 1939

Woman's Foreign Missionary Society

&

Woman's Home Missionary Society

&

Woman's Convention

&

Ladies' Aid Society

(No record of any emblem)

METHODIST EPISCOPAL CHURCH, SOUTH
1844 – 1939

Woman's Foreign Missionary Society

&

Woman's Home Missionary Society

&

Woman's Missionary Council

&

Parsonage & Ladies' Aid Societies

&

Young Women's & Business Women Circles

METHODIST EPISCOPAL CHURCH
1784 – 1939

1939

Woman's Home Missionary Society
1880

&

Woman's Foreign Missionary Society

1939

&

Wesleyan Service Guild
1921 – 1939

Ladies' Aid Society
1904 – 1939

EVANGELICAL CHURCH
1922 – 1946

Woman's Missionary Society
1884 – 1946

UNITED BRETHREN IN CHRIST
1800 – 1946

Women's Missionary Association
1875   1909

&

Home & Foreign Missionary Societies
1909–1946

EVANGELICAL UNITED BRETHREN CHURCH

Women's Society of World Service
1946

W.S.W.S.
1968–short period

THE METHODIST CHURCH
1939 – 1968

Wesleyan Service Guild Auxiliary
1939 – 1968

Women's Society of Christian Service
1968

Woman's Society of Christian Service
1939–40

Woman's Society of Christian Service
1968

Women's Society of Christian Service
1973

Emblem continued for
UNITED METHODIST WOMEN
1973–

THE UNITED METHODIST CHURCH
1968 –

Otterbein Guild
1968 –

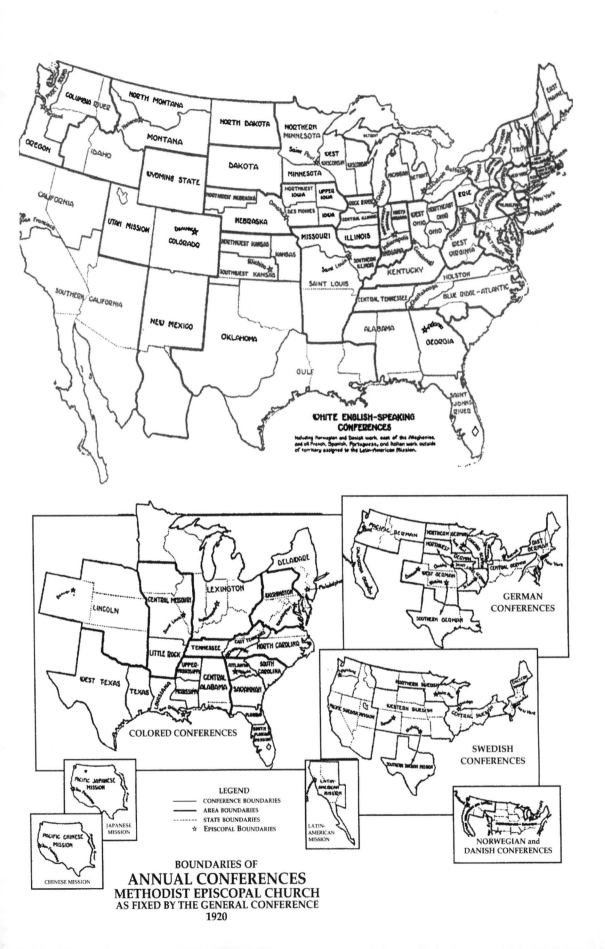

BOUNDARIES OF
ANNUAL CONFERENCES
METHODIST EPISCOPAL CHURCH
AS FIXED BY THE GENERAL CONFERENCE
1920

Proposed Jurisdictional Conference of
THE METHODIST CHURCH
Under the Plan of Union of
THE METHODIST EPISCOPAL CHURCH, THE METHODIST EPISCOPAL CHURCH, SOUTH, and THE METHODIST PROTESTANT CHURCH

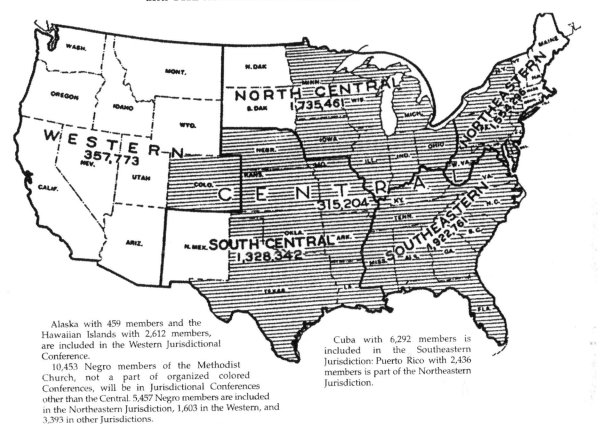

Alaska with 459 members and the Hawaiian Islands with 2,612 members, are included in the Western Jurisdictional Conference.

10,453 Negro members of the Methodist Church, not a part of organized colored Conferences, will be in Jurisdictional Conferences other than the Central. 5,457 Negro members are included in the Northeastern Jurisdiction, 1,603 in the Western, and 3,393 in other Jurisdictions.

Cuba with 6,292 members is included in the Southeastern Jurisdiction: Puerto Rico with 2,436 members is part of the Northeastern Jurisdiction.

The above map gives the outlines of the Jurisdictional Conferences of The Methodist Church as proposed for administrative purposes in the United States. The heavy lines indicate the boundaries proposed for five Jurisdictional Conferences, and the shaded portion overlying includes one Jurisdictional Conference—the Central. The work outside the United States will be administered through Central Conferences such as those now in use in The Methodist Episcopal Church.

The membership of The Methodist Church (proposed) is 7,213,837 in the United States only, and in the world it is over 8,000,000. There is also a Sunday-school enrollment of 6,437,000. These three Churches now proposing union represent over one half the communicant Methodist membership of the world and a Methodist constituency of over 30,000,000.

The membership of The Methodist Church within the Jurisdictional Conferences of the United States and territories as represented above is composed of communicants who are at present in the three uniting Churches as follows: Methodist Protestant, 191,595; Methodist Episcopal, South, 2,725,954; Methodist Episcopal, 4,296,288.

—The Christian Advocate (December 12, 1935)

LAY REPRESENTATION IN THE CONFERENCES

	GENERAL CONFERENCE			ANNUAL CONFERENCE	
	≠	=	♀	≠	=
MPC	——	1830	1892	——	1830
MECS	——	1870	1922	1854 (1/district) 1866 (4/district)	1930
MEC	1872 (2/conf.)	1990	1904	——	1932 (lay conf.)
UBC	1872 (optional) 1889 (mandatory)	1901	1893	1872 (optional) 1889 (mandatory)	
EUC	——	1894	——	——	1894
EvA	1907 (1-3 conf.)	——	——	1907 (4/district)	——
EvC	1922 (1/14 clergy)	——	1946	——	1922
MC	——	1939	1939	——	1939 (1960 up to 2/charge)
EUBC	——	1947	1947	——	1947
UMC	——	1968	1968	——	1968 (1976 1 clergy)

AUTHORIZED METHODIST HYMNALS

1780 (London) *A Collection of Hymns for Use of the People Called Methodists* ("large hymnbook")

1784 (London) *A Collection of Psalms and Hymns for the Lord's Day* (attached to *The Sunday Service of the Methodists in North America*)

1785 (London) *A Pocket Hymn Book* for the use of Christians of all Denominations, John Wesley.

1785 (York) *A Pocket Hymn Book, designed as a constant companion for the pious; collected from various authors* (compiled by Robert Spence)

The solid lines on this chart show a direct relationship and influence between the hymnals. The dotted lines indicate indirect or questionable influences.

1786 (New York) *A Pocket Hymn Book: Designed as a Constant Companion for the Pious. Collected from various authors.* 5th ed.; printed by W. Ross.

1802 (Philadelphia) *The Methodist Pocket Hymn Book, revised and improved: designed as a constant Companion for the pious of all denominations* (Revised and published by Ezekiel Cooper)

1808 (New York) *A Selection of Hymns from various authors, designed as a Supplement to the Methodist Pocket Hymn Book, compiled under the direction of Bishop Asbury and published by order of the General Conference.* (The "Double Hymn Book" J. C. Totter, printer, 1810)

The Methodist Protestant Church

1829 (Baltimore) *A compilation of Hymns, adapted to public and social Divine Worship* (compiled by John Harrod in 1828(?); adopted by the 1834 General Conference)

1821 (New York) *A collection of Hymns for the use of the Methodist Episcopal Church, principally from the Collection of the Reverend John Wesley, M.A., late Fellow of Lincoln College, Oxford* (slightly revised in 1835 and tunes cross-referenced with *The Methodist Harmonist*, 1821)

1837 *(Baltimore) Hymn Book of the Methodist Protestant Church* (compiled by Thomas H. Stockton; adapted by the 1838 General Conference)

1836 (New York) *A Collection of Hymns...* (prepared by Nathan Bangs, a supplement of 90 hymns to the 1821 *Collection*).

1859 (Baltimore) *Hymn Book of the Methodist Protestant Church* (Eastern and Southern Conferences; Josiah Varden, et al.; published by the president and director of the Book Concern)

The Methodist Episcopal Church South

1849 (New York) *Hymns for the use of the Methodist Episcopal Church; revised,* 1852; tune edition, 1857

1847 (Nashville) *A Collection of Hymns for public, social and domestic worship;* tune edition, *The Wesleyan Hymn and Tune Book,* 1860, edited by L. C. Everett.

1860 (Springfield, Ohio) *Hymn Book for the Methodist Protestant Church* (Northern and Western Conferences; compiled by George Brown; ed. by A. H. Bassett)

1851 (Nashville) *Songs of Zion: A Supplement to the Hymn Book of the Methodist Episcopal Church, South* (edited by Thomas O. Summers)

1871 (Pittsburgh) *The Voice of Praise: a Collection of Hymns for the use of The Methodist Church* (Alexander Clark, et al.; A. H. Bassett, publishing agent) Ordered by the 1867 General Conference

1874 (Nashville) *Songs of Zion* (revised and enlarged edition)

1874 (Nashville) *A Collection [of] Hymns and Tunes for Public, Social, and Domestic Worship*

1882 (Pittsburgh and Baltimore) *The Tribute of Praise and Methodist Protestant Hymn Book* (based on *Tribute of Praise,* 1874, with tunes)

1878 (New York and Cincinnati) *Hymnal of the Methodist Episcopal Church* (with tunes, liturgies, and order of worship in 1896 printing)

1880 (Nashville) *The New Hymn Book* (also published with tunes, ritual, and order of worship)

1901 (Pittsburgh and Baltimore) *The Methodist Protestant Church Hymnal* (with tunes, readings, and ritual)

1905 (New York, Cincinnati, Nashville) *The Methodist Hymnal* (produced jointly by the Methodist Episcopal Church and the Methodist Episcopal Church, South; with tunes, readings, and ritual)

1889 (Nashville) *Hymnbook of The Methodist Episcopal Church, South* (also published as *Hymn and Tune Book*)

1935 (New York, Cincinnati, Baltimore, Nashville) *The Methodist Hymnal* (produced jointly by the three churches; texts only; and with tunes, readings, and ritual)

1966 (Nashville) *The Methodist Hymnal* (with tunes, readings, and ritual)

1989 (Nashville) *United Methodist Hymnal*

AUTHORIZED HYMNALS OF THE EVANGELICAL AND UNITED BRETHREN CHURCHES

United Brethren Church in Christ

1795 *Das Aller Neuste Harfenspiel*

1808 *Lobegesange zu Ehren dem Heiligen und Gerechten in Israel*

1816 *Herzens Opfer; eine SammlungGeistreicher Lieder*

1826 *The Sacrifice of the Heart; or, A Choice Selection of Hymns*

1829 *The Sacrifice of the Heart; 2d ed.*

1830 *Eine Sammlung von Geistlichen, Lieblichen Liedern*

1835 *A Collection of Hymns, for the Use of the United Brethren in Christ; and Union Songster*

1842 *The Church Harp*

1847 *Die Kirchen-Harfe*

1848 *A Collection of Hymns, for the use of the United Brethren in Christ*

1854 *Das Gesangbuch der Vereinigten Bruder in Christo*

1858 *A Collection of Hymns, for the Use of the United Brethren in Christ*

1865 *Das Gesangbuch, der Vereinigten Bruder in Christo*

Evangelical Association

1810 *Eine Kleine Sammlung alter und neuer Geistricher Lieder*

1817 *Das Geistliche Saitenspiel*

1818 *Die Kleine Geistliche Viole*

1821 *Eine Sammlung neuer Geistlicher Lieder*

1824 *Zwen Geistreiche Leider*

1835 *A Collection of Hymns*

1846 *Hymns Selected From Various Authors*

1850 *Evangelisches Gesangbuch*

1857 *The Evangelical Hymn-Book*

1867 *The New Evangelical Hymn-Book*

United Brethren Church

1874 *Hymns for the Sanctuary and Social Worship*

1878 *Gesangbuch der Vereinigten Brüder in Christo (new ed.)*

1888 *Deutsches Gesangbuch der Vereinigten Brüder in Christo*

1890 *The Otterbein Hymnal (also published as The People's Hymnal)*

1914 *The Sanctuary Hymnal*

1937 *The Church Hymnal*

Evangelical Association

1877 *Evangelisches Gesangbuch*

1881 *Hymn-Book of the Evangelical Association*

1882 *The Evangelical Hymn and Tune Book*

1887 *Gesangbuch der Evangelischen Gemeinschaft*

1910 *Gesangbuch der Evangelischen Gemeinschaft (new ed.)*

1921 *The Evangelical Hymnal*

United Evangelical Church (1894-1922)

1897 *Evangelisches Gesangbuch*

1897 *Hymn Book of the United Evangelical Church*

The Evangelical United Brethren Church

1957 *The Hymnal*

THE FIRST WOMEN TO BE ELECTED TO THE GENERAL CONFERENCE OF THE METHODIST EPISCOPAL CHURCH

Mary C.
Nind

Amanda C.
Rippey

Francis E.
Willard

Elizabeth D.
Van Kirk

Angie F.
Newman

IN THE FIRST LAY DELEGATION, 1872

The Electoral Conferences sent a remarkable delegation to the General Conference of 1872, the first to which laymen were eligible. Each Conference was entitled to two.

HON. JAMES HARLAN
Iowa
Senator and Cabinet Officer

HON. PAUL DILLINGHAM
Vermont
U. S. Senator

WILLIAM DEERING
Maine
Manufacturer

OLIVER HOYT
Connecticut
Leather Manufacturer

JOHN B. CORNELL
New York
Iron Manufacturer

WASHINGTON C. DE PAUW
Indiana
Glass Manufacturer

HON. W. T. WILLEY
West Virginia
U. S. Senator

HON. JOHN EVANS
Colorado
Governor

HON. WILLIAM CLAFLIN
Massachusetts
Governor

ORDERS OF WORSHIP: METHODIST

COMMON HYMNAL, 1905

[MEC AND MECS]

Order of Public Worship

NOTE.—The Methodist Episcopal Church and the Methodist Episcopal Church, South, have adopted a Common Order of Worship as given below.

[PARTS IN BRACKETS MAY BE USED OR OMITTED.]

Let all our services begin exactly at the time appointed, and let all our people kneel in silent prayer on entering the sanctuary.

[I. VOLUNTARY, instrumental or vocal.]

II. SINGING FROM THE COMMON HYMNAL,
the people standing.

[III. THE APOSTLES' CREED, recited by all, still standing.]

I BELIEVE in God the Father Almighty, Maker of heaven and earth:
And in Jesus Christ, his only Son our Lord; who was conceived by the Holy Ghost, born of the Virgin Mary; suffered under Pontius Pilate, was crucified, dead, and buried; the third day he rose from the dead;
he ascended into heaven, and sitteth at the right hand of God the Father Almighty; from thence he shall come to judge the quick and the dead.
I believe in the Holy Ghost; the holy catholic Church, the communion of saints; the forgiveness of sins; the resurrection of the body; and the life everlasting. Amen.

IV. PRAYER, concluding with the Lord's Prayer, repeated audibly by all, both minister and people kneeling.

[V. ANTHEM OR VOLUNTARY.]

VI. LESSON FROM THE OLD TESTAMENT,
which, if from the Psalms, may be read responsively.*

[VII. THE GLORIA PATRI.]

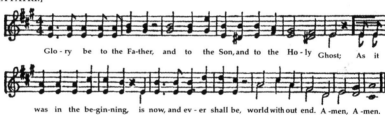

Glo - ry be to the Fa-ther, and to the Son, and to the Ho - ly Ghost; As it was in the be-gin-ning, is now, and ev - er shall be, world with out end. A -men, A -men.

VIII. LESSON FROM THE NEW TESTAMENT.

IX. NOTICES, FOLLOWED BY COLLECTION;
during after which an offertory may be rendered.

X. SINGING FROM THE COMMON HYMNAL,
the people standing.

XI. THE SERMON.

XII. PRAYER, the people kneeling.†

XIII. SINGING FROM THE COMMON HYMNAL,
the people standing.‡

XIV. DOXOLOGY AND THE APOSTOLIC BENEDICTION

(2 Cor. 13. 14)

---

*In the afternoon or evening the Lesson from the Old Testament may be omitted.
†The order of prayer and singing after sermon may be reversed.
‡An invitation to come to Christ or to unite with the Church should be given when this hymn is announced.

ORDERS OF WORSHIP: METHODIST COMMON HYMNAL, 1935

[MEC, MPC, MECS]

Order of Worship I

Let the Services of Worship begin at the time appointed, and let the People kneel or bow in silent prayer upon entering the Sanctuary.

THE PRELUDE.   The people in devout meditation.

THE CALL TO WORSHIP.   Which may be said or sung.

A HYMN.   If a Processional, the Hymn shall precede the Call to Worship, and the People shall then rise at the second stanza and join in singing.

THE PRAYER OF CONFESSION.   To be said by all, the People seated and bowed, or kneeling. The following, or other Prayer of Confession, may be said:

Our Heavenly Father, who by Thy love hast made us, and through Thy love hast kept us, and in Thy love wouldst make us perfect, we humbly confess that we have not loved Thee with all our heart and soul and mind and strength, and that we have not loved one another as Christ hath loved us. Thy life is within our souls, but our selfishness hath hindered Thee. We have resisted Thy Spirit. We have neglected Thine inspirations.

Forgive what we have been; help us to amend what we are; and in Thy Spirit direct what we shall be; that Thou mayest come into the full glory of Thy creation, in us and in all men, through Jesus Christ our Lord.   Amen.

THE SILENT MEDITATION.   The People seated and bowed, or kneeling.

THE WORDS OF ASSURANCE.   By the Minister.

THE LORD'S PRAYER.   Which may be said or sung.

THE ANTHEM OR CHANT.   Which may be the *Venite* or the *Te Deum.*

THE RESPONSIVE READING.   The People to stand and remain standing until after the Affirmation of Faith.

THE GLORIA PATRI.

THE AFFIRMATION OF FAITH.   To be said by the Minister and People.

THE LESSON FROM THE HOLY SCRIPTURES.   The Old and New Testament.

THE PASTORAL PRAYER.   The People seated and bowed, or kneeling.

THE OFFERTORY.   The Dedication of Offerings. With Prayer or Offertory Sentences.

A HYMN.   The People standing.

THE SERMON.

THE PRAYER.   The People seated and bowed, or kneeling.

THE INVITATION TO CHRISTIAN DISCIPLESHIP.

A HYMN OR DOXOLOGY.   The People standing.   The closing Hymn may be a Recessional Hymn.

THE BENEDICTION.   The People seated and bowed, or kneeling.

THE SILENT PRAYER.

THE POSTLUDE.

ORDERS OF WORSHIP: MEC
1784–1905

Italics indicates change or addition from previous order.

1784

Scripture sentences
Exhortation
General Confession (unison)
Prayer for Pardon
Lord's Prayer
Versicles & responses
Psalm with Gloria Patri
First lesson OT

Te Deum
Second lesson NT
Jubilate
Apostles' creed
Versicles & responses
Three collects (Day, peace, grace)
Prayer for Supreme Rulers
Prayer of St. Chrysostum
Grace   (2 Cor. 13:14)

1792

Singing
Prayer
Reading (1 chapter OT, 1 chapter NT)

Preaching

"On days of Administering the
Lord's Supper, the two chapters in
the morning-service may be
omitted."

1824

Singing
Prayer *concluded with Lord's Prayer*
Reading
    (1 chapter OT, 1 chapter NT)
Preaching
Dismissal   *Apostolic Benediction*

"In administering the sacraments
and in the Burial of the Dead, let
the Ritual invariably be used."

1864

Singing
Prayer with Lord's Prayer
    (congregation joining)
Reading (1 *lesson* OT, 1 *lesson* NT)
Preaching
Doxology
Dismissal   Apostolic Benediction

1868

Footnote to *Discipline* section on
Public Worship:

"Our people should be urged to
take part in the public worship of
God, first, in singing; secondly, in
prayer in the Scriptural attitude
of kneeling, and by the repetition
of the Lord's Prayer."

1888

Singing   *standing*
Prayer with Lord's Prayer, *kneeling*
Reading (1 lesson OT, 1 lesson NT
    "either of which may be read
    responsively."
Collection
Singing   sitting
Preaching
A short prayer for the blessing on the
    Word
Singing, closing with a doxology,
    the people standing
Apostolic Benediction

1896

Expanded "Order of Worship"
adopted by General Conference
1896; added opposite title-page
of new printings of 1878 *Hymnal;*
inserted in others.

1905

With minor changes 1896 order is
included in common hymnal with
MECS

[See page 33]

ORDERS OF WORSHIP: MECS
1846–1905

Italics indicates change or addition from previous order.

1846

Singing
1st prayer (concluded with Lord's
 Prayer)
Reading (1 chapter OT, 1 chapter NT)
Preaching
Dismissal (Apostolic Benediction)

1866

Singing
1st prayer (concluded with Lord's
 Prayer)
Reading (1 *lesson* OT, 1 *lesson* NT)
Preaching
Dismissal (Apostolic Benediction)

"Let the Lord's Supper be administered *monthly*, in every congregation,
wherever it is practicable, and where it
is not practicable, *at every quarterly
meeting.* Let the service preceding the
administration be so proportioned as
to admit of due time for this ordinance. . . . *Let the Ritual be invariably
used in all the offices for which it is prescribed.*"

*The Sunday Service of the Methodists in
North America* (1784) authorized for
use; reprinted 1867.

1870

Singing *standing*
Prayer (concluding with Lord's Prayer)
 kneeling
Reading (1 lesson OT, 1 lesson NT)
Singing *sitting*
Preaching
Singing *standing*
Prayer *kneeling*
Benediction (Apostolic)

"The Lord's Supper *shall* be
 administered monthly."

1905

Expanded "Order of Worship" in
common hymnal with MEC.

[See page 33]

[The 1906 MECS *Discipline*
retained the rubric concerning the
giving of an invitation to discipleship,
with the hymn following the sermon.]

ECUMENISM TIME-LINE

NATIONAL

Evangelical Alliance
(American branch) 1867
collapses in 1890s

Federal Council of Churches 1908

Foreign Missions Conference, 1893
Missionary Education Movement, 1902
Home Missions Council, 1908
National Protestant Council
  on Higher Education, 1911
United Stewardship Council, 1920
International Council on
  Religious Education, 1922
United Council of Church Women
  1941

National Association of Evangelicals 1943

National Council of Churches 1950
(Assemblies convene every three years)

North American Conference on
Faith and Order, Oberlin, 1957

Consultation on Church Union 1960
Plan of Union drafted 1970
Emerging doctrinal consensus adopted 1976
Covenanting model proposed 1979
Doctrinal consensus adopted 1984
Covenanting plan adopted & submitted
  to member churches 1988
Became Churches Uniting in
  Christ (CUiC) in 2000

Christian Holiness Association 1971

ROMAN CATHOLIC CHURCH

Vatican Secretariat for Promoting Christian Unity formed 1960

Vatican Council II convenes in Rome with Methodist observers 1962

Decree on Ecumenism 1964

INTERNATIONAL

Evangelical Alliance
London, 1846+
(World meetings held through 1896)

World Student Christian Federation
Stockholm, 1895+

World Missionary Conference
Edinburgh, 1910

churches develop common strategies along three roads:

MISSION	ACTION	DOCTRINE
International Missionary Council	**Life & Work Movement**	**Faith & Order Movement**
	Stockholm 1925	Lausanne 1927
	Oxford 1937	Edinburgh 1937
Jerusalem 1928		Utrecht 1938
Madras 1938		
Whitby 1947		
	World Council of Churches	
	General Assemblies	
	1st Amsterdam, 1948	
	2nd Evanston, 1954	Lund 1952
Willingen 1952	3rd New Delhi 1961	
Ghana 1957	"All in each place"	
	4th Uppsala 1968	Montreal 1963
Bankok 1972	5th Nairobi 1975	Lima 1982
(World Mission &		*Baptism, Eucharist &*
Evangelism)	6th Vancouver 1983	*Ministry*
	7th Canberra 1991	
	8th Harare 1998	

METHODIST

Ecumenical Methodist Conferences

1st	London 1881	5th	London 1921
2nd	Washington 1891	6th	Atlanta 1931
3rd	London 1901	7th	Springfield, MA 1947
4th	Toronto 1911	8th	Oxford 1951

World Methodist Conferences

9th	Lake Junaluska, NC 1956	14th	Honolulu 1981
10th	Oslo 1961	15th	Nairobi 1986
11th	London 1966	16th	Singapore 1991
12th	Denver 1971	17th	Rio de Janeiro 1996
13th	Dublin 1976	18th	Brighton, England, 2001

World Federation of Methodist Women 1939

World Methodist Council 1951

Commission on Ecumenical Affairs
mandated by General Conference 1964
(now General Commission on Christian Unity
and Interreligious Concerns)

Bi-lateral Conversations
Roman Catholic (USA) 1966+
Roman Catholic (international) 1967 +
Lutheran (USA) 1977+
Lutheran (international) 1979+
Anglican (international) 1988+
Anglican (USA) 1988+
Reformed (international) 1992+
Orthodox (international) 1992+
Wesleyan/Holiness Churches (USA) 1999+

Interreligious Dialogues
Jews 1972
Muslims 1976

Anglican/Methodist Unity Conversations (England)
1st extended set of talks fail in 1969
2nd set of talks fails in 1972
3rd set of wider talks fail in 1982
4th set of talks with Anglicans alone
       begin again, 1995

CIEMAL (Council of Evangelical Methodist churches in Latin America) 1969

Commission on Pan-Methodist Union (between AME, AMEZion, CME and UMC Churches in USA)
Bishops begin work 1979,
  begin collaborative planning in 1985,
  begin drafting plan of union in 1998

World Fellowship of Methodist and Uniting Church Men 2001

CONFESSIONS OF FAITH OF
THE UNITED BRETHREN CHURCH

1815
[First published in pamphlet form in 1816.]

1819
[Included in the first published edition of the UB Book of Discipline, 1819.]

1889
[Published in the 1889 UB Book of Discipline.]

In the name of God we confess before all men, that we believe the only true God, Father, Son, and Holy Ghost; That these three are one: the Father in the Son, the Son in the Father, and the Holy Ghost equal in essence with both; that this God created heaven and earth and all that in them is, visible as well as invisible, and sustains, governs, protects, and supports the same.

In the name of God we declare and confess before all men, that we believe in the only true God, the Father, Son and Holy Ghost; that these three are one, the Father in the Son, the Son in the Father, and the Holy Ghost, equal in essence or being with both.

That this triune God created the heavens and the earth, and all that in them is, visible as well as invisible, and furthermore sustains, governs, protects and supports the same.

In the name of God, we declare and confess before all men the following articles of our belief:

Article I. Of God and the Holy Trinity

[same as 1819]

Article II. Of Creation and Providence

[*1819 text+*]
. . . and governs with gracious regard for the welfare of man, to the glory of his name.

Article III. Of Jesus Christ

[same as 1819]

We believe in Jesus Christ; that he is very God and man; that he by the Holy Ghost, assumed his human nature in Mary and was born of her; that he is the Saviour and Redeemer of the whole human race, if they with faith in him accept the grace profered in Jesus; that this Jesus suffered and died on the cross for us, was buried, rose again on the third day, ascended into heaven, and sitteth on the right hand of God to intercede for us; and that he shall come again to judge the living and the dead.

We believe in Jesus Christ; that he is very God and Man; that he became incarnate by the power of the Holy Ghost in the Virgin Mary, and was born of her; that he is the saviour and mediator of the whole human race, if they with full faith in him accept the grace profered in Jesus.

That this Jesus suffered and died on the cross for us. . . .

Article IV. Of the Holy Ghost

We believe in the Holy Ghost; that he is equal in being with the Father and the Son; that he proceeds from both; that we are through him enlightened: through faith justified and sanctified.

We believe in the Holy Ghost, that he is equal in being with the Father and the Son, and that he comforts the faithful, and guides them into all truth.

We believe in the Holy Ghost; that he is equal with the Father and the Son; that he convinces the world of sin, of righteousness and of judgment. . . .

We believe that the Bible, Old and New Testament, is the word of God; that it contains the true way to our soul well-being and salvation that every true Christian is bound to acknowledge and receive it, with the influences of the Spirit of god, as his only rule and guide; and that without repentance, faith in Jesus Christ, forgiveness of sins, and following after Jesus Christ, no one can be a true Christian.

[The same as 1815 with refinement of a few words.]

Article V. Of the Holy Scriptures

We believe that the Holy Bible, Old and New Testaments, is the word of God: that it reveals the only true way to our salvation; that every true Christian is bound to acknowledge and receive it by the help of the Spirit of God as the only rule land guide in faith and practice.

Article VI. Of the Church

We believe that the doctrine which the Holy Scriptures contain, namely, the fall in Adam and salvation through Jesus Christ, shall be preached and proclaimed throughout the whole world.

We also believe, that what is contained in the Holy Scriptures to wit: the fall in Adam and redemption through Jesus Christ shall be preached throughout the world.

We believe in a holy Christian church, composed of true believers, in which the word of God is preached by men divinely called, and the ordinances are duly administered; that this divine institution is for the maintenance of worship, for the edification of believers, and the conversion of the world to Christ.

Article VII. Of the Sacraments

We believe that the outward means of grace are to be in sue in all Christian societies, namely: that baptism and the remembrance of the death of the Lord in the distribution of the bread and wine are to be in use among his children, according to the command of the Lord Jesus; the mode and manner, however, shall be left to the judgment of every one. Also, the example of feet washing remains free to every one.

[The same as 1815 but with slight verbal updating.]

We believe that the sacraments, Baptism and the Lord's Supper, are to be used in the Church, and should be practiced by all Christians; but the mode and manner of observing the Lord's Supper are always to be left to the judgment and understanding of each individual. Also the baptism of children shall be left to the judgment and understanding of each individual. Also the baptism of children shall be left to the judgment of believing parents. The example of the washing of feet is to be left to the judgment of each one, to practice or not.

[The following articles were added in the 1889 Confession of Faith. They have no previous parallels.]

Article VIII. Of Depravity

We believe that man is fallen from original righteousness, and apart from the grace of our Lord Jesus Christ, is not only entirely destitute of holiness, but is inclined to evil and only evil, and that continually; and that except a man be born again he cannot see the kingdom of heaven.

Article IX. Of Justification

We believe that penitent sinners are justified before God, only by faith in our Lord Jesus Christ, and not by works; yet that good works in Christ are acceptable to God, and spring out of a true and living faith.

Article X. Of Regeneration and Adoption

We believe that regeneration is the renewal of the heart of man after the image of God, through the word, by the act of the Holy Ghost, by which the believer receives the spirit of adoption and is enabled to serve God with the will and the affections.

Article XI. Of Sanctification

We believe that sanctification is the work of God's grace, through the Word and the Spirit, by which those who have been born again are separated in their acts, words and thoughts from sin, and are enabled to live unto God, and to follow holiness, without which no man shall see the Lord.

Article XII. Of the Christian Sabbath

We believe that the Christian Sabbath is divinely appointed; that it is commemorative of our Lord's resurrection from the grace, and is an emblem of our eternal rest; that it is essential to the welfare of the civil community, and to the permanence and growth of the Christian church, and that it should be reverently observed as a day of holy rest and of social and public worship.

Article XIII. Of the Future State

We believe in the resurrection of the dead; the future general judgment; and an eternal state of rewards, in which the righteous dwell in endless life, and the wicked in endless punishment.

[General Conference authorization:

The 1813 General Conference, on motion of the East Pennsylvania Conference, moved to include the Confession of Faith in the forthcoming Book of Discipline.]

[General Conference authorization:

The 1817 General Conference resolved the Discipline *to be printed, 300 German, 100 English editions. The* Discipline *was first published in 1819 in three formats: German only, English only, and a bilingual edition with text in German on the left and in English on the right.]*

ARTICLES OF FAITH OF THE EVANGELICAL ASSOCIATION/CHURCH

A. The Twenty-Six Articles of 1809:

A German translation of the Twenty-Five Articles of Religion of the Methodist Episcopal Church (1784) plus one new article on Eschatology, a theme omitted in the Methodist Articles. It is a paraphrase of Article XVI of the Augsburg Confession (1530) of the Lutheran family of churches. First published in the 1809 Discipline.

Jacob Albright's successor, George Miller, used a newly published German translation of the 1804 Methodist Episcopal Discipline prepared under the close supervision of Henry Boehm, Asbury's trusted adviser of German work. Completed in 1807, it was published in Lancaster in 1808 under the title: *Lehre under Zuchtordnung der Bischoflish-Methodisten Kirche.*

XXVI. Of the Last Judgment and God's Righteous Sentence of Rewards and Punishments.

We believe that Jesus Christ will come in the last day, to judge all mankind by a righteous judgment; that God will give unto the faithful, elect and godly, eternal life and happiness, everlasting rest, peace, and joy without end. But God will bid the impenitent and ungodly, depart to the Devil and his angels, to endure everlasting damnation, punishment and pain, torment and misery. Therefore we are not to concede to the doctrine of those who maintain that devils and ungodly men will not have to suffer eternal punishment and torment.

From the first English translation of the Evangelical Association Discipline *published in 1832.*

B. The Twenty-One Articles of 1816:

Elimination of five polemical Articles: "Of Works of Supererogation"
"Of Purgatory"
"Of Both Kinds"
"Of Marriage of Ministers" [all anti-Catholic]
"Of a Christian Man's Oath" [anti-Anabaptist]

C. The Thirty-Two Articles of 1839:

Slight verbal updating; for example, in Article VIII, "preventing" becomes "assisting and influencing."

D. The Nineteen Articles of 1901:

A reduction from 21 to 19 by combining some of them, but without omitting any of their original content.

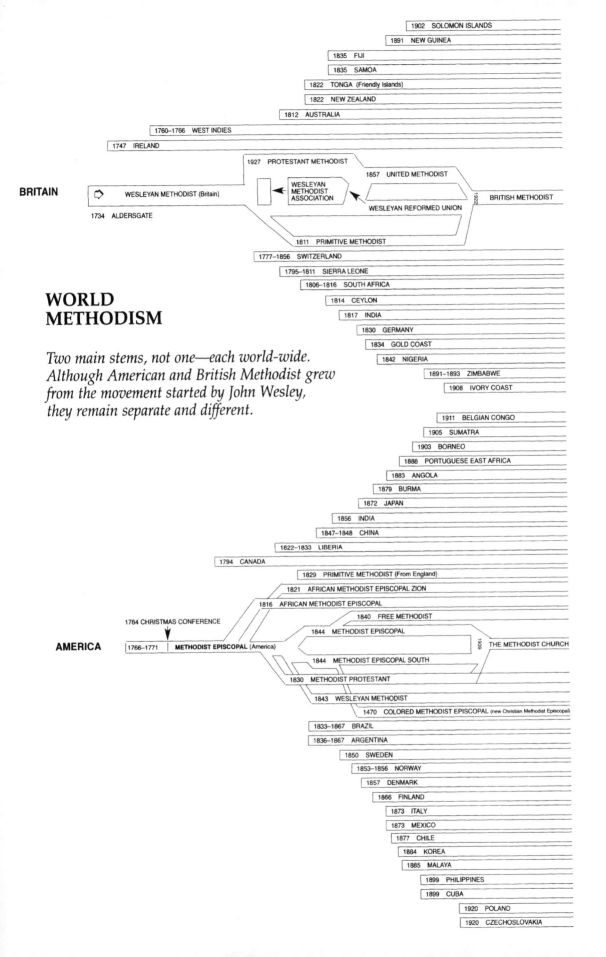

WORLD METHODISM

Two main stems, not one—each world-wide.
Although American and British Methodist grew
from the movement started by John Wesley,
they remain separate and different.

BRITAIN

AMERICA

1902 SOLOMON ISLANDS
1891 NEW GUINEA
1835 FIJI
1835 SAMOA
1822 TONGA (Friendly Islands)
1822 NEW ZEALAND
1812 AUSTRALIA
1760–1766 WEST INDIES
1747 IRELAND

1927 PROTESTANT METHODIST
1857 UNITED METHODIST
WESLEYAN METHODIST ASSOCIATION
WESLEYAN METHODIST (Britain)
BRITISH METHODIST
1734 ALDERSGATE
WESLEYAN REFORMED UNION
1922
1811 PRIMITIVE METHODIST

1777–1856 SWITZERLAND
1795–1811 SIERRA LEONE
1806–1816 SOUTH AFRICA
1814 CEYLON
1817 INDIA
1830 GERMANY
1834 GOLD COAST
1842 NIGERIA
1891–1893 ZIMBABWE
1908 IVORY COAST

1911 BELGIAN CONGO
1905 SUMATRA
1903 BORNEO
1888 PORTUGUESE EAST AFRICA
1883 ANGOLA
1879 BURMA
1872 JAPAN
1856 INDIA
1847–1848 CHINA
1822–1833 LIBERIA
1794 CANADA
1829 PRIMITIVE METHODIST (From England)
1821 AFRICAN METHODIST EPISCOPAL ZION
1816 AFRICAN METHODIST EPISCOPAL
1840 FREE METHODIST
1844 METHODIST EPISCOPAL
1784 CHRISTMAS CONFERENCE
1766–1771 METHODIST EPISCOPAL (America)
1939 THE METHODIST CHURCH
1844 METHODIST EPISCOPAL SOUTH
1830 METHODIST PROTESTANT
1843 WESLEYAN METHODIST
1470 COLORED METHODIST EPISCOPAL (new Christian Methodist Episcopal)
1833–1867 BRAZIL
1836–1867 ARGENTINA
1850 SWEDEN
1853–1856 NORWAY
1857 DENMARK
1866 FINLAND
1873 ITALY
1873 MEXICO
1877 CHILE
1884 KOREA
1885 MALAYA
1899 PHILIPPINES
1899 CUBA
1920 POLAND
1920 CZECHOSLOVAKIA

MEA I:
1760–1815

William Otterbein stresses repentance in a sermon at a conference of German Reformed preachers in Philadelphia

Source: William Otterbein, Die Heilbringende Menschwerdung und der Herrliche Sieg Jesu Christi ueber den Teufel und Tod. Germantown (Philadelphia): Printed by Christoph Sauer, 1763. English translation in J. Steven O'Malley, Early German-American Evangelicalism: Pietist Sources on Discipleship and Sanctification (Lanham, Md.: Scarecrow Press, 1995), 19, 25-28. Excerpts; footnotes omitted.

THE SALVATION-BRINGING INCARNATION AND THE GLORIOUS VICTORY OF JESUS CHRIST OVER THE DEVIL AND DEATH

Text: Hebrews 2:14-15

Since therefore the children share in flesh and blood, he himself likewise partook of the same nature, that through death he might destroy him who has the power of death, that is, the devil, and deliver all those who through fear of death were subject to lifelong bondage [RSV].

The doctrine of the redemption of the poor sinner through Jesus Christ is rightly called a gospel and a message that brings salvation and joy. By nature we are in a completely desperate condition. We are without God, and children of wrath. What a pity! So we go astray, like a sheep without a shepherd, who locate no pasture, and stand exposed to the power of Satan and sin. How amazing, that most people live totally secure and hardened in this desperate condition! Are we not destitute of all godly light and life, and without hope? Truly, this is a condition that—if we think about it—rightly drives us into a tight spot. . . .

The gospels give us a detailed account of the death of Jesus Christ. Christ died a violent and agonizing death on the cross. He has already guaranteed from eternity that this would happen for poor sinners. This death was not only prophesied through the prophets, but it was also prefigured through the sacrifices and the other ceremonies of the law. And all of this happened for our good. It was for the sake of our sins that Christ sweated blood, and out of love for us He offered His soul as a guilt offering. What a work our sins made for him! We are expensively purchased. As painful as this suffering was to the Lord Jesus, so great was the salvation that occurred from this for the poor sinner.

Paul says, "That through death He might destroy him who has the power. . . ." That was the purpose of the suffering of Jesus Christ (I John 3:8). The promise in paradise was directed toward this (Genesis 3:15). And Christ has actually carried out this promise through His death (II Timothy 1:10). That happened above all on the cross (Colossians 2:14-15). Christ here became a poison for death and destruction for hell (Hosea 13:14). Hence Paul joyfully cries out (I Corinthians 15:55-57), "Death, where is your sting?" O costly death! (Daniel 9:24). This death brings a laudable salvation. Now God is reconciled, and the way into the inner holiness is prepared, that Paul so simply expressed in his words of praise (Ephesians 1:3), "Blessed be the God and Father of our Lord Jesus Christ."

Meanwhile, with all that, the matter of our salvation is not yet fully completed. What a pity it is that people almost without exception seek a salvation that lies outside themselves. People imagine that Christ has completed all things on the cross and He has made us holy just as we are. Christ has paid, they think, and sin will be fully put away at death. Those are erroneous thoughts about Jesus' death and redemption. Almost any perverse thinker can conclude this. It is certainly more on the order of a hellish doctrine, that merely makes Christ to be a covering for sin, that also builds the devil's kingdom. . . .

Pay attention to see if you comprehend this. Through what He has done outside of us, Christ has only laid the groundwork for our salvation. He has freely reconciled His heavenly Father to us through His death. However, He has at the same time given us a picture of what He must do within us—how He must destroy the kingdom of Satan within us, even as He has destroyed this kingdom outside of us. Christ has set an example for us by His suffering (I Peter 2:21), and Paul speaks clearly about conformity with His death (Philippians 3:10). Thus, the Savior Himself urges the bearing of His cross after Him, and that is the great secret, *Christ in us* (II Corinthians 13:5). Here it becomes apparent that what Christ has done outside of us, He also completes within us. He also crushes the head of the serpent within us and with it the sin that leads to death. Paul rejoices in this (Galatians 2:19). This is true of all believers (Galatians 5:24). Christ and His death only become beneficial to us when He comes home to us in this way. On the basis of conformity with the death of Jesus Christ we receive the crown (James 1:12). Life depends on this (Romans 6:8). Upon the same agony with Jesus, there follows the same glory (Romans 2:17).

But may a person know whether Christ has killed the sin in him? Certainly, as surely as he lives. An unbroken heart, security, a worldly outlook are all genuine works of darkness, of Satan's kingdom within us. Wherever a man walks according to the lusts of his heart, while boasting that he is redeemed through Christ, he remains horribly blind, if not completely obstinate. Even the devil shudders when he thinks of God. What help is it if a man has great sorrow for his sins and yet he repeats them a hundred times? Peter describes this sort of repentance in II Peter 2:22. Where there is no true change of heart there is also no deliverance.

How, then, does a person arrive at this point of deliverance? That is God's work. No one comes to the Son until the Father draws him. As soon as God's Spirit opens a person's eyes, so that he recognizes and feels his misery, then he gets up with the prodigal son and says, "Father, I have sinned" (Luke 15:18). A person will not become disgusted with the world and sin until he recognizes in God's light that these things have brought him unhappiness. If a person comes this far by God's grace, that he despairs of himself and his efforts, he then sits down with Mary at Jesus' feet and cries.

In this way a person can easily know whether the Holy Spirit has His work in a person; it is when he knows and feels with agony his inner corruption of heart, and where this knowledge breaks, shames, and makes the heart humble before God. It is wherever a person becomes an enemy of sin, turns his back to the world, and hungers after Jesus. It is where all of this continues and grows (Hebrews 3:14). Whoever struggles here, under the discipline of the Holy Spirit, will finally be led by grace to victory. And that is the work of deliverance, *Christ in us*. The marks by which it can be recognized are where lusts and a tendency to sin are lost, where sin ceases (Romans 6:6 and verse 18). The fruit of this is holiness (Romans 6:22), the new man (Colossians 3:10-14), and a step-by-step progression toward perfection (II Corinthians 3:18).

And that is the purpose of redemption (Titus 2:14). If nothing impure can enter into the New Jerusalem (Revelation 21:27), then an impure, unregenerated sinner has no hope. God is reconciled on His side through Jesus, and where grace puts to death the carnal mind that lives in us by nature, then will we also be reconciled to God on our side. Furthermore, just as it is impossible for a doctor to cure a sick person if he has not first killed the evil that has caused the sickness and pain, so also Christ has little opportunity to save a single soul from hell where he does not eradicate the sin that brings about the hell. And is not the power of Satan over us based on the sin and evil within us? This is undeniable. Accordingly, the power of Satan over us ceases when sin also ceases within us. . . .

What counsel is there, then? It is indicated for you to make repentance, believe the gospel, search in the Scripture. There is no other way. . . . The entire word of God presses toward denial, inward renewal, and holiness. If you want Jesus to rid you of your sin, then first let your hearts break down in true repentance. You must travel this way, if you want to find mercy on that day. . . .

To be a redeemed person of the Lord—what a salvation! What a joy there will be when God sends this message to one or to another of you, saying your names are written in the book of life. You came to this place by the way of repentance. Come, then, to the One who can help you. Jesus has already saved many miserable sinners. If your salvation is important to you, join up with the prodigal son. Jesus waits upon you. The garment is already prepared. Everything is ready; come.

THOMAS TAYLOR BEGS WESLEY
TO SEND PREACHERS TO AMERICA

Source: Frank Baker, "Early American Methodism: A Key Document," Methodist History *3/2 (January 1965): 9-15. First printed in Charles Atmore,* An Appendix to the Methodist Memorial *(Manchester: W. Shelmerdine & Co., 1802), 579-82. Nathan Bangs published a variant full text of Taylor's letter in the* Methodist Magazine *(New York) 6/11 (November 1823): 427-31, and again in his 1838* History *1:52-58. The following text is from Atmore, as edited by Baker.*

New York, 11th April, 1768

Rev. and very Dear Sir [John Wesley],

I intended writing to you for several weeks past, but a few of us had a very material transaction in view. I therefore postponed writing until I could give you a particular account thereof. This was the purchasing of ground for building a preaching-house upon, which by the blessing of God we have now concluded. But before I proceed I shall give you a short account of the state of religion in this city. By the best intelligence I can collect there was little either of the form or power of it till Mr. Whitefield came over thirty years ago; and even after his first and second visit there appeared but little fruit of his labours. But during his third visit fourteen or fifteen years ago there was a considerable shaking among the dry bones. Divers were savingly converted, and this work was much increased in his last journey, about four years since, when his words were really as a hammer and as a fire. Most part of the adults were stirred up, great numbers pricked to the heart, and by a judgment of charity several found peace and joy in believing. The consequence of this work was, the churches were crowded and subscriptions raised for building new ones. Mr. Whitefield's example provoked most of the ministers to a much greater degree of earnestness. And by the multitudes of people young and old, rich and poor, flocking to the churches, religion became an honourable profession—there was no outward cross to be taken up therein. Nay, a person who could not speak about the grace of God and the new birth was esteemed unfit for genteel company. But in a while, instead of pressing forward and growing in grace (as he exhorted them) the generality were pleading for the remains of sin, and the necessity of being in darkness. They esteemed their opinions as the very essentials of Christianity, and regarded not holiness either of heart or life.

The above appears to me to be a genuine account of the state of religion in New

York eighteen months ago, when it pleased God to rouse up Mr. Embury to employ his talent (which for several years had been as it were hid in a napkin) by calling sinners to repentance and exhorting believers to let their light shine before men. He spoke at first only in his own house. A few were soon collected together and joined in a little society—chiefly his own countrymen, Irish. In about three months after brother White and brother Sause from Dublin joined them. They then rented an empty room in their neighbourhood, which was in the most infamous street of the city, adjoining the barracks. For some time few thought it worth their while to hear. But God so ordered it by His providence that about fourteen months ago Captain Webb, barrack master at Albany (who was converted about three years since at Bristol) found them out and preached in his regimentals. The novelty of a man preaching in a scarlet coat soon brought greater numbers to hear than the room could contain. But his doctrines were quite new to the hearers, for he told them point blank "that all their knowledge and profession of religion was not worth a rush unless their sins were forgiven and they had the 'witness of God's spirit with theirs, that they were the children of God.' " This strange doctrine, with some peculiarities in his person, made him soon be taken notice of, and obliged the little society to look out for a larger house to preach in. They soon found a place that had been built for a rigging-house, sixty feet in length and eighteen in breadth.

About this period Mr. Webb, whose wife's relations live at Jamaica on Long Island, took a house in that neighbourhood, and began to preach in his own house and several other places on Long Island. Within six months about twenty-four persons received justifying grace, near half of them whites, the rest Negroes. While Mr. Webb (to borrow his own phrase) was "felling the trees on Long Island," brother Embury was exhorting all who attended on Thursday evenings and Sunday mornings and evenings at the rigging-house to flee from the wrath to come. His hearers began to increase, and some gave heed to his report, about the time the gracious providence of God brought me safe to New York after a very favourable passage of six weeks from Plymouth [England]. It was the 26th day of October last when I arrived, recommended to a person for lodging. I inquired of my host (who was a very religious man) if any Methodists were in New York. He informed me there was one Captain Webb, a strange sort of man, who lived on Long Island and sometimes preached at one Embury's at the rigging-house. In a few days I found out Embury. I soon found what spirit he was of, and that he was personally acquainted with you and your doctrines, and had been a Helper in Ireland. He had formed two classes, one of the men and another of the women, but had never met the society apart from the congregation, although there were six or seven men and about the same number of women who had a clear sense of their acceptance in the Beloved.

You will not wonder at my being greatly surprised in meeting with a few here who have and desire again to be in connection with you. God only knows the weight of the affliction I felt in leaving my native country. But I have reason now to conclude God intended all for my good. Ever since I left London my load has been been removed and I have found a cheerfulness in being banished from all near and dear to me, and I made a new covenant with my God that I would go to the utmost parts of the earth provided He would raise up a people with whom I might join in His praise. On the great deep I found a more earnest desire to be united with the people of God than ever before. I made a resolution that God's people should be my people, and their God my God, and (bless His holy name!) I have since experienced more heartfelt happiness than ever I thought it possible to have on this side of eternity. All anxious care even about my dear wife and children is taken away. I cannot assist them, but I daily and hourly commend them to God in prayer, and I know He hears my prayers, by an answer of love in my heart. I find power daily to devote myself unto Him, and I find power also to overcome sin. If any uneasiness at all affects me, it is because I can speak so little of so good a God.

Mr. Embury has lately been more zealous than formerly, the consequence of which is that he is more lively in preaching, and his gifts as well as graces are much increased. Great numbers of serious people came to hear God's word as for their lives. And their numbers increased so fast that our house for this six weeks past would not contain the half of the people.

We had some consultations how to remedy this inconvenience, and Embury proposed renting a lot of ground for twenty-one years, and to exert our utmost endeavours to collect as much money as to build a wooden tabernacle. A piece of ground was proposed, the ground rent was agreed for, and the lease was to be executed in a few days. We, however, in the mean time, had two several days for fasting and prayer for the direction of God and His blessing on our proceedings—and Providence opened such a door as we had no expectation of. A young man, a sincere Christian and constant hearer, though not joined in society, would not give anything towards this house, but offered ten pounds to buy a lot of ground, (and) went of his own accord to a lady who had two lots to sell, on one of which there is a house that rents for eighteen pounds per annum. He found the purchase money of the two lots was six hundred pounds, which she was willing should remain in the purchaser's hands on good security. We called once more upon God for His direction, and resolved to purchase the whole. There are eight of us, who are joint purchasers, among whom Mr. Webb and Mr. Lupton are men of property. I was determined the house should be on the same footing as the Orphan House at Newcastle and others in England, but as we were ignorant how to draw the deeds we purchased for us and our heirs until a copy of the writings from England was sent us, which we desire may be sent by the first opportunity.

Before we began to talk of building[,] the devil and his children were very peaceable, but since this affair took place many ministers have cursed us in the name of the Lord, and laboured with all their might to shut up their congregations from assisting us. But He that sitteth in Heaven laughed them to scorn. Many have broke through and given their friendly assistance. We have collected above one hundred pounds more than our own contributions, and have reason to hope in the whole we shall have two hundred pounds: but the house will cost us four hundred pounds more, so that unless God is pleased to raise up friends we shall yet be at a loss. I believe Mr. Webb and Mr. Lupton will borrow or advance two hundred pounds rather than the building should not go forward, but the interest of money here is a great burden, which is seven per cent. Some of our brethren proposed writing to you for a collection in England, but I was averse to this, as I well knew our friends there are overburdened already. Yet so far I would earnestly beg: if you would intimate our circumstances to particular persons of ability[,] perhaps God would open their hearts to assist this infant society and contribute to the first preaching-house on the original Methodist plan in all America—excepting Mr. Whitefield's Orphan House in Georgia. But I shall write no more on this head.

There is another point far more material, and in which I must importune your assistance not only in my own name but in the name of the whole society. We want an able, experienced preacher—one who has both gifts and graces necessary for the work. God has not despised the day of small things. There is a real work in many hearts by the preaching of Mr. Webb and Mr. Embury, but although they are both useful, and their hearts in the work, they want many qualifications necessary for such an undertaking, where they have none to direct them. And the progress of the gospel here depends much on the qualifications of the preachers.

I have thought of Mr. Helton, for if possible we must have a man of wisdom, of sound faith, and a good disciplinarian, one whose heart and soul are in the work, and I doubt not but by the goodness of God such a flame would be soon kindled as would never stop until it reached the great South Sea. We may make many shifts to evade temporal inconveniences, but we cannot *purchase* such a preacher as I have described. Dear sir, I entreat you for the good of thousands to use your utmost endeavours to send one over. I would advise him to take shipping at Bristol, Liverpool, or Dublin, in the month of July or early in August; by embarking at this season he will have fine weather in his passage and probably arrive here in the month of September. He will see with his own eyes before winter what progress the gospel has made. With respect to the money for payment of a preacher's passage over, if they could not procure it, we would sell our coats and shirts and pay it.

I most earnestly beg an interest in your prayers, and trust you and many of our brethren will not forget the church in this wilderness.

I remain with sincere esteem, Rev. and Dear Sir,

Your very affectionate brother and servant,

T. T. [Thomas Taylor]

Boardman Describes the Biracial Character of Methodism in North America

Source: "Letter CCCXXIII. From Mr. Richard Boardman to the Rev. J. Wesley,"
Arminian Magazine *[London] 7/3 (March 1784): 163-64.*

New-York, Nov. 4, 1769

Rev. Sir [John Wesley],

After a nine weeks voyage of great difficulties, we safely arrived at Philadelphia. Several said there had not, in the memory of the oldest man on the Continent, been such hard gales of wind, as those for a few months past. Many vessels have been lost, while others got in with loss of masts, and much damage to their cargoes. We observed shipwrecks all along the coast of the Delaware. I never understood David's words as I now do : "They that go down to the sea in ships, that do business in great waters, these see the works of the Lord, and his wonders in the deep." In calm, serene weather, I found much exercise of mind; strong temptations, and great dejection. In rough, stormy weather, particularly when it appeared morally impossible the vessel should live long, amidst conflicting elements I found myself exceeding happy, and rested satisfied that death would be gain. I do not remember to have had one doubt of being eternally saved, should the mighty waters swallow us up. This was the Lord's doing! O may it ever be marvellous [*sic*] in my eyes!

When I came to Philadelphia I found a little Society, and preached to a great number of people. I left brother Pilmoor [Pilmore] there, and set out for New-York. Coming to a large town on my way [probably Trenton, New Jersey], and seeing a barrac[k], I asked a soldier if there were many Methodists belonging to it? "O yes, said he, we are all Methodists: that is, we should all be glad to hear a Methodist preach." "Well, said I, tell them in the barrac[k] that a Methodist Preacher, just come from England, intends to preach here to night." He did so, and the inn was soon surrounded with soldiers. I asked, "Where do you think I can get a place to preach in?" (it being then dark.) One of them said, "I will go and see if I can get the Presbyterian Meeting-house." He did so, and soon returned to tell me he had prevailed, and that the bell was just going to ring to let all the town know. A great company soon got together, and seemed much affected.

The next day I came to New-York. Our House contains about seventeen hundred hearers. About a third part of those who attend the preaching get in; the rest are glad to hear without. There appears such a willingness in the Americans to hear the word, as I never saw before. They have no preaching in some parts of the Back Settlements. I doubt not but an effectual door will be opened among them. O may he now give his Son the heathen for his inheritance.

The number of Blacks that attend the preaching, affects me much. One of them came to tell me she could neither eat nor sleep, because her Master would not suffer her to come to hear the word. She wept exceedingly, saying, "I told my Master I would do more work than ever I used to do, if he would but let me come; nay, that I would do every thing in my power to be a good servant."

I find a great want of every gift and grace for the great work before me. I should be glad of your advice. But, dear Sir, what shall I say to almost every body I see. They ask, "Does Mr. Wesley think he shall ever come over to see us?"

I am, dear Sir, your affectionate Son and Servant,

R. BOARDMAN

JOSEPH PILMORE WRITES WESLEY ABOUT BLACK CLASS MEETINGS AND THE NEED FOR ORDINATION

Source: Frederick E. Maser, "A Revealing Letter from Joseph Pilmore,"
Methodist History *10/3 (April 1972): 56-58. Notes omitted.*

New York [November 1771]

My Dear Dear Br. [Bumstead?]

You[r] much esteemed favour came safe to hand, & was made a Blessing to my Soul. Nothing gives me so much pleasure as to hear that you are well, & that the pleasure of the Lord prospers in your Hands. When we preach and live the Gospel, this must necessarily be the Case. It was the pure Doctrine & upright lives of the primitive Xtians & preachers that prevailed over all the opposition of Jews and Gentiles, & stood as a barrier against all the projects which a Subtile [*sic*] Devil could Invent. & this in all ages of the World will stand as a sure Basis, that will support every Minister of the Gospel under all his Trials and Tribulations.

From what you write of Yorkshire I am led to believe "wherein sin abounded, Grace hath much more abounded." O! Grace, Grace! Unbounded Grace! "Ho! Ye despairing Sinners, come, & trust upon the Lord."

I have been waiting with eager expectation for some of the Brethren to come over to our Macedonia & help us, but Ah me! There are so many things to give up, before one can cross the Atlantic, that it seems to be too much even for a Methodist preacher! I find by Mr. Wesley's letter that none were willing to come, so it is very uncertain whether ever we shall have an opportunity of returning to Old England or no. But blessed be God, we know what was our Intention in leaving all that was dear to us, in order to visit those dear, dear Americans: & as we came in singleness in heart, the Lord has greatly blessed us both, in N. York & Philadelphia. Our Congregations are very large, & very serious' triffling [*sic*] seems to have no place at present for Sinners are engaged about the vast important affairs of the Invisible World, even the poor Negroes are turning to God, & seeking to wash their robes and make them white in the Blood of the Lamb.

A few days ago the Lord was pleased to manifest his Love to a poor Black, her Mistress has persecuted her very much because she came to the Methodist Church, but she thought it was better to be "beaten for hearing the word of God here; than to burn in Hell to all eternity." We have about twenty Black women that meet in one Class, & I think upon the whole they are as happy as any Class we have got.

Many people of superior rank come to hear the word and are very friendly. The chief difficulty we labour under is want of Ordination & I believe we shall be Obliged to procure it by some means or other. It is not in America as it is in England, for there is no Church that is one Establish'd more than another. All Sects have equal authority with the Church of England; I do believe if we should form a Church, we should soon have the largest congregation in these two Cities. The fields are white already, but the labourers are very few, there are hundreds of Sinners in this Country who dont hear a Sermon above once a quarter & some for not half a Year, & many of them would gladly hear, if they had anybody to preach to them; but in many places they have not a Minister of any Denomination for forty or fifty miles.

What a field for Methodist preachers! Whils't I was in Pensylvania [sic] I had the favour of opening the New Methodist Church about twenty miles from Philadelphia; and what was most remarkable, the poor plain Country people have called it Bethel, i.e., *the House of God.*

I have preach'd several times in an English Church, and the people flock'd together from all Quarters in such multitudes that I was oblig'd at last to stand upon a Table in the churchyard, & to preach the Word to a crowded Multitude who stood all around under the Shady Trees.

Perhaps you will say I speak too much in favour of the Americans, but I do assure you one half is not yet tould [sic] you. And I freely wish, that you would come and prove the truth of what I say; if you will come, I assure you that you will want nothing that is good. The people here are very kind & take pleasure in provoiding [sic] for the Methodist preachers.

Robt Williams is in Maryland preaching to the poor Convicts & I trust the Lord makes him useful. Mr. Webb is now in New York. He is a genuine Wesley & labours hard to promote the Cause. His Gifts are small, but he is very zealous and honest, & that you know is very precious in a preacher.

I could still add more, but you see my paper is just done & therefore must take my leave of you for the present, wishing you an increase of every Gift and Grace necessary for that office to which the Lord has called you unto.

I am, Dear Brother, whilst yours forever,

Joseph Pilmore

Preachers in North America Gather
for Their First Conference

Source: Minutes of the Methodist Conferences, annually held in America from 1773 to 1784, inclusive *(Philadelphia: Printed by Henry Tuckniss; sold by John Dickins, 1795)*, (5)-7.

The following queries were proposed to every preacher:

1. Ought not the authority of Mr. Wesley and that Conference, to extend to the preachers and people in America, as well as in Great Britain and Ireland?

Ans. Yes.

2. Ought not the doctrine and discipline of the Methodists, as contained in the Minutes, to be the sole rule of our conduct who labour in the connection with Mr. Wesley in America?

Ans. Yes.

3. If so, does it not follow that if any preachers deviate from the Minutes we can have no fellowship with them till they change their conduct?

Ans. Yes.

The following rules were agreed to by all the preachers present:—

1. Every preacher who acts in connection with Mr. Wesley and the brethren who labour in America is strictly to avoid administering the ordinances [sacraments] of baptism and the Lord's supper.

2. All the people among whom we labour to be earnestly exhorted to attend the Church [of England], and receive the ordinances there; but in a particular manner to press the people in Maryland and Virginia to the observance of this minute.

3. No person or persons to be admitted to our love-feasts oftener than twice or thrice unless they become members; and none to be admitted to the society meetings more than thrice.

4. None of the preachers in America to reprint any of Mr. Wesley's books without his authority (when it can be gotten) and the consent of their brethren.

5. Robert Williams to sell the books he has already printed, but to print no more, unless under the above restrictions.

6. Every preacher who acts as an assistant to send an account of the work once in six months to the general assistant.

Quest. 1. *How are the preachers stationed?* [10 preachers in all]

New-York, Thomas Rankin, to change in four months.
Philadelphia, George Shadford, to change in four months.
New-Jersey, John King, William Watters.
Baltimore, Francis Asbury, Robert Strawbridge, Abraham Whitworth, Joseph Yearbry.
Norfolk [Virginia], Richard Wright.
Petersburg [Virginia], Robert Williams.

Quest. 2. *What numbers are there in the Society?*

New-York	180
Philadelphia	180
New-Jersey	200
Maryland	500
Virginia	100
	1160

Mary Evans Thorn Parker
DETAILS IMPLICATIONS OF
SOCIETY MEMBERSHIP IN PHILADELPHIA

*Source: Autograph letter. Mary Parker to Thomas Coke and Adam Clarke,
29 July 1813. Philadelphia: St. George's United Methodist Church Archives.
Photocopy in United Methodist Archives, Madison, New Jersey.*

Liverpool, 29 July 1813

Rev'd Sirs [Thomas Coke and Adam Clarke],

How ever strange it appears that I should presume to write you, yet perhaps the following will plead my apology. If any men on earth can resemble the great example who, though surrounded with a crowd of attendants and concerns, yet condescended at least to listen to the application of an individual, surely it is the venerable body of men now assembled in Mount Pleasant Chapel [Liverpool, for annual conference].

However obscure, neglected, and forgotten we are now, it was not so once. In the course of our pilgrimage in the Methodist cause, myself for forty-three years and my husband for fifty-five, it has fallen to our lot to make greater sacrifice, perhaps, than is now considered. We joined not the Methodists in their prosperity, but during their adversity, when no one would follow them for their loaves and fishes, but for their reproaches. Such it was in the time when Mr. Pilmore and Mr. Boardman planted the first Methodist Church in America [about 1769].

When, after having been a member of the Baptist Church seven years, I cried: "This people [the Methodists] shall be my people and their God, my God." This I did not for honour, since for this in their meeting, I was struck down nearly lifeless. For this at the hazard of my life, I was pitched through a glass door, and for this, when a leader of three classes, I was reproached with the name of "Mother Confessor," pelted through the streets, and stoned in effigy. It was for this that one arm'd stood behind the glass door to kill me, till the Lord smote him with a better weapon. For this cause it was that my husband, at the hazard of his life, rescued a Methodist preacher from the mob by slipping him through a window. And for this cause it was that I was soon called to make as great a sacrifice as perhaps nature can bear, to forsake a beloved father and mother for the cause of religion. My mother, alarmed because one son and two daughters were under serious [religious] convictions, in the bitterness of her soul cried out, "They will all be in bedlam." She then interposed her authority and said, "You shall either forsake the Methodists or we will forsake you and leave the country"—a day of wormwood and gall never to be forgotten. When my mind was in an agony, the word of our Lord thundered in my soul, "He that loveth father or mother more than me is not worthy of me" [Matt. 10:37]. I cried out, "It is enough, Lord, here I am: do with me as seemeth good in thy sight, only save my soul" [2 Sam. 15:26]. Thus I gave my final answer to my dear mother [and father] and never saw them more. And this I suffered only for Methodism, the only cause of offence.

Whilst a leader of three [Methodist] classes and two bands, yet I remained a member of the Baptist Church, which it may be scarce remembered was not inconsistent with Mr. Wesley's first intention for Methodism. This, however, roused the elders and deacons of the Baptist Church. As this was a community that I highly esteemed, yet for the Methodists, it was given up. They appointed persons to reason with me for three months to resign my class papers and to renounce the Methodists. At last I, with other members that had met amongst the Methodists, were summoned before the association, before whom we were called and examined singly. After having stood this trial, we were placed before the Communion Table where the ministers, elders, and deacons sat. And after an examination, ten of us, standing firm, the books were opened and with awful denunciations our names, before the whole congregation, were erased out. My heart being full, I said: "Blessed be God, ye cannot erase my name out of the Lamb's Book of Life. We know whom we worship." The Sacrament [of Holy Communion] was administered, but we were turned to the left and not suffered to partake. But I can truly say I never felt the Lord so present and precious at a sacrament as at that time. For of a truth, He broke to my soul the Bread of Life, and I could then, and I can still say, "Whom man forsakes, Thou wilt not leave; ready the outcasts to receive." This was another sacrifice for the same cause.

With a soul full of joy and sorrow I returned home and found Mr. Asbury, who said, "Now Sister, I will give you the right hand of fellowship." After this, the Rev. Wm. Percy [Baptist pastor in England and] cousin to Earl Percy, then one of the Lady Huntingdon's chaplains, was directed by the Rev'd Mr. Oliver Hart [Mary's Baptist pastor] to persuade my revolt from the Methodists. This I also withstood.

When Philadelphia was besieged by the war, the famine and the plague [1776 and following], I, as some in this kingdom yet know, took my life in my hands and by day and night visited the hospitals and the sick and the dying, whether by wounds or the plague, when often not the nearest friend would approach on account of the infection [yellow fever]. And thus, by attending them in their extremity, I sometimes had the consolation of seeing them die happy. This continued till the Methodist Chapel [St. George's] the soldiers made into a riding school and my house became their chapel. There originated my acquaintance with Capt'n [Samuel] Parker, my present husband, a friend of Mr. Thomas Rankin. When Mr. Parker's ship returned to England [1778], Mr. Rankin and two other preachers then came with us, having a present made of their passage. Thus all the way over we had singing, preaching, and class meetings.

Here I did wrong, and though at that time surrounded with war and bloodshed I should, as Mr. Asbury then did, have stood my ground and not have fled. Then come life or death, it would not have been with me as it is now, destitute and afflicted, without a friend to have compassion on me in this my poverty and old age. I was accompanied to the ship by a number of weeping friends, but where have I now one to feel for me? If I go to the rich to let them know that my poor husband, now above fourscore, is afflicted with fits and has not a bit of bread to eat, they say, "We must try to get you to the poor house." Is not this like a plaster of mustard to a bleeding wound?

At Cork [Ireland] my old friend Mr. Boardman introduced me to Mr. Wesley, with whom and [with other] Methodist preachers we lived on terms of particular intimacy, while in different circumstances. For then my poor husband was a person of property, had a good ship at sea, money in the funds, and his house, his purse, and heart were open to all the preachers and the [Methodist] cause. Mr. Wesley appointed him steward for Gravel Lane Chapel, London, and me a class leader. And so at Scarborough, Yorkshire, where my husband was steward and trustee and myself a leader of two classes. Here also [at Liverpool] and at Newby our house was a welcome and a frequent home for the preachers and their families.

Thus we went on receiving and doing all the good we could for the cause of God till providence took an awful turn. We lost ship after ship till we lost our all and were reduced to poverty. So we continue still grappling with extreme poverty and the infirmities of old age. Unable to do anything to get a bit of bread, all our dependence is on our son, who is now thrown out of business by an old concern. He has not about three publications, nevertheless he would be thankful for a situation if you have a vacancy at the [Methodist] schools, bookroom or elsewhere, to help maintain his poor old father and mother.

Now my dear honored friends, permit a poor old afflicted mother to plead for her only son, the stay and staff of our old age. For the Lord's sake and for his soul's sake, and for our sake if we can encourage him, do and you will not resent it, for he fears God and will be found faithful to the charge committed to him.

I remain in that same sentiment maintained for forty-three years, your truly respectful and attached friend,

Mary [Evans Thorn] Parker

JOHN WESLEY CAUTIONS AMERICAN COLONISTS ON THEIR PLEA FOR INDEPENDENCE

Source: John Wesley, A Calm Address to Our American Colonies *(London: R. Hawes, 1775), 3-5, 13, 17-18.*

BRETHREN AND COUNTRYMEN,

1. The grand question which is now debated, (and with warmth enough at both sides) is this, Has the English Parliament a power to tax the American colonies?

In order to determine this, let us consider the nature of our colonies. An English colony is, a number of persons to whom the King grants a charter, permitting them to settle in some far country as a corporation, enjoying such powers as the charter grants, to be administered in such a manner as the charter prescribes. As a corporation they make laws for themselves: but as a corporation subsisting by a grant from higher authority, to the control of that authority they still continue subject.

Considering this, nothing can be more plain, than that the supreme power in England has a legal right of laying any tax upon them for any end beneficial to the whole empire.

2. But you object, "It is the privilege of a freeman and an Englishman to be taxed only by his own consent. And this consent is given for every man by his representative in parliament. But we have no representatives in parliament. Therefore we ought not to be taxed thereby."

I answer, This argument proves too much. If the parliament cannot tax you because you have no representative therein, for the same reason it can make no laws to bind you. If a freeman cannot be taxed without his own consent, neither can he be punished without it; for whatever holds with regard to taxation, holds with regard to all other laws. Therefore he who denies the English Parliament the power of taxation, denies it the right of making any laws at all. But this power over the colonies you have never disputed; you have always admitted statutes for the punishment of offences, and for the preventing or redressing of inconveniences; and the reception of any law draws after it, by a chain which cannot be broken, the necessity of admitting taxation.

3. But I object to the very foundation of your plea: That "every freeman is governed by laws to which he has consented:" As confidently as it has been asserted, it

is absolutely false. In wide-extended dominions, a very small part of the people are concerned in making laws. This, as all public business, must be done by delegation. . . .

[W]ould a republican government give you more liberty, either religious or civil? By no means. No governments under heaven are so despotic as the republican; no subjects are governed in so arbitrary a manner as those of a commonwealth. . . .

14. Brethren, open your eyes! Come to yourselves! Be no longer the dupes of designing men! I do not mean any of your countrymen in America; I doubt whether any of these are in the secret. The designing men, the Ahithophels, are in England; those who have laid their scheme so deep, and covered it so well, that thousands, who are ripening it, suspect nothing at all of the matter. These well-meaning men, sincerely believing that they are serving their country, exclaim against grievances, which either never existed, or are aggravated above measure, and thereby inflame the people more and more, to the wish of those who are behind the scene. But be not you duped any longer; do not ruin yourselves for them that owe you no good-will, that now employ you only for their own purposes, and in the end will give you no thanks. They love neither England nor America, but play one against the other, in subserviency to their grand design of overturning the English government. Be warned in time; Stand and consider, before it is too late; before you have entailed confusion and misery on your latest posterity. Have pity upon your mother-country! Have pity upon your own! Have pity upon yourselves, upon your children, and upon all that are near and dear to you! Let us not bite and devour one another, lest we be consumed one of another! O let us follow after peace! Let us put away our sins! the real ground of all our calamities! Which never will or can be thoroughly removed, till we fear God and honour the King!

PREACHERS IN THE SOUTH AUTHORIZE ORDINATION

Source: "Minutes of Conference, from the year 1774, to the year 1779 (from minutes kept by Philip Gatch)," Western Christian Advocate 4/5 (26 May 1837): 18-19.

MINUTES OF A CONFERENCE HELD AT ROGER THOMSON'S IN FLUVANNA COUNTY, VA., MAY 18, 1779

Q. 1. What preachers are admitted this year?
   A. Caleb Pedicord
Q. 2. Are there any objections to any of the preachers?
   A. Examine them one by one (which was done).
Q. 3. What numbers are in Society?
   A. As follows:

Hanover	281	Charlotte	186
Frederick	480	[Brunswick]	656
Fairfax	309	Pitsylvania	500
Barkley	191	Roanoke	470
Fluvanna	300	Tarr River	455
Amelia	470	Newhope	542
Sussex	655	Charles City	77
Lunenburg	489	Buckingham	25
Total	6086		

Q. 4. Shall any of the preachers receive quarterage money, who are able to travel and do not travel?
   A. No.
Q. 5. Shall preachers reduced, or broke down by preaching, or sickness, receive any support from the society?
   A. 1st. If they are able to support themselves, they are to receive no support from the Society.
      2. If they are in real want, they are to be assisted.
Q. 6. In what light are we to look on those preachers who receive money for preaching by subscription?
   A. As excluded from Methodist connection.

Q. 7. What is the conference collection? . . .

Q. 8. How was it expended? . . .

Q. 9. What shall the preachers be allowed per quarter?

A. Something equivalent to five pounds, Virginia currency four years ago.

Q. 10. How are the preachers stationed this year? . . .

Q. 11. How are the local preachers and exhorters to be ruled . . . ?

A. Every local preacher and exhorter to go according to the direction of the assistant, where, and only where he shall direct him.

Q. 12. Is any helper to make any alteration, or appoint preaching in the circuit, or in any new place, without consulting the assistant?

A. No.

Q. 13. What directions shall this conference give the several assistants, for the promoting Discipline and order in the several rounds?

A. That the assistants require every local preacher, exhorter, or temporary traveler, to take a note from quarter to quarter; and the assistants and stewards of the societies, and the trustees of the preaching-houses, are to suffer none to preach or exhort without having such a note as aforesaid.

Q. 14. What are our reasons for taking up the administration of the ordinances [sacraments] among us?

A. Because the Episcopal Establishment is now dissolved and therefore in almost all our circuits the members are without the ordinances, we believe it to be our duty.

Q. 16. [i.e., 15] What preachers do approve of this step?

A. Isham Tatum, Henry Willis, Charles Hopkins, Frank Poythress, Nelson Reed, John Sigman, Reuben Ellis, Leroy Cole, Philip Gatch, Carter Cole, Thomas Morris, James Kelly, James Morris, William Moore, James Foster, John Majors, Andrew Yeargin, Samuel Roe.

Q. 16. Is it proper to have a committee?

A. Yes, and by the vote of the preachers.

Q. 17. Who are the committee?

A. Philip Gatch, James Foster, Leroy Cole, and Reuben Ellis.

Q. 18. What powers do the preachers rest in the committee?

A. They do all agree to observe all the resolutions of the said committee, so far as the said committee shall adhere to the Scriptures.

Q. 19. What forms of ordination shall be observed, to authorize any preacher to administer?

A. By that of a presbytery.

Q. 20. How shall the presbytery be appointed?

A. By a majority of the preachers.

Q. 21. Who are the presbytery?

A. Philip Gatch, Reuben Ellis, James Foster, and in case of necessity, Leroy Cole.

Q. 22. What power is vested in the presbytery by this choice?

A. 1st. To administer the ordinances themselves.

2d. To authorize any other preacher or preachers approved of by them, by the form of laying on of hands and of prayer.

Q. 23. What is to be observed as touching the administration of the ordinance, and to whom shall they be administered?

A. To whose who are under our care and Discipline.

Q. 24. Shall we re-baptize any under our Discipline?

A. No.

Q. 25. What mode shall be adopted for the administration of baptism?

A. Either sprinkling or plunging, as the parent or adult shall choose.

Q. 26. What ceremony shall be used in the administration?

A. Let it be according to our Lord's command, Mat. xxviii 19, short and extempore.

Q. 27. Shall the sign of the cross be used?

A. No.

Q. 28. Who shall receive the charge of the child after Baptism, for its future instruction?

A. The parents, or persons who have the care of the child, with advice from the preacher.

Q. 29. What mode shall be adopted for the administration of the Lord's Supper?

A. Kneeling is thought the most proper, but in cases of conscience, may be left to the choice of the communicant.

Q. 30. What ceremony shall be observed in this ordinance?

A. After singing, praying, and exhortation, the preacher delivers the bread, saying, "The body," &c., according to the church order [i.e., words of distribution from the *Book of Common Prayer*].

Q. 31. When and where shall our next conference be?

A. At American town, the second Tuesday in May [1780].

Virginia preachers debate ordination and administering the Sacraments

Source: William Watters, A Short Account of the Christian Experience and Ministereal [sic] Labours of William Watters, Drawn up by Himself (Alexandria, Va.: Printed by S. Snowden, 1806), 79-82.

April 24, 1780, our conference began in Baltimore for those preachers who rejected the administering the ordinances. Two of our brethren from below [from the South], [P.] Gatch and R. Ellis, who had adopted the administering the ordinances, attended to see if any thing could be done to prevent a total disunion, for they did not wish that to be the case. They both thought their brethren were hard with them, and there was little appearance of any thing but an entire separation. They complained that I was the only one who did not join them that treated them with affection and tenderness. Before conference rose [ended], it appointed Mr. Asbury, Garrettson, and myself to attend their conference below [in the South], but as nothing less than their suspending the administering the ordinances, could be the terms of our treaty with them, I awfully feared our visit would be of little consequence. Yet I willingly went down in the name of God—hoping against hope.

We found our brethren as loving and as full of zeal as ever, and as fully determined on persevering in their newly adopted mode [to baptize, and celebrate the Lord's Supper]; for to all their former arguments they now added (what with many was infinitely stronger than all the arguments in the world) that the Lord approbated and greatly blessed his own ordinances [sacraments], by them administered last year. We had a great deal of loving conversation with many tears; but I saw no bitterness, no shyness, no judging each other. We wept, and prayed, and sobbed, but neither would agree to the other's terms. In the mean time I was requested to preach at twelve o'clock. As I had many preachers and professors to hear me, I spoke from the words of Moses to his father-in-law. "We are journeying unto the place of which the Lord said, 'I will give it to you'; come thou with us and we will do thee good, for the Lord hath spoken good concerning Israel."

After waiting two days, and all hopes failing of any accommodation taking place, we had fixed on starting back each morning. But late in the evening, it was proposed by one of their own party in conference (none of the others being present) that there should be a suspension of the ordinances for the present year [1780–81], and that our circumstances should be laid before Mr. Wesley and his advice solicited in the business; also that Mr. Asbury should be requested to ride through the different circuits and superintend the word at large. The proposal in a few minutes took with all but a few. In the morning, instead of coming off in despair of any remedy, we were invited to take our seats again in conference, where with great rejoicing and praises to God, we on both sides, heartily agreed to the above accommodation. I could not but say it is of the Lord's doing, and it is marvellous [*sic*] in our eyes. I knew of nothing upon earth that could have given me more real consolation, and could not but be heartily thankful for the stand I have taken, and the part I had acted during the whole contest. I had, by several leading characters on both sides, been suspected of leaning to the opposite. Could all have agreed to the administering the ordinances I should have had no objection. But until that was the case, I could not view ourselves ripe for so great a change. In a letter I received from Mr.—— in the course of the year, he observed amongst other things, nothing shakes Bro.—— like your letters. You will I hope continue to write and spare not. We now had every reason to believe that every thing would end well, that the evils which had actually attended our partial division, would make us more cautious how we should entertain one thought of taking any step that should have the least tendency to so great an evil. It is an observation that I have seen in some of Mr. Wesley's works. None can so effectually hurt the Methodists as the Methodists. The more I know of Methodism, the more I am confirmed in the correctness of the observation. The Lord make and keep us of one heart and mind.

Thomas Ware hears moving testimony during love feast at a quarterly meeting in New Jersey

Source: Thomas Ware, Sketches of the Life and Travels of Rev. Thomas Ware *(New York: T. Mason and G. Lane, 1839), 62-69.*

Many who seemed to have forgotten that they were accountable creatures, and lived in enmity one with another on account of the part they had taken in the great national quarrel [the Revolutionary War], were brought to follow the advice of St. Paul, "Be ye kind one to another, tender-hearted, forgiving one another, even as God, for Christ's sake, hath forgiven you" [Ephesians 4:32].

Of this I saw a pleasing exhibition in a love-feast, at a quarterly meeting held by our missionary, Mr. George Mair, previous to his taking leave of his spiritual children in the north-west part of East Jersey. I saw there those who had cordially hated lovingly embrace each other, and heard them praise the Lord who had made them one in Christ. The meeting was held in a barn, attended by several preachers, one of whom opened it on Saturday, and great power attended the word; many wept aloud, some for joy, and some for grief; many, filled with amazement, fled, and left room for the preachers to have access to the mourners to pray with and exhort them to believe in the Lord Jesus, which many did, and rejoiced with great joy. Such a meeting I had never seen before.

Next morning we met early for love-feast. All that had obtained peace with God, and all who were seeking it, were invited, and the barn was nearly full. As few present had ever been in a love-feast, Mr. Mair explained to us its nature and design, namely, to take a little bread and water, not as a sacrament, but in token of our Christian love, in imitation of a primitive usage, and then humbly and briefly to declare the great things the Lord had done for them in having had mercy on them.

Mr. James Sterling, of Burlington, West Jersey, was the first who spoke, and the plain and simple narrative of his Christian experience was very affecting to many. After him rose one of the new converts, a Mr. Egbert, and said, "I was standing in my door, and saw a man at a distance, well mounted on horseback, and as he drew near I had thoughts of hailing him, to inquire the news; but he forestalled me by turning into my yard and saying to me, 'Pray, sir, can you tell me the way to heaven?' 'The way to heaven, sir! we all *hope* to get to heaven, and there are *many ways* that men take.' 'Ah! but,' said the stranger, 'I want to know the best way.' 'Alight, sir, if you please; I should like to hear you talk about the way you deem the best. When I was a boy I used to hear my mother talk about the way to heaven, and I am under an impression you must know the way.' He did alight, and I was soon convinced the judgment I had formed of the stranger was true. My doors were opened, and my neighbours invited to come and see and hear a man who could and would, I verily believed, tell us the best way to heaven. And it was not long before myself, my wife, and several of my family, together with many of my neighbours, were well assured we were in the way, for we had peace with God, with one another, and did ardently long and fervently pray for the peace and salvation of all men. 'Tell me, friends,' said he, 'is not this the way to heaven?'

"It is true, many of us were for a time greatly alarmed and troubled. We communed together, and said, It is a doubtful case if God will have mercy on us, and forgive us our sins; and if he does, it must be after we have passed through long and deep repentance. But our missionary, to whom we jointly made known our unbelieving fears, said to us, 'Cheer up, my friends, ye are not far from the kingdom of God. Can any of you be a greater sinner than Saul of Tarsus? and how long did it take him to repent? Three days were all. The Philippian jailer, too, in the same hour in which he was convicted, was baptized, rejoicing in God, with all his house. Come,' said he, 'let us have faith in God, remembering the saying of Christ, *Ye believe in God, believe also in me.* Come, let us go down upon our knees and claim the merit of his death for the remission of sins, and he will do it—look to yourselves, each man, God is here.' Instantly one who was, I thought, the greatest sinner in the house except myself, fell to the floor as one dead, and we thought he was dead; but he was not literally dead, for there he sits with as significant a smile as any one present.' " Here the youth of whom he spoke uttered the word *glory*, with a look and tone of voice that ran through the audience like an electric shock, and for a time interrupted the speaker; but he soon resumed his narrative, by saying, "The preacher bid us not be alarmed—we must all *die* to *live*. Instantly I caught him in my arms and exclaimed, The guilt I *felt*, and the vengeance I *feared*, are gone, and now I know heaven is not far off; but here, and there, and wherever *Jesus* manifests himself, is *heaven*.' " Here his powers of speech failed, and he sat down and wept, and there was not, I think, one dry eye in the barn.

A German spoke next, and if I could tell what he said as told by him, it would be worth a place in any man's memory. But this I cannot do. He, however, spoke to the following import:—"When de preacher did come to mine house, and did say, 'Peace be on dis habitation; I am come, fader, to see if in dese troublesome times I can find any in your parts dat does know de way to dat country where war, sorrow, and crying is no more; and of whom could I inquire so properly as of one to whom God has given many days?' When he did say dis, I was angry, and did try to say to him, Go out of mine house; but I could not speak, but did tremble, and when mine anger was gone I did say, I does fear I does not know de way to dat goodist place, but mine wife does know; sit down, and I will call her. Just den mine wife did come in, and de stranger did say, 'Dis, fader, is, I presume, yourn wife, of whom you say she does know de way to a better country, de way to heaven. Dear woman, will you tell it me?' After mine wife did look at de stranger one minute, she did say, *I do know Jesus*, and is not he de way? De stranger did den fall on his knees and tank God for bringing him to mine house, where dere was one dat did know de way to heaven; he did den pray for me and mine children, dat we might be like mine wife, and all go to heaven togeder. Mine wife did den pray in Dutch, and some of mine children did fall on deir knees, and I did fall on mine, and when she did pray no more de preacher did pray again, and mine oldest daughter did cry so loud.

"From dat time I did seek de Lord, and did fear he would not hear me, for I had made de heart of mine wife so sorry when I did tell her she was mad. But de preacher did show me so many promises dat I did tell mine wife if she would forgive me, and fast and pray wid me all day and all night, I did hope de Lord would forgive me. Dis did please mine wife, but she did say, We must do all in de name of de Lord Jesus. About de middle of de night I did tell mine wife I should not live till morning, mine distress was too great. But she did say, Mine husband, God will not let you die; and just as de day did break, mine heart did break, and tears did run so fast, and I did say, Mine wife, I does now believe mine God will bless me, and she did say, Amen, amen, come, Lord Jesus. Just den mine oldest daughter, who had been praying all night, did come in and did fall on mine neck, and said, O mine fader, Jesus has blessed me. And den joy did come into mine heart, and we have gone on rejoicing in de Lord ever since. Great fear did fall on mine neighbours, and mine barn would not hold all de peoples dat does come to learn de way to heaven." His looks, his tears, and his broken English, kept the people in tears, mingled with smiles, and even laughter, not with lightness, but joy, for they believed every word he said.

After him, one got up and said, For months previous to the coming of Mr. Mairs into their place, he was one of the most wretched of men. He had heard of the Methodists, and the wonderful works done among them, and joined in ascribing it all to the devil. At length a fear fell on him; he thought he should die and be lost. He lost all relish for food, and sleep departed from him. His friends thought him mad; but his own conclusion was, that he was a reprobate, having been brought up a Calvinist; and he was tempted to shoot himself, that he might know the worst. He at length resolved he would hear the Methodists; and when he came, the barn was full; there was, however, room at the door, where he could see the preacher, and hear well. He was soon convinced he was no reprobate, and felt a heart to beg of God to forgive him for ever harbouring a thought that he, the kind Parent of all, had reprobated any of his children. And listening, he at length understood the cause of his wretchedness; it was guilt, from which Jesus came to save us. The people all around him being in tears, and hearing one in the barn cry, Glory to Jesus, hardly knowing what he did, he drew his hat from under his arm, and swinging it over his head, began to huzza with might and main. The preacher saw him and knew he was not in sport, for the tears were flowing down his face, and smiling, said, "Young man, thou art not far from the kingdom of God; but rather say, Hallelujah, the Lord God omnipotent reigneth." Several others spoke, and more would have spoken, had not a general cry arisen when the doors were thrown open that all might come in and see the way that God sometimes works.

JOHN WESLEY ISSUES PASTORAL LETTER TO "OUR BRETHREN IN NORTH-AMERICA"

Source: John Telford, ed. The Letters of the Rev. John Wesley, 9 vols. (London: Epworth Press, 1931), 7:237-38.

BRISTOL, September 10, 1784.

To Dr. COKE, Mr. ASBURY, and our Brethren
in *NORTHAMERICA*.

1. By a very uncommon train of providences, many of the Provinces of *NorthAmerica* are totally disjoined from their Mother-Country, and erected into Independent States. The English Government has no Authority over them either Civil or Ecclesiastical, any more than over the States of *Holland.* A civil Authority is exercised over them, partly by the Congress, partly by the Provincial Assemblies. But no one either exercises or claims any Ecclesiastical Authority at all. In this peculiar Situation some thousands of the inhabitants of these States desire my advice; and in compliance with their desire, I have drawn up a little Sketch.

2. Lord King's *Account of the Primitive Church* convinced me many years ago, That Bishops and Presbyters are the same Order, and consequently have the same right to ordain. For many years I have been importuned from time to time, to exercise this right, by ordaining part of our travelling Preachers. But I have still refused, not only for Peace' sake; but because I was determined, as little as possible to violate the established Order of the national Church to which I belonged.

3. But the case is widely different between England and NorthAmerica. Here there are Bishops who have a legal Jurisdiction. In America there are none, neither any Parish Ministers. So that for some hundred miles together there is none either to baptize or to administer the Lord's supper. Here therefore my scruples are at an end: and I conceive myself at full liberty, as I violate no Order and invade no man's Right, by appointing and sending Labourers into the Harvest.

4. I have accordingly appointed Dr. Coke and Mr. Francis Asbury, to be joint *Superintendents* over our Brethren in NorthAmerica: As also Richard Whatcoat and Thomas Vasey, to act as *Elders* among them, by baptizing and administering the

Lord's Supper. And I have prepared a Liturgy little differing from that of the Church of England (I think, the best constituted national Church in the World) which I advise all the Travelling-Preachers to use, on the Lord's Day, in all their Congregations, reading the Litany only on Wednesdays and Fridays, and praying extempore on all other days. I also advise the Elders to administer the Supper of the Lord on every Lord's Day.

5. If any one will point out, more rational and scriptural way, of feeding and guiding those poor sheep in the wilderness, I will gladly embrace it. At present I cannot see any better method than that I have taken.

6. It has indeed been proposed, to desire the *English* Bishops, to ordain part of our Preachers for *America*. But to this I object. 1. I desire the Bishop of *London*, to ordain only one; but could not prevail: 2. If they consented, we know the Slowness of their proceedings; but the matter admits of no delay. 3. If they would ordain them *now*, they would likewise expect to govern them. And how grievously would this intangle us? As our *American* Brethren are now totally disentangled both from the State, and from the *English* Hierarchy, we dare not intangle them again, either with the one or the other. They are now at full liberty, simply to follow the Scriptures and the Primitive Church. And we judge it best that they should stand fast in that Liberty, wherewith God has so strangely made them free.

JOHN WESLEY.

Bishop Coke details his episcopal mission to North America, describes Christmas Conference in Baltimore

Source: Thomas Coke, "The Journal of Thomas Coke, Bishop of the Methodist-Episcopal Church, from September 18th, 1784, to June 3, 1785," Arminian Magazine *(Philadelphia) 1/6 (June 1789): 237-44, 290-93. Excerpts.*

September 18, 1784. At ten in the morning we sailed from *King-road* [Bristol, England], for *New York*. There was hardly a breeze of wind stirring, but the tide was in our favour. My brethren and myself retired to prayer in the cabin. Almost immediately a breeze sprung up, which carried us with the help of the tides about a hundred leagues from *Bristol* by Monday morning. St. *Austin's* meditations were this day made no small blessing to my soul.

Sunday 19. This day we intended to give two sermons to the ship's company, but all was sickness: we were disabled from doing any thing but casting our care upon GOD.

Wednesday 22. This was to me a night of trial. The storm was high: the sea frequently washed the deck. My thirst was excessive, and all the sailors at work on the deck, except a few that were gone to rest. Sleep had forsaken me, but my trust was truly in the Lord.

Thursday 23. For this and the three former days we lost several leagues, being now nearer *Bristol* considerably than on Monday morning. The storms were high and frequent, and the ship obliged to tack backwards and forwards every four hours between the coasts of *England* and *France*. It appeared doubtful for some time whether we should not be obliged to take refuge in the port of *Brest*. For the five last days my brethren and myself tasted no flesh, nor hardly any kind of meat or drink that would stay upon our stomachs. . . .

Sunday 26. This day we performed divine service both morning and afternoon, and the sailors, except those on immediate duty, attended. A *French* ship came hoisting her colours, and of course expecting the same compliment from ours, whilst I was enforcing the history and example of the trembling jailor converted by *Paul* and *Silas*, which not a little interrupted us. They appeared indeed to give close attention to Mr. *Whatcoat* in the afternoon, whilst he explained to them the wages of sin and the gift of God. But alas! I am ready to despair of our doing them any essential good. O for more faith!

Tuesday 28. For the two last days the winds were contrary, and we hardly gained a league; but now they are again favourable, and we are come about 250 leagues from *Bristol.* The sailors now attend us daily at morning prayer. For these few days past, I have been reading in my study of the life of *David Brainerd* [by Jonathan Edwards]. O that I may follow him as he followed Christ, though in some things, I believe, he ran to great extremes. But his humility, his self-denial, his perseverance, and his flaming zeal for God, were exemplary indeed.

This morning a whale played around our ship for an hour and a half: it was a noble sight indeed. And after him, an innumerable company of porpoises. How manifold are thy works, O GOD!

Friday, October 1. This morning I devoted to fasting and prayer, and found some degree of refreshment, and a sacred longing after more fervency and activity in the service of my God. . . .

Sunday 10. Mr. *Whatcoat* and Mr. *Vasey* preached this day to the sailors, and I expounded in the evening: but, alas! I do not perceive that we reach their hearts; though they now attend morning and evening on the week days.

Friday 15. For many days we had contrary winds till yesterday: but within these two days we have made a considerable progress.

Monday 18. I have now waded through Bishop *Hoadley's* treatises on conformity and episcopacy, 566 pages octavo. He is a powerful reasoner, but is, I doubt, wrong in his premises. However, he is very candid. In one place he allows the truth of St. *Jerome's* account of the presbyters of *Alexandria*, who, as *Jerome* informs us, elected their own bishops for 200 years, from the time of St. *Mark* to the time of *Dionysius.* In another, he makes this grand concession, "I think not an *uninterrupted line* of *succession* of regularly ordained *bishops* necessary." Page 489. In several other places he grants, that there may be cases of necessity, which may *justify* a *Presbyterian* ordination. But he really seems to prove one thing, "That it had been the *universal* practice of the church from the latter end of the lives of the apostles to the time of the reformation, to invest the power of ordination in a church-officer superior to the presbyters, whom the church, soon after the death of the apostles, called *bishop* by way of eminence, but who had no distinct name given him in the New Testament."

Friday 22. This day, being set apart for fasting and prayer, as also Wednesday last, I finished St. *Austin's* [Augustine's] meditations. Certainly he was a good man, however false zeal might sometimes have led him astray, or his *Manichean* principles drawn him into errors after his conversion.

We were now visited by a sparrow, which informed us we were not far from land. She probably came from *Newfoundland.*

My brethren and I spend a couple of hours or thereabouts in reading together in the evenings. The captain and his son and the mate sometimes listen to us with great attention.

The Lord has, I trust, now given us one soul among the sailors; that of *Richard Hare.* His mother lived in *Stepney*, and was a member of our society. I believe, he is in a measure awakened, blessed be God, by our ministry in this ship. . . .

Wednesday, November 3. We are now safely arrived at *New-York*, praised be GOD, after a very agreeable passage. We inquired for the Methodist preaching-house [John Street], and a gentleman, who I afterwards found had no sort of connexion with us, led us to our friend *Sands*, where we make our abode in a most comfortable manner.

I have opened Mr. *Wesley*'s plan to brother *Dickins*, the travelling-preacher stationed at this place, and he highly approves of it, says that all the preachers most earnestly long for such a reformation, and that brother *Asbury*, he is sure, will consent to it. He presses me earnestly to make it public, because, as he most justly argues, Mr. *Wesley* has determined the point, though Mr. *Asbury* is most respectfully to be consulted in respect to every part of the execution of it. By some means or other, the whole continent, as it were, expects me. Mr. *Asbury* himself has *for some time* expected me.

This evening I preached on *the kingdom of GOD within*, to a serious little congregation, the notice being very short. Thursday 4. This morning (at six o'clock, in compliance with the desire of some of our friends) I preached on "As the hart panteth," &c. and had very near as many, I think, as on the evening before.

Friday 5. This morning I enforced on the people the example of the *Rechabites*: last night the necessity of being sealed with the spirit of promise. In the afternoon I set off for *Philadelphia*. Saturday 6. I arrived at *Philadelphia*, and was received most kindly by brother *Baker*, merchant, in *Market-street*. Sunday 7. This day I preached in the morning and afternoon in St. *Paul*'s [Anglican] church, at the desire of Dr. *Magaw*, and in the evening to a large congregation in our own chapel [St. George's], on the necessity of the witness of the Spirit; after preaching, I opened to the society our new plan of church-government: and I have reason to believe, that they all rejoice in it.

Friday 12. I preached at the *Cross-Roads* in the state of *Delaware*, to a simple-hearted people. But there is no morning-preaching. Brother *Whatcoat* had almost as many to hear him in the morning, as I had in the evening. On my journey to this place, we were most sumptuously entertained at an inn *gratis*. The landlady has certainly some love for the people of GOD. Saturday 13. I was most kindly entertained at the house of Mr. *Basset*. The place where he lives, is called *Dover*: he is not in society, but is building us a large chapel. Here I met with an excellent young man *Freeborn Garretson* [*sic*]. It was this young man (though but just come out into the work) who joined himself to Mr. *Asbury*, during the dreadful dispute concerning the ordinances, and bore down all before him. He seems to be all meekness and love, and yet all activity. He makes me quite ashamed, for he invariably rises at four o'clock in the morning, and not only he, but several others of the preachers: and now blushing I brought back my alarm to four o'clock.

Sunday 14. Brother *Whatcoat* had a very good congregation in the court-house at six in the morning. About ten o'clock we arrived at *Barratt*'s chapel, so called from the name of our friend who built it, and who went to heaven a few days ago. In this chapel, in the midst of a forest, I had a noble congregation, to which I endeavoured to display to blessed Redeemer, as our wisdom, righteousness, sanctification, and redemption. After the sermon, a plain, robust man came up to me in the pulpit and kissed me: I thought it could be no other but Mr. *Asbury*, and I was not deceived. I administered the sacrament after preaching, with the aid of brother *Whatcoat*, to, I think, five or six hundred communicants, and afterwards we held a love-feast. It was the best season I ever knew, except one at *Charlemount*, in *Ireland*. After dining in company with eleven of the preachers at our sister *Barret*'s [*sic*], about a mile from the chapel, I privately opened our plan to Mr. *Asbury*. He expressed considerable doubts concerning it, which I rather applaud than otherwise; but informed me that he had received some intimations of my arrival on the continent; and as he thought it probable I might meet him on that day, and might have something of importance to communicate to him from Mr. *Wesley*, he had therefore called together a considerable number of the preachers to form a council; and if they were of opinion that it would be expedient immediately to call a conference, it should be done. They were accordingly called, and after debate, were unanimously of opinion that it would be best immediately to call a conference of all the travelling-preachers on the continent. We therefore sent *Freeborn Garrettson* like an arrow, the whole length of the continent, or of our work, directing him to send messengers to the right and left, and to gather all the preachers together at *Baltimore*, on *Christmas-Eve*. Mr. *Asbury* has also drawn up for me a route of about 800 or a 1000 miles in the mean time, which, GOD willing, I shall punctually fulfil. (He has given me his black *(Harry)* [Hosier] by name and borrowed an excellent horse for me.) I exceedingly reverence Mr. *Asbury:* he has so much simplicity, like a little child; so much wisdom and consideration; so much meekness and love; and under all this, though hardly to be perceived, so much command and authority; that he is exactly qualified for a primitive bishop. He and I have agreed to use our joint endeavours to establish a school or college on the plan of *Kingswood*-school. One of our American preachers (brother *Tunnell*) has been this year at St. *Christopher*'s, in the *West-Indies*, for his health, and the people liked him so well, that they offered him £.150 per ann. a horse, a room, and a slave, if he would stay among them; but he refused. I baptised here about 30 or 40 infants and seven adults. We had indeed a precious time at the baptism of the adults.

I am now convinced that the preachers cannot preach in the mornings early except in the towns which are very thinly scattered. Nay, they can seldom preach in the evenings. The middle of the day, even upon the week-days, is their general time of preaching throughout the whole continent, except in the large towns.

My whole plan, except one day, leads me to preach in the middle of the day; and *then only*, in general.

White's chapel, *Kent-county*, state of *Delaware*, Tuesday 16. I am now at the house of our brother *WC*, who is chief-justice of the court of common pleas, and general steward of the circuit. I preached here to a moderate congregation, and baptized many children. . . .

Thursday 16. We returned this day to brother *Dallam's*, where I preached and administered the Lord's supper to an attentive people.

Friday 17. We now set off for our friend's Mr. Gough [Maryland] His new mansion-house, which he has lately built, is reckoned one of the most elegant in the thirteen states.

Baltimore, Friday, Dec. 24–Jan. 2, 1785: On Christmas-eve we opened our conference: which was continued ten days. I admire the body of American preachers. We had had near sixty of them present. The whole number is 81. The are indeed a body of devoted, disinterested men, but most of them young. The spirit in which they conducted themselves in chusing [*sic*] the elders, was most pleasing. I believe they acted without being at all influenced either by friendship, or resentments, or prejudice, both in chusing and rejecting. One elder was elected for Antigua, Jeremiah Lamburt: two for Nova-Scotia, Freeborn Garretson and James Cromwell: and ten for the states, John Tunnell, John Haggerty, James O'Kelly, Le Roy Cole, William Gill, Nelson Reed, Henry Willis, Reuben Ellis, Richard Ivey, and Beverly Allen. They also elected three deacons, John Dickins, Caleb Boyer, and Ignatius Pigman. Brothers Tunnell, Willis, and Allen, of the elected elders, were not present at the conference; nor brother Boyer of the deacons. The Lord, I think, was peculiarly present whilst I was preaching my two pastoral sermons; the first when I ordained brother Asbury a bishop. The second when we ordained the elders. GOD was indeed pleased to honor me before the people. At six every morning one of the preachers gave the people a sermon; the weather was exceedingly cold, and therefore brother Asbury thought it best to indulge the people: and our morning congregations held out and were good to the last. At noon I preached, except on Sundays and other ordination-days, when the service began at ten o'clock, it generally lasting on those occasions four hours: and the chapel was full every time. At six in the evening, a traveling preacher preached in the Town chapel, another in the Point chapel (a chapel about half a mile out of town), and another in the Dutch church, which the pious minister (Mr. Otterbine [*sic*]) gave us the use of in the evenings during the conference. (Brother Asbury has a so high an opinion of Mr. Otterbine, that we admitted him, at brother Asbury's desire, to lay his hands on brother Asbury with us, on his being ordained bishop.) By this means the congregations were divided: otherwise we should not have had half room enough for the people, who attended in the evening. Our friends in Baltimore were so kind as to put up a large stove, and to back several of the seats, that we might hold our conference comfortably. Before I left the town, I met our principal friends, who promised me to put up a gallery in our Town church (for so we call our preaching-houses now) immediately.

One of the week-days at noon, I made a collection towards assisting our brethren who are going to *Nova-Scotia* and *Antigua,* and our friends generously gave fifty pounds currency (£. 30 sterling).

January, Monday 3, 1785. On this day I left *Baltimore,* and came to our good friend Mr. Gough's, but had the coldest ride I ever rode.

January, Tuesday 4. I rode with several of my brethren to the side of the *Chesapeake-Bay,* but found it so frozen we could not pass. Here an hospitable planter took in four of us, and kindly entertained us.

Wednesday 5. I returned to Abingdon. Brother Dallam had buried his father-in-law that very day, and his house was full of carnal relations, so I stopt at our good brother Toy's the silversmith: however, I preached the funeral sermon in Mr.

Dallam's house and was heard with great attention. I now gave orders that the materials should be got for building the college.

Friday 7. We this day came to one Barton's, a local preacher, formerly a Quaker; he is a precious old man, and loves GOD, I believe, with all his heart.

January 8-19. *Philadelphia.* In this city I find myself perfectly at home. One thing worthy of notice happened here—one of our sisters who belonged to the Dutch-church, was particularly prejudiced against our liturgy, but received whilst I was reading it, one of the greatest manifestations of GOD's love she had ever enjoyed in her life, and went away as much prejudiced in favour of it as she was before against it.

Thursday 20. *Princeton,* State of *Jersey.* I have had the pleasure of Mr. Jones's company from Philadelphia to New-York, where the congress is going to sit. He introduced me this evening to Dr. Smith, a Presbyterian minister, son-in-law to Dr. Witherspoon, a very candid, sensible, and pious man. We lie to-night at his house.

January 22-February 6. *New-York.* We expected that this society would have made the greatest opposition to our plan, but on the contrary they have been the most forward to promote it. They have already put up a reading-desk, and railed in a communion-table, and also purchased a burial-ground. I have united some bands here. The assistant has promised me to continue the morning-preaching faithfully. I have now given over all thoughts of going to the West-Indies, but have taken a ship for brother Lamburt our elder: he is an excellent young man, and will, I trust, be a great blessing in that country. Here I published, at the desire of the conference, my sermons on the Godhead of Christ. Perhaps it was in some measure expedient; as some of our enemies began to whisper that we were enemies to the doctrine of the Trinity, because we left out the Athanasian and Nicene creeds in our liturgy. The general minutes I published in Philadelphia. I took shipping for brother Garretson, to go to Halifax in Nova-Scotia, and left some money for brother Cromwell, who is soon to follow him. Our friends in Philadelphia and New York, *gave* me sixty pounds currency for the missionaries, so that upon the whole I have not been above three or four pounds out of pocket on their account.

February, Monday 7. I left *New-York*; and on Tuesday, February 8, reached *Trenton,* (state of Jersey.) In my way I dined with my kind hospitable friend Dr. Smith, he would have opened his meeting-house to me, if I could have staid [*sic*]. At Trenton I had but a small congregation and about twenty hearers in the morning.

Wednesday 9. I went to *Burlington.* Here the vestry opened to me the church.

HARRY HOSIER RIDES CIRCUITS WITH BISHOP COKE AND FREEBORN GARRETTSON

Source: Thomas Coke, Extracts of the Journals of the Rev. Dr. Coke's Three Visits to America *(London: Printed and sold at the New Chapel, City-Road, 1790), 16, 18, 19.*

Sunday [November] 14 [1784, Frederica, Delaware].—We therefore sent off *Freeborn Garrettson,* lik[e] an arrow, from North to South, directing him to send messengers to the right and left, and to gather all the preachers together at *Baltimore* on Christmas-Eve. Mr. Asbury has also drawn up for me a route of about eight hundred or a thousand miles in the mean-time. He has given me his black (*Harry* by name,) and borrowed an excellent horse for me. . . .

Monday [November] 29 [1784, Worcester City, Pocomoke County, Maryland].— I preached at one *John Purnell's* [Purnall's]. I have now had the pleasure of hearing *Harry* preach several times. I sometimes give notice immediately after preaching, that in a little time *Harry* will preach to the blacks; but the whites always stay to hear him. Sometimes I publish him to preach at candle-light, as the negroes can better attend at that time. I really believe that he is one of the best preachers in the world, there is such an amazing power [that] attends his preaching, though he cannot read; and he is one of the humblest creatures I ever saw.

Monday [December] 6 [1784, Bolingbroke, Maryland]—I had this morning a great escape in crossing a broad ferry. After setting off, *Harry* persuaded me to return back, and leave our horses behind us, to be sent after me the next day, on account of the violence of the wind. I have hardly a doubt but we should have been drowned if we had not taken that step. We were in great danger as it was; and if my heart did not deceive me, I calmly and sincerely prayed that God would take me to himself, if the peculiar work in which I am engaged, was not for his glory.

Source: Freeborn Garrettson, American Methodist Pioneer: The Life and Journals of the Rev. Freeborn Garrettson. *Introduction, biographical essay, and notes by Robert Drew Simpson (Rutland, Vt.: Academy Books, 1983), 266-70.*
Copyright held by Drew University.

Wednesday June 2d, 1790 [New York City]—Having stayed a few days in the city, on Wednesday, . . . accompanied by Harry who is to travel with me this summer, I rode as far as Miles's Square, and preached to more people than could get into the house. . . .

Thursday [Tuesday] June 8th, 1790 [Hudson Valley, New York]—[M]any more came together at brother H.'s than could crowd into the house: we had a joyful season; my own spirit is filled with sweetness. The people of this circuit are amazingly fond of hearing Harry. . . .

Thursday June 10, 1790—[T]hough a wet day, the church at ———— was well filled and I had much pleasure in describing the walk and prosperity of the blessed man, [Psalm 1:1-3], and in the afternoon the old English church was nearly filled. I showed that "He that is born of God doth not commit sin," &c. Harry, though it was a heavy cross, exhorted afterwards. . . .

Saturday [June] 19th—I rode to Mr. Herrick's, where I preached in the afternoon. I had great freedom to preach from "In hell he lifted up his eyes," &c. Harry exhorted after me with much freedom.

Wednesday [June] 23rd—I rode about twelve miles to Litchfield [Connecticut], and was surprised to find the doors of the Episcopal Church open and a large congregation waiting for me. I preached from, "Enoch walked with God," and I believe good was done. I left Harry to preach another sermon and went on to the centre of the town; the bell rang and I preached to a few in the Presbyterian meeting house, and lodged with a kind Churchman. . . .

Tuesday July 1st—[W]e rode through a very pleasant country; I never saw more elegant buildings in a country place than those that surround Cambridge [Massachusetts], and the college [Harvard] has an imposing appearance. I got into Boston, about seven o'clock, after riding forty-eight miles. I boarded Harry at the master Mason for the Africans, and I took my own lodgings with a private gentleman, who had been a Methodist in England, but has, I fear, fallen from the spirit of Methodism. . . .

Sunday [July] 11th, 1790 [Providence, Rhode Island]—With freedom I preached in the morning at six o'clock. I officiated all day for good Mr. Snow, and at six Harry preached in the meeting house to more than one thousand people. I appointed to preach the next morning at five o'clock, and I suppose three hundred people attended to hear my last sermon. I had a sweet time in Providence. I have no doubt but the Lord begun a good work in many hearts. . . .

Sunday [July] 25th—I preached in Canaan [Connecticut] to about five hundred people, from [Matt. 25:14-15], the parable of the talents. The Lord was with us: the work in this place is moving on. I have circulated a subscription for the building of a church here. Brother Bloodgood was with me; as it was too warm in the house I preached in the open air. Harry preached after me with much applause. I rode in the afternoon and preached in Salisbury, in a part of the town in which I had never before preached, and I think I have never seen so tender a meeting in this town before, for a general weeping ran through the assembly, especially while Harry gave an exhortation. The Lord is carrying on a blessed work in this town. . . .

Wednesday July 28th—I had a sweet time at the furnace, and sent on Harry to supply my afternoon's appointment. I rode twelve miles with two disciples, and had an opportunity to see a distressed woman, Mrs. L———n, who has almost lost her reason. . . .

[Thursday] July 29th—I rode to Hudson [New York], where I found the people very curious to hear Harry. I therefore declined preaching that their curiosity might be satisfied. The different denominations heard him with much admiration, and the Quakers thought that as he was unlearned he must preach by immediate inspiration.

FIRST BOOK OF DISCIPLINE PRESCRIBES DUTIES OF MEMBERS AND MINISTERS, SETS GUIDELINES FOR WORSHIP AND PREACHING, AND ESTABLISHES RULES ON SLAVERY

Source: Minutes of Several Conversations Between the Rev. Thomas Coke, LL. D., the Rev. Francis Asbury and others, at a Conference, Begun in Baltimore, in the State of Maryland, on Monday, the 27th of December, in the Year 1784 [*Philadelphia: Charles Cist, 1785*], 3-4, 9-20. *Excerpts.*

Q. 2. What can be done in order to the future Union of the Methodists?

A. During the life of Rev. Mr. Wesley, we acknowledge ourselves his Sons in the Gospel, ready in Matters belonging to Church-Government, to obey his Commands. And we do engage after his Death, to do every Thing that we judge consistent with the Cause of Religion in America and the political Interests of these States, to preserve and promote our Union with the Methodists in Europe.

Q. 3. As the Ecclesiastical as well as Civil Affairs of these United States have passed through a very considerable Change by the Revolution, what Plan of Church-Government shall we hereafter pursue?

A. We will form ourselves into an Episcopal Church under the Direction of Superintendents, Elders, Deacons and Helpers [lay preachers], according to the Forms of Ordination annexed to our Liturgy, and the Form of Discipline set forth in these Minutes.

Q. 4. What may we reasonably believe to be God's Design in raising up the Preachers called Methodists?

A. To reform the Continent, and to spread scriptural Holiness over these Lands. . . .

Q. 16. How shall we prevent improper Persons from insinuating into the Society?

A. 1. Give Tickets to none but those who are recommended by a Leader, with whom they have met at least two Months on Trial.

2. Give Notes to none but those who are recommended by one you know, or till they have met three or four Times in a Class.

3. Give them the [General] Rules the first time they meet.

Q. 17. When shall we admit new Members?

A. In large Towns, admit them into the Bands at the quarterly Love-feast following the Quarterly-Meeting: Into the Society, on the Sunday following the Quarterly-Meeting. Then also read the Names of them that are excluded.

Q. 18. Should we insist on the Rules concerning Dress?

A. By all means. This is no Time to give any Encouragements to Superfluity of Apparel. Therefore give no tickets to any, till they have left off superfluous Ornaments. In order to this, 1. Let every Assistant read the *Thoughts upon Dress* [Wesley's] at least once a Year in every large Society. 2. In visiting the Classes, be very mild, but very strict. 3. Allow no exempt Case, not even of a married Woman. Better one suffer than many. 4. Give no Ticket to any that wear High-Heads, enormous Bonnets, Ruffles, or Rings. . . .

Q. 26. What is the Office of a *Superintendent* [Bishop]?

A. To ordain *Superintendents, Elders,* and *Deacons;* to preside as a Moderator in our Conferences; to fix the Appointments of the Preachers for the several Circuits: and in the Intervals of the Conference, to change, receive or suspend Preachers, as Necessity may require; and to receive Appeals from the Preachers and People, and decide them.

N. B. No Person shall be ordained a *Superintendent, Elder* or *Deacon,* without the Consent of a Majority of the Conference and the Consent and Imposition of Hands of a Superintendent; except in the Instance provided for in the 29th Minute.

Q. 27. To whom is the *Superintendent* amenable for his Conduct?

A. To the Conference: who have Power to expel him for improper Conduct, if they see necessary.

Q. 28. If the *Superintendent* ceases from Travelling at large among the People, shall he still exercise his Office in any Degree?

A. If he ceases from Travelling without the Consent of the Conference, he shall not thereafter exercise any ministerial Function whatsoever in our Church.

Q. 29. If by Death, Expulsion or otherwise there be no Superintendents remaining in our Church, what shall we do?

A. The Conference shall elect a Superintendent, and the Elders or any three of them shall ordain him according to our Liturgy.

Q. 30. What is the Office of an *Elder?*

A. To administer the Sacraments of Baptism and the Lord's Supper, and to perform all the other Rites prescribed by our Liturgy.

Q. 31. What is the Office of *Deacon?*

A. To baptize in the absence of an Elder, to assist the Elder in the Administration of the Lord's Supper, to marry, bury the Dead, and read the Liturgy to the People as prescribed, except what relates to the Administration of the Lord's Supper.

Q. 32. What is the Office of a *Helper* [lay preacher]?

A. 1. To preach.

    2. To meet the Society and Bands weekly.

    3. To visit the Sick.

    4. To meet the Leaders weekly.

Let every Preacher be particularly exact in this, and in Morning-Preaching. If he has twenty Hearers, let him preach.

N. B. We are fully determined never to drop Morning-Preaching, and to preach at five wherever it is practicable. . . .

Q. 41. Are there any Directions to be given concerning the Negroes?

A. Let every Preacher, as often as possible, meet them in Class. And let the Assistant always appoint a proper White Person as their Leader. Let the Assistants also make a regular Return to the Conference, of the Number of Negroes in Society in their respective Circuits. . . .

Q. 42. What Methods can we take to extirpate Slavery?

A. We are deeply conscious of the Impropriety of making new Terms of Communion for a religious Society already established, excepting on the most pressing Occasion: and such we esteem the Practice of holding our Fellow-Creatures in Slavery. We view it as contrary to the Golden Law of God on which hang all Law and the Prophets, and the unalienable Rights of Mankind, as well as every Principle of the Revolution, to hold in the deepest Debasement, in a more abject Slavery than is perhaps to be found in any Part of the World except America, so many Souls that are all capable of the Image of God.

We therefore think it our most bounden Duty, to take immediately some effectual Method to extirpate this Abomination from among us: And for that Purpose we add the following to the Rules of our Society: viz.

1. Every Member of our Society who has Slaves in his Possession, shall within twelve Months after Notice given to him by the Assistant (which Notice the Assistants are required immediately and without any Delay to five in their respective Circuits) legally execute and record an Instrument, whereby he emancipates and sets free every Slave in his Possession who is between the Ages of Forty and Forty-five immediately, or at farthest when they arrive at the Age of Forty-five:

And every Slave who is between the Ages of Twenty-five and Forty immediately, or at farthest at the Expiration of five Years from the Date of the said Instrument:

And every Slave who is between the Ages of Twenty and Twenty-five immediately, or at farthest when they arrive at the Age of Thirty:

And every Slave under the Age of Twenty, as soon as they arrive at the Age of Twenty-five at farthest.

And every Infant born in Slavery after the above-mentioned Rules are complied with, immediately on birth.

2. Every Assistant shall keep a Journal, in which he shall regularly minute down the Names and Ages of all the Slaves belonging to all the Masters in his respective

Circuit, and also the Dates of every Instrument executed and recorded for the Manumission of the Slaves, with the Name of the Court, Book and Folio, in which the said Instruments respectively shall have been recorded: Which Journal shall be handed down in each Circuit to the succeeding Assistants.

3. In Consideration that these Rules form a new Term of Communion, every Person concerned, who will not comply with them, shall have Liberty quietly to withdraw himself from our Society within the twelve Months succeeding the Notice given as aforesaid: Otherwise the Assistant shall exclude him in the Society.

4. No Person so *voluntarily withdrawn,* or so *excluded,* shall ever partake of the Supper of the Lord with the Methodists, till he complies with the above-Requisitions.

5. No Person holding Slaves shall, in future, be admitted into Society or to the Lord's Supper, till he previously complies with these Rules concerning Slavery.

N. B. These Rules are to affect the Members of our Society no further than as they are consistent with the Laws of the States in which they reside.

And respecting our Brethren in *Virginia* that are concerned, and after due Consideration of their peculiar Circumstances, we allow them *two Years* from the Notice given, to consider the Expedience of Compliance or Non-Compliance with these Rules.

Q. 43. What shall be done with those who buy or sell Slaves, or give them away?

A. They are immediately to be expelled: unless they buy them on purpose to free them.

Q. 44. Are there any Directions to be given concerning the Administration of the Lord's Supper?

A. [1.] Let it be recommended to the People to receive it *kneeling:* but let them at the same time be informed that they may receive it either *standing* or *sitting.*

2. Let no Person who is not a Member of the Society, be admitted to the Communion without a Sacrament-Ticket, which Ticket must be changed every Quarter. And we empower the Elder or Assistant, and no others, to deliver these Tickets.

Q. 45. Is there any Direction to be given concerning the Administration of Baptism?

A. Let every adult Person, and Parents of every Child, to be baptized, have their Choice either of *Immersion* or *Sprinkling,* and let the Elder or Deacon conduct himself accordingly.

Q. 46. What shall be done with those who were baptized in their Infancy, but have now Scruples concerning the validity of their Infant-Baptism?

A. Remove their Scruples by *Argument,* if you can; if not, the Office may be performed by Immersion or Sprinkling, as the Person desires.

Q. 47. Shall Persons who continue to attend Divine Service and partake of the Lord's Supper with other Churches, have Liberty at the same time to be Members of our Society?

A. They shall have *full* Liberty, if they comply with our Rules. . . .

Q. 54. What is the best general Method of Preaching?

A. 1. To convince: 2. To offer Christ: 3. To build up: And to do this in some measure in every Sermon.

William Otterbein Prepares Constitution and Rules for Evangelical Reformed Church in Baltimore

Source: Arthur C. Core, Philip William Otterbein: Pastor, Ecumenist (Dayton, Ohio: Board of Publication, Evangelical United Brethren Church, 1968), 109-14.

THE CONSTITUTION AND ORDINANCES OF THE EVANGELICAL REFORMED CHURCH OF BALTIMORE, MARYLAND, 1785

By the undersigned preacher and members which now constitute this church, it is hereby ordained and resolved, that this church, which has been brought together in Baltimore, by the ministration of our present preacher, W. Otterbein, in future, consist in a preacher, three elders, and three deacons, an almoner and church members, and these together shall pass under and by the name—The Evangelical Reformed Church.

2d. No one, whoever he may be, can be preacher or member of this church, whose walk is unchristian and offensive, or who lives in some open sin—(1 Tim. iii: 1-3; 1 Cor. v.: 11-13).

3d. Each church member must attend faithfully the public worship on the Sabbath day, and at all other times.

4th. This church shall yearly solemnly keep two days of humiliation, fasting, and prayer, which shall be designed by the preacher; one in the spring, the other in the autumn of the year.

5th. The members of this church, impressed with the necessity of a constant religious exercise, suffering the word of God richly and daily to dwell among them,—(Col. iii.:16. Heb. iii.: 13;—x: 24, 25)—resolve that each sex shall hold meetings apart, once a week, for which the most suitable day, hour, and place, shall be chosen, for the males as well as the females: for the first, an hour in the evening, and for the last, an hour in the day time, are considered the most suitable. In the absence of the preacher, an elder or deacon shall lead such meetings.

(a) The rules for these special meetings are these: No one can be received into them who is not resolved to flee the wrath to come, and, by faith and repentance, to seek his salvation in Christ, and who is not resolved willingly to obey the disciplinary rules, which are now observed by this church, for good order, and advance in godliness, as well as such as in the future may be added by the preacher and church Vestry; yet, always excepted, that such rules are founded on the WORD OF GOD which is the only unerring guide of faith and practice.

(b) These meetings are to commence and end with singing and prayer; and nothing shall be done but what will tend to build up and advance godliness.

(c) Those who attend these special meetings but indifferently, sickness and absence from home excepted, after being twice or thrice admonished, without manifest amendment, shall exclude themselves from the church (*versammlung*).

(d) Every member of this church (who is the head of a family) should fervently engage in private worship; morning and evening prayer with his family; and himself and his household attend divine worship at all times.

(e) Every member shall sedulously abstain from all backbiting and evil-speaking, of any person, or persons, without exception, and especially of his brethren in the church.—(Rom. xv:1-3; 2 Cor. xii:20; 1 Peter ii:1; Ja. iv:11). The transgressor shall, in the first instance, be admonished privately; but, the second time, he shall be openly rebuked in the classmeeting.

(f) Every one must avoid all worldly and sinful company, and, to the utmost, shun all foolish talking and jesting—(Ps. xv:4; Eph. v:4-11). This offense will meet with severe church censure.

(g) No one shall be permitted to buy or sell on the Sabbath, nor attend to worldly business; not to travel far or near, but each spend the day in quietness and religious exercises—(Isa. lviii:13, 14).

(h) Each member shall willingly attend to any of the private concerns of the church, when required so to do, by the preacher or Vestry; and each one shall strive to lead a quiet and godly life, lest he give offense, and fall into the condemnation of the adversary—(Matt. v:14-16. 1 Pet. 11:12).

6th. Persons expressing a desire to commune with us at the Lord's table, although they have not been members of our church, shall be admitted by the consent of the Vestry, provided that nothing justly can be alleged of their walk in life; and more especially when it is known that they are seeking their salvation. After the preparation sermon, such persons may declare themselves openly before the assembly; also, that they are ready to submit to all wholesome discipline; and thus they are received into the church.

7th. Forasmuch as the difference of people and denominations end in Christ—(Rom. x:12; Col. iii:11)—and availeth nothing in Him but a new creature—(Gal. vi:13-16)—it becomes our duty, according to the gospel, to commune with, and admit to the Lord's table, professors, to whatever order, or sort, of the Christian church they belong.

8th. All persons who may not attend our class-meetings, nor partake of the holy sacrament with us, but attend our public worship, shall be visited, by the preacher, in health and in sickness, and on all suitable occasions. He shall admonish them, baptize their children, attend to their funerals, impart instructions to their youth; and, should they have any children, the Church shall interest herself for their religious education.

9th. The preacher shall make it one of his highest duties to watch over the rising youth, diligently instructing them in the principles of religion, according to the word of God. He should catechise them once a week; and the more mature in years, who have obtained knowledge of the great truths of the gospel, should be impressed with the importance of striving, through divine grace, to become worthy recipients of the holy sacrament. And in view of church membership, such as manifest a desire to this end, should be thoroughly instructed for a time, be examined in the presence of their parents and the Vestry, and, if approved, after the preparation sermon, they should be presented before the church, and admitted.

10th. The church is to establish and maintain a German school, as soon as possible; the Vestry to spare no effort to procure the most competent teachers, and devise such means and rules as will promote the best interests of the school. . . .

12th. No preacher shall stay among us who is not in union with our adopted rules, and order of things, and class-meetings, and who does not diligently observe them.

13th. No preacher can stay among us who teacheth the doctrine of predestination (*Gnadenwahl*) or the impossibility of falling from grace, and who holdeth them as doctrinal points.

14th. No preacher can stay among us who will not, to the best of his ability, CARE for the various churches in Pennsylvania, Maryland, and Virginia, which churches, under the superintendence of William Otterbein, stand in fraternal unity with us.

15th. No preacher can stay among us who shall refuse to sustain, with all diligence, such members as have arisen from this or some other churches, or who may yet arise, as helpers in the work of the Lord, as preachers and as exhorters, and to afford unto them all possible encouragement, so long as their lives shall be according to the gospel.

16th. All the preceding items (*punckte*) shall be presented to the preacher chosen, and his full consent thereto obtained, before he enters on his ministry. . . .

24th. All offenses between members shall be dealt with in strict conformity with the precepts of our Lord—(Matt. xviii:15-18). No one is, therefore, permitted to name the offender, or the offense, except in the order prescribed by our Savior.

25th. No member is allowed to cite his brother before the civil authority, for any cause. All differences shall be laid before the Vestry. . . .

26th. The elders [lay] and deacons [lay] shall meet four times in the year, viz.: the last Sabbath in March, the last Sabbath in June, the last Sabbath in September, and the last Sabbath in December, in the parsonage house, after the afternoon service, to take the affairs of the church into consideration.

27th. This constitution and these ordinances shall be read every New Year's day, before the congregation, in order to keep them in special remembrance, and that they may be carefully observed, and no one plead ignorance of the same.

28th. We, the subscribers, acknowledge the above-written items and particulars, as the ground-work of our church, and we ourselves, as co-members, by our signatures, recognize and solemnly promise religious obedience to the same.

William Otterbein, *Preacher.*

Lehard Herbach, Henry Weitner, Peter Hofman, [Lay] *Elders.*

Philip Bier, William Baker, Abraham Lorsh, [Lay] *Deacons.*

Baltimore, January 1st, 1785.

Elizabeth McKean details membership at St. George's Church, Philadelphia

Source: Elizabeth McKean, "An Extract from the Diary of Elizabeth McKean," The Methodist Magazine (Philadelphia) 1/5 (May 1797): 227-30.

An Extract from the Diary of Elizabeth McKean, *afterwards the Wife of Alexander Cook; who having experienced the Cares of a Family, for several Years, died in the Lord, at Philadelphia, on the 12th Day of April, 1796, and is now at Rest in Abraham's Bosom.*

Monday, October 1st, 1785. My mind was uncomfortable all the morning; but in the evening I felt the Lord's goodness in a wonderful manner: my tongue cannot express the joy that I had, and the love which I felt to God.

Monday, October 8th. I was much cast down all day. This being my class night, I find it a great cross to attend, and yet I dare not stay away; to neglect it, would be acting contrary to my conscience. Thou, O God, knowest the thoughts and intentions of my soul!

Thursday, 11th. When I awoke this morning, my thoughts were drawn out to God in a wonderful manner. I arose and went to prayer, and find great comfort in early rising, and morning devotion. It is not so agreeable to flesh and blood, to rise on a cool morning before it is light; but if I gain spiritual warmth and light to my soul, in the duty, surely it is worth while to take up the cross. In the after-part of the day my mind was drawn after the things of this world. May the Lord give me to see, how vain all things are here below! Without divine assistance, I am weak as helpless infancy.

Sunday, 21st. This morning I made it my earnest prayer to God, that he would enable me to spend the day to his glory. I attended morning preaching, and the word came with power to my heart—the text was, I Peter, ii, 7. *Unto you, therefore, which believe, he is precious.* This day I received the sacrament, with thanksgiving and great joy: the language of my heart was,

> None but Christ to me be given,
> None but Christ in earth or heaven.

Monday, 22d. I felt a deadness in duty, and discovered that all evil tempers were not subdued. The enemy with his fiery darts attacked me. O Lord, give me to see the sinfulness of my heart, and enable me when trials come, to look to thee by faith, in humble love! And, for Jesus' sake, may I see and feel the tempter fly!

Wednesday, 24th. This morning I had power, and experienced great sweetness in private prayer. My mind was much composed through the day—But in the evening Mrs. V——— was on a visit at my mother's, and her conversation rather drew me into such a trifling spirit, that I almost forgot myself. The Lord pity and forgive me.

Monday, 29th. In the evening I enjoyed a peace of mind that the world knows nothing of. And what added to my joy, was, that this evening two of my sisters joined in class with me. What reason I have to be thankful to God, who has answered prayer in behalf of my dear sisters? It gives me more joy than I can express! O Lord, may they and I have true faith and holiness; without which none can see thy face!

Wednesday, 31st. This morning I awoke just as the clock struck five. My mind was filled with thoughts concerning my never-dying soul. O what a merciful God I have, to shew me, in some measure, what I am by nature and what I must be by grace! I continued in contemplation, and when the clock struck six, thought I, another hour is past and gone for ever. O how am I indebted to my great Redeemer and Lord for health and strength, food and raiment; and for tender parents and other comforts: But above all, what obligations I am under to Christ, who suffered and died for me and all mankind. Was there ever love like this! May I take thy yoke, and learn of thee, my Lord; without which, there is no rest to my soul. O God, increase my desires!

Saturday, November 3d. I was rather in a cold, lifeless frame. A lukewarm spirit I find to be an inlet to wrong tempers, and, of consequence, must be hurtful to me, and displeasing to God.

Sunday, November 4th. This morning, before preaching, my soul was greatly drawn out in prayer for faith, which I know to be the gift of God. I think that I had a clearer discovery of my heart, than ever I had before. Blessed be God who gives me to see the sinfulness of my nature, before it was too late. What judgments have I deserved—but what mercies have I received. In private prayer the language of my mind was,

> Thy resurrection's power impart,
> And rise triumphant in my heart.

Saturday, 10th. This morning I attended preaching; but did not find much life in the duty. My brother and I were set out to-day on a visit, which thought so much of, that I almost forgot I was in the presence of God. After returning from preaching, I went to prayer, with an earnest desire that the Lord would put a stop to our journey, if it was not pleasing to him. After breakfast, brother Joseph and I set out for Ann's-Mount. My aunt and cousins received us with great emotions of pleasure. I pray that the Lord may protect me, until I return home, from the dangers of visiting.

> Keep me, keep me, gracious Lord,
> And never let me go.

Monday, 19th. I returned home after an absence of nine days. What a pleasure it gave me to meet my mother and sisters once more. O may we all meet my mother and sisters once more. O may we all meet at last around the throne of God! What inexpressible gladness there, where pain and parting will be no more.

January 1st, 1786. I rose this morning under great indisposition of body; but, through the mercy of God, I went to preaching, and was much comforted under the word. What reason have I to be thankful, that the goodness of God has preserved unworthy *me* to see the beginning of another year. Many have been cut off in the last year, and have entered on their unalterable fate. O Lord, grant that I may for the future so live, in all diligence to make my calling and election sure, that when I am called away, I may go in peace and meet thy saints in glory!

CATHERINE LIVINGSTON NARRATES HER CONVERSION IN EXEMPLARY METHODIST STYLE

Source: Autobiography, 1817. Catherine Livingston Garrettson papers.
United Methodist Archives, Madison, N.J.

In the city [New York] I found many interruptions. I therefore determined to go and spend time with my sister [Gertrude] Lewis, a mile out of the bustling busy town. There I spent a most delightful fortnight in the enjoyment of God and the impartation of His peace, and had a most remarkable answer to prayer. But alas! alas!—Cards went out from my sister Lewis's for a private ball. My particular friends and favorites were asked. Good manners I thought demanded my presence. Other inducement I had none, and I was so ignorant on the subject of my new attainments that I saw not the gulf into which I was about to precipitate myself. That worldly wisdom which brought me into such company obliged me to dance, but it was all dull work. The same carriage that brought my sisters from town to the ball took me back with them to the city house. And thus ended my present journey in the paradise of peace and heavenly mindedness. I was left in darkness, in dullness, in heaviness. I might no doubt have regained my peace had I pursued right methods, but I consulted no one. All was locked up in my own breast. Retirement no longer yielded me peace nor pleasure, and by degrees I forsook it for the world and its polluted enjoyments, and was content with a form of religion, such I mean as passes current in the present day. I could go to public amusements, not a week before but a week after the sacrament with a good conscience. Twice dead. What a mercy that in this awful state the Lord did not cut off the withered branch. . . .

In the summer we retired into the country, and blessed be the Lord He did not leave me to my own ruin. He visited me, and I had many serious reflections. But on my return in the autumn to the city, hurry, fashion, and company spoiled all again—but I was to be brought in only by affliction and humiliation, and they were preparing for me. . . . Another afflictive stroke followed, in the loss of a most dear friend, for whom I had the tenderest affection. Her death was a solemn warning not only to me but the whole city. On Saturday she was well; on Sunday at 2 o'clock I saw her a pale corpse. And the hopes of parents, husband, friends all blasted in a moment. . . . I soon after left New York for Clermont [the Livingston home near Rhinebeck, New York]. . . .

Friday and Saturday, October 11 and 12th, 1787, were two dismal days. I took a retrospective view of my life; it seemed crowded with painful circumstances. My convictions were deep, I felt pained beyond expression. On Saturday night I sat up in the dining room at my brother Chancellor Livingston's till all the house were in bed and asleep. I then in anguish of heart walked softly upstairs, and casting myself on my knees, prayed fervently. My plea was, Lord, thine arm is not shortened that it cannot save, nor thine ear heavy that it will not hear. A gleam of light broke in upon my soul, and a measure of confidence and peace sprung up into my heart. It seemed to be saying to me, lie down and take your rest. I did so. My mind was sweetly composed and I fell asleep and did not awake until morning.

On Sunday October 13, 1787, I arose early with a heart full of expectation, bolted down to breakfast, took a cup of tea and then retired to my room, bolted the door, and opening my prayer-book (for we had then, only preaching [once] in three weeks) I read over the Church Service on my knees with clasped hands and uplifted eyes. I prayed, "By thine agony and bloody sweat; by thy cross and passion, by thy glorious resurrection and ascension, and by the coming of the Holy Ghost." Scarce had I pronounced those words, when I was received and made unspeakably happy. A song of praise and thanksgiving was put in my mouth—my sins were pardoned, my state was changed, my soul was happy. In a transport of joy, I sprang from [my] knees, and happening to see myself as I passed the looking glass, I could not but look with surprise at the change in my countenance. All things were become new.

Philip Bruce reports large numbers of African American converts in Virginia

Source: "An Extract of a Letter from Philip Bruce, Elder of the Methodist Episcopal Church, to Bishop Coke, Dated Portsmouth, Virginia, March 25, 1788," The Arminian Magazine (Philadelphia) 2/11 (November 1790): 563-64.

Reverend and very dear Sir,

'Tis with pleasure I take my pen to write to you, brother, an account of GOD's gracious dealings with us in these parts of the Lord's vineyards; for certainly the work has been extraordinary: vast numbers flocking into the fold of Christ from every quarter. In many places in this circuit, as soon as the preacher begins to speak, the power of GOD appears to be present; which is attended with trembling among the people, and falling down; some lie void of motion or breath, others are in strong convulsions: and thus they continue, till the Lord raises them up, which is attended with emotion of joy and rapture. When one gets happy, it spreads like a flame: so that one after another, they arise to join in the praises of their loving Redeemer.

But the greatest work in many parts of this circuit is among the blacks. In some places it seems as if they would all turn unto the Lord. The following is only a specimen. A few nights past we held a night-meeting for the negroes in the *Isle of Wight* county. Soon after preaching began, there arose a cry among the poor slaves (of which there was a great number present) which in a short time drowned the preaching: a number was on the floor crying for mercy, but soon one and another arose praising GOD. Those who were happy, would surround those who were careless, with such alarming exhortations, as appeared sufficient to soften the hardest hearts. If they could get them to hang down their heads, they would begin to shout and praise GOD, and the others would soon begin to tremble and sink. I saw a number (some who at first appeared to be most stubborn) brought to the floor, and there lie crying till most of them got happy. But the conversion of the poor blacks gives huge offence to the rich and great. I suppose if they dared, they would tear us in pieces: but through the grace of GOD, we regard them not, and had rather offend one half of the world to save the other, than let them all go quietly to hell together. The work has been chiefly carried on, by the instrumentality of brother *Jackson*, in this circuit.

But great as the work is with us, it loses all report; the work above us is so far superior to what it is here, especially in *Sussex* and *Brunswick*. Brother *Cox* informs me, that between twelve and fifteen hundred whites have been converted in his circuit, besides a great number of blacks. Here liberty prevails. A friend informed me that at the *February* court in *Sussex*, the Methodists manumitted above an hundred, at that one court.

Brother *Easter* informs me, that by the best account he can make, there have been two thousand whites converted in his circuit this past year. The work has likewise spread very considerably in other circuits to the Southward and Westward. Great is the joy, great is the glory. Surely *America* will become the mart of nations for piety. I remain your affectionate brother in Christ.

PHILIP BRUCE.

Bishop Asbury makes his episcopal rounds in Maryland and Delaware

Source: Francis Asbury, Journal and Letters of
Francis Asbury (Nashville: Abingdon Press, 1958), 1:612-15.

MARYLAND

Saturday, [November] 7, [1789]. At Annamessex quarterly meeting the Lord was amongst the people on the first day. On *Sunday,* at the love feast, the young were greatly filled, and the power of the most high spread throughout. It appeared as if they would have continued till night if they had not been in some measure forced to stop, that we might have public worship. I stood near the window, and spoke on Isaiah 64:1-5 ["1. O that thou wouldst rent the heavens, that thou wouldst come down, that the mountains might flow down at thy presence. 2. As when the melting fire burneth, the fire causeth the waters to boil, to make thy name known unto thine adversaries, that the nations may tremble at thy presence! 3. When thou didst terrible things which we looked not for, thou camest down, the mountains flowed down at thy presence. 4. For since the beginning of the world, men have not heard, nor perceived by the ear, neither hath the eye seen, O God, besides thee, what he hath prepared for him that waiteth for him. 5. Thou meetest him that rejoiceth and worketh righteousness, those that remember thee in thy ways: behold, thou art wroth; for we have sinned: in those is continuance, and we shall be saved."] There was a stir, and several sinners went away. There were very uncommon circumstances of a supernatural kind said to be observed at this meeting. The *saints of the world* are dreadfully displeased at their work; which, after all, is the best evidence that it is of God.

The preachers urged me to preach at Princess Anne. I did so, and many poor, afflicted people came out. I trust some will be able to say of Christ, "He is altogether lovely!"

I felt uncommon power in preaching at Thomas Garrettson's. Surely the Lord is at work.

At the quarterly meeting I did not speak the first day. The second, I preached on Romans 10:14-15 ["14. How then shall they call on him in whom they have not believed? And how shall they believe in him of whom they have not heard? And how shall they hear without a preacher? 15. And how shall they preach, except they be sent? As it is written, How beautiful are the feet of them that preach the gospel of peace, and bring glad tidings of good things!"] There was a little stir; yet this is said to be the dullest, or one of the dullest places in the peninsula.

DELAWARE

Thursday, [November] 12, [1789] was a warm day, and we had a heavy ride to the Line Chapel. There were but few hearers, owing to the great affliction that prevails. The influenza and other complaints carry off many people; and it is an awful time.

Friday, [November] 13, [1789]. Came to Broad Creek chapel, where some of the wicked had broken the windows. There had been a stir at the quarterly meeting, and a testimony borne against their revellings, and it was judged, that on this account the injury was committed on the house. My throat was sore, and my testimony feeble on 2 Corinthians 6:1. ["1. We, then, as workers together with him, beseech you also that ye receive not the grace of God in vain."] I rode to the head of Nanticoke, where brother Whatcoat preached a warm sermon.

Saturday, [November] 14, [1789]. Preached at Brown's Chapel: the general affliction hindered many from attending: but we were happy together, and it was a strengthening, confirming time to many tired souls.

Sunday, [November] 15, [1789]. The people were shouting the praise of God when I came. After the noise and fervour had subsided, I preached on the men of Nineveh's repenting at the preaching of Jonah [Jonah 3]; and the work sunk into some hearts.

Monday, [November] 16, [1789]. We had a noble shout, and the people rejoiced in the Lord.

Friday, [November] 20, [1789]. Being the day of our quarterly fast, we strove to keep it as well as our feeble bodies would admit.

Saturday and *Sunday,* [November] 21-22, [1789]. There was a shaking among the people; some were alarmed; some professed to be justified, and others sanctified; whilst the wicked brought with them much of the power of Satan. I received some relief for my poor orphans. For some days past I have been kept in an humble, living, holy, conquering frame [of mind].

Monday, [November] 23, [1789]. Although the north-west wind blew very strong, we crossed Choptank River, and came to Bolingbroke. Here we had loud shouts and living testimonies from many of our oldest members, whilst some of our gay young Methodists were mute. Being a day of public thanksgiving, I rode to Wye, where there is a good new chapel. The rain hindered, so that we had but few hearers. Came through the rain to Tuckahoe.

Friday, [November] 27, [1789]. There was a good move [meeting?] at Choptank Bridge. I ordained five persons to the office of deacon.

Saturday, [November] 28, [1789]. Preached with some freedom at Dover.

MARYLAND

Sunday, [November] 29, [1789]. I preached at Duck Creek. Stopped and gave them a discourse at Middletown; and spent the evening with a worthy, kind friend. A number of dear old brethren accompanied me to Cokesbury [College], where we had an examination of the boys, and stationed eleven on charity. Thence we hastened on to Baltimore.

Thursday, December 3, [1789]. Our Council was seated, consisting of the following persons, viz. Richard Ivey, from Georgia; Reuben Ellis, South Carolina; Edward Morris, North Carolina; Philip Bruce, North district of Virginia; James O'Kelly, South district of Virginia; Lemuel Green, Ohio; Nelson Reed, Western Shore of Maryland; Joseph Everett, Eastern Shore of Maryland; John Dickins, Pennsylvania; James O. Cromwell, New Jersey; and Freeborn Garrettson, New York. All our business was done in love and unanimity. The concerns of the college were well attended to, as also the printing business. We formed some resolutions relative to economy and union, and others concerning the funds for the relief of our suffering preachers on the frontiers. We rose [ended our meeting] on the eve of Wednesday following. During our sitting we had preaching every night; some few souls were stirred up, and others converted. The *presence* of some had stilled the noisy ardour of our young people; and it was difficult to re-kindle the fire. I collected about twenty-eight pounds for the poor suffering preachers in the West. We spent one day in speaking our own experiences, and giving an account of the progress and state of the work of God in our several districts; a spirit of union pervades the whole body, producing blessed effects and fruits.

Thursday, [December] 10, [1789]. This and the two following days were spent in writing, and other necessary business. I also preached at town [Lovely Lane Chapel] and [Fells] Point [Strawberry Alley Chapel].

Sunday, December] 13, [1789]. I delivered some alarming truths at our meeting house with some life. I preached at the German Church [William Otterbein's Evangelical Reformed Church] in the afternoon; and in the evening I spoke on "The men of Nineveh shall rise up in judgment against the men of this generation, and condemn it," &c. [Matt. 12:41].

Bishops Coke and Asbury exchange letters with President Washington

Source: Thomas Coke and Francis Asbury, "Address of the Bishops,"
Arminian Magazine (Philadelphia) 1/6 (June 1789): 284-86.

The address of the BISHOPS of the Methodist-Episcopal Church
To the President of the United States.

SIR,—

We, the bishops of the Methodist-Episcopal Church, humbly beg leave, in the name of our society, collectively, in these United States, to express to you the warm feelings of our hearts, and our sincere congratulations on your appointment to the presidentship of these states. We are conscious, from the signal proofs you have already given, that you are a friend of mankind; and under this established idea, place as full a confidence in your wisdom and integrity, for the preservation of those civil and religious liberties which have been transmitted to us by the providence of God, and the glorious revolution, as we believe, ought to be reposed in man.

We have received the most grateful satisfaction, from the humble and entire dependance [*sic*] on the Great Governor of the universe which you have repeatedly expressed, acknowledging him the source of every blessing, and particularly of the most excellent constitution of these states, which is at present the admiration of the world, and may in future become its great examplar for imitation; and hence we enjoy a holy expectation, that you will always prove a faithful and impartial patron of genuine, vital religion,—the grand end of our creation and present probationary existence. And we promise you our fervent prayers to the throne of grace, that God Almighty may endue you with all the graces and gifts of his Holy Spirit, that he may enable you to fill up your important station to his glory, the good of his Church, the happiness and prosperity of the United States, and the welfare of mankind.

Signed in behalf of the Methodist-Episcopal Church,

THOMAS COKE,
FRANCIS ASBURY.

New-York, May 29, 1789.

To which the President was pleased to give the following Answer:
To the Bishops of the Methodist-Episcopal church in the United States of *America*.

Gentlemen,—

I return to you individually, and (through you) to your society collectively in the United States, my thanks for the demonstrations of affection, and the expressions of joy offered in their behalf, on my late appointment. It shall still be my endeavour to manifest the purity of my inclinations for promoting the happiness of mankind; as well as the sincerity of my desires to contribute whatever may be in my power towards the preservation of the civil and religious liberties of the *American* people. In pursuing this line of conduct, I hope, by the assistance of Divine Providence, not altogether to disappoint the confidence which you have been pleased to repose in me.

It always affords me satisfaction, when I find a concurrence in sentiment and practice between all conscientious men, in acknowledgments of homage to the Great Governor of the universe, and in professions of support to a just civil government. After mentioning that I trust the people of every denomination, who demean themselves as good citizens, will have occasion to be convinced, that I shall always strive to prove a faithful and impartial patron of genuine vital religion; I must assure you in particular, that I take in the kindest part the promise you make of presenting your prayers at the throne of grace for me, and that I likewise implore the Divine benediction on yourselves and your religious community.

G. WASHINGTON.

Bishop Coke conducts secret negotiations with Episcopalians

Sources: John Kewley, An Enquiry into the Validity of Methodist Episcopacy, *with an Appendix Containing Two Original Documents Never Before Published (Wilmington: Joseph Jones, 1807), Appendix No. 2.; William White,* Memoirs of the Protestant Episcopal Church in the United States of America *(Philadelphia: S. Potter & Co., 1820), 430-31.*

Richmond, Va.
April 24, 1791

To Bishop William White, Philadelphia

Right Reverend Sir,

Permit me to intrude a little on your time upon a subject of great importance.

You, I believe, are conscious that I was brought up in the Church of England, and have been ordained a Presbyter of that Church. For many years I was prejudiced, even I think to bigotry in favour of it: but through a variety of causes or incidents, to mention which would be tedious and useless, my mind was so exceedingly biased on the other side of the question. In consequence of this, I am not sure but I went further *in the separation* of our Church in America, than Mr. Wesley, from whom I had received my commission, did intend. He did indeed solemnly invest me, *as far as he had a right so to do,* with Episcopal authority, but did not intend, I think, that an entire separation should take place. He, being pressed by our friends on this side of the water for ministers to administer the sacraments to them, (there being very few clergy of the Church of England then in the states), *went farther, I am sure, than he would have gone if he had foreseen some events which followed.* And this I am certain of—*that he is now sorry for the separation.*

But what can be done for a re-union, which I much wish for; and to accomplish which Mr. Wesley, I have no doubt, would use his influence to the utmost? The affection of a very considerable number of the preachers and most of the people, is very strong towards him, notwithstanding *the excessive ill-usage he received from a few.* My interest also is not small; and both his and mine would readily and to the utmost be used to accomplish that (to us) very desirable object; if a readiness were shown by the bishops of the Protestant Episcopal Church to re-unite.

It is even to *your church* an object of great importance. We have now above 60,000 adults in our society in these states, and about 250 travelling ministers and preachers; besides a great number of local preachers, very far exceeding the number of travelling preachers; and some of those local preachers are men of very considerable abilities. But if we number the Methodists as most people number the members of their church, viz. by the families which constantly attend the divine ordinances in their places of worship, they will make a larger body than you possibly conceive. The Society, I believe, may be safely multiplied by five on an average to give us our stated congregations; which will then amount to 300,000. And if the calculation which, I think, some eminent writers have made, be just, that three-fifths of mankind are un-adult (if I may use the expression) at any given period, it will follow that all the families, the adults of which form our congregations in these states, amount to 750,000. About one fifth of these are blacks.

The work now extends in length from Boston to the south of Georgia; and in breadth from the Atlantic to Lake Champlain, Vermont, Albany, Redstone, Holstein, Kentucke, Cumberland, &c.

But there are many hindrances in the way. Can they be removed?

1. Our ordained Ministers will not, ought not, to give up their right of administering the sacraments. I don't think that the generality of them, perhaps none of them, would refuse to submit to a re-ordination, if other hindrances were removed out of the way. I must here observe that between 60 and 70 only out of the two hundred and fifty have been ordained presbyters, and about 60 deacons (only). The presbyters are the choicest of the whole.

2. The other preachers would hardly submit to a re-union, if the possibility of their rising up to ordination depended on the present bishops in America. Because though they are *all* I think I may say, zealous, pious and very useful men, yet they are not acquainted with the learned languages. Besides, they would argue,—If the present bishops would wave [waive] the article of the learned languages, yet their sucessors might not.

My desire of a re-union is so sincere and earnest that these difficulties almost make me tremble: *and yet something must be done before the death of Mr. Wesley, otherwise I shall despair of success:* for though my influence among the Methodists in these states as well as in Europe is, I doubt not, increasing, yet *Mr. Asbury, whose influence is very capital, will not easily comply: nay, I know he will be exceedingly averse to it.*

In Europe, where some steps had been taken, tending to a separation, all is at an end. Mr. Wesley is a determined enemy of it, and I have lately borne an open and successful testimony against it.

Shall I be favoured with a private interview with you in Philadelphia? I shall be there, God willing, on Tuesday the 17th. of May. If this be agreeable, I'll beg of you just to signify it in a note directed to me at Mr. Jacob Baker's, merchant, Market Street, Philadelphia . . . and I will wait upon you with my friend Dr. Magaw. He can then enlarge on these subjects.

I am conscious of it, that secrecy is of great importance in the present state of the business, till the minds of you, your brother bishops, and Mr. Wesley, be circumstantially known. I must therefore beg that these things be confined to yourself and Dr. Magaw, till I have the honour of seeing you.

Thus, you see, I have made a bold venture on your honour and candour, and have opened my whole heart to you on the subject as far as the extent of a small letter will allow me. If you put equal confidence in me, You will find me candid and faithful. . . .

I will intrude no longer at present. One thing only I will claim from your candour—that if you have no thoughts of improving this proposal, you will burn this letter, and take no more notice of it (for it would be a pity to have us entirely alienated from each other, if we cannot write in the manner my ardent wishes desire). But if you will further negotiate the business, I will explain my mind still more fully to you on the probabilities of success.

In the mean time, permit me, with great respect, to subscribe myself,
RIGHT REVEREND SIR,
Your very humble servant in Christ,

THOMAS COKE.

[Bishop White's Reply]

[Philadelphia, late April/early May, 1791]

[To Thomas Coke]

REV. SIR,
My friend, Dr. Magaw, has this day put into my hands your letter of the 24th of April, which I trust, I received with a sense of the importance of the subject and of the answer I am to give to God, for the improvement of every opportunity of building up his church. Accordingly, I cannot but make choice of the earliest of the two ways you point out to inform you, that I shall be very happy in the opportunity of conversing with you at the time proposed.

You mention two difficulties in the way of the proposed union. And there are further difficulties which suggest themselves to my mind. But I can say of the one and of the other, that I do not think them insuperable provided there be a conciliatory disposition on both sides.—So far as I am concerned, I think that such a disposition exists.

It has not been my temper, Sir, to despond in regard to the extension of christianity in this new world: And in addition to the promises of the great head of the church, I have always imagined that I perceived the train of second causes so laid by the good Providence of God, as to be promoting what we believe to be his will in this respect. On the other hand, I feel the weight of most powerful discouragements, in the increasing number of the avowed patrons of infidelity, and of others, who pretend to confess the divine authority of our holy religion while they endeavour to strip it of its characteristic doctrines. In this situation, it is rather to be expected, that distinct churches, agreeing in fundamentals, should make mutual sacrifices for a union, than that any church should divide into two bodies, without a difference being even alleged to exist, in any leading point. For the preventing of this, the measures which you may propose cannot fail of success, unless there be on one side, or on both, a most lamentable deficiency of christian temper. . . .

Therefore, with assurance of the desired secrecy, and with requesting you to accept a like promise of candour to that which I credit from you, I conclude myself at present—

Your Brother in Christ, and very
   Humble servant,

W. W. [William White]

JACOB ALBRIGHT EXPERIENCES RELIGIOUS CONVERSION AND BEGINS TO PREACH

Source: George Miller, The Life of Jacob Albright, translated and edited by James D. Nelson (Dayton: The Center for the Study of Evangelical United Brethren History, 1985), 17-31. First published in German in Reading, Pennsylvania, in 1811. Excerpts.

[As a young man] I wandered carelessly on the path of life, was joyful with those who were joyful, and thought little of the purpose of human existence. I did not heed the duties of a human being, much less of a Christian. I lived as if this brief time would last forever and committed many sins for which God has promised a severe punishment. . . .

I was horrified with myself. God's judgments stood before my imagination. My spirit felt deep depression which no external stimulation of the senses could dispel. The feeling of my unworthiness increased day by day until at last in my thirty-second year [1791], on a particular day in the month of July, it had risen to such a state that it bordered on despair. I felt myself so small, and my sins so great that I could not comprehend how the righteous Judge who judges on the basis of merit would not be forced to dash me into the abyss of damnation. My heart's anxiety increased with every moment, so that I could have cried out, "Ye mountains fall upon me and ye hills cover me" [Rev. 6:15-17]. I thought, oh, if only I had my life to live again, . . . how entirely differently would I organize my behavior!

This incessant and warm supplication at last brought me nearer and nearer to my enlightenment. I felt the power to consecrate myself to the good and to surrender my will entirely to God's will. I heard the voice of comfort in my inner self [Rom. 7:22], for I learned to comprehend and became convinced that since God does not desire the destruction of the sinner [1 Tim. 1:15]—but that he be converted and live—he would regard my honest remorse, repentance and contrition of my heart with gracious eyes; and that the merit of my Redeemer, of his bitter suffering and death, would fulfill the task.

I now constantly continued steadfastly and fervently to entreat the grace of God, to plead for the assistance of His Spirit, that He gave to me the power to battle against sin and at last to gain the victory [Rom. 6:8]. I watched scrupulously over every one of my actions, over each thought, over every impression made upon my heart by any sort of outward matter. Through this incessant striving, I finally managed to release myself entirely from the way of the flesh and to look only to that which is above [Eph. 2:1-6]. Into the place of all sensuality there stepped a holy love toward God, toward His Word and toward all true children of God. Little by little all the dread and anxiety of my heart disappeared; comfort and blessed peace in God inspired my breast. God gave witness to my spirit that I had become a child of God [Rom. 8:16; Gal. 4:6]. One glad sensation after another and such blessed joy coursed through my innermost self as no human pen can describe, nor the mouth of a mortal express. In contrast to this, all the fullness of earthly joys, which I had theretofore enjoyed, even unto the highest order of the same, were merely wretchedness and miserable deception [Phil. 3:7]. Now my prayer was no longer a mere supplication. Praise and hearty thanks, accompanied by tears of joy, were also brought as sacrifice to the Giver of all that is good.

No longer was the practice of good a burdensome business to me. I was now inclined to hate sin and every evil. It was my joy to serve God and I had a sense of blessedness when I could converse with my God in prayer. . . .

Since I had now attained the grace of justification [Rom. 5:1-6], I soon perceived that the easiest and surest way to progress in clearing the path for salvation of one's soul and to be always ready to fight a good fight [2 Tim. 4:7] would be to take one's part in the cross [Gal. 6:14] in community with other pious Christians, to pray and to watch with and for each other, and to edify one another through an instructive example in the service of God [1 Cor. 12-14].

There was at that time no class of Christian confessors known to me that seemed to me more lively and active in the good and whose excellent discipline and order pleased me better than the Methodists. Therefore I adhered especially to them and received among them occasion to obtain great blessing and profit for my soul. At that time much about their practices still remained obscure to me because they were then conducted in the English language, and I was not all that well versed in that. So I applied myself diligently to learning it, and soon progressed far enough that I could acquaint myself with the articles of their faith-teaching and their disciplinary order. I was greatly pleased with these. I scrupulously governed myself in accordance with their prescriptions and arranged my service of God accordingly. I sought to persevere in restraint and practiced much in fasting and prayer [1 Cor. 7:5], which I always found the best means in times of trial. I then had heavy and hard temptations and inner trials, and since I did not know whether I could or dared accept the counsel of others, I held constantly and persistently to prayer, which always helped me to overcome. Yet I must confess that often pious and true servants of God, through their well-intended admonition and faithful counsel, which were founded on grace and experience, were likewise a support for me to lean on.

In this way I became ever more practiced in the knowledge of God. Through battle in testings and victory which the grace of the Lord granted me, my faith and commitment to goodness grew more steadfast. And through steadfast and fervent prayer I constantly gained a greater trust. Through all this my joy in God grew from day to day and I obtained power to pray forcefully in the public meetings, this to my own edification and that of others. In this I continually gained more and more strength, and upon the request of my fellow Christians I now and then delivered an exhortation which did not remain fruitless. By nature I had no gift for speaking at all and must freely confess that I was less suited for it than anyone else who might have stood up. But when I felt myself transported by the Spirit of God, when prayer had brought my soul closer to my Redeemer, when I was on fire with abhorrence toward sin, when the righteousness of a severely testing Judge stood before my eyes and I at the same time also felt His overwhelming love toward His fallen creatures, then I was grasped by an inspiration that unlatched my mouth so that eloquence streamed from my lips and God's grace worked through my words to the conversion of fallen and unconverted Christians and to the edification of the faithful [1 Cor. 14:26].

Thus I spent some years in the state of grace. I served the Lord with gladness and felt his blessing in the attainment of the knowledge of His Being; a fervent inward love dwelt in my breast toward my Creator, toward the true children of God and toward my fellow humans in general. Through this love, which poured the peace with God into my soul [Rom. 5:1], it then also came about that I saw in what great ruin true Christianity was with the German nation in America. This affected me very deeply. I recognized in all persons, even in the fallen, the creative hand of the Almighty. I saw in them my brethren, and my love wished them to be just as happy as myself. In this mood I often flung myself upon my knees and pled with hot tears that the Lord might yet lead all my German brethren on the way of knowledge and bring them to the knowledge of truth [1 Tim. 2:4], that He would present them good examples and give them true teachers who proclaim the Gospel in its power [Rom. 1:16-17; 1 Thess. 1:5] among them, in order to awaken the dead and drowsy Christians among them out of their sleep of sin [1 Thess. 5:5-7] and to bring them once more to the true life in godliness, wherewith they also may become partakers in the blessed peace with God and of the communion of the saints. . . .

I thought, "I am an entirely uneducated and incapable person. How many men of greater gifts and learning there are who would be better instruments for this than I, and who have more authority and possess more impressiveness." With such reflections my courage often failed me, and then I most fervently prayed to God that He might after all give this commission to another who would be more able and more worthy of it than I, the incompetent one. To such objections, however, the voice of my conscience persistently answered me, that on my part I must merely trustfully obey without scrupling; God's grace would do the rest. It equips those whom He has selected as the instruments of His all encompassing love with power from on high [Acts 1:8] and lends blessing and prosperity to their undertakings. . . .

In this chastisement I now saw more than ever the finger of God [Luke 11:20], and learned with the uttermost conviction that a person can do no better thing than to surrender entirely to the will of his Creator and to obediently follow His calling, neither looking forward nor backward. Even as miserable as my condition was, the Lord still had such unmerited compassion for me that He maintained me in the state of grace. I therefore constantly persisted in prayer, humbled myself before His throne [Revelation 4 and 5], pled with hot tears for pardon and promised most solemnly, and fixed the firm resolve that if I should become well once more, I would follow His call—and that at once—by preaching throughout the country, proclaiming His Gospel everywhere. He might send me wherever it pleased Him if only He would be with me [Matt. 28:18-20].

As soon as this firm decision was established in my heart, it was as if a heavy burden rolled from my soul. I felt an utter relief and peace in my breast once more restored with my own self. Just as the repose of my soul was restored, so also the pain of my body soon disappeared. My powers soon returned, new life permeated my members, and in a short time I was entirely restored.

As soon as this had taken place I immediately readied myself to travel and prepared myself in such a way as I regarded appropriate. Qualification to proclaim the Gospel I sought only from the Lord, in incessant prayer and in searching in His revealed Word. I also sought to consecrate my body entirely to the service of the Lord, and so to prepare it that no passion, desire, nor love of comfort might limit or hinder my career. . . .

In possession of such grace, which was a gift of the Lord, equipped with the power of His righteousness and holiness, sealed with His Spirit [Eph. 1:13-14], in love, faith, and hope [1 Cor. 13:13], I set out on the itinerant ministry in the year 1796, in the month of October, in order to obey the call of God in the revelation of His holy will through the Gospel.

I travelled through a large part of Pennsylvania and Virginia, and the Lord so lent me His blessing that I was welcomed so that I was able to preach in churches, schoolhouses, and private houses. I also received here and there some support, so that I could continue to travel, for my ministry through the Gospel was fruitful [John 15:1-8] so that through it many sinners were awakened and converted to God.

Since I had preached for about four years and had especially devoted myself to proclaiming the Gospel at those places where the life from God and Christian order and discipline were yet unknown, I also sought through grace that had come down to me from on high [Acts 1:8] to give appropriate direction to the awakened and converted souls as to how they might work out their souls' salvation [Phil. 2:12] in communal practice, and in the unity of faith edify themselves according to the precept of Christ and His Apostles. And God so granted His blessing to this, my undertaking, that through the aid and assistance of this communal unification among one another the light of truth arose for many souls that had before lived in darkness and ignorance [John 1:5; 1 Thess. 5:5]. And God, my Helper and Supporter, also strengthened my heart and understanding with His grace so that I not only preached a pure doctrine to the souls that He had entrusted to me, but I sought to confirm them through my mode of life.

ELIZABETH SINGER ROWE'S DEVOTIONAL CLASSIC TEACHES METHODIST WOMEN TO PRAY FOR SANCTIFICATION

Source: Elizabeth Singer Rowe, Devout Exercises of the Heart, in Meditation and Soliloquy, Prayer and Praise. *Abridged for the use of the Methodist Society (Philadelphia: Printed by Parry Hall and sold by John Dickins, 1791), 160-65.*

XXV. A PRAYER FOR SPEEDY SANCTIFICATION

O LORD GOD, great and holy, all-sufficient, and full of grace, if thou shouldst bid me form a wish, and take whatsoever in heaven or earth I had to ask, it should not be the kingdoms of this world, nor the crowns of princes; no, nor should it be the wreaths of martyrs, nor the thrones of archangels: my request is to be made holy: this is my highest concern. Rectify the disorders sin has made in my soul, and renew thy image there; let me be satisfied with thy likeness. Thou hast encompassed my paths with mercy in all other respects, and I am discontented with nothing but my own heart, because it is so unlike the image of thy holiness, and so unfit for thy immediate presence.

Permit me to be importunate here, O blessed God, and grant the importunity of my wishes; let me be favoured with a gracious and speedy answer, for I am dying while I am speaking[.] [T]he very breath with which I am calling upon thee is carrying away part of my life: this tongue that is now invoking thee must shortly be silent in the grave; these knees that are bent to pay thee homage, and these hands that are now lifted to the most high God for mercy, must shortly be mouldering to their original dust: these eyes will soon be closed in death, which are now looking up to thy throne for a blessing. Oh! prevent [anticipate] the flying hours with thy mercy, and let thy favour outstrip the hasty moments.

Thou art unchanged, while rolling ages pass along; but I am decaying with every breath I draw[.] [M]y whole allotted time to prepare for heaven is but a point, compared with thy infinite duration. The shortness and vanity of my present being, and the importance of my eternal concerns, join together to demand my utmost solicitude, and give wings to my warmest wishes. Before I can utter all my present desires, the hasty opportunity perhaps is gone, the golden minute vanished and the season of mercy has taken its everlasting flight.

Oh God of ages! hear me speedily, and grant my request while I am yet speaking.

My frail existence will admit of no delay; answer me according to the shortness of my duration, and the exigence of my circumstances. My business, of high importance as it is, yet is limited to the present now, the passing moment; for all the powers on earth cannot promise me the next.

Let not my pressing importunity, therefore, offend thee[.] [M]y happiness, my everlasting happiness, my whole being is concerned in my success, as much as the enjoyment of God himself is worth, is at stake.

Thou knowest, O Lord, what qualifications will fit me to hold thee; thou knowest in what I am defective; thou canst prepare my soul in an instant to enter into thy holy habitation. I breathe now, but the next morning may be death: let not that fatal moment come before I am prepared. The same creating voice that said, "Let there be light, and there was light," can, in the same manner, purify and adorn my soul, and make me fit for thy own presence; and my soul longs to be thus purified and adorned. O Lord, delay not, for every moment's interval is a loss to me, and may be a loss unspeakable and unrepairable. Thy delay cannot be the least advantage to thee; thy power and thy clemency are as full this present instant as they will be the next, and my time as fleeting, and my wants as pressing.

Remember, O eternal God, my lost time is for ever lost, and my wasted hours will never return[.] [M]y neglected opportunities can never be recalled; to me they are gone for ever, and cannot be improved; but thou canst change my sinful soul into holiness by a word, and set me now in the way to everlasting improvement.

O let not the Spirit of God restrain itself, but bless me according to the fullness of thy own being, according to the riches of thy grace in Christ Jesus, according to thy infinite inconceivable love manifested in that glorious gift of thy beloved Son, wherein the fullness of thy Godhead was contained; it is through his merit and mediation I humbly wait for all the unbounded blessings I want or ask for.

JAMES O'KELLY PROTESTS APPOINTIVE POWER OF BISHOPS

Source: James O'Kelly, The Author's Apology for Protesting *Against the Methodist Episcopal Government.* Published by the author. *(Richmond: John Dixon, 1798), 1:32-39. Excerpts.*

ADVERTISEMENT.

If Christians are free citizens of Zion, they should prize those liberties, seeing they were purchased with the precious blood of Christ.

By adding reproaches to oppression, can never tend to heal a distressed mind.

If my narrative is thought destitute of merit, I can give no preface that can possibly grace it.

The Author.

[First General Conference of Methodist Episcopal Church, Baltimore, November 1-15, 1792, Thomas Coke, Presiding]

CHAP. XIII.

6 And it came to pass on the morrow, that conference met persuant [*sic*] to adjournment [Friday, November 2].

7 Then arose Thomas [Coke], the president, and reported to conference the resolves of the committee, &c.

8 Moreover, Thomas continued his speech and said, "The members of this conference are the representatives of the people;

9 "And we are to all *intents* the *legislature* of the Methodist Episcopal Church: and the government is *Aristocratical.* You may call me a weather-cock."

10 This speech effected many minds, because they justly expected the affairs of the council to have come before them; *that* being the business for which they were called together.

11 Some of the members at sundry times would interrogate the president, after this manner;

12 But where is the council affairs, &c? That being the cause of this meeting.

13 Thomas would arise and warmly oppose, and demand silence on the subject: And silence it was.

14 In our debates, if at any time we were led to speak of the conduct of Francis [Asbury], he would leave the house.

15 The debates of the synod turned chiefly on episcopal dignity.

16 The Virginians, for a while did distinguish themselves in defending their ecclesiastical *liberties*, but they fainted in the struggle.

17 Richard Ivey, exceeded himself, he spake with tears, and in the fear of God, and much to the purpose; crying popery, &c.

18 If at any time a minister would move to abridge (in any degree) the bishop's power,

19 The defenders of that faith, would not oppose the motion, but would charge the member with something like treason, as it were.

20 We still complained heavily of such illegal and radical alterations. Their cry was, "Every general conference is possessed of a right to form their own preliminaries."

21 Thus we see, the government is subject to perpetual innovations.

CHAP. XIV.

The same continued.

It would have been an unspeakable blessing to the Methodist church, if we had been allowed to have done the business for which we met;

2 Because it would have necessarily led us into the very merit of the cause, or a full investigation of church government.

3 I began to see that equity and gospel simplicity would be obliged to retreat, for power and policy would overcome the minority.

4 I feared the ministers were carried away by an adventurous leader.

5 I then arose, and stood before the assembly with the New Testament of our Lord Jesus, in my hand,

6 And spake after this manner; Brethren, hearken unto me, put away all other books, and forms, and let this be the only *criterion*, and "that will satisfy me."

7 I thought the ministers of Christ, would unanimously agree to such a proposal. But alas, they opposed the motion!

8 A certain member whose name was John [Dickins], withstood me, and spake after this manner; The scripture is by no means a sufficient form of government. . . .

9 "The Lord has left that business for his ministers to do, Suitable to times and places," &c. I withstood him for a season, but in vain; the motion was lost.

10 I now saw, that moderate Episcopacy was rising to its wanted and intended dignity. I discovered also, that districts had lost their suffrage.

11 I considered that the stations of the Lord's ministers rested entirely with Francis [Asbury]; so, that unless that absolute power could be abridged, the best of men might ever be injured, and run out of the connection.

12 I now moved again, after this manner; Let a preacher who thinks himself injured in his appointment, have an appeal to the district conference.

13 The motion was seconded, and warmly debated. William McKendree, with several more, did, with holy zeal strive with me for liberty.

14 Conference adjourned until the second day of the next week [Monday, November 5]: at which time they reassumed the debate with double vigour.

15 Some professed fears, that if an appeal was allowed, it would reflect on the wisdom, and goodness of the bishop, &c.

16 Others saw, or thought they saw, that such liberty would be injurious to the church, because preachers would ever be appealing;

17 And they would take each others' part; so that easy and wealthy circuits, would be crowded with preachers, while poor circuits would be left desolate.

18 Heavy reflections on the conference; had any other people said as much, it would have been thought hard persecution. Was this ignorance, or policy?

19 It was urged by several, that the bishop always appointed well, as far as they knew. I prayed them not to arrogate infallibility to the bishop:

20 For in my judgment, he made many injudicious appointments.

CHAP. XV.

Same subject continued. . . .

15 The debates were more powerful than ever, yet with a deal of Christian moderation. I was entirely silent.

16 Hope Hull, a worthy Elder, sounded a proper alarm! He exceeded himself by far: I could wish his words were written in a book.

17 He spake after this manner; O Heavens! Are we not Americans! Did not our fathers bleed to free their sons from the British yoke? and shall we be slaves to ecclesiastical oppression?

18 He lift up his voice, and cried, "What no appeal for an injured brother? Are these things so? Am I in my senses?"

19 Henry [Willis] arose, and displayed his political abilities, exclaiming against a balance of power; with an essay on church history.

20 Stephen Davis, in whom was the spirit of wisdom, withstood the celebrated Henry, assuring of us, that the last arguments were badly founded. "We are far gone into POPERY!"

21 Quickly after this, the votes were taken; ah fatal hour, the motion was lost; and out of an hundred, and more, we had a small minority.

22 Some withdrew from that hour, resolving to enjoy their liberties at the expense of society: and hold fast faith, and a good conscience.

23 Will not these words cause the ears of an American to tingle. "Shall an injured man have no appeal? No!"

CHAP. XVI.

Some left conference, and no more returned—Their distress of Soul—A committee sent, &c.

It was surely a very fatal hour of papal darkness, in which a law passed, that an injured brother and minister in the church of Christ, should have no redress! . . .

6 I spent great part of that night in groans and tears! On the morrow I implored the God of heaven to give me understanding. I consulted my friends, and in the fear of God, resolved not to return to conference. . . .

RICHARD ALLEN LEADS BLACK METHODISTS OUT OF ST. GEORGE'S CHURCH, PHILADELPHIA

Source: The Life Experience and Gospel Labors of the
Rt. Rev. Richard Allen *(Nashville: Abingdon Press, 1960), 15-35.
First published in Philadelphia in 1833. Excerpts.*

I was born in the year of our Lord 1760, on February 14th, a slave to Benjamin Chew, of Philadelphia. My mother and father and four children of us were sold into Delaware state, near Dover; and I was a child and lived with him until I was upwards of twenty years of age, during which time I was awakened and brought to see myself, poor, wretched and undone, and without the mercy of God must be lost. . . . I joined the Methodist Society and met in class at Benjamin Wells's, in the forest, Delaware state. John Gray was the class leader. I met in his class for several years.

My master was an unconverted man, and all the family, but he was what the world called a good master. He was more like a father to his slaves than anything else. . . . At length, our master said he was convinced that religion made slaves better and not worse, and often boasted of his slaves for their honesty and industry. Some time after, I asked him if I might ask the preachers to come and preach at his house. He being old and infirm, my master and mistress cheerfully agreed for me to ask some of the Methodist preachers to come and preach at his house. . . . Preaching continued for some months; at length, Freeborn Garrettson preached from these words, "Thou art weighed in the balance, and art found wanting." In pointing out and weighing the different characters, and among the rest weighed the slaveholders, my master believed himself to be one of that number, and after that he could not be satisfied to hold slaves, believing it to be wrong. And after that he proposed to me and my brother buying our times, to pay him 60£. gold and silver, or $2000, Continental money, which we complied with in the year 17————. . . .

I was after this employed in driving of wagon in time of the Continental war, in drawing salt from Rehoboth, Sussex County, in Delaware. I had my regular stops and preaching places in the road. I enjoyed many happy seasons in meditation and prayer while in this employment.

After peace was proclaimed, I then travelled extensively, striving to preach the Gospel. My lot was cast in Wilmington. Shortly after, I was taken sick with the fall fever and then the pleurisy. September the 3rd 1783, I left my native place. After leaving Wilmington, I went into New Jersey, and there travelled and strove to preach the Gospel until the spring of 1784. I then became acquainted with Benjamin Abbott, that great and good apostle. He was one of the greatest men that ever I was acquainted with. He seldom preached but what there were souls added to his labor. He was a man of as great faith as any that ever I saw. The Lord was with him, and blessed his labors abundantly. He was a friend and father to me. I was sorry when I had to leave West Jersey, knowing that I had to leave a father. . . .

December 1784, General Conference sat in Baltimore, the first General Conference ever held in America. The English preachers just arrived from Europe were, Rev. Dr. Coke, Richard Whatcoat and Thomas Vassey. This was the beginning of the Episcopal Church amongst the Methodists. Many of the ministers were set apart in holy orders at this conference, and were said to be entitled to the gown; and I have thought religion has been declining in the church ever since. There was a pamphlet published by some person, which stated, that when the Methodists were no people, then they were a people; and now they have become a people they were no people; which had often serious weight upon my mind.

In 1785 the Rev. Richard Whatcoat was appointed on Baltimore circuit. He was, I believe, a man of God. I found great strength in travelling with him—a father in Israel. In his advice he was fatherly and friendly. He was of a mild and serene disposition. My lot was cast in Baltimore, in a small meeting-house called Methodist Alley. I stopped at Richard Mould's, and was sent to my lodgings, and lodged at Mr. McCannon's. I had some happy meetings in Baltimore. I was introduced to Richard Russell, who was very kind and affectionate to me, and attended several meetings. Rev. Bishop Asbury sent for me to meet him at Henry Gaff's. I did so. He told me he wished me to travel with him. He told me that in the slave countries, Carolina and other places, I must not intermix with the slaves, and I would frequently have to sleep in his carriage, and he would allow me my victuals and clothes. I told him I would not travel with him on these conditions. He asked me my reason. I told him if I was taken sick, who was to support me? and that I thought people ought to lay up something while they were able, to support themselves in time of sickness or old age. He said that was as much as he got, his victuals and clothes. I told him he would be taken care of, let his afflictions be as they were, or let him be taken sick where he would, he would be taken care of; but I doubted whether it would be the case with myself. . . . I travelled several months on Lancaster circuit with the Rev. Peter Morratte and Irie Ellis. They were very kind and affectionate to me in building me up; for I had many trials to pass through, and I received nothing from the Methodist connection. My usual method was, when I would get bare of clothes, to stop travelling and go to work, so that no man could say I was chargeable to the connection. My hands administered to my necessities. . . . The elder in charge in Philadelphia frequently sent for me to come to the city. . . . My labor was much blessed. I soon saw a large field open in seeking and instructing my African brethren, who had been a long forgotten people and few of them attended public worship. I preached in the commons, in Southwark, Northern Liberties, and wherever I could find an opening. I frequently preached twice a day, at 5 o'clock in the

117

morning and in the evening, and it was not uncommon for me to preach from four to five times a day. I established prayer meetings; I raised a society in 1786 for forty-two members. I saw the necessity of erecting a place of worship for the colored people. I proposed it to the most respectable people of color in this city; but here I met with opposition. I had but three colored brethren that united with me in erecting a place of worship—the Rev. Absalom Jones, William White and Dorus Ginnings. These united with me as soon as it became public and known by the elder who was stationed in the city. The Rev. C——— B——— opposed the plan, and would not submit to any argument we could raise; but he was shortly removed from the charge. The Rev. Mr. W——— took the charge, and the Rev. L——— G———. Mr. W——— was much opposed to an African church, and used very degrading and insulting language to us, to try and prevent us from going on. We all belonged to St. George's church———Rev. Absalom Jones, William White and Dorus Ginnings. We felt ourselves much cramped; but my dear Lord was with us, and we believed, if it was his will, the work would go on, and that we would be able to succeed in building the house of the Lord. We established prayer meetings and meetings of exhortation, and the Lord blessed our endeavors, and many souls were awakened; but the elder soon forbid us holding any such meetings; but we viewed the forlorn state of our colored brethren, and that they were destitute of a place of worship. They were considered as a nuisance.

A number of us usually attended St. George's church in Fourth street; and when the colored people began to get numerous in attending the church, they moved us from the seats we usually sat on, and placed us all around the wall, and on Sabbath morning we went to church and the sexton stood at the door, and told us to go in the gallery. He told us to go, and we would see where to sit. We expected to take the seats over the ones we formerly occupied below, not knowing any better. We took those seats. Meeting had begun, and they were nearly done singing, and just as we got to our seats, the elder said, "Let us pray." We had not been long upon our knees before I heard considerable scuffling and low talking. I raised my head up and saw one of the trustees, H——— M———, having hold of the Rev. Absalom Jones, pulling him up off of his knees, and saying, "You must get up—you must not kneel here." Mr. Jones replied, "Wait until prayer is over." Mr. H——— M——— said "No, you must get up now, or I will call for aid and force you away." Mr. Jones said, "Wait until prayer is over, and I will get up and trouble you no more." With that he beckoned to one of the other trustees, Mr. L——— S——— to come to his assistance. He came, and went to William White to pull him up. By this time prayer was over, and we all went out of the church in a body, and they were no more plagued with us in the church. This raised a great excitement and inquiry among the citizens, in so much that I believe they were ashamed of their conduct. But my dear Lord was with us, and we were filled with fresh vigor to get a house erected to worship God in. Seeing our forlorn and distressed situation, many of the hearts of our citizens were moved to urge us forward. . . . I hope the name of Dr. Benjamin Rush and Robert Ralston will never be forgotten among us. They were the first two gentlemen who espoused the cause of the oppressed, and aided us in building the house of the Lord for the poor Africans to worship in. Here was the beginning and rise of the first African church in America. But the elder of the Methodist Church still pursued us. Mr. John McClaskey called upon us and told us if we did not erase our names from the subscription paper, and give up the paper, we would be publicly turned out of meeting. We asked him if we had violated any rules of discipline by so doing. He replied, "I have the charge given to me by the Conference, and unless you submit I will read you publicly out of meeting." We told him we were willing to abide by the discipline of the Methodist Church, "And if you will show us where we have violated any law of discipline in the Methodist Church, we will submit; and if there is no rule violated in the discipline we will proceed on." He replied, "We will read you all out." We told him if he turned us out contrary to rule of discipline, we should seek further redress. . . .

We bore much persecution from many of the Methodist connection; but we have reason to be thankful to Almighty God, who was our deliverer. The day was appointed to go and dig the cellar. I arose early in the morning and addressed the throne of grace, praying that the Lord would bless our endeavors. Having by this time two or three teams of my own—as I was the first proposer of the African church, I put the first spade in the ground to dig a cellar for the same. This was the first African Church or meetinghouse that was erected in the United States of America. We intended it for the African preaching-house or church; but finding that the elder stationed in this city was such an opposer to our proceedings of erecting a place of worship, though the principal of the directors of this church belonged to the Methodist connection, the elder stationed here would neither preach for us, nor have anything to do with us. We then held an election, to know what religious denomination we should unite with. At the election it was determined—there were two in favor of the Methodist, the Rev. Absalom Jones and myself, and a large majority in favor of the Church of England. The majority carried. Notwithstanding we had been so violently persecuted by the elder, we were in favor of being attached to the Methodist connection; for I was confident that there was no religious sect or denomination would suit the capacity of the colored people as well as the Methodists; for the plain and simple gospel suits best for any people; for the unlearned can understand, and the learned are sure to understand; and the reason that the Methodist is so successful in the awakening and conversion of the colored people, the plain doctrine and having good discipline. But in many cases the preachers would act to please their own fancy, without discipline, till some of them became such tyrants, and more especially to the colored people. They would turn them out of society, giving them no trial, for the smallest offense, perhaps only hearsay. They would frequently, in meeting the class, impeach some of the members of whom they had heard an ill report, and turn them out saying, "I have heard thus and thus of you, and you are no more a member of society"—without witnesses on either side. This has been frequently done, notwithstanding in the first rise and progress in Delaware state, and elsewhere, the colored people were their greatest support; for there were but few of us free; but the slaves would toil in their little patches many a night until midnight to raise their little truck and sell to get something to support them more than what their masters gave them, but we used often to divide our little support among the white preachers of the Gospel. This was once a quarter. It was in the time of the old Revolutionary War between Great Britain and the United States. The Methodists were the first people that brought glad tidings to the colored people. I feel thankful that ever I heard a Methodist preach. We are beholden to the Methodists, under God, for the light of the Gospel we enjoy; for all other denominations preached so high-flown that we were not able to comprehend their doctrine. Sure am I that reading sermons will never prove so beneficial to the colored people as spiritual or extempore preaching. I am well convinced that the Methodist has proved beneficial to thousands and ten times thousands. It is to be awfully feared that the simplicity of the Gospel that was among them fifty years ago, and that they conform more to the world of the fashions thereof, they would fare very little better than the people of the world. The discipline is altered considerably from what it was. We would ask for the good old way, and desire to walk therein.

In 1783 a committee was appointed from the African Church to solicit me to be their minister, for there was no colored preacher in Philadelphia but myself. I told them I could not accept of their offer, as I was Methodist. . . . I bought an old frame that had been formerly occupied as a blacksmith shop, from Mr. Sims, and hauled it on the lot in Sixth near Lombard street, that had formerly been taken for the Church of England. I employed carpenters to repair the old frame, and fit it for a place of worship. In July 1794, Bishop Asbury being in town I solicited him to open the church for us which he accepted. The Rev. John Dickins sung and prayed, and Bishop Asbury preached. The house was called Bethel, agreeable to the prayer that was made. Mr. Dickins prayed that it might be a bethel to the gathering in of thousands of souls. My dear Lord was with us, so that there were many hearty "amen's" echoed through the house. This house of worship has been favored with the awakening of many souls, and I trust they are in the Kingdom, both white and colored. Our warfare and troubles now began afresh. Mr. C. proposed that we should make over the church to the Conference. This we objected to; he asserted that we could not be Methodists unless we did; we told him he might deny us their name, but they could not deny us a seat in Heaven. . . . We agreed to be incorporated. He offered to draw the incorporation himself, that it might save us the trouble of paying for to get it drawn. We cheerfully submitted to his proposed plan. He drew the incorporation, but incorporated our church under the Conference. . . . We labored about ten years under this incorporation, until James Smith was appointed to take charge in Philadelphia; he soon waked us up by demanding the keys and books of the church, and forbid us holding any meetings except by orders from him; these propositions we told him we could not agree to. He observed he was elder, appointed to the charge, and unless we submitted to him, he would read us all out of meeting. We told him the house was ours, we had bought it, and paid for it. He said he would let us know it was not ours, it belonged to the Conference; we took counsel on it; counsel informed us we had been taken in; according to the incorporation it belonged to the white connection. We asked him if it couldn't be altered; he told us if two-thirds of the society agreed to have it altered, it could be altered. He gave me a transcript to lay before them; I called the society together and laid it before them. My dear Lord was with us. It was unanimously agreed to, by both female and male. We had another incorporation drawn that took the church from the Conference, and got it passed, before the elder knew anything about it. This raised a considerable rumpus, for the elder contended that it would not be good unless he had signed it. The elder, with the trustees of St. George's, called us together, and said we must pay six hundred dollars a year for their services, or they could not serve us. . . .

Mr. Samuel Royal being appointed to the charge of Philadelphia, declared unless we should repeal the Supplement, neither he nor any white preacher, travelling or local, should preach any more for us; so we were left to ourselves. . . . [A]n edict was passed by the elder, that if any local preacher should serve us, he should be expelled from the connection. John Emory, then elder of the Academy, published a circular letter, in which we were disowned by the Methodists. A house was also hired and fitted for worship, not far from Bethel, and an invitation given to all who desired to be Methodists to resort thither. But being disappointed in this plan, Robert R. Roberts, the resident elder, came to Bethel, insisted on preaching to us and taking the spiritual charge of the congregation, for we were Methodists he was told he should come on some terms with the trustees; his answer was, that "He did not come to consult with Richard Allen or other trustees, but to inform the congregation, that on next Sunday afternoon, he would come and take the spiritual charge." We told him he could not preach for us under existing circumstances. However, at the appointed time he came, but having taken previous advice we had our preacher in the pulpit when he came, and the house was so fixed that he could not get but more than half way to the pulpit. . . .

The next elder stationed in Philadelphia was Robert Birch, who, following the example of his predecessor, came and published a meeting for himself. But the method just mentioned was adopted and he had to go away disappointed. In [the] consequence of this, he applied to the Supreme Court for a writ of mandamus, to know why the pulpit was denied him. Being elder, this brought on a lawsuit, which ended in our favor. Thus by the Providence of God we were delivered from a long, distressing and expensive suit, which could not be resumed, being determined by the Supreme Court. For this mercy we desire to be unfeignedly thankful.

About this time, our colored friends in Baltimore were treated in a similar manner by the white preachers and trustees, and many of them driven away who were disposed to seek a place of worship, rather than go to law.

Many of the colored people in other places were in a situation nearly like those of Philadelphia and Baltimore, which induced us in April 1816, to call a general meeting, by way of Conference. Delegates from Baltimore and other places which met those of Philadelphia, and taking into consideration their grievances, and in order to secure the privileges, promote union and harmony among themselves, it was resolved: "That the people of Philadelphia, Baltimore, etc., etc., should become one body, under the name of the African Methodist Episcopal Church."

We deemed it expedient to have a form of discipline, whereby we may guide our people in the fear of God, in the unity of the Spirit, and in the bonds of peace, and preserve us from that spiritual despotism which we have so recently experienced— remembering that we are not to lord it over God's heritage, as greedy dogs that can never have enough. But with long suffering and bowels of compassion, to bear each other's burdens, and so fulfill the Law of Christ, praying that our mutual striving together for the promulgation of the Gospel may be crowned with abundant success.

BISHOPS COKE AND ASBURY PUBLISH ANNOTATED BOOK OF DISCIPLINE

Source: Thomas Coke and Francis Asbury, The Doctrines and Disciplines of the Methodist Episcopal Church, in America *(Philadelphia: Henry Tuckniss, 1798), 38-53, 146-48. Excerpts.*

SECTION IV.

Of the Election and Consecration of Bishops, and of their Duty.

NOTES.

In considering the present subject, we must observe that nothing has been introduced into Methodism by the present episcopal form of government, which was not before fully exercised by Mr. Wesley. He presided in the conferences; fixed the appointments of the preachers for their several circuits; changed, received, or suspended preachers, wherever he judged that necessity required it; travelled through the European connection at large; superintended the spiritual and temporal business; and consecrated two bishops, Thomas Coke and Alexander Mather, one before the present episcopal plan took place in America, and the other afterwards, besides ordaining elders and deacons. But the authority of Mr. Wesley and that of the bishops in America differ in the following important points:

1. Mr. Wesley was the patron of all the Methodist pulpits in Great Britain and Ireland *for life,* the sole right of nomination being invested in him by all the deeds of settlement, which gave him exceeding great power. But the bishops in America possess no such power: The property of the preaching-houses is invested in the trustees; and the right of nomination to the pulpits, in the general conference—and in such as the general conference shall, from time to time, appoint. This division of power in favour of the general conference was absolutely necessary. Without it the itinerant plan could not exist for any long continuance. The trustees would probably, in many instances, from their *located* situation, insist upon having their favourite preachers stationed in their circuits, or endeavour to prevail on the preachers themselves to *locate* among them, or choose some other settled minister for their chapels. In other cases, the trustees of preaching houses *in different circuits* would probably insist upon having the *same* popular or favourite preachers.

Here, then, lies the grand difference between Mr. Wesley's authority, in the present instance, and that of our American bishops. The former, as (under God) the father of the connection, was allowed to have the *sole, legal, independent* nomination of preachers to all the chapels: the latter are *entirely dependent* on the general conference.

But why, may it be asked, does the general conference lodge the power of stationing the preachers in the episcopacy? We answer, On account of their entire confidence in it. If ever, through improper conduct, it loses that confidence in any considerable degree, the general conference will, upon evidence given, in a proportionable degree, take from it this branch of its authority. But if ever it evidently betrays a spirit of tyranny or partiality, and *this* can be proved before the general conference, the whole will be taken from it: and we pray God, that in such case the power may be invested in other hands! And alas! who would envy any one the power? There is no situation in which a bishop can be placed, no branch of duty he can possibly exercise, so delicate, or which so exposes him to the jealousies not only of false but of true brethren, as this. The removal of preachers from district to district and from circuit to circuit, very nearly concerns them, and touches their tenderest feelings: and it requires no small portion of grace for a preacher to be *perfectly* contented with his appointment, when he is stationed in a circuit, where the societies are small, the rides long, and the fare coarse. Any one, therefore, may easily see, from the nature of man, that though the bishop has to deal with some of the best of men, he will sometimes raise himself opposers, who, by rather overrating their own abilities, may judge him to be partial in respect to their appointments: and these circumstances would weigh down his mind to such a degree, as those who are not well acquainted with the difficulties which necessarily accompany public and important stations among mankind, can hardly conceive.

May we not add a few observations concerning the high expediency, if not necessity, of the present plan. How could an itinerant ministry be preserved through this extensive continent, if the yearly conferences were to station the preachers? They would, of course, be taken up with the *sole* consideration of the spiritual and temporal interests of *that part* of the connection, the direction of which was intrusted to them. The necessary consequence of this mode of proceeding would probably, in less than an age, be *the division of the body* and *the independence* of each yearly conference. The conferences would be more and more estranged from each other for want of a mutual exchange of preachers: and *that grand spring, the union of the body at large,* by which, under divine grace, the work is more and more extended through this vast country, would be gradually weakened, till at last it might be entirely destroyed. The connection would no more be enabled to send missionaries to the western states and territories, in proportion to their rapid population. The grand circulation of ministers would be at an end, and a mortal stab given to the itinerant plan. The surplus of preachers in one conference could not be drawn out to supply the deficiencies of others, through declensions, locations, deaths, &c. and the revivals in one part of the continent could not be rendered beneficial to the others. *Our grand plan,* in all its parts, leads to an *itinerant* ministry. Our bishops are *travelling* bishops. All the different orders which compose our conferences are employed in the *travelling line;* and our local preachers are, *in some degree,* travelling preachers. Everything is kept moving as far as possible; and we will be bold to say, that, next to the grace of God, there is nothing *like this* for keeping the whole body alive from the centre to the circumference, and for the continual extension of that circumference on every hand. And we verily believe, that if our episcopacy should, at any time, through tyrannical or immoral conduct, come under the severe censure of the general conference, the members thereof would see it highly for the glory of God to preserve the present form, and *only* change the men.

2. Mr. Wesley, as the venerable founder (under God) of the whole Methodist society, governed without any responsibility whatever; and the universal respect and veneration of both the preachers and people for him, made them cheerfully submit to this: nor was there ever, perhaps, a mere human being who, used so much power better, or with a purer eye to the Redeemer's glory, than that blessed man of God: But the American bishops are as responsible as any of the preachers. They are *perfectly subject* to the general conference. They are indeed conscious that the conference would neither degrade nor censure them, unless they deserved it. They have, on the one hand, the fullest confidence in their brethren; and, on the other, esteem the confidence which their brethren place in them, as the highest earthly honour they can receive.

But this is not all. They are subject to be tried by seven elders and two deacons as prescribed above, for any immorality, or supposed immorality; and may be suspended by two-thirds of these, not only from all public offices, but even from being private members of the society, till the ensuing general conference. This mode subjects the bishops to a trial before a court of judicature, considerably inferior to that of a yearly conference. For there is not one of the yearly conferences which will not, probably, be attended by more presiding elders, elders, and deacons than the conference which is authorized to try a bishop, the yearly conferences consisting of from thirty to sixty members. And we can, without scruple, assert, that there are no bishops of any other episcopal church upon earth, who are subject to so strict a trial as the bishops of the Methodist episcopal church in America. We trust, they will never *need* to be influenced by motives drawn from the fear of temporal or ecclesiastical punishments, in order to keep *from vice:* But if they do, may the rod which hangs over them have its due effect; or may they be expelled from the church, as "salt which hath lost its savour, and is thenceforth good for nothing but to be cast out, and trodden under the foot of men!"

3. Mr. Wesley had the entire management of all the conference funds and the produce of the books. It is true, he expended all upon the work of God, and for charitable purposes; and rather than appropriate the least of it to his own use, refused, even when he was about seventy years of age, to travel in a carriage, till his friends in London and Bristol entered into a private subscription for the extraordinary expense. That great man of God might have heaped up thousands upon thousands, if he had been so inclined; and yet he died worth nothing but a little pocket money, the horses and carriage in which he travelled, and the clothes he

wore. But our American bishops have no probability of being rich. For not a cent of the public money is at their disposal: the conferences have the entire direction of the whole. Their salary is sixty-four dollars a year; and their travelling expenses are also defrayed. And with this salary they are to travel about six thousand miles a year, "in much patience," and sometimes, "in affliction, in necessities, in distress, in labours, in watchings, in fastings," through "honour and dishonour, evil report and good report: as deceivers, and yet true; as unknown, and yet well known; as dying, and behold," they "live; as chastened, and not killed; as sorrowful, yet always rejoicing; as poor, yet making many rich; as having nothing, yet possessing all things;" and, we trust, they can each of them through grace say, in their small measure, with the great apostle, that "they are determined not to know any thing, save Jesus Christ, and him crucified; yea, doubtless, and count all things but loss for the excellency of the knowledge of Christ Jesus their Lord: for whom they have suffered the loss of all things, and do count them but dung, that they may win Christ."

We have drawn this comparison between our venerable father and the American bishops, to shew to the world that they possess not, and, we may add, they aim not to possess, that power which he exercised and had a right to exercise, as the father of the connection: that, on the contrary, they are perfectly dependent; that their power, their usefulness, themselves, are entirely at the mercy of the general conference, and, on the charge of immorality, at the mercy of two-thirds of the little conference of nine.

To these observations we may add, 1. That a branch of the episcopal office, which, in every episcopal church on earth, since the first introduction of christianity, has been considered as essential to it, namely, *the power of ordination*, is *singularly* limited to our bishops. For they not only have no power to ordain a person for the episcopal office till he be first elected by the *general* conference, but they possess no authority to ordain *an elder or a travelling deacon*, till he be first elected by a *yearly* conference; or a local deacon, till he obtain a testimonial; signifying the approbation of the society to which he belongs, countersigned by the general stewards of the circuit, three elders, three deacons, and three travelling preachers. They are, therefore, not under the temptation ordaining through interest, affection, or any other improper motive; because it is not in their power to do. They have, indeed, authority to suspend ordination of an elected person, because they are answerable *to God* for the abuse of their office, and the command of the apostle, "Lay hands suddenly on no man," is absolute; and, we trust, where conscience was really concerned, and they had *sufficient reason* to exercise their power of suspension, they would do it, even to the loss of the esteem of their brethren, which is more dear to them than life; yea, even to the loss of their usefulness in the church, which is more precious to them than all things here below. But every one must be immediately sensible, how cautious they will necessarily be, as men of wisdom, in the exercise of this suspending power. For unless they had such weighty reasons for the exercise of it, as would give some degree of satisfaction to the conference which had made the election, they would throw themselves into difficulties, out of which they would not be able to extricate themselves, but by the meekest and wisest conduct, and by reparation to the injured person.

2. . . .

Some may think, that the mode of travelling, which the bishops are obliged to pursue, is attended with little difficulty, and much pleasure. Much pleasure they certainly do experience, because they know that they move in the will of God, and that the Lord is pleased to own their feeble labours. But if to travel through the heat and the cold, the rain and the snow, the swamps and the rivers, over mountains and through the wilderness, lying for nights together on the bare ground and in log-houses, open to the wind on every side, fulfilling their appointments, as far as possible, whatever be the hinderance,—if these be little difficulties, then our bishops have but little to endure.

We have already quoted so many texts of Scripture in defence of episcopacy and the itinerant plan, that we need only refer our reader to the notes on the 1st and 3rd sections. The whole tenor of St. Paul's epistles to Timothy and Titus clearly evidences, that *they* were invested, on the whole, with abundantly more power than our bishops: nor does it appear that *they* were responsible to any but God and the apostle. . . . [T]he *general itineracy* would not probably exist for any length of time on this extensive continent, if the bishops were not invested with that authority which they now possess. They alone travel through the whole connection, and, therefore, have such a view of the whole, as no yearly conference can possibly have.

One bishop, with the elders present, may consecrate a bishop who has been previously elected by the general conference. This is agreeable to the Scriptures. We read, 2 Tim. i. 6. "I put thee in remembrance, that thou stir up *the gift* of God *which is in thee*, by the putting on of *my* hands:" here we have the imposition of the hands of the apostle. Again we read, 1 Tim. v. 14. "Neglect not *the gift that is in thee*, which was given thee by prophecy, with the laying on of the hands of *the presbytery*:" here we have the laying on of the hands of *the elders*. And by comparing both passages, it is evident that the imposition of hands was, both in respect to the apostle and the elders, *for the same gift*. Nor is the idea, that three bishops are necessary to consecrate a bishop, grounded on any authority whatever, drawn from the Scriptures, or the practice of the apostolic age.

The authority given to, or rather declared to exist in, the general conference, that in case there shall be no bishop remaining in the church, they shall elect a bishop, and authorize the elders to consecrate him, will not admit of an objection, except on the supposition that the fable of an uninterrupted apostolic succession be allowed to be true. St. Jerome, who was as strong an advocate for episcopacy as perhaps any in the primitive church, informs us, that in the church of Alexandria (which was, in ancient times, one of the most respectable of the churches) the college of presbyters not only elected a bishop, on the decease of the former, but consecrated him by the imposition of their own hands *solely*, from the time of St. Mark, their first bishop, or the time of Dionysius, which was a space of about two hundred years: and the college of presbyters in ancient times answered to our general conference.

127

SECTION V.

Of the Presiding Elders, and of their Duty.

Quest. 1. By whom are the presiding elders to be chosen?

Answ. By the bishop.

Quest. 2. What are the duties of a presiding elder?

Answ. 1. To travel through his appointed district.

2. In the absence of a bishop, to take charge of all the elders, deacons, travelling and local preachers, and exhorters in his district.

3. To change, receive, or suspend preachers in his district during the intervals of the conferences, and in the absence of the bishop.

4. In the absence of a bishop, to preside in the conference.

5. To be present, as far as practicable, at all the quarterly meetings: . . .

Quest. 4. How long may the bishop allow an elder to preside in the same district?

Answ. For any term not exceeding four years successively.

Quest. 5. How shall the presiding elders be supported?

Answ. If there be a surplus of the public money, in one or more circuits in his district, he shall receive such surplus. . . .

NOTES.

[W]e have texts which indubitably prove that there were *presiding, superintending,* or *ruling* elders (the words bear the same meaning) in the church in the apostolic age, and that this office is fully warranted by the Word of God. Thus we read in Acts xx. 17–28. "From Miletus he [Paul] sent to Ephesus, and called the *elders* of the church. And, when they were come to him, he said unto them, Take heed—unto yourselves, and to all the flock over the which the Holy Ghost hath made you OVERSEERS," &c. The word *overseers* in this place signifies, as it does every where, persons who had a considerable degree of superintendency over the work in which they were employed. . . .

On the principles or data above-mentioned, all the episcopal churches in the world have, in some measure, formed their church-government. And we believe we can venture to assert, that there never has been an episcopal church of any great extent, which has not had *ruling* or *presiding* elders, either expressly *by name* as in the apostolic churches, or otherwise in *effect.* On this account it is, that all the modern episcopal churches have had their *presiding* or *ruling* elders under the names of grand vicars, archdeacons, rural deans, &c. The Moravians have presiding elders, who are invested with very considerable authority, though we believe they are simply termed elders. And we beg leave to repeat, that we are confident, we could, if need were, shew that all the episcopal churches ancient and modern, *of any great extent,* have had an order or set of ministers corresponding, more or less, to our presiding or ruling elders, all of whom were, more or less, invested with the superintendence of other ministers.

Mr. Wesley informs us in his works, that the whole plan of Methodism was introduced, step by step, by the interference and openings of divine Providence. This was the case in the present instance. When Mr. Wesley drew up a plan of government for our church in America, he desired that no more elders should be ordained in the first instance than were absolutely necessary, and that the work on the continent should be divided between them, in respect to the duties of their office. The general conference accordingly elected twelve elders for the above purposes. Bishop Asbury and the district conferences afterwards found that this order of men was so necessary, that they agreed to enlarge the number, and give them *the name* by which they are at present called, and which is perfectly scriptural, though not *the word* used in our translation: and this proceeding afterwards received the approbation of Mr. Wesley.

In 1792 the general conference, equally conscious of the necessity of having such an office among us, not only confirmed everything that bishop Asbury and the district conferences had done, but also drew up or agreed to the present section for the explanation of the nature and duties of the office. The conference clearly saw that the bishops wanted assistants; that it was impossible for one or two bishops so to superintend the vast work on this continent as to keep everything in order in the intervals of the conference, without other official men to act under them and assist them: and as these would be only the agents of the bishops in every respect, the authority of appointing them, and of changing them, ought, from the nature of things, to be in the episcopacy. If the presiding or ruling elders were not men in whom the bishops could fully confide, or on the loss of confidence, could exchange for others, the utmost confusion would ensue. This also renders the authority invested in the bishops of fixing the extent of each district, highly expedient. They must be supposed to be the best judges of the abilities of the presiding elders whom they themselves choose: and it is a grand part of their duty, to make the districts and the talents of the presiding elders who act for them, suit and agree with each other, as far as possible: for it cannot be expected, that a sufficient number of them can at any time be found, *of equal talents*, and, therefore, the extent of their field of action must be proportioned to their gifts.

From all that has been advanced, and from those other ideas which will present themselves to the reader's mind on this subject, it will appear that the presiding elders must, of course, be appointed, directed, and changed by the episcopacy. And yet their power is so considerable, that it would by no means be sufficient for them to be responsible to the bishops *only* for their conduct in their office. They are as responsible in this respect, and in every other, to the *yearly* conference to which they belong, as any other preacher; and may be censured, suspended, or expelled from the connection, if the conference see it proper: nor have the bishops any authority to over-rule, suspend, or meliorate in any degree, the censures, suspensions, or expulsions of the conference.

Many and great are the advantages arising from this institution.

1. It is a great help and blessing to the quarterly meetings respectively, through the connection, to have a man at their head, who is experienced not only in the ways of God, but in men and manners, and in all things appertaining to the order of our church. Appeals may be brought before the quarterly meeting from the

judgment of the preacher who has the oversight of the circuit, who certainly would not be, in such cases, so proper to preside as the ruling elder. Nor would any local preacher, leader, or steward be a suitable president of the meeting, as his parent, his child, his brother, sister, or friend, might be more or less interested in the appeals which came before him: besides his *local* situation would lead him almost unavoidably to *prejudge* the case, and, perhaps, to enter warmly into the interests of one or other of the parties, previously to the appeal. It is, therefore, indisputably evident, that the *ruling elder* is most likely to be impartial, and, consequently, the most proper person to preside.

2. Another advantage of this office arises from the necessity of changing preachers from circuit to circuit in the intervals of the yearly conferences. Many of the preachers are young in years and gifts; and this must always be the case, more or less, or a fresh supply of travelling preachers in proportion to the necessities of the work could not be procured. These young men, in general, are exceedingly zealous. Their grand *forte* is to awaken souls; and in this view they are highly necessary for the spreading of the gospel. But for some time their gifts cannot be expected to be *various*; and, therefore, half a year at a time, or sometimes even a quarter, may be sufficient for them to labour in one circuit: to change them, therefore, from circuit to circuit, in the intervals of the yearly conferences, is highly necessary in many instances. Again, the preachers themselves, for family reasons or on other accounts, may desire, and have reason to expect, a change. But who can make it in the absence of the bishops; unless there be a presiding elder appointed for the district? . . .

3. Who is able properly to supply the vacancies in circuits on the *deaths* of preachers, or on *their withdrawing* from the travelling connection? Who can have a thorough knowledge of the state of the district, and of its resources for filling up such vacancies, except the presiding elder who travels through the whole district? And shall circuits be often neglected for months together, and the flocks, during those times, be, more or less, without shepherds, and many of them, perhaps, perish for want of food, merely that one of the most scriptural and useful offices among us may be abolished? Shall we not rather support it, notwithstanding every thing which may be subtilly [*sic*] urged by our enemies under the cry of tyranny, which is the common cry of restless spirits even against the best governments, in order that they may throw every thing into confusion, and then ride in the whirlwind and direct the storm?

4. When a bishop visits a district, he ought to have one to accompany him, in whom he can fully confide; one, who can inform him of the whole work in a complete and comprehensive view; and, therefore, one who has travelled *through the whole*, and, by being present at all the quarterly meetings, can give all the information, concerning every circuit in particular, and the district in general, which the bishop can desire. Nor is the advantage small that the bishops, when at the greatest distance, may receive from the presiding elders a full account of their respective districts, and may thereby be continually in possession of a more comprehensive knowledge of the whole work, than they could possibly procure by any other means.

5. The only branch of the presiding elder's office, the importance and usefulness

of which is not so obvious to some persons, but which is, at the same time, perhaps the most expedient of all, is *the suspending power*, for the preservation of *the purity* of our ministry, and that our people may never be burdened with preachers of insufficient gifts. Here we must not forget, that the presiding elder acts as agent to the bishops; and that the bishops are, the greatest part of their time, at a vast distance from him; he must, therefore, exercise episcopal authority (ordination excepted) or he cannot act as their agent. All power may be abused. The only way which can be devised to prevent the abuse of it, if we will have a good and effective government, is to make the executive governors completely responsible, and their responsibility within the reach of the aggrieved. And, in the present instance, not only the general conference may expel the presiding elder—not only the episcopacy may suspend him from the exercise of his office—but the yearly conference may also impeach him, try him, and expel him: and such a threefold guard must be allowed, by every candid mind, to be as full a check to the abuse of his power, as, perhaps, human wisdom can devise.

But is it not strange, that any of *the people* should complain either of *this* or of the *episcopal* office? *These offices* in the church are peculiarly designed to meliorate the severity of christian discipline, as far as they respect *the people.* In them the people have a refuge, an asylum to which they may fly upon all occasions. To them they may appeal, and before them they may lay all their complaints and grievances. The persons who bear these offices are their fathers in the gospel, ever open of access, ever ready to relieve them under every oppression. And we believe we can venture to assert, that the people have never had even a *plausible* pretence to complain of the authority either of the bishops or the presiding elders.

6. We may add, as was just hinted above, that the bishops ought not to enter into *small details.* It is not their calling. To select the proper men who are to act as their agents—to preserve in order and in motion the wheels of the vast machine—to keep a constant and watchful eye upon the whole—and to *think deeply* for the general good—form their peculiar and important avocation. All of which shews the necessity of the office now under consideration. . . .

We will conclude our notes on this section with observing, that there is no ground to believe that the work of God has been injured, or the numbers of the society diminished, by the institution of this order, but just the contrary. In the year 1784, when the presiding eldership did, *in fact,* though not in *name,* commence, there were about 14,000 in society on this continent; and *now* the numbers amount to upwards of 56,000: so that the society is, at present, four times as large as it was twelve or thirteen years ago. We do not believe that the office now under consideration was the *principal cause* of this great revival, but the Spirit and grace of God, and the consequent zeal of the preachers in general. Yet we have no doubt, but the full organization of our body, and giving to the whole a complete and effective executive government, of which the presiding eldership makes a very capital branch, has, under God, been a grand means of preserving the peace and union of our connection and the purity of our ministry, and, therefore, *in its consequences,* has been a *chief instrument,* under the grace of God, of this great revival. . . .

SECTION II

Of Class-Meeting.

Quest. 1. How may the leaders of classes be rendered more useful?

Answ. 1. Let each of them be diligently examined concerning his method of meeting a class. Let this be done with all possible exactness, at least once a quarter. In order to this, take sufficient time.

2. Let each leader carefully inquire how every soul in his class prospers: Not only how each person observes the outward rules, but how he grows in the knowledge and love of God.

3. Let the leaders converse with those who have the charge of their circuits, frequently and freely.

Quest. 2. Can any thing more be done in order to make the class-meetings lively and profitable?

Answ. 1. Change improper leaders.

2. Let the leaders frequently meet each other's classes.

3. Let us observe which leaders are the most useful: And let these meet the other classes as often as possible.

4. See that all the leaders be not only men of sound judgment, but men truly devoted to God.

Quest. 3. How shall we prevent improper persons from insinuating themselves into the society?

Answ. 1. *Give tickets to none until they are recommended by a leader, with whom they have met at least six months on trial.*

2. Give notes to none but those who are recommended by one you know, or until they have met three or four times in a class.

3. Read the rules to them the first time they meet.

Quest. 4. How shall we be more exact in receiving and excluding members?

Answ. The official minister or preacher shall, at every quarterly meeting, read the names of those that are received and excluded.

Quest. 5. What shall we do with those members of society, who willfully and repeatedly neglect to meet their class?

Answ. 1. Let the elder, deacon, or one of the preachers, visit them, whenever it is practicable, and explain to them the consequences if they continue to neglect, viz. Exclusion.

2. If they do not amend, let him who has the charge of the circuit exclude them in the society; shewing that they are laid aside for a breach of our rules of discipline and not for immoral conduct.

NOTES

1. [W]e may observe, how careful our ministers should be in their choice of leaders. For our leaders under God are the sinews of our society, and our revivals will ever, in a great measure, rise or fall with them. Our ministers and preachers should

therefore consider no time better employed than that which they bestow on the leaders, in examining them, directing them, and stirring them up to their holy and momentous duty.

2. We have made many remarks in the course of our work on the necessity of christian fellowship: but this cannot be carried on to any considerable advantage without stated solemn times of assembling. The meetings held for this purpose must have a name to distinguish them. We call ours *Class-meetings,* and *Band-meetings;* . . . Here we must notice, that it is *the thing itself, christian fellowship* and not the name, which we contend for. . . . [W]e have rarely met with one who has been much devoted to God, and at the same time not united in close christian fellowship to some religious society or other. Far be it from us to suppose that no fellowship-meetings, except ours, are owned of God: so illiberal a sentiment never entered our minds. . . .

We have no doubt, but meetings of christian brethren for the exposition of scripture-texts, may be attended with their advantages. But, the most profitable exercise of any is a free inquiry into the state of the heart. We therefore confine these meetings to *christian experience,* only adjoining singing and prayer in the introduction and conclusion. And we praise the Lord, they have been made a blessing to scores of thousands. . . . In short, we can truly say, that through the grace of God our classes form the pillars of our work, and, . . . are in a considerable degree our universities for the ministry. Mal. iii. 16, 17. "Then they that feared the Lord, spake often one to another, and the Lord hearkened, and heard it, and a book of remembrance was written before him for them that feared the Lord, and that thought upon his name. And they shall be mine, saith the Lord of hosts, in that day when I make up my jewels, and I will spare them as a man spareth his own son that serveth him." . . . Matt. xviii. 20 "Where two or three are gathered together *in my name,* there am I in the midst of them."

GENERAL CONFERENCE ISSUES
PASTORAL LETTER ON SLAVERY

Source: The Address of the General Conference of the Methodist Episcopal Church, to all their Brethren and Friends in the United States. Broadside. *Philadelphia: Printed for Ezekiel Cooper, 1800. Reprinted in World Parish 7/2 (August 1959): 58-60.*

DEAR BRETHREN,

WE, the members of the General Conference of the Methodist Episcopal Church, beg leave to ADDRESS you with earnestness on a subject of first importance.

WE have long lamented the great national evil of NEGRO-SLAVERY, which has existed for so many years, and does still exist in many of these United States. We have considered it as repugnant to the unalienable rights of mankind, and to the very essence of civil liberty, but more especially to the spirit of the Christian religion.

FOR inconsistent as is the conduct of this otherwise free, this independent nation, in respect to the slavery of the Negroes, when considered in a civil and political view; it is still more so, when examined in the light of the gospel. For the whole spirit of the New Testament militates in the strongest manner against the practice of slavery and the influence of the gospel wherever it has long prevailed (except in many of these United States) has utterly abolished that most criminal part of slavery, the possessing and using the bodies of men by arbitrary will and with almost uncontrollable power.

THE small number of adventurers from Europe, who visit the West Indies for the sole purpose of amassing fortunes, are hardly worth our notice, any farther than their influence reaches for the enslaving and destroying of the human race. But, that so large a proportion of the inhabitants of this country, who so truly boast of the liberty they enjoy, and are so justly jealous of that inestimable blessing, should continue to deprive of every trace of liberty so many of their fellow-creatures equally capable with themselves of every social blessing and of eternal happiness—is an inconsistency which is scarcely to be paralleled in the history of mankind!

INFLUENCED by these views and feelings, we have for many years restricted *ourselves* by the strongest regulations from partaking of "the accursed thing"; and have also laid some very mild and tender restrictions on our society at large. But at this General Conference we wished, if possible, to give a blow at the root to the enormous evil. For this purpose we maturely weighed every regulation which could be adopted within our own society.—All seemed to be insufficient. We therefore determined at last to rouse up all our influence, in order to hasten, to the utmost of our power, the universal extirpation of this crying sin. To this end we passed the following resolution:—

"THAT the Annual Conferences be directed to draw up ADDRESSES for the gradual emancipation of the slaves to the Legislatures of those states, in which no general laws have been passed for that purpose: that these Addresses urge in the most respectful but pointed manner the necessity of a law for the gradual emancipation of the slaves: that proper Committees be appointed out of the most respectable of our Friends for the conducting of the business: and that the Presiding Elders, Elders, Deacons and Travelling Preachers, do procure as many proper signatures as possible to the Addresses, and give all the assistance in their power in every respect to aid the Committees, and to further this blessed undertaking. And that this be continued from year to year, till the desired end be fully accomplished."

WHAT now remains, dear Brethren, but that *you* coincide with us in this great undertaking, for the sake of God, his church and his holy cause, for the sake of your country, and for the sake of the miserable and oppressed. Give your signatures to the addresses; hand them for signatures to all your acquaintants and all the friends of liberty; urge the justice, the utility, the necessity of the measure: persevere in this blessed work, and the Lord, we are persuaded, will finally crown your endeavours with the wished-for success. O what a glorious country would be ours, if equal liberty were every where established, and equal liberty every where enjoyed!

WE are not ignorant that several of the Legislatures of these States have most generously stepped forth in the cause of liberty, and passed laws for the emancipation of the slaves. But many of the members of our societies, even in *those* States, may be highly serviceable to this great cause by using their influence by writing or otherwise with their friends in *other* states, whether those friends be methodists or not.

COME then, Brethren, let us join hand and heart together in this important enterprize. God is with us, and will, we doubt not, accompany with his blessings all our labours of love.

WE could write to you a volume on the present subject; but we know that in general you have already weighed it; and we have great confidence that your utmost assistance will not be wanting, and we promise to aid you with zeal and diligence.

THAT our gracious God may bless you with all the riches of his grace, and that we

may all meet where perfect liberty and perfect love shall eternally reign, is the ardent prayer of
Your affectionate Brethren,

Signed in behalf and by order of the General Conference.

Bishops: THOMAS COKE,
FRANCIS ASBURY,
RICHARD WHATCOAT.

The Committee: EZEK. COOPER,
WILLIAM MCKENDREE,
JESSE LEE.

THE UNITED BRETHREN RECORD EARLY ANNUAL AND GENERAL CONFERENCES

Source: Minutes of the Annual and General Conferences of the
Church of the United Brethren in Christ, 1800–1818, *Augustus W. Drury,*
trans. and ed. (Dayton: Published for the United Brethren Historical Society, 1897),
9-12, 17-21, 65-67. Order of conferences altered. Excerpt.

[1800 Frederick County, Maryland]

September 25, 1800, the following preachers assembled at the house of Frederick Kemp in Frederick County, Maryland: William Otterbein, Martin Boehm, John Hershey, Abraham Troxel, Christian Krum, Henry Krum, George Pfrimmer, Henry Boehm, Christian Newcomer, Dietrich Aurand, Jacob Geisinger, George Adam Geeting, Adam Lehman.

Each person spoke first of his own experience, and then declared anew his intention with all zeal, through the help of God, to preach untrammeled by sect to the honor of God and [the good] of men.

1. Resolved that two preachers shall go to Smoke's and investigate whether D. Aurand should baptize and administer the Lord's supper.

2. Resolved that yearly a day shall be appointed when the unsectarian [*unpartheiische*] preachers shall assemble and counsel how they may conduct their office more and more according to the will of God, and according to the mind of God, that the church of God may be built up, and sinners converted, so that God in Christ may be honored.

3. The meeting was opened with prayer, then a chapter read, a short discourse delivered by Brother Otterbein, and then again closed with prayer.

[1801 Frederick County, Maryland]

September 23, 1801, we again assembled at Peter Kemp's in order to counsel together and instruct one another how we might be pleasing to God and useful to our fellow men.

The following preachers were present: William Otterbein, Martin Boehm, Christian Newcomer, Daniel Strickler, George Adam Geeting, Peter Senseny, John Neidig, David Long, Abraham Mayer, Frederick Schaffer, Jacob Geisinger, John

Hershey, Thomas Winter, Ludwig Duckwald, David Snyder, Peter Kemp, Kessler, Christian Krum, Abraham Hershey, Michael Thomas.

1. After prayer, Otterbein gave a discourse. He said that salvation depends on Christ alone and his mercy, and that whoever here becomes free from sin and a party spirit has God to thank. Thus he declared his mind, and then each of the preachers spoke of his experience, and then was the following resolved.

2. A letter was read from Rev. Pfrimmer, and it was resolved to make no answer, because that seemed right to every one.

3. A letter was received from Aurand at Smoke's, and resolved to grant his desire and to notify him through Christian Newcomer.

4. Today's session closed with song and a hearty prayer that God would bless us and make us true and faithful laborers in his vineyard. Oh, that the Lord would send upon us all his Holy Spirit, that we might proclaim with power the word of God. Amen.

1. The 24th of September, 1801, we again assembled in God's name in Peter Kemp's house; and first a chapter of the Revelation of John was read, namely, the fourteenth chapter. Then followed singing and hearty prayer that each one might be willing to preach the gospel and that he also be careful, and that he also so walk as he preaches to others.

2. The preachers were examined as to whether they are willing according to their ability to labor in the work of the Lord, through the grace of the Lord.

3. It was asked who are willing to take charge of a circuit and preach at the appointed places. Then the following preachers offered themselves: Christian Newcomer, David Snyder, Michael Thomas, Abraham Hershey, Daniel Strickler, Abraham Mayer, Frederick Schaffer, David Long, John Neidig, Peter Kemp.

4. Resolved that each preacher, after the sermon, shall hold conversation with those who would be converted, be they who they may, if they are determined from the heart to give themselves to God.

5. Resolved that the preachers shall be brief and avoid unnecessary words in preaching and in prayer; but if the Spirit of God impels, it is their duty to follow as God directs. O God, give us wisdom and understanding to do all things according to thy will. Amen.

1. At nine o'clock we again came together. We began the session again with singing and hearty prayer that God would bless us with wisdom and understanding and with hearty love to God and one another. Amen.

2. Resolved that our preachers' meeting (conference) next year shall be October 5, 1803, at David Snyder's and whoever of the preachers cannot come shall write to the conference.

3. Resolved that the last Sunday in August a great meeting shall be held at Sleepy Creek.

4. Our present meeting was now closed; and indeed with a hearty prayer, which may the Lord out of grace grant for Jesus' sake. Amen.

Martin Boehm.
William Otterbein.
George Adam Geeting.

[1802 Frederick County, Maryland]

At Cronise's, in Frederick County [Maryland], we, the following preachers, came together to hold counsel: William Otterbein, Martin Boehm, Christian Newcomer, John Hershey, Christopher Grosh, Abraham Troxel, Henry Krum, Michael Thomas, Dietrich Aurand, David Snyder, Peter Kemp, Matthias Kessler, George Adam Geeting.

We began our meeting with singing, then with right hearty prayer to God that the kingdom of God might come and the will of God be done on earth as in heaven. May God will to send us preachers the grace of love to love God and all men.

2. Each of the preachers spoke of his condition, how it is with him in his preaching and how his purpose is further to do in his office, to call heartily upon God for his help, and that ever he might through humility give to another higher esteem than to himself. May God give to us preachers grace that we may become very humble to the honor of God and the good of men.

3. Resolved that Valentine Flugle have a certificate from us that he is allowed to exhort and persuade the people that they be converted. The Lord give him his blessing.

4. Resolved that we write to Pfrimmer that for the present we will have nothing to do with him.

5. At the close of the session Ludwig Duckwald and William Ambrose from Sleepy Creek, Virginia, arrived.

6. October 7, the sermon began, which was preached by Otterbein and Boehm, on Hebrews 13:17, with great blessing. To God be all the glory for this. May the sermon never be forgotten by us preachers and all the hearers.

7. The first thing that was taken up was that John Miller with our approval shall exhort the people to incite them to good works as much as he can through God's grace.

8. It appeared that in the matter of the recording of names, twelve votes were in favor and nine against. It therefore with consent laid over for the present.

9. The preachers shall establish prayer-meetings where they preach, if it is possible.

10. It is permitted to Ludwig Duckwald to baptize and to administer the outer signs of the Lord's supper according to God's Word.

11. On the 26th of September there was a sermon preached by our Brother Otterbein from the fourteenth verse to the end of the Epistle of Jude, and that with great blessing. In the afternoon our consultation was resumed.

12. A proposal was made relating to the collecting of a sum of money for poor preachers. Nothing, however, was done.

13. Resolved that if a preacher does anything wrong or scandalous, the nearest preacher shall go and talk with him alone. If he refuses to hear or heed, said preacher shall take with him one or two more preachers. If he refuses to hear them, he shall be silent till the next conference.

14. Resolved that George Adam Geeting in the spring and fall shall visit the societies on Frederick Circuit.

15. Resolved that Christian Newcomer visit Cumberland Circuit twice yearly.

16. Resolved that Martin Boehm twice yearly visit the circuits in Pennsylvania beyond the Susquehanna, to ascertain the condition of things in their societies.

17. Resolved that Jacob Baulus and Valentine Baulus shall make house-visits in Middletown and Fredericktown and their vicinity.

18. Further, it is laid down as a rule [*vest gesetzt*] that when one of our superintendents [or elders, *eltesten*] dies, namely Otterbein or Martin Boehm, who now are appointed to the place [*gesetzt sind*], then shall another always be chosen in his stead. This is the wish of both, and all of the preachers present unanimously consent and are agreed that it be thus.

Now for this time is the session closed in God's name.

Martin Boehm.
William Otterbein.

This yet here to mention: Peter Senseny, Ludwig Duckwald, John Neidig, are authorized to baptize and administer the Lord's supper, with all belonging thereto.

[1803 Cumberland County, Pennsylvania]

1. October 5, 1803, as assembled at David Snyder's in Cumberland County, Pennsylvania. The preachers present were the following: William Otterbein, Martin Boehm, Christian Newcomer, David Snyder, John Hershey, Peter Kemp, Abraham Mayer, Christopher Grosh, Christian Krum, Valentine Flugle, John Winter, Frederick Schaffer, George Adam Geeting, George Benedum. We began the session with the reading of the second chapter of First Timothy, and then with singing some verses of a hymn, and with prayer. Thou, dear Savior, bless our coming together to the honor of thy name and to the edification of us all. O Lord, answer us for Jesus' sake. Amen.

2. Each one of the preachers spoke as to his condition, how it stood with him; and of his renewed determination in upright love with all, with earnest determination in uprightness toward one another, and bound together in love, to walk in the ways of God; to preach the gospel through the power of Jesus. Amen.

3. Resolved that Daniel Strickler and Christian Krum shall call the preachers in Virginia together and with one another determine how they should preach and rightly arrange their plan. The Lord give them wisdom and power from above.

4. October 6, at two o'clock, our session again began with the reading of a chapter and with prayer. In the forenoon there was preaching by Otterbein and Boehm.

5. The work in Maryland was considered. It was left to the preachers in Maryland themselves to arrange.

6. Resolved that Martin Boehm and Grosh place the preachers in order in Pennsylvania as may tend most to the honor of God and the benefit of the hearers and the bettering of the church of God.

7. Resolved that David Snyder and Abraham Mayer and Benedum shall make

their own arrangement, how they shall serve their preaching place, as may be best for the kingdom of God. May the Lord help them. Amen.

8. It is order that Christian Newcomer and Henry Krum go to Christian Berger's and preach the gospel in his part of the country wherever they can find an entrance to the praise of our Lord Jesus Christ.

9. Resolved that the preachers names shall give to Christian Berger authority to baptize, but nothing more at this time.

10. October 7, we began our session again with the reading of the Fourteenth Psalm, and very hearty prayer.

11. Concerning Brother Flugle it was resolved that Brother Hershey visit his place to administer the Lord's supper.

12. There being a complaint against D. Aurand, resolved that Brother Snyder and Brother Neidig should go thither and make an investigation.

13. Resolved that our next conference again be held at David Snyder's, if Lord will, the first Wednesday in October, 1804, and a great meeting Saturday and Sunday following. The Lord grant it his blessing.

At length it was resolved that concerning the recording of the people's names every one has the freedom to do according to his understanding, and that they love one another as brethren. Further, it was resolved that the preacher after the sermon should converse with awakened souls as in the circumstances it might seem proper.

Wm. Otterbein.
Martin Boehm.
George Adam Geeting.

[1804 Cumberland County, Maryland]

October 3, 1804, the conference met at David Snyder's. Few preachers came, however, on account of the prevailing sickness and mortality. Present, Christian Newcomer, Martin Boehm, Frederick Schaffer, David Snyder, Matthias Bortsfield.

They counseled together and resolved, the Lord willing, that the next conference be held near Middletown, Maryland, on Wednesday before Whitsunday, 1805.

[1805 Middletown, Maryland]

1. May 29, 1805, we, the following preachers, assembled at the house of Christian Newcomer. Both our [superintendents] were present—Otterbein and Boehm. John Hershey, George Adam Geeting, Daniel Strickler, Frederick Schaffer, Peter Kemp, Lorenz Eberhart, George Benedum, David Snyder, Christian Krum, Frederick Duckwald, William Ambrose, Jacob Baulus, Jacob Geisinger, Christian Berger, Abraham Mayer, Christian Newcomer.

2. We began the session with hearty prayer. Otterbein gave a short address. May the Lord Jesus grant his blessing to the same. Amen.

3. The assembled preachers resolved through the grace of Jesus Christ to urge forward the work of God with more earnestness than ever before. O dear Saviour, help us, poor and unworthy, for the sake of they suffering and death. Amen.

4. According to the confession of the preachers the grace of God was with them and their work. May the Lord bless them in their office. The Lord make each one very faithful.

5. Pfrimmer received permission to preach among us.

6. The following preachers arrived: Ludwig Duckwald, Daniel Troyer, Jacob Dehof.

7. At eight o'clock, May 30, we again assembled. A portion from God's Word was read, followed by prayer to God in the name of Jesus, and thus the session began.

8. With the advice and consent of the preachers Newcomer determined to preach the whole year in Maryland and a part of Pennsylvania; and Christian Krum in Virginia. Resolved that each receive forty pounds yearly.

9. Resolved that George Adam Geeting shall be present at the usual great meetings in Maryland and on this side of the Susquehanna in Pennsylvania.

10. It was decided by the preachers' meeting that Geeting should not take up his residence at Hagerstown, but that Hagerstown should be served by our preachers.

11. The preachers who preach where they desire, according to their inclination, shall have no compensation. When, however, they receive money, they shall bring the same to the conference, to be given to the regular preachers.

12. It is allowed in our preachers' meeting that Frederick Duckwald of Sleepy Creek, and Christian Berger, of Westmoreland, baptize, administer the Lord's supper, and solemnize marriage.

13. The conference will be held next year at Lorenz Eberhart's, the Tuesday before Whitsunday, 1806, and that there on the Saturday following a great meeting shall begin. May the Lord be with us.

14. With this the session was brought to a close after the reading of a chapter and an exhortation that we should live to the honor of God.

William Otterbein.
Martin Boehm.

[1806 ? Maryland?]

May 21, 1806, we held our conference for this year at Lorenz Eberhart's. The following preachers were present: John Neidig, Lorenz Eberhart, Joseph Hoffman, Peter Kemp, Christian Krum, Michael Thomas, John Hershey, Christian Newcomer, Jacob Baulus, Henry Krum, George Adam Geeting. O God, make thy servants very faithful.

2. Each preacher present spoke of his condition, how he stands with God, how it goes with him in his office, and his purpose henceforth to be faithful through our Jesus Christ.

3. On the 22nd of May we came together again. The question arose whether the preachers stand united in love. They all declared that they stand in hearty love, not only with one another, but also toward all men, whoever they may be.

4. Resolved that Joseph Hoffman and Christian Krum shall and will take their circuit to serve the societies for a year, if the Lord shall grant life and health.

5. Resolved that the Pennsylvania brethren shall be written to.

6. Resolved that our next annual conference shall be held in Pennsylvania, beginning the Tuesday before Whitsunday, a great meeting following on Saturday and Sunday.

7. Great meetings shall be held at the school-house on the Antietam on Whitsunday, 1807; at Lemaster's, June 15; at the Spring [Rocky Spring], June 22; at Baulus's, October 4 and 5; at Hohmann's, in Virginia, September 24 and 25. The good Jesus bless his work. Amen.

George Adam Geeting.
Christian Newcomer.

[1807 Lancaster County, Pennsylvania]

1. We held our conference May 13, 1807, at Christian Herr's in Pennsylvania. The following preachers were present: Martin Boehm, Christian Newcomer, David Snyder, Isaac Niswander, Abraham Mayer, Christian Krum, John Neidig, Frederick Schaffer, Christian Smith, Joseph Hoffman, George Adam Geeting, David Long, Christian Hershey, Abraham Hershey.

2. The session was opened with prayer; then every one spoke of his condition; afterward Brother Martin Boehm gave a short exhortation. The fourth chapter of First John was read. Would God that he would make of us all useful instruments. . . .

7. It was again laid down as a rule that a married preacher shall receive per year forty pounds, and a single preacher twenty-four pounds, if he travels regularly. . . .

Martin Boehm.
George Adam Geeting.

[FIRST GENERAL CONFERENCE, 1815, Mount Pleasant, Pennsylvania]

This, the 6th of June, 1815, the following preachers assembled for the General Conference, near Mount Pleasant, Westmoreland County, Pennsylvania:

1. Christian Newcomer.	8. Henry Spayth.
2. Abraham Hiestand.	9. John Snyder.
3. Andrew Zeller.	10. Abraham Mayer.
4. Daniel Troyer.	11. Henry Kumler.
5. George Benedum.	12. Abraham Troxel.
6. Christian Krum.	13. Christian Berger.
7. Isaac Niswander.	14. Jacob Baulus.

Those persons were elected from the various districts to the General Conference.

Brother Abraham Hiestand was chosen to assist the bishop in the conference.

The conference was opened with the reading of the fifth chapter of First Peter, then singing, and then prayer by the most of the members.

Then proceeded to business.

There was misunderstanding and prejudice on the part of some, but this was removed in part.

A letter from Christopher Grosh, coming from their so-called conference, was read. It was evident therefrom that they had not considered the matter of which they wrote.

Brother Newcomer was accused by Bonnet that he was untruthful. The matter was investigated by three presiding elders, and it was found that there was only a misunderstanding.

He was in nothing liable to accusation.

John Baulus, *Secretary*

[SECOND GENERAL CONFERENCE, 1817, Mount Pleasant, Pennsylvania]

Proceedings of the Second General Conference, held at Mount Pleasant, Pennsylvania, June 2, 1817.

The United Brethren in Christ assembled in a general conference.

The following preachers were present:

1. C. Newcomer.	7. Jacob Dehof.
2. Andrew Zeller.	8. L. Kramer.
3. Abraham Mayer.	9. D. Mechlin.
4. Joseph Hoffman.	10. H. G. Spayth.
5. John Snyder.	11. C. Roth.
6. H. Kumler.	12. H. Ow.

1. The conference was opened with the reading of the fourth chapter of Ephesians, singing, and prayer.

2. Andrew Zeller was chosen associate chairman, and H. Spayth secretary.

3. Two letters were read, one from brethren in Washington County, Pennsylvania, and the other from brethren in New Philadelphia, Ohio. Resolved to give them a brotherly answer.

Closed for this day, with hearty prayer, till tomorrow at eight o'clock.

June 3, opened with the reading of the second chapter of Ephesians, singing, and prayer.

4. Resolved to give to Brother Abraham Forney license. To this end he was solemnly ordained to the ministerial office by Brothers C. Newcomer and A. Zeller with the laying on of hands. Further,

5. Brother C. Newcomer and Brother A. Zeller were, according to the Discipline, chosen bishops.

Adjourned at noon with prayer.

At two o'clock the thirteenth chapter of Hebrews was read, then singing and prayer, and again closed with prayer till next day.

June 4, at the opening the ninth chapter of Romans was read, then singing and prayer.

6. Resolved that the next General Conference shall be held at Dewalt Mechlin's, in Pleasant Township, Fairfield County, Ohio, beginning May 15, 1821.

7. Resolved that an annual conference shall be held in the Muskingum District, beginning June 1, 1818.

8. Resolved that three hundred Disciplines be printed in the German language, and one hundred in the English language.

The conference again closed with preaching and hearty prayer.

CLASS LEADERS MONITOR MEMBERS IN JOHN STREET CHURCH, NEW YORK CITY

Source: Samuel A. Seaman, Annals of New York Methodism Being a History of the Methodist Episcopal Church in the City of New York *(New York: Hunt & Eaton, 1892), 464-66. Notes indicating erasures omitted.*

LIST OF THE CLASSES, LEADERS' NAMES, AND WHEN THEY MEET, TAKEN SEPTEMBER 8 1802, BY THOMAS MORRELL

There are forty-six classes (No. 35 being repeated), and as at the preceding Conference 937 members were reported—this will give an average of rather more than twenty to a class. All, with two exceptions, were exclusively either male or female. Both of these were at the two-mile stone, and have the same leader—Vark. Besides these there were, of the whites, 13 composed of men and 23 of women; of colored, 4 of men and 7 of women—in both cases nearly twice as many female as male classes. Five leaders have each two classes. About one third of them also meet at private houses, and only five were held in the evening. Twenty-four met on Sunday; one at 6 A.M. and three at 7 A.M.

WHITE CLASSES.

No.	Days of Meeting.	Leader's Names.	Sex.	Time and Place of Meeting
1	Sunday..........	Van Wyck........	Male.	Old church, 7 o'clock, morning.
2	".............	Cooper..........	"	His work-shop, Bowery, 9 o'clock, morning.
3	"	Davis...........	Female.	Corner of Fayette & Henry Street, 9 o'clock, morning.

No.	Days of Meetiing.	Leader's Names.	Sex.	Time and Place of Meeting.
4	"	Gilman...........		Bowery school-house, 9 o'clock, morning.
			Male.	
5	"	Hick.............	"	Division Street, 9 o'clock, morning.
6	"	Praul...........	"	At Bro. Jaquish's, 9 o'clock.
7	"	Mead.............	"	At Bro. Lion's, 9 o'clock.
8	"	Ketchum..........	"	North Church, 9 o'clock.
9	"	Henry............	"	Bowery school, noon.
10	"	Jeffery..........	"	Bowery church, noon.
11	"	Russell..........	"	John Street church, noon.
12	"	Elsworth........	"	North church, noon.
13	"	Carpenter........	"	John Street Church, 4 o'clock, afternoon.
14	"	Vark.............	"	2 mile stone.
15	Sunday..........	Praul...........		Bowery church, 4 o'clock
			Female	
16	"	Lion.............	"	Second Street, at Forrest's, 1 o'clock
17	Monday..........	Cooper...........		Bro. Lyons, Fisher Street, 3 o'clock.
			Women	
18	"	Dugalls..........	"	Pump Street, 4 o'clock.
19	"	Smiths..........	"	Old church, 4 o'clock.
20	"	Barney..........	"	North church, 3 o'clock.
21	"	Hick.............	"	Davis's, 3 o'clock.

No.	Days of Meeting.	Leader's Names.	Sex.	Time and Place of Meeting
22	"	Sayres...........	"	No. 5 Barclay Street.
23	Tuesday.........	Stilwell.........	"	Harman Street, Price's, 3 o'clock.
24	"	Fowler...........	"	Bowery Church, 4 o'clock.
25	"	Browers..........	"	Old Church, 3 o'clock.
26	Wednesday.......	Arcularius.......	"	Old Church, 4 o'clock.
27	"	Knight...........	"	North church, 5 o'clock.
28	"	Stagg...........	"	No. 91 Harman Street, 4 o'clock.
29	"	Bonsall..........	"	Old church, 3 o'clock.
30	"	Dawson...........	"	Bowery Church, 3 o'clock.
31	Thursday........	Gilman's.........	"	North Church, 2 o'clock.
32	"	Mead's...........	"	Bowery Church, 4 o'clock.
33	"	Preacher's.......	"	Old church, 3 o'clock.
34	Friday..........	Marsh...........	"	Old church, evening, after preaching.
35	"	Vark............	"	Meets at church 2 mile stone, evening.
			Both.	

COLORED CLASSES.

No.	Days of Meeting.	Leader's Names.	Sex.	Time and Place of Meeting
35	Sunday	Sipkins..........	Men.	Old church, 6 o'clock, morning.
36	"	Pointers.........	"	Peter Williams, 7 o'clock, morning.
37	"	Thompsons........	"	African church, 7 o'clock, morning.
38	"	Cooks............		Evans, near African Church, 4 o'clock, afternoon.
			Women.	

No.	Days of Meeting.	Leader's Names.	Sex.	Time and Place of Meeting
39	"	Collins..........	"	School-house. No. 13 Barclay Street, 4 o'clock, afternoon.
40	"	Miller...........	"	African Church, 4 o'clock, afternoon.
41	"	Scott............	Men.	African Church, noon.
42	"	Marsh............		No. 45 Ann Street, Dinah Forbes, 4 o'clock, afternoon.
43	Tuesday.........	Matthison........	Women.	Old church, evening.
44	"	Parks............	"	Bowery church, evening.
45	Thursday........	Barney...........	"	Old church, evening.

FANNY LEWIS DESCRIBES
CAMP MEETING NEAR BALTIMORE

Source: Fanny Lewis, "[Letter], Baltimore, October 1803," Extracts of Letters Containing Some Account of the Work of God Since the Year 1800, written by the Preachers and Members of the Methodist Episcopal Church to their Bishops *(New York: Published by Ezekiel Cooper and John Wilson for the Methodist Connection in the United States, 1805), 88-91.*

Baltimore, October 1803

I hasten to give you some account of our glorious camp-meeting; but alas! all description fails. It would take an Addison or a Pope to give you even an idea of the lovely grove, particularly in the night, when the moon glimmered through the trees, and all was love and harmony. The [preaching] stand was placed at the bottom of several small hills, on which our tents and waggons [*sic*] were placed. The meeting began on Saturday, and was very lively.

On Sunday morning, Mr. S——— called his family to prayer-meeting. At ten o'clock public preaching began, and great was the power of God. There was scarce any intermission day or night. It looked awful and solemn to see a number of fires burning before the tents, and the trees with lanterns and candles suspended to them. No sound was heard except Glory to God in the highest! or, mercy! mercy! Such a night, my father, I never saw or felt before. Many souls were converted, and many witnessed that God was able to cleanse from all sin.

On Monday morning there was such a gust of the power of God that it appeared to me the very gates of hell would give way. All the people were filled with wonder, love and praise. Mr. S——— came and threw himself in our tent, crying, "Glory! glory! this is the happiest day I ever saw." He says he never knew such a continual power and increase of the love of God for three days and nights. We call it, "the happy Monday." Yes, it was a happy, happy Monday! a day long to be remembered, and a night never to be forgotten. O! how I longed for you, that you might share in the happiness of your unworthy child. Nor was our parting less glorious than our meeting; for several received perfect love after the congregation broke up. They were under the necessity of dismissing the people for want of preachers; all that were present were worn out. Truly the harvest was great, but the labourers were few.

Those who were absent, know not what they have lost; nor can they form any idea of what we enjoyed. It was none other than the gate of heaven.

Where! O! where shall we begin to praise redeeming love, for the peace and comfort and assurance our souls felt in realizing the promises of an unchangeable Jehovah? Camp-meeting! Why the very name thrills through every nerve! and almost makes me think I am in the charming woods. Every foot of ground seemed to me sacred. I saw nothing, heard nothing to molest my peace, not one jarring string. Every thing seemed to combine together to promote the glory of God and his Gospel.

Such indeed, my dear father, was our meeting; and I can but lament my inability to give you an account of it; but it was better felt than expressed. Sometimes you would see more than one hundred hands raised in triumphant praise with united voices, giving glory to God, for more than one hour together, with every mark of unfeigned humility and reverence.

The time between services was not taken up with "what shall we eat, or what shall we drink," but in weeping with those that wept, and rejoicing with those that rejoiced, and that had found the pearl of great price.

The preachers all seemed as men filled with new wine. Some standing crying, others prostrate on the ground, as insensible to every earthly object; while the master of assemblies was speaking to the hearts of poor sinners, who stood trembling under a sense of the power and presence of a sin-avenging God. They seemed unwilling to move from the spot where they stood, with their eyes fixed on them that were rejoicing in God their Saviour.

After all was over, I walked over the ground by moon-light—the scene was solemn and delightful. When I left the place, I cannot describe the emotion I felt. It was something like parting with all that was dear to me. My foolish heart kept saying, adieu ye sacred grove, adieu—never, never shall I see you more.

I am your dutiful
And affectionate daughter,
FANNY LEWIS

THE EVANGELICAL ASSOCIATION RECORDS EARLY ANNUAL AND GENERAL CONFERENCES

Source: S. C. Breyfogel, Landmarks of the Evangelical Association *(Reading, Pa:
Eagle Book Print, 1888), 13-14, 16-18, 24-25, 28-31. Excerpts.*

1807.
The First Annual Conference.

The first regular Annual Conference session of the Association was held at
Muehlbach, Dauphin (now Lebanon) Co., Pa., on the 15th and 16th of November,
1807. The session was opened with a season of prayer during which we implored the
divine blessing upon our transactions. Our membership had now reached a total of
220, nearly all of whom professed conversion. The following were the traveling
preachers: Jacob Albright elder, and John Walter and George Miller in full connection. John Dreisbach and Jacob Frey were newly received on trial. The local preachers were Charles Bisse, Conrad Phillips, and Solomon Miller. The class leaders and
exhorters present numbered twenty, making a total attendance of twenty-eight.

Jacob Albright was elected *Bishop* and George Miller, *Elder* by a majority of votes.
The Conference appointed Jacob Albright to prepare and publish a brief com-
pendium of church rules—a Discipline—for the instruction and edification of the
societies. The fields of labor were then assigned to the preachers, after which the
session closed with prayer. . . .

1809.
The Second Annual Conference.

The April of 1809 the second regular Annual Conference was held in Albany
Twp., Berks Co., Pa. The session was opened with prayer for the divine blessing to
rest upon the transactions. The membership of the Association was reported to be
426. One preacher was expelled on account of immoral conduct. The traveling
preachers on record were George Miller elder, John Walter and John Dreisbach in
full connection, and John Erb on trial. Matthew Betz and Henry Niebel were newly
received on trial. John Walter and John Dreisbach were elected to the office of

Elder and afterwards ordained as such. After the circuits had been arranged the preachers were appointed to their various fields.

Geo. Miller was directed to travel and to preach as much as his health would allow. He was also instructed to write upon such subjects as might prove edifying to the Association. Owing to the failing health and early decease of Albright, the preparation of Articles of Faith and of a Discipline was accomplished by Geo. Miller. The Conference instructed the latter to publish the work at his own expense. It was resolved that the official documents of the Association shall hereafter be published under the title of "The so-called Albrights." John Dreisbach was instructed to publish for the use of the Association a small catechism which he had translated from the English. The Conference gave John Walter $42.72 out of the subsidiary collection, for the purchase of a horse. The session closed with prayer. . . .

1813.
The Sixth Annual Conference.

President, George Miller.
Secretary, John Dreisbach.

On the 21st of April, 1813, the members of Conference assembled in Buffalo Valley, Pa., Northumberland Circuit, and continued in session three days. The proceedings were opened with prayer and supplication for the divine blessing. G. Miller was elected chairman, and J. Dreisbach, secretary. Two preachers were expelled from the Association on account of immoral conduct. G. Miller and J. Erb located on account of bodily infirmities. M. Betz and H. Niebel were ordained to the office of Elder; D. Yerlitz and L. Zimmerman to the office of Deacon. Abraham Buchman, John Kleinfelter, John Stambach, Adam Henig, Jacob Kleinfelter, and John Walter, Jr., were newly received on trial. A committee, consisting of G. Miller, J. Walter, and J. Dreisbach, was appointed to assign the different circuits to the preachers. The highest amount of salary received by a traveling preacher was $64.81. . . .

Geo. Miller and J. Erb promised Conference to attend the extra meetings and to travel as much as God would grant them strength. The former promised also to complete the supplement to our Church Discipline provided God give them grace to do so. The preachers received their licenses and gave their successors a list of appointments, the class books, and correct information concerning the state of affairs on the respective fields. With a resolution of consecration to the service of God and of reliance upon him the Conference adjourned. . . .

1816.
The Ninth Annual Conference.

President, John Dreisbach.
Secretary, Henry Niebel.

Conference convened in Dry Valley, Pa., Union Circuit, on June 11th, 1816, and continued its sessions until June 13th. The transactions were preceded by the customary religious exercises. J. Dreisbach was elected chairman, and H. Niebel, secretary. The conduct of the preachers was investigated. . . .

It was resolved that hereafter itinerant preachers shall receive annually in addition to their salary an allowance of $56 for clothes, provided the Conference find itself able to do so. At this time there were 41 local preachers in the Association.

The Conference appointed J. Dreisbach and H. Niebel to secure a printed form of license for preachers, J. Dreisbach promising to procure a suitable conference seal. These two brethren were also instructed to unify and edit our Discipline and to compile a good and suitable collection of hymns. It was unanimously agreed that local preachers who have stood their probation for six years shall, upon the recommendation of twelve itinerant preachers, be ordained. The Conference elected a Chief Book Commission, empowered to superintend for the Evangelical Association the printing establishment and book bindery with all their appurtenances, as long as the Conference shall see proper. The commission was instructed to hold an annual meeting for consultation in order to secure proper management, and also to make a correct annual statement of all the publishing interests. This first Book Commission consisted of J. Dreisbach, H. Niebel, Solomon Miller, A. Ettinger, Dan'l Bertolet, P. Breidenstein, and Chr. Spengler.

It was resolved that the next General Conference be held on Union Circuit, October 14th, 1816. The delegates appointed to constitute that body were: J. Dreisbach, H. Niebel, J. Walter, L. Zimmerman, J. Erb, J. Stambach, John Kleinfelter, S. Miller, J. Dehoff, D. Thomas, A. Ettinger, and J. Frueh.

J. Dreisbach, Jac. Kleinfelter, H. Niebel were instructed to visit A. Henig and F. Shauer on their fields of labor during the year. Each preacher received his license and gave his successor all needed information. The Conference adjourned with prayer and the customary resolution of sanction to the proceedings and of diligence in the work. . . .

1816.
The General Conference.

President, John Dreisbach.
Secretary, Henry Niebel.

The General Conference of the Evangelical Association convened in Buffalo Valley, Union Co., Pa., on the 14th day of October, 1816, and continued in session until the 17th. J. Dreisbach was elected chairman, and H. Niebel, secretary. Solomon Miller was elected general book agent, and H. Niebel, assistant.

It was resolved to meet in Social Conference with the United Brethren in Christ, at Conococheague, Maryland, on Feb. 14th, 1816; the object of this conference being an attempt to unite the two denominations, if such be the will of God. The delegates chosen to represent the Evangelical Association were: J. Dreisbach, H. Niebel, Solomon Miller, John Kleinfelter, D. Thomas, and A. Ettinger.

The Discipline—re-arranged and improved by the brethren J. Dreisbach and

154

H. Niebel—was examined and approved. Its publication was deferred until after the meeting of the Social Conference, with instructions that, if no union be effected by that body, fifteen hundred copies of the revised Discipline be published as soon as possible. The new hymn book *"Das Geistliche Saiten Spiel"* was examined and approved. Fifteen hundred copies were ordered to be published at once. The General Conference adjourned with the customary resolution of sanction to the proceedings, of reliance upon God and diligence in his service. Attached to the proceedings are the following names: J. Dreisbach, H. Niebel, J. Erb, J. Stambach, J. Kleinfelter, S. Miller, D. Thomas, J. Dehoff, J. Frueh, and A. Ettinger.

GENERAL CONFERENCE FASHIONS A "CONSTITUTION" FOR THE NEW CHURCH

Source: Methodist Episcopal Church, The Doctrines and Discipline of the Methodist Episcopal Church. *Published by John Wilson and Daniel Hitt for the Methodist Connection (New York: Printed by J. C. Totten, 1808), 14-15.*

Section III
Of the General and Yearly Conferences.

It is desired that all things be considered on these occasions, as in the immediate presence of God: That every person speak freely whatever is in his heart.

Quest. 1. How may we best improve our time at the conferences?

Answ. 1. While we are conversing, let us have an especial care to set God always before us.

2. In the intermediate hours, let us redeem all the time we can for private exercises.

3. Therein let us give ourselves to prayer for one another, and for a blessing on our labour.

Of the General Conference.

Quest. 2. Who shall compose the general conference, and what are the regulations and powers belonging to it?

Answer 1. The general conference shall be composed of one member for every five members of each annual conference, to be appointed either by seniority or choice, at the discretion of such annual conference: Yet so that such representatives shall have travelled at least four full calendar years from the time that they were received on trial by an annual conference, and are in full connection at the time of holding the conference.

2. The general conference shall meet on the first day of May, in the year of our Lord 1812 in the city of New-York, and thenceforward on the first day of May once in four years perpetually, in such place or places as shall be fixed on by the general conference from time to time: But the general Superintendants, with or by the

advice of all the annual conferences, or if there be no general Superintendant, all the annual conferences respectively shall have power to call a general conference, if they judge it necessary, at any time.

3. At all times when the general conference is met, it shall take two-thirds of the representatives of all the annual conferences to make a quorum for transacting business.

4. One of the general Superintendants shall preside in the general conference; but in case no general Superintendant be present, the general conference shall choose a president pro tempore.

5. The general conference shall have full powers to make rules and regulations for our church, under the following limitations and restrictions, viz.

[The Restrictive Rules]

1. The general conference shall not revoke, alter, or change our articles of religion, nor establish any new standards or rules of doctrine contrary to our present existing and established standards of doctrine.
2. They shall not allow of more than one representative for every five members of the annual conference, nor allow of a less number than one for every seven.
3. They shall not change or alter any part of rule of our government, so as to do away Episcopacy or destroy the plan of our itinerant general superintendency.
4. They shall not revoke or change the general rules of the United Societies.
5. They shall not do away the privileges of our ministers or preachers of trial by a committee, and of an appeal: Neither shall they do away the privileges of our members of trial before the society or by a committee, and of an appeal.
6. They shall not appropriate the produce of the Book Concern, or of the Charter Fund, to any purpose other than for the benefit of the travelling, supernumerary, superannuated and worn-out preachers, their wives, widows and children. Provided nevertheless, that upon the joint recommendation of all the annual conferences, then a majority of two-thirds of the general conference succeeding, shall suffice to alter any of the above restrictions.

FANNY NEWELL EXPERIENCES CALL TO PREACH

Source: Fanny Newell, Memoirs of Fanny Newell, Written by Herself.
Published by O. Scott and E. F. Newell (Springfield:
Merriam, Little & Co., 1832), 52-145. Excerpts.

June 9, 1809.

I set out in company with Br. Isaac Steadman and his wife to attend a camp-meeting, which was to be holden in Monmouth. At the same time and place the annual New England Conference was holden by the Methodist Episcopal Church. . . .

Sabbath morning, I attended prayer meeting at the stand, O! what a struggle I felt for the perfect love, that casteth out fear. . . . The kind Redeemer condescended to grant me the spirit of faith by which I laid hold on the blessing, and held it fast. O! what an enjoyment of God my soul was favored with. . . . O my soul!—this is a season never to be forgotten, whilst sense or reason lasts. O! what words can paint the glorious views, which perfect love unfolds. . . .

Tuesday. The circuit preacher, E. F. Newell came to my father's house to preach for the first time. His text was Psalms cxxii. 1, "I was glad when they said unto me, let us go up to the house of the Lord"; and he added, I also am glad that I have been brought here safe. Glory be given to God for the same. I added in my heart, Amen, if reformation attends your labor among us. Before he got through his sermon I had strong faith to believe that God would revive his work among us, and my little vessel was, like David's cup, running over; and I lost my bodily strength, for awhile, and the Lord revealed his glory and power to me, and I prophesied reformation. When the meeting was closed, I had the boldness of the lion; cheerfully took up my cross, and passing through, talked with every person in the room, warning and exhorting, and the Spirit of the Lord was upon me to help and strengthen me in this duty. I could say, "the Lord is my helper, of whom shall I be afraid." . . .

After commending myself to the care of my constant preserver, I lay down to sleep, and had a dream, which I think proper to relate. My mind was in the sweet composure when I gave myself up to sleep.

THE DREAM.

On a sudden fear came into my mind, lest I should not hold out to the end, and be faithful unto death. If I come short of heaven, I thought I should never see my beloved father in Christ, Henry Martin. This caused me to cry to the Lord to help my infirmities, and keep me as the apple of his eye. I fancied that I fell into a deep sleep, and dreamed that a woman who had been dead, came to me and said, "Fanny, I am sent with an errand from Brother Henry Martin to you. . . . He has sent me to tell you, that you must take his gown, and wear it; and when you die you must leave it where he left it." On which I awoke and exchanged my pillow for my knees. I thought on Elijah and Elisha, and was prepared to say, "behold the hand-maid of the Lord, let the mantle of an Henry, or rather Elijah, rest on me." The morning flows in, but goodness and mercy flow more delightfully. This is one of my good mornings. I believe the Lord is about to send us reformation. . . .

Last night in my sleep my thoughts were again occupied in preaching to perishing sinners. When awake, the subject rests upon me, and I am brought to wonder, why my mind is so much on preaching, both day and night, sleeping and waking, seeing I am but a feeble woman. At times I think I will go and join the people called Quakers or Friends, because they approbate females to preach amongst them. Travelling and visiting from house to house is all my delight, and the joy of my heart. Notwithstanding I have labored to collect all the objections that could be made against a woman's speaking in public, on any occasion whatever, to excuse myself, and then owning that it was my youth and ignorance that had pushed me forward,—after all my labor, I could not ease my conscience, or obtain peace of mind; therefore I must go in that way where I can find peace with God; for if God frowns upon me, who can appease his wrath? Yet it is so crucifying to my proud nature, that I too often neglect my duty, framing some excuse; but find by sad experience that it will not do. I have again and again given myself unreservedly to the Lord; and at times I am perfectly willing that he should do with me what seemeth good in his sight; for although I am *weak*, yet he is strong—he will help all my infirmities. . . .

My mind was sweetly exercised, even in sleep;—one night I fancied that I was in a large assembly preaching from these words, "Repent, for the kingdom of heaven is at hand." Could I preach as well when awake as when asleep, I should think "wo [*sic*] is me, if I preach not the Gospel";—and even now if I was a man, I should think it was my duty, and should be willing to go and preach Jesus, and hold a bleeding Saviour up to view before a guilty world of sinners. O Saviour! thou art calling me to something, I know not what; but my concern is so great for my fellow-mortals, that I could willingly do or suffer whatever the good Lord should be pleased to lay upon me. . . .

When Br. Newell came to his appointment, he asked me if I had weighed those questions, and was prepared to give any answer. I replied, Not fully; but am willing to relate some of the exercises of my mind, which I did. When he had prayed with the family, he went on his way, and in one week returned, took dinner, joined with

159

us to sing and pray, and as he was going away he gave me a paper, and said, "Sister Fanny, I wish you to watch and be much in prayer to God"; and then left me. On the paper he had written a sketch of his former character, his experience, and call to the ministry; and then asked me this question, "could you join such an one in marriage, and help him in the great work of saving souls?" He added, "I cannot advise one of your tender age and delicate constitution to join, and engage in so arduous a work, with one who has no worldly property or prospect to present to you for comfort; having nothing, yet possessing all things; but if you are convinced, that the Lord has called you to this great work, and I could be so happy as to have your help, I would receive you as a tender lamb to my bosom, and by the grace of God, be a guard to you; while you might labor with me in the gospel. May the Lord give thee understanding in all things. Farewell. E. F. N." . . .

From this time until we were married, which was not until the following October, we had very little private conversation. For a number of weeks I have had daily communion with God. Doubts, fears, temptations, and trials, all shrink before the breath of prayer. . . .

November 10th.

Mr. Newell returned, and on the 11th I started with him on a tour round his circuit, and in this journey I was more than ever confirmed, that I was in the work, for which the Lord had by painful scenes for several years been preparing me. Yes, blessed be God, for he does confirm his word with signs following. At every appointment the melting power of God was more or less experienced. . . .

On the evening of the 4th of December, 1811, my first born was introduced to the joy of all present. I said in my heart, he shall be called Ebenezer; for hitherto the Lord has helped me. Three days after, by means of neglect, I took a violent cold, and a fever followed. O what a wonder that I am alive on the shores of time. I am a miracle of grace, and am thankful for this instance of mercy; for I would rejoice in the will of my Heavenly Father, and to have it more than my meat and drink to do his will. For me it would have been better to have departed, and then I should have been with Christ. O yes, the delightful prospect which I had of heaven and glory still rests within my heart. On the eighth day my body sunk in a measure under my disease, and for several days I had little knowledge of what passed around me. The terror of death was upon me, and I expected soon to pass its dismal vale. My mind was resigned to give up my friends, and to die in a strange land, yet to leave a dear afflicted husband and tender son, were painful thoughts to me. I began now to examine myself, and sought earnestly for full resignation to the will of God—and I found what I sought. The Lord delivered me from the terrors of death, and enabled me to give up all, and I felt fully resigned to go.

Then an awful, glorious, interesting scene was open to my view; and whether I was in the body or out of the body, I cannot tell; God knoweth. This one thing I know, that I had no knowledge of anything, that transpired below the sun on this earth. Neither did I see anything with my natural eyes; for they were covered with several thicknesses of cloth, to protect them from the light, which gave me pain. In the first of my vision I thought, that I had taken leave of all earthly friends, and was taken up a little from the earth; from thence looking down I saw my body, from which my spirit had so lately taken her flight. I saw also my companion and friends weeping around the poor lifeless clay, and thought God had taken natural affection from me, for I felt no degree of sorrow. My stay here was short; for I beheld a path like stairs leading from earth to Heaven, and immediately was on the stairs ascending up to Heaven. I observed that there were multitudes of people behind and before me, who were ascending the same stairs. . . .

Rising from my knees, and looking most earnestly across the gulf, I beheld the gate thrown wide open, and a man standing full in the gateway. I raised up both my hands, and cried out, that is my Saviour, Christ the Lord. O how unspeakable was the joy that filled my soul. Immediately he spoke and said, "Fanny, you must not come yet; thou shalt not die, but live, and declare the works of the Lord to the children of men. Go back to yonder earth." When these words were spoken, I was turned about. . . . [W]ith them a divine power of reconciliation so filled my heart, that all was peace; and such a view of different parts of the earth, islands, new settlements, and large towns, and villages, was given to me that, when I came to myself, I called for Mr. Newell. He sat by me (as he afterwards told me, waiting to see what the Lord was about to do with me, and had my hand in his), and pressing my hand gently said, I am here. I answered, I shall not die, but live, and declare the wonderful works of God to the children of men. . . .

June, 1818.

The New England Conference is at Bowman's Point, in Hallowell. I contemplate to attend the preaching, and my desire has been, that the Lord would make the sitting of the Conference a blessing to the people, the preachers be filled with the power of the Holy Ghost, and perishing souls experience the salvation of God. O Lord, be with the preachers in conference, give them wisdom from above, that they may be directed aright in all their deliberations, and every preacher's appointment wind up in thy glory and the best welfare of souls. . . .

Sabbath. A trying day for me, on account of a new opening for preaching on St. Croix river. A proposal is made by conference for a volunteer, and Mr. Newell wishes to go, if I feel free to go with him; and here is a new trial. I know not what will be for the best.—I am *willing* he should go, and have a desire that he should go; but shrink back from accompanying him; for I have had such a scene of sufferings that my feeble nature shrinks at the prospect. I have a comfortable place to live in, and my children are with me and tender; and to think of launching out again into the open world, to face the storms, and plunge through mud and snow in those wild regions, and to experience heat and cold, I am ready to say, have me excused, I cannot go. With these discouragements, I go to meeting, and my love for souls increaseth; and as the cry of those destitute regions sounds louder and louder, my objections give way, and I begin to feel, like one of old, when he saw the miseries of a ruined people, "here am I, send me." After meeting I gave my companion some encouragement. . . .

Sabbath.—This has been a wearisome week to me. I have had but little rest, day or night, since my companion left home; for I am convinced that it was my duty to go with him, but the path seems to be hedged up with briars and thorns; yet it is the plain and right path for me to follow. That vision, which I had in Vermont on my sick bed six years ago, comes fresh to my mind. What were my feelings then, when my Saviour waved his hand, and said to me, "Fanny, go back," and pointed my course to this wilderness world! O how dreary did the earth appear to me then, when in sight of that celestial city, just across the fiery gulf. My feelings are much the same now as they were then. I am concerned lest I do the things I ought not to do, and leave undone the things which I ought to do. . . .

At evening I met my dear husband in peace and saluted him in these words, you have come back for help, have you not? He answered, "Woman's help." These words went to my heart, and my cry was, Lord how can I go? it looks like too great a work for me. . . .

The thought of leaving Gardiner is painful; for the providence of God seemed to cast my lot there. It was pleasant to me, and my mind became more composed, and willing to cease travelling than it had ever been before, since I was married. I thought, here my usefulness may be as great as any where else. But now all these pleasant prospects are blasted. . . . He does not bid me stop travelling yet; therefore I have no business with house or home at present. . . .

My spirit is so stirred within me at the sight of the people in destitute places, and the missionary spirit takes such hold of me, that hard things look easy; and I am willing to encounter difficulties, to spend and be spent in the service of God; for it is better to wear out than to rust out. O Lord, keep me humble.—While Mr. Newell was preaching, my heart was warm with the love of God, which more than compensated me for all my pain and fatigue of body. After sermon I arose to deliver my message [*sic*], "What came ye out for to see? a reed shaken with the wind?" &c. were my first words; and I had great liberty in pointing them to Christ, as a strong refuge in the day of trouble. . . .

Tuesday. Visited St. David's (New-Brunswick,) and a precious time it was. I do not regret my fatigue, although the enemy tried to disturb me with thoughts like these; Woman, you are not in the way of your duty—God has never called you to go to this and that place, or to speak in public—it is your own enthusiastic notion, and not from God. My mind replied, these thoughts are very congenial with my natural feelings, for I never sought, neither did I desire to be the wife of a preacher, much less an exhorter. My husband preached, and much power attended the word. Near the close, a few fragments fell into my mind, and such a sense of eternity rolled upon me, that I said, O Lord! I will attempt to speak once more, if thou wilt speak through this poor feeble instrument to the awakening of some poor soul. Blessed be God for that peace, that overflowed my heart. One man was there, who was heard to say, "I have heard preaching in almost every clime, and men of different orders and distinguished talents, but never shed tears under any one's word before." O Lord, make it for his everlasting good. Thanks be to God for the many tears and sighs, which I have witnessed in almost all congregations, which I have attended round these settlements.

Daniel Coker dialogues with slave master from Virginia

Source: Daniel Coker, A Dialogue Between a Virginian and an African Minister *(Baltimore: Joseph James, 1810), 5-8, 18-22. Excerpts.*

Virginian. Sir, I have understood that you have advanced an opinion that it would be just in our legislature to enact a law, for the emancipation of our slaves that we hold as our property; and I think I can convince you, that it would be wrong in the highest degree.

Minister. Sir, I will hear you with pleasure.

Virginian. You will observe sir, in the first place, that negroes were made slaves by law; they were converted into property by an act of the legislature, and under the sanction of that law, I purchased them; they therefore become my property, and I have a legal right to them. To repeal that law in order to annihilate slavery, would be, violently to destroy, what I legally purchased with my money or inherited from my father. It would be equally unjust with dispossessing me of my horses, cattle or any other species of property. To dispossess me of their children, would be equally unjust with dispossessing me of the annual profits of my estate.

Minister. That is an important objection and it calls for a serious answer. The matter seems to stand thus. Many years ago, men being deprived of their natural rights to freedom, and made slaves, were by law converted into property. This law, it is true, was wrong; it established iniquity; it was against the law of humanity, common sense, reason and conscience. It was, however, a law, and under the sanction of it, a number of men, regardless of its iniquity, purchased these slaves, and made their fellow men their property. But the question is concerning the liberty of man. The man himself claims it as his own property. He pleads, (and I think in truth) that it was originally his own; that he has never forfeited, nor alienated it; and therefore, by the common laws of justice and humanity, it is still his own. The purchaser of the slave claims the same property. He pleads that he purchased it under the sanction of the law, enacted by the legislature, and therefore it became his. Now, the question is, who has the best claim? Did the property in question belong to the legislature? Was it vested in them? I answer, no; it was not in them collectively; and therefore they could not convey it to those they represent. Now, does the property belong to him, who claims it from the legislature that had it not to give, or to the original owner who has never forfeited, nor alienated his right? For instance; should a law pass to sell a man's head, and should I purchase it, have I, in consequence of this law and this purchase, a better claim to this man's head than himself? Therefore, freeing men, in my opinion, is not depriving any one of their property, but restoring it to the right owner; it is suffering the unlawful captive to escape. *"Turn again our captivity O Lord, as the streams in the south."* Psal. cxxvi. 4. It is not wronging the master, but doing justice to the slave, restoring him to himself. The master, it is true, is wronged, he may suffer, and that greatly; but this is his own fault, and the fault of the enslaving law, and not of the law that does justice to the oppressed. You say, a law of emancipation would be unjust, because it would deprive men of their property; but is there no injustice on the other side? Let us consider the injustice on both sides, and weigh them in an even balance. On one hand, we see a man deprived of all property; of all capacity to possess property; of his own free agency; of the means of instruction; of his wife and children; and, of almost every thing dear to him: on the other, a man deprived of eighty or one hundred pounds. Shall we hesitate a moment to determine who is the greatest sufferer, and who is treated with the greatest injustice? The matter appears quite glaring, when we consider that *"neither this man nor his parents had sinned."* John, ix. 3. that he was born to these sufferings; but the other suffers altogether for his own sin, and that of his parents or predecessors. . . .

Minister. You will grant me the scriptures to be of Divine authority; you will also grant, that they are consistent with themselves, and that one passage may help to explain another: grant me this, and then I reply to your argument in favor of slavery.

Virginian. By all means.

Minister. In the thirteenth verse of the seventeenth chapter of Genesis, we find that Abraham was commanded to circumcise all that were born in his house or bought with money: we find in the sequel of the chapter, that he obeyed the command without delay, and actually circumcised every male in his family who came under this description. This law of circumcision continued in force, it was not abrogated, but confirmed by the law of Moses. Now, to the circumcised, were committed the oracles of God; and circumcision was a token of that covenant, by which (among other things) the land of Canaan, and various privileges in it, were promised to Abraham and his seed, and to all that were included in that covenant. All were included, to whom circumcision (which was the token of the covenant) was administered, agreeably to God's command. By Divine appointment, not only Abraham, and his natural seed, but he that was bought with money, of any stranger that was not of his seed, was circumcised. Since the seed of the stranger received the token of this covenant, we must believe that he was included and interested in it; that the benefits promised, were to be conferred on him. These persons bought with money, were no longer looked upon as uncircumcised and unclean; as aliens and strangers; but were incorporated with the church and nation of the Israelites, and became one people with them; became God's covenant people. Whence it appears, that suitable provision was made by the divine law, that they should be properly educated, made free, and enjoy all the common privileges of citizens. It was, by the divine law enjoined upon the Israelites, thus to circumcise all the males born in their houses; then, if the purchased servants in question had any children, their masters were bound by law to incorporate them into their church and nation. The children then were the servants of the Lord, in the same sense as the natural descendants of Abraham were; and therefore, according to the law, Lev. xxv. 42, 54. they could not be made slaves. *"For they are my servants, which I brought forth out of the land of Egypt: they shall not be sold as bondmen. And if he be not redeemed in these years, then he shall go out in the year of Jubilee, both he, and his children with him."* The passage of scripture under consideration was so far from authorizing the Israelites to make slaves of their servants' children, that they evidently forbid it; and therefore, are so far from proving the lawfulness of your enslaving the children of Africans, that they clearly condemn the practice as criminal. These passages of sacred writ have been wickedly pressed into the service of mammon perhaps more frequently than others. But does it not now appear, that these weighty pieces of artillery may be fairly wrested from your minister, and turned upon the hosts of the mammonites, with very good effect? The minister you speak of, who plead for slavery from this passage of scripture, should have observed, that in the law Moses referred to, there is not the least mention made of the children of these servants; it is not said they should be servants or any thing about them. No doubt some of them had children; but it was unnecessary to mention them, because they were already provided for, by the law of circumcision. To extend the law of Moses to the children of these servants, is arbitrary and presumptuous; it is making them to include much more than is expressed or necessarily implied in the text. And, it is not binding on me to prove how these persons were made servants at first; nor is it necessary we should know whether they were persons who had forfeited their liberty by capital crimes; or whether they had involved themselves in debt by folly or extravagance, and submitted to serve during their lives, in order to avoid a greater calamity; or whether they were driven to that necessity in their younger days, for want of friends to take care of them. We are not informed, whatever may be conjectured. This, however, we may be certain of, that the Israelites were not sent by a divine mandate, to nations three hundred miles distant, who were neither doing, nor meditating any thing against them, and to whom they had no right whatever, in order to captivate them by fraud or force; tare [*sic*] them away from their native country, and all their tender connections; bind them in chains and fetters; crowd them into ships, and there murder them by thousands, for want of air and proper exercise; and then doom the survivors and their posterity to bondage and misery forever.

JOHN TOTTEN PUBLISHES APOLOGY
FOR CAMP MEETINGS

Source: An Apology for Camp-Meetings, Illustrative of Their Good Effects, and Answering the Principal Objections Urged Against Them. *New York: John C. Totten, 1810*.

If then, we would justify those meetings, it is necessary to clear them from the charge of evil, and prove them productive of good only: and by the same rule would we condemn and explode them, we must shew that they are the cause of evil, rather than good: for of both they cannot be; and which of the two is the truth, I shall now proceed to inquire. And, [*sic*]

First, What is a Camp-Meeting? It is a body of christians, christian ministers, preachers and exhorters, assembled in an appointed grove, or some other convenient place, where they form a regular encampment, for the express purpose of spending a few days and nights together, in preaching, exhortation, hearing the word of life, prayer, praise, and other religious exercises; which are allowed by all sects and denominations of christians under heaven, to be means of grace, instituted by Christ himself, for the promotion of his own kingdom, in the awakening, conversion, edification, and sanctification of the souls of men, in order to their being prepared for heaven, as well as for usefulness in this life: and none dispute their natural tendency thereto, who believe the divinity of the gospel of Christ Jesus. . . .

There are many, who, for various reasons, seldom, and some perhaps never see the inside of a house of worship; some, because they have no relish for religious exercises; others, because they are irksome to them; not a few, because they cannot attire themselves in a manner judged suitable by their pride, to appear in a gay, modish congregation; and many more, because of their avowed enmity to Jesus Christ and his religion. But Camp-meetings attract the attention, and draw together some of all these, and many other characters and descriptions of men and women; as well as Christians of different sects and persuasions, from some motive or other; if not christians, often curiosity; fondness or novelty; inquisitive speculations; philosophical, religious, or literary criticism; sectarian opposition; romantic disposition; and a propensity to trifle with, and ridicule sacred things; but none of those motives as unworthy and sordid as they are, furnish an effectual barrier against the first operations of truth and grace, in the awakening of sinners, however they may resist and stifle it afterwards, for in this respect it is as irresistable, and often sudden as the darted lightning, and not unfrequently, where the subjects of it were as pre-resolved against the religion of Jesus, as was Saul of Tarsus, . . . nor is it uncommon for the same effects and fruits to follow, as did in his case, for like him, many of them immediately begin to preach the same Jesus they before persecuted.

How many Christians whose hearts had grown cold in the frozen regions of worldly business and cares of life, so that, their careless hands began to hang down in the ways of godliness, and their feet to loiter in the heavenly race, have, by retiring from the bustle of the world, and spending a few days in those exercises, melted into contrition again under the baptizing fire of the Holy Ghost; and returned home, strong in the Lord and in the power of his might; thus, being saved from further apostasy, and prepared for future usefulness, both in the church of Christ, and society at large. . . .

That at those Camp-meetings, every exertion is made, not only to prevent the commission of evil among those who are disposed for it, but to bring sinners to repentance, and to provoke Christians to live and good works, no one will deny who has ever attended them, nor that the good effects above stated have uniformly followed those exertions; of the truth of which, thousands are this day the living witnesses, many of whom attended from no better motives than those already mentioned.

What greatly adds to the weight of argument in favour of those meetings, is, that the good effects produced by them at the time, is not circumscribed to, nor does it end with them. Not to mention those who have died happy in the Lord; having been awakened, converted, or sanctified on some of those occasions, but to notice the subsequent good which society at large has derived from them; for, not only have the neighborhoods in their vicinity experienced religious revivals, as the fruits of them, but more or less has the same effect followed in many other parts of the country, far distant from the places where they have been held, through the instrumentality of those who had been blessed under this institution. . . .

But it is objected, that, "admitting much good to have resulted from Camp-meetings, yet much more might have been done, had it not been prevented by the wild proceedings of the preachers and other members of those meetings, by such loud passionate characterising discourses and exhortations, the noisy prayers, cries, groans, shouts, falling, and odd gestures of the people." As those extraordinaries complained of are not peculiar to Camp-meetings only, but common on other religious occasions, where the power of grace is displayed, I shall take no other notice of them in this little work, than as far as they stand related to the objection raised upon them. . . .

It will be asked, however, if there are no counterfeits among those who make so much ado about religion? I grant there may be, and no doubt is. But what then? Does it prove that the work is not in general genuine? . . . And such has generally been the proof of the genuineness of the work; although it is much to be lamented, that some have fallen away; yet their number is small compared with those who have continued, and still continue to persevere in religion; to say nothing of those who have died happy in God, as the fruit of camp-meetings.

It is objected, however, that, "For people to conduct in this manner, is highly enthusiastic." . . .

If this, or any thing that resembles it, is enthusiasm, them, not only Christ, but the prophets, apostles, and primitive christians, were enthusiasts. "Clap your hands," says the Psalmist, "all ye people; shout unto God with a voice of triumph. God is gone up with a shout, the Lord with the sound of a trumpet." Psalm xlvii. 1, 5. Says Isaiah, "Cry out and shout, thou inhabitant of Zion, for great is the Holy One of Israel in the midst of thee." Isaiah xli. 6. And again, chap. xlii. 11. "Let the inhabitants of the rock sing; let them shout from the top of the mountains."

The same may be said with respect to people's loosing their animal strength, and falling prostrate on the earth under those religious exercises, apparently lifeless, or in great agitations, both of body and mind. The very enemies and persecutors of Christ, with all their hardihood, have not been able to withstand the divine power, which, on certain occasions, accompanies his word and presence. . . .

The scriptures do not, however, confine this extraordinary experience to sinners under the influence of the awakening power of God: but mention some of the most eminent saints, as having been affected in the same manner, on particular occasions: of which I shall state but two cases. . . .

Nor can any solid arguments be urged against those meetings, from the loud, pointed, characterizing, passionate discourses, common on such occasions, (though bitterly complained of) so long as it is written, Isaiah lviii. 1. "Cry aloud, spare not; lift up thy voice like a trumpet, and shew my people their transgressions, and the house of Jacob their sins," . . .

It is said that "The most ridiculous confusion reigns at Camp-meetings, occasioned by a variety of religious exercises intermixing with each other; as preaching, praying, shouting, crying for mercy, &c.; which renders it difficult for a person to attend (rationally) to any thing serious, if disposed for it." It is certain that nothing can be confusion, only as it is conceived of by, and affects the mind; . . . The only confusion then that exists, is in the minds of those who raise the objection, and is the offspring of a dissipated, unstable mind, or a certain prejudice of education, which takes it for granted, that no religious exercises can be right, or agreeable to the order of God, but such as correspond with the straight laced regulations of modern decorum: the moral sense of which, differs but very little from supposing, that a man cannot worship God as acceptably in the habit of a common labourer, as in a richer dress, because out of the line of common custom; and would generally produce as much confusion (tho' of another kind) in the minds and conduct of a proud congregation of Sunday, meeting-house Christians, to witness such an innocent, indifferent circumstance, as do the extraordinary exercises of Camp-meetings.

What would those objections have said, had they been present on the day of Pentecost? When the newly inspired disciples of Jesus, altogether, in no less than fifteen different languages, spake forth the wonderful works of God, Acts. ii. 9, 10, 11. . . .

[T]he objection which says, that the intermixing of so many different religious exercises at camp-meetings, either prevents good from being done, or that there would be more effected, if it were otherwise, is altogether falacious, so long as it is undeniably manifest, that all those different exercises are sanctioned by the divine presence, and saving grace of the Son of God: for while the different groups of Christians, in their several little circles and tents, are all at once engaged, within hearing of each other, in prayer, praise, exhortation, &c. at all these sinners are awakened, souls converted, backsliders reclaimed, the lukewarm quickened, believers sanctified, and the work of God in general revived; the fruits of which are long afterwards witnessed by the world, and are incontestible proofs that God was among the people, and approved their religious proceedings.

It is further objected, that "Camp-meetings occasion a waste of time, and unnecessary expence [*sic*]." To this, no other reply is necessary, than (what no man of common sense will dispute) that the time employed in promoting the eternal welfare of our own souls, and the souls of others, is so far from being wasted, that it really is the only part of our time which is properly saved, or redeemed from the consumption of worldly cares, and the business of life; . . .

It has often been said that, "Camp-meetings are the cause of, or afford an opportunity for an illicit intercourse of the sexes; by which they have become the fruitful source of illegitimate children, and consequently great personal and social evils." . . .

That many of this character attend those meetings is unquestionable, (as well as every other description of sinners, among us) and numbers of them have been awakened and converted to God, who are now faithful, and worthy members of the church of Christ, who, like Mary Magdalene, (once a Jewish harlot) now set at the feet of Jesus, to hear his gracious words, and live upon his approbating smiles; while the less degraded and less penitent Martha's, are accosted by the Saviour in the reprehending language of, "Martha! Martha! thou art careful and troubled about many things; but one thing is needful: and Mary hath chosen that good part, which shall never be taken away from her."

So that Camp-meetings, instead of being the cause of female degeneracy, are the means of lessening the number of common prostitutes, and of restoring the self-degraded daughters of our mother Eve, to the lost favour, both of God and man, to useful membership in society, and if faithful to death, to the eternal enjoyment of virgin honours of Paradise. . . .

The next objection I shall notice is, that "Camp-meetings furnish an opportunity for avaricious persons, to avail themselves of the institutions of religion, for the purpose of carrying on an iniquitous speculations, to the prejudice of individuals and society at large; by retailing spirituous liquors from tents and hovels, erected for that purpose, . . . I may confidently challenge the world to produce a single instance, of a person, who before was strictly temperate, that has become a drunkard from attending Camp-meetings; or to prove that any drunkard from attending who has there been intoxicated, would have been sober had he been at home, or any where else, in possession of the means to procure the intoxicating fluid: . . . No new evil therefore exists on this account, but only an old one is removed from one place, or part of society to another, by which their families and neighbours enjoy a short respite from the plague of having them drunk at home, and the Methodists, and other religious people who may unite with them at those seasons, are obliged for the time being, to bear the burden for them. For I make no hesitation to say, that, the man who exposes himself in the debauchery of intemperate drinking, before a household of thousands, is a sottish drunkard in his own house, or his fathers.

The last objection I shall notice is, that, "Camp-meetings are unnecessary and unscriptural." They are said to be "unnecessary because there is no want among us, of houses of public worship, whereas, if it were otherwise, or if Christians were so persecuted in our towns and cities, that they could not there enjoy the gospel in peace, it would furnish a plausible excuse for retiring to the wilderness for that purpose; but since none of those difficulties exist, there is no necessity for it." . . .

That we are under the highest obligations to worship and adore the Supreme Being, no man of sense will pretend to deny; and a number of reasons have already been offered, to shew that, the circumstances and exercises of Camp-meetings, have a direct tendency to inspire the minds of the truly pious, with more sublime views of the Divine majesty, and purer strains of undissembled adoration, than any other religious institution among us; and God is undoubtedly worthy to receive our most sublime homage, and ourselves are bound to offer it to him. It is therefore necessary that we should attend to those means, which have the greatest tendency to excite it, in the highest degree.

We are likewise under moral obligations, as we have opportunity, to do all the good we can to our fellow-creatures. The greatest possible good we can do them, is to be instrumental in leading them to God, and the knowledge of his salvation: and no institution affords so great an opportunity for this as camp-meetings: nor, (as heretofore observed,) is any other in general so notable for the awakening and conversion of sinners, the reclaiming of backsliders, quickening the lukewarm, and for reviving the work of God in all its branches, and of course promoting the general good of society. . . .

Whether camp-meetings are unscriptural or not, does not so much depend upon their being enjoined by a divine command, as upon, whether they are forbidden: and that they are, no one who has ever read the Bible will pretend to maintain. . . .

But what need of abstract reasoning, in support of the scripturality of an institution, which has for its basis the precedency of the example of Jesus Christ. For whoever reads the fourteenth and fifteenth chapters of St. Matthew's gospel, cannot but be convinced that, he was no wise strenuous for confining the public worship of God within the walls of temples; but on certain occasions, chose rather to transfer it to a solitary mountain or desert; where he detained thousands of men, women and children for several days at a time. . . .

JARENA LEE HEARS A CALL TO PREACH

Source: Religious Experience and Journal of Mrs. Jarena Lee, Giving
an Account of Her Call to Preach the Gospel. Revised and
Corrected from the Original Manuscript, Written by Herself
(*Philadelphia: Printed and published for the author, 1849*), 10-18. *Excerpts.*

My Call to Preach the Gospel

Between four and five years after my sanctification, on a certain time, an impressive silence fell upon me, and I stood as if some one was about to speak to me, yet I had no such thought in my heart. But to my utter surprise there seemed to sound a voice which I thought I distinctly heard, and most certainly understood, which said to me, "Go preach the Gospel!" I immediately replied aloud, "No one will believe me." Again I listened, and again the same voice seemed to say, "Preach the Gospel; I will put words in your mouth, and will turn your enemies to become your friends."

At first I supposed that Satan had spoken to me, for I had read that he would transform himself into an angel of light, for the purpose of deception. Immediately I went into a secret place, and called upon the Lord to know if he had called me to preach, and whether I was deceived or not; when there appeared to my view the form and figure of a pulpit, with a Bible lying thereon, the back of which was presented to me as plainly as if it had been a literal fact.

In consequence of this, my mind became so exercised that during the night following, I took a text and preached in my sleep. I thought there stood before me a great multitude, while I expounded to them the things of religion. So violent were my exertions and so loud were my exclamations, that I awoke from the sound of my own voice, which also awoke the family of the house where I resided. Two days after, I sent to see the preacher in charge of the African Society, who was the Rev. Richard Allen . . . to tell him that I felt it my duty to preach the gospel. But as I drew near the street in which his house was, which was in the city of Philadelphia, my courage began to fail me; so terrible did the cross appear, it seemed that I should not be able to bear it. . . . [A]s soon as I came to the door, me fears subsided, the cross was removed, all things appeared pleasant—I was tranquil.

I now told him that the Lord had revealed it to me that [I] must preach the gospel. He replied by asking, in what sphere I wished to move in? I said, among the Methodists. He then replied, that a Mrs. Cook, a Methodist lady, had also some time before requested the same privilege; who it was believed, had done much good in the way of exhortation, and holding prayer meetings; and who had been permitted to do so by the verbal license of the preacher in charge at the time. But as to women preaching, he said that our Discipline knew nothing at all about it—that it did not call for women preachers. This I was glad to hear, because it removed the fear of the cross—but no sooner did this feeling cross my mind, than I found that a love of soul had in a measure departed from me; that holy energy which burned within me as a fire, began to be smothered. This I soon perceived.

O how careful ought we to be, lest through our bylaws of church government and discipline, we bring into disrepute even the word of life. For as unseemly as it may appear nowadays for a woman to preach, it should be remembered that nothing is impossible with God. And why should it be remembered that nothing is impossible with God? And why should it be thought impossible, heterodox, or improper for a woman to preach, seeing the Saviour died for the woman as well as the man?

If the man may preach, because the Saviour died for him, why not the woman, seeing he died for her also? Is he not a whole Saviour, instead of a half one, as those who hold it wrong for a woman to preach, would seem to make it appear?

Did not Mary *first* preach the risen Saviour, and is not the doctrine of the resurrection the very climax of Christianity—hangs not all our hope of this, as argued by St. Paul? Then did not Mary, a woman, preach the gospel? For she preached the resurrection of the crucified Son of God. . . .

My Marriage

In the year 1811, I changed my situation in life, having married Mr. Joseph Lee, Pastor of a Coloured Society at Snow Hill, about six miles from the city of Philadelphia. . . .

For six years from this time I continued to receive from above such baptisms of the Spirit as morality could scarcely bear. About that time I was called to suffer in my family by death—five, in the course of about six years, fell by his hand; my husband being one of the number, which was the greatest affliction of all.

I was now left alone in the world, with two infant children, one of the age of about two years, the other six months, with no other dependence than the promise of Him who hath said, "I will be the widow's God, and a father to the fatherless." Accordingly, he raised me up friends, whose liberality comforted and solaced me in my state of widowhood and sorrows. I could sing with the greatest propriety the words of the poet.

> He helps the stranger in distress,
> The widow and the fatherless,
> And grants the prisoner sweet release.

I can now say even now, with the Psalmist, "Once I was young, but now I am old, yet I have never seen the righteous forsaken, nor his seed begging bread." I have ever been fed by his bounty, clothed by his mercy, comforted and healed when sick, succored when tempted, and every where upheld by his hand.

The Subject of My Call to Preach Renewed

It was now eight years since I had made application to be permitted to preach the gospel, during which time I had only been allowed to exhort, and even this privilege but seldom. This subject now was renewed afresh in mind; it was as a fire shut up in my bones. About thirteen months passed on, while under this renewed impression. During this time, I had solicited of the Rev. Bishop Richard Allen, who at this time had become Bishop of the African Episcopal Methodists in America, to be permitted the liberty of holding prayer meetings in my own hired house, and of exhorting as I found liberty, which was granted me. By this means, my mind was relieved, as the house was soon filled when the hour appointed for prayer had arrived. . . .

Soon after this, as above related, the Rev. Richard Williams was to preach at Bethel Church, where I with others were assembled. He entered the pulpit, gave out the hymn, which was sung, and then addressed the throne of grace; took his text, passed through the exordium, and commenced to expound it. The text he took is in Jonah, 2d chap. 9th verse,—"Salvation is of the Lord." But as he proceeded to explain, he seemed to have lost the spirit; when in the same instant, I sprang, as by an altogether supernatural impulse, to my feet, when I was aided from above to give an exhortation on the very text which my brother Williams had taken.

I told them that I was like Jonah; for it had been then nearly eight years since the Lord called me to preach his gospel to the fallen sons and daughters of Adam's race, but that I had lingered like him, and delayed to go at the bidding of the Lord, and warn those who are as deeply guilty as were the people of Ninevah.

During the exhortation, God made manifest his power in a manner sufficient to show the world that I was called to labour according to my ability, and the grace given unto me, in the vineyard of the good husbandman.

I now sat down, scarcely knowing what I had done, being frightened. I imagined, that for this indecorum, as I feared it might be called, I should be expelled from the church. But instead of this, the Bishop rose up in the assembly, and related that I had called upon him eight years before, asking to be permitted to preach, and that he had put me off, but that he now as much believed that I was called to that work, as any of the preachers present. These remarks greatly strengthened me, so that my fears of having given an offense and made myself liable as an offender subsided, giving place to a sweet serenity, a holy job of a peculiar kind, untasted in my bosom until then.

The next Sabbath day while sitting under the word of the gospel, I felt moved to attempt to speak to the people in a public manner, but I could not bring my mind to attempt it in the church. I said, Lord, anywhere but here. Accordingly, there was a house not far off which was pointed out to me; to this I went. It was the house of a sister belonging to the same society with myself. Her name was Anderson. I told her I had come to hold a meeting in her house, if she would call in her neighbours. With this request she immediately complied. My congregation consisted of but five persons. . . . At this place I continued to hold meetings about six months. During that time I kept house with my little son, who was very sickly. About this time I had a call to preach at a place about thirty miles distant, among the Methodists, with whom I remained one week, and during the whole time not a thought of my little son came into my mind; it was hid from me, lest I should have been diverted from the work I had to do, to look after my son. Here by the instrumentality of a poor coloured woman, the Lord poured forth his spirit among the people. Though, as I was told, there were lawyers, doctors, and magistrates present to hear me speak, yet there was mourning and crying among sinners, for the Lord scattered fire among them of this own kindling. The Lord gave his handmaiden power to speak for his great name, for he arrested the hearts of the people, and caused a shaking amongst the multitude, for God was in the midst.

I now returned home, found all well, no harm had come to my child, although I left it very sick. Friends had taken care of it which was of the Lord. I now began to think seriously of breaking up housekeeping, and forsaking all to preach the everlasting Gospel.

Methodists Gather for Quarterly Conference at Smithfield, New York

Source: William Warren Sweet, ed., Religion on the American Frontier, *1783–1840 (Chicago: University of Chicago Press, 1946), 4:562-67. Excerpts. Spelling in the source document is highly irregular. Bracketed notes or corrections derive from Sweet.*

Minutes of a Qrt. Conference held at Smithfield May 25th 1811

Qust 1st Who are the members of this Conference
Ans [List of names given.]

2d The Members of this Conference were particularly examined one by one in each of the following Christian ordinances and Practice—1st Baptism both Adult and the rite of Infants—2d The Lords supper—3d of Labor in their Calling—4th Experience—5th Practise viz Family Devotion and Instruction—6 Family Habits viz Drinking spiritous liquor; Wearing of Gold and ornimintal apparal—7th Fasting—8th Support of the Gospel—9th Privileges of the Church such as Love feasts & Class meetings

3d Br. Reuben Haight and Br. Isaac Pierson have their Preaching Licence Renewed

4th Brethren Timothy Pratt, Martin Pierson, Thomas Grimes, Enoch Wilcox, & Sylvester Morris, have their Exhorting licence Renewed

5th Br Ebenezer Doolittle receivd. Licence to Preach—

6th Br. Isaac Clark Received Licence to Exhort—

7th Voted to Recommend Br Orrin Doolittle unto the Annual Conference as a Propper person to Join the Traviling Connection

8th Acording to appointment of the Qrt. Conference

We entered on our labor with Br. James Annis on Monday 11th March and Report that after requesting him (Br. Annis) to go aside with us where we first prayed to God for him and bles[s]ing on our labor we then asked Br. Annis if he did not think he had done wrong in praying the Curses of God on his Neighbor he answered that he Did not feel guilty and had no confession to make We then proved to him from our saviours words that instead of Cursing he ought to bless them that curse us to which he made no particular answer, but said he had Done the man no wrong and would make no Confession; We

175

then informed him that he was suspended and Cited him to appear at the next conference for his trial.

Wm. Case

9th This Conference Consider that the case of Br. Annis in his praying the Curses of God on his Neighbor to be very unchristian and his giving no satisfaction notwithstanding an affectionate Labor of his Brethren We therefore in the fear of God expell him from our Church

10th Voted that we have Camp Meeting at our next Qrt. At Br. O'Ferrils in Pompey—

Neh. Batcheller *Secretary*

At Qt. Conference held in Smithfield March 12th 1814

Members Present [List follows.]

2d Members examined.—

3d An appeal presented to this Conference by Br. Benjamin Morse of Eaton.—

4# the Accusation; Falsehood.—

5# Jehial Clark deposeth that about six weeks ago he was at Br. Mors's to borrow an auger and got Br. Stewarts auger which was dull he also told Br Morse he would bring it home at which Br. Morse told him he need not bring it home for he was going over to his house and would git it himself.

7# Br. Stewart deposeth.—that in the fore part of the winter he carried an auger to Br Morse's to be fixed and that Br Morse charg'd one Shilling for Repairing the auger in answer to which he told him he ought to have Damages inasmuch as the auger was broken he also saith that Brother Clark told him that he fill'd [*sic*] the auger and broke it. also that Brother Morse told him that he fill'd the auger himself Br. Clark saith that Br. Morse lent him the auger.

8# Br Bayley saith that he conciv'd that Br. Morse me[a]nt Br Clark should have the auger.

9# Br. Stewart saith that Br Morse told him that he had Nothing to do with the auger for Br. Clark took it with liberty.

10# Br Fowler saith that Br. Morse told him that it was his intention that Br. Clark should have the auger.

11# Resolved that this Conference Refer the Case of Br. Morse to a Committee of three to wit Brethren Timothy Dewey, John Pratt, & Isaac Pierson.—

12# From the testimony it appears to us that Br Morse is guilty

| Report of the Comm. | } | of falsehood yet it may be possible that he did not design to tell a falsehood but we cannot call it any thing than Evation— |

13# Resolv'd therefore that Br Morse acknowledges to Br. Clark and the Society that he has given reason to believe that he intended falsehood and that he be

Suspended three Months from the privileges of the Church and put back on triall for Six Months

14# Br Morse being cal[l]ed and the Judgement read was asked if he Conceded to it to which he replied in the Negative and Conference then Voted that three weeks be allowed him ti make his Confession but if he did not in that time he should be expel[l]ed

15# Resolv'd that we advise Br Case to discharge Br Doolittle from travailing the Circuit

16# Resolv'd that we have Camp Meeting in Sept. Next—

17# Resolv'd that our next Qrt. Meeting be at the Meeting house in Lenox—

Neh. Batcheller *Secretary*

Bishop McKendree delivers first Episcopal Address to the General Conference

Source: Robert Paine, Life and Times of William McKendree, Bishop of the Methodist Episcopal Church *(Nashville: Lamar & Barton, 1922), 160-62.*

To the General Conference of the Methodist Episcopal Church, now assembled in the city of *New York.*

Dear Brethren: My relation to you and the connection in general seems in my opinion, to make it necessary that I should address you in some way by which you may get possession of some information perhaps not otherwise to be obtained by many of you.

It is now four years since, by your appointment, it became my duty jointly to superintend our extensive and very important charge. With anxious solicitude and good wishes, I have looked forward to this General Conference. The appointed time has come, and the Lord has graciously permitted us to meet according to appointment, for which I hope we are prepared jointly to praise and adore his goodness.

Upon examination, you will find that the work of the Lord is progressing in our hands. Our important charge has greatly increased since the last General Conference. We had an increase of upward of 40,000 members. At present we have upward of 2,000 local preachers, about 700 traveling preachers, and about 190,000 members. And these are widely scattered over seventeen States, besides the several territorial settlements and the Canadas.

Thus situated, it must be expected in the present state of things that the council and direction of your united wisdom will be necessary to preserve the harmony and peace of the body, as well as the cooperation of the teaching and local ministry in carrying on the blessed work of reformation which the Lord has been pleased to effect through our instrumentality. To deserve the confidence of the local ministry and membership, as well as to retain confidence in ourselves and in each other, is undoubtedly our duty. And if we consider that those who are to confide in us are a collection from all classes and descriptions and from all countries of which our nation is composed, scattered promiscuously over this vast continent, men who were originally of different educations, manners, habits, and opinions, we shall see the difficulty as well as the importance of this part of our charge.

In order to enjoy the comforts of peace and union, we must "love one another." But this cannot abide where confidence does not exist; and purity of intention, manifested by proper actions, is the very foundation and support of confidence. Thus "united we stand," each member is a support to the body and the body supports each member, but if confidence fail, love will grow cold, peace will be broken, and "divided we fall." It therefore becomes this body, which by its example is to direct the course of thousands of ministers and tens of thousands of members, to pay strict attention to the simplicity of gospel manners and to do everything as in the immediate presence of God. If we consider the nature of our business, our natural imperfections, and the history of the Church in all its attempts to reform the world, it is scarcely to be expected, in so large a body, that all will be as strictly evangelical as they should be. But it is to be hoped that such failures will be prevented as far as possible by both your action and your example.

Standing in the relation I do to you and the connection generally, I feel it a part of my duty to submit to your consideration the appointment of the Genesee Conference. And perhaps it may be for the general good if in your wisdom you should think proper to take into consideration a division of the work in the western country, and a proper arrangement of the work in general; and the magnitude and extent of the work which the Lord has graciously pleased to prosper in our hands, may make it proper for you to inquire if the work is sufficiently under the oversight of the superintendency, and to make such arrangements and provision as your wisdom may approve. I would also suggest the necessity of keeping in view not only the traveling, but the relation and situation also of our local brethren, and to pursue that plan which may render the whole more useful. It may also be proper to bring into view any unfinished business of the last General Conference. Hitherto, as a body, we have been preserved by our well-digested system of Rules, which are as sinews to the body, and form the bond of union; but it is evident, both from experience and Scripture, that even good men may depart from first principles and from the best of rules: it may therefore be proper for you to pay some attention to the administration, to know the state both of the traveling and local ministry, as it relates to doctrine, discipline [*sic*], and practice.

Before I conclude, permit me, my dear brethren, to express a few thoughts concerning the view I take of the relation in which I stand to this body. It is only by virtue of a delegated power from the General Conference that I hold the reins of government. I consider myself bound, by virtue of the same authority, to exercise discipline in perfect conformity with the Rules of our Church, to the best of my ability. I consider myself justly accountable, not for the system of government, but for my administration, and ought therefore to be ready to answer in General Conference for my past conduct and be willing to receive information and advice to perfect future operations. I wish this body to exercise their rights in these respects.

I take pleasure here in presenting my grateful acknowledgments for the high degree of confidence which my beloved brethren have placed in me and especially for the able council and seasonable support afforded by many, which has, I believe, with the divine aid, preserved and supported me.

Dear brethren, such are the effects of our high responsibility connected with a consciousness of my insufficiency for so high a task that I move with trembling. Your eyes and the eyes of the Lord are upon me for good. We shall rejoice together to see the armies of our Israel wisely conducted carrying the triumphs of the Redeemer's kingdom to the ends of the earth, and the Lord will rejoice to "make his ministers a flame of fire."

In you I have confidence and on you I depend for such aid as the wisdom of men can give, and, above all, I trust in divine aid. Influenced by these considerations, with my situation in full view, I cannot entertain a thought of bearing such awful responsibility longer than I am persuaded my services are useful to the Church of God and feel a confidence of being aided by your counsel and support, which is for you to give in any way or form you may see proper. And while I join with you, my dear brethren, in pure gospel simplicity to commit and recommend ourselves and our several charges to the special care of the great Head of the Church, I remain, with sentiments of love and confidence, your servant in the gospel of Christ.

New York, May 5, 1812. WILLIAM McKENDREE.

BISHOP ASBURY ENCOURAGES ANN WILLIS TO PERSIST IN BEING A MOTHER IN ISRAEL

Source: Francis Asbury, The Journal and Letters of Francis Asbury: In Three Volumes *(Nashville: Abingdon Press, 1958), 3:465.*

UNION CAMPMEETING, [PENNSYLVANIA]
September 7, 1812

[*To Mrs. Ann Willis*]

My dear Sister:

Grace, peace, prudence, courage be with thee. As I feel a Christian confidence and partiality for you three, I hope, widows indeed in Israel; I have written one line to each, so to thee also. Be a mother in Israel; pray on this coming, as well as the past winter. May you have souls not only justified, but sanctified in your house, this fall, and winter. Camp meeting has been blest to my mind, preaching every day. I am paid for the desperate roads and 5000 miles riding this year; but hope it will be 6000 next. Only let me retreat at night and I am ready by grace for duty every day, 2 campmeetings, all and conference in less than a month; help me sister by your prayers.

I live for millions of sons and daughters of Adam, and of God. I fear you will slack your hands, watch on, pray and suffer on, believe on, fight on, like a *woman! Like a man for God.* When I saw you stemming the weather up the hill like an heroine or shining mite riding on, stop not to get to the ———; be Frank's *sister* and his *mother* and prompter to all good. The borough of Pipe Creek shall be ours, we will not, if God is with us leave a hoop behind. I shall keep the campmeeting in mind. If the Lord spares us we will settle at conference, if not we, our spiritual children, by these campmeetings. We Bishops are seen by thousands that only wish to see, and hear us a little.

I am most sincerely to you, mother and children

Asbury

P.S. Take my Soul, and ———, and some of your *paperbark.* If I recommend you to read any Book but the Bible it will be Fletcher's Life by Joseph Benson which I have nearly read during this campmeeting.

UNITED BRETHREN ADOPT RULES

Source: Disciplines of the United Brethren in Christ, *Augustus W. Drury, ed.*
(Dayton: United Brethren Publishing House, 1895), 4-6.

RULES OF THE UNITED BRETHREN IN CHRIST, 1813

Article 1. Only such brethren shall be acknowledged as preachers by the United Brethren in Christ, who have been proposed at the conference or a great meeting and by the same have been regularly examined and have answered the following questions: whether he believes in Christ, whether he has received the forgiveness of his sins, whether he follows after peace and holiness, whether the salvation of his soul, along with the salvation of his fellow men, lies on his heart, whether he will submit himself to the counsels of his brethren. Such persons shall receive a written permission [to preach among us.]

Art. 2. Such preachers shall, at the conference, every three years, elect bishops by a majority of votes.

Art. 3. What are the duties of a bishop? (1) To preside at the conference. (2) He shall have the right, with the consent of the conference, to act. (3) By the consent of the conference he has the liberty to choose elders.

Art. 4. To whom are the bishops, elders, and preachers answerable for immoral conduct? To the general conference. But where the conduct is contrary to the Bible and the evidence is sufficient, the one to whom the case is known shall take other preachers with him and investigate the case. If it is found to be contrary to the Bible, then shall the accused remain silent till the conference.

Art. 5. Every preacher shall use diligence to build up the Church, as far as possible, by doctrine and life, by prayer and a godly walk. He shall seek to become acquainted with all the members of his society, so that he can call the same by name, and when it is possible, to talk with them about the salvation of their souls.

Art. 6. In each society leaders shall be chosen, whose duty it shall be to open and close the prayer-meetings, and private meetings; also to visit the sick, and to exhort and keep in love every member of the society, and to keep a watch upon themselves.

Art. 7. Every member of the Church shall confess that he receives the Bible as the word of God; that from now on he will strive from his heart to seek his welfare in Christ, and to work out his salvation with fear and trembling, and flee the eternal wrath of God.

Art. 8. Every member shall endeavor to lead a strict and godly life, to be diligent in prayer, especially in private, and whenever possible, to be present at all meetings, both public services and prayer-meetings, for his own edification.

Art. 9. Heads of families should never omit to pray with their families morning and evening and to set them a good example in all Christian virtues.

Art. 10. Every member shall endeavor to walk circumspectly as in the presence of God, to habituate himself to communion with God in his business occupations, to practice love toward friend and foe, to do good to the poor, and seek to be a follower of Jesus Christ indeed.

Art. 11. Every member shall abstain from strong drink, and use it only on necessity as medicine.

Art. 12. Every member shall abstain from ordinary occupations on Sunday, buying or selling, but spend the time in devotion, in singing songs to the [honor] and glory of God.

Art. 13. Every member of this Church shall contribute quarterly, with a free will, as much as his circumstances will allow, for the support of the traveling preachers.

Art. 14. It is the duty of every member of this Church to live a peaceable, quiet, and godly life in his intercourse with all men, as it behooves a Christian to live in peace; especially, shall each one be obedient to the government and the laws of the land, for government is ordained of God.

Art. 15. If disputes should arise between two or more brethren of the Church concerning debts, or any other cause, and the disputing parties cannot come to an agreement, then the preacher who has the oversight of the society shall investigate the matter, and shall recommend to the disputing parties a reference to a committee, which shall consist of three members of the society, of whom the plaintiff shall choose one, the defendant another, [and these two a third], and these three shall settle the difficulties. In case, however, one of the contending parties shall be dissatisfied with the decision, he may appeal to the next general meeting, by making this known to the preachers, to have a second settlement. If the preachers find sufficient reason therefor, a second settlement shall be allowed, in which case each of the parties shall choose two members of the Church, and these four a fifth, who shall decide the difficulties fully. If one of the persons should still not be satisfied with this decision, he thereby excludes himself from the Church. If a member of the Church should refuse, in case of debts or other difficulties, to allow the matter to be settled, after this has been recommended to him by the preachers who have oversight of the society, or should a member of the church bring suit before the civil court before the foregoing regulations have been followed, he shall be expelled from the Church, unless the difficulties are of such a kind that they demand and justify a legal decision.

Christopher Grosh and Christian Newcomer

AILING ASBURY INSTRUCTS HIS
SUCCESSORS ON HOW TO RUN THE CHURCH

Source: Francis Asbury, *"Valedictory Address to William McKendree,"*
The Journal and Letters of Francis Asbury
(Nashville: Abingdon Press, 1958), 3:475-92. Excerpts.

[*To William McKendree*]

Speaking to the Genesse [New York] Annual Conference in your presence on the subject of apostolical, missionary Methodist Episcopal Church government, I was desired to commit my thoughts to writing. I feel the more disposed to do this, that I may leave a written testimony which may be seen, read, and known when your friend and father is taken from the evil to come. . . .

I am bold to say that the apostolic order of things was lost in the first century, when Church governments were adulterated and had much corruption attached to them. At the Reformation the Reformers only beat off part of the rubbish, which put a stop to the rapid increase of absurdities at that time; but how have they increased since! Recollect that state of the different Churches as it respects government and discipline in the seventeenth century [i.e., eighteenth century] when the Lord raised up that great and good man John Wesley, who formed an evangelical society in England. In 1784 an apostolical form of Church government was formed in the United States of America at the first General Conference of the Methodist Episcopal Church held at Baltimore, in the State of Maryland. . . .

Comparing human Church history with the Acts of the Apostles, it will manifestly appear that the apostolic order of things ended in about fifty years. With the preachers and people of that day, the golden order was lost. But we must restore and retain primitive order; we must, we will, we have the same doctrine, the same spirituality, the same power in ordinances [sacraments], in ordination, and in spirit. . . .

You will say if our Church were as pure as the primitive Church, will it not, may it not, like other modern [Churches], decline? I answer, We live in a purer age and in a free country. If discipline be maintained, men that carry sand rather than salt for the sheep will be constrained soon to leave us, to join some more honorable, but perhaps fallen, Church where they can have more ease and greater emoluments. We have lived to see the end of such persons who left us and set up for themselves—witness Hammett and O'Kelly. . . .

This leads me to conclude that there were no local bishops until the second century; that the apostles, in service, were bishops, and that those who were ordained in the second century mistook their calling when they became local and should have followed those bright examples in the apostolic age. . . .

We have a few more thoughts to add. It is my confirmed opinion that the apostles acted both as bishops and traveling superintendents in planting and watering, ruling and ordering the whole connection; and that they did not ordain any local bishops, but that they ordained local deacons and elders. I feel satisfied we should do the same. . . .

My dear Bishop, it is the traveling apostolic order and ministry that is found in our very constitution. No man among us can locate without order or forfeit his official standing. No preacher is stationary more than two years; no presiding elder more than four years, and the constitution will remove them; and all are movable at the pleasure of the superintendent whenever he may find it necessary for the good of the cause.

(Source: Francis Asbury, "Address, Counsel and Advice to the General Conference of the Methodist Episcopal Church, 1816," Journals and Letters of Francis Asbury *[Nashville: Abingdon Press, 1958], 3:532.)*

[Near Charleston, South Carolina] January 8, 1816

[To the members of the General Conference]

Most dearly beloved in the Lord:

My loving confidential Sons in the Gospel of the grace of God, in Christ Jesus; great grace rest upon you! The God of glory cover your assembly and direct all your acts and deliberations for the Apostolic order and establishment of the Church of God in holy succession to the end of time. Only recollect as far as your observation or information will go, what God hath done by us . . . in about 70 years in Europe and less than 50 years in America, and what wonderful things he may do for us and our successors in future years if we stand fast in the Gospel doctrine and pure Apostolic ordination, discipline and government into which we have been called and now stand.

We are prepared, and if called upon, to prove and demonstrate even in your assembly, not from uncertain Church Histories and testimonies, but from the pure Oracles of the New Testament,—Three distinct ordinations, their distinct powers rising in gospel order by constituted degrees, one over another, and under the government, and distinct in names, that is to say Apostles, Elders, and Deacons. We will enter the sanctuary of divine truth, here we shall stand, this is our ground.

[Francis Asbury]

CHRISTIAN NEWCOMER TAKES LEADERSHIP AMONG THE UNITED BRETHREN

Source: Christian Newcomer, The Life and Journal of the Rev'd Christian Newcomer, Late Bishop of the Church of the United Brethren in Christ. Written by Himself. *Transcribed, corrected, and translated by John Hildt (Hagerstown: Printed by F. G. W. Kapp, 1834), 216-27. Excerpts.*

[Lancaster County, Pennsylvania]

[*August 1813*]

19th—I visited [Martin] Landis, his wife was sick; staid for the night with his brother-in-law. 20th—I preached at Martin Landis's; rode to old Mr. Stocker's and staid for the night. 21st—Today a sacramental meeting commenced at Peter Seitz's, I spoke first, from Psalm 130, v. 7; at night I preached again from Psalm 40, v. 2, 3, 4.

Sunday 22d—An uncommonly large congregation had this day collected; I preached with great liberty from 1st Peter 5, v. 5 to 9. I was followed by a brother in the English language; a vast number came to the Lord's table, and we had a melting time. At night I preached again at John Buck's; here we again had a soul-reviving meeting; nearly every person present melted into tears; some cried for mercy, others shouted and praised God. 23d—This forenoon we held our Love-feast; we had truly a day of Pentecost: all the glory be to our God. I lodged with Rodebach. 24th—I reached Henry Keller's, and staid for the night. 25th—I preached at old Mr. Mohn's, from Psalm 34, v. 20; rode to Peter Seitz's, where our Conference is to be held. 26th—This forenoon the session of our Conference commenced; upwards of twenty preachers were present; poor unworthy me was elected their president. The Conference continued until the 28th; all things were done in brotherly love, and the greatest unanimity prevailed throughout the sessions: bless the Lord, O my soul! for all his mercy. The Conference was concluded, and I rode 11 miles yet to Jacob Hautz's.

[Ohio]

Sunday 29th—This forenoon I preached in Lyday's school-house, in the German and English language; in the afternoon I spoke in Middle-town. 30th—To-day I stopped for refreshment with Henry Huber; rode to Zanesville and lodged at a public house. 31ˢᵗ—This evening I stopped with a Quaker family and lodged with them for the night.

September 1—This evening I reached Steubenville; having no acquaintances in the place, I stopped at a public house. 2d—The Ohio Conference is here in session. I went this morning to pay a visit to Bishop Asbury, who is present; he lodges with Mr. Wells, where we took breakfast together; I went with him to Conference, and delivered a communication from our Conference. Here I found several brethren to whom I was known; was cordially invited to lodge at Br. Noland's, during my stay, which invitation I cheerfully accepted.

Sunday 5ᵗʰ—Bishops Asbury and McKendree both preached to-day to a congregation estimated at more than 2000 persons. 6ᵗʰ—This forenoon I received a communication from the Conference to the Brethren in our next Conference which is to assemble in Montgomery county, Ohio. After taking an affectionate farewell of the two Bishops and the other Brethren, I dined once more with my kind host Br. Wm. Noland; commended him and his amiable family to God in prayer, and set out at three o'clock in the afternoon; crossed the Ohio river, and staid for the night in a little village. . . .

[Pennsylvania]

10ᵗʰ—I preached at Mr. Dietz's, to an attentive congregation, from Luke 19, v. 5, 6; Br. Louis Fechtig followed me; we had a blessed time, particularly in class meeting. Rode to old Br. Abr Draksel's, where I staid for the night. 11ᵗʰ—This day a Sacramental meeting commenced in Mount Pleasant; I spoke first, from Psalm 40, v. 6; Br. Fechtig followed me. At night I preached in Bonnet's school-house, from Acts 16, v. 30, 31, and lodged at Worman's.

Sunday 12ᵗʰ—This forenoon Christian Berger spoke first, then Jacob Winter. I preached again, from John 3, v. 6, 7; lodged with Sloderbeck. 13ᵗʰ—This forenoon we held our Love-feast; in the afternoon I rode 17 miles and staid for the night at a public house. 14ᵗʰ—This morning I set out before day, stopped at Jacob Blauch's and took some refreshment; rode to Casper Stadtler's, where I lodged with Romer. 16ᵗʰ—It rained incessantly; I stopped in Mercersburg with Br. King, and rode to my son David's.

[Maryland]

17ᵗʰ—This day I returned home and found the family all well: bless the Lord for all his mercies.

18ᵗʰ and Sunday 19ᵗʰ—We held a Quarterly meeting in Hagers-town; we had a blessed time; I lodged with John Hershey. 20ᵗʰ—To-day we had a meeting at Joel Newcomer's. 21ˢᵗ—At John Knegi's, in Frederick county. 22d—This forenoon we preached at Sauder's; in the evening at Frederick-town; lodged with Byerly. 23d— I attended the funeral of Sister Simon Cronise; the Rev. Mr. Helfenstein preached first, in the German language, from Revelation 21, v. 7; I followed him in the English language, and spoke from Psalm 40, v. 1; rode to Witter's and staid for the night. 24th—We had meeting at Schnebly's; Br. Hauser, from Kentucky, and Neidig, spoke with uncommon power and unction from above; it was a blessed time.

25th, and Sunday 26th—We had a glorious Quarterly meeting in Middle-town; I spoke from Acts 16, v. 30. 29th—Br. Joseph Hoffman came this morning to my house, on his way to Baltimore, and requested me to accompany him. In a short time I got ready; we rode to Frederick-town and lodged with the widow Byerly. 30th—We reached Mr. Yundt's, four miles from the city, where we were received in the most friendly manner.

October 1st—This morning we came to Baltimore; old father Otterbein is very weak and feeble in body, but strong and vigorous in spirit, and full of hope of a blissful immortality and eternal life. He was greatly rejoiced at our arrival, informed me that he had received a letter from the Brethren in the west, wherein he was requested to ordain me, by the laying on of hands, to the office of elder and preacher of the gospel, before his departure: adding, "I have always considered myself too unworthy to perform this solemn injunction of the Apostle, but now I perceived the necessity of doing so, before I shall be removed." He then requested to know whether I had any objection to make, and if not whether the present would not be a suitable time. I replied, that I firmly believed solemn ordination to the ministry had been enjoined and practiced by the Apostles; therefore, if in his opinion the performance of the act should be thought necessary and beneficial, I had no objection to make whatsoever, but would cheerfully consent; only one observation I wished to make; as Brs. Joseph Hoffman and Frederick Shaffer were present, that he should ordain them at the same time. To this he readily assented, and immediately appointed the following day to the solemn performance of this duty. 2d—This forenoon the Vestry and several other members of the church, assembled at the house of father Otterbein. The old man addressed us in so spiritual and powerful a manner, that all behold him with astonishment. It appeared as if he had received particular unction from above, to perform this solemn act. After addressing a throne of grace with great fervency for a blessing, he called on Br. Wm. Ryland, an Elder of the Methodist Episcopal church, (who had been invited for the purpose,) to assist him in the ordination; we were accordingly ordained to the office of Elders in the ministry, by the laying on of hands. John Hildt, a member of the Vestry, had been appointed Secretary. He executed certificates of Ordination to each of us, in the German and English languages. Which certificates were then signed by father William Otterbein and delivered to each of us. At night we preached in the church; I lodged with Otterbein.

Sunday 3d—This forenoon Br. Hoffman preached first, I followed him; Br. Shaffer assisted in the administration of the Lord's Supper. A great many persons came to the table of the Lord with contrite hearts and streaming eyes; this was truly a day of grace to many souls: unto God be all the glory. 4th—We visited several of the friends in the city. Towards evening we left Baltimore, rode to Mr. Yundt's, where we staid for the night. 5th—This evening we reached Valentine Daub's. 6th—

This day I arrived at home. 7th—This morning I rode to Sharpsburg, where I met Br. Hoffman; we dined at Br. Beeler's, rode in the afternoon to my son Jacob's, where we lodged for the night. 8th—We came to Jacob Hess's. 9th, and

Sunday 10th—We had a Sacramental meeting at Shauman's church; Hoffman and John Sneider rode home with me, where we had a blessed meeting by candle-light. 16th, and

Sunday 17th—We had a Sacramental meeting at Leonard Middlekauff's; at night we had a blessed meeting at Henry Kumler's. Several were in great distress, and some obtained peace with God in the pardon of their sins. 18th—I returned home.

Sunday 25th—I preached at Peter Newcomer's. 30th, and

Sunday 31st—We had a two-day's meeting at J. Huber's; the Lord was with us in his convicting and converting power.

November 2^d—This day Br. Chambers arrived at my house. 3^d—To-day we set out early on our journey: may the Lord accompany us. Rode to Samuel Brandt's, and staid for the night.

[Pennsylvania]

4th—We had meeting at Flickinger's; at night in Chambersburg. I lodged with Mr. Johns. 6th—To-day we had meeting at Rhodes'.

Sunday 7th—This forenoon we preached at David Sneider's. 8th—At Joseph Hoffman's. 9th—This forenoon we had meeting at Christian Straub's; rode to Carl Walter's, on Middle Creek. A numerous congregation had assembled here; Jacob Bowlus addressed the people, from Romans 8, v. 12, 13, I followed him. It appeared as if the word spoken had some effect. 10th—This forenoon we had meeting at John Walter's; at night I reached at Mr. Mack's, near New Berlin, from Psalm 34, last four verses. 11th—This purpose of our journey to this place was to try whether a union could not be effected between the society of the United Brethren in Christ, and the people denominated the Albright Brethren. This forenoon the following Brethren were present, viz: Chr. Crum, Joseph Hoffman, Jacob Bowlus and myself of our society; and Miller, Walter, Dreisbach and Niebel, of the Albright Brethren. Our consultation continued until the 13th, but we were not able to effect a union. The greatest stumbling block appeared to be this, that according to our discipline our local preachers have a vote in the Conference as well as the travelling preachers; this was a sine qua non which the Albright Brethren could or would not accede to; so we parted and came at night to Youngman'stown where we lodged. . . .

[Maryland]

Sunday [March] 13th [1814]—I preached a funeral discourse; D. Newcomer's wife was buried. 14th and

15th—I preached at two funerals. 16th—I set out for Baltimore; rode to Middletown and lodged with Valentine Bowlus. 17th—I rode in company with Jacob Bowlus; we staid for the night at a public house 21 miles from Baltimore. 18th—We arrived in the city; the Methodist Conference is in session here. 19th—We attended the Conference and delivered a communication from our Conference.

Sunday 20th—This forenoon Jacob Gruber preached in Otterbein's church; in the afternoon, Jacob Bowlus; I spoke at night. . . . 23d—This day the Conference came to a close; in the forenoon Bishop Asbury preached a funeral discourse for the late Wm. Otterbein, from Revelation 3, v. 10, 11. The congregation was so numerous, that the church was much too small to contain all the people. Here were ministers of different persuasions assembled to pay the last tribute of respect to this servant of the Most High; Methodists, United Brethren, Lutherans, Presbyterians, and Episcopalians,—all mingled together to pay homage to departed worth. Bishop McKendree closed the service with fervent prayer. . . .

Sunday [April] 3d—I attended a meeting of the Albright Brethren. . . .

Sunday 10th—I attended meeting with the River Brethren. . . .

[May] 24th—This day our Conference commenced in Hagers-town, and continued until the 27th. More preachers were present than at any Conference before. The Brethren elected poor unworthy Christian Newcomer as Bishop and Superintendent, for three years. May God have mercy on me, and grant me his assisting grace to discharge my duty faithfully. 28th and Sunday, 29th—We had a Sacramental meeting at the Antietam. . . .

[August] 22d—I arrived at Br. Andrew Zeller's, where our Conference is to be held. 23d—This morning the Conference is to commence. O! may the Lord take the helm into his own hands, grant us grace and wisdom to transact our business, patience and brotherly love to bear one with another, that all we do may be according to His will and tend to His glory: Amen.

As president, I opened the session with prayer. The Conference continued until the 27th. We had considerably less difficulty than I expected. The session closed in great harmony and unity. Praise the Lord for it.

Sunday, 28th—Today I preached from 2d. Peter 1, v. 5 to 8; had great liberty to declare the counsel of God; lodged with Frederick Wolf. 29th—We had a meeting again and administered the Sacraments. After meeting the preachers dined once more together at Br. Andrew Zeller's. We then bid each other an affectionate farewell and departed to our respective fields of labor. . . .

[August] 10th, and Sunday 11th—We had a two days' meeting at Dewalt Mechlin's; a great number of people assembled. I spoke from Luke 24, v. 47. The Lord's Supper was administered, and we had a blessed time; I lodged with Jacob Mechlin. 12th—The meeting continued today; in the morning we had our Love-feast; many praised God and confessed what the Lord had done for their souls. . . .

African American layman John Stewart begins mission to Wyandott Indians in Ohio

Source: James B. Finley. "Account of the Work of God Among the Wyandott Indians at Upper Sandusky," Methodist Magazine 3/11 (November 1820): 431-37. Excerpts.

Extract of a letter from Rev. James B. Finley to the Editors.

Ridgeville, August 30, 1820.

Dear Brethren,

Through the mercy of God, I am still on the shore of mortality, and hoping for a better world, whenever I am called to leave this. In many sections of our country, religion is reviving, and in some places is rapidly advancing. We have had some as prosperous times, at the close of our last Conference year, as I have ever witnessed. Many profess to have experienced a divine change of heart, and have been added to the Church.

Believing it will be pleasing to many of your readers to know of the progress of the mission among the Indians at Sandusky, I send you a short account of it, with the address of the Wyandotts to the Ohio Conference. Perhaps it may be expedient to notice the manner in which the gospel of Christ was first introduced among them.

John Steward [Stewart], a coloured man, but born free, and raised in the state of Virginia, Powhattan county, having been brought to the knowledge of salvation by the remission of sins, and become a member of the Methodist Episcopal Church, at Marietta, Ohio, being divinely impressed, as he supposed, the latter end of the year 1815, went among these people, with a view to impart to them a knowledge of the true God. Unauthorised by any body of Christians, he went of his own accord, under, however, a persuasion that the Holy Spirit had moved him to it; nor did he stop except for rest and refreshment, until he arrived at Upper Sandusky, where dwelt the Indians to whom he believed God had sent him. He was first directed to Jonathan Pointer, a coloured man, who had been taken a prisoner when young, and adopted by them as one of their nation. After making known his mind to this man, he prevailed on him to become his interpreter; and he accordingly introduced Steward to the Indians as their friend. They were at that time amusing themselves in dancing, and they seemed at first very indifferent in respect to the message of their strange visitor. He, however, requested as many as were willing, to come together and hear the word of the Lord. To this they all consented by giving him their hands.

Accordingly the next day was appointed for the meeting, at the house of the interpreter; but, instead of a numerous assembly, which might have been expected, only one old woman attended. Not discouraged at this, Steward preached, (as Jesus had done before him to the woman of Samaria) the gospel to her as faithfully as if there had been hundreds. He appointed to preach again the next day at the same place, when his congregation was increased by the addition of one old man. To these two he preached, and it resulted in their conversion to God. Next day being the Sabbath, preaching was appointed in the Council-house. Eight or ten attended this time, some of whom appeared deeply affected. From this time the work of God broke out rapidly, and meetings were held every day in the several cabins, and on Sabbath-days in the Council-house. Many were convicted of the sinfulness of their hearts and lives, which they frankly confessed; and they seemed astonished that the preacher should know what was in their hearts; and their concern for salvation became general. The consequence was, that crowds flocked to hear the word, to learn to sing, and likewise began to pray in private and public for salvation in the name of Jesus. Such, indeed, was their deep solitude for the salvation of their souls, that their secular concerns, for a season, seemed entirely neglected. This afforded an occasion for the mercenary traders to reproach them, and to accuse Steward of injuring the nation by keeping them from hunting, and thereby starving them; though it was manifest their chief concern was, that the Indians would not furnish themselves with fur to purchase their goods, of which they stood in no need.

To intimidate Steward, these traders threatened him with imprisonment. He however gave them to understand that he should not desist from his labours; and even if he went to prison, the Indians would follow him, and he should have an opportunity to preach Christ to them there.

After continuing among them about three months, he proposed to return to Marietta, promising to come back when the corn should shoot. Accordingly he appointed a farewell meeting in the Council house, at the close of which there was an universal weeping among the people; and such was their affection for him, who had been instrumental of their conversion to Christianity, that crowds of them followed him some distance when he took his departure. He stopped at their sugar works several days, which were spent in prayer, and in praising God for his mercies in sending them the good word by their brother Steward. At length he left them. During his absence, they continued their meetings, being aided by the interpreter, who united with them, in praying for the prosperity of religion; so that on Steward's return, he found some added to the number of believers.

His return was hailed by many, and they were now fully confirmed in his faithfulness. After his departure many slanderous reports had been circulated respecting him, which tended to excite suspicions in some of their minds; but these suspicions were soon removed after his return among them. It is to be lamented that certain mercenary men opposed this gracious work, and even succeeded in enticing some back to their old practices, who, in their turn, became persecutors of their brethren. After some time, Steward proposed leaving them again, but a circumstance occurred which prevented it for the present. A certain woman of some note among them, and who was a violent persecutor of the Christians, was suddenly arrested so powerfully that she lay some time senseless and motionless. When recovered, she declared she had been warned in a vision, that she was in the way to destruction; and also that Steward was sent from God to teach the people the right way. She yielded to her convictions, and exhorted others who were unfriendly to the Christians, to repent and to believe. The work now revived and progressed rapidly for some time.

Steward, like the first apostle to the Gentiles, who taught from house to house, went from cabin to cabin, and from camp to camp; and with Jonathan the interpreter, who had now become an experimental Christian, exhorted them to embrace the gospel of Jesus Christ. They thus laboured for two years with success, without any assistance of either a temporal or spiritual nature, except now and then a transient visit from some white preachers, which was of but little use. After this Steward made a visit to Urbanna, Champaign county, Ohio, where he became acquainted with a coloured man, who was a member of the Methodist Church, and persuaded him to accompany him to Sandusky. Shortly after he returned with a request of Steward to the Quarterly Meeting Conference of Mad-river circuit to afford him some assistance and counsel. In compliance with this request, Moses Hinkle, junior, volunteered his services, and went to Upper Sandusky. He was highly gratified in beholding the reformation which had been effected among the Wyandott Indians. At the next Quarterly Meeting Conference held at Urbanna, Steward attended, presented his certificate from his society at Marietta, and received a license as a local preacher, and was appointed as a missionary among the Indians at Upper Sandusky, where he continues to labour as a faithful servant of God. His excessive labours have induced various afflictions of body, so that he seems daily declining in health. Frequent fasting, sometimes watching all night, long and loud speaking and singing, have contributed to lay foundation, if not of premature death, yet of great debility. . . .

MEA II:
1816–65

Daniel Coker celebrates liberation of Bethel Church, Philadelphia, from control of white conference

Source: Daniel Coker, "Sermon Delivered Extempore in the African Bethel Church in the City of Baltimore, on the 21st of January, 1816, to a numerous concourse of people, on account of the Coloured People gaining their Church (Bethel) in the Supreme Court of the State of Pennsylvania." A Documentary History of the Negro People in the U.S., Herbert Aptheker, ed. (New York: Citadel Press, 1951), 1:67-69.

The Jews in Babylon were held against their will. So were our brethren. But how, it will be asked, were your brethren bound?

1. By the deed. 2. By the charter of their church. (To whom were they bound? To the conference. For how long were they bound? Answer. It was supposed by the ecclesiastical expounders of the law, that it would be till the last trump should sound!) But it will be asked, were they not at liberty to go from under the control of the conference when they thought proper? In answering this we shall disclose a paradox, viz. The conference (as I have understood) have said repeatedly, that the coloured societies were nothing but an unprofitable trouble; and yet, when the society of Bethel Church unanimously requested to go free, it was not granted, until the supreme court of Pa, said it should be so. But again, it will be asked, who could stop them, if they were determined to go. None—Provided they had left their church property behind; to purchase which, perhaps many of them had deprived their children of bread.—And this in my opinion, would have been about equal to captivity!

2. Those Jews as above stated, had not equal privileges with the Babylonians, although they were governed by the same laws, and suffered the same penalties. So our brethren were governed by the same church law, or discipline, and suffered all its penalties. But it is evident, that here was a difference made between the colored members and those of a superior colour (vulgarly so called) in point of church privileges; and it is evident that all this distinction was made on account of the complexion. Is this denied? . . .

And how many of you, (I had like to have said) have acted the hypocrite, and mocked God. For while you have prayed that Ethiopia might stretch out her hands unto God, now when God seems to be answering your prayers, and opening the door for you to enjoy all that you could wish, many of you rise up and say, the time is not yet come; and it is thought by some a mark of arrogance and ostentation, in us who are embracing the opportunity that is now offered to us of being free. May the time speedily come, when we shall see our brethren come flocking to us like doves to their windows. And we as a band of brethren, shall sit down under our own vine to worship, and none to make us afraid.

Ministers belonging to the *African Bethel Church*, who have withdrawn from under the charge of the Methodist Bishops and Conference, but are still Methodists:—

> Richard Allen, ordained by bishop Asbury
> James Champin, ordained by bishop Asbury
> Jacob Tapsico, ordained by bishop Asbury
> Jeffrey Bulah, ordained by bishop Asbury

And five or six local preachers, and about fourteen hundred members, who are now, by the decision of the Supreme Court, placed under the charge of Richard Allen.

> Daniel Coker, ordained by bishop Asbury
> Richard Williams, local preacher
> Henry Harden, local preacher
> Abner Coker, local preacher
> Charles Pierce, local preacher
> James Towson, local preacher
> James Coal, local preacher

And several hundred members.
At Elkridge [Maryland] we have a Church and a growing Society.

N.B. Contrary to the predictions of many, we have found to our great consolation, that the wholesome and friendly laws of our happy country will give us protection in worshipping God according to the dictates of our own conscience.

And my prayer is, that we, the descendants of Africa, may enjoy, and not abuse our glorious privileges: and always retain a high sense of our obligation of obedience to the laws of our God, and the laws of our land.

African American Methodists in New York
Search for Ordination and Organization

Source: Christopher Rush, A Short Account of the Rise and Progress of the African M.E. Church in America *(New York: Published by the author, 1843), 60-65. For a variant transcript, see "Black Methodists Request the Formation of a Black Conference, 1821," Discovery, vol. 1 (Spring 1963): 3-5.*

To the Bishops and Preachers of the Philadelphia and New York Conference assembled.

Respected Brethren:

We, the official members of the African Methodist Zion and Asbury Churches in the City of New York, and of the Wesleyan Church in the City of Philadelphia, on behalf of our coloured brethren, the members of the aforesaid Churches, likewise, of a small society at New Haven, and some of our coloured brethren on Long Island, beg the favor of addressing you on a subject, to us, of great importance, and, we presume not a matter of indifference to you.

In the first place, suffer us to beg you will accept of our humble and sincere thanks for your kind service to us when, in our infant state, trusting that the Great Head of the Church, the all-wise and gracious God has, and will continue to reward you for your labours among us, having made you the instruments of bringing us from darkness to light, and from the power of sin and Satan, to him, the true and living God.

In the next place we proceed to say: When the Methodist Society in the United States was small, the Africans enjoyed comfortable privileges among their white brethren in the *same meeting-house,* but as the whites increased very fast, the Africans were pressed back; therefore, it was thought essentially necessary for them to have meeting houses of their own, in those places where they could obtain them, in order to *have more room to invite their coloured brethren yet out of the Ark of safety to come in;*—and it is well known that the Lord has greatly enlarged their number since that memorable time, by owning their endeavors in the conversion of many hundreds. Many preachers have been raised up among them, who have been very useful in a located state; but they have been hitherto confined; they have had no opportunity to travel, being generally poor men, and having no provisions made for them to go forth and dispense the Word of Life to their brethren, their usefulness have been greatly hindered, and their coloured brethren have been thereby deprived of those blessings Almighty God might have designed to grant to their instrumentality.

And now, it seems, the time is come, when something must be done for the prosperity of the ministry amongst our coloured brethren; and how shall this be accomplished?—for we have not the least expectation that African or coloured preachers will be admitted to a *seat and vote in the Conferences of their white brethren,* let them be how much soever qualified for the work of the ministry; nor do we desire to unite with our Brother Richard Allen's connexion, being dissatisfied with their general manner of proceedings (for our brethren, the members of the Wesleyan Church in Philadelphia withdrew from them to build their present house of worship named as above); therefore, our brethren in the City of New York, after due consideration, have been led to conclude that to form an itinerant plan and establish a Conference for African Methodist preachers, *under the patronage of the white Methodist Bishops and Conference,* would be the best means of accomplishing the desired end, believing that such an establishment would tend greatly to the prosperity of our coloured brethren in general, and be the means of great encouragement to our preachers now in regular standing in connection with the White Methodist Episcopal Church in the United States, and also to such as may be hereafter raised up among us, who may be disposed to join the said Conference and enter on the travelling plan.

And in order to commence this great work, the two societies in the City of New York united and agreed that the title of the connection shall be "The African Methodist Episcopal Church in America," and has selected a form of discipline from that of the mother (white) church, which, with a little alteration, we have adopted for the government of the said connection, and to which we beg to refer you.

After the perusal of our selection and consideration of our case, should our proceedings meet your approbation and you should be disposed to patronize the same, we stand ready, and shall be glad to receive such advice and instructions as you may think proper to give us through our father in the Lord, Bishop McKendree, or any other person the Conference may be pleased to appoint.

On the subject of ordination to Eldership (a privilege which our preachers have been long deprived of) permit us to say that we might have obtained it from other sources, but we preferred and determined to follow the advise of Bishop McKendree, given to our brethren in New York the last time he was with them, and wait until the meeting of your Annual Conference, in this, and in the District of New York, in order to understand what encouragement we might look for from the mother church.

But in consequence of some uneasiness in the minds of some of our members in New York, occasioned by our brother Richard Allen's determination to establish a Society of his connection in that city, our brethren there, have under the *necessity of solemnly electing* three of their Deacons to the office of Elders and some of their preachers to the office of Deacons, to act *only in case of necessity,* and to show to our people that our preachers can be authorized to administer the Sacrament of the

Lord's Supper, as well as those of our Brother Richard Allen's connexion, that thereby they might keep the body together,—and we believe it has had the desired effect, for very few have left the Societies there, notwithstanding the efforts made to induce them to leave us.

We expect that our first Yearly Conference will be held in the City of New York on the 14th day of June next [1822], at which, we hope to have the happiness of hearing that our Father in the Lord, Bishop McKendree, presided, and commenced his fatherly instructions in an African Methodist Conference, formed under the patronage of The Methodist Episcopal Church in the United States of America. With this hope we shall rest, waiting your answer; meanwhile praying that the Great Shepherd and Bishop of Souls, and our most Merciful Father, will be pleased to bless and guide you in your deliberations on our case, so that your conclusions may be such as shall be pleasing in his sight and tend most to the prosperity of his kingdom amongst the Africans, and consequently prove an everlasting blessing to many precious souls.

N.B. Should the above address be sanctioned by your respected body, and you should be pleased to act upon it, we will thank you to transmit the same to the New-York Annual Conference for their consideration, and should the *time appointed* for the sitting of the *African Conference* be inconvenient for the person who may be appointed to organize the same, we are willing that it should be altered to a few days sooner or later, provided you will please to give us timely notice of said alteration. But should you be disposed *not to favor* the said address in any respect, you will please have the goodness to return it to the bearer.

Signed in behalf of the official members at a meeting called specially for that designed purpose, composed of Preachers, Trustees, Class Leaders, and Exhorters of both societies in the City of New York, March 23d, 1821.

Of New York   James Varick, President
                        George Collins, Secretary

signed in behalf of the Wesley Church

Of Philadelphia   Cyrus Potts, President
                        Robert Brown, Secretary

WILLIAM STOCKTON PROPOSES LAY REPRESENTATION IN THE GOVERNING CONFERENCES

Source: [William S. Stockton], "On Church Government," The Wesleyan Repository, and Religious Intelligencer 1/8 (19 July 1821): 126-27.

No one ought to be surprized [sic] or alarmed, if Americans, as such, prefer respectful petitions, declaring their dissatisfaction with every vestige of former ecclesiastical tyrannies. It can answer no good purpose to hold up excommunication in terrorum, as the scourge of complaint. Especially, when in our day, and under our form of political government, the people have witnessed the very absurdity of absurdities; namely, A man who professes to be the servant of all, took it into his head to imagine, that he, as an individual, was invested with supreme authority! Another man, (who had received a gratuitous, in addition to a previous and ample compensation) refused an office of high trust and widely extended prerogative, merely because his former equals and coadjutors refused to submit to certain wild pretensions and assumptions of arbitrary powers. The first man held his sceptre as a legitimate successor; that is, his right to arbitrary rule was derived in the common routine of succession! The second man thought himself as surely in the succession as the first! But in very truth, John Wesley was no pope! how highly soever some persons may pretend to value the authority said to be derived from him. Mr. Wesley never pretended to be an infallible being. He was the highly honored instrument of infinite good to hundreds of thousands; but it seems rather ridiculous to expect that men of another generation should be invested with all the powers, and more powers too, than John Wesley ever had, or than ever fell to the lot of the twelve apostles. But if Mr. Wesley had even been a pope, I, for one, would claim the privilege of clinging to the apostles, who were not popes. The Divine Master of the household informed his family—"Ye are brethren, and one is your Master, even Christ." Brethren have the same rights, privileges, and immunities.

The supreme rulers in our church, pretend to have inherited absolute power, as the lawful heirs of Mr. Wesley. But when or where did Mr Wesley appoint them his successors over men of another generation and country? After this is proved, it would seem expedient to prove, that Mr Wesley had authority to deprive some of their inalienable rights, and to confer enormous and incompatible powers on others. I should be glad to be informed of any passage in the New Testament, if such passage there be, in which the laity were derived of an elective or representative privilege. Such a deprivation is not to be found in the first chapter of Acts, nor in the 15th chapter of the same book. And if the people may be allowed to read the history of the early ages of the church, and after having read, to form an opinion of their own, they must be confirmed in their belief, that absolute power never was, as a sacred deposit, committed to the gospel ministry. (I call *legislation*, without *representation*, absolute power.) Every one knows, that an extended itinerant ministry cannot be governed as a local body. Nor can a large local body be governed as an itinerant ministry. There should be a representation of both, if an identity of interests is to be maintained. But it will be asked, why need the people burden themselves with a lay-representation? And then we are referred to our unexampled prosperity as a people! I cannot now take time to examine all that has been said against a lay-delegation, nor attempt to prove its necessity. This may be done hereafter, when it will, perhaps, appear that no form of church government is adapted to our state of society, but such an one as will promote the general prosperity, by securing the rights and promoting the prosperity of each individual. We have much to be thankful for, many reasons to rejoice, and not a little to amend.

A METHODIST.
[William S. Stockton]

PETER CARTWRIGHT PRESIDES
AT QUARTERLY MEETING IN KENTUCKY

Source: Peter Cartwright, Autobiography, *Centennial edition (Nashville: Abingdon Press, 1956), 158-60. Excerpts.*

We had a very interesting quarterly meeting the past spring in Russellville [Kentucky], and a considerable number in the higher and wealthier walks of life, especially among the ladies, gave signs of repentance, and a disposition to devote themselves to a religious life. I had given them a special and pressing invitation to attend our camp-meeting, and accordingly they came, and there was a glorious work going on in the congregation from time to time. Many came to the altar as penitents, and sought and found mercy of the Lord. And although these wealthy ladies would weep under the word, yet we could not get them to the altar, and I was afraid it was pride that kept them back, and frankly told them so, assuring them, if this was the case, they need not expect to obtain religion.

They told me that it was not pride that kept them away, but that the altar was so crowded not only with mourners, but idle professors and idle spectators, and that in many instances the mourners were unceremoniously trodden on and abused, and the weather being very warm, the mourners in the altar must be nearly suffocated. These were the reasons why they did not come into the altar as seekers, and not pride; and I assure the reader I profited very much by these reasons given by those ladies, for I knew all this and much more might, with great propriety, be said about our altar operations. So I determined, at all hazards, to regulate, renovate, and cleanse the altar of God, and turn out, and keep out, all idle, strolling, gaping lookers-on; and when the evening sermon closed, I rose in the stand, and I told them all these objections of the ladies, and I deliberately indorsed them as valid objections to our altar exercises, and told them I was going to invite every seeker of religion to come into the altar, and assured them they should be protected from these abuses; and in order to a fair start, I invited all to rise up and retire out of the altar except seekers; and directed that the avenues leading to the altar be kept clear at all times; that there was to be no standing on the seats, and no standing up around the pales of the altar; that no person whatever could come into the altar unless invited, and that no person was to talk to, or pray with, the mourners uninvited, unless they got very happy. I appointed and named out my men to keep order. Thus arranged, and our large altar being cleared, and the aisles kept open, I invited the mourners to come as humble penitents, and kneel in the altar, and pray for mercy; and we all were astonished at the number that distinguished themselves as seekers. I suppose there were not less than one hundred, and almost all of them professed comfort that night, and among the rest, many of those fine, wealthy ladies from town. It was supposed that this was one among the best camp-meetings ever held in Logan County, where there had been many, very many, glorious camp-meetings, where camp-meetings started in modern times [at Cane Ridge]; and they had been in progress for twenty-two years, every year more or less. The fruits of this camp-meeting I hope to see with pleasure in vast eternity.

The Methodist Church received an impetus and strength at this meeting, that vastly increased her usefulness, her members, and religious respectability. . . .

During my presidency on this district up to the fall of 1824, there was a blessed revival in many parts of the district, and many joined the Methodist Episcopal Church. . . .

New York City church tries and expels Parmelia Olmstead and John Hoare for breach of discipline

Source: New York City Circuit, Methodist Episcopal Church. Record of the Proceedings in the Trial of Members, 1824–1827 *(Manuscript).* United Methodist Archives, Drew University, Madison, N.J., *22-24.*

Thomas Truslow [class leader] in behalf of the Church
vs John Hoare

New York, October 4, 1824

Presiding : Peter P. Sandford [pastor]; [Select] Committee [of triers]: Simon Price, J. Buckmaster, T. Fairweather, Abrm. Riker, N. C. Hart.

John Hoare had been duly notified but did not appear. Complainant [Truslow] charges John Hoare with neglect of duty and immoral conduct.

As to [the first charge] neglect of duty, his [class] leader states that he had not attended his class for about one year, that he has called on him and requested him to attend his class, which he promised to do, but did not fulfill his promise. He [Truslow] then reported him to Bro. Sandford [pastor]. P. P. Sandford states that he called on J. Hoare and conversed with him on the subject & informed him of the consequences of continuing to neglect [attending class]; then [Hoare] promised that he would go to class that night. Bro. Truslow says that he has not been to class since.

On the second charge [immoral conduct], Bro. Truslow states that John Hoare's son, who is a member of the church, informed him that his father drinks to excess frequently, & often uses wicked and profane language. Bro. Sandford states that he conversed with John Hoare on his intemperance, which he acknowledged had been the case frequently.

The Committee are of the opinion that John Hoare is guilty of both charges.

Signed: Simeon Price, John Buckmaster, Thomas Fairweather, Abraham Riker, and N.C. Hart.

He is expelled from the Methodist E. Church, New York, October 6, 1824, P. P. Sandford.

The Church vs. Parmelia Olmstead, formerly P. Barrows

New York, February 28, 1825

Presiding, Peter P. Sandford [pastor]; John Bailey, Samuel Williams, Michael Dixon. [Select] committee [of triers].

Charge: Breach of Rules. 1. Neglect of Duty. 2. Marrying an irreligious man.

She [Olmstead] was notified to attend [trial] by David Keys, who carried to her an open letter from [pastor] P. P. Sandford and read it to her. Letter stated the charge with its specifications.

She [Olmstead] does not appear. D. Keys says he did not think at the time she intended to appear.

Specification 1: Was last a member of Br. Rudman's class. Has not attended her class for more than a year and six months. Last fall professed to be reclaimed from a backslidden state. Talked of wishing to get into another class, but neglected to do so. Has not attached herself to any class.

Specification 2: David Keys states that he cautioned her [Olmstead] against keeping company with and marrying the man to whom she was afterwards married [Mr. Olmstead]. She paid no regard to it. Finally married him. [Keys] found a change in her conduct for the worse immediately after her marriage. Her husband told her of his attachment to another girl. She threatened to take Laudanum [a solution of opium in alcohol] to destroy herself. Returned to brother [x, employer?]. Was unsteady. Finally demanded all her wages that night, though her month was not up. Left the house promising to return in half an hour. Never returned until [Keys] sent her to inform her to appear on her trial. The man to whom she married is of bad character, plays cards, &c.

The judgement of the committee is that she is unworthy to be a member of the Methodist E. Church, having forfeited her membership by her improper conduct.—John Bailey, Michael Dixin, Samuel Williams.

She is expelled from the Methodist E. Church.—P. P. Sandford.

MISSISSIPPI CONFERENCE ADDRESSES SPIRITUAL AND TEMPORAL CONCERNS IN PASTORAL LETTER

Source: "Address of the Mississippi Annual Conference, to the members within its bounds," Christian Advocate (New York) (22 February 1828): 98.

DEAR BRETHREN:—Your pastors and "servants for Christ's sake," wish you grace, mercy, and peace, from God the Father, through our Lord Jesus Christ. Our king heavenly Father has permitted us once more to assemble, to confer on the interests of His church. . . .

We are happy to learn, that union of sentiment and of effort, generally prevails throughout our widely extended conference; and that peace has been restored in some places, where the demon of discord had, for a time, interrupted it. Many of our societies, in the last year, have been favoured with special outpourings of the Holy Spirit, and with considerable accessions to their numbers; while, in other places, we have either maintained our ground steadfastly, or moved on with a slow but steady step. Upon the whole, at no period of our history, have our prospects been more flattering than at the present time; all which we ascribe to the free grace of God; and we would magnify the riches of that grace which has made use of *such earthen* vessels in furthering the Redeemer's kingdom.

We lay before you the state of our finances, not in the language of complaint, but merely for your information. After applying all our disposable funds to the making up of the allowances of the preachers, there is a deficit of $736[.]07. . . .

One means of removing the above mentioned deficiencies, we will suggest the providing of parsonage houses, and furnishing of them, according to Discipline, on all the circuits and stations. We are happy to learn, that our address to you last year, has been noticed in many places; and that measures are in operation to carry into effect this important provision of our Discipline. We hesitate not to give it as our decided opinion, that such a provision for the support and comfort of the itinerant ministry, will be one of the most efficient auxiliaries to the stability and strength of your ecclesiastical institutions. . . .

In the present state of things, there has been some just cause for a dislike to receive married men on the circuits. This arises entirely from the fact, that they have not been so punctual in attending their appointments, as have single men.

This, we are persuaded, has arisen in most instances, from the embarrassment of their circumstances, and not from a want of zeal. . . .

We wish, brethren, to call your attention to sabbath schools; and, if possible, to wake up a lively interest in the mind of every Methodist, for the rising generation. It has been the glory of the Methodists, in many places, that they have been foremost in works of mercy like this; but we are forced to acknowledge, that in many places, within the bounds of this conference, we have been rather backward. . . . Might there not be a sabbath school, either small or great, in almost every society? In this, as in all other matters, we should recollect, God regards the day of small things. Wherever it is practicable, we would advise the formation of Sunday school societies, auxiliary to the Sunday School Union of the Methodist Episcopal Church. . . . We think it unnecessary to dwell for a moment on the importance of the institution; we only refer you to the pages of all our religious periodicals; and, especially, of the Christian Advocate and Journal.

But here, brethren, permit us to invite your attention to a field of labour, in this department of our Lord's plantation, which is too much overlooked or neglected;—we mean the religious cultivation of your slaves. This is thought, by many, too delicate a subject to be handled by us with safety; and, indeed, some seem to think that no one has a right to interfere with the master in regard to the treatment of his slave. Such was not the opinion of St. Paul, or he would not have given such special directions to both master and servant; clearly recognising the authority of the master, and requiring the submission of the slave, as well as defining the obligations arising from these relations respectively. Hence on the same authority with which we enjoin servants to obey their masters in all things lawful, we demand of the masters to render to their servants that which is just and equal; and in this demand we think is included the means of religious instruction. And here, brethren, permit us to call your attention to a passage in the latest edition of our Discipline, where it is strongly recommended to the members of our society, to have their servants taught to read. By this means, the volume of divine revelation would be opened to them; and surely, if it was important that God should give a revelation, it is important that men should be able to read it. We cannot conceive that men can be placed in any situation in which it would be improper for them to read God's holy word; and even should we not attempt to teach our servants to read we could engage for a few hours in oral catechising on the sabbath. In this way, many of us may find a field of labour in our own families; and who would not engage in the delightful task? We should recollect, that all souls are the purchase of the Redeemer's blood.

We speak to you, brethren, freely and plainly on this subject. We are all your fellow citizens, having common interests with you; and many of us are involved in the same responsibility. We are sometimes pained, after riding a considerable distance to preach to a small congregation, to find that our brethren, who live near at hand, do not bring their servants with them, if it happens to be in the week; and even in some instances, when we preach in their houses, they do not call their servants from the field, to hear the word of life. We make not these observations to bear on extreme cases of business, but on ordinary occasions. These things ought not to be so.

Before we close this address, permit us to suggest our fears that there is not that strict attention to class meetings, in many parts of our work, that there should be. Some have, not improperly, called this distinguishing feature in our institutions the soul of Methodism. If class meetings ever fall into disuse, we shall sustain an irreparable injury. It will be found, on observation, that wherever class meetings are most esteemed, and best attended, there religion revives and flourishes most. It has become a practice among some of our brethren, if there is preaching anywhere in reach, to leave their class meeting to attend the preaching. Now, though we would by all means urge you not to neglect the word preached[,] yet we believe that, *on all ordinary occasions*, it is your duty rather to attend *your class meeting*, than preaching at any other than your own regular place of worship. . . .

"Finally, brethren, whatsoever things are pure; whatsoever things are lovely; whatsoever things are of good report; think on these things" [Phil. 4:8]. Our conference has sat in great peace—we go to our stations, we trust, determining to know nothing among you, save Jesus Christ, and him *crucified*. The grace of our Lord Jesus Christ, and the love of God, and the communion of the Holy Ghost, be with you all! Amen.

WILLIAM WINANS, *Secretary.*
Natchez, Mi., Dec. 27, 1827.

REFORMERS PETITION GENERAL CONFERENCE TO ADMIT LAY MEMBERS TO CONFERENCES

Source: Methodist Episcopal Church. General Conference Papers, 1828.
United Methodist Archives, Madison, N.J. Full transcript in
Proceedings of the General Convention of Delegates from the Members
and Local Preachers of the Methodist Episcopal Church Friendly to Reform
Assembled in the First Evangelical Lutheran Church, in the City of Baltimore,
Nov. 15, 1827 (Baltimore: John D. Toy, 1827), 17-23.

Memorial of the General Convention of Delegates from the Members
and Local Preachers of the Methodist Episcopal Church Friendly
to Reform, Baltimore, November 15, 1827, to the 1828 General
Conference of the Methodist Episcopal Church

To the Bishops and Delegates of the Annual Conferences in General Conferences Assembled:

Respected Brethren,

1. We beg leave to inform you that we have assembled together in this city (Baltimore), in virtue of an appointment by our brethren, the members and local preachers of the Methodist Episcopal Church friendly to reform, in the neighbourhoods and districts where we severally reside, for the purposes of petitioning and memorializing the General Conference upon the subject of lay and local representation in the legislative department of the church, and certain other matters. We have therefore, taken the title of, The General Convention of Delegates of the Members & Local Preachers of the Methodist Episcopal Church, Friendly to Reform; and you will please to consider us as addressing you, not in our own names only, but in behalf of our brethren who appointed us, or approved of our appointment.

2. We wish it to be distinctly understood, that we do not intend to use any word or phrase, calculated to wound the feelings of any member of the General Conference, or of the travelling connexion.

3. All our brethren who have made known to us their opinions and desires respecting the subject of reform, or changes in the government of the church generally agree that a representation of the lay members and of the local preachers, in the General Conference, or the legislative department of our government, is by far the most important. We speak advisedly, when we say, the opinion is daily gaining

ground among our personal friends and correspondents, that *the extension of the principle of representation to the members and the local preachers of the church by the General Conference, in compliance with a petition of this kind, at this conjuncture of time, would do more towards conciliating good feeling, restoring lost confidence among brethren, and confirming wavering minds, on all sides, than any other measure which can be adopted.*

4. The subject of lay and local representation, may be considered as a matter of right and as a matter of liberty. The members of this Convention are aware that much exception has been taken to the claim of right, and that it has been frequently argued, and attempted to be proved that the members and local preachers have no right to seat in the legislative department of the government.... *To suppose that there is no analogy between a civil and a religious government, is just as erroneous as to suppose that there may be a sacred and a profane system of arithmetick* [*sic*], or system of numbers by which to estimate religious things, independently of the axioms, that the whole is greater than a part, and that all the parts are equal to the whole. The principles of addition and subtraction may be made as applicable to estimates of ecclesiastical power as to civil power. In both cases, when all is assumed nothing remains, and when any part is granted the whole is so much diminished. When all the legislative power in a state is in the hands of a monarch, or the nobles, or in both conjointly, none is left for the people. So likewise in a church, when all its legislative power is in the hands of the bishops, or the bishops and a particular order of ministers, none remains to the members, or to any other order of ministers, and any portion of power which may be granted to the people in a state, or to the members in a church diminishes to that amount the sum which was in the hands of the civil or religious ruler or rulers....

5. Are not the subject of the most absolute religious sovereigns and the members of the Methodist Episcopal Church, while destitute of legislative power, equally alike, applies to the legislative department of those governments? Not only can no ingenuity of the human mind alter this law of cause and effect, but we cannot conceive of any power that can alter it. To our apprehension it is not only like the principle of universal gravity, which operates upon all bodies according to the quantity of matter contained in them, but like absolute necessity itself; it is so and it must be so, and it cannot be otherwise—that, while all the legislative power is in the hands of the travelling preachers, none can be in the hands of the members of the church and the local preachers. *Monarchy, or absolute sovereignty, by the very nature of its existence excludes liberty*—they cannot remain together at the same time and place. Were we to make these statements of civil government only, all persons in the General Conference, and out of it, we are persuaded, would instantly and universally admit them. How is it, then, that no sooner than we refer to the liberties of the church, we are met with the strange prejudice about the want of analogy between civil and religious liberty; as though men might possess religious liberty of legislation under an exclusive sovereignty, in which all the legislative power is in the hands of the travelling preachers....

7. *It is legislative liberty, brethren, that we want;* and the liberty, so far as we understand the New Testament, is not forbidden to us by it—nor can we conceive how

any portion of that sacred book can be construed by the General Conference, so as to amount to an interdiction of the grant of it on your part. . . .

8. But it is within our knowledge that some of the itinerant brethren do hold lay and local representation to be lawful, but *not expedient*; and the knowledge of this fact seems to justify us in offering a few remarks upon the subject of expediency. . . . Nothing, we think, is more susceptible of proof than that all the great hierarchies, as well as the great monarchies have been remarkable for the prevalence of ignorance and vice: and that in almost every country and in every age men have improved in knowledge and virtue in proportion to the advancement of legislative liberty among the people in church and state. Was not the Reformation expedient? Would it not have been expedient had it commenced sooner? . . .

9. . . . We ask for no distinct representation of the local preachers, and only require that the *number of lay-delegates and local preachers chosen by their joint ballot should be equal to the whole number of the travelling preachers in General Conference.*

10. Recent circumstances, in the highest degree painful to our feelings, induce us to urge upon the General Conference an immediate attention to the third paragraph of the Discipline, . . . respecting *"endeavoring to sow dissensions,"* which we are persuaded has been misconstrued; . . . *This objectionable paragraph, as it now stands in the Book of Discipline, has been made to cooperate even in the hands of sincere and well-meaning men, who are not apprized of the consequences, so as to produce great injustice and oppression.*

Another subject of great importance in the estimation of this Convention is the invaluable institution of *trial by jury.* . . .

In conclusion, we would respectfully call the attention of the General Conference to the Office of *Presiding Elders,* which the members of this Convention think should be *either abolished, or so altered so as to make them elective by the Annual Conferences.*

Signed: Wm R. Stuart

President of the General Convention of Methodists Favourable to Reform
Baltimore, Maryland   November 15, 1827

GENERAL CONFERENCE MAJORITY DENOUNCES REFORM MOVEMENT

Source: Methodist Episcopal Church, Journal of the General Conference *[1828], 355-56.*

[Friday Morning, May 23, 1828
Pittsburgh, Pennsylvania
Bishop Enoch George, presiding]

J[ohn] Emory [New York Conference] moved the adoption of the following resolutions, to wit:—

Whereas, an unhappy excitement has existed in some parts of our work, in consequence of the organization of what have been called "Union Societies," for purposes and under regulations believed to be inconsistent with the harmony and peace of the Church, and in relation to the character of much of the matter contained in a certain periodical publication called the "Mutual Rights [of the Ministers and Members of the MEC]," in regard to which certain expulsions from the Church have taken place; and whereas, this General Conference indulges in a hope that a mutual desire may exist for conciliation and peace, and is desirous of leaving open a way for the accomplishment of so desirable an object on safe and equitable principles, therefore,

Resolved, 1. That in view of the premises, and in the earnest hope that this measure may tend to promote this object, this General Conference affectionately advises that no further proceedings may be had, in any part of our work, against any minister or member of the Methodist Episcopal Church, on account of any past agency or concern in relation to the above-named periodical, or in relation to any Union Society as above-mentioned.

Resolved, 2. If any persons expelled as aforesaid feel free to concede that publications have appeared in said "Mutual Rights," the nature and character of which were unjustifiably inflammatory, and do not admit of vindication, and that others, though for want of proper information, or unintentionally, have yet, in fact, misrepresented individuals and facts, and that they regret these things; if it be voluntarily agreed also, that the union societies above alluded to shall be abolished, and the periodical called "Mutual Rights" be discontinued at the close of the current volume, which shall be completed with due respect to the conciliatory and pacific design of this arrangement, then this General Conference does hereby give authority for the restoration to their ministry or membership, respectively, in the Methodist Episcopal Church, of any person or persons so expelled as aforesaid, provided this arrangement shall be mutually assented to by any individual or individuals so expelled, and also by the quarterly meeting conference, and the minister or preacher having the charge in any circuit or station within which any expulsion may have taken place; and that no such minister or preacher shall be obliged, under this arrangement, to restore any such individual as leader of any class or classes, unless, in his own discretion he shall judge it proper so to do; and provided, also, that it further be mutually agreed, that no other periodical publication to be devoted to the same controversy shall be established on either side, it being expressly understood at the same time, that this, if agreed to, will be on the ground, not of any assumption of rights to require this, but of mutual consent for the restoration of peace, and that no individual will be hereby precluded from issuing any publication which he may judge proper on his own responsibility. It is further understood that any individual or individuals who may have withdrawn from the Methodist Episcopal Church on account of any proceedings in relation to the premises, may also be restored by mutual consent under this arrangement, and the same principles as above stated.

Signed, J. Emory [and] H. G. Leigh [Virginia Conference].

The question was then taken on the adoption of the foregoing resolutions, and decided in the affirmative.

The conference then adjourned [for lunch].

CHEROKEE CONVERTS IN NORTH CAROLINA
HOLD CAMP MEETING

Source: John B. M'Ferrin, *"Cherokee Mission,"* Christian Advocate
(New York) (13 November 1829): 42.

[To Nathan Bangs, New York]
New-Echota, Cherokee Nation, Oct. 7, 1829.

DEAR BRETHREN:—Our camp meeting at Chattooga, Cherokee nation, closed on Monday, the 5th inst. And inasmuch as our superintendent was not present, I embrace the privilege of letting you and all the friends of our mission know, that we had an interesting and glorious time. Early last spring we were solicited by our Cherokee brethren to hold a camp meeting some time during the year at Chattooga. We consented, and appointed the meeting to commence on the first day of October. Considerable interest was soon awakened, and the Cherokees, as soon as they were done working on their farms, collected together, and, under the superintendence of brother Garrett, erected a large and commodious shelter, and built a number of fine tents, or rather houses. This work was all done at their own expense. On the first day of the meeting all the tent holders were present with their families. Indeed some who lived at the distance of twenty or thirty miles were on the ground some days before the meeting was to commence, making every arrangement for the worship of God. On Thursday evening, just as the sun was setting, I reached the camp ground. As soon as I came in view of the consecrated spot, my soul was filled with expectation. I saw the Cherokees coming from every direction, and many already present. Every thing seemed to declare that God was at work with the people.

Early in the evening the meeting commenced, and from that time until Monday ten o'clock, we had regular service, at stated hours, around the altar of our God, which we erected here in the wilderness. There was supposed to be a larger collection of Cherokees at this meeting than was ever assembled for religious purposes in this nation before. I have attended many camp meetings among the whites, but I never witnessed more order or deeper solemnity in all my life than I witnessed on this occasion. "The power of the Most High overshadowed us."

Worship was generally conducted in Cherokee. We had several Cherokee laborers with us, who manifested much zeal and concern for the souls of their brethren of the forest. While they addressed the congregation on the subject of religion, they frequently made their appeals with tears. Mourners were often invited to the altar, and a large number generally came forward weeping, trembling, and crying for mercy; and no doubt many found the pearl of great price. Thirty-one were baptized, including infants and adults; twenty-nine joined society, and 125 communed at the Lord's table. Our sacrament was administered on Sunday evening, at candle light. O it was an interesting scene to behold the Lord's Supper administered in the silent grove to the tawny sons of the forest. We could truly say—"The desert does rejoice and blossom as the rose."

On Monday morning, about the time we were to separate, we had one of the most solemn and joyful seasons I ever witnessed. We opened a door at this hour for the reception of members, and several of respectability came forward and gave us their names, among whom were Mr. John Ross, the principal chief of the nation, and his brother, Mr. Andrew Ross, one of the supreme judges of the nation.

We hope to see the fruits of our meeting hereafter.—We have had two camp meetings in the nation previously to this, this year. They were times of refreshing from the presence of the Lord. But you have doubtless heard from them by our superintendent. Indeed, brethren, the work is going forward in this nation; and if the Indians only remain here in peace, they will soon be a wise and happy nation. May God bless and preserve this people.

My second year among the Cherokees, as a missionary is almost at a close. I have seen many happy seasons here, all of which I cannot tell you in a short letter.

Yours affectionately,

JOHN B. M'FERRIN.

SALLY THOMPSON TRIED AND EXPELLED FOR PREACHING

Source: Sally Thompson. Trial and Defence of Mrs. Sally Thompson, on a Complaint of Insubordination to the Rules of the Methodist Episcopal Church, Evil Speaking and Immorality, held before a Select Committee of said church in Cherry Valley (New York), June 10, 1830, to which is annexed an Exposition of some facts relating to her former movements and encouragement in said society. *West Troy, N.Y. Printed by W. Hollands, 1837. Excerpts.*

Minutes of evidence in the case of Mrs. Thompson, arraigned on charges and specifications annexed, before a committee of triers, by the Methodist Episcopal Society, in Cherry Valley, [New York] on the 18th of June, 1830. Her written answers are also annexed. Br. Bodice was called on to take the minutes of evidence; Br. Grant acted in support of the charges; Br. E. Hall, chairman.

Sally Thompson ads.[i.e., vs.] Daniel Wright. Charged as follows, viz:

1st charge—For insubordination to the church in its economy. 1st. In repeatedly appointing directly or indirectly, and carrying on meetings. 2d. For inducing one class leader to go into the bounds of another class, to aid you in your operations at the time of the regular class meetings, but in a different place, twice, viz., Br. Burrett's class, and once in Br. Peaslee's class.

2d charge—For sowing discord among brethren and evil speaking. 1st. For saying "Br. Grant is my enemy, and an enemy to the work of God"; 2d. "Br. Bodice is a snake in the grass." —3d. "Br. Bates is a spy."

3d charge—For immorality. 1st In saying you should take your own way, or old way, and then denying it. 2d For saying that Br. Bates could have the Lancaster [school], and afterwards denying it. 3d. For saying to Br. Diefendorf and others that you had never spoken before on the subject of the prodigal son, and afterwards denying the same.

Sister Sally Thompson, you are hereby requested to appear at the house of J. C. Hall in Cherry-Valley, on Thursday the 10th of June next, at one o'clock P.M. to answer to the above charges.

Cherry-Valley [New York], May 24th 1830. Ephraim Hall.

The parties having adjourned from J. C. Hall's to the Lancasterian [*sic*] schoolhouse, Br. E. Hall addressed the throne of grace, after which the following committee was called and took their seats, viz: J. C. Hall, G. Tailor, T. Tailor, J. Nichols, R. Herdman, J. Stonemetz, J. B. Jones.

On the charges being read to Sister Thompson, she was about to make the following reply, but was prevented by Br. Hall, chairman, who commanded her to be silent. She here takes the liberty to insert it.

"As it regards the first allegation, and the specification under it, if there be sin or insubordination in what I have done, I am wholly unconscious of it, and it is extraordinary at this late period, to call my course in question, when if I had not authority for what I have done in the example of Mrs. Fletcher, a luminary of magnitude in the pure and early days of Methodism, and in the sanction of her cause, by the father of the order himself, Wesley. Some of my triers, and others, who hear me this day, have heretofore given me their countenance, approbation, and support, in all that I have publicly done in my feeble but honest efforts to reform and convert the children of men. My whole course has been open to the world. I have studied no concealment, and have enveloped my conduct in no mystery. Could I under these circumstances say that I had done wrong? The guilt of falsehood would crimson my cheek, and I should justly stand before you publicly accused and self-convicted.

"To the 2d charge, I would say as before, that I am wholly unconscious of ever having made use of the language respecting either Brs. Grant, Bodice, or Bates, imputed to me. I would further say, that I would be the last, if I know my own heart, to sow discord among brethren. To evil speaking I am equally an enemy. It is possible, however, in all that has been told of me of opposition to my conduct, arising from Br. Grant, and others of similar sentiments, regarding female rights, that I may have spoken lightly of him—and if I have done so further than justice, courtesy or piety will warrant, I am heartily sorry for it, and will make any apology or acknowledgment that Christian discipline or wisdom may dictate.

"To the 3d charge I can, with the same freedom and self-consciousness of right, *respond not guilty.* To some even of the brethren, the specifications under this charge would not seem to be heinous or aggravated, yet falsehood of the slightest hue, or even prevarication, to my mind, implies great guilt. I therefore trust, with trembling anxiety, that no proof will be found to warrant or support these specifications, and that I shall be wholly acquitted of them before the public, as I am in my own mind. Whatever may be the result here—the searcher of all hearts, our final Judge, I feel, will acquit me. For his justice, enlightened by omniscience, renders it impossible for him to find guilt or inflict punishment where there is no consciousness of crime or evil intention."

[Reports of testimony on the first charge follow, for example:]

Brother How, class leader, says, that he has heard Br. Grant say that Mrs. Thompson was useful in moving in her proper sphere. He thought that she moved in too large a sphere. She asked his advice. He said he thought she ought to conform to the discipline of the society. She said she would take her old course; thinks she has given out meetings. He gave notice of a prayer meeting at her request. She said she would continue her old course. He understood her that she would continue her appointments. . . .

To the 2d charge—Br. Bates, and Br. Bodice, Mrs. Nichols, two Messrs. Butlers, were called, and testified to nothing. . . .

[Reports of testimony on the 3d charge follow, for example:]

Br. B. Diefendorf, local preacher, says that he heard Mrs. Thompson preach on the parable of the Prodigal Son. The same day after sermon, being pleased with the discourse, he spoke to her on the subject at Br. Ferris'. She said that she had never before spoken or so fully spoken on the subject. He never heard her deny that she had told him so. It was a year ago last summer. . . .

Br. Hill, class leader, says that Mrs. Thompson was often requested to hold forth at Bowman's Creek. She was often invited to preach at his house. Br. Wallace, preacher in charge of circuit, spoke highly of her and praised her. Meetings were appointed, and it was said she would be at them. The salaries of the preachers have been raised or increased in consequence of her labors. She has done well. He never heard her speak on the parable of the Prodigal Son, though he has been present at all her meetings at his own house. . . .

Br. Harris ceased that when Mrs. Thompson came to Cherry-Valley, the congregation was small. It immediately increased after she commenced her labors. He invited her to attend meetings, and she did so.

James Brackett says that he has frequently attended the meetings when Mrs. Thompson exhorted, and thinks that she has been the instrument of great good to Cherry-Valley,

Having taken minutes at the trial, having looked them over, and taxed my recollection as to the facts testified on the occasion, I think the above a true history of the same.

Dated October 1830. James Brackett

Having heard the testimony of witnesses, the committee retired and in a short time returned with a verdict of "NOT GUILTY."

Br. Ephraim Hall, chairman, then arose and appealed the case to Quarterly Conference next to be held in Worcester. A short time after which, the following expressive letter was received by sister Sally Thompson, viz:

"Mrs. Thompson, This is to inform you that according to a decision of the Quarterly Conference in your case, this day, you are no longer a member of the Methodist Episcopal Church.

George Harmon, P. Elder
Worcester, August 14th, 1830."

In addressing myself to the public, I do not with the spirit of rebellion, or censure, but considering that my course of life, manner of movement in the Methodist

Society, may be, and in fact actually is, misrepresented abroad. I feel it a duty which I owe to myself, my friends, and most of all, to the cause of God which I have espoused, to state some simple facts, which are not generally known and which, to an impartial mind, will justify my manner of proceeding for several years past. I do it not for self aggrandizement, but that the world may know that I do not wish to screen my conduct from the public eye.

More than five years have passed since I left Boston where I enjoyed many religious principles. I was embosomed in the hearts of an experienced and humble society of Methodist brethren, to whom I looked for counsel and instruction, and from whom I received all the instruction that could be expected from finite creatures. O! thrice precious brethren, you still live in my memory, and while I write, my eyes overflow with tears and my soul looks forward to that auspicious morning where I hope to meet you and share in the joy of the first resurrection.

While I lived in Boston and Cambridge, many of the brethren, (preachers and others) pressed me forward into public duty. Soon after I went to Boston, brother T. Merrit, who was then the stationed preacher in that city, called on me, and requested me to hold meetings at my house, and to exhort the people, that I might thereby gain confidence to speak in a more public manner. I observed to him that my embarrassments were many, and I felt a diffidence in going forward in a more public manner. I brought up some of the more generous objections to females speaking or preaching. His answer was, that the life of Mrs. Fletcher was coming out, and that she was a preacher among the Methodists. This was the first time I had ever heard of her. From that time, he encouraged me to go forward. And obtaining the help of God, I have continued until this day, witnessing none other things than what the prophet Joel said should come to pass, "that in the last days, God would pour out his spirit on his servants and handmaids, and they should prophesy." And adored be the mercy of God, he has, in answer to the prayers of his people, blessed my feeble, but honest efforts to the awakening and conversion of hundreds of my fellow creatures. And many of them are, I trust, this day living witnesses of God's power to save returning sinners. And no doubt, as soon as these lines shall fall into their hands, will witness to the facts I have stated.

Some time after complying with the request of brother Merrit, I was invited by brother W. Fisk, to visit the people under his charge in Charlestown (Mass.) And soon after by brother J. Horton, to visit Lynfield, Saugus, and Marblehead, and likewise Marshfield, Disbar, and Salem, and by brother V. R. Osborn, who was the year before one of our stationary preachers in Boston, to visit Needham circuit, and then by brother B. Otheman, stationed preacher in Providence [Rhode Island], to visit his charge, and then by brother J. McKee, to Northridge. And many other preachers and brethren invited me to visit their stations, circuits, and neighborhoods, which places I visited, and saw the power of God displayed in the conversion of souls.

When the preachers were present, I generally spoke after them. If not present, I usually requested some brother to open the meeting. If no class leader was present, and others declined, I went forward with much fear and trembling, relying upon the promise of our blessed Saviour, "Lo, I am with you always, even unto the end of the world." Many of the preachers said unto me, "Be of good courage, and fail not to cast in your mite to help forward the cause of God."

From many I received this and other necessary counsel and encouragement, viz: brother Otis, then Presiding Elder; brothers Linsey, Pickering, E. T. Taylor, and J. Maffitt; and as I have letters from some of the preachers, I will here insert extracts from them.

[Nine letters follow: from J. Horton, Marblehead, September 3, 1831; V. R. Osborn, Needham, January 29, 1821; B. Otheman, Providence, February 15, 1821; J. W. McKee, Northbridge, March 19, 1821; and Stonington, April 1, 1822; T. Merrit, Springfield, August 11, 1828; J. Horton, Jr., Boston, September 4, 1820; W. Fisk, July 3, 1821; and V. R. Osborn, Asburnham, June 9, 1821.]

Extract of a letter from V. R. Osborn to Mrs. Sally Thompson, Boston, dated at Asburnham, 9th June 1821.

Dear Madam—

Not having the privilege of visiting Boston this Spring, I take the opportunity of conversing with you, as I only design benefitting you, and aiding you in the way to heaven. I have not a doubt but God has called you to exercise your talent publicly, and if you intend to reach heaven, you must continue to exercise it; notwithstanding all the opposition with which you meet. Your visit to Northbridge was an incalculable blessing to me, and doubtless was to others. According to the testimony of the brethren, many will be as stars in your crown of rejoicing in the day of the Lord. Remember God is on your side. However, be prudent. Receive reproof with thankfulness. If any think you have done wrong, or are doing wrong, receive the admonition friendly. But I entreat you never yield to the desires of your friends nor enemies, as it relates to your ceasing from travelling wherever God in his providence opens the door for you. Your case is not forgotten by me. Neither can I bear that you should cease from your public labors. God will give you wisdom and prepare the way before you. I believe you have the prayers as well as the confidence of some as able and pious ministers as we have in our church. And to fill up the rear, you have the confidence and prayers of him who subscribes himself the feeblest of God's ministers.

V. R. Osborn

Soon after I came from Boston into the town of Russia, Herkimer county, N.Y. It pleased God, in answer to the prayers of this people, to convert a multitude of precious souls in that place, and the adjoining towns. . . . I labored day and evening in the revival, until I was invited to visit Floyd. I went, and met with no repulses from the preachers there.

Not long after, I was invited by brother Wallace, preacher in charge of the Herkimer circuit, to visit the lower part of his circuit. I did, in Salisbury, Manheim, and many other towns. . . .

I was invited to hold meetings in Cherry-Valley village, by brother L. Ferris . . . and likewise by some good Presbyterian brethren. In the fear of God I complied. . . .

Brs. Grant and Bowdish were put on the circuit, and I learned that brother Grant was opposed to me before he came on the circuit. . . . Some weeks after brother Grant came to our house, and I waited for him to introduce the subject, but he did not. . . . However, I soon, learned the arm of ecclesiastical power was lifted up against me. And knowing that the Presiding Elder, brother G. Harman . . . was opposed to me, I strove by fasting and prayer to commend my cause to God as into the hands of a faithful creator. About this time, perceiving that the visage of brother Hall was changed, and his conduct towards me very different from usual, I asked him of it, and why the preachers were opposed to my labors? He answered, "If I was on a circuit, I should not want you on it." I replied, why, brother, I do not take the liberty that Doct. A. Clarke gives females in his commentary, nor the liberty that Mrs. Fletcher took. He replied sternly that I did, for, said he, Mrs. Fletcher supported herself and you do not. At which my heart sickened, and my spirit fainted within me.

After this, a quarterly meeting was held at Clarkes-Ville, and resolutions passed by the Preachers, *that none of the brethren should convey me to or from a meeting; no collection or subscription should be taken up for me; that no meeting should be appointed for me, and that they should not tell the people I would be there.*

Meanwhile the cry of brethren and seeking mourners was "come and help us." Not long after this, I was informed by brother E. Hall, that he must labor with me, for there were charges delivered to him by brother Dan. Wright, a local preacher in Maryland, Otsego County [New York] against me. He then took up a paper and read the foregoing charges, after which I asked him what I could do under the existing circumstances. He said that I would be restored on trial, on the promise of reformation, if I would desist from my former course of going from place to place, as I had done when invited by my brethren, for said he, *"they* have no *right* to invite you, nor have *you* any *right* to go; and furthermore, we are *determined* to frown down females' preaching in our conference." I then replied that I should submit my case to a trial before my class in Cherry-Valley village. He said he would not allow it; but I must select a committee out of the class or he would, for he had power to deal with me authoritatively. I therefore selected the foregoing committee. I availed myself of means to have my trial public, and God in his infinite mercy granted it. The committee convened at brother Hall's from whose house it was adjourned to the Lancasterian [*sic*] school-house in Cherry-Valley village in the presence of probably two hundred and fifty or three hundred persons. Brother Grant came forward as counsellor for brother Wright, and Brother Bowdish, his colleague, was called on to take minutes of the trial. I had previously requested lawyer Brackett of Cherry-Valley village to do the same.

Thus, dear reader, whoever you are, I have given you a statement of a few facts which have transpired within a few years past. Whether you have ever seen me or ever will see me in this world, God only knows, but be this known unto you, that at the bar of God we *shall* meet, there to give an account of the deeds done in the body. Therefore if you are a lover and follower of the Lord Jesus Christ, I exhort you to "stand fast in the liberty wherewith Christ has made you free, having on the breast-plate of righteousness, and for a helmet, the hope of salvation." And I here beg an interest in all your prayers, that I may not put away a good conscience, nor make a shipwreck of faith. But dear reader, if you are still in the gall of bitterness, and bonds of iniquity, I exhort you, as one who loves your soul, to flee from the wrath to come to the outstretched arms of bleeding mercy, that you may find a sure safety and defence in "that day when God shall come to judge the world in righteousness, by the man Christ Jesus, whom he hath appointed." That this may be your happy lot, is the earnest and sincere prayer of your unworthy friend,

Sally Thompson

MISSIONARIES AMONG CHEROKEES IN GEORGIA PROTEST REMOVAL

Source: Dickson C. M'Leod, "To the Editors of the Christian Advocate and Journal,"
Christian Advocate (New York) (29 October 1830): 34.

Dear Brethren:—It having been made my duty to transmit to you the following preamble and resolutions for publication, permit me to assure you, that the members composing the meeting acted from the most pure and conscientious motives in what they have done. Under existing circumstances, very peculiar in themselves, they unfeignedly believed, that to remain silent any longer would be criminal. The public will hereafter be more fully apprized of the *reasons* why the missionaries in this nation have come out in this manner.

Your brother in the kingdom of Christ Jesus,

Dickson C. M'leod.

Coosawatee, C. N., Sept. 30, 1830.

———

At a meeting of the Methodist missionaries in the Cherokee nation, held at Chattooga camp ground, on Saturday evening the 25th of September, 1830, the Rev. Francis A. Owen was appointed to the chair, and the Rev. Dickson C. M'Leod was appointed secretary;—after which the following resolutions were unanimously adopted:—

Resolved, That it is the sincere opinion of this meeting that the present oppressed condition of our brethren, the Cherokees, and the future prosperity of the missionary cause among them, do most importunately solicit from the Tennessee Annual Conference a public and official expression of sentiment on the subject of their grievances.

Resolved, That the present missionaries in the Cherokee nation, and belonging to the Methodist Episcopal Church, give, as soon as practicable, a public detail of the civil, moral, and religious condition of this nation, and embody their several accounts in one condensed, general report.

Resolved, That all the missionaries, in their detailed accounts, unequivocally testify that it is abundantly evident, that the Cherokee nation is firmly resolved not to remove from their present homes, unless forced so to do, either by power or oppression.

Resolved, That it is the unanimous opinion of this board of missionaries, that a removal of the Cherokees to the west of the Mississippi would, in all probability, be ruinous to the best interests of the nation.

Resolved, That whereas it has been stated to the public that the missionaries in this nation are associated with, and under the controlling influence of, the principal men of the nation, merely in order the more effectually to extend our missionary operations here, we do hereby solemnly and unhesitatingly deny the charge. It is unanimously resolved, by this missionary convention, that the present aggrieved condition of the Cherokees, in this nation, loudly calls for the sympathy and religious interposition of the Christian community in these United States, together with all the true and faithful friends of humanity and justice.

Resolved, That the secretary of this meeting forward the above resolutions to the editor of the Cherokee Phoenix, and to the editors of the Christian Advocate and Journal, for publication. Signed,

FRANCIS A. OWEN, *President.*

GREENBERRY GARRET.

JACOB ELLINGER.

JOSEPH MILLER.

WM. M. M'FERRIN.

NICHOLAS D. SCALES.

JAMES J. TROTT.

DICKSON C. M'LEOD, *Secretary.*

AFRICAN AMERICAN MEMBERS IN PHILADELPHIA FAVOR APPOINTMENT OF BLACK PREACHERS

Source: Methodist Episcopal Church, General Conference Papers, 1832. United Methodist Archives, Madison, N.J. Spelling in the source document is highly irregular.

To the General Conferance in Philadelphia assembled

Gentlemen:

We the undersined being Deuly Sencilbe of the great increase boath in membership and congregation in our churches and concquently our Ministers in many places from the Press Of Business among the whits they have not time to Devote to the Sattisfaction and general Benefit of the coloured Congregations—And as their are many of our coloured Bretherin in the ministery of a congregation.—and many of them where it is Practicable would be willing to Receive sutch an appointment.

Therefore your humble petitioners sincearly pray that you would add to the Discipoline so as to give the Bishop power to appoint Ministers of colour to coloured congregations when asked for and when it is Practicable to Remain with sutch congregation as long as the discipoline may Direct—they being held ameanable as you in your wisdom may Direct. Believeing as we do that sutch an alteration would be conducive to mutch good to many of our congregations and our Brethern having sutch a field of labour opened to them would be Induced to seek for that knowledge so necessary for the gospel Ministery and we have too no doubt that it would be a final preventive to sutch a secation [i.e., secession] among the ministers as hertofore all of which we respectfully submit to your honours.

signed on Behalf of the Peopel
of colour in the Philadelphia charge,

Simon Murray, Pres., attested
Cyrus B. Miller Secret.

Philadelphia   April 23, 1832

HENRY BASCOM PROMOTES GOALS AND RAISES FUNDS FOR THE AMERICAN COLONIZATION SOCIETY

Source: Henry B. Bascom, "Claims of Africa; or an Address in Behalf of the American Colonization Society, delivered in Wilmington, Del., April 2, 1832, in Dover, Del., April 6, 1832, in St. Louis, Mo., March 4, 1833, in Louisville, Ky., March 17, 1833, and in various other places at different times," Posthumous Works of the Rev. Henry B. Bascom, *Thomas N. Ralston, ed. (Nashville: Published by E. Stevenson & F. A. Owen, book agents of the M.E. Church, South 1856), 2:251-52, 280-82, 289-90. Excerpts.*

The American Colonization Society was projected and gotten up by the friends of humanity some fourteen or fifteen years since [1816]. Its one great, engrossing, and exclusive object as shown by its constitution and the records of its operation accessible to all is to colonize and settle comfortably on the western coast of Africa the free people of color in the United States who may be disposed to go. No compulsion is used.—None is allowed.—All is voluntary.... With the subject and system of domestic slavery as they exist in this country sanctioned by law, we have nothing to do in any *direct* form. In view of all the aggressive efforts and provisional relations of the society, slaves and their masters are apart from our enterprise altogether. We are confidently assured, however,... that the successful operations of the society whose cause we plead, will in all moral likelihood, have a serious and, we hope, a redeeming reflex bearing upon this very delicate, much contested question of America... policy. And the remedy we propose is, perhaps, the only discovered hope of the country on this subject, as it consults the rights and promotes the interests of every portion of the Union. It is alike advantageous to the free and the slave-holding states.

We have in the United States at this time exceeding three hundred thousand free persons of color. They exist here a separate caste—an anomalous, alien portion of society, necessarily subjected to legal disabilities and social degradation. Our object is to give them a home—a comfortable, an independent, a veritable home such as they have not, and judging the future from the past, cannot have among us.... Many of them are willing and anxious to go. We confidently believe it would be best for them to go. We are able to send them.... And we take signal pleasure and pride in saying it is the sole aim of the Colonization Society... to promote this grand national charity—an enterprise destined, in or judgment, to bless... both the continents concerned.

XI. *The good that is to come to Africa*
The prospect already affords direct encouragement. Civil and religious liberty

may be hereby given to an entire continent; together with a reversion to national consequence, glory and grandeur. All the arts of civilized life, all the means of religious instruction, will go with the colonists. It will be a signal advantage to those who *go* as well as the *native* African. . . .

Liberia is even now a Pharos' light to Western Africa and points to the hopes of philanthropy to her approaching enfranchisement and civilization; which are to be viewed as an event of more general importance than anything that has occurred during the last century, except the universal emancipation of the Western Continent.

XII. *It may prevent mischief and ruin to this country, and finally save it from premature decay and ultimate overthrow, or at least from internal civil dissensions.*

Our free people of color are mocked when we call them citizens. We disown them as our fellows and peers and yet refuse them the protection afforded to slaves. . . . They are *natives* but still *strangers* and *aliens*! We brutalize them and then urge this brutality in bar to the grant of their rights! This state of things has rendered this portion of our population a *cancer* in the body politic—living, contagious pestilence! Virtue and enterprise are left without motive, because in this country they can have no reward. And hence this unhappy people . . . are rapidly spreading a fearful taint—an alarming virus that runs through all the relations of general society. This taint, this virus, not only affects the morals, but even the blood—the genealogy of the nations. O my country! where is thy blush! . . .

XIV. *We urge it on the score of Duty.*

You owe it to yourselves, to your country, to humanity and religion. God requires it in every language earth can understand. . . .

XXI. *Once more and finally, we base our plea upon the Prophetic Assurances of the Bible, and urge it upon Christian and Missionary principles in hope of the world's conversion.*

God is interested in our cause. Messiah is engaged for the success of our enterprise and the Holy Spirit will cooperate with our efforts. Address yourselves then to the task and let your eye, penetrating into the future, roll ardent over the gladdening scene of a regenerated continent; for, in the certainty of prophetic vision, it is done! Ethiopia, from the rock-bound shores of the Mediterranean to the mountains of Good Hope, is "stretching out her hands to God." Africa is redeemed, her deserts are blooming, her hamlets and cities are rising, the seats of science and the temples of piety adorn her Congo and her Senegal, while the Niger and Gambia are everywhere wafting the floating monuments of her commerce! We see, O God! what a vision! the captive mother of a thousand generations bought and sold at the caprice of fortune, casting away from her the blood-encrusted fetters of slavery, and the tattered insignia of pauperism, and *once* more linking herself in confederation with her Maker!—God is in her midst with a shout!—she joins the family of the first born, and takes her rank, her elevated rank, among the Nations of the earth! Come forward then, in the name of God, every one of you—

man, woman and child, and pour your patriotic and pious offerings into Heaven's Exchequer for the relief of humanity, and having done so, draw your bills on futurity, and we pledge the truth of all history and the veracity of Heaven, your drafts shall be honored; and you, instead of disappointment, shall repose in the consummation of your wishes!

WILLIAM CAPERS PUBLISHES SPECIAL CATECHISM FOR USE IN SLAVE MISSIONS

Source: William Capers, Catechism for Little Children and for Use on the Missions to the Slaves in South-Carolina *(Charleston, S.C.: Printed by J. S. Burges, 1833), 3-16. Excerpts.*

LESSON I.

Minister. My good children, tell me, Who made you?
Children. God. He made all things.
  {Who made all things?}
M. What did God make man out of?
C. The dust of the earth.
M. What should this teach you?
C. To be humble.
M. What else should you learn from it?
C. To remember I must die, and my body turn to dust again.
  {What ought you to be?}
  {What ought you to remember?}
M. Did God make man's soul out of the dust?
C. No. Only man's body was made out of dust.
  {What was made out of dust?}
M. Will your soul turn to dust with your body when you die?
C. No. My soul will go to Heaven, or to Hell.
M. What sort of place is Heaven?
C. A place of light and glory.
M. What sort of place is Hell?
C. A bottomless pit, full of fire and brimstone.
M. Who will go to Heaven?
C. Good men and infants.
M. Who will go to Hell?
C. The wicked, and all who forget God.

{This may be said or sung.}
Boys. Alas, how soon we have to die.
Girls. We fear to think of death so nigh!
Boys. Our bodies dust, our lives a breath!
Girls. Alas, how soon we sink in death!
Boys. But let us humbly trust the Lord.
Girls. And love his grace, and mind his word.
Boys. The dust can rise, and death can be.
Girls. The gate of Heaven to you and me.

LESSON II.

Minister. My good children, you told me that God made man's body out of the dust of the earth; but can you tell me how he made man's soul?
Children. The Lord God breathed into his nostrils, the breath of life, and man became a living soul.
 {What did the Lord do?}
 {What did man become?}
M. Was man good or bad when he was first made?
C. He was made in the image of God: very good. . . .

The Lord's Prayer

LESSON III.

Minister. Where did God put the first man and woman?
Children. In the garden of Paradise.
M. Were they happy in Paradise?
C. Yes, they were very happy and holy.
M. How did they come to lose it?
C. By sin.
M. What is sin?
C. The doing what God has said we must not do.
M. What was the sin of the first man and woman?
C. God forbid them to eat the fruit of the tree of the knowledge, but they did eat of it.
 {What did God forbid them?}
 {What did they eat of?}
M. How did they eat of it?
C. The devil tempted the woman; and she did eat, and gave to her husband, and he did eat.

{Who did the Devil tempt?}
{What did the woman do?}
{What did the husband do?}

M. *What happened to them on account of their sin?*

C. They lost the image of God, and became very miserable.

{What did they lose?}
{What did they become?}

M. *What else happened to them?*

C. They were driven out of the garden of Paradise; and the ground was cursed for their sake.

M. *Did anything else happen to them?*

C. They were doomed to labor, and sorrow and death. . . .

CAPERS PUBLISHES EXPANDED SLAVE CATECHISMS IN 1837 AND 1847

(Source: No separately printed copy of the second, expanded 1837 edition survives. However, a full text was published in a Charleston, South Carolina, Methodist newspaper that Capers edited: Capers, Williams, "A Catechism for the Use of the Methodist Missionaries in Their Godly Work of Instructing the Negroes," Southern Christian Advocate [Charleston, S.C.] 1/18 [October 21, 1837], 69-70. Copies of several printings of the third edition survive, since it was kept in print by the publishing house of the Methodist Episcopal Church, South, from 1847 until 1918. Capers, William, Catechism for the Use of the Methodist Missions: First Part, 3d. ed. Louisville. Published by John Early for the Methodist Episcopal Church, South [1847], 2, 6-7, 14-15, 20. Excerpts.)

PREFACE TO THE THIRD EDITION

The author of this humble work begs leave to accompany it with a few brief remarks to those of his brethren who may think proper to use it.

1. It is believed that a Catechism for the mass of colored people, whether

children or adults, had better be confined to the rudiments of Christian knowledge, simply, than diffused through a wide range of Scripture topics, doctrinal, historical, biographical, &c.; our object being not barely to communicate knowledge, but such as tends most to the glory of God—the knowledge of salvation.

2. The present little work has been composed under a persuasion that the persons to be instructed can more easily conceive the truth than comprehend the terms in which it is apt to be expressed. We have therefore discarded all hard words, and aimed to present truth in a guise so simple as to suit their capacities. This however is very difficult; we can only say, we have done what we could.

3. It is not pretended that this catechism contains all that ought to be taught; and yet, we fear, it will be found too full for many learners. It is designed as a *help* to the Missionary in his truly Christian work of directing the untutored mind to the knowledge of God. The questions and answers may sometimes need explanation, and will often serve as a text for farther instructions and exhortations.

W. C. [William Capers]

CHAPTER X.

PARTICULAR DUTIES.

What is your duty to God?
To love him with all my heart, and soul, and strength, and so to worship him, and serve him.

What is a child's duty to his father and mother?
To love them, honor them, comfort them, and mind what they say.

What is a servant's duty to his master and mistress?
To serve them with a good will heartily, and not with eye-service.

What is the duty of a husband to his wife?
To love her, and cherish her, as Christ loves the church.

What is the duty of a wife to her husband?
To honor and love him, as her head.

What is the duty of brothers and sisters?
To be patient, kind, and loving to one another.

What is your duty to your enemies?
To love them, and pray for them.

What is your duty to them that do you any wrong?
To forgive them, as I pray God to forgive me.

What is the duty of parents to their children?
To be tender to them, and bring them up in the fear of God. . . .

SELECT PASSAGES OF SCRIPTURE.

THE DUTY OF SERVANTS.

Servants, be obedient to them that are your masters according to the flesh, with fear and trembling, in singleness of your heart, as unto Christ. Not with eye-service as men pleasers, but as the servants of Christ, doing the will of God from the heart. *Ephesians* vi, 5, 6.

Let as many servants as are under the yoke count their own masters worthy of all honor, that the name of God, and his doctrine, be not blasphemed. And they that have believing masters, let them not despise them because they are brethren, but rather do them service because they are faithful and beloved, partakers of the benefit. These things teach and exhort. 1 *Tim.* vi, 1, 2.

Abolitionist clergy in New England urge immediate end to slavery

Source: Zion's Herald *(Boston) (4 February 1835), insert. Italics in original. Reprinted in full as document 16 in Charles Elliott,* History of the Great Secession from the Methodist Episcopal Church in the Year 1845 *(Cincinnati: Swormstedt and Poe, 1855), 858-78.*

Zion's Herald Extra

Appeal to the Members of the New England and New Hampshire Conferences of the Methodist Episcopal Church.

Dear Brethren—

If any apology be necessary for our troubling you in this manner, we trust a sufficient one may be found in the importance of the subject upon which we address you.

It is a command of the infinite God, that we should "open our mouths and plead a righteous judgment for the poor and the needy, who are dumb, and appointed to destruction" (Prov. xxxi.9); and it is in obedience to this command that we now appeal to you in behalf of more than two millions of our fellow citizens, who, we know, are made *poor* and *needy* by the bondage which they are compelled to suffer, and who are *dumb* [silent] in a most affecting sense, inasmuch as they are not, and never have been, permitted to speak for themselves.

On the subject of Negro Slavery, as it exists in the United states, we think we can say, that we have bestowed the most serious attention for a number of years past. It has interested our sincerest sympathies and prayers, both for the enslaver and the enslaved; nor are we conscious of having neglected any means which might serve to afford us a consistent and enlightened view of the question which we now wish to propose for your consideration.

But it is not the cause of two millions five hundred thousand slaves that we plead merely, nor yet the millions of their posterity which are yet to live and endure the evils of an unjust and violent bondage; but we plead for the Methodist Episcopal Church, of which we are, unworthy indeed, but we trust devoted members. We feel that we should prove ourselves utterly unfit for the relation which we sustain to this Church, either as members or ministers, were we longer to keep silence and do nothing to avert the dreadful evils with which Slavery threatens, so evidently, our peace and prosperity. We cannot look on with indifference and see some of the plainest rules of her discipline outraged and set at defiance, though we were to leave out of the account the part which so many of her members and ministers have taken in the unnatural and anti-Christian work of Slavery.

In approaching this subject we are conscious of no unkind feelings towards any who may differ from us in opinion; we wish to "speak the truth in love," to discharge a solemn duty which we owe to God our maker, to the church of which we are members, and to the thousands of poor slaves from whose minds the light of science and religion are shut out, and who are held in a bondage more oppressive and cruel in many respects, than any other kind which ever prevailed among men.

It is not necessary that we should here enter into a detailed account of the evils of Slavery, or that we should attempt a particular discussion of its principles; nor is it our design to answer all the apologies which have been made by professing *Christians* and *Christian ministers* for the system. We wish simply to mention some of the most prominent features of the system of Slavery as it exists in the Methodist Episcopal Church, and to lay before you some of the reasons which force upon our minds the solemn conviction, that as a church and as individuals, we are far behind our duty in relation to this thing; that no man has, or can have, a right to hold a fellow man for one moment in bondage as a piece of merchantable property, to take the hire of his labor against his will, or to refuse him the means of social, moral and intellectual improvement; that personal liberty, that is, liberty to enjoy the fruits of one's own labor, is the inalienable gift of the infinite God to every human being; therefore to take away this liberty where no crime has been committed, is a direct violation of a right which belongs to God alone. Hence, every American citizen who retains a fellow being in bondage as a piece of property, and takes the price of his labor without his consent, is guilty of a *crime* which cannot be reconciled with the spirit of the Christian religion; and it is the more criminal for a professing Christian or Christian minister to do this, because they thus afford their support to an unjust and violent system of oppression; a system which always has been, is now, and always will be, the unyielding enemy of virtue, knowledge and religion; a system which leaves more than one sixth of the citizens of these United States without any adequate protection for their persons; a system which opens the way for and fosters the worst of passions and crimes—such as prostitution, adultery, murder, discord, theft, insurrection, indolence, insensibility to the claims of justice and mercy, pride and a wicked contempt for the rights and feelings of a large proportion of our fellow men. Its natural tendency upon all who become the victims of its oppression, is to benumb the sensibilities of the mind, to corrupt and deaden the conscience, and to kill the soul. Hence we say the system is *wrong*, it is *cruel* and *unjust*, in all its parts and principles, and that no Christian can consistently lend his influence or example for one moment in support of it, and consequently it should be abandoned NOW and FOREVER.

In this view of the subject we shall show you that we are not alone, but we are most firmly supported by the Bible, by the discipline of the Methodist Episcopal Church, by the opinions of [John] Wesley, of Dr. [Adam] Clarke, of [Richard] Watson, and by the testimony of the British Conference, and the unanimous voice of the Wesleyan Connection in England, including the whole of the preachers and people. We choose to confine ourselves to the above named testimonies, not indeed because there are not a multitude of other collateral ones, but rather because we wish to examine the subject in *connection with the Methodist Episcopal Church.* Hundreds of her ministers and thousands of her members are enslavers of their fellow men, as they have been for years. They hold the bodies and the souls of men, women and children,—many of whom are members of the same church with themselves—in abject slavery, and still retain their standing without any censure on this account. Nay, we shall show you that the *Christian Advocate and Journal,* the official organ [weekly periodical] of this Church, apologizes for the crimes of the enslaver of the human species, and attempts to justify the system! . . .

> [Numerous texts from the Bible, from the 1804 *Discipline,* resolutions of the Methodist conference in England, and Methodist authors abhorring slavery, including large excerpts from Wesley's *Thoughts Upon Slavery* and his famous letter to Wilberforce, follow.]

It is well known that the laws of the United States declare the African slave-trade to be *piracy,* and punishable by death; but what can render the foreign slave-trade so much worse than the same kind of trade carried on under circumstances a thousand times more aggravating within the bounds of the United States? And yet the traffic in human souls is carried on among us in these *free* and Christian states, with the very same kind of violence, kidnapping and fraud which was ever perpetrated upon the coast of Africa. Thousands are bought and sold and transported from one place to another in this country every year. For evidence of this part of the subject, see the Doings of the N.E. Anti-Slavery Convention, held in Boston in May last.

Now in view of these appalling facts, you will naturally be led to inquire,—"What can we do?" To this inquiry we beg leave respectfully to answer, and to suggest a few things which we humbly conceive every Christian, and especially every Christian minister, is at this time more than ever deeply concerned to do.

1. We should make ourselves well acquainted with the state of Slavery in this country, especially as it is connected with the Christian church. . . .

2. There is another thing which God himself commands us to do:— *"Remember them that are in bonds, as bound with them: them which suffer adversity, as being yourselves also in the body."* Heb xiii.3. Two millions five hundred thousand of our fellow citizens or brethren are "in bonds," even in this land of boasted freedom. Do we remember them at the family altar? Do we remember them at the monthly concert for prayer? * Do we remember that the greater proportion of them are in their sins, going down to hell; that it is the grand policy of most of their masters to degrade and brutalize their minds, by withholding from them all knowledge; and consequently, if there be any one class of human beings upon the face of the globe who have a higher claim than all the rest for our sympathies and missionary labors, the two millions five hundred thousand slaves in our own land are that class? And we should remember, too, that these miserable beings are increasing at the rate of from sixty to seventy thousand every year, or about two hundred are added to the number every day!

3. "But when should the System of Slavery cease?" We answer, if, as we trust it has been fully made to appear in the foregoing remarks, Slavery is one general system of violence, robbery, injustice, vice and oppression, then it is a sin in the sight of Heaven, and ought to cease at once, NOW and FOREVER. But mark us here. We do not mean by this that all the slaves should be thrust out loose upon the nation like a herd of cattle, nor that they should be immediately invested with all political privileges and rights, nor yet that they should be banished from the land of their nativity to a distant clime. But we mean that the slaves should immediately be brought under the protection of suitable laws, placing them under such a supervision as might be adapted to their condition; one which would secure to them, by adequate and impartially administered laws, the right of enjoying the fruits of their own labor, and the privilege of obtaining secular and religious instruction. And nothing in the world hinders the enactment of such laws, by which the slaves might be made free with all imaginable safety immediately, but the *wickedness* of those who hold them in bondage. . . .

We leave it to your own consciences and the providence of God to dictate to you the course of your duty. But we would respectfully suggest whether the true friends of Methodism and the church of Christ, will have done their duty, if the next general conference [1836] is suffered to pass without having heard from our congregations and conferences upon this momentous subject. Why should we be so very far behind our [Methodist] brethren in England, in relation to this thing? Why should we be at all behind any of the good and faithful in this country, in our efforts to relieve the Church of so "great" an "evil?" How can we stand still and pause, when God and the cause of bleeding humanity have claims so high!

Permit us to subscribe ourselves, dear brethren, with due respect and sincere affection,

Yours affectionately,

SHIPLEY W. WILLSON
ABRAM D. MERRILL
LA ROY SUNDERLAND
GEORGE STORRS
JARED PERKINS

Boston Dec. 19, 1834

P.S. Perhaps we should add here, that we know a number of brethren, members of the same Conference with ourselves, who agree with the foregoing views of Slavery, and we have no doubt but they would give their names to this Appeal if we could have an opportunity of consulting them.

* The last Monday night in each month has been observed recently in many places as a *concert* for prayer for the slaves in this country and their masters. We hope it will yet be observed by *all* who desire to obey the above command of God.

South Carolina Conference Upholds Slavery and Promotes Plantation Missions

*Source: William M. Wightman, Life of William Capers
(Nashville: J. B. M'Ferrin, 1858), 295-96. Excerpt.*

REPORT OF THE SOUTH CAROLINA CONFERENCE MISSIONARY SOCIETY

by William Capers

[1.] We regard the question of the abolition of slavery as a *civil* one, belonging to the State, and not at all a *religious* one, or appropriate to the Church. Though we do hold that abuses which may sometimes happen, such as excessive labor, extreme punishment, withholding necessary food and clothing, neglect in sickness or old age, and the like, are immoralities, to be prevented or punished by all proper means, both of Church discipline and the civil law, each in its sphere.

2. We denounce the principles and opinions of the abolitionists *in toto*, and do solemnly declare our conviction and belief, that whether they were originated, as some business men have thought, as a *money speculation*, or, as some politicians think, for *party electioneering purposes*, or, as we are inclined to believe, in a *false philosophy*, overreaching and setting aside the Scriptures, through a vain conceit of a higher refinement, they are utterly erroneous, and altogether hurtful.

3. We believe that the Holy Scriptures, so far from giving any countenance to this delusion, do unequivocally authorize the relation of master and slave: 1. By holding masters and their slaves alike, as believers, brethren beloved. 2. By enjoining on each the duties proper to the other. 3. By grounding their obligations for the fulfillment of these duties, as of all others, on their relation to God. Masters could never have had their duties enforced by the consideration, *"your* master who *is in heaven,"* if barely being a master involved in itself any thing immoral.

Our missionaries inculcate the duties of servants to their masters, as we find those duties stated in the Scriptures. They inculcate the performance of them as indispensably important. We hold that a Christian slave must be submissive, faithful, and obedient, for reasons of the same authority with those which oblige husbands, wives, fathers, mothers, brothers, sisters, to fulfil the duties of these relations. We would employ no one in the work who might hesitate to teach thus; nor can such a one be found in the whole number of the preachers of this Conference.

Preacher's Wife, Mary Orne Tucker, details hardships of circuit life in Massachusetts

Source: Mary Orne Tucker, Itinerant Preaching in the Early Days of Methodism, by A Pioneer Preacher's Wife. *Edited by her son, Thomas W. Tucker. Boston. B. B. Russell (1872), 97-100, 107-9, 136-38.*

Our next station [appointment] was Holliston, Mass., to which place we removed in 1839. Upon our arrival we found, as in many other places, that no provision had been made for our accommodation, and that we were to "trust to luck" for a tenement. The omission of stewards in the various places where itinerant preachers with their families are sent, to provide suitable tenements for their use, is a "crying evil" to which I beg to call attention. Every Methodist society should have a parsonage, not costly but comfortable, in which to install their newly arrived minister. It is too much to expect that every appointment can afford the outlay for such an establishment; but with the growing prosperity of our societies, much can be done in that direction. Few persons inexperienced in such matters can imagine the discomfort of many of our most worthy preachers and their families, for the want of a suitable tenement to receive them and their humble stock of house-keeping goods upon arrival in a new place. . . . I have often been subjected to positive suffering on this account, so that I can speak as "one having authority" on this subject.

During our residence in Holliston I made, in quite an unexpected manner, my *debut* as a public speaker. The circumstances were these: An organization had been formed in the place called the "Female Moral Reform Society," which consisted of one hundred and thirty ladies, mostly members of the different religious societies in the town. I was complimented by being chosen its president, although I should have been better pleased with a more humble position. At our first meeting the question came up for discussion, whether it would be proper and expedient to invite gentlemen to lecture before the society. My opinion being asked, I replied that I thought it hardly proper for a gentleman to lecture to ladies exclusively, adding rather jocosely, that as the society was conducted by females, the lecturing might as well be done by themselves. At our next meeting I found, to my surprise and chagrin, that the members had adopted my advice by unanimously choosing me to deliver a lecture at the next quarterly meeting. My first impulse was to decline the honor, but upon reflecting a little I thought that *example* ought to agree with *precept,* and decided to make the attempt. I prepared my lecture, and delivered it to a large audience to general acceptance, although my embarrassment on facing the assembly was at first rather disastrous to my elocution.

Mr. Tucker labored hard and earnestly in this place, but failed in securing that co-operation of the leading members so vitally necessary to success. It is a severe burden for the preacher to carry the sins of the ungodly upon his heart and the church upon his back.

This year (1840) Mr. Tucker was appointed to labor half time at Framingham, and the other half at Needham and Natick, the latter to be our place of residence. This is said to be a "world of change." To a Methodist minister's family it is indeed so. No sooner are we comfortably settled and pleasant acquaintances formed than the inevitable fiat is received from Conference, the result of which is to "stand not upon the order of your going, but go at once." Many a year of experience has hardly reconciled me to the trials of an itinerant life. It is a gypsy sort of life, yet it has its compensations. . . .

July 20, 1843.—We bid farewell to Sudbury in the morning, and took our journey to Grafton [Massachusetts]. Although our circle of acquaintance in Sudbury had been a limited one, yet we have found, as in other places, some good and true souls whose kindness we can truly appreciate. When we arrived in New England Village, we found, as usual, that no tenement had been provided, and we accepted the hospitality of Brother John Phillips until a place of shelter was provided. As before remarked in these pages, it is one of the peculiar sins of omission on the part of our societies that no provision is made to accommodate the preacher and his family upon their arrival at a station. Men hardly treat dumb animals so badly; for there is always a stable and something to eat for a horse, but the preacher has to shift for himself—a very easy thing for a single man, but hard when encumbered with wife and children. New England Village is a manufacturing place, and like all places of this kind, the population is migratory. The society is small but vigorous for its size, and the people seem kindly disposed.

Monday, July 29 [1843].—We have succeeded in finding a tenement, such as it is. A sort of tenement house, as it already contains several families. It cannot be said that we are not "getting up in the world"; for our back chambers are six stories from the ground. I have been accustomed to these "moving scenes" for so many years that I seldom complain; yet I was so weary and wretched when arranging my household goods in this place that I could not help remarking to a brother who was assisting us that I was getting tired of this travelling life, when he rather coarsely replied, "Wal, what did you git intew it for? Yew knew what it was afore you commenced. Yew oter got used tew it before this." In reply to this rather rude speech, I said, "Friend, did you ever have the toothache?" —"Yes," said he. "Well," said I, "was it any relief to your suffering that you knew beforehand the nature of toothache?" Scratching his head thoughtfully a moment, he replied, "Sister Tucker, I guess I'll drop the subject." . . .

Feb. 21, 1846 [Dorchester, Massachusetts].—Brother T. C. Pierce, our Presiding Elder, is with us. It is his last quarterly meeting in this part of his district for the year.

He has travelled the district during the past four years to the acceptance of the preachers, and to the great satisfaction of the people under his charge. He possesses in a large degree good, strong common sense, combined with wisdom and moderation. He is also a staunch, firm friend. Mr. Tucker and myself always felt a strong attachment for him, growing stronger with advancing years. My husband and Brother Pierce were boys together in Boston; early professing piety and commencing their labors in the itinerant field about the same time—thirty-five years ago. We regret to part with him in this field, but go where he will, our prayers and best wishes will follow him. Our parting is lightened by the expectation that when we are done with the things of time, we shall meet him in a blissful eternity, recounting the joys and sorrows we experienced on the earth we have left behind.

Feb. 25. —A "donation party" took possession of our humble tenement this evening, numbering some three hundred persons, bringing a profusion of eatables, besides some presents of a more substantial character. It was a most happy meeting of true and congenial souls, and the kind remembrances of these beloved brethren and sisters were gratefully appreciated by Mr. Tucker and myself. Such pleasant occasions are like the oasis in the desert, refreshing to the wearied traveller in his Master's vineyard, who for many long wearisome years travel from place to place, trusting in Providence, with no abiding place to call his own, and expecting no rest from his labors until his tired body finds it in the lowly grave.

It is not because of the temporal benefits conferred upon the preacher and his family by these friendly gatherings that I prize them so highly. I value them for that blessed exhibition of love and friendship which is far more precious than earthly gifts, and more enduring than the perishable things of time and sense. Many long years ago when I left the comfortable home of my youth to wander I knew not whither, I little thought that my young heart would so often sigh for the warm sympathy and kindly smile which had made bright my girlhood days. Since those halcyon days, my dear partner and myself have been called to endure fatigue, privations, and, I may add, sometimes hunger. This however was the lot of all of those preachers who traveled extensively in the earlier days of Methodism in New England, breaking up the fallow ground and planting the seed which has since ripened into a rich harvest.

Our solace in these weary journeyings, aside from the divine trust, has been the true friendships we have formed with loving hearts in many places where our tent has been pitched. Yet these choice gifts of heaven were enjoyed but for a brief season; the inevitable parting day brooked no delay, when, with heaving bosom and weeping eyes, I exchanged the last farewell with dear and well-tried friends to seek in other untried scenes, new friendships and loving hearts.

George Cookman Celebrates Achievements at Centennial

Source: George G. Cookman, Speeches Delivered on Various Occasions (New York: George Lane for the MEC, 1840), 124, 127-37. Excerpts.

It is not my intention to pronounce any panegyric on Mr. Wesley, but rather to glorify the grace of God in him. We regard him as an eminent instrument employed by divine Providence for the good of mankind. The history of Methodism as identified with that of John Wesley is a bright page in the mysterious book of Providence. Was it not providential that he was born *when* he was, *where* he was, *what* he was? . . .

And in all his subsequent history, in his expulsion from the Established Church, in his out-door and field preaching, in the origin of class-meetings, the employment of lay preachers, the settlement of the poll deed, securing the chapels for ever to the *itinerancy of Methodism*, thus perpetuating the system, *binding it equally* upon preachers and people, we see not the wisdom and policy of man, but the wisdom and power of God.

But what is Methodism? To this oft-repeated question, and to the many explanations which have been offered, permit us to give a definition of our own. And, first, we would answer the question negatively, by remarking, *Methodism, so called, is not a sect.* The announcement of Mr. Wesley at the outset of his career was *anti-sectarian*, and has been fulfilled to the very letter, "THE WORLD IS MY PARISH." . . . Our *pulpits and altars are anti-sectarian*, admitting *all* evangelical ministers to the *former*, and members of other churches to the *latter*, setting forth on this subject an *example of Christian liberality* which it would be well for *some* churches to *imitate* who charge us continually with sectarianism.

Methodism is not a form. It has always adapted itself to providential circumstances, and practised the doctrine of Christian expediency. Less anxious about nonessentials, it has laboured at the substance of religion. It has waived a controversy about forms, but contended manfully for the power of godliness. . . . And here let me animadvert upon a certain class of *deplorable croakers*, who, looking at mere forms, are for ever complaining about departures from what they are pleased to call good *old* Methodism. *Good old Methodism, indeed!* And is good old Methodism susceptible of no improvement? If our noble fathers, in the days of their poverty, *walked*, is that any sufficient reason why we, their sons, now that we can afford it, should not *ride?* What! sir, shall we be so wedded to *old* prejudices that we must travel in the *old* Pennsylvania wagon, at the rate of two miles an hour, when all the world is flying by steam? . . .

Methodism is not an opinion. It demands no previous test of opinions, but one only condition, "a desire to flee from the wrath to come, and to be saved from sin." The magnanimous language of Mr. Wesley was, "Away with opinions; if *thy* heart is as *my* heart, give me *thy* hand."

What, then, is Methodism? And we answer,

Methodism is a spirit. It is the spirit of Bible truth and Christian charity imbodied and defined in the mind, the heart, the character, the habits, the labours of that remarkable man, John Wesley, and from him expanded to upward of a million other minds and hearts, making upon them the imprint of his sentiments and doctrines, the light of his example, the impulse of his zeal.

And what is this spirit? We answer, "Now the Lord is *that* Spirit, and where the Spirit of the Lord is there is liberty." *That,* sir, is Methodism.

What is Methodism? Methodism, sir, is a *revival of primitive New Testament religion*, such as glowed in the bosom and was seen in the lives of the apostles and martyrs.

It is a *revival of the vital, fundamental doctrines of the Christian faith.*

It is a *revival of the original New Testament organization*, particularly in restoring the itinerancy and brotherhood of the ministry, and the *right* administration of church discipline.

It is a *revival of the social spirit*, the free and ancient manner of social worship.

It is, above all, a *revival of the missionary spirit*, which, not content with a mere *defensive* warfare upon Zion's walls, goes forth *aggressively*, under the eternal promise, to the conquest of the world. . . .

If, then, sir, this be a true version of Methodism, and I am still pressed with the question, "What is the grand characteristic, the distinctive peculiarity of Methodism?" I would answer, It is to be found in one single word, ITINERANCY. Yes, sir, *this*, under God, is the mighty spring of our motive power, the true secret of our unparalleled success. *Stop the itinerancy, let congregationalism prevail for only twelve months,—Samson is shorn of his locks, and we become as other men.* . . .

In considering, some time ago, that beautiful text, "All things work together for good," I found the apostle explaining, in a previous chapter, *how* the "all things" *worked.* He says, "Tribulation *worketh* patience, and patience experience, and experience hope." Now, sir, it occurred to me that these things all *worked* to a delightful result, after the manner of *wheels* in beautiful co-operation, as in Ezekiel's vision. *Tribulation* may be compared to the *great iron wheel*, where, by the divine blessing, the gracious power is first felt and attained. To this *great iron wheel* there is attached a smaller *brazen wheel*, which we may denominate *patience*, and as the great iron wheel moves around, lo, the brazen wheel begins to move also; to this we see a *bright silver wheel*, which is styled *experience*, which, moved by the two former, commences and continues its bright and rapid revolution; and yet, beyond all these, there is a *splendid golden wheel*, which is fitly styled *hope*, and over this is thrown the gospel rope of exceeding precious promises, upon which, if a man hold fast and never let go, it will wind him up to glory. Now, sir, let us apply this to Methodism. The *great iron wheel* in the system *is itinerancy*, and truly it grinds some of us most tremendously; the *brazen wheel*, attached and kept in motion by the former, is the *local ministry*; the *silver wheel*, the *class leaders*; the *golden wheel*, the *doctrine and discipline of the church*, in full and successful operation. Now, sir, it is evident that the entire movement depends upon keeping the *great iron wheel of itinerancy* constantly and rapidly rolling around. But, to be more specific, and to make an application of this figure to American Methodism. Let us carefully note the admirable and astounding movements of this wonderful machine. You will perceive there are "wheels within wheels." First, there is the great outer wheel of episcopacy, which accomplishes its entire revolution *once* in *four* years. To this there are attached *twenty-eight smaller wheels*, styled *annual conferences*, moving around *once a year*, to these are attached *one hundred wheels*, designated *presiding elders*, moving *twelve hundred other wheels*, termed *quarterly conferences*, every *three* months; to these are attached *four thousand wheels*, styled *travelling preachers*, moving round *once a month*, and communicating motion to *thirty thousand* wheels, called *class leaders*, moving round *once a week*, and who, in turn, being attached to between *seven and eight hundred thousand wheels*, called *members*, give a sufficient impulse to whirl them round *every day*. O, sir, what a machine is this! This is the machine of which Archimedes only dreamed; this is the machine destined, under God, to *move the world, to turn it upside down*. But, sir, you will readily see the whole success of the operation depends upon keeping the *great iron wheel of itinerancy* in motion. It must be as unincumbered and free as possible. To accomplish this has ever been our main difficulty and hindrance, and if ever this machine stop it will be because the *great wheel* is clogged. The provision for the support of the ministry is insufficient, the funds for the support of the worn-out preachers meagre, the temptations to location strong and pressing.

EDITOR THOMAS BOND PONDERS GROWING PRACTICE OF STATION VERSUS CIRCUIT APPOINTMENTS

Source: Thomas E. Bond, "Itinerant Arrangements—Stations and Circuits,"
Christian Advocate *(New York) (27 October 1841): 42. Excerpts.*

[T]he question for consideration now is, whether the division of circuits into sabbath day appointments, and the multiplication of small stations, has not been carried to an injurious extreme? An extreme, onerous to many of the smaller stations, and inflicting a privation of the word of life upon those who reside in the country?

First, onerous to stations. Many of these, in order to provide themselves with a regular ministration of the word, and a constant pastoral oversight, make, it is known, extraordinary exertions. Churches are often embarrassed with debt; always a lamentable state of things to a people who acknowledge the authority of the command, "Owe no man any thing, but to love;" [Romans 13:8] and a state of things which, among us, often imposes heavy burdens upon those who are less able, though more willing, to bear it, than other brethren. The wealthy are often less liberal than those of scantier means.

But this is not the worst of it. A society in debt have a never failing excuse for not contributing to any purpose abroad. Their contributions for the support of the preacher and family might be found not utterly to exhaust their liberality, but then there is the interest on the church debt to be annually provided for. The trustees being looked to for this annual payment, are naturally on the *qui vive* [alert] to prevent any drains from abroad; the adage "Charity begins at home," is always at hand. It is, as Mr. [Richard] Watson says, "a neat little pocket edition of selfishness," which a man may always carry about with him; and hence the membership, generally, are soon provided with it. Yet it is strange that few are satisfied unless they are allowed to supplement to it. They improve upon the proverb, and their charity leaves off where it begins.

But whether there be any church debt or not, it is often found that it is hard work for the small society in a village to support the preacher and his family, and pay the current expenses of the church. The preacher is often compelled to talk about money [more] than is profitable, either to himself or the people of his charge, though we admit he ought steadfastly to maintain, and enforce the declaration, that "if we are unfaithful in the unrighteous mammon, God will not give us true riches" [Luke 16:11]. But it is desirable that his ministrations should never appear to be influenced by selfish, nor even by any pecuniary considerations. Money is not *the one thing needful,* though it is *one needful thing.* Every measure, therefore, should be avoided which would unnecessarily give a tinge of worldly-mindedness to the duties and ministrations of the preacher. It should always *appear,* as it is always *the fact,* that his great business is to save souls.

We ask, then, is it impossible so to connect circuits with the smaller stations, as to multiply the tributary streamlets of benevolence, and lessen the burden of contribution which rests so heavily on weak Churches? We have before said, we are not able to decide this question. Our situation does not command a view of the whole ground. Let it be calmly and dispassionately considered, beforehand, by the preachers in consultation with the more experienced of their lay brethren, and then discussed and determined in the annual conferences.

Hitherto we have chiefly considered the financial bearing of the question. Yet there are more serious matters to be taken into the account. Has the arrangement we have alluded to had no unfriendly influence on the spiritual state of the Churches, and of the ministry? Will a preacher lose nothing of his zeal, and spiritual fervor, by being compelled to preach to the same congregation constantly for two years? Mr. Wesley thought he could preach both himself and his congregation asleep in less time [John Wesley, letter to Samuel Walker, 3 September 1756, *Letters* (Telford) 3:195]. It will be acknowledged that a preacher, who serves the same people every sabbath, and twice or three times a day on the sabbath, will be under the necessity of studying hard to supply the necessary variety. But will not this variety be purchased by an unprofitable breaking up of discourses into fragments, and presenting the great truths of the Gospel in a detached and isolated manner? Not only giving the doctrine of repentance in one sermon, faith in another, and holiness in a third, but dividing these fundamental doctrines into an infinite number of sections, or points of discussion; so that the combined influence they exert, when presented together, will be lost upon the hearers? Indeed, in order to afford the necessary variety, there is a constant temptation to divide the law from the Gospel; both of which we are instructed to preach in every sermon. Who has not heard a sermon on a single moral obligation; and who has not heard even such a sermon divided, so as to give part in the morning, and part in the afternoon, or evening? Under such preaching the congregation will seldom be profited, and the zeal of the preacher will inevitably evaporate. He will not expect to awaken and convert sinners; and according to his faith so shall it be unto him.

But this is not all. It is reported that, in order to keep up the congregations, dangerous compliances are made with the world. It is said that people are retained in society who seldom come to class! And that lovefeasts are held with open doors! Thus, neither the pastor nor the class leader knows the spiritual condition of those under his charge; and in lovefeast, that which is holy is given to the dogs, and the pearls are cast before swine, who trample them under their feet, and turn again and rend the Church; they make a mock of religious experience, which they have no taste to enjoy, or improve.

Meantime the country people are left to themselves. It is in vain to say they are generally within reach of the village churches, and might go to them if they would. The very fact that they do not come to us, is the most urgent reason why we should go to them. They do not know, or sufficiently appreciate, the value of the Gospel, and never will, until they hear it. To wait until they seek it is to wait until they sink into hell. It is the calling of the Methodists to carry the Gospel to those who are too ignorant to desire it, or too poor to pay for it—nay, to those who will persecute the messengers of mercy bearing to them the glad tidings of salvation. From the beginning we set out on entirely different principles from other denominations, in respect to our mode of dispensing the word of life. In other religious communities the people call the preacher; among us the preacher calls the people. O, let us not forget our calling, brethren. Our eyes should be steadily fixed on this peculiarity of our economy. We are persuaded it is fundamental, and indispensable. This was perhaps the chief, at least it is the most obvious, design of God in raising up the Methodists; and when we choose another way, and frustrate this benevolent design, there will be little use for us as a separate division in the Christian army; and God will assign our work, and give our crowns to others. He who could of stones raise up children unto Abraham, will not lack instruments to fulfill his glorious purposes; but the reward will be unto them who are faithful to their calling.

Ladies' Repository celebrates pious life and happy death of Caroline Pilcher

Source: Caroline Matilda Pilcher, journal extracts in "The Christian in Death," Ladies' Repository 1/2 (February 1841): 59-61.

It was Monday, July 18, 1831, when, for the first time, the light of God shone into my benighted mind. O, what joy then filled my heart! All was happiness within, and I felt truly like a *new creature*. The consideration that God was reconciled almost overwhelmed my soul. Strange, indeed, did it seem to me, that God should even observe one so unworthy. I felt, indeed, that I had been ungrateful to him for the Holy Spirit, which had been so often sent to convince me of my sins—the remembrance of which was grievous to me. Then I *humbly* repented before God—I believed then that there was efficacy in the blood of Christ to take my sins away. . . .

Feb. 25, 1834.—I feel that I am in the hands of God. I am toiling to be directed by him; for he will do all things for my good. It fills my soul with joy when I think that, after I have passed the sorrows of life, I shall see "those who have come up through great tribulation, and have washed their robes and made them white in the blood of the lamb."

May 24 [1834].—I look forward with a pleasing hope that one day I shall gaze upon the beatific beauties of my King, and swell the notes of the heavenly choir. Yes, on the other side of Jordan, with the saints of God, I hope to cast my crown at the feet of my Savior, and cry, "*Holy, holy* is the Lord God of hosts!" O, how pleasing is the hope of the Christian! He knows that this world is not his abiding home; but he seeks a city out of sight. He is only a sojourner here, hastening to a land where everlasting spring abides.

> No chilling winds nor pois'nous breath
> Can reach that healthful shore;
> Sickness and sorrow, pain and death,
> Are felt and fear'd no more.

May 25 [1834.—] I do realize my unworthiness this day in the sight of God, but I *do trust* that he is fashioning me after his own likeness, and humbling me at the foot of the cross. O, that I might there remain, until the all-cleansing blood of the Savior shall be applied to my heart, and wash away all my sins!

> 'Tis all my hope and all my plea,
> For me the Savior died.

O, for a dedication of my soul and body to the service of God!

July 19, 1834.—I must expect to be separated from the friends I love. Yes, we meet and part here below, but will soon reach heaven. *Glory* to God, *there* is a resting place! God will take care of me. I wish to feel a cheerful resignation to his will in all the dispensations of his providence, and then I shall be happy. I *do rejoice* in God.

February 1840.—O, heavenly treasure, guide of my youth, my solace in the hour of affliction, and blessed beacon, which points my souls to a land where I shall flourish in immortal youth! I return *thee* to that *dear one* who has been the partner of my joys and sorrows, but who will shortly be left to feel that his *little boy* is motherless, and he, himself, is bereft of the *companion* of his early days. Then, O! then, my dear *Elijah*, open this book and read for your consolation, of that *glorious morn*, when the *trumpet shall sound*, and we shall be raised incorruptible, to be separated no more.

Till then adieu!

CAROLINE

[February 24, 1840].—This is a scene of conflict all through; but I feel that the almighty Arm on which I lean, will carry me safely through.

[February 26, 1840].—When I pass through the waters, they shall not overflow me. Deep—deep! the waters below appear deep and dark, but the sky above is clear and glorious, and I shall rise above all. Sometimes I fancy I have been [on] a long sea-voyage all alone, tossed and driven by the wind and waves; sometimes almost at the port, then driven away again upon the ocean. Thus I have struggled with the wind and tide, but now I feel as if I was near the port, and every wave carries me nearer.

March 25 [1840].—God only takes from you what he lent. You have been a kind father, but I ask one favor. When I am done breathing, I wish you would see that this wreck be deposited where some of the family will lie; have no pomp, but mark the spot with a tree, vine or shrub, (I was always fond of something green) that my *little son* may be pointed to the spot.

April 3 [1840].—I would willingly *suffer* on my three-score years and ten, if it would be for the glory of God. I am just ready and waiting. Halleluiah, *halleluiah*, HALLELUIAH! I never expected such a halo of glory! What unfading glory waits for me! O, that *ineffable* glory! it almost bursts this tenement of clay. My heart is so full, my head rings every moment with *halleluiahs*! No wonder so many have shouted *glory* when leaving this world. I feel I have no longer to dread suffering, but to praise and dwell in his presence for ever. O, glory! Never was language formed full enough to tell what I feel. Where shall I find words to express it? I expect to walk the golden streets above, and eat of the tree of life. My palsied tongue almost fails me to speak of that which my heart can hardly contain.

CHIPPEWA CONVERT PETER MARKSMAN
NARRATES HIS CONVERSION AND CALL TO PREACH

Source: Peter Marksman, "The Indian Convert,"
Ladies' Repository *2/12 (December 1842): 361-63. Excerpts.*

My Dear Brother,—I write a few lines to you to tell you the salvation of God towards me since I cast away my blanket from my body, and my images, or gods, before mine eyes, whom I worshiped many days, and served them with much prayer and fasting. While I set in darkness, and in the shadow of death, I heard a voice, saying, *"Behold, I bring you good tidings of great joy!"* [Luke 2:10]. Then I beheld the man. Behold, he points to heaven, saying, *"Repent, for the kingdom of heaven is at hand"* [Matt. 4:17]. Then I repent of my sins. It was a bitter medicine I ever tasted. Then I cried out before the man of God the language of every poor sinner, "O Lord, *what* must I do to be saved?" The good man told me, saying, "Believe in the Lord Jesus Christ, and thou shalt be saved" [Acts 16:30]. Then I believed in the Lord Jesus, my Savior. As soon as I believed, my sorrowful heart was turned into great joy. I went home rejoicing and praising God on the way. I took my images, the gods of my father, and I did burn and destroy them; and I said, "I know now my Redeemer liveth" [Job 19:25]. My poor soul was happy in God—my heart was filled with the love of God. Then I had a clear evidence that I was a child of God. I felt to tell all men what great things God has done for me; but I was too young to leave my parents. However, I put my trust in God, knowing that he is an eternal being. O, God, thou art from everlasting to everlasting! I could not help of thinking that it was my duty to go and tell my fellow men to come to Christ, that they may have a new heart, and be saved from their sins by the blood of the Lamb. The Spirit of God told my poor heart to ask God, through Jesus Christ, that the favor of God might fill my heart. While I prayed to the God of heaven and earth, he blessed me. My vessel filled with the love of God—it run over. O, what a glorious feeling was this! Then I arose from the bosom of my dear parents, and felt willing [to] *"go into all the world, and preach the Gospel to every creature"* [Mark 16:15], and point sinners to *"the Lamb of God that taketh away the sins of the world"* [John 1:29].

O, my brother, while I am writing, the missionary spirit burns in my poor heart. O, how can we be idle, while the wide field is opened before us! My fellow laborer in the

Gospel, how do you feel about the glorious work of God? Ah, brother, I know you are happy in God. Your heart is filled with the love of God. I tell you, my brother, what I feel when the missionary spirit burns in my poor heart. O, sometimes makes me to jump out of my chair. What is it for? Why, I see so many poor souls who starve for want of living bread, And one missionary ask me (his name was John Clark) that if I was willing to follow him in his missionary labor. I told him I was willing to go. Then I told my father and mother what I heard from the missionary. As soon as I had made an end of speaking, they say, "My son, you cannot go away, because you are too young to leave us, and you cannot take care of yourself well; and if you are sick no body will take care of you." Then I told them, "My dear parents, is God too unkind to take care of me wherever I go—to give me favor in my young days, or is God too thoughtless to forget me: if I fall in sickness, will he not take good care of me? Surely he will show me his great kindness even on my dying bed." And my mother told me again, "My son, how can your father and myself let you go? You are younger than the rest of my family. We love you. Why will you forsake us! We are getting old, thou knowest. We shall die soon; then you will go wherever you please." And I told my mother, "O, dear parent, I know you cannot let me go; but God knows that how he can let me go. O, the God of heaven and earth will bless you. I command you to trust in God; then we shall see each other in heaven before the dazzling throne of God." Then my mother wept, and she beheld me weeping, tears on her cheek, and said, "My dear son, the Lord will bless you. I let you go, for God calls you into the ministry. Be faithful."

I have been traveling since that time from place to place, and along the shore of Lake Superior, calling my fellow men to come to Christ by faith, and be saved. O how often I have a glorious time! My poor soul praised the Lord—my poor heart was filled with the love of God. O what a glorious cause! although I often have been tired, not only in preaching but in foot traveling. When the snow is deep in the winter time, when I walked so many days that my feet bled, I was very tired, hungry, and cold. Sometimes I am thinking of brethren's house, if I could stay to-night, how comfortably I will be; but I must dig the snow, and make my nest in a cold place to lodge in during night. It was a cold night. Ah! "the foxes have holes, and the fowls of the air have nests, but the Son of man had no place to lay his head" [Matt. 8:20]. O, ye missionaries, be not discouraged, but "rather rejoice, because your names are written in heaven." O what encouragement is this: "Be thou faithful unto death, and I will give thee a crown of life" [Rev. 2:10]. O, what a glorious company will that be; when all faithful missionaries cease from their labor, we shall wear the dazzling crown upon our own heads! . . .

And after I spent number of days at the mission, we started, brother John Kahbege and myself and three other Indian brethren at the mission, coming down to Sault de St. Marie mission. We got a very large canoe; and I thought I had quite good company this time. And after we got at Sault de St. Marie mission, I stayed a few days in that place, waiting for the arrival of brother Wm. H. Brockway from conference, the superintendent at Sault de St. Marie and Kah-ke-wa-oo-naun missions; and he told me that I was appointed by the conference to Lakeville mission, where I am now.

I was willing to leave my native country and come down to the place where I was appointed, knowing that God sending his unworthy servant where he may be useful. God forbid that I ever feel to make my choice of the place where I shall labor! My brethren, if you send me in the woods with my old dull axe and piece of bread, I shall try to be faithful and cut down the trees as many as I can, "God being my helper." And when I come to the place where I have been laboring this year, I was pleased with the country and the inhabitants. And I have found some of the Lakeville Indians loving Jesus Christ as their Savior. They were kind to me after they learned that I was their preacher for this year. I immediately commenced preaching and visiting from lodge to lodge. The Lord blessed the poor Indians, who once laid along the streets of white men, who are part of them black men in their hearts! And now the Indians are praising God in the streets and roads of white men. Now poor whisky, or fire-water traders are ashamed; for the Indians have joined the temperance society, and keep their pledges. Now soon these poor fire-water traders will hide themselves in their whisky barrels. Lord, find them out in their fire-water barrels!

Soon we have large society among the Indians, and many of them experienced the religion of Jesus Christ[.] I believe all the Lakeville Indians embraced Christianity. Sometime, after I was done preaching, the Indians rejoicing and praising their God with a loud voice as they returned home. I have kept school in three months. I had thirty-six scholars regularly. Some of them are now gone as far as three or four syllables. When I first commenced the school, I found two of the boys knowing letters, from Ke-che-moo-koo-maun-un, which signifies, persons who have a great knife, and rest of them they have learned since that time.

And during this spring I have visited Nebeseeng Indians in Genesee county, Michigan, about thirty-four miles northwest from Lakeville mission. I continued visiting them three times. The last visit I made, the Lord blessed this band of Oo-je-bwais. These poor Indians, while they sat in *"darkness, and in the shadow of death"* [Luke 1:79], they saw a great light, the light of the Gospel, and salvation from God. Marvelous, O, marvelous light of the Gospel of Christ! He poured down his Holy Spirit upon this tribe, to convict them that they were "very far gone from original righteousness." I took the text from St. Luke xv, 18: *"I will arise and go to my Father, and will say unto him, Father, I have sinned against heaven, and before thee."* As I went along, explaining my text, I saw the poor Indians listening very attentively, some of them their tears running down on their cheeks. Poor *"prodigal son!"* As soon as I had done preaching I asked them, who *"will arise and go to his Father?"* And they all, men, women, children, rose up, saying, "We will arise up and embrace Christianity!" And, Monday morning, they all brought their images and bad medicines to me. I took them all, and piling up those images and bad medicines, I did burn and destroy them before their eyes. Those Indians requested some one to labor with them, and I told them I will, God being my helper. But O, God, *"send more laborers into thy vineyard!"* And now, of these Indians, sixty-nine have been baptized, with their children. O this is glorious tidings in the ears of the bright angels of God, who rejoice before the dazzling throne of God and of the Lamb, when one sinner repenteth of his sins, and coming home to God. And also this is encouragement and glorious news to the saints of God who pray day and night for the prosperity of Zion.

Pray for your unworthy brother and laborer in the Gospel,

MA-DWA-GWUN-A-YAUSH,
alias,
PETER MARKSMAN.
Lakeville Mission [Minnesota], *August,* 1842.

ABOLITIONIST CLERGY ISSUE PUBLIC LETTER OF WITHDRAWAL

Source: Orange Scott, The Grounds of Secession from the M.E. Church; or, Book For The Times, being an Examination of her Connection with Slavery, and also of her Form of Government to which is added Wesley Upon Slavery, *revised and corrected (New York. Published by C. Prindle for the Wesleyan Methodist Connection of America 1848), 3-16. Excerpts. Italics in original.*

WITHDRAWAL OF JOTHAM HORTON, ORANGE SCOTT AND LAROY SUNDERLAND

With the date of this communication, closes our connection with the Methodist Episcopal Church. We take this step after years of consideration, and with a solemn sense of our responsibility to God—we take it with a view to his glory and the salvation of souls.

Twenty years and upwards of the best part of our lives has been spent in the service of this church—during which time we have formed acquaintances which have endeared to our hearts multitudes of Christian friends. Many of these are true kindred spirits, and we leave them with reluctance. But the view we take of our responsibility is not local in its bearings, nor limited in its duration. While we live, and when we die, we wish to bear a testimony which shall run parallel with coming ages; nay, with the annals of eternity. Many considerations of friendship as well as our temporal interests, bind us to the church of our early choice. But for the sake of a high and a holy cause, we *can* forego all of these. We wish to live not for ourselves, nor for the present age alone, but for all coming time; nay, for *God and Eternity.* We have borne our testimony a long time against what we considered wrong in the M.E. Church. We have waited, prayed, and hoped until there is no longer any ground for hope. Hence we have come to the deliberate conclusion that we must submit to things as they are, or peaceably retire. We have unhesitatingly chosen the latter.

It is however, proper, in leaving the church, that we assign our reasons. These are, mainly, the following:—

1. The Methodist Episcopal Church, is not only a slaveholding, but a *slavery defending church.* . . . She allows her members and ministers *unrebuked,* to hold innocent human beings in a state of hopeless bondage—nay, more, she upholds and

defends her communicants in this abominable business! All her disciplinary regulations which present a *show* of opposition to slavery are known and acknowledged to be a dead letter in the South. And they are as dead in the North as in the South. Even the General Rule [on Slavery] has been altered, either through carelessness or design, so as to favor the internal slave trade; and yet the last General Conference [1840] refused to correct the error, *knowing it to be such!*

This church has defended in a labored argument, through some of her best ministers, the *present rightful relation of master and slave*—in that she has never called them to account for putting forth such a document.

She has exhorted, through her regularly constituted agents and highest officers, the trustees of Methodist churches to close their pulpits against Methodist anti-slavery lecturers.

She has refused, in numerous instances, through her bishops, to entertain, in the annual conferences, motions expressive of the sinfulness of slave-holding—motions for the appointment of committees on slavery—motions for the adoption of reports on slavery; and that, because those motions and reports contained the sentiment, that *slaveholding is sin*—which, it was alleged, is contrary to Methodism, which recognizes and approves of the relation of master and slavery under some circumstances.

She has refused, through her bishops, to *hear* the prayers of scores and hundreds of her members *against* slavery, in some of the annual conferences.

She has said, through some of her annual conferences, that slavery is not a moral evil—while she has repeatedly refused, through her bishops, to allow other annual conferences to express the opposite sentiment. . . .

2dly, The government of the M.E. Church contains principles not laid down in the Scriptures, nor recognized in the usages of the Primitive Church—principles which were subversive of the rights, both of ministers and laymen.

While we admit that no *form* of church government is laid down in the Scriptures, we contend that *principles* are laid down which are in direct contravention with some of the existing forms. . . .

The power which our bishops claim and exercise in the annual conference is contrary to the plainest principles of Christian responsibility. . . . Another serious objection to Methodist Episcopacy is the election of bishops for life. . . .

We will mention but one thing more. And that is that feature in the economy of the M.E. Church, which gives the power to the preacher of excluding almost any member *he* may wish to get rid of. True, the Discipline requires the forms of trial, in case of expulsion; but as the preacher has the sole power to appoint the committee, and that without giving the accused any right of challenge, it is not, in general, difficult, for a preacher to punish whom he pleases. . . .

Such, in brief, are some of our reasons for leaving the Methodist Episcopal Church.

We wish it to be distinctly understood that we do not withdraw from anything essential to *our Wesleyan Methodism*. We only dissolve our connection with

Episcopacy and Slavery. These we believe to be anti-Scriptural, and well calculated to sustain each other. . . .

Though but three of us sign this document, scores if not hundreds, to our certain knowledge, might easily have been obtained. . . .

And now, dear brethren of the M.E. Church, we bid you farewell. Many of you we know and love. And while we do not impeach your motives or honesty, we hope in turn you will not treat us as barbarians. There is room enough for us all. Let us have no *unchristian* contention.

Jotham Horton
Orange Scott
LaRoy Sunderland

Providence, RI, November 8, 1842

Ann Wilkins Describes Difficulties of Missionary Labors in Liberia

Source: Ann Wilkins papers. Missionary Correspondence.
United Methodist Archives, Madison, N.J.

Millsburgh [Liberia], June 20th, 1842

My Dear Sister [Mary] Mason [New York City]:—
Having received very short notice of an opportunity for sending letters to America, I can only write a few hasty lines at present, to tell you that I am keeping house and teaching school in Millsburgh, though I have not yet got any native girls under my care. Brother Chase directs the little girls at White Plains to be given over to me, but the good folks who have the care of them objected on account of their contract with the parents of the girls. But Bro. Chase wrote me that he had instructed ———— to let those parents know that if those girls cannot be subject to his control, he should pay for nothing for their support, and so he expected to hear something further about them soon. This, I think, was about two weeks ago. I have not heard anything on the subject since. I have myself spoken to several natives whom I have accidently seen about this school, setting forth its advantages to them as a people, and endeavoring to persuade them to send their daughters &c, to persuade their friends to send theirs. Some have promised to bring their own; and others who said they had none of their own, and whom I requested to use their influence with their friends, replied, "I'll try." How far their promises are to be relied on is yet to be seen.

The great difficulty in the way of obtaining female scholars more than male, lies in the fact of their being contracted for, for wives at a very early age, and I have heard since my return to this country, often in infancy, and sometimes even before they are born—see [*Africa's*] *Luminary* of Nov. 19th 1841 under the head, "Manners and Customs of Native Africans." Our greatest hope is from among the converts to Christianity. Both Bro. Chase and myself have requested the preachers who are employed out among natives, to use their influence with the people of their charges in behalf of the Female School. I hope that some scholars may be obtained, after a time, for this as well as all else that is desirable. My only trust is in the Lord, and my prayers are daily poured out before him for help and direction in what is right. I wish not to move a step out of *his* way. I know it does not become me to be easily discouraged, but I sometimes almost fear I have mistaken the path of duty, and done wrong in coming here this time; and yet I see the wonderful goodness of the Lord in his preservation of my life where many others die. Already one of the dear young ladies who accompanied us out the last voyage is dead—two of the Presbyterian Missionaries down the coast, and the wife of one of them has died since our arrival. O I think what great cause have I to admire and adore the goodness that preserves me, unworthy me. I find that many things are not yet wanted for the purposes of the school if we can but make up one of the character designed, which I may make a list of and send by the next vessel either to you or the Ladies in Philadelphia. I do not know that I could recollect half.

What are the Ladies doing for the school? I hope they still keep it in mind and not only think, but *act* in favor of it. And what are the auxiliaries doing? Have you heard anything from them? O that Christians everywhere were properly awake to the importance of their duty of sending the blessed Gospel among the heathen!

Please present my grateful love to all the Board of the Female Missionary Society, and tell them I would delight in writing to many of them if I had a little more time, and will be grateful for letters from any of them, or all of them.

With much love to yourself and all your family, especially your daughter Elizabeth, who, I suppose, has left your home for another one of her own, and Anna. I am, though in great haste,

Yours affectionately,
Ann Wilkins

Millsburgh [Liberia] Oct. 18th, 1849

My dear Sister Mason,

I was very sorry that I could not get even a *little* time to write to you before Sister Brush left here, to send by her, especially as I felt so much indebted to you for your kind letter, as well as attention to business I had committed to you. I hope your kindness will forgive, and accept this late expression of my thanks for your favors. I am glad to be assured that I am remembered in the supplications of the Female prayer meetings which you have mentioned, and doubtless I am remembered in prayers which are offered oftener than that meeting takes place, even in the morning, noon and evening private prayers of faithful Christians, who wish prosperity to the work I have in hand. And still I beseech all to *pray*, if possible with more *faith* and *fervency*, that the way of the Lord may be prepared in the wilderness, as well as that grace and wisdom may be given to me, suitable to my calling and responsibility. Without an immediate interposition of Divine influence we can not expect native Africans, in their own countries, to become Christians; or, if they become converted under the preaching of the Gospel attended with the manifestation of the Holy Spirit and power, on some suddenly exciting occasion. They need special aid from on high to keep them Christians. There is so much and so strong contrary influence around them. Our brethren who are sent out to preach and teach among them find great discouragements. Beside the strong laws that are opposite in their tendency to the pure principles of the Gospel, polygamy, and the ceremonies of the devil bush, the frequent rumors of *war* that distract the minds of the people are a great hindrance to the attention necessary to be given to religion by those to whom it is preached. Teachers too find great discouragements in our work. Many who have been taught to read and something of Grammar, Arithmetic, Geography and Writing have gone back to their country habits again, mostly by the control of their parents,

But a few we may hope will turn out to be good and useful persons; and it may be the Lord will yet cause his precious word sown in the hearts of those who have gone, to spring up and bring forth fruit of righteousness that may glorify his name, only the more for being scattered. . . .

I know you will praise the Lord for his goodness to us on this distant shore, and pray that those converted may be steadfast, and that the good work may extend out among the natives. O! if I had not the Lord to trust in, dear sister, I could not remain here. But blessed be his holy name, he is a strong tower to those who trust in him.

Please give much love from me to your family and to the dear sisters of the Board, and all kind sisters who may inquire about me, and accept a heart full for yourself,

Yours affectionately,
Ann Wilkins

Phoebe Palmer models "The Way of Holiness"

Source: Phoebe Palmer, The Way of Holiness, with Notes by the Way; Being a Narrative of Experience Resulting from a Determination to Be a Bible Christian *(New York: Piercy and Reed, 1843), 5-10, 33-38. Excerpts.*

IS THERE NOT A SHORTER WAY?

SECTION I.

"Be always ready to give an answer to every man that asketh you a reason of the hope that is within you, with meekness and fear." —*Peter* [1 Pet. 3:15].

"I have thought," said one of the children of Zion to the other, as in love they journeyed onward in the way cast up for the ransomed of the Lord to walk in; "I have thought," said he, "whether there is not a *shorter way* of getting into this way of holiness than some of our * * * brethren apprehend?"

"Yes," said the sister addressed, who was a member of the denomination alluded to: "Yes, brother, THERE IS A SHORTER WAY! O! I am sure this long waiting and struggling with the powers of darkness is not necessary. There is a shorter way." And then, with a solemn responsibility of feeling, and with a realizing conviction of the truth uttered, she continued to say, "But, brother, there is but one way."

Days and even weeks elapsed, and yet the question, with solemn bearing, rested upon the mind of that sister. She thought of the affirmative given in answer to the inquiry of the brother—examined yet more closely the Scriptural foundation upon which the truth of the affirmation rested—and the result of the investigation tended to add still greater confirmation to the belief, that many sincere disciples of Jesus, by various needless perplexities, consume much time in endeavoring to get into this way, which might, more advantageously to themselves and others, be employed in making progress in it, and testifying from experimental knowledge of its blessedness.

How many, whom Infinite Love would long since have brought into this state, instead of seeking to be brought into the possession of the blessing at once, are seeking a preparation for the reception of it! They feel that their *convictions* are not deep enough to warrant an approach to the throne of grace, with the expectation of receiving the blessing confidently *now*. Just at this point some may have been lingering months and years. Thus did the sister, who so confidently affirmed "there is a shorter way." And here, dear child of Jesus, permit the writer to tell you just how that sister found the "shorter way."

On looking at the requirements of the word of God, she beheld the command, "Be ye holy." She then began to say in her heart, "Whatever my former deficiencies may have been, God requires that I should *now* be holy. Whether *convicted*, or otherwise, *duty is plain.* God requires *present* holiness." On coming to this point, she at once apprehended a simple truth before unthought of, i.e. *Knowledge is conviction.* She well knew that, for a long time, she had been assured that God required holiness. But she had never deemed this knowledge a sufficient plea to take to God— and because of present need, to ask a present bestowment of the gift.

Convinced that in this respect she had mistaken the path, she now, with renewed energy, began to make use of the knowledge already received, and to discern a "shorter way."

Another difficulty by which her course had been delayed she found to be here. She had been accustomed to look at the blessing of holiness as such a high attainment, that her general habit of soul inclined her to think it almost beyond her reach. This erroneous impression rather influenced her to rest the matter thus:— "I will let every high state of grace in name alone, and seek only to be *fully conformed to the will of God, as recorded in his written word.* My chief endeavors shall be centered in the aim to be an humble *Bible Christian.* By the grace of God, all my energies shall be directed to this one point. With this single aim, I will journey onward, even though my faith may be tried to the uttermost by those manifestations being withheld, which have previously been regarded as essential for the establishment of faith."

On arriving at this point, she was enabled to gain yet clearer insight into the simplicity of the way. And it was by this process. After having taken the Bible as the rule of life, instead of the opinions and experience of professors, she found, on taking the blessed word more closely to the companionship of her heart, that no one declaration spoke more appealingly to her understanding than this: "Ye are not your own, ye are bought with a price, therefore glorify God in your body and spirit which are his" [1 Cor. 7:23].

By this she perceived the duty of *entire consecration* in a stronger light, and as more sacredly binding, than ever before. Here she saw God as her Redeemer, claiming, by virtue of the great price paid for the redemption of body, soul, and spirit, the *present and entire service* of all these redeemed powers.

By this she saw, that if she lived constantly in the entire surrender of all that had been thus dearly purchased unto God, she was but an unprofitable servant; and that, if less than all was rendered, she was worse than unprofitable, inasmuch as she would be guilty of keeping back part of that price which had been purchased unto God: "Not with corruptible things, such as silver and gold, but by the precious blood of Jesus" [1 Pet. 1:18]. And after so clearly discerning the will of God concerning her, she felt that the sin of Annanias [*sic*] and Sapphira would be less culpable in the sight of Heaven than her own, should she not at once resolve on living in the *entire* consecration of all her redeemed powers to God.

Deeply conscious of past unfaithfulness, she now determined that the time past should suffice; and with a humility of spirit, induced from a consciousness of not having lived in the performance of such a "reasonable service" [Rom. 12:1], she was enabled, through grace, to resolve, with firmness of purpose, that entire devotion of heart and life to God should be the absorbing subject of the succeeding pilgrimage of life. . . .

IS THERE NOT A SHORTER WAY?

SECTION VI.

"He staggered not at the promise of God, through unbelief, but was strong in faith, giving glory to God; being fully persuaded that what he had promised he was able also to perform."—*The word of God.* [Rom. 4:20]

> "Faith in thy power thou seest I have,
> For thou this faith hast wrought,
> Dead souls thou callest from the grave,
> And speakest worlds from nought.
>
> In hope against all human hope,
> Self-desperate, I believe,
> Thy *quickening word shall raise me up,*
> Thou shalt thy spirit give.
>
> The thing surpasses all my thought,
> But faithful is my Lord:
> Through unbelief I stagger not,
> For *God hath spoke the word.*"

[Charles Wesley, "Father of Jesus Christ my Lord," *A Collection of Hymns for the use of the Methodist Episcopal Church* (1836), no. 362, pp. 311-12. Full original text in John Wesley, *Works* (Bicentennial edition), 7:515-16.]

From the preceding views she discerned clearly, that *one* more step must be taken ere she had tested fully the faithfulness of God. "Faithful is he who hath called you, who also *will do* it," [1 Thess. 5:24] was now no longer a matter of opinion, but a truth confidently believed, and she now saw that she must relinquish the confident expression before indulged in, as premising something in the *future*, "Thou *wilt* receive me," for the yet more confident expression, implying *present* assurance, "Thou *dost* receive!" It is, perhaps, almost needless to say, that the enemy who had heretofore endeavored to withstand every step of the Spirit's leadings, now, with much greater energy, withstood; the suggestion that it was strangely presumptuous to believe in such a way, was presented with a plausibility which only Satanic subtilty could invent; but the resolution to believe had passed; and then the Spirit most inspiringly said to her heart, "The kingdom of heaven suffereth violence, and the violent take it by force" [Matt. 11:12].

And now realizing that she was engaged in a transaction eternal in its consequences, she here, in the strength, and as in the presence of the Father, Son, and Holy Spirit, and those spirits that minister to the heirs of salvation, said, "O, Lord, I now call heaven and earth to witness that I *now lay body, soul, and spirit, with all these redeemed powers, upon thine altar, to be for ever* thine! 'Tis done! Thou hast promised to receive me! Thou canst not be unfaithful! *Thou dost receive me now!* From this time henceforth I *am thine—wholly thine!"*

The enemy suggested, " 'Tis but the work of your own understanding—the effort of your own will." But the spirit of the Lord raised up a standard which Satan, with his combined forces, could not overthrow. It was by the following presentation of truth that the Spirit helped her infirmities. "Do not your perceptions of right— even your *own understanding*—assure you that it is matter of *thanksgiving to God* that you have been thus enabled to present your all to him?" "Yes," responded her whole heart, "it has been all the work of the Spirit. I will praise Him! Glory be to God in the highest! Worthy is the Lamb to receive glory, honor, and blessing! Hallelujah! the Lord God Omnipotent reigneth! Yes, thou dost reign unrivalled in my heart! Thou hast subdued all things to thyself, and now thou dost reign throughout the empire of my soul, the Lord God of every motion!" The Spirit now bore full testimony to her spirit of the Truth *of* the word! She felt in experimental verity that it was not in vain that she had believed; her very existence seemed lost and swallowed up in God; and she seemed plunged as it were, into an immeasurable ocean of love, light and power, and realized that she was encompassed with the "favor of the Almighty as with a shield, and felt assured, while she continued thus to rest her entire being on the faithfulness of God, she might confidently stand rejoicing in hope," and exultingly, with the poet, assure her heart—

> "My steadfast soul from falling free,
>   Shall now no longer rove,
> But Christ be all in all to me,
>   And *all my soul be* LOVE."

[Charles Wesley, "My God, I Know, I Feel Thee Mine," *A Collection of Hymns for the Use of the Methodist Episcopal Church* (1836) No. 318, pp. 274-75. Full original text in John Wesley, *Works* (Bicentennial edition), 7:517-18.]

She now saw infinite *propriety, comprehensiveness,* and *beauty,* in those words of DIVINE *origin* from which she had before indulged a shrinking, as implying a state too high and sacred for ordinary attainment or expectation.

HOLINESS, SANCTIFICATION, *perfect love,* were now no longer so incomprehensible, or indefinite in nature or bearing, in relation to the individual experience of the Lord's redeemed ones. She wondered not that it should be said, in reference to the "WAY OF HOLINESS," "The *ransomed of the Lord shall walk there!*" She now perceived that these terms were most significantly expressive of a state of soul in which *every* believer should live, and felt that no words of mere earthly origin could embody to her own perceptions, or convey to the understanding of others, half the comprehensiveness of meaning contained in these significant expressions, which stand forth so prominently in the word of God, thereby assuring men that they are given by the express dictation of the Holy Spirit.

She now thought of her former peculiar scruples in reference to the *use* of these words of divine origin, as in a degree partaking of the sin of Uzzah, implying, as she now clearly discerned, an *unwarrantable* carefulness about the ark of God, as though infinite wisdom had not devised the most *proper mode of expression*; for she well remembered how often her heart had risen against these expressions, as objectionable, when she had heard other travellers in the "way of holiness" use the terms as expressive of the state of grace into which the Lord had brought them; the very same words which she now saw were infinitely expressive of the state into which the Lord had brought *her* own soul.

But she now felt such a mighty increase of confidence in God, that she hesitated not in trusting the entire management of his own cause in his own hands, and was willing, ay, even desirous, to become an instrument through which he might show forth his power to save unto the uttermost; desirous to be accounted of no reputation—to be but as a *"voice"* to sound forth the praise of the "Almighty to save;" willing that the instrument should be despised and rejected, only so that the voice of God should be heard, and the Saviour honored and accepted.

267

GENERAL CONFERENCE CONSIDERS RESOLUTIONS ON SLAVE-HOLDING BISHOP ANDREW

Source: Methodist Episcopal Church, Journal of General Conference *(1844), 63-66. Excerpts.*

[May 22, Bishop T. A. Morris, presiding]

The Committee on Episcopacy, to whom was referred a resolution, submitted yesterday, instructing them to inquire whether any one of the Superintendents is connected with slavery, beg leave to present the following as their report on the subject. . . .

A. Griffith and J. Davis [both Baltimore Conference] offered the following preamble and resolution, which were read and debated:—

"Whereas, the Rev. James O. Andrew, one of the Bishops of the M. E. Church, has become connected with slavery, as communicated in his statement in his reply to the inquiry of the Committee on the Episcopacy, which reply is imbodied in their report, No. 3, offered yesterday; and whereas it has been, from the origin of said Church, a settled policy and the invariable usage to elect no person to the office of Bishop who was embarrassed with this 'great evil,' as under such circumstances it would be impossible for a bishop to exercise the functions and perform the duties assigned to a general Superintendent with acceptance, in that large portion of his charge in which slavery does not exist; and whereas Bishop Andrew was himself nominated by our brethren of the slaveholding states, and elected by the General Conference of 1832, as a candidate who, though living in the midst of a slaveholding population, was nevertheless free from all personal connection with slavery; and whereas, this is, of all periods in our history as a Church, the one least favourable to such an innovation upon the practice and usage of Methodism as to confide a part of the itinerant general superintendency to a slaveholder; therefore,

"Resolved, That the Rev. James O. Andrew be, and he is hereby affectionately requested to resign his office as one of the Bishops of the Methodist Episcopal Church. . . ."

[May 23, Bishop Hedding presiding]

J. B. Finley [Ohio Conference] offered a substitute for the resolution, in the following words, viz.:—

"Whereas, the Discipline of our church forbids the doing anything calculated to destroy our itinerant general superintendency, and whereas Bishop Andrew has become connected with slavery by marriage and otherwise, and this act having drawn after it circumstances which in the estimation of the General Conference will greatly embarrass the exercise of his office as an itinerant general Superintendent, if not in some places entirely prevent it; therefore,

"Resolved, That it is the sense of this General Conference that he desist from the exercise of this office so long as this impediment remains.

J. B. FINLEY,
J. M. TRIMBLE [Ohio Conference]."

General Conference Delegates
Debate Slavery and Episcopacy

Source: Report of Debates in the General Conference of the Methodist Episcopal Church, Held in the City of New-York, 1844, Robert Athow West, reporter for the MEC (New York: G. Lane & C. B. Tippett, 1844), 148-50, 172-77. Excerpts.

[Monday, May 27, Morning Session, Bishop Joshua Soule, presiding]

Bishop Andrew then rose, evidently labouring under powerful emotion, and spoke as follows:

Mr. President,—I have been on trial now for a week, and feel desirous that it should come to a close. For a week I have been compelled to listen to discussions of which I have been the subject, and I must have been more than man, or less than man, not to have felt. Sir, I have felt and felt deeply. I am not offended with any man. The *most* of those who have spoken against me, have treated me respectfully, and have been as mild as I had any right to expect. I cherish no unkind feelings toward any. I do not quarrel with my abolition brethren, though I believe their opinions to be erroneous and mischievous. Yet so long as they conduct themselves courteously toward me, I have no quarrel with them. It is due that some remarks should be made by me, before the conference come to a conclusion upon the question, which I hope will be speedily done, for I think a week is long enough for a man to be shot at, and it is time the discussion should terminate.

As there has been frequent reference to the circumstances of my election to the episcopal office, it is perhaps proper that I give a brief history of that matter. A friend of mine (brother Hodges) now with God, asked me to permit myself to be put in nomination for that office. I objected—the office had no charms for me. I was with a conference that I loved, and that loved me. What was I to gain to be separated from a happy home—from a wife and children whom I loved more than I did my own life? But my friend urged me; he said my election would, he believed, tend to promote the peace of the Church, and that he believed it would be especially important to the prosperity of Methodism at the south. Finally I consented, with the hope of failure; but I was nominated and elected. I was never asked if I was a slaveholder—no man asked me what were my principles on the subject—no one dared to ask of me a pledge in this matter, or it would have been met as it deserved.

Only one man, brother Winans, spoke to me on the subject: he said he could not vote for me because he believed I was nominated under the impression that I was not a slaveholder. I told him I had not sought the nomination, nor did I desire the office, and that my opinions on the propriety of making non-slaveholding a test of qualification for the office of bishop were entirely in unison with his own. Sir, I do not believe in this matter of secret will as a rule of action, either in the revelations of the Bible, or in the prescriptions of the book of Discipline. I believe in the revealed will of God, and in the written law of the Church as contained in the book of Discipline. I took office upon the broad platform of that book, and I believe my case is covered by it. It was known that I was to reside at the south; I was elected in view of that very thing, as it was judged important to the best interests of the Church that one of the bishops should reside in that section of the work, and it was judged that I could be more useful there than elsewhere. Well, what was I to do then? I was located in a country where free persons could not be obtained for hire, and I could not do the work of the family—my wife could not do it—what was I to do? I was compelled to hire slaves, and pay their masters for their hire; but I had to change them every year—they were bad servants, for they had no interest in me or mine—and I believe it would have been less sin before God to have bought a servant who would have taken an interest in me and I in him: but I did not do so. At length, however, I came into the possession of slaves; and I am a slaveholder, (as I have already explained to the conference,) and I cannot help myself. It is known that I have waded through deep sorrows at the south during the last four years; I have buried the wife of my youth and the mother of my children, who left me with a family of motherless children, who needed a friend and a mother. I sought another: (and with this the conference has nothing to do:) I found one, who, I believed would make me a good wife, and a good mother for my children. I had known her long—my children knew and loved her. I sought to make my home a happy one—and I have done so. Sir, I have no apology to make. It has been said, I did this thing voluntarily, and with my eyes open. I did so deliberately and in the fear of God—and God has blessed our union. I might have avoided this difficulty by resorting to a trick—by making over these slaves to my wife before marriage, or by doing as a friend who has taken ground in favour of the resolution before you suggested: "Why," said he, "did you not let your wife make over these negroes to her children, securing to herself an annuity from them?" Sir, my conscience would not allow me to do this thing. If I had done so, and those negroes had passed into the hands of those who would have treated them unkindly, I should have been unhappy. Strange as it may seem to brethren, I am a slaveholder for conscience' sake. I have no doubt that my wife would, without a moment's hesitation, consent to the manumission of those slaves, if I thought proper to do it. I know she would unhesitatingly consent to any arrangement I might deem it proper to make on the subject. But how am I to free them? Some of them are old, too old to work to support themselves, and are only an expense to me; and some of them are little children: where shall I send these, and who will provide for them? But, perhaps, I shall be permitted to keep these; but, then, if the others go, how shall I provide for these helpless ones? and

271

as to the others, to what free state shall I send them? and what would be their condition? Besides, many of them would not go—they love their mistress, and could not be induced, under any circumstances, to leave her. Sir, an aged and respectable minister said to me several years ago, when I had stated just such a case to him, and asked him what he would do,—"I would set them free," said he, "I'd wash my hands of them, and if they went to the devil, I'd be clear of them." Sir, into such views of religion or philanthropy my soul cannot enter. I believe the providence of God has thrown these creatures into my hands, and holds me responsible for their proper treatment. I have secured them to my wife by deed of trust since our marriage. The arrangement was only in accordance with an understanding existing previous to marriage. These servants were hers—she had inherited them from her former husband's estate—they had been her only source of support during her widowhood, and would still be her only dependance if it should please God to remove me from her. I have nothing to leave her. I have given my life to the Church from the days of my youth, (and I am now fifty,) and although, as I have previously remarked, she would consent to any arrangement I might make, yet I cannot consent to take advantage of her affection for me to induce her to do what would injure her without at all benefiting the slaves.

Sir, I do not for a moment believe that this body of grave and reverend ministers would make this a subject of serious discussion. I thought it likely that there might be some warm ultra brethren here who would take some exception to my course, and on that account I did not make the deed of trust before marriage, lest some should suppose I designed to dodge the responsibility of the case. Those who know me must know that I could not be governed by the mere matter of dollars and cents. What can I do? I have no confession to make—I intend to make none. I stand upon the broad ground of the Discipline on which I took office, and if I have done wrong, put me out. The editor of the Christian Advocate has prejudged this case. He makes me the-scape goat of all the difficulties which abolition excitement has gotten up at the north. I am the only one to blame, in his opinion, should mischief grow out of this case. But I repeat, if I have sinned against the Discipline, I refuse not to die. I have spent my life for the benefit of the slaves. When I was but a boy, I taught a Sunday-school for slaves, in which I taught a number of them to read; and from that period till this day I have devoted my energies to the promotion of their happiness and salvation; with all my influence in private, in public, with my tongue, with my pen, I have assiduously endeavoured to promote their present and eternal happiness. And am I to be sacrificed by those who have done little or nothing for them? It is said, I have rendered myself unacceptable to our people. I doubt this: I have just returned from Philadelphia, where they knew me to be a slaveholder; yet they flocked to hear me, and the presence of God was with us; we had a good, warm, old-fashioned meeting. I may be unacceptable in New-York, yet from the experience I have had, I doubt even that. To whom am I unacceptable? Not to the people of the south—neither masters nor slaves. Has my connection with slaves rendered me less acceptable to the coloured people of the south—the very people for whom all this professed sympathy is felt? Does the fact-that I am a slaveholder make me less acceptable among them? Let those who have laboured long among them answer the question. Sir, I venture to say, that in Carolina or Georgia I could to-day get more votes for the office of bishop from the coloured people, than any supporter of this resolution, let him avow himself an emancipator as openly as he pleases. To the coloured people of the south there, and to their owners,—to the entire membership of the slaveholding conferences, I would not be unacceptable—but, perhaps, they are no part of "our people"; in short, sir, I believe that I should not be acceptable to one half of the connection—but on this question I have nothing to say. Should the conference think proper to pass me, there is plenty of ground where I can labour acceptably and usefully. The slaveholding conferences will present a field sufficiently large for me, should I live to the age of Methuselah, and the bishops, in arranging the work, will certainly have discretion enough not to send me where I would not be received; nor would I obtrude myself upon any conference, or lay my hands upon the head of any brother who would feel himself contaminated by the touch. However, on this subject I have nothing to say. The conference can take its course; but I protest against the proposed action as a violation of the laws of the Discipline, an invasion of the rights secured to me by that book. Yet let the conference take the steps they contemplate; I enter no plea for mercy—I make no appeal for sympathy; indeed, I love those who sympathize with me, but I do not want it now. I wish you to act coolly and deliberately, and in the fear of God; but I would rather that the conference would change the issue, and make the resolution to depose the bishop, and take the question at once, for I am tired of it. The country is becoming agitated upon the subject, and I hope the conference will act forthwith on the resolution. . . .

AFTERNOON SESSION

[May 27]

Dr. [John] Durbin [Philadelphia Conference] rose, and alluded to the disadvantage of his position in making an after-dinner speech; but, as it could not be avoided, he would make the best of it. . . .

We of the north have been repeatedly taunted on this floor with our differences of opinion on the subject of slavery. Sir, whatever other differences of opinion there may be among us, on one point there is none. Our minds, and hearts, and feelings, are all united on this *one* point at least—*that the episcopacy of the Methodist Episcopal Church ought not to be trammelled with slavery.* On that point, sir, our minds are as the mind of one man, and the brethren of the south will find it so. Nor is this any sudden purpose. It is the ground we have always held, and we shall be found standing up for it, shoulder to shoulder, to the end of the battle. We have also been told, sir, that the early Methodists, in their protest against slavery, went further than Christ and his apostles had done. Nay, sir, we have had arguments to-day drawn from the Bible to sustain slavery. What do brethren mean, sir? Is it their *intention* to plead the word of God in defence of slavery? Do they really believe, with the brother from South Carolina, who spoke this morning, that the system of slavery is to find its authority in the Decalogue, written by God's own hand? Sir, they cannot mean this, they will not affirm this. And yet we are gravely told that because the commandment speaks of the ox, and the ass, and the man-servant, and maid-servant, in the same connection, that therefore the right of property was assumed on the same ground for the latter as for the former. As well go a little further, and assume that the *wife* too was a chattel, according to the intent of the commandment. O! sir, I hope we shall never be compelled to hear the Bible—the record of God's truth—the charter of human freedom and human rights—appealed to in support of American slavery.

We have had some strange statements here in regard to the legislation of the Church on the subject of slavery. Brethren have tried to make the impression, to use one of their own figures, that the north has been putting the screws on the south, and continually pressing them harder, until at last the compression can be endured no longer. Sir, the facts in the case are just the reverse of all this. The history of the Church shows this point indisputably, that the highest ground that has ever been held upon the subject, was taken at the very organization of the Church, and that concessions have been made by the Church continually, from that time to this, in view of the *necessities* of the south; that while the anti slavery principle has never been abandoned, our rules have been made less and less stringent, and our language less and less severe,—because experience has shown it to be *absolutely necessary* for the welfare of the Church in the south—and these concessions have been made, too, while the power of the Church has been continually passing from the slaveholding to the non-slaveholding states. I trust brethren will bear this in mind. Without laying stress upon Mr. Wesley's vehement denunciations of slavery, what was the declaration of the Church in 1780? *"We pass our disapprobation on all our friends who keep slaves, and advise their freedom."* The language of 1784, when the Church was organized, was equally bold. All *private members* were required to emancipate their slaves in those states where the laws allowed of manumission. The action taken was too strong, sir, and in six months it was suspended, in accordance with the genius of Methodism, which does not all the good she would, but all she can. The Church then made a concession to the south on the score of *necessity*. Even the language of the question on slavery was mitigated. In 1796 it was, "What regulations shall be made for the extirpation of the crying evil of African slavery?" In 1804 it was, "What shall be done for the extirpation of the evil of slavery?" In 1808 all that relates to slaveholding among private members was stricken out, and no rule on the subject has existed since. I might advert to other points to show the truth of my position, that the Church has gradually made concessions to the necessities of the slaveholding states, until our brethren from the south say they stand firmly on the ground of Discipline. But I forbear: it will not be denied by any who are conversant with the history of the Church. Is it necessary to make still another concession, and allow slavery to connect itself with our episcopacy?

Now, sir, I do not mean to say that these concessions ought not to have been made. Our fathers wisely made them, on the ground of necessity. The Methodist

Church could not have existed at all in the south without them. This should be a rebuke to our abolition brethren everywhere who would urge this question to extremities. I take my stand on the *conservative* ground of the Discipline, as far from extreme opinions in the north as in the south. I have no sympathy with either. I would not, dare not, urge on our southern brethren to a position where they cannot stand. The Discipline has placed the Church in the proper relation to slavery in the south. She does not propose to disturb the relations of our southern brethren on the question of slavery in the south, but to leave them free to contend with the evil in the best manner they can under the laws of their several states. But while I stand up firmly for their rights and privileges, and shall be ever ready to lend what weight I can to protect them if assaulted, I must beg our brethren of the south not to return the question of slavery upon the north in connection with our general superintendency. This is the real question, Shall slavery be connected with our episcopacy, which is common to all parts of our Church, the north as well as the south, and thus cause the Church to give her example in favour of the "great evil of slavery," in a form which will be pleaded as decisive of her judgment on the general question, and in those parts of the country where no necessity exists for such a declaration, and where it will fearfully agitate our societies? There is no necessity in the south for any one of our bishops to hold slaves in order to do his work there. This is admitted on all hands; while it is as readily admitted, even by the south, that there are many conferences "in which his connection with slavery would render his services *unacceptable.*"

I come now, sir, with as much delicacy as possible, to examine the question of the power of the General Conference over the bishops. It has been maintained here, sir, that the General Conference has no power to remove a bishop, or to suspend the exercise of his functions, unless by impeachment and trial, in regular form, for some offence regularly charged. If this be true, sir, I have greatly misunderstood the nature of our episcopacy. From whence is its power derived? Do we place it upon the ground of divine right? Surely not, sir. You do not plead any such doctrine. Whence, then, is it derived? Solely, sir, from the suffrages of the General Conference. There, and there only, is the source of episcopal power in our Church. And the same power that conferred the authority can remove it, if they see it necessary. Nor is this a new doctrine, sir. The Minutes of 1785 declare that at the organization of the Church, the "episcopal office was made elective, and the elected superintendent or bishop amenable to the body of ministers and preachers." The Notes to the Discipline assert that the bishops are *"perfectly subject* to the General Conference—their power, their usefulness, themselves, are entirely at the mercy" of that body. Again, sir, I bring you the authority of a witness sanctioned by the conference of 1792, and by Bishop Asbury, and whose doctrine on this subject is endorsed by our late beloved Bishop Emory. I do not mention these venerated names for the mere purpose of awaking the feelings of brethren.

I would not call the sleeping dead from their honoured graves, as some have done on this floor. No, sir; they are escaped from all our strifes and warfare. Let them rest, sir—let them rest. They never saw the Methodist Church threatened with so fearful a storm as that which now hangs over us; I know not what they would say or do were they with us now. But hear my witness. Rev. John Dickens, the most intimate friend of Bishop Asbury, in a pamphlet, published in 1792, as already stated, with the sanction of the General Conference, thus answered a question put by Mr. Hammett, in reference to this very point. "Now whoever said the superiority of the bishops was by virtue of a separate ordination? If this gave them their superiority, how came they to be removable by the conference?" "We all know Mr. Asbury derived his official power from the conference, and, therefore, his office is at their disposal." "Mr. Asbury was thus chosen by the conference, both before and after he was ordained a bishop; and he is still considered as the person of their choice, by being responsible to the conference, who have power to remove him, and to fill his place with another, if they see it necessary. And as he is liable every year to be removed, he may be considered as their annual choice." Bishop Emory states that this may be considered as expressing the views of "Bishop Asbury in relation to the true and original character of Methodist episcopacy"; and gives it the sanction of his own authority, by quoting and using it in the twelfth section of the "Defence of our Fathers."

I have thus, sir, expressed, and, I trust, maintained, my views of the authority of the General Conference, in regard to the episcopal office. I am sorry, sir, that this opinion differs somewhat from your own (if I may be permitted to address you personally), knowing, as I do, that my judgment, thrown into the opposite scale to yours, is but as a feather against a thousand pounds weight. Still, sir, I must hold my opinion.

A few words now in regard to the application of this power in the present instance. The action that is proposed to be taken in the case of Bishop Andrew is contained in the substitute now before us. We are told that it is in fact a proposition to *depose* Bishop Andrew. Sir, we do not so regard it. The venerable man who moved it does not so regard it. I am sure he does not: I know him well—he has called me "John," sir, from my boyhood,—and on the day when he offered this substitute, he called to me across the pews—"John, explain this for me." Understanding his view of the substitute, I now propose to explain it—having the opportunity of doing so for the first time. It reads: . . .

"Resolved, That it is the sense of this General Conference, that he desist from the exercise of his office so long as this impediment remains."

Now, sir, this action is *not* contemplated without cause. The preamble states the ground of the action clearly and distinctly, in a statement of undisputed and indisputable facts. And what does the resolution propose? Expulsion? No, sir. Deposition? No. If I am pressed to a decision of this case in its present form, I shall vote for that substitute, and so will many others; but if, after we *have* voted for it, any man should come and tell us personally that we have voted to *depose* Bishop Andrew, we should consider it a personal—shall I say—insult, sir? The substitute proposes only to express the sense of this conference in regard to a matter which it cannot, in duty and conscience, pass by without suitable expression; and having made the solemn expression, it leaves Bishop Andrew to act as *his* sense of duty shall dictate. Will any of the brethren on the other side of the house tell us that if such is our deliberate sense, and we deem it our duty to the Church to say so, we ought to suppress it? . . . In passing this substitute—if we do pass it—we make a clear declaration against the connection of slavery with our episcopacy—a declaration which we cannot avoid making if we would, and ought not if we could:—a declaration, sir, which the world will approve. . . .

I have read in the public reports of the proceedings during my absence some things that gave me great pain. Mention has been made here of proceedings at law—of the possibility of obtaining an "injunction" upon the Book Concern, and stopping our presses. I am sorry that such words have been uttered here. Perhaps such an injunction might be issued. I do not know but a judge or a chancellor might be found (though I do not believe it) wicked enough to rejoice in our difficulties, and exult over our strife. Ah! sir, wicked men would, indeed, exult in it: Satan would exult in it—perhaps, I say, such an injunction might be obtained[,] but what then? You may lay an injunction upon types, and presses, and newspapers; but, thank God, no injunction can be laid upon an honest conscience and an upright mind. The Book Concern! There is no man here, I am sure, whose soul is so mean and paltry as to be influenced by such a motive. Sir, that Book Concern was burned down *once*, and I grieved over its destruction; but gladly would I see it destroyed again this night—gladly would I welcome the first flash of light that might burst into that window—even though in the conflagration buildings, types, presses, paper, plates, and all, were this night to be destroyed if it could place the Church back where she was only six months ago.

Before I sit down, I desire to call the attention of the conference to a proposition made by the brethren from the south in the Committee of Pacification. The language of part of that proposition was "that Bishop Andrew shall not be required to preside in any annual conference in which his connection with slavery would render his services unacceptable." Now, sir, here was a clear admission of the fact that Bishop Andrew's position did render him unacceptable to many of the conferences, and a proposition founded upon it. Keeping the admission in mind, and recollecting that we are forbidden by the constitution to do anything that shall impair our itinerant general superintendency, I beg the conference to look at the bearing of this proposition, and of similar ones that have been made here from time to time. It is wrong to do that for one of the bishops which, if done for all, would be destruction to the system. Now, sir, suppose that you should become an abolitionist, and on that account you could not go to the south—for the same reasons precisely a resolution might be brought here to confine your services to the east. Suppose some similar contingency to continue another bishop in the north, and another in the west—is not our itinerant general superintendency effectually destroyed? Assuredly it is—and it seems to me that we cannot take the first step toward such a result without violating the constitution as it now stands.

I am free to declare that I do not wish to come to a direct vote on this momentous question; I have looked long and earnestly for some way to escape. I have hoped our brethren of the south could agree to say to this conference, "Brethren, we have been very unexpectedly and unintentionally the occasion, in the person of our beloved bishop, of bringing the Church into great danger; we had not apprehended such a cloud as now covers our Zion; we have stood up for what we believed to be our rights and the interests of the Church in the south; we have heard you feelingly and plainly declare the certain danger which threatens you in the north; the sacrifice of the peace and unity of the Church is too costly a sacrifice to be made almost by accident; postpone all proceedings in this unfortunate case, and we will see that the Church shall suffer no further harm." Such an announcement as this would come upon the conference and the Church like a message from heaven; and no man would ask you, how, when, or where are you going to deal with the case. This conference and the Church would trust your word and your religion in the case, and ask you no questions. I will conclude, sir, by saying, a few days ago brother Early, from Virginia, threw out a suggestion at the close of the session, viz.: *might* not this matter be referred back to the Church or the conferences? This course was distinctly advised by yourself, sir, this morning, in your address to the conference. These weighty facts led me to believe that the north would meet the south on the following resolution, which I would willingly offer if I had the least intimation that our brethren from the south would meet us on it, viz.:—

"Resolved, That the case of Bishop Andrew be referred to the Church, and that the judgment of the next General Conference be deemed and taken to be the voice of the Church, whether Bishop Andrew shall continue to exercise his functions as a general superintendent in the Methodist Episcopal Church, while he sustains the relation to slavery as stated in his communication to the conference, as reported to the conference by the Committee on the Episcopacy."

GENERAL CONFERENCE DELEGATES ADOPT "PLAN OF SEPARATION"

Source: Methodist Episcopal Church, Journal of General Conference (1844), 135-37. *Excerpts.*

[June 8, Bishop T. A. Morris, presiding]

"The select committee of nine to consider and report on the declaration of the delegates from the Conferences of the slaveholding states, beg leave to submit the following report:

"Whereas, a declaration has been presented to this General Conference, with the signatures of *fifty-one* delegates of the body, from thirteen Annual Conferences in the slaveholding states, representing that, for various reasons enumerated, the objects and purposes of the Christian ministry and church organization cannot be successfully accomplished by them under the jurisdiction of this General Conference as now constituted; and

"Whereas, in the event of a separation, a contingency to which the declaration asks attention as not improbable, we esteem it the duty of this General Conference to meet the emergency with Christian kindness and the strictest equity; therefore,

"Resolved, by the delegates of the several Annual Conferences in General Conference assembled,

"1. That, should the Annual Conferences in the slaveholding states find it necessary to unite in a distinct ecclesiastical connection, the following rule shall be observed with regard to the northern boundary of such connection:—All the societies, stations, and Conferences adhering to the church in the South, by a vote of a majority of the members of said societies, stations, and Conferences, shall remain under the unmolested pastoral care of the Southern Church; and the ministers of the Methodist Episcopal Church shall in no wise attempt to organize churches or societies within the limits of the Church South, nor shall they attempt to exercise any pastoral oversight therein; it being understood that the ministry of the South reciprocally observe the same rule in relation to stations, societies, and Conferences adhering, by vote of a majority, to the Methodist Episcopal Church; provided also, that this rule shall apply only to societies, stations, and Conferences bordering on the line of division, and not to interior charges, which shall in all cases be left to the care of that church within whose territory they are situated.

"2. That ministers, local and travelling, of every grade and office in the Methodist Episcopal Church, may, as they prefer, remain in that church, or, without blame, attach themselves to the Church South.

"3. Resolved, by the delegates of all the Annual Conferences in General Conference assembled, That we recommend to all the Annual Conferences, at their first approaching sessions, to authorize a change of the sixth restrictive article, so that the first clause shall read thus: 'They shall not appropriate the produce of the Book Concern, nor the Chartered Fund, to any other purpose other than for the benefit of the travelling, supernumerary, superannuated, and worn-out preachers, their wives, widows, and children, and to such other purposes as may be determined upon by the votes of two-thirds of the members of the General Conference.'

"4. That whenever the Annual Conferences, by a vote of three-fourths of all their members voting on the third resolution, shall have concurred in the recommendation to alter the sixth restrictive article, the Agents at New-York and Cincinnati shall, and they are hereby authorized and directed to deliver over to any authorized agent or appointee of the Church South, should one be organized, all notes and book accounts against the ministers, church members, or citizens within its boundaries, with authority to collect the same for the sole use of the Southern Church, and that said Agents also convey to the aforesaid agent or appointee of the South all the real estate, and assign to him all the property, including presses, stock, and all right and interest connected with the printing establishments at Charleston, Richmond, and Nashville, which now belong to the Methodist Episcopal Church.

"5. That when the Annual Conferences shall have approved the aforesaid change in the sixth restrictive article, there shall be transferred to the above agent of the Southern Church so much of the capital and produce of the Methodist Book Concern as will, with the notes, book accounts, presses, &c., mentioned in the last resolution, bear the same proportion to the whole property of said Concern that the travelling preachers in the Southern Church shall bear to all the travelling ministers of the Methodist Episcopal Church; the division to be made on the basis of the number of travelling preachers in the forthcoming Minutes. . . .

"9. That all the property of the Methodist Episcopal Church in meeting-houses, parsonages, colleges, schools, Conference funds, cemeteries, and of every kind within the limits of the Southern organization, shall be for ever free from any claim set up on the part of the Methodist Episcopal Church, so far as this resolution can be of force in the premises.

"10. That the church so formed in the South shall have a common right to use all the copy-rights in possession of the Book Concerns at New-York and Cincinnati, at the time of the settlement by the commissioners.

"11. That the Book Agents at New-York be directed to make such compensation to the Conferences South, for their dividend from the Chartered Fund, as the commissioners above provided for shall agree upon.

"12. That the Bishops be respectfully requested to lay that part of this report requiring the action of the Annual Conferences before them as soon as possible, beginning with the New-York Conference."

[The first resolution was adopted 135 yeas to 18 nays; the second, 139 to 17; the third, 147 to 12; the fifth, 153 to 13; and the others without a division.]

Bishop Morris Convenes Organizing Session of Oklahoma Indian Mission Conference

Source: Thomas A. Morris, "Indian Mission Conference," Western Christian Advocate (November 29, 1844), 131.

Brother [Charles] Elliott [editor],—

The Indian Mission conference commenced its first session at Riley's Chapel, near Tahlequah, in the Cherokee nation, on Wednesday, 23d of October, 1844. The name of the house [of worship] is intended, I learn, to perpetuate the precious memory of the first Cherokee converted to Christianity. It is a respectable frame building for a frontier country. There are in this conference 17 elders, all of whom were present but 1, 6 deacons, and 4 licentiates: total, 27 and all tried men in the Indian work. About one-fourth of them are native preachers. There are also several natives not yet admitted into the conference, who act as helpers and interpreters on the circuits. The conference, as a whole, will compare well with other conferences in point of ministerial qualification, in proportion to their numbers. This little band of missionaries live and labor together in the bonds of Christian affection. All their work is missionary; and, consequently, there is no scrambling for popular appointments, or city stations. After arranging the work for the ensuing year, we stationed the whole conference in less than two hours, and had no occasion afterward to change a single appointment, nor did any complain that his lot was hard. The religious exercises at the opening of each day's session were conducted in English, and at the close of the session, in Choctaw or Cherokee. We reached the point of final adjournment on Saturday afternoon, all the business having been fully considered and done up, except to ordain the preachers, which was done on the Sabbath. Two of those ordained were full-blooded Choctaws, and one of them, being a good English scholar, interpreted the questions to the other in the presence of the congregation.

As this was the commencement of a new state of things in the Indian missionary work, the conference thought it best to take decisive measures at once, being determined not to encourage or countenance any mere hangers on, or inefficient men, who might desire, under the name of traveling preachers, to be employed as teachers of neighborhood or government schools, not under the control of the conference. And though they gave a supernumerary relation to one brother in feeble health, it was without claim on the missionary funds. Any brethren who may wish to become identified with the Indian Mission conference must calculate to go in for the work, the whole work, and nothing but the work, or to be furnished with "walking papers" in short order. So it should be in every conference. And the fear expressed by some that the missionaries, when once the power was put into their own hands, would make a prodigal use of the missionary funds, is perfectly groundless. On the contrary, the mission committee of five leading men, whose report of estimates was cordially approved by the conference, and concurred in by myself, manifested a scrupulous regard to economy. The whole amount appropriated for all the conference this year, is $14,490[.]32. And this, let it be observed, is not only to support the twenty-seven missionaries and their families, (for most of them have families, and all of them should have,) but also their helpers, interpreters, teachers, to pay for necessary improvements, and feed, clothe, lodge and educate the children in the mission schools. Three of these schools alone required $7,000, nearly half of the whole amount. It is worthy of remark, that the appropriation for the Indian work, this year, is less than it usually was when connected with the other conferences. And yet much fear is entertained, that in the present excited state of the Church [i.e. plan of separation], the means [money] may not come into the hands of the Assistant Treasurer to take up the drafts, without difficulty. Still we hope better things, though we thus speak. The conference organized itself into a Conference Missionary Society, auxiliary to the Parent Society of the Methodist Episcopal Church, and reported $217 and some cents, obtained during the year, and at the first meeting. They will more than double this sum next year, I presume.

Now if any one doubts the propriety of expending so much money on the Indians, to effect their conversion from heathenism and sin to civilization and Christianity, let him visit the work, make observation for himself, and his doubts will be removed. If he cannot do this, we refer him to the official minutes of the Indian Mission conference, where he will see that, beside a few white and some hundreds of colored members, (for some of the Indians are extensive slaveholders, and are likely to become liberal supporters of the missionary cause,) we have nearly 3,000 Indian Church members. Moreover, we have very many of the children in a course of training in day schools and Sabbath schools. But while much has been done, much remains to be done. Thousands are yet heathen sinners and perishing for the bread of life. We owe them much, as an injured people. The land is before us. Great and effectual doors are open unto us; and there are many adversaries. Some of these doors may be shut, or entered by others, while we delay operations. The far-famed Nannawarrior fund has slipped out of our hands. By official action of the Choctaw council, it has been diverted to other channels not under our control. And from the best information we can obtain, this movement was intended by the leading men before they requested us to postpone our operation in the premises last spring. After all, it is questionable whether we shall have lost much in the end, as there is some prospect of other and more inviting fields of labor. In such an enterprise as that of converting the heathen, there will always be difficulties and discouragements, beyond what may be reasonably expected in our ordinary circuit work among our own countrymen; and these difficulties have been increased by the system of connecting the Indian missions with ordinary work in the conferences, which has led to frequent changes both of men and measures. We trust, however, the difficulties will be relieved in part by the organization of the Indian Mission conference, which will certainly afford those having the management of the missions more time and better means of information, in arranging and carrying out their plans of usefulness. Another thing greatly to the advantage of the work was ordered by the late [1844] General conference, namely, the appointment of a superintendent to reside in the Indian country, overlook all the missionary interests, and act as an agent for the Church to negotiate with Indian councils and the government of the United States, in regard to Indian education funds, &c., as occasion requires. As the bishops were charged with the responsibility of making such appointments, both for the slave missions in the south and Indian missions in the southwest, they met in New York the day after General Conference adjourned, and appointed Rev. William Capers to the former, and Rev. Jerome C. Berryman to the latter. Brother Berryman had long been identified with the Indian Missions, and was already a citizen of the Missouri territory, within the bounds of the mission conference, which gave him some advantage in his new office. He entered upon his work immediately, and before the conference met, had been to nearly every mission in its bounds. Those who know him best, think he is the right sort of a man for the work; and I trust he will make full proof of his ministry.

Upon the whole, Mr. Editor, I am much pleased with my visit to the Indian Mission conference. And it would be ungrateful in me not to acknowledge the kindness which I have constantly received. I was not only conveyed by the brethren to conference, as I have elsewhere explained, gratuitously, but was subsequently sent by the hospitable family, who had the trouble of entertaining me, in a fine, close carriage, with handsome match horses, driver and escort, nearly forty miles to this neighborhood, where I can obtain a stage to Van Buren, and thence to Little Rock. Such kindness I shall never forget, nor cease to acknowledge with gratitude.

Yours respectfully,

THO. A. MORRIS.

ROBERT MACLAY REPORTS PROGRESS
OF MISSION IN CHINA

Source: Robert S. Maclay, "Letter to Cor. Sec, Miss. Soc., M.E. Church,"
Missionary Advocate 6/6 (September 1850): 48. Excerpts.

Fuh-Chau, China, April 30, 1850

To the Cor. Sec. Miss. Soc. M.E.Church [John P. Durbin]:

Dear Brother:
With profound gratitude we recognize and acknowledge the protection and guidance of a covenant-keeping God. Deeply conscious, as from our circumstances we must be, how greatly we need, and how entirely we are dependent upon the Divine blessing, it is to us a source of indescribable consolation and encouragement to know that under its gracious influence, we go forward.

Temporal Benefits. Temporal mercies have been largely granted to us. We continue to enjoy quiet and comfortable homes. The people render us every service we desire. We have been favoured with good servants and capable teachers. Our tables have been bountifully supplied with the necessaries of life. We obtain readily whatever the market affords. In private we enjoy very pleasant intercourse with the native members of our respective families. In public we associate freely and safely with the people. Nothing has occurred during the period under review to interrupt this interchange of kind offices and good feeling. We are much gratified to discover the increasing respect and kindness of the people as they gradually come to understand our character and purpose. In many ways we observe with much pleasure the confidence reposed in us by those with whom we have intercourse. We have been untrammeled by government restrictions; we know nothing of those petty and vexatious annoyances to which foreigners have sometimes been subjected by the Chinese. . . .

Spiritual Privileges. We would not forget to notice those religious privileges which we here enjoy. The blessed Bible is ever with us. The closet affords us many seasons every day for precious communion with the Lord. We possess too a family altar, where the morning and evening sacrifice [prayer and praise] is offered. On

Wednesday afternoon of each week we meet all our missionary friends in social prayer. At the same hour, on the first Monday of each month, we hold our concert of prayer in behalf of missions. On Sabbath we hear a discourse preached by one of our brethren; and on the first Sabbath of each month we celebrate the sufferings and death of our Divine Redeemer [Lord's Supper].

Mode of Work. Our work continues to be in the main one of preparation. We have no election in this matter: if we hope ever to preach Christ in the dialect of this people we must prepare ourselves by patient, persevering study. Without this we cannot do the work of a missionary to the Chinese. It may be an irksome task, chafing to our spirits, and our burning zeal may cry out against it, but still it must be done. The sounds and variations of sounds in this dialect must be thoroughly studied by every missionary student. This will give much quietness and monotony to the first years of his life in the mission field, and his eager soul may pant for the stirring excitement of direct conflict with these powers of darkness, but stern necessity will prepare his back for the burden.

Schools. We have not, however, confined ourselves exclusively to [language] study. Just as ability was granted we have entered on our public duties. Our schools have been in operation for about two years. We have two under our control. They have done and still promise well. One school under the charge of Brother [Judson] Collins is located in Nantai, about midway on the great thoroughfare leading from the river to the south gate of the city. For the present this school has been transferred to Tong-chin, the island where several of the missionaries live. This change is only temporary, designed to continue only until other and more suitable accommodations can be procured in Nantai. We hope soon to effect this. The number of scholars has been about twenty-five and an a large proportion attend with great regularity. The other school has been under my care. The number of scholars is twenty-five, most, if not all of them, being the children of parents living in the immediate vicinity. This school has grown steadily from the beginning. Just as the prejudices of the parents yielded, the number of scholars increased. I know of no instance of dissatisfaction. Not one scholar has been removed by his parents. This is to us full of encouragement. We try to deal faithfully with them, urging them to seek God in the pardon of their sins, and reproving them for their faults. Their progress in the studies assigned them is very gratifying. We most earnestly commend these youth to the prayers of the Church.

Extending Influences. We take frequent opportunities for visiting the villages surrounding the city. During these excursions we distribute Christian books, and converse, so far as we can, with the people. We are thus extending our influence beyond this city. The books we distribute penetrate the dark places of the empire, from which as yet the missionary is excluded. We now have two rooms for conversation with the people. Brother Collins' room, however, is for the present given up. It was small and not well adapted to our purpose. We have consequently ceased to rent it, and hope in a short time to procure a better situation. A room has been procured near my residence and we now have frequent opportunities for public conversation with the people. This room is on the street and very well answers our purpose. Our exercises in it have been interesting. We are much encouraged by the respectful attention of our hearers. Our message is a strange thing to their ears, and our imperfect acquaintance with the dialect prevents us from explaining and enforcing it as we desire, but still they listen. We painfully feel our own weakness. Our work, with its responsibilities, presses heavily upon us. Do we err when cheering our hearts with the assurance that we, as missionaries, are remembered among the tents and altars of our Israel in America? We do thus bear up our faith. Friends of Jesus, we commend to your sympathies and prayers these precious yet perishing heathen. . . .

Yours in the fellowship and faithfulness of Christ,

R.S. Maclay

Roman Catholic convert Benigno Cardenas preaches sermon in Santa Fe

Source: Thirty-fifth Annual Report of the Missionary Society of the Methodist Episcopal Church *(New York, 1854)*, 86-89.

NEW-MEXICAN MISSION

Nearly four years ago, a mission was projected at Santa Fé, New-Mexico, and Rev. E. G. Nicholson and family were sent out to commence it. Brother Nicholson remained in Santa Fé and vicinity for some time, and a small Church was organized, chapel fitted up, and a small congregation collected, composed wholly of Americans residing in Santa Fé, or connected with the army. Shortly after this the head-quarters of the army were removed, and with it, of course, those hearers who are connected with the army. This curtailed the business of the city, and further reduced the American population, and very much lessened the number attending upon divine service in the mission. About the same time the health of Mrs. Nicholson failed. All these things taken together rendered the mission to the American population, speaking the English language, of less value than was expected; and Brother Nicholson returned home, chiefly on account of the health of his wife, and the mission was suspended.

In the course of the year after his return, the question of a mission to the Spanish population of New-Mexico was agitated. It seems scarcely right that our Church, or, indeed any of the Protestant Churches, should wholly neglect a large territory within the limits of our own country. While this question was being considered, two things transpired which hastened its solution in favour of sending a mission of exploration or observation to the Spanish population, as well as to the American, in New-Mexico. The results will determine whether the mission shall be permanently established or not.

1. There was a young brother connected with our Swedish mission in New-York, who could speak Spanish pretty well; well enough, it was thought, to enable him to preach, if but imperfectly at first, until he could become more perfect in it. Besides, he had for a long time desired to go to Mexico as a missionary.

2. During brother Nicholson's residence at Santa Fé, he had become acquainted

with an intelligent, well-educated Roman Catholic priest, of much influence in the country, and very eloquent withal. His name is Benigno Cardenas. He came to brother Nicholson, expressing dissatisfaction with the Roman Catholic Church, and with the bishop; but Brother Nicholson fearing that it might be a matter of personal quarrel, after considering the case, gave him no encouragement. Shortly thereafter Cardenas left New-Mexico for Rome, there to complain of the treatment he had received from the bishop. He obtained redress, and left Rome with all his papers in order under seals, (as we ourselves have seen,) and with due passports as a Roman Catholic priest, and arrived in London. His visit to Rome seems to have completely opened his eyes, and fixed his purpose to forsake their communion. He called on Rev. Mr. Rule in London, who had long been a resident Wesleyan missionary in Spain. Mr. Rule took Cardenas into his family, and for ten weeks carefully observed him and instructed him in evangelical views of religion. When Cardenas left London, Mr. Rule gave him letters of introduction and confidence to us at New-York. Upon his arrival we treated him kindly, and had much intercourse with him through interpreters. Our confidence grew slowly, but surely, and we put him in communication with the bishops, then reported to the Board. About this time brother Nicholson visited the East at the instance of Bishop Waugh; and at the New-York Conference in Kingston, in consultation with Bishop Janes and Simpson, and brother Nicholson and the Corresponding Secretary, Bishop Waugh determined, with the consent of the Board, to renew the New-Mexican Mission, and enlarge its aims so as to include the Spanish population, should the project, upon observation in the territory, be found practicable. The Board concurred, and the mission was organized by the appointment of Rev. E. G. Nicholson superintendent and Rev. W. Hansen assistant. At the same time, brother Nicholson was authorized to take along with him Benigno Cardenas, and to receive him into the Church in the mission in New-Mexico, and employ him in the mission as an assistant, under conditions plainly set forth to him and to Cardenas. The main conditions were: if Cardenas, after arriving in New-Mexico, should apply publicly to the mission for admission and service; and his spirit and conduct should be satisfactory to brother Nicholson, the superintendent.

Under these conditions and arrangements the mission departed for New-Mexico early in autumn, 1853, and arrived safely at Santa Fé in due time. An opportunity offering for brother Hansen to open a school in a populous district, in which he might visit the towns, and preach, and thus perfect himself in the Spanish language, it was judged best that he should do so. Brother Nicholson and Brother Cardenas proceeded to Santa Fé. The Roman Catholic bishop has heard that Cardenas had renounced his Church, as was expected in New-Mexico, and intended to speak to the people; and he denounced him in advance, privately, publicly, and from the altar in the church. The public mind was much excited, and awaited with much anxiety the arrival of the Cardenas, to see what he would do. Indeed, it was predicted that he would be assassinated on his way from Tucolate to Santa Fé. But this was a mistake; no one disturbed him. Brother Nicholson reports him to be of a gentle and devout spirit, and passionately attached to New-Mexico, and declares that she [New Mexico] is blighted by the influence of the priesthood, while the United States have been made what they are by Protestantism. They reached Santa Fé November 10, and after resting a week to recruit, brother Nicholson says, under date of *Santa Fé*, Nov. 19:—

> Cardenas is to preach his first public discourse, as a Protestant, to-morrow, on the public square, under the portals of the palace. The friends of the bishop are quite excited about it. They have torn down my printed notices of the meeting, and some persons think we will be pelted with stones if we attempt to hold service on the plaza. But the die is cast: no building can be obtained; the plaza is public ground; the governor does not object to us standing so near his palace; and as the Constitution of the United States and God's word grant us freedom of speech, we intend to utter our sentiments and offer up our prayers on the plaza to-morrow, though priests rage and stones fly thick as hail about us.
>
> The bishop denounced Cardenas from the altar last Sabbath. He told the people they must not hear him or look at him, as he was an apostate, and his very looks might contaminate them. He said he did not object to their hearing the other gentlemen, as they had been brought up Protestants. (He knew neither of us could use the tongue of the people as Cardenas can.) But he required them, under penalty of excommunication, not to hear Cardenas, and to refuse him admission to their houses.
>
> *Nov.* 20—This has been a day of much interest to the few Protestants in this city. We had fixed on the hour of eleven o'clock for our service in the plaza, intending to begin as soon as the service at the bishop's chapel should be over; but the bishop protracted his service, and, at the close, denounced Cardenas again, appealed to their superstitious feelings, and warned them not to hear him, not even look at him, but to stop their cars, avert their faces, and go immediately to their homes. Then the bells were made to keep up a clatter till long after the bishop, priests, and nuns had crossed the plaza and entered their house. But it would not go. These attempts to interrupt our service, and prevent a freeman from being heard by a few people, excited indignation. The people who had listened to the bishop lingered about the chapel a long time; many went to their homes without looking toward Cardenas; some came under the portal of the palace; others came forward and filled the seats; others squatted on the ground, and a great many gathered in groups about the plaza, within hearing of the preacher. Cardenas spoke with force and clearness. He had the unbroken attention of the people, and uttered his reasons for renouncing the dogmas and legends of Rome and embracing the faith and worship of Protestants in a most noble and touching manner.
>
> The subject of his discourse was REPENTANCE as connected with the justification of man. It was apostolic and catholic in its sentiments, well suited to the occasion, and its illustration was marked by a simplicity and propriety that

made it captivating and singularly interesting to all present. At the close of the service Cardenas announced me to the people as the reverend superintendent of the Methodist mission in New-Mexico; and, after unfolding and explaining his parchments and letters of ordination and character, as a presbyter or priest in the Church of Rome, and missionary apostolical to New-Mexico, he placed them one by one in my hands, expressing, as he did so, a desire to be connected with our mission, and to be authorized to officiate as a minister among us. I have his papers in my possession, and, should nothing occur to change the good opinion I have formed of him, I will employ him in this field, and issue a certificate of his position among us.

His conduct in public and private since we have been together has been blameless, and such as becomes a servant of God. We pray, alternately, twice a day, in all the families where we stay; and we never omit to ask God's blessing at table, and to return thanks for our food. We rise early and spend some time in reading the Spanish version of the Vulgate. Then we visit families who are willing to be visited by us. Wherever we go his theme is religion—the religion of Jesus—the only true catholic religion as found in the gospel of Christ.

Monday, Nov. 20, brother Nicholson administered the sacrament of baptism, in the Senate Chamber, to the children of Mr. and Mrs. Spencer. The sponsors were Spaniards, reputable and influential members of the Roman Catholic Church. They told brother Nicholson the next day, that the bishop had required them to make satisfaction to the Church within fifteen days, or he would excommunicate them. Brother Nicholson does not think that they will submit.

Cherokee Preacher Walter Duncan Reports on his Ministry in the Cherokee Nation

Source: Ninth Annual Report of the Missionary Society of the Methodist Episcopal Church, South (*Louisville, Ky.: Morton & Griswold, 1854*), 102-4.

Cherokee Nation, Dec. 14th, 1853

E[dmund] W. Sehon, D. D.
[General Secretary, Missionary Society of the MECS, Louisville, Kentucky]

Dear Dr. Sehon: . . .

The work on my Mission is not in as good a condition as I would like to see it, still we are advancing a little. Indeed, when I contemplate what little good I seem to do, compared with what others might do, I would willingly resign my post to one more competent; not that I desire to quit the field, but that the greatest blessing might accrue to the people. The people seem to receive the word.

The first quarterly meeting for Salisaw Mission the present year was held last Saturday and Sabbath at Canaan Camp Ground. This is a place that in a few years has grown up into a flourishing society, who have erected suitable buildings for worship. They have a good log church and have a prosperous school supported at the public expense. Our laborious and beloved Presiding Elder, Rev. D[avid] B. Cumming, was present. He stood, as he has always stood, in the front of the battle. May the Lord still spare and support him. We had quite an interesting meeting. Two [native converts] were admitted on trial. It seemed that the Holy Spirit had taken deep hold upon them.

Our efforts in the line of Sunday schools and Bible classes are greatly embarrassed for the want of books and suitable teachers. There are on my Mission hundreds of children that might be worked into Sunday schools if we had the proper books translated into Cherokee. We have not a line, save a very few copies of a very small part of our Discipline, translated. The American [i.e., Congregational and Presbyterian] and Baptist [mission] boards have translated parts of the Holy Scriptures, together with a few other sketches. And, as for myself, I have always thought that we ought to have at least our Discipline and the Wesleyan Catechisms

Nos 1 and 2 translated. Why may not this be done? What an amount of Scriptural instruction might be gained by the Cherokees from this Catechism? These translations would not only enable us to success in our Sunday schools but would be the means of greatly assisting our Cherokee preachers in the acquisition of a knowledge of the Scriptures.

The Cherokees have a passion for information which seems natural with them. If you meet one on the way he will ask you where you are going, what after, and when you will return, &c.; and if you could speak in the Cherokee, they would set a whole day without getting the least wearied and hear you tell of travels, scenes and incidents, or explain the principles of science. Then, if we could only get the Wesley Catechism printed in the Cherokee, if it even were impossible to have any more done, I should feel that we had a sword unsheathed before the sweep of which the gordian knot of ignorance and superstition would yield like threads before the wind.

I was so situated I could not attend the Anniversary of our Conference Missionary Society as I much desired. Our excellent brother Harrell was kind enough to act as Secretary of the meeting and will furnish you with the annual report.

Yours truly,

W[alter] A[dair] Duncan
Elysian Fountain, Cherokee Nation

James Strong favors a central theological seminary

Source: James Strong, "A Central Theological Seminary for Our Church," Christian Advocate *(New York) (22 December 1853), 201. Excerpts.*

I have been a long time waiting for some one among our leading men to broach this subject in our public papers, but as no one seems inclined to do more than hint at it, I have resolved to venture my views upon it, and leave them to the consideration of the Methodist community. . . .

1. *The necessity of such an institution.* I do not purpose here to enter into any abstract discussion of the propriety of such schools in themselves, or their compatibility with former views and customs, whether in our own Church or in apostolic times. It is sufficient for my present purpose that they do not appear to be repugnant to any clear doctrine of Scripture, nor necessarily heretical in their influence. The fact that the apostles were favoured with direct and plenary inspiration in their ministry, is no reason why modern teachers of Christianity should neglect to avail themselves of every aid likely to qualify them more effectually for their work. It is admitted on all hands, in our Church at least, that preachers must study in order to this; and the question simply is, How, and where, and when can they do so to the best advantage? Methodism has always been distinguished for its eminently *practical* policy, and to this it owes its hitherto unrivalled success. It is only by pursuing the same line, adapting itself to the varying exigencies of the times, that it can retain its hold upon the popular mind, and continue to be useful. It first derived its name from its *method* in this adaptation, and we hope the day will never be suffered to come when it will cease to have a method of meeting fully the demands of the age, and circumstances in which it may be found.

The demand for superior theological training in our Church shows itself in a two-fold form, arising from the upward tendency of Methodism, like any other successful and progressive principle, from the lower to the higher stratum of society. As our congregations increase in number and wealth, they naturally increase likewise in intelligence, either by a gradual improvement in the mental culture of the mass, or by the introduction among them of persons of more than ordinary learning and refinement. These congregations cannot now be satisfied with the quality of preaching, in a literary point of view, with which they once were; the preacher must keep pace with his people in this respect, or, rather, in advance of them. Even congregations of very moderate capacity in this respect have listened to good preaching, and have learned to appreciate it; so that they too are no longer content with the literary standard which once sufficed. We may exclaim against this tendency as being due to "itching ears," and lecture the people about "plain practical sermons" as long as we please: there the fact stands, and all we can say in this way will not mend it. The people are hungry for a higher style of sermonizing, and they will have it, or leave our communion. Under the strong excitements of a revival they may remain attached to the public services of the sanctuary, and the young converts especially cling around the pastor to whom they owe their spiritual enlightenment; but when things return to their wonted level, and when that preacher is succeed by a stranger, these associations no longer bind the members to the Church, and multitudes decline in their attendance and religious feelings, and presently withdraw to other Churches, where they are favoured with preaching more congenial to their minds. New residents coming into a place find an indifferent man occupying the pulpit, and they join some other Church, where a superior preacher officiates. We thus yearly lose large numbers of those whose intelligent influence we need the most. We train up children in the bosom of the Church, who leave us at the very time they are prepared for usefulness. They are the sons and daughters of Methodist parents, the members of our Sunday schools, nay, the very probationers among our converts, that go to swell the ranks of other denominations. I think it is no exaggeration to estimate that *one-half* of all those who are brought to Christ through the instrumentality of Methodism, in this way finally go over to other denominations, or back again into the world. Of these I am firmly persuaded the larger proportion leave us from disaffection, growing out, in one way or another, of the very lack of theological qualifications in our ministers of which I am speaking. And they are often the flower of the flock; they are usually such as, if retained, would become the best and most useful members of our society. *We cannot afford to lose them. . . .*

Finally,—and this point must be conclusive of the argument, whatever be thought of the foregoing,—a few of these college graduates, seeing that their preparation for the work of the ministry is still incomplete, wisely determine to finish it before entering fully upon their work. They look around for a theological seminary in which to perfect their education, so far as books and scholastic discipline can do it. But they find none in our own Church adequate to their wants, or even up to the literary standard that they have already attained. We have no institution corresponding to those of other denominations for this purpose. Hence they are compelled to enter these latter institutions, or wholly forego the further culture that they seek. This they actually do, and in very considerable numbers. Six members out of a single class that graduated at the Wesleyan University, within my knowledge, entered theological seminaries belonging to other denominations, for the purpose of completing their studies preparatory to the Methodist ministry. Almost every graduating class has more or less instances of the same kind. Similar facts occur at Dickinson College, and doubtless at all our Methodist colleges. Such cases are numerous enough every year to form a respectable class for a theological seminary, if we had one of the proper grade to receive them. We may argue as we will about the necessity or propriety of this course on the part of these young men, but all our arguments will not lessen the fact. Nor ought we to excuse the Church from the duty of providing for them, from any views or notions of our own on the subject; they are surely the best judges of the preparation requisite in their own case, and it would be the height of folly to dictate to them in this matter. Many a fine young man has been dwarfed for life by the misjudged officiousness of older advisers among us in similar cases. We have shown why our young preachers need such additional preparation, and it is proof of good sense in them to seek it. We may point them to Concord or elsewhere within our own denomination to attain it; but they feel even these institutions to be inadequate: they will have to compete with ministers in other denominations, who have been trained in thorough theological seminaries, and nothing short of a similar training will suffice for themselves. The plain practical question, therefore, is, Shall we compel them to seek this training in seminaries established and controlled by other Churches, or will we furnish it ourselves? This is the real issue, and we must meet it.

The effect upon young men of inquiring minds, subjected daily to the influence of choice intellects and profound learning occupying the preceptor's chair, and insidiously instilling the dogmas and spirit of another denomination, can readily be imagined. They soon cease to be Methodists, and are lost to our Church. Probably not one-half of those who pass through these seminaries ever occupy Methodist pulpits afterward. Those who are firm in their denominational views, find these institutions so uncongenial to their tenets, and are so constantly brought into collision with the views around them, and advanced by their teachers, that they are disgusted with their position, and leave the institution in despair of obtaining the preparation they need. Indeed, this is their only mode of self-protection. Now shall we leave these pious, sincere youths to this perilous alternative? After we have spent so much on their education up to this point, shall we at last throw them into the hands of other denominations? *Least of all, can we afford to lose these?* And yet this is done every year. I could, at this moment, mention not a few young men who have been lost to our Church in this very way. It has pierced my heart with grief as I have heard them describe their difficulties, as I have been compelled to acquiesce in their selection of such institutions, and as I have at last vainly argued against their decision, which was the result of such a selection, and seen them leave our communion forever. Was it thus that the broad-souled Wesley cared for the education of his people—his children? Our Church has unnaturally refused to provide literary food for her most promising sons, and then upbraids them because they cling to the foster-mother that took them up. It is not enough that we have colleges, as a denomination; we must also have theological seminaries, and that for the same reason. Indeed, it is even more important, for it immediately affects our religious interests and prospects.

I know it will be said that the course of study required of preachers after joining the conference is intended and sufficient to supply the special theological preparation needed. This is no doubt to a great extent the object of this prescription; but any one who has the slightest opportunity of observing how hastily these studies are gone through by the candidate, and how superficially he is generally examined upon them, will at once perceive how indifferently this method meets the requirements of the case. Very few who enter upon them are prepared, by previous study, for a thorough theological routine; and those who are, find the prescribed course altogether too popular and circumscribed for their advanced position. It is idle to propose the meager outline appended to the Discipline as an adequate course of theology for the present day. But even this the young preacher does not find time to master fully. Preparation for the pulpit (if he is conscientious and improving in this respect) and pastoral labour, to say nothing of the thousand and one extra calls and enterprises which he is expected personally to attend to, leave him neither leisure nor strength to keep up any regular system of study, or even of reading. The result is, that he makes but little literary progress, and continues a theological dwarf all his career; and this for the want of having a sufficient start to enable him to keep in advance of his pulpit and other theological draughts, and from the absence of a fund of this kind of thought and information previously accumulated. One in a thousand may, by dint of uncommon talent and diligence, acquire a tolerable acquaintance with the original languages in which the Scriptures were written; but the mass are unable even to undertake the task. It is a notorious and inevitable fact, that the vast majority of our preachers have no more—and many of them have less—proper theological knowledge and discipline at fifty than they had at thirty years of age; they are compelled to repreach the same stale, stereotyped common-place from station to station, till they themselves lose all interest in their sermons, and their ministrations leave their hearers to snore over the insipid exercises of the Sabbath. Can we wonder, then, that our young graduates seek a more complete equipment before they engage in the actual and incessant duties of the ministry? Can we blame them for so doing? Is it not rather our duty to encourage and enable them to do so, instead of thrusting them out, half-armed and half-trained, into the conflict?

In every point of view, therefore, whether as respects the preachers or the people, we must conclude that theological seminaries are the great desideratum among us; they are essential to our growth and permanence as a denomination; they are downright necessary in simple self-preservation. Indeed, it is doubtful whether any want among us be more pressing just now than this. Nor are these views of this want at all novel in our community; they have already begun to be acted upon in various quarters. A Biblical or theological department has been organized, or is about to be organized, in nearly all our colleges, both on the Atlantic shore and in the West, and measures are in contemplation to secure, as far as such a means can do it, the advantages of this additional training to our youth. But these means, we claim, are inadequate to meet the want. It is not merely a *department*, added as a supplement to the regular college course, under a single professor, and crowded into the time allotted to the proper academic studies, that is demanded. We need a separate and full course of theological instruction, with a competent faculty, and organized on a scale corresponding with those of other denominations. Nothing short of this will either satisfy students or fulfil the ends aimed at. Such departments added to our present colleges may be useful, as far as they go, and I would not by any means discourage them; but, at the same time, we must have a seminary proper for those who, after having gone through college, still feel the need of further and more direct preparation for the pulpit. We have also a Biblical Institute at Concord, and the brethren and friends concerned in establishing and maintaining that pioneer institution in our Church deserve great praise for their liberal views and self-denying exertions. I heartily bid them God speed. I would not throw a straw in the way of their success. At the same time they will not take it ill of me, when I say that there is room and demand for another institution, in view of the following particulars, which I suggest as needful to be combined in order to its full utility.

2. *Scope, location, &c., of the proposed institution.* It will be seen, from the foregoing remarks, that such a seminary as will answer the purpose designed must not stop short of the standard adopted by other denominations. It must be prepared to take students who have regularly graduated at college, and carry them forward through a full course of Biblical and theological study. I would exclude all who do not design to go through such a course, or who are not prepared to enter upon it. It will not do to spend time there, to any great degree, in laying the foundation, which ought to have been acquired elsewhere, of preliminary classical or scientific study. A thorough academic preparation must be insisted on as a condition of admission. All who enter, of course, would have the ministry more or less distinctly in view; but I would not require the students to be absolutely exhorters or preachers, or to be recommended as such by a quarterly conference. Many young men would be desirous of availing themselves of the advantages of such an institution, whose views and purposes might not be mature on this point; they may have a call to preach, but wish to satisfy themselves more fully on this point before they positively commit themselves to the work. This I know is the situation of many at the time of their graduation in college; and to force them to a final determination at this time might be fatal to their impressions and prospects in that direction. They ought to come with a certificate of a good religious character, and there is no objection to their being recommended by a suitable ecclesiastical authority; but, beyond this, each student ought to be unfettered. At the same time every facility ought to be given to those who already hold or wish a license, and opportunities, as well as encouragements, ought to be afforded them to preach regularly or occasionally, so that they may become familiar, practically as well as theoretically, with the duties of the pulpit.

Such an institution ought to be located in the vicinity of New-York, our great commercial metropolis. The literary and other operations of our Church are concentrating more and more around this city, and any other location would necessarily have too much local character to promise success. There would be some advantages in a connexion with one of our colleges, but this would also produce rivalry, and be more than counterbalanced by a loss of interest in our community as a whole. No other position, I am persuaded, can secure the general sympathy of our Church. It is not necessary, however, that it should be located within the immediate precincts of the city itself; indeed, this would be objectionable to many, on the score of economy, health and morality. The benefits of proximity to the city might be secured, and its disadvantages avoided, by selecting some place removed a few miles, but easily accessible. If the villages in the environs may be brought into competition for this honour, I would propose Flushing as being as suitable a candidate as any that could be selected. But the immediate locality is comparatively unimportant, provided it be in itself not unsuitable, and adjoin the city. This latter point, the vicinity to New-York, I regard as essential to the success of the project. We cannot dispense with the aid and influence of the Methodists of this region, and these, I apprehend, cannot be effectually secured on any other terms.

The institution will of course be denominational in its character, but it ought not on that account to be bigoted. I do not see that it need have a sectarian front and title, or any other guarantee for its Methodism than the patronage of our Church. These and other minor details, however, can better be discussed when the enterprise comes to be taken in hand.

3. *The feasibility of the project.* For one, I do not entertain a doubt that it will eventually be realized, and at no very distant day; but I also firmly believe that it can be accomplished at once, if the leading members of our Church will but lend their united co-operation to it. Ten or fifteen thousand dollars would purchase a sufficient quantity of land, and erect buildings upon it that would answer present purposes. I think it would not be difficult to find so many wealthy members of our Church, even in this section along, who would be willing to do themselves the credit of giving a thousand dollars each for this noble object; this would be better, as well as easier, than to raise the necessary sum by driblets. When the enterprise should be under successful operation, others would readily contribute for its support, enlargement, and endowment. For the present the expenses would have to be kept low, and these the bills of the students would probably meet. Tuition ought to be fixed at a merely nominal sum. Three or four professors would be sufficient to impart it, but they must be well qualified and industrious. There is no lack of such men now in our Church, and some of them would be willing to engage in the work and trust to Providence for their reward. I have myself heard two preachers of distinguished position and literary qualification, (D. D.'s both of them,) volunteer their services, gratis, till the institution should be established; and I know of another, a layman, who would be willing to give his aid in the Biblical department on the same terms. The *salaries*, therefore, could easily be provided for at the outset. The state might perhaps afford some pecuniary aid at the time of conferring a charter; or some individual may yet feel his heart prompted to make a liberal donation or bequest in its behalf. At any rate, the plan above sketched seems practicable for the commencement, and I cannot believe that our Church would suffer it to languish or fail, when once undertaken and in operation. Is it not at least worth the effort the attempt the enterprise on this basis, or some other equally simple?

My sincere anxiety to see something of the kind done, has led to these suggestions, and I hope others will take up the matter, with voice, and pen, and act, until the attention of the Church is fully aroused to its necessity, and engage in its accomplishment.

In concluding, I would therefore suggest the propriety of a general meeting of the friends of the enterprise in our Church, both preachers and laymen, at the Book Concern in Mulberry-street, at an early day, to discuss the subject and take measures for its realization.

Flushing, Dec. 12, 1853.

JAMES STRONG.

WILLIAM SMITH OFFERS BIBLICAL, HISTORICAL, AND THEOLOGICAL RATIONALE FOR SLAVERY

Source: William Smith, D.D., Lectures on the Philosophy and Practice of Slavery, as Exhibited in the Institution of Domestic Slavery in the United States: With the Duties of Masters to Slaves *(Nashville: Stevenson and Evans, 1856), 11-13, 208-9, 276-78. Excerpts.*

The great question which arises in discussing the slavery of the African population of this country—correctly known as "Domestic Slavery"—is this: *Is the institution of domestic slavery sinful?*

The position I propose to maintain in these lectures is, that slavery, *per se*, is right; or that the great abstract principle of slavery is right, because it is a fundamental principle of the social state; and that domestic slavery, as an *institution*, is fully justified by the condition and circumstances (essential and relative) of the African race in this country, and therefore equally right.

I confess that it is somewhat humiliating to discuss the question enunciated—Is the institution of domestic slavery sinful? The affirmative assumes that an immense community of Southern people, of undoubted piety, are, nevertheless, involved in great moral delinquency on the subject of slavery. This is a palpable absurdity in regard to a great many. For nothing is more certain than this, that if it be sinful, they either know it, or are competent to know it, and hence are responsible. And as no plea of necessity can justify an enlightened man in committing known sin, it follows that all such Southern people are highly culpable, which is utterly inconsistent with the same admission that they are pious. To say, as some are accustomed to do, that "slavery is certainly wrong in the *abstract*," that is, in plain terms, in itself sinful, but that they cannot help themselves, appears to me wholly unfounded. It assumes that a man may be absolutely compelled to commit sin. This certainly cannot be true. All candid minds will readily allow, that so far as Deity has yet explained himself, he has in no instance enjoined upon man the observance of any principle as his duty, which he may be compelled, in the order of his providence, to violate. It is equally false in fact, for it is not true that we are absolutely compelled to be slaveholders. If government be, as it undoubtedly is, the agent of the people, and the people choose, they are certainly competent by this agent to free themselves from this institution. True, the immense cost of such an enterprise would be the least in the catalogue of evils resulting from it; for the total ruin of the African race in this country may be put down among the rest. But what of all this? Nothing can justify an enlightened and civilized people in committing sin. No; not even the sacrifice of life itself. Withal, if the civil society refuse to make so costly a sacrifice to avoid sin, there is nothing that can compel any individual citizen to remain a slaveholder. He can live in the community, as some do, without even hiring or owning a slave; or he can remove to one of the so-called free States. We should give no countenance, therefore, to any such mere attempts to *apologize* for domestic slavery. The conduct of bad men may sometimes find apologists. The conduct of good men always admits *of defence.* . . .

On the general question, Is the system of domestic government existing among us, and involving the abstract principle of slavery, justified by the circumstances of the case, and therefore right? we reach an affirmative conclusion, for the reasons:

I. That the Africans are a distinct race of people, who cannot amalgamate to any material extent with the whites, and who, therefore, must continue to exist as a separate class.

II. That they are, as a class, decidedly inferior to the whites in point of intellect and moral development, so much as to be incompetent to self-government. Although they have shared largely in the progress of civilization, they have not reached this point. The proof is:

1. Such is the almost universal opinion of the most intelligent and pious communities throughout the whole Southern country, who certainly are well acquainted with their character and capabilities, and therefore fully competent to judge in their case.

2. The experiments at domestic colonization which have been made in this country prove it.

3. The experiments in the case of the free colored population spread through the country are equally in proof.

4. The colonization experiment on the coast of Africa is still more conclusive.

III. That domestic slavery is the appropriate form of government for a people in such circumstances, is fully exemplified by the Divine procedure in the case of the heathen subdued by the ancient Israelites.

We infer:

1. That they have no right to social equality or to political sovereignty—that to accord them either, in their present moral condition, would be a curse instead of a blessing. It would in all probability lead to the extermination of the race, and inflict a deep injury both upon the moral and physical condition of the whole country.

2. That every consideration of humanity and prudence requires that, until a better form of subordinate government shall be devised, they must be continued under the system of domestic slavery now in operation. . . .

It has been shown in previous lectures that the principle of slavery accords fully with the doctrine of abstract rights, civil and social; and that a system of domestic slavery in the United States is demanded by the circumstances of the African population in the country. But it by no means follows that the conduct of all masters, in the exercise of their functions as masters, is proper, any more than that the conduct of all parents, or the owners of apprentices, is such as it should be. The opinion is entertained that the domestic government of children does not more than approximate propriety as a general thing; and that the government of apprentices and of African slaves falls far short of what is proper. In this lecture it is proposed to deal with the relations of masters to slaves, that is, the duties they owe them. The doctrine that the system of domestic slavery assumes that the slave is a "mere machine—a chattel," has been fully exploded. The Bible particularly regards the slave an accountable being. It requires him to yield a willing obedience to his master, and teaches him that such service is accepted of the Lord as service done unto himself, Ephesians vi. 5-8; and in the 9th verse, the master is required to "do the same things unto them, forbearing threatening: knowing that your Master also is in heaven." And again, (Colossians iv. 1,) "Masters, give unto your servants that which is just and equal." Hence, in the strictest sense, religion holds the scales of justice between masters and slaves. Each one is held to a strict accountability for the faithful performance of his duty, the one to the other—"for there is no respect of persons with God."

It behooves us, then, who are masters, or who expect to become masters, to inquire into the duties of this relation. The master who does not inform himself on this subject, and endeavor conscientiously to do his duty, is strangely wanting in importance elements of Christian character, and, indeed, even in some of those attributes which enter materially into the character of a good citizen.

A most fanatical spirit is abroad in the land on the subject of domestic slavery. The inhumanity of masters at the South is greatly exaggerated. (Instances in which the institution of slavery is abused no doubt contribute to this excitement.) Even those who are deficient in the duties they owe their domestics and apprentices— quite as much so as is common at the South with the masters of African slaves— lend a willing ear to political denunciations of the South. Want of sympathy for hired servants, and instances in which they are overreached and oppressed beyond the means of legal redress, are as common in certain quarters as are the cases of inhumanity to the slaves at the South. But this does not help the matter. Evils of this kind are to be deplored whether they occur at the North or the South. The injunction of the apostle reaches every case of the kind—"Masters, give unto your servants that which is just and equal: knowing that ye also have a Master in heaven."

ALICE COBB DELIVERS STUDENT ADDRESS AT WESLEYAN FEMALE COLLEGE COMMENCEMENT

Source: Mary Culler White, The Life-Story of Alice Culler Cobb *(New York: Fleming H. Revell, 1925), 41-43.*

Gentlemen of the Board of Trustees

It is no doubt a pleasure and gratification to you, as well as a duty, to preside over the interests of our noble college.

It was through your influence that this college was organized: —the first, not only in Georgia and in the United States but in the world, where a regular college course was imparted to females. Through your influence, directly or indirectly, *woman* has been gradually brought to a knowledge of the revealed truths of science, and elevated to the high position which she now occupies in society.

Georgia has taken the lead in female education. You, her high-born sons, conceived the practicability of extending the benefits and privileges of collegiate training and culture to the female as well as to the male. When first the plan proposing such a benefit to our sex was made known to the public, it was ridiculed upon the one hand as a mere Utopian fancy; while upon the other it was roundly repudiated upon the baseless assumption that its tendencies would prove injurious. Notwithstanding, however, the strength and the prevalency of the opposition to this new theory of Female Education, and well nigh fatal apathy and penuriousness of its friends, it survived—and survived to die never.

Doubtless the present mode of imparting instruction will be subject to some changes and modifications, but the ground gained will never be given up while man has a head to think, a heart to feel, and a hand to execute.

It received its first experimental and practical development in the institution now well and extensively known as the Wesleyan Female College. Only twenty years have been thrown into the past since the strange intelligence was heralded through the country that a veritable Female College, chartered by the State legislature [of Georgia], had really gone into operation. But it had scarcely gone into operation before its practical working was admired, and its utility acknowledged. With it the spell was broken.

Since then what an astonishingly rapid change has taken place in the public mind! The errors, prejudices, and ignorance which had so long seemed to present an invincible barrier to a proper appreciation of women's education wants were attacked and dissipated; and if they still have an existence, they are only as the fragmentary mists of the morning—hovering over a land gilded by the increasing brilliance of an ascendant sun!

Beloved Companions

Allow me to congratulate you upon your enviable position and your exalted privileges. It was formerly regarded by the masses as a matter desirable, though not really necessary, that the male be subjected to a rigid intellectual training, in order that he might be fitted and qualified for the arduous duties and responsibilities of life; while the hapless female was supposed to be well freighted for times hazardous voyage if she possess a knowledge of the lower branches of an English education, could "finger well" upon a stringed instrument, "construct a flower," paint and sketch. But, thank Heaven! that time with many of its mischievous errors and pernicious prejudices has passed away! And a brighter day is dawning. Its morning light has already spread upon the mountain. The assumption that there is a radical difference in the mental endowment of the sexes has been refuted, and woman is no longer denied her right and title to the thorough cultivation and development of her intellectual faculties.

Let me point you onward, then, to the completion of your education; not that you are to attempt a thorough exploration of all the fields of literature, science and art. To attempt that would be vain; to accomplish it, impossible. Life is too short, ability too meager, but the mind, the whole mind, should be educated. Of what use could half an arch be, or three-quarters, or nine-tenths? Could it support anything? The taste, the imagination, the fancy, the memory, the judgment, the reasoning powers—these, and still more than these, combine in the constitution of the human mind. If they are all brought out in bold, strong and beautiful harmony and proportion, they shall form an intellectual arch whose key-stone shall be piety and whose culminating point shall be Heaven. Possessed of minds thus developed, mingling the resplendent rays of piety with the charms of genius and the blazing lights of science, you will inevitably be useful in society, and a blessing to the world.

Respected Auditory

This is and *ought* to be a glad day to the citizens of Macon and surrounding country. This is *ought* to be a joyous assemblage. And why not joyous? Within these halls dedicated to science, literature, and religion; fatherly dignity, matronly tenderness, maiden modesty and beauty, youthful pride and manhood, childhood's innocence and loveliness, all mingle and blend in sweet concord of sentiment and feeling.

All bespeak either in word or in approving smile, approbation of the manner in which this institution has been conducted and gratitude to God for the very encouraging success that has marked its history. As Georgians, in viewing this broad commonwealth—its inexhaustible agricultural and mineral resources; the facilities which it affords its inhabitants for the procurement of life's comforts and luxuries; its bright skies, grand, beautiful and richly varied scenery; salubrious climate; and health-giving waters—our hearts dilate with gratitude to God for having cast our lot in such a goodly heritage. The increase of our population in number, wealth, and influence in the galaxy of states forming this great Confederacy, is matter of gratulation in popular assemblies, and furnishes the staple of many a public harangue. When the statesman, the stump orator, or the political demagogue would flatter the vanity, foster the pride, and cater to the tastes of our money-loving, money-getting, money-keeping people, he dwells with velvet lip and dulcet tongue upon magnificent internal improvements that have been projected and carried into effect by our industrious enterprising and preserving citizens.

Mind is excited, imagination fired, and fancy winged, when he speaks of our extensive and extending railways, valuable stocks, reliable banking companies, increasing exports, flourishing commerce, growing and fast multiplying towns and cities, wealthy mines, and richly waving harvests. And truly the abundant bequests of nature and of providence for us as the constituency of a free state, and the industry, progress and achievements of the generation past, and of those now occupying the stage, appear worthy of the poet's lyre and of the orator's tongue. We would not paralyze the one or strike dumb the other; but we would and do claim moral and intellectual progress and achievements as furnishing the theme for the poet's highest rhapsody, and orator's warmest, boldest, sublimest flight.

What are sunny skies, purling fountains, enchanting and richly varied scenery, agricultural and mineral resources, vast and increasing wealth, extensive railroads and flourishing towns and cities, in comparison with cultivated minds and correct morals? The one is as far superior to the other as the substance is to the shadow, as the mind is to matter, as the Creator is to the creature.

The genial sky, the streamlet with music in its flow, the ever changing landscape spread out in all the gorgeousness and delicacy of nature's own painting, the fertility of soil and treasures of the mine are only appreciated and rendered subservient to the temporal happiness, and eternal well-being of man by the conquest of the mind over matter, actuated and controlled by correct moral views and principles. The commencement of all the great enterprises of the state, which are looked upon as our boast and our glory, are traceable to that period in our history at which the public mind was awakened to a sense of the importance of building up seminaries of learning at home—in the South; and educating well and wisely the sons and daughters of our land in the midst of circumstances and influences calculated to foster a love of our peculiar social and civil institutions.

I have said that this is and *ought* to be a glad day to the citizens of Macon. I repeat it: the institution which we now represent is one of the noblest monuments of your benevolence, your intelligence, and your enterprise. Rally to it. Patronize it. Support it. The cradle of its infancy was rocked by prejudices and opposition, and had it been born to die, its funeral obsequies would long since have been performed, and its epitaph would have been oblivion.

Wesleyan has survived all its embarrassments, and now unencumbered it leans upon your arm, and moves forward under your fostering care. Contribute to it money and prayers; increase its facilities; enlarge its influence and elevate its character; give to its teachers an opportunity of shaping for your daughters a brilliant career and a high destiny; and then shall the institution ever be what it is now—an honor to the state, and a fruitful source of blessing to the people.

Visitor details country Sunday school

Source: An Hour and a Half in a Country Sunday School, Being a
Picture of the Practical Working of a Successful Country
Sunday School (*New York: Published by Carlton & Porter for the
Sunday-school Union of the Methodist Episcopal Church, 1858), 32-188. Excerpts.*

CHAPTER III. THE SCHOOL-ROOM

How the Room Appeared Inside

We entered the Sunday-school room by the door on the side of the meeting-house, and found it nearly filled with happy-looking children.

As we were quite early enough, I had time to observe how everything was arranged. The room wore a very cheerful aspect. The sunlight came so soft through the tinted glass, and made such bright shadows on the wall from the crimson flowers on the corners of the panes; the [plaster] wreath on the ceiling seemed ready to drop down on the head of the best scholar; the seats were so substantial in form and appearance; the row of doors, with "Library," "Infant Class," "Bible Class" painted over them, were so suggestive of convenience and thoughtful care; the little clock ticking musically over the infant-class door, told so plainly of punctuality and order; all these, with the host of cheerful faces before me, told very clearly that it was a most lovable place.

I walked around through the aisles into the rooms, and behind the railing, looking at everything, with inquiring and delighted eyes, Jimmy pleasantly leading the way, and pointing out the various objects of interest. I was very much pleased with the library and wanted to stop to see how the librarian disposed so soon of the stream of boys and girls coming with their returned books, for, though the school had not yet begun, the librarian was in the library room receiving the books of the scholars. . . .

CHAPTER IV. OPENING THE SCHOOL

Something About the Minister

Jimmy, who, after he had taken his book to the librarian, had been pointing out all the beauties of the rooms, now looked up to the small clock which was over the infant-class room door, and seeing the hands pointing to nine o'clock, quietly left me seated on the wall seat behind the stove, and took his place in the class.

At the same moment the door opened, and a gentleman entered the room, followed by a boy of about ten or twelve years, leading a little girl of about five years who looked like his sister. The boy, after guiding his charge to the front seat, returned up the aisle to the seat Jimmy was sitting on, and sat down by him.

The gentleman passed down the aisle slowly, and as he reached the [altar] railing which surrounded the platform at the end of the aisle, the superintendent rose as if he had expected him, and they shook hands heartily. He then passed inside of the railing and seated himself in a chair behind the desk [pulpit].

His face wore a pleasant expression, and he smiled as he looked around on the bright faces before him; and, from what Jimmy had said to me, and from his present appearance and position, I thought he must be the minister.

Getting Ready to Sing

The superintendent now came forward to the desk, and taking a small bell from one of the shelves inside of the desk, rung a few strokes, which fixed the attention of every one in the room upon him.

After waiting a minute for all to get quiet, he pleasantly said: "I am pleased to see so many of the school present at the time: I hope the session will be an agreeable and profitable one."

Reciting the Hymn

He then rang the bell another stroke, and the whole school rose. He now recited two lines of the opening hymn, which the school repeated after him; then he recited two lines more, and they repeated them also. Thus he continued to recite, and the school to repeat, to the end of the hymn.

After they had repeated it slowly, and in equal time, observing the pauses, and getting the meaning of the words of the hymn, the superintendent drew from his vest pocket a tuning fork, which, after striking it a slight blow across his forefinger, he applied to his ear.

The sound of the fork gave him the pitch of the key note in the music, and as the children and teachers were quite ready, he sang—the whole school joining—in a very animated manner the words they had just repeated, to the tune given on the next page, where the hymn is given also.

[Here follows text and tune "Hear Our Song of Gladness."]

What I Thought About the Singing

I was well prepared to be pleased with everything about this Sunday School; but I think if I had been in a very unhappy state of mind, the singing would have cheered my feelings. Such a hearty union of sweet voices, and such a volume of cheerful harmony—it was easy to see that they loved the singing. . . .

The minister joined with a full, clear bass; the women on the side seats who belonged to the Bible class made the alto; the men belonging to the Bible class who were on the other side seats sang the tenor and bass, and even the infant scholars who were placed on the front seats raised their sweet little voices; and although I am not a very great singer, yet I could not help joining too, especially after a blushing little maid had stepped from her seat just before singing began and kindly given me a card with the music and hymn printed on it. . . .

About the Minister's Prayer

As soon as the singing was ended, the minister stepped to the railing, still wiping his eyes; the superintendent then touched the bell, and all kneeled down for prayer.

The minister began in a very low tone, for his voice was a little broken by the singing; but the school was very still, and as he went on in his prayer the words became smooth, and his heart became engaged in thoughts of God. He seemed to speak the wants and emotions of the children, and teachers, and parents, all out to the blessed father in heaven, just as if he were the children, and teachers, and parents all in himself.

I would be glad to give all the words of the prayer; but I cannot do this. I can only give you the breathing thoughts as he poured them out for the school to the God who hears and answers prayer. . . .

The Lord's Prayer

The minister ceased without saying the "Amen," and I was about to rise, thinking the prayer was ended; but in a moment the superintendent began to say the Lord's Prayer very slowly and distinctly, the whole school joining him in repeating it.

When it was ended, and "Amen" was said, all rose quietly from their knees, and took their seats. . . .

CHAPTER V. PREPARING FOR THE LESSONS

More Singing

As soon as the school was still, which it was in a minute, the superintendent drew a small tune-book from the shelf inside of the desk and gave out the one hundred and fortieth page.

Many of the scholars and teachers had books of the same kind, and after they had turned to the page, he struck the tuning-fork again on his forefinger, and after placing it to his ear and making two or three sounds with his voice to get the right pitch of the key-note, he touched the bell again and the school all rose up. He then sang the Sunday-school song, which you will find on the next page, the school all joining with hearty spirit. . . .

[Text and tune of hymn "Here We Throng" follows.]

When they had sung through the first verse, the superintendent said he had noticed some scholars who did not sing the whole of the verse. . . . "If any new scholars do not know the words and have not a book, I will give you a card with the hymn printed on it, if you will come to the desk." . . .

After singing all the verses of the "joyous song," at a stroke of the little bell the school was again seated. . . .

Calling the Roll

While the superintendent was speaking to me in a low tone of voice [welcoming me to the school], the secretary of the Sunday school had taken a registry book from the shelf in the desk and, standing up by the railing, he called the names of the officers and teachers beginning with the superintendent and ending with the minister.

All answered to their names as they were called, except one; and when her name was called, a teacher rose and made an excuse for her. She had been taken down by sickness the day before and could not be present.

The Largest and Smallest Classes Go Out

When the secretary had called all the names and marked them in his book the minister rose from his seat and passed into the Bible-class room. The men and women who were seated on the seats at the sides of the platform followed him. This was the Bible class and the minister was the teacher.

At the same time that the minister and Bible class went out, the teacher of the infant class rose also and went to the infant-class room. The little boys followed close behind her, two by two, with hands joined; and the little girls followed them in the same manner.

There were about twenty boys and nearly the same number of girls in the infant class, and they looked very beautiful as they marched so prettily through the aisle to their own room.

Teachers Prepare to Hear the Lessons

As soon as the Bible class and the Infant class had left the room, the teachers of the remaining classes turned the backs of the seats so as to bring two seats between two backs; and then, after changing seats so as to make room for all, the teachers seated themselves before their classes and began to hear the scholars recite their lessons.

BISHOP ANDREW OUTLINES CHANGES
IN THE DUTIES OF A BISHOP

Source: James O. Andrew, *"Bishop Asbury (part one of a three-part review of Thomas O. Summers' new book* Biographical Sketches of Eminent Itinerant Ministers*),"* Quarterly Review of the Methodist Episcopal Church, South *13/1 (January 1859), 10-11.*

We have sometimes heard the example of [Bishop] Asbury and his associates contrasted with the character and doings of our modern Bishops, quite to the disadvantage of the latter. Now, so far as we are individually concerned, we have no disposition to claim any sort of equality with our fathers in talents, or labors, or sufferings; yet that some of the present board of Bishops possess the same spirit of zeal and self-sacrifice, and the same willingness to do or to suffer which animated Asbury and McKendree, we have not the least doubt. There is no use for a Methodist Bishop to go on horseback or in a sulky now, when everybody else goes by steam [train], and when the Bishop can reach more points, and do so more comfortably and cheaply, than in the old way. Nor did the Bishops of olden time, after all, do so much more work than their modern descendants do annually. Perhaps Bishop Asbury visited more Annual Conferences than we do; but presiding in an Annual Conference then was a much lighter task than it is now. When we first visited an Annual Conference, the most we had to do was to examine the characters of the preachers, take the numbers, attend to the finances, (a very small business about those times,) and read out the appointments, and go home. We had no schools or colleges, no Tract, Missionary, or Sunday-school Societies to manage. We had not a dozen associations whose complicated machinery requires several days to adjust and keep in proper order. Now we have so many things before us at our Conferences that it is impossible to do anything well without a longer time than we can usually bestow on any one Conference. And then, as to stationing the preachers in the early times, most of the preachers were single men, whose removal from post to pillar could be accomplished without much difficulty; but how is it now? The removal of a preacher in these days involves very often the affliction of a wife and half-a-dozen children. This is quite a different affair from stationing young men with no encumbrance.

But there is another point of difference. Bishop Asbury was regarded with almost boundless reverence by the early preachers: his word was law; and when the old gentleman had repeatedly prayed over his plan, and it was complete, it was generally received as all right, and as being, in some sort, the work of God's providence: so, as a general thing, the preachers received it, and usually went to their work cheerfully. But the Bishops of this day are regarded not so much in the light of fathers as of elder brothers. We could not now, if we would, do as Bishop Asbury might do in his day; nor could Bishop Asbury, if now living, do as he did in those days. The oft-repeated saying, that power is constantly stealing from the many to the few, is reversed in reference to us. The Bishops of the Methodist Church have less power by far than they had forty years ago; and it might be very appropriately said that power has been constantly flowing from the few to the many; and it is no doubt right enough that it should be so. In the early days of the Church it required just such an administration as was that of our fathers. Then we were in childhood: now the Church has reached her manhood. It is proper that there should be a more general diffusion of power among the preachers and the laity. For our part, we have no fear of either, so long as we mutually, preachers and people, sustain the simplicity and purity of the gospel of Jesus Christ. . . .

Phoebe Palmer asserts biblical and historical support for women's right to preach

Source: Phoebe Palmer, Promise of the Father; or, A Neglected Speciality of the Last Days *(Boston: Henry V. Degen, 1859), 21-24, 29-31, 329-30, 341-42.*

Did the tongue of fire descend alike upon God's daughters as upon his sons, and was the effect similar in each?

And did all these waiting disciples, who thus, with one accord, continued in prayer, receive the grace for which they supplicated? It was, as we observed, the gift of the Holy Ghost that had been promised. And was this promise of the Father as truly made to the daughters of the Lord Almighty as to his sons? See Joel ii. 28, 29. "And it shall come to pass afterward, that I will pour out my Spirit upon all flesh; and your sons and your daughters shall prophesy, your old men shall dream dreams, your young men shall see visions. And also upon the servants, and upon the handmaidens in those days will I pour out my Spirit." When the Spirit was poured out in answer to the united prayers of God's sons and daughters, did the tongue of fire descend alike upon the women as well as upon the men? How emphatic is the answer to this question! "And there appeared unto them cloven tongues, like as of fire, and it sat upon *each of them.*" Was the effect similar upon God's daughters as upon his sons? Mark it, O ye who have restrained the workings of this gift of power in the church. "And they were *all* filled with the Holy Ghost, and began to speak as the Spirit gave utterance." Doubtless it was a well nigh impelling power, which was thus poured out upon these sons and daughters of the Lord Almighty, moving their lips to most earnest, persuasive, convincing utterances. Not alone did Peter proclaim a crucified risen Saviour, but each one, as the Spirit gave utterance, assisted in spreading the good news; and the result of these united ministrations of the Spirit, through human agency, was, that three thousand were, in one day, pricked to the heart. Unquestionably, the whole of this newly-baptized company of one hundred and twenty disciples, male and female, hastened in every direction, under the mighty constrainings of that perfect love that casteth out fear, and great was the company of them that believed.

And now, in the name of the Head of the church, let us ask, Was it designed that these demonstrations of power should cease with the day of Pentecost? If the Spirit of prophecy fell upon God's daughters, alike as upon his sons in that day, and they spake in the midst of that assembled multitude as the Spirit gave utterance, on what authority do the angels of the churches restrain the use of that gift now? Has the minister of Christ, now reading these lines, never encouraged open female testimony, in the charge which he represents? Let us ask, What account will you render to the Head of the church, for restricting the use of this endowment of power? Who can tell how wonderful the achievements of the cross might have been, if this gift of prophecy in woman had continued in use as in apostolic days? Who can tell but long since the gospel might have been preached to every creature? Evidently this was a *speciality* of the last days, as set forth by the prophecy of Joel. Under the old dispensation, though there was a Miriam, a Deborah, a Huldah, and an Anna who were prophetesses, the special outpouring of the Spirit upon God's daughters as upon his sons seems to have been reserved as a characteristic of the last days. This, says Peter, as the wondering multitude beheld these extraordinary endowments of the Spirit, falling alike on all the disciples—this is that which was spoken by the prophet Joel, "And also upon my servants and upon my handmaidens will I pour out my Spirit."

And this gift of prophecy, bestowed upon all, was continued and recognized in all the early ages of Christianity. The ministry of the Word was not confined to the apostles. No, they had a laity for the times. When, by the cruel persecutions of Saul, all the infant church were driven away from Jerusalem, *except the apostles*, these scattered men and women of the laity "went off every where *preaching the word*," that is, proclaiming a crucified, risen Saviour. And the effect was that the enemies of the cross, by scattering these men and women who had been saved by its virtues, were made subservient to the yet more extensive proclamation of saving grace.

Impelled by the indwelling power within these Spirit-baptized men and women, driven by the fury of the enemy in cruel haste from place to place, made all their scatterings the occasion of preaching the gospel everywhere, and believers were everywhere multiplied, and *daily* were there added to the church such as should be saved. . . .

A large proportion of the most intelligent, courageous, and self-sacrificing disciples of Christ are females. "Many women followed the Saviour" when on earth; and, compared with the fewness of male disciples, many women follow him still. Were the women who followed the incarnate Saviour earnest, intelligently pious, and intrepid, willing to sacrifice that which cost them, something, in ministering to him of their substance? In like manner, there are many women in the present day, earnest, intelligent, intrepid, and self-sacrificing, who, were they permitted or encouraged to open their lips in the assemblies of the pious in prayer, or speaking as the Spirit gives utterance, might be instrumental in winning many an erring one to Christ. We say, were they permitted and encouraged; yes, encouragement may now be needful. So long has this endowment of power been withheld from use by the dissuasive sentiments of the pulpit, press and church officials, that it will now need the combined aid of these to give the public mind a proper direction, and undo a wrong introduced by the man of sin centuries ago.

But more especially do we look to the ministry for the correction of this wrong. Few, perhaps, have really intended to do wrong; but little do they know the embarrassment to which they have subjected a large portion of the church of Christ by their unscriptural position in relation to this matter. The Lord our God is one Lord. The same indwelling spirit of might which fell upon Mary and other women on the glorious day that ushered in the present dispensation still falls upon God's daughters. Not a few of the daughters of the Lord Almighty have, in obedience to the command of the Saviour, tarried at Jerusalem; and, the endowment from on high having fallen upon them, the same impelling power which constrained Mary and the other women to speak as the Spirit gave utterance impels them to testify of Christ.

"The testimony of Jesus is the spirit of prophecy." And how do these divinely-baptized disciples stand ready to obey these impelling influences? Answer, ye thousands of Heaven-touched lips, whose testimonies have so long been repressed in the assemblies of the pious! Yes, answer, ye thousands of female disciples of every Christian land, whose pent-up voices have so long, under the pressure of these man-made restraints, been uttered in groanings before God.

But let us conceive what would have been the effect, had either of the male disciples interfered with the utterances of the Spirit through Mary or any of those many women who received the baptism of fire on the day of Pentecost. Suppose Peter, James or John had questioned their right to speak as the Spirit gave utterance before the assembly, asserting that it were unseemly, and out of the sphere of woman, to proclaim a risen Jesus, in view of the fact that there were *men* commingling in that multitude. How do you think that he who gave woman her commission on the morning of the resurrection, saying, "Go, tell my brethren," would have been pleased with an interference of this sort?

But are there not doings singularly to these being transacted now? We know that it is even so. However unseemly on the part of the brethren, and revolting to our higher sensibilities, such occurrences may appear, we have to know that they are not at all unusual in religious circles [today]. . . .

One would regret more deeply than ourselves the error of writing one line that might seem to diminish the influence of an officially ordained ministry; yet it has for many years been our belief that the modern ideas of preaching, and apostolic preaching, differ greatly.

What is meant by preaching the Gospel? Says the devoted Dr. [Francis] Wayland, "The word *preach* in the New Testament has a different meaning from that which at present commonly attaches to it. We understand by it the delivery of an oration, or discourse on a particular theme, connected more or less closely with religion. It may be the discussion of a doctrine, an exegetical essay, a dissertation on social virtue or vices, as well as a persuasive unfolding of the teaching of the Holy Ghost. No such general idea was intended by the word as it is used by the writers of the New Testament. The words translated *preach* in our [King James] version are two. The one signifies simply to herald, to announce, to proclaim, to publish. The other, with this general idea, combines the notion of good tidings, and means to publish, or be the messenger of good news." And in this exposition of the word, we believe most, and perhaps all other Bible expositors agree. And if this be the Scriptural meaning of the word *preach*, then where is the Christian, either of the clergy or laity, but would have every man, woman or child, who had an experimental knowledge of the saving power of Christ, herald far and near the tidings of a Saviour willing and able to save? When the ten lepers were healed, how reasonable it would have been, if they had neighbors or friends afflicted in the same manner, to have hastened with the glad tidings to them! And thus either men or women who prove the power of the heavenly Healer, the first impulse of their renewed nature is to proclaim the good news, so that all may be induced to come to the divine Restorer.

If this be the true Scriptural idea of *preaching*, to this we believe *every* individual called, whether male or female, who has been brought to an experimental knowledge of the grace of Christ, as the Saviour of sinners. And it is thus only that the command *can* be obeyed, and the gospel preached to every creature. How varied are the processes of grace on the human heart in leading it from sin to holiness! And just so diversified and correspondingly varied in interest, would be the proclamation of the healing, saving power of Christ in the assemblies of the saints, if the same ideas of preaching now prevailed as in the primitive days of Christianity. . . .

I have often thought, since then, how cruel to woman it is to compel her to stifle her convictions, to grieve the Holy Spirit, to deny the Saviour the service of her noble gifts, because the pleasure of the church (not surely the world, for it favors woman's liberty) must be regarded above that of God.

The church in many places is a sort of potter's field, where the gifts of woman, as so many strangers, are buried. How long, O Lord, how long before man shall roll away the stone that we may see a resurrection?

The church is a potter's field where the gifts of women are buried! And how serious will be the responsibilities of that church which does not hasten to roll away the stone, and bring out these long-buried gifts! Every church community needs aid that this endowment of power would speedily bring. And what might we not anticipate as the result of this speedy resurrection of buried power! Not, perhaps, that our churches would be suddenly filled with women who might aspire to occupy the sacred desk. But what a change would soon be witnessed in the social meetings of all church communities! God has eminently endowed women with gifts for the social circle. He has given her the power of persuasion and the ability to captivate. Who may *win* souls to Christ, if she may not?

And how well nigh endless her capabilities for usefulness, if there might only be a persevering effort on the part of the [ordained] ministry to bring out her neglected gifts, added to a resolve on the part of woman to be answerable through grace to the requisition! [The Church is] the only place where woman's gifts are unrecognized; that is, the church estranges herself from woman's gifts. To doubt whether woman brings her gifts into the church would be a libel on the Christian religion.

Benjamin T. Roberts laments Methodism's upward mobility

Source: B. T. Roberts, "Free Churches," The Earnest Christian 1/1 (January 1860): 6-10. Excerpts.

Mankind need nothing so much, as the universal prevalence of the Christian religion, in its purity. This would allay the evils under which humanity is groaning, by removing their cause. It would bring Paradise back to earth. For the blessings of the Gospel of Christ there is no substitute. . . .

The question of free churches derives its importance from its influence upon the purity and the progress of Christianity. It has a greater bearing upon both, than many imagine. The world will never become converted to Christ, so long as the Churches are conducted upon the exclusive system. It has always been contrary to the economy of the Methodist church, to build houses of worship with pews to sell or rent. But the spirit of the world has encroached upon us by little, and little, until in many parts of the United States, not a single free church can be found in any of the cities or larger villages. The pew system generally obtains among all denominations. We are thoroughly convinced that this system is wrong in principle, and bad in tendency. It is a corruption of Christianity. . . .

Free Churches are essential to reach the masses.

The wealth of the world is in the hands of a few. In every country the poor abound. . . .

The provisions of the gospel are for all. The "glad tidings" must be proclaimed to every individual of the human race. God sends the TRUE LIGHT to illuminate and melt every heart. It visits the palace and the dungeon, saluting the king and the captive. . . . To civilized and savage, bond and free, black and white, the ignorant and the learned, is freely offered the great salvation.

But for whose benefit are special efforts to be put forth?

Who must be *particularly* cared for? Jesus settles this question. He leaves no room for evil. When John sent to know who he was, Christ charged the messengers to return and show John the things which they had seen and heard. "The blind receive their sight, and the lame walk, the lepers are cleansed, and the deaf hear, the dead are raised up," and as if all this would be insufficient to satisfy John of the validity of his claims, he adds, "AND THE POOR HAVE THE GOSPEL PREACHED TO THEM. This was the crowning proof that he was the ONE THAT SHOULD COME." It does not appear that after this John ever had any doubts of the Messiahship of Christ. He that thus cared for the poor must be from God.

In this respect the Church must follow in the footsteps of Jesus. She must see to it, that the gospel is preached to the poor. With them, peculiar pains must be taken. The message of the minister must be adapted to their wants and condition. . . .

Thus the duty of preaching the gospel to the poor is enjoined, by the plainest precepts and examples. This is the standing proof of the Divine mission of the Church. In her regard for the poor, Christianity asserts her superiority to all systems of human origin. The pride of man regards most the mere accidents of humanity; but God passes by these, and looks at that which is along essential and imperishable. In his sight, position, power, and wealth, are the merest trifles. They do not add to the value or dignity of the possessor. God has magnified man by making him free and immortal. Like a good father, he provides for all his family, but in a special manner for the largest number, and the most destitute. He takes the most pains with those that by others are most neglected. . . .

[Roberts then quotes from his teacher, Stephen Olin, president of Wesleyan University:]

"There is precisely one gospel for all; and that is the gospel that the poor have preached to them. The poor are the favored ones. They are not called up. The great are called down. They may dress, and feed, and ride, and live in ways of their own choosing; but as to getting to heaven, there is only God's way, the way of the poor. They may fare sumptuously every day, but there is only one sort of manna.

"That *is* the gospel which is effectually preached to the poor, and which converts the people. The result shows it. It has demonstration in its fruits. A great many things held, and preached, may be above the common mind—intricate—requiring logic and grasp of intellect to embrace them. They may be true, important, but they are not the gospel, not its vital, central truths. Take them away, and the gospel will remain. Add them and you do not help the gospel. That is preached to the poor. Common people can understand it. This is a good test. All the rest is, at least, not essential.

"There are hot controversies about the true Church. What constitutes it, what is essential to it, what vitiates it? These may be important questions, but there are more important ones. It may be that there cannot be a Church without a bishop, or that there can. There can be none without a gospel, and a gospel for the poor. Does a church preach the gospel to the poor—preach it effectively? Does it convert and sanctify the people? Are its preaching, its forms, its doctrines, adapted *specially* to these results? If not, we need not take the trouble of asking any more questions about it. It has missed the main matter. It does not do what Jesus did, what the Apostles did. Is there a church, a ministry, that converts, reforms, sanctifies the people? Do the poor really learn to love Christ? Do they live purely, and die happy? I hope that Church conforms to the New Testament in its government and forms, as far as may be. I trust it has nothing anti-republican, or schismatic, or disorderly in its fundamental principles and policy. I wish its ministers may be men of the best training, and eloquent. I hope they worship in goodly temples, and all that; but I cannot think or talk gravely about these matters on the Sabbath. They preach a saving gospel to the poor, and that is enough. It is an Apostolic church. Christ is the corner stone. The main thing is secured, thank God."

If the gospel is to be preached to the poor, then it follows, as a necessary consequence, that all the arrangements for preaching the gospel, should be so made as to secure this object. There must not be a mere incidental provision for having the poor hear the gospel; this is the main thing to be looked after.

There is a feeling of independence in man that prompts him not to go where he fears he shall be regarded as an intruder. This is especially true of our American people. They will not accept as a gratuity, what others claim as a right. Their poverty does not lessen their self-respect. Let them be treated at a social visit as objects of charity, rather than equals, and they will not be very likely to repeat it. Hence, houses of worship should be, not like the first class car on a European railway, for the exclusive, but like the streets we walk, free for all. Their portals should be opened as wide for the common laborer, or the indigent widow, as for the assuming, or the wealthy. All who behave themselves in a becoming manner, should feel at perfect liberty to attend on all occasions of public worship.

The requirement of the gospel is not met by setting apart a certain number of free seats, for those who are too poor, or too indifferent to rent or purchase. . . .

The pew system, wherever it prevails, not only keeps the masses from attending church, but alienates them, in a great degree, from Christianity itself. They look upon it as an institution for the genteel, and the fashionable; and upon Christians as a proud and exclusive class. "When I came to this city," said a respectable mechanic, "I was a member of a Christian church. I rented a seat, and attended worship regularly. But I found that I could not hire a seat, and attend church at an expense of less than fifty dollars a year, without having my family looked down upon with contempt. This expense I could not afford; so we do not any longer attend religious meetings." His experience is that of multitudes. Many who, on going to the cities, are favorably inclined to religion, finding themselves virtually excluded from the churches, become at first indifferent, and then ready to drink in any error that comes along. Hence the ease with which the advocates of Millerism, and Spiritualism have found hearers and converts. . . .

Friends of Jesus, we call upon you to take this matter into serious consideration. The Gospel is committed to your trust. Your business is to save souls—first your own, then the souls of others. You are to dig for rough diamonds amid the ruins of fallen humanity, and polish them up for jewels in the crown of your Redeemer. The church edifice is your workshop. Do not, we beseech you, convert it into a show room, to display, not the graces of Christians, but the vain fashions of the world.

Politicians teach us an important lesson. How do they reach the masses? The places for their public gatherings, often rough and uncomfortable, are always free. The rich and poor associate as equals. What party could long survive, should they build splendid temples for the propagation of their principles, and then sell, at a high rate, the right to the occupancy of their seats? It is no feeble proof of the Divine origin of Christianity, that it has been able to survive a practice so absurd. But it can never spread with the rapidity with which we are authorized—from its sublime doctrines affecting man's highest interests for time and for eternity, from the beneficent influence it ever exerts upon society, and from the gracious efficacious assistance which God has promised to those who labor, as He directs, for its promotion—to expect it should, until all its houses of worship are free.

LAYMEN'S CONVENTION ADDRESSES MEC GENERAL CONFERENCE ON DESIRE FOR LAY REPRESENTATION

Source: Methodist Episcopal Church, "Address of the Laymen's Convention," Journal of the General Conference (1864), 407-11. *Excerpts*.

ADDRESS OF THE LAYMEN'S CONVENTION.

TO THE GENERAL CONFERENCE OF THE METHODIST EPISCOPAL CHURCH.

[Delivered by Professor James Strong, Drew Theological Seminary a layman.]

Fathers and Brethren,—The laymen of the Methodist Episcopal Church accepted with gratitude the resolution adopted in the General Conference of 1860, declaring the assent of that body to the principle of lay representation, and its willingness to admit lay delegates as associate members. The language of the pastoral address, in which it was said, *"The discussion of the question led us to approve the principle of lay delegation* in the General Conference," was hailed as the expression of a conciliatory spirit, and the recognition of the scriptural right of the laity to participate in the general administration of the Church. The reference of the question to the vote of the male members was not, however, asked by us, nor did we ourselves regard it as expedient. There were in our minds serious objections to such a process of legislation, and these, with our observations upon the vote as taken, we beg leave to present to your consideration.

1. A popular vote upon any question of connectional interest is without precedent in the history of American Methodism. The facilities for *adequately* employing this method of ascertaining the popular judgment do not as yet exist. Whether the vote should be properly taken depended solely upon the fidelity and care of the pastors. In our opinion the preachers should have been required to notify the people by reading the resolutions of the General Conference, and the passage of the pastoral address which touches upon lay delegation from their pulpits, and not by verbal statement; and the General Conference papers should have been directed to publish the same resolutions conspicuously a certain number of times during the period appointed for the taking of the vote.

2. In point of fact the vote was very imperfectly, and in some churches irregularly taken. In some instances preachers neglected or wholly refused to present the subject to their congregations; in other cases that have come to our knowledge the people were requested to give their judgment upon the admission of laymen to the Annual Conferences as well as the General Conference, thus having before them a question totally different from that which was by your order presented to their consideration. . . .

3. The breaking out of war which is now raging has withdrawn the attention of our members from this subject, and rendered its proper consideration difficult, if not impossible. . . . Yet, despite these disadvantages, the vote, as summed up, shows a degree of favor for lay representation which induces us to believe that had the subject been presented to the people under more favorable circumstances it would have received their unqualified approval.

In the Conferences situated east of the Allegheny Mountains, embracing the New England states, the central states, and the eastern border states, making nineteen conferences in all, the sum total of the votes cast gives a majority of over one thousand for lay delegation. These are the original seats of Methodism. In these regions our Church had its early home, and in them first grew to vigor and power. They are Conferences whose lay members may be taken to represent the most advanced consciousness of the wants of Methodism. The people in this important part of the territory of Methodism have spoken thus emphatically for the admission of laymen into the General Conference, we feel warranted in urging the subject afresh upon your consideration. . . .

Our Church in the order of Providence has an important part to perform in the moral culture of the American people, yet we do not see how it can find that acceptance with the people which we desire for it, and *retain* its hold upon them, if it shall be decided that, in its form of government, it is to be so far unlike the Protestantism of the whole world as to remain *permanently* under the sole government of the clergy. With the habits of American Christians, as they are habits acquired under the forms of a free political commonwealth, it is not likely that they will regard with abiding favor a Church purely hierarchical in its structure.

To resist the claim of the laity to participate in the general administration of the Church is, as it seems to us, a resistance of the whole tendency of the Christian life in this our age. In all the Protestant Churches of the world—unless our own be the sole exception—a more perfect association of the ministry with the laity in the administration of the interests of the kingdom of Christ is forming. . . .

But we are told that the Methodist system is peculiar, unique, and will not safely admit a sharing of the responsibilities of a General Conference between the ministry and the laity. We answer that the admission of laymen to the General Conference will not interfere with any essential peculiarity of Methodism. The administration will still remain in the hands that hold it now. Bishops will still appoint preachers to their stations; itinerant ministers and itinerant presiding elders will still revolve in their fixed orbits as they have revolved heretofore. The composition of the General Conference will be modified, but we are bold to say that the laity will be found as staunch in their adherence to all the essentials of Methodism as the ministry. The experience of this General Conference proves that the passion for innovation is already strongly developed in our preachers. . . . The experience of all ecclesiastical bodies in which laymen are members is, that the laity are more prone to resist than to encourage innovation, and that they consent with reluctance to the removal of old landmarks. . . .

There is another consideration to which we attach much importance. The proposal is, on our part, an offer that the ministry shall take into more perfect association with them all the resources of the Church. It is substantially an offer of partnership. So long as the General Conference is a purely clerical body, it cannot act with sufficient decision in founding and conserving the great charitable endowments which are, in our day, a part of the working force of an earnest Christianity. . . . As now constituted, the Conference cannot command the resources of the Church as it would be able to do were the laity to be united with the ministry in the expression of its supreme legislative will. . . .

We are met, however, with the declaration, that the ministers have managed the Church well, and that we should "let well enough alone." . . . But prudence suggests that every system should be provided with the checks and balances which are requisite to secure stability. And we should give heed to the teachings of Church history, which has demonstrated the fact, that a government of the clergy alone develops in time the most fearful evils—evils which, when they have become inveterate, are well nigh incurable. And we should never forget that the great reformation was just as much a reform of the *polity* of the Church, by the distribution of its powers between the clergy and the laity, as it was a revival of the Christian life. American Methodism should here, as well as elsewhere, follow the great lines of Protestant development.

But are we doing well enough now? Let our failure to keep pace with the growth of our large cities and towns answer. Witness again the numbers of youth who, nourished in the lap of Methodism, yet if they embrace religion at all so often join other communions where the lay element is more influential. Are our literary institutions adequately endowed? Where are our munificent foundations for the education of the ministry? . . .

We are gratified to find, fathers and brethren, that in urging our claim we are occupying the doctrinal ground of the greatest teachers of Methodism. The prince of Methodist theologians, Richard Watson . . . fully concedes that the *consent of the people through their representatives* is essential to the right ordering of the Church. We stand then firmly on Methodist ground; we stand on Protestant ground; we stand on the sure ground of Scripture. What we seek is in harmony with the New Testament, accords with primitive usage, and is the distinctive mark of Protestant Christianity. Lay representation in the General Conference once accomplished, the laity and the ministry will be more firmly bound to each other; the tie that unites them will be indissoluble. The Church will then have given to the Christian world a new guaranty of its perpetuity. American Methodism has, in our judgment, acquired the maturity which makes the union of the laity with the ministry, in its general government, both wise, safe, and necessary.

We leave it to you, fathers and brethren, to note the signs of the times, confident that in your mature deliberation this important and growing want of Methodism will receive from you the attention which the magnitude of the question demands. With sincere respect and affection, in behalf of the Laymen's Convention,

JAMES STRONG, *Secretary.*   THOS. KNEIL, *President.*
PHILADELPHIA, *May 18th, 1864.*

GENERAL CONFERENCE WRITES TO PRESIDENT LINCOLN, AND HE THANKS METHODISTS FOR THEIR SOLDIERS, NURSES, AND PRAYERS

Sources: Methodist Episcopal Church, Journal of the General Conference (1864), 155, 378-80. Also in Abraham Lincoln, The Collected Works, Roy P. Basler, ed. (New Brunswick, N.J.: Rutgers University Press, 1953), 7:350-51.

TO HIS EXCELLENCY ABRAHAM LINCOLN, PRESIDENT OF THE UNITED STATES.

The General Conference of the Methodist Episcopal Church, now in session in the city of Philadelphia, representing nearly seven thousand ministers and nearly a million of members, mindful of their duty as Christian citizens, takes the earliest opportunity to express to you the assurance of the loyalty of the Church, her earnest devotion to the interests of the country, and her sympathy with you in the great responsibilities of your high position in this trying hour.

With exultation we point to the record of our Church as having never been tarnished by disloyalty. She was the first of the Churches to express, by a deputation of her most distinguished ministers, the promise of support to the Government in the days of Washington. In her Articles of Religion she has enjoined loyalty as a duty, and has ever given to the government her most decided support.

In this present struggle for the nation's life many thousands of her members, and a large number of her ministers, have rushed to arms to maintain the cause of God and humanity. They have sealed their devotion to their country with their blood on every battle-field of this terrible war.

We regard this dreadful scourge now desolating our land and wasting the nation's life as the result of a most unnatural, utterly unjustifiable rebellion, involving the crime of treason against the best of human governments and sin against God. It required our government to submit to its own dismemberment and destruction, leaving it no alternative but to preserve the national integrity by the use of the national resources. If the government had failed to use its power to preserve the unity of the nation and maintain its authority it would have been justly exposed to the wrath of heaven, and to the reproach and scorn of the civilized world.

Our earnest and constant prayer is, that this cruel and wicked rebellion may be speedily suppressed; and we pledge you our hearty co-operation in all appropriate means to secure this object.

Loyal and hopeful in national adversity, in prosperity thankful, we most heartily congratulate you on the glorious victories recently gained, and rejoice in the belief that our complete triumph is near.

We believe that our national sorrows and calamities have resulted in a great degree from our forgetfulness of God and oppression of our fellow-men. Chastened by affliction, may the nation humbly repent of her sins, lay aside her haughty pride, honor God in all future legislation, and render justice to all who have been wronged.

We honor you for your proclamations of liberty, and rejoice in all the acts of the government designed to secure freedom to the enslaved.

We trust that when military usages and necessities shall justify interference with established institutions, and the removal of wrongs sanctioned by law, the occasion will be improved, not merely to injure our foes and increase the national resources, but also as an opportunity to recognize our obligations to God and to honor his law. We pray that the time may speedily come when this shall be truly a republican and free country, in no part of which, either state or territory, shall slavery be known.

The prayers of millions of Christians, with an earnestness never manifested for rulers before, dayly ascend to heaven that you may be endued with all needed wisdom and power. Actuated by the sentiments of the loftiest and purest patriotism, our prayer shall be continually for the preservation of our country undivided, for the triumph of our cause, and for the permanent peace, gained by the sacrifice of no moral principles, but founded on the word of God, and securing in righteousness liberty and equal rights to all.

Signed in behalf of the General Conference of the Methodist Episcopal Church. Respectfully submitted,

JOSEPH CUMMINGS, *Chairman.*

PHILADELPHIA, *May* 14, 1864.

Gentlemen,—In response to your address, allow me to attest the accuracy of its historical statements; indorse the sentiment it expresses; and thank you, in the nation's name for the sure promise it gives.

Nobly sustained as the government has been by all the Churches, I would utter nothing which might in the least appear invidious against any. Yet without this it may fairly be said that the Methodist Episcopal Church, not less devoted than the best, is, by its greater numbers, the most important of all. It is no fault in others that the Methodist Church sends more soldiers to the field, more nurses to the hospitals, and more prayers to heaven than any. God bless the Methodist Church! bless all the Churches! and blessed be God! who in this our great trial giveth us the Churches!

May 18, 1864.

A. LINCOLN

United Brethren Conference in Ohio pledges loyalty to the Union

Source: Minutes of the Fifty-fifth Session of the Miami Annual Conference of the United Brethren in Christ, Held at Union Chapel, Montgomery Co., Ohio, August 25-28, 1864 *(Dayton: United Brethren Printing Establishment, 1864), 11.*

ON THE STATE OF THE COUNTRY.

Resolved, That we disapprove of the act of Congress, refusing to pass the "Bill" for the amendment of the Constitution abolishing slavery, and we call upon all good and patriotic citizens to rebuke their time-serving policy and their respect for the "Relic of Barbarism" and cruel oppression—slavery—by ejecting them from place and power at the coming election.

2d. That we believe it a grievous wrong and wickedness for citizens in free States, who have been educated under the benign influences of liberty, to so far forget the rights and privileges of others as to unite with the oppressor to bind chains upon the limbs of others, and aid in their elevation to place and power by giving them their suffrages at the polls. But how much more grievously wicked it is for members of our church—a church always anti-slavery—to forget their religious obligations, as well as their political duties and sense of patriotism.

3d. That it is the duty of every good citizen to sustain the Administration in its efforts to suppress the rebellion; and every effort to distinguish between the Administration and the Government, denying the supremacy of the former while acknowledging the latter, is the mark of a traitorous heart, with a design of over-throwing the authority of the Administration, and with it the nation.

4th. That it is the duty of all citizens and Christians, but more especially members of the United Brethren church, to strengthen the hands of the President in every effort for the overthrow of slavery.

5th. That we behold with wonder and astonishment the development of a secret order, known as the "Sons of Liberty," whose malicious designs are nothing less than the inauguration of civil war in the free States, for the sole purpose of the overthrow of the national authority, and the division of this government into independent sovereignties, that the present unholy rebellion may succeed in its wicked efforts, and that slavery may be established upon a surer foundation. We beseech every lover of this country, and especially the members of our church, to have no communion or connection whatever with a political organization capable of such depravity and malicious wickedness.

6th. That we believe that if all the people outside of the so-called Confederate States had, from the beginning of this war, been in *earnest sympathy* with the Government, peace might, ere this, have been restored. God has a controversy with this nation, because of her obstinate wickedness and sympathy with slavery and rebellion. We are doubly guilty before God for resistance to his will, and for the blood now being shed, both for and against the nation.

7th. That we hereby express our heartfelt sympathy for the soldiers in the field, the hospitals and rebel prisons; for our brethren in the laity and in the ministry, especially those of this conference. We will remember them in our affections and in our prayers, that God may preserve their lives, their health and their morals, and that he will restore them to the embraces of home and the church.

B. W. Day,
C. W. Miller, } Committee
H. Garst,

Adopted.

CHOIR CONVENTION IN NEW YORK CITY ENDORSES IMPROVED STANDARDS FOR CHURCH MUSIC

Source: Erastus Wentworth, "Methodists and Music," Methodist Quarterly Review (New York) 47/3 (July 1865), 375-78.

To the General Conference of the Methodist Episcopal Church, held in Philadelphia, May, 1864, this Memorial of Choristers and others is respectfully presented:

BRETHREN AND FATHERS,—The place which music has ever held in the Church, and the part it has performed in the success of Methodism, establishes its importance.

While some denominations of Christians, by artistic skill unattainable by the masses, have excited admiration, it has been the purpose of the Methodist Church that music should be the medium and instrument of fervent spiritual devotions, adapted to all.

In this, as in other matters of Church polity, our puritanic affinities have caused us to lean too strongly away from ceremonials, and thus we have not sufficiently cherished the science of music, or kept pace with the advanced state of society.

It is true we have not been without efforts, which have at least fixed the love of music and sacred song in the affections of our people stronger perhaps, and more widely diffused than in any other body of Christians; yet it is apparent that we are, as a denomination, without a musical literature or satisfactory professorship.

We need music of an elevated and devotional character, wedded to our incomparable poetry, by which both shall be engraven upon the memory of our people, producing a oneness of taste and practice. Then shall we accomplish the prophetic desire: "Let the people praise thee, O God; let *all* the people praise thee!" [Ps. 67:5].

The efforts hitherto made have been diverse and sectional, and have not secured the regard and sympathy of our wide-spread membership. A more extensive movement is now contemplated. Already a society has been formed and is in successful operation, designing to associate the choirs of the Methodist Episcopal Church of New York and vicinity, and also extend its correspondence and sympathies throughout our connection.

This society of the "Associated Choirs" is about to call a Convention of choristers and others interested in the music of the Church, by which a concord of views may be had, and plans devised which may obtain the desired results.

Promotive of such purposes, the society respectfully asks that a committee may be appointed by the General Conference of the Methodist Episcopal Church to co-operate with said society and convention, by which the prestige of official sanction may be given to such measures and publications as may have its approval.

For such purpose the subscribers hereto append their names.

JOHN STEPHENSON, *President of the Associated Choirs.*
L. A. BENJAMIN, *Conductor.*

NEW YORK, *May* 2, 1864.

[Resolutions of a choir convention that met in New York City for ten days in October 1864.]

Resolved, 1. That singing is an important element of divine worship; it is, therefore, our duty to aim at its highest perfection.

2. That singing is the part of public worship in which the whole congregation can unite, and therefore the assignment of this service to a select few, practically to the exclusion of the congregation, is at variance with the spirit of divine worship, and subversive of its purposes.

3. That singing is a religious exercise commanding our entire faculties, and is the mode by which many of our noblest aspirations and holiest feelings find expression.

4. That in churches of non-liturgical observances singing is the only opportunity for a common declaration of faith and public general confession.

5. That this Convention express as its conviction that the authorized version of hymns in use among us should be sacredly guarded from displacement in our public worship by a loose sentimental literature.

6. That a selection of hymns for Sunday-school purposes be embodied in the Church Hymn-Book, and engrossed in the general index.

7. That singing is a part of divine worship, in which instrumental music, when employed, should be subordinate—an accompaniment, not a substitute.

8. That the human voice is the standard of perfection in music; and as accompaniment, not supersedure, of the vocal powers is the object of instrumental music in sacred worship, and as the modern organ, in its genera, combines in one instrument the excellences for such purpose, we therefore recommend the organ as the most suitable instrument.

9. That the importance of singing points to the necessity of regarding the wise counsel of our revered founder: "Let all the people be diligently instructed in singing;" we therefore recommend to pastors and Church officiaries that their sev-

eral congregations be regularly assembled for practice in Church music, and our people are earnestly urged to attend thereto as a religious duty.

10. That in the attainment of science an educated professorship is a necessity; it is therefore recommended that we cherish those engaged in the profession of music, and that our Churches make more liberal appropriations for that part of Church service.

11. That while we fully recognize the importance of musical knowledge, and ability to sing "with the understanding," we are also persuaded that this is of secondary importance in the worship of God, and that the primary injunction to "sing with the spirit" should cause us to commit the direction of such service to those who have also been divinely instructed.

12. That the best form of book for congregational singing is that with hymns and tunes on the same page; and for compactness, the four parts written on two staves.

13. That, in such book, each meter should have a preponderance of tunes selected from those already in use, and most approved by our Churches.

14. That, for congregational music, tunes of extreme intervals or complicated harmony are not desirable.

BISHOP SIMPSON SEES GUIDING HAND OF GOD IN THE CIVIL WAR

Source: Matthew Simpson, "Our National Conflict," in George R. Crooks The Life of Bishop Matthew Simpson of the Methodist Episcopal Church (New York: Harper & Brothers, 1880), 379-83. Excerpts.

An address first delivered 3 November 1864.

I would stand . . . far above all party; I have no epithets for any of my fellow-citizens. . . . *First:* It is a possible result of this conflict that we may become a prey to some foreign powers and be reduced under their control. There is a second possible result of this contest: that the nation may be divided into two or more separate confederacies. There is a third possible issue: that the nation may remain united, but with its present institutions overthrown, and Southern institutions and Southern ideas established. The fourth and last possible issue is that our nation, having passed through this fiery ordeal, may come out of it purer, stronger, and more glorious than ever before. At this point I will simply say that I believe it to be the design of Providence to secure the last result. . . . No great nation has, in all history, risen and fallen in a single century. [Illustrated by examples.] Moreover, there are indications to show that this is destined to be a great nation in the earth. The discovery of America by Columbus, at the time thereof, was opportune. This nation has done more than any other to fulfil a great destiny. One thing it has done towards the accomplishment of its work is the education of the masses. In this land all may rise to the highest offices. The humblest cabin-boy may lead our armies, and the poor hostler may sit in the Senate. Who has not heard of Henry Clay, the Mill-boy of the Slashes, and Jackson, the child of poor Irish parents; and some may have heard that even a rail-splitter may become president. [Applause.] Again, this nation is an asylum for all the nations of the earth. There is no large migration to any other land, but men come here from all parts of the world. I have no feeling of sympathy with any person who will seek to exclude from free national association all who may come. We have broad acres for them to cultivate, schools for their children and churches for themselves, and a Constitution broad enough, thank God! and strong enough for all the world to stand upon. This nation has the sympathy of the masses all over the earth, and if the world is to be raised to its proper place, I would say it with all reverence, God cannot do without America.

Then comes the second question—Shall the nation be divided? If we divide, where shall we divide? We have no mountain-chains, no great natural landmarks, to separate us into two, and if we divide must it not be into several confederacies? If you allow the South to go, then the Northwest will become a separate confederacy; and when the Northwest undertakes that, the people of the Pacific coast will set up for themselves, and you will lose all that gold-bearing country. I tell you here to-day, I would not give one cent on the dollar for your national liabilities if you allow a single dividing line to be run through your country from the Atlantic to the Pacific. [Applause.] I deprecate war, it is terrible; much of the best blood of the nation has flowed, and more, possibly, will moisten the earth; but if we should divide this land into petty sections, there will come greater strife, which will waste the blood of your children and grandchildren, and there will be sorrow and wailing throughout the generations to come. When I look at this dark picture, much as I dislike war, I yet say, better now fight for twenty years and have peace than stop where we are. [Tremendous applause.] If any peace is had, I want a peace which shall be lasting, so that I can leave my wife and children safe when I die, and that can only be by our remaining a united nation. We have glorious boundaries on the north and the south, on the east and the west, and when I look at those boundaries I say: "Palsied be the hand which shall try to wrest from us one foot of this domain." [Applause.]

Then the question comes, "Shall our form of government be changed?" This is what Mr. Davis expects: he can hardly suppose the South will live in separation. They at the South expected that this great city would declare itself independent; but this city has a heart that throbs in sympathy with the nation, and stands out, as it ought, as the national metropolis. The South hopes for a monarchy, but this nation will never tolerate a monarchy.

If these three results are not likely to happen, then shall we, as a people, emerge from this contest purer and more glorious than before. The nation must be purified, and for that we are going through the war. The war is nothing new; the South has been preparing for it for thirty years. At the same time a series of providences has appeared, which shows the hand of God. [The bishop here gave a review of the timely discovery of fresh resources for the increase of national wealth, and dwelt on the incidents of the war which appeared to him to have a Providential meaning. A high tribute was paid to Grant and his tenacity of purpose. He then turned his attention to slavery.]

I have one more impression, that if this war lasts much longer slavery will be damaged. [Loud applause.] It is seriously damaged now, and I hope and desire that it may pass away quickly and let us see the last of it. [Loud applause.] Do you ask what has been accomplished? The District of Columbia has been made free [Applause], and this week—on last Tuesday—the sun, as it rose, shone for the first time on the glorious free State of Maryland. [Great applause.] West Virginia, from her mountain home, echoes back the shouts of freedom. But this war ought not to be carried on for the purpose of restoring the authority of our government. But if, while we are striking blows at freedom. Let the children of these poor slaves have the chance to look back not only to Fort Pillow, but to battles fought and won in front of Petersburg and Richmond, and they will feel that they, too, are worthy of freedom. It has been demonstrated in this war that a blue coat can make a hero even of a sable skin. The black men have long ago learned to follow the stars; they have followed the North Star successfully, and now it is shown that they can follow, as well as any others, the stars that are set in our glorious flag. [Loud applause.]

Your Fifty-fifth Regiment carried this flag [taking up a war-worn, shot-riddled flag, which was greeted with tremendous cheers]; it has been at Newbern, and at South Mountain, and at Antietam. The blood of our brave boys is upon it; the bullets of rebels have gone through and through it; yet it is the same old flag. [Most enthusiastic applause, the audience rising and giving three rousing cheers.] Our fathers followed that flag; we expect that our children and our children's children will follow it; there is nothing on earth like that old flag for beauty. [Long and loud cheering.] Long may those stars shine! Just now there are clouds upon it and mists gathering around it, but the stars are coming out, and others are joining them. And they grow brighter and brighter, and so may they shine till the last star in the heavens shall fall! [Great cheering and waving of handkerchiefs and hurrahing.]

METHODISTS IN MISSOURI DECLARE
SOUTHERN CHURCH WILL REORGANIZE AND CONTINUE

Source: William H. *Lewis*, The History of Methodism in Missouri:
A Decade of Years from 1860 to 1870 *vol. 3 (Nashville:*
Publishing House of the M.E.C., South, 1890), 175-78.

[Committee on the State of the Church, Conference of Preachers and
Laymembers of the Methodist Episcopal Church, South, within the bounds of the
Missouri Conference, Palmyra, Missouri, June 22, 1865]

Your committee, in considering "the importance of maintaining our separate
and distinct ecclesiastical organization," beg leave to present the following resolution and accompanying paper:

Resolved, that we consider the maintenance of our separate and distinct ecclesiastical organization as of paramount importance and our imperative duty.

The reasons are many and obvious. While we have maintained a separate and distinct ecclesiastical organization for twenty years, yet we claim original paternity and
co-existence as a Methodist Church with the other branches of the great Methodist
family in the country. Facts will not permit us to yield to any other Church of that
name priority of age; nor in any other light than as an attempt to deceive the unsus-
pecting among our people can we regard the specious claims urged to the confidence and patronage of the Methodist public under the name of "Old Church."

In contravention to the Plan of Separation agreed upon by the General
Conference of 1844—the legitimacy and binding force of which were recognized
by the Supreme Court of the United States—the Northern wing of the Church has
acted in bad faith toward us in many ways.

And since that Church was forced by law to give to our Church her *pro rata* share
of property—which she was too mercenary to do without an appeal to the highest
judiciary of the country—she has persisted in an unprovoked and undesired war
upon us—a war which has aggravated the questions of difference, widened the
breach, and produced an estrangement of feeling and a destruction of fellowship
for which she alone is responsible, and which we cannot even seek to remedy without compromising principles and yielding all self respect.

Those who publish to the world that all differences between us are swept away with the institution of slavery are either ignorant of the facts or are trying to mislead the public. The question upon which the Church divided was not whether the institution of slavery was right or wrong, *per se,* but whether it was a legitimate subject for ecclesiastical legislation. The right or wrong of the institution, its existence or non-existence, could not affect this vital question. It is now abolished by Federal and State legislation, which event we accept as a political measure with which we have nothing to do as a Church. And it remains for us to demonstrate our ability to exist without the institution of slavery, as we have existed with it, which we have already done in California and other places.

Now, if we go into the Methodist Episcopal Church, we will by that act yield the position we have so often taken, admit the charges we have so often refuted, and by accepting political tests of Church-fellowship, stultify ourselves and compromise the essential principles of the Gospel. If we seek an alliance with or permit our Church to be swallowed up by any other ecclesiastical body so as to destroy our separate existence as a distinct organization, we admit the charge that with the institution of slavery we stand or fall.

The subject of Church reconstruction or consolidation has been widely discussed by the press and the ministry of the Methodist Episcopal Church (North), and reasons, both political and ecclesiastical, are urged with an ill-disguised pertinacity why we should consent to an absorption of our entire ecclesiastical body by that Church.

It cannot be disguised that what they failed to accomplish during the war by military order and authority, they now seek to effect by ecclesiastical strategy and diplomacy—that is, to get possession of our Church property, and rather than recognize us now as a Christian Church entitled to their ecclesiastical fellowship and Christian fraternity (which they by formal vote of their General Conference refused to do in 1848) and in that way, and with a Christian spirit, seek to offer negotiations upon the subject, they prefer to ignore our existence, or, which would suit their purpose better, pronounce us disloyal to the government, and per consequence not entitled to an existence at all; then invade us and by misrepresentations seek to disaffect our people, disintegrate our church, and inaugurate an ecclesiastical strife that will involve the third and fourth generations.

The only consolidation or reconstruction they would accept would be that we turn over to them our church property and interests and influence; yield the whole field; confess that we have been in the wrong; endorse the politics of their Church as a condition of membership; and become political hucksters instead of Gospel ministers; then even our motives would be suspected, and we looked upon with contempt for our cowardly truckling to party and power.

Again we affirm that our itinerant system has become a great moral agency in elevating the masses of the people, preaching the Gospel to the poor, and "spreading Scriptural holiness over these lands." Under its wide-spread operations we have gathered the people together, planted Churches, organized Sabbath-schools, acquired Church property, built up and endowed institutions of learning, and become a moral and religious element of the country at least equal to any other Protestant Church.

The people have learned to look to our ministry for the Gospel, to our Churches and Sunday-schools for religious instruction, and to our influence in restraining vice, encouraging virtue, maintaining law and order, and promoting the well-being of society. We cannot, therefore, abandon our Church and people, or betray the interests and trusts committed to us as a Church, without a plain and culpable disregard of duty that would subject us to the contempt and derision of the Christian public.

We are not at liberty to dissolve our ecclesiastical organization or permit our Church to be absorbed by any other, even should we desire to do so, for our people have been consulted as far as practicable, and they are unwilling to seek any other Church connection, but with great unanimity demand at our hands the maintenance of our Church organization intact.

It is, therefore, due the great mass of the people who oppose the prostitution of the pulpit to political purposes, it is due to our large membership who have been converted and gathered into the fold of Christ under our ministry, and who love our Church doctrines and discipline too fondly to seek any other fold now—it is due to every principle of self-respect and ecclesiastical propriety that we maintain, with firm reliance upon the help of the Great Head of the Church, our organization without embarrassment or compromise.

While these are some of the many reasons why we should adopt the above resolution, we desire most ardently to cultivate fraternal relations with all the evangelical Churches, and "as much as in us lies live peaceably with all men" [Romans 12:18].

Wm. M. Leftwich, Chairman; John D. Vincil, Wm. N. Newland.
[all clergy members]

HISTORIAN ABEL STEVENS URGES "IMPROVEMENT" OF CHURCH ARCHITECTURE

Source: Abel Stevens, The Centenary of American Methodism (New York: Carlton & Porter, 1865), 233-36. Italics in original.

Methodism should feel itself responsible to minister hereafter, to the public culture, by the improvement of its church architecture. During most of its history, [Methodism] has had to extemporize its temples. Within the last twenty-five years it has been providentially enabled to renew a large proportion of them, to give them better locations, better internal accommodations, and better architectural style; so that in some of the principal cities, Boston, New York, Newark, Philadelphia, Wilmington, Chicago, Cincinnati, its places of worship are rapidly taking rank with those of older denominations. It has need, indeed, of caution against excess in this respect, but it has more need of liberal taste than of caution, for its error has been in the opposite direction, if not in the opposite extreme. It should bear in mind that its permanent hold upon its congregations, especially in the larger communities, will depend much upon the convenience and even the elegance (the just elegance) of its churches; that there can be no moral objection to good taste and genuine art; and that the monuments of religion deserve such tributes above all other structures. The taste of the Church has advanced much in this respect, more, perhaps, than its liberality; but it needs further training in both. It needs to be reminded that true taste and true art are not adventitious things, much less the products of pride or luxury; that they are founded in original laws, that is to say, divine laws of human nature, and therefore meet a natural want of man; that even the strictest "utilitarianism" cannot rationally condemn them, for beauty is often the highest utility, ministering, in art, to our higher wants in a manner incomparably more utilitarian, than the service of the lower or "practical arts" to our lower nature. God has written its vindication over all his works, for whatever may be their mechanical processes and directly utilitarian designs, he has decorated them everywhere with beauty or sublimity, and their very first appeal is to our minds rather than to our physical necessities. The heavens by day and by night, the mountains and valleys, the streams and seas, and most living things, are made by him pictures for the soul before they can be made by us tributary to our material wants. He permits not the vegetable world to yield us bread, till it has first yielded beauty through the eye, to the mind. The blossom precedes the fruit. True art should be recognized as one of the noblest handmaids of religion; elevating impressions and associations, through the senses in our temples, may ennoble even divine worship; and imposing monuments of taste, consecrated to piety, are among the highest means of national culture, and the highest proofs of advanced civilization. It is a sacred peculiarity of architectural art that, unlike painting and sculpture, it will not lend itself to vice; its severe and stately beauty disdains effeminate or voluptuous tastes. It is the most sublime, the most religious, of the works of man.

On really utilitarian grounds, then, may we plead for religious art. Yet we may plead for it also on really economical grounds. The most expensive temple is usually the most economical. The Church that builds its edifice in the most eligible locality and in the most attractive style, almost invariably finds its expense the best reimbursed, by its command of the people, their attendance, their intelligence, and their money. A well located, substantial, and commanding temple aids much in giving security to a Church, and is cheap in this respect. The stability of the religions of the old world, their power over local populations, are owing largely to their grand edifices. Methodism should not despise this power. It must still throw up hastily, especially in its frontier fields, temporary "meeting-houses," shanties, or log-cabins; it should multiply greatly its cheap suburban temples; but it should make all prudent haste to supersede these by better structures. Consulting always, and primarily, practical convenience in its buildings, it should also endeavor liberally to ennoble the house of God by every aid of genuine taste and art. It will not be able to justify itself against the claims of public opinion and public taste upon it if, with its great prosperity, it should fail to have within the next twenty-five years the most approved and most commodious churches of the nation.

HISTORIAN ABEL STEVENS TOUTS CENTENARY FUND AND CONNECTIONALISM

Source: Abel Stevens, The Centenary of American Methodism *(New York: Carlton & Porter, 1865), 225, 266-68. Italics in original. Excerpts.*

The capabilities of American Methodism, for continued and increased usefulness, have already been shown in the historical view of its practical methods, its theological teachings and its actual results. It stands strong to-day in its essential doctrines and methods; and it has the additional ability and responsibility of greater financial resources than it has ever had before. Its people, originally the poorest of the land, have become, under its beneficent training, perhaps the wealthiest. Not only has it more diffused wealth than any sister denomination, but its cases of individual opulence have, within the last quarter of a century, greatly multiplied. As the leading Church of the country, it bears, before God and man, the chief responsibility of the moral welfare of the nation. *The better consecration of its wealth to the public good is therefore one of its principal responsibilities of its future. . . .*

The sum of two millions is here named as the lowest mark at which the Church should aim in its Centenary offerings of gratitude. It is believed that this *minimum* will be largely transcended; and indeed, that the final summing up will be nearer to four millions than two. And without pretending to dictate to the ministry or the membership of the Church, we feel it our duty to make the following concluding suggestions:

1. One great object of the Centenary movement should be to promote the Connectional spirit of Methodism, and to bind anew, in cords of fraternal love and of devotion to the common cause, the East, the West, the North, and the South. So let us rebuke, by the grand unity of our vast societies, the spirit of secession, whether in Church or State. Unity in Christ is one of the needful marks of the true Church, and to promote the unity of the American people is one of the obvious functions of the Church in this country. We trust that this mark and function of the Church will be dwelt on in every pulpit of Methodism at some period of the Centenary celebration.

2. One of the most signal and obvious ways of showing our Connectional spirit will be to contribute to the Centenary Educational Permanent Fund, and to the

other Connectional objects named by the General Conference and its committees. As we have said, the whole Church, and at the same time every locality within its bounds, is interested in these objects.

Local objects will doubtless be urged, with earnestness and pertinacity, by those interested in them. We do not wish to overshadow these objects so as to hinder their success. At the same time let us remember that these objects are always with us, always at our doors, and therefore always with likely to be taken care of. But our Permanent Fund is to be the great mark and proof of our connectional feeling as demonstrated by our Centenary gifts. Let the Centenary year be our Sabbath of Church fellowship; one year, at least, out of the century, in which we shall rise above all local and sectional thoughts, feelings and interests, into the higher atmosphere of our Unity in the Church, and in Christ the Head of the Church.

MEA III:
1866–83

EDITOR GILBERT HAVEN PLEADS FOR "NO CASTE IN THE CHURCH OF GOD"

Source: Gilbert Haven, "No Caste in the Church of God," Zion's Herald and Wesleyan Journal (10 April 1867), 57.

Adopted by the N.E. [New England] Conference. March 30th, 1867.

DEAR BRETHREN AND SISTERS:—We desire to set before you, as your faithful pastors and affectionate brethren, a duty which, in our most solemn judgment, we believe God calls upon his churches, in this hour and land, to boldly perform; a duty in this discharge of which he especially requires this Conference to lead the way, by virtue of her whole history of zeal for his cause in all departments of human as well as heavenly salvation. As it is one which we cannot discharge without your co-operation, we are constrained to issue this appeal.

Three years ago we admitted to our membership a well known and able minister of our church, whose services in the local ranks had made him popular and believed in many of our churches. But solely on account of his complexion, he could not be received by the charge to which he was sent, which even complained that its character had been damaged by having his name, only, thus officially connected with its own. No complaint was made of his abilities, which were unquestioned, and which, under other circumstances, they would have been proud and glad to have enjoyed as their own. They revolted from him solely because of the color of his skin. We do not say this to condemn them, but as a necessary ground for our appeal. They will yet be proud of having this first official connection of any white church in America with a colored minister. May it soon be renewed. They yielded to what doubtless at the time seemed to them an absolute necessity. They thought perhaps that the church could not be sustained under such ministrations. We believe in this they erred, and that the church, as well as the unconverted community, would have responded to a courageous conquering of unchristian prejudices. Yet we consider that in this matter they were on a level with their sister churches, and cannot be held to have indulged in different sentiments, or to have pursued a different course from their brethren. He would as surely probably have been despised and rejected by every other church.

In consequence of this feeling, the Conference could not proceed as they wished in the great work of practicing, as well as preaching the brotherhood of believers, the equal rights and perfect unity of the ministers of our church. They had welcomed him to their companionship, and would have delighted to honor him with their favors, but they could not compel a church to receive him as a pastor. He could be admitted to serve, perhaps, as a missionary in a distant field. But if that privilege were allowed, the necessity of it would still be a humiliation to which a minister of Jesus Christ should not be subjected. We asked for his return, pledging ourselves to go upon circuits with him, if in no other way the churches could be induced to accept him as a pastor.

But the time has come, in our judgment, when a yet more broad and just course should be pursued. We do not plead for this or any other brother in particular, but for all those whom God has called to his ministry; whom you would gladly recommend, and we would gladly admit to our Conference. We plead for risen and rising men of power, that are now shut out from the full exercise of divinely given endowments by the prevalence of this most unchristian prejudice. We entreat you to open your hearts and consent to the opening of your pulpits to their official ministrations.

Our reasons for this entreaty are manifold. Be pleased to listen to a few of them:

First, The spirit of the age demands it of us. Everywhere the chains of caste are falling. In India and England, in the South and the North man is beginning to see "brother" written in the face of him whom he lately loathed, and his heart is yearning toward him. The haughty descendant of haughty Frederic throws open his Parliament to universal suffrage; so that peasants in Germany are now the equals of princes, and may supplant them in seats of power. Italy is yet more enthusiastic in this feeling. So is France. Even England is stirring with the strange emotion. Our own land has grown in stature and wisdom in this duty day by day since the war began. Shall not our churches in their sphere be equally faithful and progressive? Shall we keep up barriers that are everywhere else disappearing?

Second. But we should do this because of its relations to our political duties. Our State long since abolished all distinctions among its citizens based on color. And now, in consequence of faithfulness, on the part of a few men, another few, equally faithful, have made their fellow citizens place in her seats of legislation those who prove to all the world that Daniel Webster's appeal is at last reached, and Massachusetts has conquered her prejudices! The United States is becoming equally true to principle, and in her late acts has completely abolished the whole iniquity of caste from national legislation. Shall the church wear these chains after the State has dropped them from her limbs? Shall she presume to look a minister of Christ in the face and reject him as her pastor, when the world around her will readily make him, its representative? If we would have any direct and ecclesiastical share in this divine work, we must hasten to avow our victory over this sin: our readiness to treat all God's ministers and people as one with us and one in the Lord.

Third. This is especially needed in view of our consistency as well as our relation to the work elsewhere. As a Conference, upheld, we rejoice to say, by our churches, for more than a generation we have plead with the church and the nation to abolish this iniquity of slavery. We have been in a minority often, and long, but have suffered and served till the church and the nation obeyed the voice of God and proclaimed his law. To-day we have been equally earnest in imploring the church to disregard all distinctions among her members and ministers based on color; to abolish separate Conferences, schools and churches; to fully and faithfully recognize and act up to the most evident will of God written in his word, in the hearts of his disciples, in the history of his church. But we are answered, "Physician heal thyself!" [Luke 4:23]. Will your churches accept a colored man as a pastor? What right have you to demand more of us than you will do yourself? How shall we answer them? We must be dumb and open not our mouths. Will you not allow us the proud privilege of replying; "we ask only that you *follow* us, as we are following Christ? We have swept the distinction from our Conference. Our brethren have swept it from our churches. They accept the pastor that is sent them whatever his complexion, and honor and love him as their shepherd in the Lord." Only by *doing* this can we remove this reproval from us. Will you not then join with us in thus giving New England her old and just leadership in the renewal of the face of the church and the land.

Fourth. But, lastly, the Spirit of God demands that we do this duty because of the brethren whom he has called to his ministry, and the souls he has filled with his salvation. They are trammeled and oppressed by our unbrotherliness. There are heavier claims than those that drag down the body. The proud man's scorn, the rich man's contumely [reproach] are harder to be borne than any fetters of iron. Put yourself in the place of these brethren. Bear their burdens in your feelings, thankful that you may thus fulfill the law of love. How would you feel if having been called of God to preach, knowing that it was not from men nor by men, but from the Lord Jesus Christ and God the Father, if when you begin to fulfill your ministry, multitudes of your brethren, churches upon churches should look with loathing upon you because of certain characteristics given you by God? Though they might be willing to hear you, and even glad to hear you, they would not let you take your place among your brethren, but compelled you to serve those affected like yourself, who had also been driven as lepers from their society. How would your soul have then suffered many martyrdoms. Such has been, such is their condition. So have they been hated and cast out by their brethren. So have their hearts been riven with anguish unutterable. The times of our ignorance God hardly winked at. Our dread chastisement was its legitimate punishment; and now every ear hears him call us everywhere to repent. Will you enable us to show our repentance by hastening to do the most just and most brotherly work of welcoming all these ministers as our own believed kindred, like Christ himself, of our own body, of our flesh, of our bones? Will you assure our Presiding Elders that you are willing to accept brethren of this hue as your pastors? Ministers of talent, attainments and piety are waiting the opening of this door. Will you respond to this request of God, spoken in your conscience, spoken by his angel in the ear of all his churches, and invite them to come in? So doing, the Master who is with them will enter as never before into our temples and hearts.

We have departed somewhat from our usual course in making this appeal. We have never before submitted to the churches questions connected with the admission of brethren to our Conference. Our Bishops, for nearly the seventy years of our existence as a Conference, have had no difficulty in finding churches willing to receive as pastors those whom we had admitted to our body; never, except in the memorable instance which compels this appeal. That instance we saw was only an exponent of a general feeling. We are therefore constrained to entreat you to aid us in our efforts to emancipate our Conference, our church, our nation from this sin. You can by resolution approve the sentiments of this appeal. You can declare your detestation of caste, and willingness as a body of believers to act up to your convictions, by ignoring color in your membership and pastorship. You can declare to your elder, through your Quarterly Conference, your readiness to receive brethren as pastors irrespective of complexion.

Thus acting, you will encourage us in our efforts to purge the church, and society of this most unrighteous leaven, and hasten forward the kingdom of our Saviour and Father, whose love embraceth all in equal ardor, patience and perfection.

We request that this appeal be read in all our churches, and that such action be taken upon it, after seeking counsel of God, as shall in your judgment, most redound to his glory, the purity, unity and fellowship of his church, and the more speedy subjugation of the world to his gospel.

George Hughes describes National Holiness Camp Meeting in Vineland, New Jersey

Source: George Hughes, *"The Vineland Encampment,"* Guide to Holiness 52/17 (September 1867), 91-93. *Italics in original.*

A great battle has been fought and a great victory won. The Lord hath triumphed gloriously. The voice of rejoicing and praise is in the tabernacle of the righteous. Heaven has kept jubilee. Every harp of immortality and the melodious voices of the blood-washed hosts before the throne have been engaged in the triumphal song. Satan has suffered loss: Messiah has had accessions of strength. The salvation of the Lord has come out of Zion. "The Lord will count, when he writeth up the people, that this and that man were born in her" [Psalm 87:6]. Glory, glory to the Lamb!

From the very inception of this meeting until its grand termination, it has been evident to faithful ones that God was in the movement. Despite the fears of the timid, and among them some who were the friends of holiness, the courageous sons and daughters of Zion saw the Lord leading his chosen people to certain victory. The preliminary meeting in Philadelphia was a baptismal time. The broad seal of Heaven was placed upon the enterprise then. Those who were present will never forget the approving tokens.

The meeting opened on Wednesday July 17, [1867] under the brightest auspices. The presiding elder of the Bridgeton [NJ] District, Rev. A. E. Ballard, being thoroughly in sympathy with the objects of the meeting, greatly inspirited ministers and people in their holy work. His clear and manly utterances at the very outset opened a wide and effectual door. The Banner was nobly flung to the breeze, bearing the grand inscription, *"Holiness to the Lord."* The first day, "the promise of a shower" was given. The morning was devoted to a prayer-meeting in one of the large tents. The Lord poured out his Spirit. In the afternoon the ground was formally dedicated; the services being in the hands of Rev. J. S. Inskip. Scriptural selections appropriate to the hour were read by Rev. A. Cookman. Then followed stirring addresses by Brothers Inskip, B. M. Adams of Brooklyn, and R. V. Lawrence of New Brunswick, NJ. The dedicatory prayer by Brother Inskip was divinely indited; it manifestly reached the throne. God's hands were open,—the Shechinah [*sic*] was revealed—the presence of the Triune God was demonstrated. From that hour it was unmistakable that every foot of that consecrated enclosure was *holy ground,* covered with the divine panoply.

The evening was given to exhortation and prayer. Penitents were bowed there seeking pardon while believers were panting for the rest of faith. *The seal of awakening and converting power* was thus affixed in the opening services. The simple testimonies of the afternoon, bearing upon the great theme, smote hearts with conviction which had resisted the most powerful preaching, the most searching pulpit appeals. This was especially gratifying, and in exact accord with the anticipations of the friends of the meeting. They have learned that the divine order is *the sanctification of believers, the conversion of sinners,*—this the great gospel conjunction. These two are so joined in the economy of grace, and especially illustrated in Methodist history, as to afford the highest demonstration of the wisdom of God; and "what God hath joined together, let no man put asunder" [Matt. 19:6].

Brother Horne of New York gave the keynote in the pulpit on Thursday morning, selecting as his text that beautiful passage in John [1 John 1:7], *"And the blood of Jesus Christ, His Son, cleanesth from all sin."* The word, as subsequently delivered by chosen ambassadors of the cross, was indeed in demonstration of the spirit and with power. One of the clearest and most effective expositions of the doctrine of entire sanctification was by Rev. Mr. Johnson, pastor of the Presbyterian Church, Fairton, NJ. It was full of unction and made a deep impression upon the [large] and attentive congregation in attendance.

Rev. Brothers Coleman of Troy Conference, B. M. Adams, New York East, R. V. Lawrence of New Jersey, J. Parker of New York, L. C. Matlack of Philadelphia Conference, J. S. Inskip of New York, J. A. Wood of Wilkes-Barre [Pennsylvania], J. R. Daniels, Newark Conference, Barnitz of East Baltimore, Rose of Troy, French of South Carolina, L. R. Dunn of Newark Conference, Clemm of Baltimore, Wells of Troy, A. Cookman of Philadelphia, Browning of New York, Pomroy of Troy, and B. W. Gorham of Pittsburgh, severally occupied the stand. They were one and all clothed with power.

A wonderful scene attended and followed the preaching of Brother [Lucius] Matlack. He was so affected that it was difficult for him to open his discourse. The strong man bowed himself. Leaning his head for a time upon the [pulpit] desk, he wept freely and the whole audience was brought to tears. He referred with deep feeling to his former experience of intimate communion with God and his desire for its happy return. At the close the whole congregation was called to kneel before the Lord in solemn, earnest prayer. That was a time of holy wrestling at the mercy seat—a lifting-up of holy hands. Several led in prayer. Brother Cookman made a solemn and most earnest approach to the audience-chamber divine. Wave after wave of power rolled over the assembly. I confess I was momentarily looking for a prostration upon the ground of the whole congregation, ministers and people. It was a hour of prayer never to be forgotten. Another great occasion at the stand was under a thrilling sermon by Brother Wells of Troy [New York] on Ezekiel's sublime vision of the cherubim touching his lips with the live coal. God was marvelously present. The effect was heightened by a soul-moving exhortation by Bishop [Matthew] Simpson. The whole audience was moved to tears, and shouts of praise emanated from many lips. The bishop himself was bathed in tears, and his whole nature was surcharged with holy fire. He had been pouring out floods of tears over the head of his darling son, who had been kneeling as a humble penitent at the footstool of mercy. His words will not be forgotten. They sank deep into many hearts. He thoroughly indorsed [sic] the meeting and its objects. Not in vain did the bishop and his family tent with the devoted worshippers on that memorable ground. The conversion of his son, and a rich baptism upon himself and beloved companion and the son's wife, will render *"Vineland Encampment"* a spot of precious memory. God bless them, and lead them on to altitudes of surpassing light!

This encampment had some peculiar features which are worthy of mention. One was the rule that each day at one o'clock the curtains of the tents should be dropped and the occupants be engaged in *private prayer.* Persons coming on the ground at that hour of private prayer and finding the tents closed and all holding audience with the Deity were awed by the solemnity of the scene.

Another feature of exceeding interest was the large enclosure which was aptly styled *"The Bower of Prayer."* It was a space which had been devoted to *dancing* purposes by citizens of Vineland. Brother W. B. Osborn, to whom we are largely indebted for the excellent arrangements, conceived the idea of transforming it into *a praying circle,* having it roofed over with brush. It was a delightful place for meetings; and, oh how honored! It was a common remark that heaven was very near that spot. After our good friends, Dr. and Mrs. Palmer arrived on the ground, the meetings there were placed under their superintendence. The people stood around in large masses, and listened with profoundest interest to the words of his honored servant and handmaid. Their labors, I believe, were greatly blessed. Many souls will, I am sure, in the judgment rise up and shower benedictions on them.

I shall never forget one scene in that *"Bower of Prayer."* After a number of thrilling testimonies had been given, and the invitation was tendered to seekers to present themselves, Brother Clemm of Baltimore asked for earnest prayer in his behalf, that he might be endued with power. He came and prostrated himself at the [anxious] bench, and was followed by about one hundred others. Oh, what a time of divine visitation! Heaven and earth were in glorious contact. The roll of the fully saved was greatly increased. The recording angel made numerous entries. The song of triumph was lifted heavenward.

One of the honored workers on this occasion was "Father [Seymour] Coleman," a venerable member of the Troy Conference. He preached at an early period in the meeting; and his message was so full of Gospel simplicity and divine unction that all were impressed. He labored continuously in the prayer-meetings, pointing seekers of pardon and purity to their bleeding Lamb. He frequently led in prayer, and carried the people with him into close fellowship with the Father of mercies. . . .

Another striking feature of the meeting was the fact that so many Christian denominations were represented. Presbyterians, Baptists, Episcopalians, Lutherans, Friends, and Methodists were all dwelling together in sweetest harmony. Never was there a more beautiful illustration of the Psalmist's declaration,—"Behold, how good and how pleasant it is for brethren to dwell together in unity!" [Ps. 133:1]. . . .

But it is utterly impossible in the limited space allotted to this article adequately to portray the scenes of this modern Pentecost. A more extended history will be written. And yet no pen is capable at this time of writing the results of this meeting. The influence will run parallel with the sweep of all succeeding ages, and roll up in the final day an aggregate which will, I believe, astonish men and angels. It has been estimated that about five hundred souls were sanctified, and not less than two hundred sinners converted. In one *private* tent alone twenty-five were reported as being sanctified; and in the public tents, in the "Bower," and at the altar.

The work went steadily forward, increasing day by day, until on the last day a climax was reached. What a day of power! How the legions of witnessing angels must have exulted! In the morning love-feast in two hours, three hundred and twenty-five testified; and, if the meeting had been extended, I doubt not one thousand testimonies would have been recorded. It was wonderful. Tears, songs, shouts were prevalent; hundreds rose and, in token of realizing in that moment full salvation, lifted up their right hand. In the afternoon, after the sermon, ministers and people prostrated themselves at the altar in living consecration, and the fire descended. One minister was cast down upon the ground under the mighty working of the Holy Ghost, and many others felt a shock from the battery. . . .

In the evening, a deeply solemn scene was presented. The sacrament of the Lord's Supper was administered, eight hundred participating. The multitude looked on, were awed, were melted. A canopy of celestial glory covered the encampment. Then the people, headed by the ministers, marched around the ground singing triumphal songs. They returned to the altar-work. About one hundred, the larger part penitents, knelt before the altar. The power was again manifested gloriously. Not less than fifty, I judged, were converted. The battle was prosecuted all night in the tents, each hour signalized by new victories.

Thus ended the most memorable encampment of modern times. Ended, did I say? Its result shall never end. The tide of salvation thus set in motion will sweep over the States of our great Union, and even visit distant lands, bearing upon its bosoms a rich fruitage of Gospel blessing. Brothers, sisters in Christ Jesus, what shall we say in view of this marvelous triumph of holiness? We will take up the sublime doxology of the great Apostle to the Gentiles: *"Now unto Him that is able to do exceeding abundantly above all that we ask or think, according to the power that worketh in us—unto Him be glory in the Church by Christ Jesus, throughout all ages, world without end. Amen"* [Eph. 3:20-21].

I close this imperfect sketch by humbly invoking every friend of holiness, in grateful commemoration of this *Jerusalem-manifestation,* at the earliest moment after reading these lines, to enter into the closet, and upon their knees, with a fervent heart, breathe into the ear of Heaven the above apostolic doxology; and let the united company of the saved say, *"Amen!"*

Newark, NJ, July 29, 1867

MISSION SUPERINTENDENTS AND
LAY OBSERVER COMMEND BEGINNING OF
SPANISH-LANGUAGE MINISTRY IN LATIN AMERICA

Source: William Goodfellow, "South America," Missionary Advocate 23/5
(20 August 1867): 39.

Buenos Ayres [*sic*], Argentina
May 29, 1867

On last Sunday night Brother [John F.] Thomson delivered his first sermon in
this city in Spanish. The church was full. Of course not many of our own people
[English-speaking foreign nationals] were present, but a large number of natives
were there who heard their first Protestant sermon. There was marked attention
and every prospect of good.

We have no Spanish Hymn Book, but we had the hymns printed on slips of paper
as a programme, and the organ and choir led the large concourse to the tunes of
Hebron, Mozart, and Old Hundred. Brother Thomson's fluency and self-
command with a new language on his lips surprised every one, and only the most
critical could detect the fact that he was not using his native language. Next Sunday
night is our missionary meeting night, and after that we hope to occupy Sunday
evening with Spanish preaching. . . .

WILLIAM GOODFELLOW

Source: William Goodfellow, "South America," Missionary Advocate 23/12
(17 March 1868): 92.

Buenos Ayres, Argentina
[Fall 1867/Spring 1868]

The Spanish service in Buenos Ayres has grown steadily since the first prayers
were offered in its behalf. At the first communion nine natives joined on proba-

tion, and others have been added since. The service in the Spanish language has been very largely attended on Sunday evenings. The Spanish ladies are attracted to them, which to them are new services in their own language. . . .

WILLIAM GOODFELLOW

Source: "Report from South America," Methodist Episcopal Church, Foreign Missionary Society, Annual Report (1870), 39.

Buenos Ayres, Argentina
December 31, 1870

In arranging the [Spanish] work at the beginning of the year it was thought best that Brother Thomson should reside in Montevideo [Uruguay] and devote most of his time to that city, making a visit to Buenos Ayres twice each quarter. A Spanish priest, Brother [Jose J.] Rial, who has been converted and has united with us, is preaching to the Spanish congregation here during the interval of Brother Thomson's visits. By this arrangement the interest here has been maintained, and the mission in Montevideo has been made a success.

The Spanish congregations are large, and appear to be deeply interested. A number have united with the Church on probation, and others, having served out their probation, have been admitted to full membership. At the last sacramental service there were not less than sixty communicants.

In our quarterly love-feasts we unite the English and Spanish charges, and give permission to each one to speak in whatever language he chooses. The speaking is principally in English and Spanish, though now and then an experience is related in French or Italian. The singing is in English and Spanish. This mingling of tongues produces no distraction or confusion, but rather reminds one of the day of Pentecost, when each one heard the Gospel in the tongue wherein he was born. These meetings have proved exceedingly pleasant and profitable to us all.

In connection with the Spanish charge is a Sabbath-school with an average attendance of about sixty, about half of whom are adults. . . .

HENRY G. JACKSON

Source: "Report from South America," Methodist Episcopal Church, Foreign Missionary Society, Annual Report (1872), 50.

Montevideo, Uruguay
"To a Lady in Massachusetts"
[Late 1871/Early 1872]

You will understand that for me to be extremely interested in a Methodist minister, he must be something more than common, and Mr. Thomson is something more than common. He is one of the most sincere Christians, one of the most hard-working missionaries, I ever saw or heard of. And, moreover, he is a most eloquent and powerful preacher. No man could be more perfectly fitted for the place than he, for he is exactly suited, and the work he has done proves it. He speaks most perfect Spanish, and fully understands the people among whom he labors. When he first came here and thundered forth his denunciations against the corruptions of the Church of Rome, his life was threatened, poison was tried, and in front of my own house a pistol was snapped at him; but he grappled with the man, and almost unassisted, had him taken to the lock-up. Nothing of this intimidated him; he worked on, and has achieved a great victory. He has not only built up quite a Church, but he has largely changed public opinion. From time to time he has had public discussions with the most learned priests here; and, at first, he was the one disturbed and hissed, but now all that is changed. Only last evening he had another such discussion with three priests, and he carried them with him as the wind sways a tree. The applause was tremendous, and the priests only obtained a hearing at the most earnest intercession of Mr. Thomson himself. The influence of the Church of Rome here received a heavy blow last night.

Now I see by the papers that the interest in Foreign Missions has greatly abated in the United States, and I have heard that they contemplate giving up this [mission]. There could be no greater mistake. Fifty missionaries in Asia or Africa could not do the real service Mr. Thomson is doing here. He has mixed a leaven that is surely leavening the whole lump, and this is a Spanish Catholic place.

UNIDENTIFIED LAY WOMAN/MAN

EDITOR DETAILS TUESDAY MEETING AT THE PALMER HOME IN NEW YORK CITY

Source: "The Tuesday Meeting," Guide to Holiness 54/1 *(July 1868): 33-35.*

Meeting for the Promotion of Holiness at the residence of Dr. Palmer, 23 Saint Mark's Place [New York City], near the Bible House, at 2.30 o'clock every Tuesday afternoon.

The meeting as usual was largely attended, every available spot of hall and stairway being occupied at an early hour. After the usual opening exercises, [hymn/s, prayer, Scripture, possibly Luke 24:44-53 or Acts 1:1-8]

SISTER P.[Palmer] said she had a very special desire, and had presented a very special prayer, that that meeting might be under the direction of the Holy Spirit; so that they might realize as they sung "Spirit of burning come." That spirit is here. Would every one be answerable to the direction of the Spirit without questioning? It might not be amiss to say, then, that the meeting was free for all, but yet there were boundaries which the Spirit would set, such as that we should confine ourselves to the object of the meeting, and perhaps it would not be in accordance with the Spirit for any one to occupy a long time. They came there, she thought, as did the disciples of whom they read in the opening lesson from the Scriptures, for the outpouring of the Holy Spirit, for we live under the dispensation of the Spirit. Christ commanded those disciples to tarry till the Holy Spirit should come. How long may we have to tarry? They had to tarry for a special reason, which may not apply to us. The types and shadows had to be completed. As soon as the day of Pentecost was come, the Holy Ghost came. There is now no reason on the part of God for delay. If there is any delay, it must be on the part of the creature. When He [Christ] bowed His head and died, it was for every one. They might interfere and prevent the answer to prayers. Will that fire consume the sacrifice? Will it be accepted unless they bind the sacrifice to the altar? They could bring the lame, the torn, or the blind. Let all ask God to look through them with His flaming eyes, and be very careful what we ask, and expect to have what they asked for.

> "Look through me with thine eyes of flame,
> The clouds and darkness chase,
> And tell me what by sin I am,
> And what I am by grace."

["Come, thou omniscient Son of Man," Charles Wesley, *A Collection of Hymns for the use of the Methodist Episcopal Church* (1836), no. 327, pp. 282-83. Full original text in John Wesley, *Works* (Bicentennial edition), 7:675-76.]

She believed the prayer that had been offered was from the inspiration of the Spirit. A man who was very seriously diseased, applied for relief to several physicians and surgeons, and there seemed but one voice, that he was incurable, except he should submit to a very serious, and what might be a fatal, surgical operation, he could not live. The surgeons were so fearful that it might be fatal, that they did not advise him to submit to the operation; but nature clings to life, and there was no hope of living without it. The surgeons understood it, and told him, if they paused at any point in the operation, he might know it was fatal, but for some unforeseen circumstance they did pause, he fully expected to die. But when they began again, though it caused the most excruciating agony, he said it was the most luxurious feeling he ever experienced. The result was he recovered.

> "The sharpness of that two-edged sword,
> Enable me to endure;
> Till bold to say my hallowing Lord,
> Hath wrought a perfect cure."

["Deepen the wound thy hands have made," Charles Wesley, *A Collection of Hymns for the use of the Methodist Episcopal Church* (1836), no. 363, pp. 312. Full original text in John Wesley, *Works* (Bicentennial edition), 7:528.]

Let all get the offering on the altar. Sacrifice meant something, and that which costs nothing does not sacrifice. Let them look upon the entire life, and present it to God. She would have them put every motive of earthly ambition; she would look ahead and see all the future of earthly existence, and then put all upon the altar. They might pray and ask amiss. O, that this might be a time of special consecration. A sister said one week before, "That they were all on common ground. None could save themselves, not one of them for one moment, but through Christ." They could not be saved for five minutes to come, any more than they could inhale the vital air, and breathe for five minutes to come. Let us remember Christ will not accept an imperfect sacrifice. Do not mock God by bringing such an one. Get such an offering on the altar as will please him. Put your reputation on the altar. You say, "I can't be singular for Christ;" or "I can't endure what others may say." O, may you be consciously answerable to all the demands of the Spirit upon you.

A BROTHER D. did not rise to tell them of his happiness, but he was at rest. Two weeks ago he left his missionary work to come to the meeting, because, "Man's extremity is God's opportunity." When there he desired not to go away until God had sanctified him by the power of the holy Ghost, and he now arose to say God gave it to him that afternoon. He did not seek it for happiness' sake, but to be fitted for the Master's work. While going from garret to cellar his heart was filled with love, so that he could have thrown his arms around the dear, erring souls. He left that he must come here to tell of the reality of this experience, and he desired prayer for his wife, who did not believe in this blessing, that her heart might be broken to pieces, and that she may be led to go from place to place, showing what a dear Saviour we have found.

SISTER R. said there were some passages that our blessed Saviour spake that seem like diamonds. There is so much in a diamond that worldly people say it is useful to own them. They had been living where the diamonds lay, though we may never have known it before. It is perfectly safe to venture all on Christ. He says, "If thine eye be single, thy whole body shall be full of light" [Matthew 6:22]. That had been a diamond to her that day. It had been as he said it. She had but one eye; and but one being to please, and that was Jesus; only one person to serve, here or hereafter, that is Jesus, and in doing so found perfect rest, not one of sitting down, but when going out and coming in. She took just what God gave her.

Those of them who were parents knew how their love went forth to the children, for God's love stretches out further than any other, for she did not know of any parent who would dare to trust a child with "more than you can ask or think" [Ephesians 3:20]. She thought it the leaven of which Br. B. spoke had been spreading, and her heart said, "I don't want to go to heaven alone." O, that every one there would just take Jesus that hour. She went into a meeting the other day where she sat pretty much alone, except one or two lovely spirits, and a room full of others, and said, "Lord, fortify thy truth and stop all wrong willings of these souls. But how can it be done? By Jesus' own words." If they would be fed, they must take the word of Jesus. In some respects all had been taught wrongly, and in many things were believing what the Devil said,—an instance of which was that a soul is really waiting for God. She might be standing on the sidewalk and trying to get into a stage, but she must go forward to get in. Thus with an old lady at the meeting referred to, who said to her, "I am now old, and for many years have been looking and looking, and thought I was waiting for God to come; but I have been misapprehending God, and do not give up to him;" and then she said, "I will, I will." At first she could not say this, because she thought she must wait for God. But God was *beseeching* us: He *wants* to save us. He wants us to be in a salvable condition. He only wants us to accept the offers of Divine mercy. The terms are, "My oxen and fatlings are killed, will you come and eat?" [Matthew 22:4].

WOMEN CIRCULATE "APPEAL TO THE LADIES OF THE MEC" REGARDING FOREIGN MISSIONS

Source: "Appeal to the Ladies of the Methodist Episcopal Church," The Heathen Woman's Friend. *1/1 (June 1869): 1-3.*

An earnest desire to develop among the ladies of our Church greater interest and activity in our Missions, together with the firm conviction that the pressing needs of our Foreign Missions demand our immediate attention, led, in the month of March, to the organization of the Women's Foreign Missionary Society.

The object of this Society is to meet, as far as possible, the great want experienced by our Eastern Missionaries, of Christian women to labor among the women of those heathen lands. Few of us have ever realized how complete is the darkness which envelopes them, and how insufficient have been the efforts hitherto made to admit the light of the Gospel to their benighted hearts and homes. Forbidden by the customs of their country to seek for themselves this light, or to receive instruction at the hands of our missionaries, they are accessible only to Christian teachers of their own sex. The wives of our missionaries have done all that they could. Many of them, in addition to their own families, have the care of large zenana schools, which they have organized and in which they are daily busied; still they have made earnest endeavors to carry the knowledge of Christ to their sisters by personal visits and labors at their homes. What wonder that, in so many instances, physical strength has failed under such constant and great exertions, and the oppressing consciousness of the magnitude of the work. Their labors have been, however, by no means without reward. Many of their heathen sisters are awaking from their ignorance and apathy, and are eagerly asking after the way of life. These calls for help our missionaries are often utterly unable to answer, because they are already over-burdened.

Dear Sisters! shall we not recognize, in this emergency, God's voice as speaking to us—for who can so well do this work as we? Does it not seem as though the responsibility were thus laid directly upon us? And shall we shrink from bearing it?

We well know how close is the relation of the mother to the child, and how important it is that the mother's heart be filled with love and grace of God if her child is to grow up under Divine influence and be guided by Divine wisdom. How then can we more successfully coöperate with our missionaries, and better insure the rapid extension of the knowledge of the truth as it is in Jesus, than by opening the hearts of the mothers to the purifying and saving influences of God's love? We know too how inestimable is the value, and how incalculable the influence of a pure Christian home; and if the influences of such homes are so indispensable in a Christian land, what must be their importance among a people, the depth of whose degradation is, as we are often assured, altogether beyond our realization?

There are many encouraging indications that the Lord has prepared the way for the commencement of this work. Wherever the idea has been suggested, East or West, it has met with a cheerful and ready response. Through the agency of Brother and Sister E. W. Parker, of our Mission in India, who are shortly to return to their chosen field, auxiliary societies have been organized in several places, and the work entered upon with hearty zeal. At the first regular meeting of the parent Society after the adoption of the Constitution, subscriptions to the amount of one hundred and ninety-three dollars were reported. Of this sum, fifty dollars were contributed by one lady for the support of a Bible reader in India for one year. Prominent friends of the missionary cause throughout the Church, have hailed the movement with joy, and given it a hearty God-speed. From these and many similar facts, it seems evident that in the good Providence of God, the mind and heart of the Church are ripe for the movement now undertaken.

The present time seems also eminently favorable for such an undertaking. The discussions and exertions of the Church during its centenary year, brought home to us all an unwonted realization of its magnitude and power, and our proportionate responsibilities. The associations then formed by the ladies were most admirably adapted to train them for subsequent harmonious coöperation in other Christian labors.

In like manner, the efforts of our sex during our late war exhibited, as never before, their latent and unemployed power to plan and labor for great and noble ends. These labors being now so happily terminated, Providence has freed our hands for new and yet grander undertakings.

If further encouragement were needed, it would be abundantly supplied by the striking success of similar organizations in other denominations. Such societies have been in operation in other countries for over thirty years, and one in this country, organized in 1861, has now in its service no less than seventy-five Bible readers, has eight hundred pupils under instruction in zenanas, and fourteen schools for girls. Another, organized a little more than a year ago, has already raised over five thousand dollars, and is supporting seven missionaries and eleven Bible readers, in fields occupied by the American Board. If in churches of less membership than our own, so much has been achieved by woman's hand, may not we, by united prayerful effort and God's blessing, accomplish a glorious work?

Christian sisters, may we not count upon your coöperation in carrying forward this great work? We believe that God will bless it to the uplifting, enlightenment, and salvation of thousands now in the shadow of death. The prime and immediate necessity is the organization of branch societies throughout the country, wherever our churches have a female membership sufficiently large to sustain an association. Accompanying this appeal will be found the draft of a constitution for such auxiliary societies. Let every reader of these lines take counsel with her own heart and with those around her, and determine to do her utmost in thus furthering Christ's cause. Limited means need be no obstacle in the way of joining in this enterprise, for surely there can be but very few among us who cannot contribute two cents weekly to aid its progress. But let it be clearly understood that on no account ought the regular Church missionary contribution be lessened. Not one dollar should be taken from those, for the constantly increasing wants of our missions are yearly rendering a larger sum necessary for distribution through the Society at New York. A moment's reflection must show, however, that too many of us have been personally interested. How few of us have ever practiced self-denial in our personal expenditures, in order to add our share to the support of the missionary work!

Apart from all considerations of duty to others, it will be profitable to ourselves to unite together in such associations as are contemplated by this Society. No one can feel an active interest in any matter with which they are not familiar. The stated meetings of our auxiliary societies, if properly conducted, cannot fail to impart to the members much information respecting different mission fields. To aid in furnishing such information for the use of such societies, it is proposed by our Executive Committee to issue a monthly paper, containing the latest intelligence from our missions, and particularly contributions respecting the claims, methods, and progress of the work among heathen women. Several of the wives of our missionaries have expressed their readiness, and indeed their desire, to assist us by their communications. This organ will be published at a low rate, in order that it may find the widest possible dissemination. Any information respecting this paper or any interest of the Society, will be gladly communicated on application to either of the Corresponding Secretaries.

Our appeal is now before you. We commend it to your prayerful attention. We are confident that you will cordially welcome and heartily participate in this movement. Sustained by your coöperation and earnest prayers, we cannot fail to achieve glorious results.

"God be merciful unto us and bless us; and cause his face to shine upon us;
"That thy way may be known upon earth, thy saving health among all nations.
"Let the people praise thee, O God; let *all* the people praise thee.
"God shall bless us, and all the *ends* of the *earth* shall fear him."

[Psalm 67:1-3, 7]

EDITOR GILBERT HAVEN COMMENDS MAGGIE NEWTON VAN COTT AS LICENSED PREACHER

Source: Gilbert Haven, "Rev. Mrs. Van Cott,"
Zion's Herald (28 October 1869): 510.

It is a coincidence worthy of note that the first regular preacher in the Methodist Episcopal Church began her work in the Centenary year [i.e., 1866]. It is the beginning of a new era, or is it an exuberance that must disappear as soon as it appears, "sicken, or ere it blossoms?" This question cannot be fully answered yet. The presence of this lady creates debate. Her success, and that of her following sisters, will conclude it. She came to this city [Boston] on invitation of Rev. J. N. Mars, whose Christian hospitalities she has enjoyed during her visit. Her personal appearance is prepossessing. She is large, well formed, with finely chiseled features, a soft, light eye, that under the excitement of discourse, flames with an unusual brilliancy; a voice of great volume for a lady, though not unlike Fanny Kemble's in strength and tone. She is dressed in plain black, wears a widow's hat of black and in her costume, as well as manners, bespeaks the lady of breeding. She is as energetic and demonstrative as an actress, and has much dramatic power. This is her forte as a popular speaker. She uses her arm and foot, and even fist, as freely as the most earnest of her pulpit brothers, and her words of rebuke ring out sharp and hot, while those of entreaty are soft and cooing as a mother's over a babe. She reads her hymns or declaims them with immense energy; sometimes with more than is needful. But one has rarely known their fullness of meaning till they hear her pronounce them. "Jesus, lover of my soul," is addressed to Him with streaming eyes and a tearful voice. "O for a faith that will not shrink," rings like a trumpet from her lips. In the flights of her passionate declamation or fervid description, she reminds one of Jean d'Arc. As she said, "I could die for Christ." It was easy to see in her rapt eye, firm lip, thin, yet strong nostril, and poised form, the inspired leader of the French armies, with the fagots piled around her, awaiting the torch and crown. She carries through all the exercises, directing the prayer-meeting, going through the congregation, imploring sinners to come to Jesus. She is much in prayer, and her bearing at home, and in public, is quiet and lady-like, except that in her discourse she is no more humble-voiced and meek-gliding than is Fanny Kemble in reading "Lady

Macbeth," or Parepa singing the "Star Spangled Banner," or Jenny Lind, or Ristori, or Rachel, or Anna Dickinson, or any other great public woman. She, then, is set for success. She will win, if possible, souls to Christ. Her success is great. One soon forgets whether she is a man or woman. It is an earnest pleader for Christ with sinners to whom he is listening. Men and women yield to her burning entreaties. A judge's lady knelt by the side of her colored brothers and sisters at the altar, seeking a common Saviour. She rises magnificently above the mean prejudice whose mud and miasma are not yet abated. When a colored youth came trembling forward, "Come, my son," is the inviting welcome he receives from her lips. She has done great service to the cause of Christ in this city by this contempt of its unchristianity—a victory over herself the more remarkable, in that she is of New York birth and breeding, and hence is naturally more bound with this chain [racism] than those living in this atmosphere. She preached in the Union Church, Charlestown, to a great multitude and with almost unanimous approval. To all who object to her ministry, it is enough to say, that God evidently does not object to it. He has already honored her in the few years of her labor with hundreds of converts. His sons whom He calls, desert His work for the insurance office, the lumber mill, and the broker's curb-stone. It is time that He thrust out his daughters. In this age, when all the world runs after great female actors, singers and talkers, when even false religions are putting their female teachers into the pulpit, and Spiritualists are bewildering thousands every Sabbath with their abominable sophistries, we rejoice that God has raised up this woman, and sent her forth, against her protest, with His message to sinful man and woman, "Repent, and believe on the Lord Jesus Christ, and ye shall be saved." A new thing is again come to pass: "A women shall compass a man" [Jer. 31:22]. The very appeals of this preacher, strange as it may appear, are more effective upon the male portion of her congregation than upon the female. When her voice says, "My son," it sounds to many a wanderer like the voice of his mother. The problem how to bring men to Christ may yet be solved in this way by the Holy Ghost. The very preponderance of women in our churches may be due to the fact that all our preachers are men. If God shall raise up Deborahs and Lydias in equal numbers, the balance may be restored. "Send by whom Thou wilt send," should be every honest Christian's cry. Let no one worry if God's ark does not rock as he may approve. To New York Methodism the Church may yet owe a new debt of gratitude. Out of her hearty faith comes this messenger of salvation. The Presiding Elder, Rev. Mr. Ferguson, who had the courage to change "his" to "her" in the certificate of a local preacher, and thus dare the frowns of his [New York] Conference [colleagues], will yet receive their blessing for his courage to see and follow the will of God. Many of the ministers have cordially welcomed her, and several engagements with our leading churches are already made. May she be kept humble and holy, and do yet greater things for her Lord and Master.

JENNY FOWLER WILLING PONDERS WHAT AMERICAN WOMEN SHALL DO NEXT

Source: Jenny Fowler Willing, "What Shall American Women Do Next?" Zion's Herald *(26 May 1870): 242.*

The first generation of American women helped immensely at the work of conquering homes from the wilderness, and laying the foundations of the New World civilization. There were giantesses of energy and patient endurance in those days, as well as in the later time, when the base stones of the Great Republic were laid. It would be impossible to estimate the part the women of our day have borne in the Herculien [*sic*] labor of clearing the land of "the sum of all villainies" [slavery].

Women have measureless energy. Their moral sentiments, usually active and earnest, crowd them to do something to make the world better. Only God knows the bitterness of the secret cry that goes up from the heart of thousands of women. The shipwrecked going down, within call! The breakers beating them to death, under our eyes, and we so helpless to help them! Christ pity us!

Conventionalisms hedge women in. Society offers a premium for fine toilets and superficial culture, soft hands and hard hearts. She is a brave woman who can play Arnold von Winkelried [legendary Swiss warrior] upon the pikes of public opinion. She is a strong woman who does not make herself ridiculous in the attempt. She is a womanly woman who will not snarl at the mean men who sneer at her, or claw the silly women who make faces at her. He is an idiot who would ignore or deny woman's energy and capabilities with the statistics of the Sanitary Commission [predecessor of the American Red Cross] staring him in the face. The [Civil] War was an immense liberating scheme, partially unfettering two sets of people. Those described in the Emancipation Proclamation [black Americans] are free in form. They will be free in fact when society lifts from them the nightmare of caste. In its sore need the country was driven to recognize the worth of woman's work. The war was not a bad investment, though it cost fearfully. Yet we shall not get the good God means to come of it till we work into our national life the meaning of that saying of Paul "There is neither bond nor free, there is neither male nor female, for ye are all one in Christ Jesus" [Galatians 3:28].

The question is fairly before us. What shall American women do next? Fidgety conservatives may flutter and worry. It is quite too late to turn women back to their frizzing and ruffling and gossip. The spirit of work has been raised: it cannot be laid [aside] by frowns, scolding, or candies. The *role* of [the] pretty plaything is at an end. Work is the word, and work it must be. It was thought well enough for women to seize the ropes, grasp the pump handles and throw every ounce of strength upon them, when the ship was aleak and drifting upon the rocks. No matter then about the women keeping silence in the churches. Their voices might be heard the wide land over reading, singing, talking, pleading for the soldiers. Now that the peril is past, it is not so easy to hush them down to parlor warblings and nursery lyrics. The elephant is drawn. What next? Beat his brains out? Not easily done. And then we can't afford it. A thousand times better train him to work. When a force breaks loose upon the world, it is well if the Church has the sense and strength to master it, give it Christian baptism, and see it at work for Christ.

The questions that stir the world's pulses now are all moral questions. Conquest, lust for gold, commercial rights have had each its turn at the lever that upheaves social systems. The issues of the hour are not high or low tariff, finance, or national prowess. They are such as these: shall men poison each other at so much a glass? Sabbath or no Sabbath; relating to civilization, human rights, Christianity; of necessity laying their hand upon the life of the Church. For self-defense (which means aggression), she [the church] needs every help she can conscript. She cannot afford to dispense with one iota of the energies of her women. Let her face this matter fairly. Let her open avenues for the capabilities of women. Let her utilize their energy lest it overleap the barriers conservative croakers would build before it, and become a harm instead of a blessing. The Methodist Church, by giving women a vote upon the Lay Delegation question [in 1869], recognizes their individual interest in Church progress, their right to an opinion, and the incompetency of men to express it for them. I think some members of the [1868] General Conference who voted for this [church-wide referendum including women] with a laugh at the novelty or nonsense of the thing, were working better than they dreamed. And the end is not yet. There is plenty of Church work that women can do as well as, or better than, men. Their tact and intuitions specially fit them for religious visiting, personal efforts to lead people to Christ, the instruction of children, and the care of young converts. They can be Bible readers, missionaries, class-leaders, and Bible class teachers. Where God has endowed them with the dignity to command attention, the voice and language to embody their pity for the perishing, they certainly can speak [preach] to the starving masses about the great Salvation. There is enough Church and Scripture precedent for all this to satisfy any who are fearful of the innovation.

Christian men and women may do far greater work for the Master than they have ever yet dreamed of. It is high time they awake to understand this. Too many of us have bounded our sympathies and efforts by our own little Church records. Our prayers for the conversion of the world have been "the drowsy mutterings of half-awakened souls talking in their sleep." Infinite resources are within our grasp. In the name of God, let us lay hold of every right thing that has power in it, and use it to conquer the world for our King, even Jesus.

Otis Gibson Begins Mission to Chinese Americans in San Francisco

Source: "Chinese Domestic [Mission]," Fifty Second Annual Report of the Missionary Society of the Methodist Episcopal Church for the Year 1870 (New York: Printed for the Society, 1871), 123-27. Excerpt.

Commenced 1867.

During some twenty-three years or more last past but four hundred and fourteen Chinese have come into the port of New York, and, being scattered in various obscure localities of the great metropolis, have received but comparatively little notice except from our city missionaries and occasional visits from Rev. M. [Moses] C. White, whose old love for these people impels to their abodes whether "naked, sick, or in prison," for in all these conditions he has sought and found them in his visits to New York.

California is the field of our actual Church mission-work to these people. In the city of San Francisco, according to latest statistics, there are between eleven and twelve thousand of them. For the purpose of effectually prosecuting our work in that city an edifice is now completed of which we insert . . . a description from Rev. O. Gibson, missionary. This building is intended to be a center and home for the mission. According to the rule for administering Domestic Missions, it will be under the care of the California Conference, within whose bounds it lies. The eyes of different Churches in America are turned toward these strange people—still more strange in our land than in their own—and there is a strong spontaneous movement toward sending Christian missionaries to them. Our Church has made a well-directed beginning, as will be seen above. This new missionary movement ought to increase the missionary spirit of our Churches, and increase also the con-tributions to our missionary treasury. Brother Gibson's original plan was:

1. To organize every-where Sunday and evening schools for gratuitous instruc-tion in the English language.

2. To open a central school in San Francisco, in which the Chinese can secure a complete English education under positive religious influence.

3. The engraving represents "The Chinese Mission Institute," for the use of our mission in San Francisco, on Washington-street, between Stockton and Powell. The

building is fifty-six feet from on Washington-street, seventy feet deep, and three stories high above the basement. The basement will be for rental purposes. On the main floor there are three school-rooms, nineteen by thirty-five feet, with folding-doors between, so that when desirable they can all be thrown into one room for general school exercises or religious services.

On the second floor there are two school-rooms, with folding-doors between, a long corridor, rooms for the family of the native assistant, and a library.

The third floor is designed for a female department. There are also a parsonage for the family of the superintendent, and . . . rooms for the assistant teachers. The lot is fifty-six by one hundred and thirty-seven and a half feet, and has a narrow street on either side, running through to Jackson-street. The location is favorable for the work designed.

Our friends have noticed that one of our native preachers has been transferred from the Chinese work at Foochow to minister to his countrymen under the supervision of Brother Gibson. He arrived in San Francisco on the 16th day of January, 1871. On the 2d day of January, 1871, Brother Gibson opened a school in the new building, and wrote as under date of the 19th of the same month:

Up to this time our numbers have been small, but a considerable interest is awakened in the public sentiment, and, after the Chinese New Year, we hope to have an increased number of scholars.

In his Annual Report Brother Gibson says:

The various Sunday-schools for Chinese have been prosecuted with more or less vigor, and with encouraging results. Many of the scholars are now able to read portions of the Bible, hymns, etc. Some of them repeat in English the Lord's Prayer, Ten Commandments, Apostles' Creed, and portions of the Scriptures. This branch of labor suffers for want of regular, devoted teachers.

Carrying out Bishop Kingsley's plan, the native preacher, Hu Sing Mi, transferred to this work by Bishop Ames, has arrived, and entered upon his work. We hope that his wife may be of some service among the Chinese women of this country.

[Brother Gibson makes a tender allusion to the removal of a lamb—"Eddie"— from his flock by the Good Shepherd. We sigh with him.] The report goes on to say:

We hope to make the schools a great power, but these must be developed from small and slow beginnings. With regard to school enterprise, Dr. H. N. Scudder, at the late session of the Presbyterian Synod in San Francisco, said: "We Presbyterians ought at once to have a Chinese school or college in this city costing not less than $50,000. The Methodists, with Rev. O. Gibson as missionary and agent, have set us a good example, and I rejoice in their prosperity and in his success."

I ask the prayers of the Church for the special outpouring of the Holy Spirit upon this mission during the year.

FORMER SLAVE MEMBERS OF THE MECS REQUEST PERMISSION TO ORGANIZE SEPARATE CHURCH

Source: Othal Hawthorne Lakey, The History of the CME Church, rev. ed.
(Memphis, Tenn.: CME Publishing House, 1996), 733-34.

Report of the Committee on Church Organization of the organizing General Conference of the Colored Methodist Episcopal Church in America, submitted December 16, 1870, by I. H. Anderson

The Committee on Church Organization beg leave to report that they have had the subject under careful consideration, and they are unanimously of the opinion that while we gratefully acknowledge the obligations we are under to the white brethren of the M.E. Church, South for what they have done for us, as a people (who by service to the country have brought them under reciprocal obligation); yet the time has come in our history when we believe it will be for the glory of God and the best interest of the Church we represent that we have a distinct and independent organization—this having been amply provided for by the General Conference of the M.E.Church, South in 1866, resolving that: "When two or more Annual Conferences shall be formed, let our Bishops advise and assist them in organizing a separate General Conference jurisdiction for themselves if they so desire and the Bishops deem it expedient in accordance with the doctrines and discipline of our Church and bearing the same relation to the General Conferences as the Annual Conferences do to each other."

Five Annual Conferences having been formed and the Bishops in their address to the General Conference in 1870 said, "It is our purpose unless otherwise ordered by your body to call a General Conference to be held next winter for the purpose of organizing them [African American preachers and lay members] into an entirely separate Church and thus enable them to become their own guides and governors." This General Conference at Memphis, Tennessee in 1870 resolved that the action of the last General Conference in reference to an ultimate organization of the Colored People is complete and therefore no additional legislation is necessary to the end intended. They therefore appointed this, the 16th day of December, 1870, for the meeting of this General Conference.

Whereas the Methodist Episcopal Church in America was the name first given to the Methodist Church by its Founder Mr. John Wesley; and

Whereas we are a part of that same Church never having seceded or separated from the Church but in the division of the Church by the General Conference in 1844 we regularly belonged to the South, and now as we belong to the Colored race, we simply prefix our color to the name as we are in fact a part of the original Church and as old as any in America.

Therefore, Resolved that our name be the Colored Methodist Episcopal Church in America.

Resolved 2nd, That while we thus claim for ourselves an antiquity running as far back as any other branch of the Methodist Family on this side of the Atlantic Ocean, and while we claim for ourselves all that we concede to others of ecclesiastical and civil rights, we shall ever hold in grateful remembrance what the M.E. Church, South, has done for us, that we shall ever cherish the kindest feelings toward the Bishops and General Conference for giving us all that they enjoy of religious principles, the ordination of our Deacons and Elders, and at this General Conference one Bishop or Bishops will be ordained by them to the highest office known in the Church. No other Colored organization has thus been established in this land. We most sincerely pray, earnestly desire, and confidently expect that there will ever be the kindest feelings cherished toward the M.E. Church, South, and hope that our conduct will be such as to merit and receive the warmest sympathy and support of the Church which acted so kindly toward us in aiding us in this our time of need.

Resolved 3rd, That we request the Bishops to organize our General Conference, upon the basis of the *Discipline of the M. E. Church, South* in its entire doctrine, discipline, and economy, making only such verbal changes as may be necessary to conform to our name and peculiarities of our condition.

I. [Isaac] H. ANDERSON, Chairman

GENERAL CONFERENCE ASSUMES OVERSIGHT OF GENERAL AGENCIES

Source: "The Report of the Special Committee on the Relation of Benevolent Institutions of the Church to the General Conference," Methodist Episcopal Church, Journal of the General Conference (1872), 295-99. Excerpts.

[May 21, 1872, fourth day, Bishop Matthew Simpson, presiding.]

REPORT OF COMMITTEE ON BENEVOLENT SOCIETIES.

The special Committee "appointed to consider and report concerning the relations of our various benevolent societies to the authorities of the Church, and whether any action is necessary, and if so what, to place them under the full control of the General Conference," has considered the subject stated, and now

REPORT

that there are five benevolent societies which have received the sanction of the General Conference, and with which it is more or less remotely connected, to wit:

1. The Missionary Society of the Methodist Episcopal Church, incorporated by the Legislature of New York;

2. The Church Extension Society of the Methodist Episcopal Church, incorporated by the Legislature of Pennsylvania;

3. The Board of Education of the Methodist Episcopal Church, incorporated by the Legislature of New York;

4. The Sunday-School Union of the Methodist Episcopal Church, incorporated by the Legislature of New York; and,

5. The Tract Society of the Methodist Episcopal Church, incorporated by the Legislature of New York.

The corporation organized under a general law of Ohio, known as the Trustees of the Methodist Episcopal Church of the United States, does not seem to come within the inquiry directed to be made by the Committee.

The two corporations, constituting what is known as "the Book Concern," do not fall within the inquiry directed to be made by the Committee.

The Chartered Fund is controlled by a corporation, but it is not a benevolent society within the meaning of the resolution under which the Committee was appointed.

The "Freedmen's Aid Society of the Methodist Episcopal Church," incorporated under a general law of the State of Ohio, is a benevolent society, but it is not in any respect under the jurisdiction or control of the General Conference.

THE BOARD OF EDUCATION

The government of the corporation known as "The Board of Education of the Methodist Episcopal Church," and the management of its property, business, and affairs, are vested in a board of twelve trustees, of whom six are by its charter required to be ministers, including two Bishops, and six to be laymen, all so arranged that the terms of office of four of the trustees expire and are to be filled by the General Conference at each quadrennial session. This arrangement, secured by the charter, places the corporation under full control of the General Conference, and no further action is necessary for that purpose.

THE MISSIONARY SOCIETY.

The management and disposition of the affairs and property of the corporation known as "The Missionary Society of the Methodist Episcopal Church" are by its charter vested in a Board of Managers to be annually elected at a meeting of the Society, to be called for that purpose, and held in the City of New York at such time and on such notice as the Board of Managers, for the time being, shall previously prescribe.

The members of the Board are elected by members of the Society, and the members of the Society are those persons who become such by the payment of twenty dollars or more to its funds.

The General Conference has no legal connection with the Society, except only that by the charter it is provided that the Corresponding Secretaries of said Society shall be elected by the General Conference; and shall hold their offices for four years, and until their successors are elected, and that in case of vacancy the Bishops shall elect their successors to hold till the ensuing General Conference.

But as the whole management is vested in the Board elected by members of the Society, the Corresponding Secretaries are powerless to represent any interest of the Church or of the Conference independent of the will of the Board. It is evident, too, that the multitude of members of the Society, scattered widely in all parts of the country, either cannot or will not participate in the election of a Board of Managers. It is equally evident that local combinations are liable to be formed each year to change the management of the corporation, and obtain control of its great resources. We do not express or intimate any doubt of the judicious and faithful management of the Society, but it is high time to close the door against the possibility of danger in the future. . . .

The General Conference, as the supreme legislative authority of the Church, and having in charge all its great interests for the diffusion of Christian civilization, should have a controlling power in all the missionary operations carried on in the name and behalf of the Church. The act of incorporation is subject to a general law, which declares that "the charter of every corporation that shall hereafter be granted by the Legislature shall be subject to alteration, suspension, and repeal, in the discretion of the Legislature." To place this corporation under the control of the General Conference, it will be proper to procure an act of the Legislature to amend the charter so as to provide that the Board of Managers shall be elected by the General Conference. In this respect the charter of the Board of Education furnishes a model which would seem to secure stability and proper management.

THE CHURCH EXTENSION SOCIETY.

. . . .

The mode of electing the Board of Managers has all the objectionable features of elections in the Missionary Society, and the plan of filling vacancies in the office of Corresponding Secretary is complicated and unsatisfactory, since neither the Bishops nor any representatives of Church authority controls it.

We have no reason to doubt the judicious and faithful management of this corporation. But it is practically independent of all Church authority in the management of its affairs.

The remedy is an amendment of the Charter so as to provide that the General Conference shall elect and perpetuate a Board, and for the filling of vacancies in the recess of the Conference by the appointment of the Bishops. To this the existing corporation would doubtless consent. If difficulties are found in the way in this respect, an independent corporation can be created subject to the General Conference.

THE TRACT SOCIETY.

The organization and management of the Tract Society are regulated by a charter and constitution substantially similar to the Missionary Society. The same objections exist alike to both, and the same remedy should be alike applied.

THE SUNDAY-SCHOOL UNION.

The Sunday-School Union is in the same condition substantially as the Missionary Society, and the same remarks are equally applicable to both.

The Committee are required by the resolution appointing them "to *consider* and report concerning the relations of our various benevolent societies to the authorities of the Church," etc.

We have done so.

We find that the powers of some of these benevolent corporations might be profitably enlarged and liberalized. Under proper limitations, they might be made more useful if authorized to receive money on payment of life annuities.

The right to hold certain offices is limited to laymen and ministers. No law of the Church prohibits women from being ministers. As such they can hold offices to which ministers are eligible. But women should be equally eligible to all offices to which laymen are eligible.

The time has gone by when persons should be excluded from Church offices on account of race, color, or sex. And when women are admitted to office in Church corporations, the way will be open to give them a just share of the employment in every department of the Book Concern, and in all the enterprises which promote temporal and spiritual good.

The Committee recommend the adoption of the following:

Resolved, That the Bishops are hereby directed to take such measures as they may deem proper to secure by law such form of organization of the various benevolent corporations of the Methodist Episcopal Church as will place all under the full control of the General Conference.

Daniel Curry [clergy, New York Conference] moved that this same Special Committee be instructed to report to this Conference full Boards of Directors for the various benevolent societies, as provided for in the report.

Wm. Lawrence [lay, East Ohio Conference] moved as an amendment that the Bishops, instead of the Special Committee, shall make these nominations.

D. Curry moved to lay this motion on the table, but it did not prevail.

The amendment then prevailed, and the original motion, as amended, was carried.

Susanna Fry Alerts Women to Ancient and Modern Sisterhoods

Source: Susanna Fry, "Ancient and Modern Sisterhoods," Ladies' Repository 32/10 (October 1872), 244-45. Excerpts.

It has been said that the Roman Catholic and Greek Churches have had the good sense to turn to account and assimilate to themselves a force which Protestant Churches allow to lie dormant [religious orders for women]. . . . If husband and children demand a woman's time, then may she prepare levers wherewith the world may be moved. If the powerful engine called *home* be but well oiled with human love and sympathy, clean, bright, and glittering, swept and garnished by the Spirit, and shone upon by the Sun of Righteousness, moving without jar or friction, controlled by an engineeress who understands her business, it will knock down and demolish many of the strongholds of sin and Satan that stand on its track; and pick up and anoint with the oil of consolation many wounded and borne down in the battle of life. But woman should be not only a teacher and cherisher of home, but also a purifier of society.

There are orphaned daughters, maiden women, and desolate widows among us, deprived of the sweet ties and duties of home, who would gladly make for themselves homes in the hearts of the people by deeds of love and charity. In New York city alone there are thirty thousand women without protector, guide, or help, who swell the miserable ranks of needle-women, who seldom receive more than thirty-three cents from twelve to fifteen hours labor. Why may not some of these be *educated* for nurses? We need not only amateur charity ladies, but an organized force trained in those ministering functions which have their root in woman's nature. Why may *we* [Protestants/Methodists] not have trained women in our prisons, penitentiaries, asylums, poor-houses, reformatories, and hospitals, who shall have at heart, not the saving of souls to the Roman Church faith, but the saving of souls from sin and suffering here, and the pangs of a death that never dies, hereafter?

The evils arising from paid, drunken nurses; the need of softening, elevating Christian influence in work-houses, prisons, and reformatories; the succoring of friendless work-house girls and domestic servants, and female prisoners just restored to liberty; and the renovating of squalid abodes of disease and misery, can only be effectually met and accomplished by a thoroughly organized and trained force of women. It is only from such a *steady, continuous* contribution of living human love and labor can flow. Such a force, freed from the deadly errors of Romanism, would open the gates of heaven to many a waiting soul, heal many of the wounds of society, and prove a "polished shaft" [Isa. 49:2] in the subduing of all nations to our Lord and Christ, "who accepts the services, not only of men, but also of women."

Where is there a broader field, or more legitimate work for women than in the ministration of love? And if so much is accomplished by the desultory labors of Protestant women, how much greater success would crown concerted action! Nor would this necessitate veils or vows, or labor by women separate and independent of men; but shall she not, indeed, be a *help-meet* to the fullest of her capacity?

Looking at the [Roman Catholic] sisterhoods, we can not fail to see that their success lies not in celibacy, but in system; not in monachism [monasticism] but in organization; not so much in blind devotion as in *thorough training*. When shall the question cease to be asked, "Why can not Protestant women do what these Roman Catholic women do?" Not that we do not do as much as they, in other channels, perhaps, and unknown to the world; but that we fall so far short of what might be done, and, we may add, *ought* to be done. Because Rome once, with a great maelstrom of denunciation, swept in all the free bands of women devoted to the service of Christ and humanity, and degraded them to mere propagandizing forces, shall we fail to oppose an equal barrier to her success? Yea, a more than equal: for so soon as Protestant women *systematically* undertake the good works humanity so loudly demands, not as "engines of religious propagandism," but simply showing their faith by their works, Rome's most powerful weapon passes from her hands. Already in all Europe the crown of victory is settling on the brows of Protestant nurses and teachers—thanks to the efforts of Mrs. Fry, Pastor Fliedner, and others.

When shall the women of America awake to a sense of their responsibility? And what great soul, filled with love to God and man shall open the way and prepare the means whereby we may be enabled to compete successfully with our sisters of Rome, not only as general charity women, educators, and succorers of the unfortunate, but especially as nurses of the sick—a department of such great good to soul and body, yet so long allowed to be monopolized by the daughters of Rome?

Earnest thinkers upon the subject of "Woman's Work in the Church," are looking to the Quakers and Methodists to move forward in God's name, smiting the waters of blind prejudice, and lead their daughters into the full possibilities of an entirely devoted Christian womanhood.

A TEACHER DESCRIBES A MODERN SUNDAY SCHOOL IN SESSION

Source: Pamela Helen Goodwin, "Methodist Episcopal Sunday-School, Akron, Ohio," Normal Class 1/3 (March 1875): 100-109. Excerpts.

"I should like very much to see your Sabbath-school. Can you not give me such a description as will enable me to form a clear idea of its rooms and workings?"

You require a difficult task. Of course, it is not hard to give dimensions, form, enrollment, or statistics, but these are too likely to be as the dry bones in the valley, giving little idea of the draperied living form. However, yield to your imagination and my direction, and the structure and school, however inadequate to express the reality, shall rise before you to be examined by your thought. . . .

Let us follow the children as they assemble some Sabbath morning. We enter upon the south side into an ample vestibule, but do not enter the large folding doors that open at once into the main room for the simple reason that they are locked. This precaution is scarcely necessary except for adults or strangers, for there is another attraction that draws the feet of the children—the library, a few feet to the east. Here the scholars exchange their books before entering their classes. . . . As we pass into the [main Sunday-school] room we notice the convenient post-office, which opens by a window into the school-room and by another into the vestibule, and from which lesson-papers, *Sunday School Advocates,* journals, tickets, etc. are dispensed. We are distinguished visitors, and will take our seat on the sofa back of the superintendent's stand.

The light streams in through those tall upper windows robbed of its dazzling brilliancy but not of its abundant purity. Before us is the fountain, sending up delicate sprays of water that fall with tinkling cadences on the leaves and flowers that, in harmony with the changing seasons, decorate the figures of the fountain. Arranged in concentric semi-circles are the classes of the Youth Department grouped in chairs, with the teacher, around a little table containing singing-books, lesson-papers, Bibles, etc. Beyond and on each side are class-rooms with their members seated toward the front ready for participation in the opening exercises; while between on either hand are clustered hundreds of little faces—the most beautiful bouquet of flowers. The perspective closes with the class-room walls tastefully adorned with pictures, statues, brackets and other furniture, both useful and ornamental, which the scholars of the class have contributed. Above, and not at all concealed from view by the delicate iron-work of the balustrade, are members of the various Bible classes, some with chairs seated on the balcony, others within their rooms a step higher, so to all the view of the superintendent is unobstructed. Between the platform and fountain is a fine Chickering piano, donated by a "friend." The floors of all the rooms are covered by a green and black carpet of neat design, and the walls of the main room are tastefully frescoed, terminating above, at a height of nearly fifty feet, in the blue of the starry dome.... Pictures, mottoes, and adornments varying with the season of the year, being now wreaths of evergreens twining around the columns and hanging in graceful festoons from the frame-work of the gallery, looped by baskets of living green, with here and there a gilded cage with its merry little prisoner, complete the embellishments of the main room; while frescoed in German-script above the heads of all, yet beneath the light that streams in from the outer heavens, is the motto of the school silently falling on us, like the ever-present benediction of the Master: "And they searched the scriptures daily, whether those things were so" [Acts 17:11].

A bell from the desk rings. It is nine o'clock. The teachers rise in their places and respond to their names called by the secretary. Another tap from the bell; the singing-books are taken from the desks without confusion; the page is announced by the chorister; the piece is played by the pianist, and the school rises for the opening song. It may be "Hail, holy Sabbath!" Tell me, as the voices of hundreds of children and adults ring out, joined by the happy carols of the little birds half-hidden in the green, does it not send a thrill of joy through your heart, seeing a foretaste of the time when "the redeemed of the Lord shall return and come with singing unto Zion; and everlasting joy shall be upon their heads; and sorrow and mourning shall flee away" [Isa. 35:10]?

Between each song that is sung, during the fifteen minutes devoted to that purpose, the door into the library is opened, permitting those whose books are exchanged to enter without disturbing the exercises. The singing and the scholars assembled, the school is opened, sometimes with devotional exercises in each room, but more frequently with a single voice leading, and then the entire school from lisping children to trembling age, joining in the Lord's Prayer; after which the Infant, Intermediate, and Normal [teacher training] classes close their doors, and the other classes read the lesson for the day responsively with the superintendent, and recite the subject, topic, and text. Sometimes the hymn from the lesson-paper is devoutly sung, and after another signal all of the doors are closed, a few chairs are turned around, and the teaching proper begins.

For a few minutes we will notice the different grades, having special permission to pass into the rooms, while ordinary visitors can only look in through the ample glass windows [in the class-room doors]. In the Infant Department over a hundred bright faces greet us, varying from three to eight years. Active, restless, but sparkling, they are waiting the fulfillment of the Saviour's command, "Feed my lambs" [John 21:15]. There is no routine of recitation here. If you notice carefully the method of developing the lesson on one Sabbath, you may be sure the method will be varied on the next. The children are entertained and rested by singing, in which they can engage without disturbing the rest of the school. The theme for instruction is the same as that of the entire school, only the milk of the Word is given by their judicious teacher.

Passing to the Intermediate Department, we find a grade of scholars from eight to twelve that are taught, in addition to the regular lessons, the main truths of the church catechism; it being the superintendent's opinion that here the general doctrines of the church can be indelibly impressed on the child's memory, although it may be years before they are fully understood.

The Youth Department consists of two grades, one occupying the main room, where there are about eight pupils in a class, and the other occupying eight of the class-rooms, and varying in number from twelve to twenty. These divisions differ only in the age of the pupils and method of instruction.

The Normal Department, but recently organized, numbers fifty young ladies and gentlemen. They have commenced the course prepared by Dr. Vincent, and not only the diploma he awards to the successful student, but one that is to be specially engraved for the Akron school. After graduation, if there is no class ready for them to teach, they will pass into the Adult Bible Department, which is composed of three classes—one for young people, two for those more advanced in life, the fathers and mothers in Israel.

After forty minutes for the special work of the teachers has passed, a signal [bell] calls the attention to the [superintendent's] desk. The doors are folded back, the few chairs are turned, and in from one to two minutes, without confusion, the school is ready for closing exercises. These consist in questions and answers concerning the [uniform] lesson; an appropriate black-board exercise; reviews, remarks from visitors, pastor or superintendent; a song from the school, or from a class appointed for that purpose; and, it may be, the reading of an obituary of some loved member taken later to the upper congregation. The secretary then reports the number of male and female pupils, respectively in each department, and the number of teachers, officers and visitors. Doxology and benediction follow, and the large doors are thrown open, permitting the scholars to pass out with ease and quietness. The average attendance for the past year was five hundred and five.

In conclusion, I will give a brief outline of the course of study to which Mr. Miller is trying to bring the school. All classes study the International Series [of uniform lessons]. In the Infant Class, special attention is given to the [Bible] story, the pupils remaining there four years. In the Intermediate, the historical parts are dwelt upon in connection with the catechism, pupils remaining three years. Four years are allotted to the first division of the Youth Department, where the lesson with all its contexts is read. Three years for the second division, where various analyses of the lesson are produced. Then the pupils at the average age of eighteen years, have gone through the Bible twice, enter the Normal Class, where methods and outside evidences are taught. Then those not having classes pass into the Bible Department, which is synthetical in its character, including all of the preceding in its search for the deep things of God. In all departments the practical truths of the lesson that tend to make the learner wise unto salvation are pressed home upon the consciences.

Evangelical Association laywoman Savilla Kring experiences Christian fulfillment

Source: Savilla Kring, "Experience of Savilla Kring," Voices on Holiness from the Evangelical Association, comp. H. J. Bowman (Cleveland: Publishing House of the Evangelical Association, 1882), 222-23. Excerpts.

I had an intense longing to see God, and at times, I earnestly desired to be released from this body, that I might know how to worship Him more perfectly. Time's swift wings had carried me to November 1876. . . . The first Sabbath morning of the meeting dawned beautifully, and I went to the house of God with a full heart. Oh, memorable day! In the morning, "the tide [of holiness] was already very high," and it continued to rise all day. In the evening people from every direction gathered in, and the house was filled to overflowing. After the sermon an invitation was given, and penitents pressed to the mercy-seat. Being directed to offer encouragement to penitents, I knelt down, and, after a few words of prayer for the mourner, I again went to the Father, saying, "Now please, for dear *dear* Jesus' sake, *now* supply *my* need!" At any cost? Yes, at *any* cost. Then followed a searching time. This body must be presented a *living* sacrifice in a sense vastly beyond the power of description. I was in the presence of the Most High, sinking lower in humility before Him. Every member was being singled out. These eyes to see for Jesus. . . . These ears to be closed to every vain or vulgar sound. . . . These feet, willing to walk in paths where the Father would have me go. This heart to be His royal throne.

I was growing faint with His loveliness, but I whispered, "Yes, yes, yes." That I was not yet quite conscious of the import of these questions was revealed to me when the Master softly asked me, "Will you give your tongue to 'tell it all'?" I was startled, and exclaimed, "Dearest Father, I cannot 'tell it.' " "Will you try?" "Oh, but I am so timid—I am so young. If I were a man, I'd try; but I'd be called a 'woman preacher' or an 'evangelist.' Oh, I cannot; my associates would all leave me. I might have to arise before great multitudes. I have not the necessary qualifications, and I could not bear the criticisms. I fear public opinion. All our people, from the Bishop down, would oppose me." It seemed to me I must be dying. I *was* dying to self, and the struggle was severe. "For the sake of perishing souls, will you 'tell it'?" Once more I faintly whispered, "God helping me, I *will*!" Once more—oh, has the end not yet come? "Your body, soul, and spirit; your memory, mind, and will; all your days, and all your hours—you have given to God to be used by Him *anywhere, every-where?*" "Oh, but I cannot leave home! . . . I'll 'tell it,' only let me 'tell it' here." Now Jesus stands before me, a halo of glory encircling Him, His locks wet with the dews from the rugged mountain, where He sought the wanderer. His face, beaming with heavenly radiance, is bruised and stained with tears and blood. His hands are extended, and from the wounds which the nails have made, the crimson drops are falling. . . . Hush! He speaks—"For *thee,* for *thine,* I have suffered *all* this. Will you *go* and *tell it?*" "He that loveth father or mother more than me is not worthy of me" [Matt. 10:37]. "O my adorable Redeemer," exclaimed my heart, "I love Thee more than all else, by Thy grace I *will tell it anywhere, everywhere.*"—"Tis done." *Glory be to the Father! Glory to the Son! Glory to the Holy Ghost!*—The last "shore line" was cut, and borne upon the billows of His love I floated out, *out* in this boundless, bottomless ocean. . . . Yea, I had "crossed the Jordan," I was resting upon the bosom of my Saviour, with his arms folded about me, and he whispered into my soul, words of heavenly love. I was inhaling the fragrance of the flowers, and feasting upon the delicious fruits growing near the entrance to "Beulah Land." The sweetness of heaven was flowing over me, and permeating my whole being. I cannot tell how long this season of thus communing with God continued, but when I again opened my eyes to earthly surroundings, only "the little company" was present. Tears fell silently from the eyes of smiling ones around me, a "weight of glory" rested upon all. A holy hush pervaded the house. All felt it. My own soul was too full to speak audibly, but the language was: " 'Tis Holiness! 'Tis Perfect Love."

BLACK POLITICIAN AND PREACHER HIRAM REVELS PROTESTS RACIAL SEPARATION IN THE CHURCHES

Source: Hiram R. Revels, "We Ought Not to Separate," Southwestern Christian Advocate *(New Orleans) (4 May 1876): 1.*

Mr. Editor—. . . . When the Methodist Episcopal Church,—our church—during and after the [Civil] War, turned her attention to the condition of the unavoidably poor, and ignorant colored people of the South, I greatly rejoiced, and the wisdom of our church in the adoption of that course, may be seen in the fact that she could have done nothing in the line of Christian duty that would have been more productive of great[er] good in the highest sense of the word. As the result of the late war, about four millions of human beings, emerged from slavery in poverty and ignorance, and knowing as our church did, that they never could be enlightened, and intelligent, and valuable and useful citizens, without pecuniary aid—literary, moral and religious instruction, she chose the Southern States as a part of the field of her future operations, and sent some of her ablest ministers to her new work, by whom that work has been ably and successfully prosecuted. As the result of this, there are in Mississippi and other States hundreds of regularly organized and prosperous churches, in which thousands of colored people and their children statedly meet, worship God, and receive enlightening instruction from preachers, many of whom are advancing in mental culture, and the acquisition of useful knowledge. . . .

If it be asked why the Mother Church [Methodist Episcopal Church] has so large an influence with the colored people [in the South], the answer is, that when she came among them to do good—she showed no pride and offishness toward them on account of their color and previous condition of servitude, but treated them kindly and affectionately, taking them by the hand and conducting them into the same fold or church with themselves. The fact of our church making my people a part of herself, instead of organizing so many of them as would unite with her into [separate] churches and conferences [as the Methodist Episcopal Church, South, had done in 1870], and then leaving them to themselves to organize and conduct churches and conferences, when they themselves were ignorant of the true principles of church government, and management, has led them fully to believe that she has for them the most kindly and friendly christian feeling. The wisdom of our church in *establishing mixed churches and conferences in the Southern States* is seen in the fact, that it has had the happy effect of leading the colored people to abandon the belief that because they are of a colored, enslaved race, they are so degraded, it would be vain for them to try by any means to become the equals of their more favored white neighbors in intelligence, pure morals and the adorning virtues of life. They have also been benefitted by coming in contact with their more learned and intelligent white brethren in the transaction of church business, and in divine worship. In view of these indisputable facts, the important question is, will the M. E. Church recede one step from the high christian ground which she took in the commencement of her Southern work, and which has given her such a powerful influence with the colored Southern people, and enable her to be a source of so many blessings to them? As our church has been blamed for making her colored members a part of herself, or, for making no distinctions on account of race or color in organizing churches and conferences on Southern soil, would not an action of the general conference, dividing the conference and churches on the color line be a virtual acknowledgment that our church has greatly erred, that those who have censured her for her course, were in the right and she in the wrong? Since conference I have visited nine or ten counties in this State, and conversed with quite a number of my people relative to the separation in question, and they declare to me that their earnest hope and prayer is, that the dear mother M. E. Church, which has done so much for them in ways already named, will not now abandon that recognition of them which has so much endeared her to them, and led them to hurl from their minds the degrading recollections of slavery, and prompted them to labor for their own and their children's elevation as otherwise they would not have done. The election of a colored Bishop, is a small matter with them, compared with the question of division on the color line. Seeing them as I do, that the separation in question will retard the great work which our church is accomplishing among the poor needy colored Southern people, I am among those who will work and pray against the same. Our white brethren who are now laboring in the South will not be harmed by continuing in the same relation to their colored brethren that now exists between them. But the sundering of that relation would afford the opponents of our church an opportunity of charging them and the M. E. Church generally with having been insincere toward the colored people *abinitio* [from the beginning]. I know that it is said by some that the colored people's want of intelligence and refinement in worship, is so clearly seen and felt, that their intelligent white brethren cannot pleasantly and profitably worship with them[.] [A]nd in reply I would say, that this circumstance only affords intelligent Christians an opportunity to do good by going among them and so instructing them by example and otherwise, that they shall abandon what is on Christian grounds, objectionable in their manner of worship. There are colored churches in Mississippi where you will find[,] as the result of intelligent instruction and leadership[,] the same order and decorum in worship that you will find in any white church. In this connection I would say that if preachers of learning and intelligence would point out to their colored hearers their notions and habits which are not essential to divine worship, but are the results of ignorance, and exhort them to abandon the same, they would[,] as a general thing[,] heed their advice. In most of the colored churches the majority of the members are opposed to what is objectionable in worship, but they can do nothing to remedy this state of things, while the Presiding Elders and Pastors are silent on the subject. In conclusion I would say that I conscientiously believe that the Head of the church led the [M. E.]Church to enter upon her Southern work, and that with his approval she cannot abandon it. Then my humble opinion is, that the safe and wise course for our church to pursue, as regards her Southern work, is to adhere to the plan on which she commenced that work, and on which she has succeeded in doing great good. "Let well enough alone."

Holly Springs, Miss., April 17th, 1876.

EDITOR CHARLES FOWLER AGONIZES OVER CUSTER'S DEFEAT BY SIOUX

Source: Charles W. Fowler, "The Indian War," Western Christian Advocate (19 July 1876): 228.

There was fought on Sunday, June 25th, a terrible battle, between the United States forces led by General Custer on the one side, and a village of Sioux Indians on the other. The engagement took place in the eastern portion of Montana, at a point between the Yellow Stone River and the Big Horn Mountains, east of the Big Horn River, and near the banks of the Little Big Horn River. This was familiar ground to the braves. The warriors of the same tribe had fought a victorious battle nine years before near the same locality, with the United States forces under General Fetterman. But the battle of the last Sunday in June will be distinguished from all other Indian battles. The troops engaged were of high standing in the service, and were skilled in border warfare, and they fought bravely, and did all within their power, but were every one sacrificed in the engagement. Fortunately the loss was not so heavy as it would have been if the reserve companies had been in the fight, for the Indians had evidently prepared to slaughter all whom they could engage. As it is, the loss is very severe. Of the five companies of the Seventh Cavalry led by the daring Custer, not a man survived. The seven companies led by Major Reno also suffered terribly in battle and retreat. The Indian loss is reported at seventy dead, among whom are many of their best chiefs.

But we have no heart to dwell on this sickening disaster. Unfortunately, as this battle did not begin, so it does not end, the cause of this Indian war. Now that we have had time to recover from the shock of this fearful calamity, and before we shall become too excited with a desire to revenge the blood of our fallen heroes to be capable of dispassionate reasoning, let us reflect upon the moral questions involved in this contest. The blood of these brave men will not have been shed in vain, if the shock of defeat shall serve to induce the country to think upon the character of this warfare against the Indians. Before we give wild shouts of encouragement to a war of extermination, let us calmly look at its justice and necessity.

A leading daily newspaper says, "It is not a question of morals." If not, why not?

What is it that lifts this subject out of the domain of moral questions? What are the facts about this contest for the possession of a given territory?

Assuming that these natives had no rights to the territory which they originally held, and that the country belonged to the United States Government, it was most clearly and positively given to them by that Government in the treaty made and signed in 1868, at Fort Rice, in Dakota, Generals Harney, Terry, and Sherman, as military commissioners on the part of the United States, being present and assisting. According to that treaty the Indians were to have all the country extending from the Running Water north to fifteen miles above Heart River, east of the Missouri River, including the whole of the Black Hills country. Its terms also called for an annuity of provisions, clothing, agricultural implements, and trainers to teach such as would come down and live at the agencies, [learn] the art of farming for a livelihood, as do the whites. Those who preferred to remain on their reservations were to be allowed to do so, and receive a smaller annuity. The treaty was accepted in good faith. Most of the Indians came into the different agencies. The Government showed its faith and good intentions by abandoning Forts Reno, Pail, Kearney, and C. F. Smith, after, as it said, having spent more than a million dollars in establishing them. Sitting Bull was the only chief who remained hostile, and whose lead was followed by forty or fifty warriors. These natives, however, carried on against the whites no open, systematic warfare, but indulged in neighborhood depredations, occasional attacks on passing soldiers, and the occasional shooting of adventurers in the Yellowstone country. Such was the general condition of things for several years, and might have so continued, with a fair prospect of improvement, had not the United States sent an exploring expedition into this country, which had been secured to the Indians by treaty. The reports of that expedition, published broadcast, put in circulation the most romantic and exciting accounts of its attractions and richness in gold ores, and started out a class of enterprising—and, in many instances, lawless—adventurers, on the move to the Black Hills.

The Indians complained to the United States of the invasion, and asked to be protected. The Government recognized their right to protection, and forbade all parties from going into this reservation. But the Government had kindled the excitement, and the prohibition came too late. It was not now to be so easily extinguished. In fact, only a feeble show of military force was made to turn the invaders back, and then the attempt was abandoned. The President [Ulysses S. Grant] then issued his proclamation that, while the invaders had no right to enter the territory of the Sioux tribes, and were violating the treaties of the United States in doing so, yet the Indians must not molest them, nor seize any provisions in transit for them. This was a remarkable proclamation. It was, in effect, saying to all invaders, "Go on, the Government is powerless to prevent you."

The Indians were quick to understand the situation—that if their possessions were to be defended they must do it themselves. Their lands were their own, as really as any settler owns the homestead given him by the United States Government. Their only possible chance of retaining their homes for themselves and their children was by driving off these bands of intruders. In their condition would not we

385

have done the same thing? Are we to expect in the Indian a better code of procedure than we should have practiced? Through the crookedness of our dealings the Sioux were absolutely forced to defend their country, or see it overrun by lawless invaders. And yet, forsooth, in doing this they incur the displeasure of the United States. For doing for themselves what the Government had undertaken to do, and had failed to perform, the Government sends out its army under command of General Terry, the hero of Fort Fisher, to punish them. A war department that could not get an army out there to prevent lawless freebooters from overrunning the reservation, can quickly get an army there to exterminate the savages that resisted the encroachment of those invaders.

Is the course of the Government right? When was it right? In opposing the invasion, or when it opposes resistance to the invasion? Its present course is a disgraceful *repudiation* of its treaty promises. Upon the honorable observance of these treaty stipulations the security of life and property in all that region of country for years to come is depending. The honor of the nation is involved. The helplessness of the other party to the contract only makes it the more dishonorable to take advantage of them. Are there none to speak for their [Native American] rights, whose voices can be heard in high places? There will be a dust-throwing effort to blind the eyes to the real moral question involved in this attack on the Sioux nation, by pointing to the flowing blood of our soldiers, and a furious outcry against the barbarous warfare of these savages will be raised, but there ought to be enough enlightened Christian sentiment in the country to stay this murderous, and wicked policy; and to settle matters in dispute according to the claims of right and law. This war has already been costly, both in treasure and blood. But its continuance, as begun, will be at a fearful expense. It is likely to swallow up many millions of dollars and hundreds more of human lives.

DIVIDED METHODISTS SEEK "FRATERNITY" AND ISSUE ADDRESS

Source: Formal Fraternity: Proceedings of the General Conference of the Methodist Episcopal Church and of the Methodist Episcopal Church, South, in 1872, 1874, and 1876, and of the Joint Commission of the Two Churches on Fraternal Relations, at Cape May, New Jersey, August 16-23, 1876 (New York: Nelson & Phillips. Nashville: A. H. Redford, 1876), 77-83. Excerpts.

ADDRESS
TO THE BISHOPS, THE MINISTERS, AND THE MEMBERS OF THE METHODIST EPISCOPAL CHURCH, AND OF THE METHODIST EPISCOPAL CHURCH, SOUTH.

DEAR FATHERS AND BRETHREN: We, the Commissioners appointed by authority of the General Conferences, respectively, of the above named Churches, to remove all obstacles to formal fraternity, and to adjust all existing difficulties between them, deem it proper, in advance of our report to the General Conferences of our respective Churches, to communicate to you, in general terms, the results of the recent harmonious session of our Joint Commission.

Pursuant to previous appointment, the Commissioners convened at Cape May, N.J., on the 16th day of August 1876, and were favored by the attendance of all the members of both Boards.

After a written communication from the Commissioners of the Methodist Episcopal Church, South, was received and answered by the Commissioners of the Methodist Episcopal Church, both Boards met in joint session, the labors of which were continued during seven days.

We have had a full and free conference and interchange of views respecting the important matters that claimed our united consideration.

If any in the Churches entertained the fear, previous to our meeting, that we could not attain complete harmony of sentiment touching the momentous questions to be determined, they will be rejoiced to learn, that after having given due attention to all questions involved in the proper construction of a platform of complete fraternity between the two great Branches of Episcopal Methodism in the United States, we have arrived at the settlement of every matter affecting, as we suppose, the principles of a lasting and cordial adjustment.

We have the satisfaction to declare that our aspirations for harmony of views on vital points have been realized. By Divine guidance, as we trust, we have been able, after a frank interchange of views, and prayerful endeavor, to harmonize all differences, and to arrive at the desired consummation of a unanimous agreement of complete fraternity. We believe that no principle of honor, on either side, has been invaded. We struck the key-note of brotherly love till it sounded high and clear, and so have been enabled to reach the elements of perfect harmony. No divergence of sentiment mars the complete unanimity of the Joint commission touching the essential principles of fraternization.

At the beginning of our consultations one great question seemed to overshadow all others. It concerns to relation of the two Churches to each other and to Episcopal Methodism. To this important matter our most earnest thought and prayerful deliberation were first directed, and the result attained occasioned the interchange of rejoicing congratulations between the members of the Joint Commission.

The Commissioners adopted, without a dissenting voice, the following:

DECLARATION AND BASIS OF FRATERNITY.

Status of the Methodist Episcopal Church, and of the Methodist Episcopal
Church, South, and their Coordinate Relation
as legitimate branches of Episcopal Methodism.

Each of said Churches is a legitimate Branch of Episcopal Methodism in the United States, having a common origin in the Methodist Episcopal Church organized in 1784; and since the organization of the Methodist Episcopal Church, South, was consummated in 1845 by the voluntary exercise of the right of the Southern Annual Conferences, ministers, and members, to adhere to that Communion, it has been an Evangelical Church, reared on scriptural foundations, and her ministers and members with those of the Methodist Episcopal Church, have constituted one Methodist family, though in distinct ecclesiastical connections.

It was next incumbent on us to consider the questions concerning conflicting claims to Church Property, and some special cases that could not conveniently be referred to the operation of a general rule.

There were two principal questions to be considered with regard to the Church Property in dispute between local Societies of the two Churches.

First. As to the legal ownership of said property.

Second. As to whether it will consist with strict equity, or promote Christian harmony of the cause of religion, to dispossess those Societies now using Church property which was originally intended for their use and occupancy, and of which they have acquired possession, though they may have lost legal title to it by their transfer from the one Church to the other.

We have considered the papers in all cases that have been brought to our notice. These arose in the following States: Virginia, West Virginia, Maryland, Tennessee,

Louisiana, North Carolina, and South Carolina. In respect of some of these cases we have given particular directions; but for all other cases the Joint Commission unanimously adopted . . . Rules for the Adjustment of Adverse Claims to Church Property [omitted]. . . .

In order to further promote the peaceful results contemplated by this Joint Commission, and to remove as far as may be all occasion, and especially to forestall all further occasion, for hostility between the two Churches, we recommend to members of both, as a wise rule of settlement where property is in contest, and one or both are weak, that they compose their differences by uniting in the same communion; and in all cases, that the ministers and members recognize each other in all relations of fraternity, and as possessed of ecclesiastical rights and privileges of equal dignity and validity. They should each receive from the other ministers and members in good standing with the same alacrity and credit as if coming from their own Church, and, without interference with each other's institutions or missions, they should, nevertheless, co-operate in all Christian enterprises.

It is not to be supposed, in respect of some matters of mere opinion, that all ministers and members in either Church will be in accord; but we trust and believe that a spirit of fellowship and mutual regard will pervade the reconciled ranks of the entire ministry and membership of both Churches. . . .

We cannot restrain the expression of our united congratulations to both of the great Churches whose Commissions we have executed, in uniting between them the broken cords of affectionate and brotherly fraternization. Henceforth they may hail each other as from the auxiliary ranks of one great army. The only differences they will foster will be those friendly rivalries that spring from earnest endeavors to further to the utmost the triumphs of the gospel of peace. Whatever progress is made by the one Church or by the other will occasion general joy. They will rejoice in each other's success as a common good; and, amid the thousand glorious memories of Methodism, they will go forward devoted to their one work of spreading Scriptural holiness over these lands.

Astronomers tell us of dual-stars revolving together in mutual relations and harmony, whose differing colors are so much the complement of each other as to produce a pure white light of exceeding brilliancy. These dual-Churches of American Methodism will henceforth revolve in mutual fellowship and harmony, so much the complement of one another as together to produce the pure and blended light of Christian charity and fraternal love. These fraternized Churches have no further occasion for sectional disputes or acrimonious differences. They may henceforth remember their common origin, pursue their fruit-bearing work and rejoice in their own and each other's success, while engaged in the same great mission of converting the world to Christ.

Distinctive features of profession and polity are bound up with the name of Episcopal Methodism. That form of Christian propagandism and ecclesiastical economy has peculiar elements of power and qualities of attraction that commend its efficiency in proclaiming a pure Gospel to the world. Its cardinal doctrines of free salvation by faith, and of the witness of the Spirit; its scriptural articles of

Christian belief; its primitive system of Church government; its sententious demand of those who would join its societies; its itinerant plan of preaching the Gospel; its Wesleyan simplicity and orthodoxy; its urgency of the practice of a holy life; its liberal and systematic benevolence; its support of educational institutions; its promotion of Sabbath-school instruction; its vigilant care for the deserving poor; its provision for superannuated ministers, their widows and children; its worldwide missionary enterprise; and its general activity in the dissemination of Gospel truth, are one and the same in the Methodist Episcopal Church and in the Methodist Episcopal Church, South.

For away in dark portions of the earth, to which their missionaries have penetrated, a divine light is breaking on the long night of paganism. For the elevation of humanity, it is more than the wand of an enchanter. There, as well as here, Methodist doctrines and usages wear their own peculiar and heaven-blessed distinctiveness, and seem to presage the dawn of that ear of gladness when the claims of universal brotherhood will commingle with the full glory of the millennium. Episcopal Methodism was never more strong and influential, and never appeared to feel more the quickening impulse of its glorious destiny, than it does at the present day.

It is eminently fit, therefore, that in its native home and wide-extended realm in these United States, whence its spirit and power go forth like swelling anthems of gladness to bless mankind, it should bear along the blended sweetness of fraternal harmony. . . .

In the bonds of the Gospel of peace,
　　　Your brethren and servants,

MORRIS D'C CRAWFORD,　　　　　EDWARD H. MYERS,
ENOCH L. FANCHER,　　　　　　　ROBERT K. HARGROVE,
ERASMUS Q. FULLER,　　　　　　　THOMAS M. FINNEY,
CLINTON B. FISK,　　　　　　　　DAVID CLOPTON,
JOHN P. NEWMAN,　　　　　　　　ROBERT B. VANCE,
Commissioners M.E. Church.　　　*Commissioners M. E. Church, South*

CAPE MAY, N.J., *August 23, 1876.*

ANNA OLIVER SEEKS PERMISSION FROM GENERAL CONFERENCE TO BE ORDAINED

Source: Anna Oliver, "Test Case" on the Ordination of Women (New York: Wm. W. Jennings, 1880), 1-8. Excerpts.

Miss Anna Oliver was recommended for Deacon's Orders in the Methodist Episcopal Church at the last session of the New England Conference. The Bishop [Edward G. Andrews] declined to submit the matter to the vote of the Conference, because, in his judgment, the law of the Church does not authorize the ordination of women. From this decision Presiding Elder [Lorenzo R.] Thayer took an appeal to the ensuing General Conference.

Miss Oliver asks for ordination. Ought she to be ordained?

The Church tacitly allows women to preach and labor as evangelists. For this ordination is not thought necessary. But here is a woman who believes herself called not to evangelistic work, but to the pastorate. The following are

MISS OLIVER'S REASONS FOR THIS BELIEF,

substantially as expressed before the New England Conference:

"I am sorry to trouble our dear mother Church with any perplexing questions, but it presses me also, and the Church and myself must decide something. I am so thoroughly convinced that the Lord has laid commands upon me in this direction, that it becomes with me really a question of my own soul's salvation. If the Lord commands me to just the course I am pursuing, as only they that do His commandments have right to the tree of life, I have no alternative.

Among other reasons, the following induce me to hold that I am called to pastoral and not evangelistic work:

I. I do not believe in evangelistic work as usually carried on, i.e. to warm up cold churches and *start* revivals. The legitimate sphere of an evangelist, in my understanding, is to assist an overworked minister and church, while the revival is advancing. But the only invitations I received were of the first description. I have served about two years thus, with what others call success.

II. The work of an evangelist is unsuited to women—certainly to me. It is contrary to the instincts of my nature. An evangelist has no home, is tossed from place to place. Advertisements, embracing personal descriptions are used, with other sensational methods, to draw together the people. The evangelist arrives and is thrust before a crowd of strangers. As soon as she becomes a little acquainted, and forms some attachments, her time expires. She is torn away and thrust before another crowd of strangers. Women are said to be timid and shrinking, and will our good mother Church take these shrinking, delicate, modest, sensitive, home-loving, nestling, timid little things, and toss them about from Maine to California, or send them as missionaries to wild and naked barbarians, at the same time forbidding them to engage in the motherly work of the pastorate?

III. Pastoral work is adapted to women, for it is motherly work. The mother has her little group, the pastor the flock. As a mother spreads her table with food suited to the individual needs of her family, so the pastor feeds the flock. Each knows the sick ones, the weak ones, those that must be carried in the arms, and those strong enough to help others. I recognize this field as suited to my natural qualifications.

IV. My interest begins with conversions. Then an evangelist leaves. And I always felt as though a whole nursery full of my own little ones were being turned over to the care of strangers. The experience was, in a word, fearful.

V. I cannot endure to preach old sermons. I have subjects in my mind that will not let me rest until I work them up. To do so would be better for my present and future usefulness, and for my own growth in grace. But a person who is preaching every night in the week, cannot prepare new subjects.

VI. The longer I preached as an evangelist, the less interest I felt—no matter how crowded the houses, nor what the apparent success—until I became convinced that, if the pastorate were unalterably closed, the Lord had released me from preaching. But just at this point pastoral work opened to me.

VII. As a pastor my interest daily increases. I would rather toil quietly in a corner with a handful of persons, seeing believers sanctified, and families transformed, than with the greatest eclat otherwise.

VIII. In evangelistic work I always saw some harm done, even where the most good was accomplished. But in regular labor, however small the gains, there is no discount of harm.

In this connection I may mention, that as an evangelist, my own spiritual growth was hindered, and had I long continued, I am convinced I would have backslidden. On the other hand, in my present charge, and in Passaic, the Lord has visited me with wonderful manifestations of his presence, and I realize in myself spiritual progress.

IX. When the Lord calls one to preach, He always calls persons to hear. So in this case. Others beside myself have recognized my adaptation to the pastorate. In less than two years thirteen churches desired me for their pastor. But the ecclesiastical authorities refused to appoint a woman, *preferring in some instances to close or sell the church buildings.*

X. God sanctions my pastoral work. In proof of this I appeal to the record in Passaic, N. J., and Brooklyn, N. Y. But it may be said, notwithstanding the reasons just given, that I am

MISTAKEN

in my call. Then it is a very great pity *for myself* that I cannot be convinced that I am mistaken—a pity that I have lived in this delusion all these years. I have made almost every conceivable sacrifice to do what I believe God's will. Brought up in a conservative circle in New York City, that held it a disgrace for a woman to work, surrounded with the comforts and advantages of ample means, and trained in the Episcopal Church, I gave up home, friends and support, went counter to prejudices that had become second nature to me, worked for several years to constant exhaustion, and suffered cold, hunger, and loneliness. The things hardest for me to bear were laid upon me. For two months my own mother did not speak to me. When I entered the house she turned and walked away. When I sat at the table she did not recognize me. I have passed through tortures to which the flames of martyrdom would be nothing, for *they* would end in a day. And through all this time and to-day, I could turn off to positions of comparative ease and profit. However, I take no credit to myself for enduring these trials, because at every step it was plain to me, that I had no alternative but to go forward or renounce my Lord.

Now is it possible that I am, that I have been all these years mistaken? Is it possible that our Father would either lead or leave a child of His in such a delusion?—a child whom He knows, as He knows my heart, desires nothing else so much as to learn the Father's will *to do it.* In fact He has really given constant evidence that He sanctions my course. At every step He has met me. He opened avenues of self-support while I was pursuing my studies. When I resigned loved ones, the joy of His presence more than compensated, so that trials have been no trials, for at all times He has given me the victory. I have been enabled through all, to rejoice evermore, and in everything to give thanks. And now He has restored all my friends. My family, who once thought I disgraced them, are proud of me now. My parents love me to-day, as I am sure they would never have done had I obeyed them instead of God. Does God thus encourage fanatics or enthusiasts?

The Methodist Episcopal Church is the church of

MY CHOICE

I have no one under God with whom to advise but the Bishops and Brethren of our Church. Therefore I ask you, Fathers and Brethren, tell me, what would you do, were you in my place? Tell me, what would you wish the Church to do toward you were you in my place? Please only apply the Golden Rule, and vote in Conference accordingly.

Finally, let not the sympathies of my friends in the Conference be taxed, imagining that I am, or under any circumstances will be, in the least discouraged. I encourage myself in the Lord my God.

NO ONE AND NOTHING CAN HARM ME

In all I am more than conqueror through Him to whom be all the glory [Rom. 8:37]. In the future, I intend in the strength of God to go forward as in the past, *joyfully.* If helped by you, my Brothers, then God bless you! If hindered by you, my Brothers, the Lord forgive you! (I know He will, for I'll ask Him to.) But whether helped or hindered, with God's grace I will stand where He commands me to stand, I will speak what He commands me to speak, because I can do no otherwise, and God takes all the responsibility.

MARY GRIFFITH APPEALS TO GENERAL CONFERENCE DELEGATES ON THE "POSITION OF WOMEN IN THE MEC"

Source: Mary L. Griffith, "The Position of Women in the Methodist Episcopal Church: A Statement and Appeal to the General Conference," Daily Christian Advocate *(Methodist Episcopal Church) 9/21 (25 May 1880): 88.*

Our Church is composed of men *and women.* Trite as this sentence is, its truth is constantly ignored. There are at least twice as many women as men in the average membership. In this two-third majority resides a moral, spiritual, social, and financial power, without which we can hardly imagine the Church existing at all; yet all through our economy, outside the higher places of privilege, opportunity, and power for good, there is a sex-line drawn, shutting women out. If there is friction here, who are at fault but those who made the line? If foam breaks against the wall, the builder is responsible, not the sea.

It is historic that women have done much for Methodism. To-day they are doing more than ever, and yet in the whole constitution and organization of the Church women are ignored—not as lacking, or being in fault, but simply as women. . . .

Women are abundant in labors, in all personal and spiritual work—in the care of the poor and sick, in supporting and encouraging the pastor; yet no woman is made steward. They have the tact and tenderness, the personal sympathy, the intense spiritual life, which should mark a good class-leader, yet very seldom does the Church avail herself of such leaders. The bulk of our Sunday-school work is done by women (and surely, as teachers of the young, women need no recommendation), yet the superintendency is scarcely ever filled by a woman, and it is only the "male" superintendent who is eligible to a seat in the quarterly conference. In all this, the Church is losing—losing both directly, by failing to put the best talent in the best places, and indirectly, because the women members—the two-thirds of the Church—are not brought out, strengthened, and made to grow. . . .

All the benevolent enterprises of the Church, which are recognized and supported as such, are officered by men. Women contribute to these, as do other members of the Church, but when they desire to put their hearts and brains into a plan of work, they must organize an independent society, which must be supported by their own separate contributions and labors. The Church is losing immeasurably by this. Methodism may well look about her in alarm, for *her women are being forced out into undenominational unions.* The fire will burn, and if Methodism will not make a place for it, it will warm another hearth. Can we afford this loss?

So far we have confined ourselves to the consideration of women as lay members. Now, as to their being licensed and ordained as exhorters, local preachers, and ministers in regular standing. This is, perhaps, a more difficult and solemn question than any of the preceding. Certainly, a more solemn one could not be presented to any body of men. It is a question that the Methodist Episcopal Church must speedily settle. Women are rising up all over the land who feel moved by the Holy Ghost to preach. They are flocking into our theological schools as fast as the doors are opened; and the Church must face their plea. . . .

[T]he final test of this question lies in the *call* of a woman to preach. As Methodists we believe in the direct operation of the Holy Spirit on the mind. Now, numbers of women testify that they have this burning zeal for souls, that constraining desire to tell the love of Christ, that sense of condemnation in silence, and all those other indications and impressions which in *men* are recognized as a call to preach. They are also led providentially into those paths of usefulness, they speak with that acceptability, they realize that success, they are sealed with that evident approval of God—both upon their own consciousness and in outward results—which in a *brother's case,* would bring him help, encouragement, opportunities of education, and finally license and ordination. Have these women "gifts, grace and usefulness"? We will risk the answer with all those who have made any considerable observation on the success of women's Gospel work; and in addition, will beg to remind you that hitherto women have worked without any special training or education, in the face of many difficulties.

To deny that many women realize the call of God to preach or speak the Gospel is to put away all faith in the conscious impressions of the Holy Spirit on the mind. Then, if God calls, how can the Church refuse to call without coming into controversy with the Divine Master? License and ordination are merely the Church's seal of approval on what it recognizes as God's will and plan. They are right and necessary for the success and convenience of the workman. If women are called they need these seals of approval as much as men do, and for the same reasons.

It may be said, "Women *are* permitted to speak and preach freely in the Methodist Episcopal Church; and since the work is the main thing why ask for office and recognition?" It is true that women have great liberty with us as compared with other Churches. Thank God, they are not doomed to utter silence! Our Methodism is grandly in advance on this line, as it is on most others. We have had women preachers since Wesley's time. Probably not one who reads this will deny that women may and should deliver the Gospel message in one way or another. Why deny as a Church what we admit as individuals? Why not, at least, grant the exhorter's or local preacher's license?

Is it not a solemn and fearful thing—is it not cruel beyond compare—to hinder a soul that is called of the Holy Ghost? Can the Church afford this loss? Are the fields no longer white, and are the laborers so many, that we can spurn any away, especially when the Master summons? We ask license and ordination for women because it is necessary for them and for the work. . . .

The Church is supposed to be founded upon *spiritual* principles. Measured by a spiritual standard, women are the equals of men. In Christ's kingdom is neither bond nor free, male nor female. Does his Church on earth fairly represent that kingdom when its constitution ignores women, and its customs shut her out of its highest places of privilege?

It rests with you, members of the General Conference, to remedy these evils, in great part at least. You best know how it should be done. Will you not examine the Discipline and determine that this May, of 1880, shall see the end of some of these harmful distinctions?

As women we have no representatives in your midst. What can we do but appeal to your sense of truth and righteousness? Surely our blessed Methodism is too pure—the heroic age of our history too fresh upon us—to let us appeal to a lower motive.

The masculine nouns and pronouns are used, throughout the Discipline, in referring to those holding office—either lay or clerical—in the Church. This is said to shut women out of all these offices. But these principles would also shut them out of Church membership altogether, for the General Rule declares the Church to be "a company of men." It would exclude them from the kingdom of heaven, for the Master said, *"Him* that cometh to me I will in no wise cast out" [John 6:37].

However, in order that the matter may be clearly understood, we ask you to formulate the principle, in legal, disciplinary enactment, that the masculine nouns and pronouns, used in the Discipline of the Methodist Episcopal Church, in referring to trustees, stewards, Sunday-school superintendents, class-leaders, exhorters, and preachers—itinerant and local—shall not be construed as excluding women from these offices; and, further, that the word "male" be expunged entirely from the Discipline.

We also ask that the General Conference shall recommend all our Churches to devise or alter their constitutions and charters, so that the disabilities of women in all business meetings may be removed.

Mrs. MARY L. GRIFFITH

Mauch Chunk [now Jim Thorpe], Pa.

NEW YORK CONFERENCE OF THE METHODIST PROTESTANT CHURCH ORDAINS ANNA HOWARD SHAW

Source: Nancy N. Bahmueller, "My Ordination: Anna Howard Shaw,"
Methodist History 14/2 (January 1976):126-31. Excerpts.

I applied for ordination about the same time as Miss O[liver, i.e 1880]. . . .

At the time I entered the [Boston University] theological school [1875] the Bishop of the New England Conference [Gilbert Haven] was very favorable to women and had promised to ordain me, but, unfortunately, he died before I graduated and the new Bishop [Edward G. Andrews] was bitterly opposed to women ministers. So we knew we shouldn't be ordained and it was a great mistake to really try it, for the first time sets such a precedent. But the head of the Boston [District, Lorenzo R. Thayer] was favorable to us, and recommended us for ordination to the New England Conference. . . . I came out top of the examination and Miss [Oliver] was second above all the men. I suppose that was natural because we were far more careful and we knew it was doubtful whether we should be ordained, so that we were anxious to have every chance.

Well, they examined us and then they refused to ordain us. And when they came to read out the names and all the young men went up to be ordained they read out our names and the Bishop refused them. Then afterwards we went to him and asked what we could do. We said we had been trained for the ministry and that we believed the Lord intended us to preach and that the church refused to ordain us: we both had parishes where they were perfectly satisfied with us, except that we could not baptize or marry them, and we had to be ordained to do that; and what were we to do[?] He said we had better get out of the church. I asked what kind of encouragement would he think that was to a young man who had spent years preparing for the ministry to be told to get out of the church! He said he was sorry but that was all he could say. And I said I would get out: that it was hard enough to get on anyhow and I wouldn't waste my strength trying to fight the Church too, that I was going to be ordained and if they wouldn't ordain me, I'd go where they would. But Miss O[liver] said she wouldn't, that she was going to be ordained [and] that she was going to stay in and fight the Church. And she did. . . . But I didn't stay in and fight the church. I knew it would be no use. There was a young man, Mark T., in my class, who took a great interest in women getting into the ministry, and he advised me to go to the Methodist Protestants and said he thought I could get in there. So I did, and I applied to their Boston Conference for ordination. Well, of course, they were a very inferior body to the Methodist Episcopalians and I didn't have to pass any examination or anything, for what I'd already done was so far superior to what they required. So all I had to do was send in my application and they had to interview me. And when they do that they generally discuss the person's character afterwards while he leaves the room. And so after they had seen me and asked me a few questions about what I had studied and the parish work I had done and so on[,] they asked me to leave the room. I thought they would be about ten minutes and then ask me to come back, and so I walked up and down for a couple of hours. Then I went off downtown and bought some things and came back and they were still discussing my character. They took two days to do it. The next day they had me come back and they asked me a whole lot of questions. The first ones they asked were about [Saint] Paul of course. Did I know what Paul said and did I believe it. And I said yes. Then they said what did I [think] about his having said "Wives obey your husbands." So I told them . . . and they hadn't heard of that. Then I added, but even if he did mean as they said, it didn't apply to me for I had no husband to obey. But they said I might have. I said I might have but if they believed in Paul the only thing for them was to ordain me, for I might have a husband who ordered me to preach and if they would ordain me now I could, whereas if they ordained me and he ordered me not to preach I could stop if I married. Well, of course that made them terribly mad. . . .

Oh, they asked me all sorts of questions of that sort, but I had the best of them, for they were not educated people at all, and of course I was straight from studying the Bible in the Hebrew and knew a great deal about it. And then of course I'd taken special pains with that part of the subject and knew all about it.

Well, then they were afraid a woman minister wouldn't do because so many of the difficulties that ministers had to settle were matrimonial difficulties, but I said there were not likely to be so many matrimonial difficulties with a woman minister, and of course that made them mad. And then I said if there were, a woman was just as good to settle them as a man, especially as it was generally the woman who had to complain and she would often go to another woman sooner than to a man.

Then they were very much afraid they would have to support me and said there was no use ordaining me because no church would have me if it could pay a salary. And I said they were not to [worry] about that, I already had a church where the people were perfectly satisfied, and a church that was not in their jurisdiction so that I was not taking away places from them, that I would never apply to them for a church, and if I couldn't get one by myself, I'd do something else. . . . They asked me a lot of foolish questions. . . . [F]inally when they put it to the vote they carried it by a pretty good majority, eight to four I think, or something like that.

Well, it had taken them so long that this was only on Saturday night and the ordination was to be on Sunday. Then I found out, or at least my friend did, that they had a most ingenious plan to defeat me after all, for I had made the great mistake of applying for ordination without being a member of their church! Well, of course, that gave them a very good excuse to refuse me. So my friends hustled around to call the council together again, and I sent an application for immediate admission to the church. But that was Saturday night and they refused to come together. . . . [S]o the men were all ordained and I was not. But on Monday they met and voted for my admission and my ordination. . . . I was scared and hated the whole thing. But when it was settled the very ones who opposed it most, Brother A and Brother B, were the ones to insist on making it a great occasion. They decided to do it at an open meeting and have as big a crowd as they could and have a public service and a sermon and a collection for the super-annuated preacher's fund. They insisted upon this and got a very good collection, I believe, for of course the church was packed with people who came out of curiosity. I nearly died of shame. I was the only one being ordained and when I had to stand up there all alone I thought I should faint. The wife of Mark T., such a tiny little woman she was, just about a head and shoulder shorter than I, saw how I felt . . . and she came and stood with me and held my hand. I thought it was so nice of her. I've never forgotten it, it was one of the kindest things anyone could do. And she was an Episcopalian, too!

Well, then after that I went to the Conference all through the week, and there were a whole set of young men who set out to make themselves disagreeable. [W]henever I made any motion or did anything in the conference they questioned my right to do it and threw difficulties in the way and laughed and jeered and were just as insulting as could be. But I was perfectly polite and quiet till the end, and then I got up and said that I had attended to the business of the conference all week and had done my best to be helpful, but that there was a crowd of young men present who had persistently insulted me all the week and questioned my right to be a member of the conference and that in consequence I would never attend another conference or help them in any way until I received a formal apology. And I never have. Every year they write and beg me to come and preach the conference sermon or something, and I always refuse. One time, a few years ago, I wrote and told them why I refused and of course they'd forgotten all about it, and so the next time they sent an apology. But I don't go because I am too heterodox and I haven't any sympathy with it anymore. One time, a few years ago, they wrote to say they were going to drop me from their lists because I never came. And I replied that just as soon as they got ready to drop me, they were at liberty to do so. They haven't yet. But I don't care. I'd be glad if they would, for I don't believe in the churches at all as I did. Sometimes, I think I ought to resign. But it does no harm that I can see, after all.

So that's how I was ordained. It wasn't very glorious. It was rather like sneaking into the ministry by the back door. But if they won't open the front door to you, what else can you do? Some day they'll open all the front doors and make a proper use of the enthusiasm for service that women have got—not only in the ministry but everywhere. But until then we've got to keep climbing in the best ways we can. And there's good deal of fun to be got out of it if you can keep from being bitter and angry.

EDITOR ATTICUS HAYGOOD PROMOTES
A NEW VISION OF THE SOUTH

Source: Atticus Haygood, The New South: Gratitude, Amendment, Hope. A
Thanksgiving Sermon *(Oxford, Ga.: Published by the author, 1880)*,
8-12. Excerpts.

[T]here is one great historic fact which should, in my sober judgment, above all
things, excite everywhere in the South profound gratitude to Almighty God: I
mean the abolition of African slavery.

If I speak only for myself, (and I am persuaded that I do not,) then be it so. But I, for
one, thank God that there is no longer slavery in these United States! I am persuaded
that I only say what the vast majority of our people feel and believe. I do not forget the
better characteristics of African slavery as it existed among us for so long a time under
the sanction of national law and under the protection of the Constitution of the United
States; I do not forget that its worst features were often cruelly exaggerated, and that its
best were unfairly minified; more than all, I do not forget that, in the providence of
God, a work that is without a parallel in history was done on the Southern planta-
tions—a work that was begun by such men as Bishop Capers, of South Carolina, Lovick
Pierce and Bishop Andrew, of Georgia, and by men like-minded with them—a work
whose expenses were met by the slaveholders themselves—a work that resulted in the
Christianizing of a full half-million of the African people, who became communicants
of our Churches, and of nearly the whole four or five millions who were brought largely under the all-pervasive and redeeming influence of our holy religion.

I have nothing to say at this time of the particular "war measure" that brought
about their immediate and unconditioned enfranchisement, only that it is history,
and that it is done for once and for all. I am not called on, in order to justify my position, to approve the political unwisdom of suddenly placing the ballot in the hands
of nearly a million of unqualified men—only that, since it is done, this also is history
that we of the South should accept, and that our fellow-citizens of the North should
never disturb. But all these things, bad as they may have been and unfortunate as they
may yet be, are only incidental to the one great historic fact, that *slavery exists no more.*
For this fact I devoutly thank God this day! And on many accounts:

1. For the negroes themselves. While they have suffered and will suffer many
things in their struggle for existence, I do nevertheless believe that in the long run

it is best for them. How soon they shall realize the possibilities of their new relations depends largely, perhaps most, on themselves. Much depends on those who, under God, set them free. By every token this whole nation should undertake the problem of their education. That problem will have to be worked out on the basis of co-operation; that is, they must be helped to help themselves. To make their education an absolute gratuity will perpetuate many of the misconceptions and weaknesses of character which now embarrass and hinder their progress. Much also depends upon the Southern white people, their sympathy, their justice, their wise and helpful co-operation. This we should give them, not reluctantly, but gladly, for their good and for the safety of all, for their elevation and for the glory of God. How we may do this may be matter for discussion hereafter.

2. I am grateful that slavery no longer exists, because it is better for the white people of the South. It is better for our industries and our business, as proved by the crops that free labor makes. But by eminence it is better for our social and ethical development. We will now begin to take our right place among both the conservative and aggressive forces of the civilized and Christian world.

3. I am grateful because it is unspeakably better for our children and children's children. It is better for them in a thousand ways. I have not time for discussion in detail now. But this, if nothing else, proves the truth of my position: there are more white children at work in the South today than ever before. And this goes far to account for the six million bales of cotton. Our children are growing up to believe that idleness is vagabondage. One other thing I wish to say before leaving this point. We hear much about the disadvantages to our children of leaving them among several millions of freed-men. I recognize them, and feel them; but I would rather leave my children among several millions of free negroes than among several millions of negroes in slavery. . . .

In conclusion, I ask you to indulge me in a few reflections that are, I believe, appropriate to this occasion.

And first of all, as a people, let us of the South frankly recognize some of our faults and lacks, and try to reform and improve. I know this is a hard task. And it is all the harder because we are the subjects of so much denunciation and misrepresentation by our critics of the Northern States, and of other countries. Much of this comes through sincere ignorance; much of it through the necessities of party politics; some of it, I fear, through sinful hatred; and much of it through habit. Many have so long thrown stones at us that it has become a habit to do so. The rather Pharisaic attitude that many public men at the North have assumed toward us has greatly embarrassed and arrested our efforts to discover our faults and to amend them. But all this only furnishes a reason for beginning the sooner and trying the harder. What is really good—and there is much that is good—let us stand by, and make it better if we can.

There are some unpleasant things that ought to be said. They are on my conscience. Will you bear with me while I point out some of the weaker points in our social make-up—some of the more serious lacks in our development?

First, then, let us endeavor to overcome our intense provincialism. We are too well satisfied with ourselves. We think better of ourselves than the facts of our history and our present state of progress justify. Some of us are nearly of the opinion that the words "the South" is a synonym for universe. As a people we have not enough felt the heartbeat of the world outside of us. We have been largely shut off from that world. Slavery did this; and this suggests another reason for gratitude that it exists no more. On this point I will add only one word more. Had we been less provincial, less shut in by and with our own ideas, had we known the world better, we would have known ourselves better, and there would have been no war in 1861.

Secondly, there is a vast mass of illiteracy among us. There is white as well as black illiteracy. There are multiplied thousands who can neither read nor write. They must be taught.

Thirdly, let us recognize our want of a literature. We have not done much in this line of things. It is too obvious to dispute about, it is too painful to dwell upon.

Fourthly, let us wake up to our want of educational facilities. Our public school system is painfully inadequate. Our colleges and universities are unendowed, and they struggle against fearful odds in their effort to do their work. We are one hundred years behind the Eastern and Middle States. We are also behind many of the new States of the West.

Fifthly, consider how behindhand we are with our manufacturing interests. And remember that nature never did more to furnish a people with the conditions necessary to successful manufactures. Does any one say, we lack capital? I answer, No, my friend, it was always so. It was so when we had capital. I have thought of these things a great deal. I have been placed where I was obliged to think of them, and I have reached this conclusion with perfect confidence of its correctness: Our provincialism, our want of literature, our lack of educational facilities, and our manufactures, like our lack of population, is all explained by one fact and one word—slavery. But for slavery, Georgia would be as densely peopled as Rhode Island. Wherefore, among many other reasons, I say again, I thank God that it is no more among us!

I mention, lastly, some traits of character we should cultivate.

First, the humble but all-prevailing virtues of industry and economy in business. There should be no non-producing classes among us—no wasting classes. The Northern people have more money than the Southern people, chiefly for the reason that they work more and save more.

Secondly, let us cultivate the sentiments and habits of political and social toleration. This is sorely needed among us. We need to feel that a man may vote against us and be our friend; we need to feel that we can be his friend although we vote against him.

Thirdly, let us cultivate respect for all law and authority as God's appointment. This is not a characteristic quality of our people. The educating influences of many generations have been unfavorable to the development of this sentiment as a mental habit, or, rather, as a mental characteristic. We must plant ourselves and bring up our children on the platform of St. Paul and St. Peter, as read and considered in the beginning of this discourse. Law, authority, we must reverence and obey as the ordinance of God.

Finally, let us cease from politics as a trust and a trade. Our duty of citizenship we must perform, but we should look no longer to political struggles as the means of deliverance from all our difficulties. If we succeed we would be disappointed. Political success may enrich a few place-hunters, who ride into office upon the tide of popular enthusiasm; but it will bring little reward to the masses of the people. There is no help for it; if we prosper, we must work for it. Our deliverance will come through millions of hard licks, and millions of acts of self-denial, through industry, economy, civil order, and the blessing of God upon obedience.

Secondly, let us look forward. Hitherto I have spoken before some of you of the South of the future. Again I say, Look forward! I do the heroic dead no injustice. But the only rational way in which we can emulate their virtues is to live for the country they died for. We are not called on to die for it, but to live for it; believe me, good friends, a much harder thing to do.

We should not forget what General Lee said to our General Gordon when it was all over: "We must go home and cultivate our virtues." Lee did that. He forthwith set himself to doing good. It is a good example. We are to do the work of today, looking forward and not backward. We have no divine call to stand eternal guard by the grave of dead issues. Here certainly we may say, "Let the dead bury their dead."

My friends, my neighbors, and my pupils, I declare to you today my hope is, that in twenty years from now, the words "the South" shall have only a geographical significance.

If any ask, "Why do you say such things here today?" I answer, Because I remember who are here, and I consider what they are to do and to be when we are gone hence.

I have spoken what I solemnly believe to be the truth. Moreover, the time has fully come when these truths should be spoken by somebody; and I try to do my part, persuaded that before many years there will happily be no longer any occasion or need for them to be spoken.

There is no reason why the South should be despondent. Let us cultivate industry and economy, observe law and order, practice virtue and justice, walk in truth and righteousness, and press on with strong hearts and good hopes. The true golden day of the South is yet to dawn. But the light is breaking, and presently the shadows will flee away. Its fullness of splendor I may never see; but my children will see it, and I wish them to get ready for it while they may.

There is nothing weaker or more foolish than repining over an irrevocable past, except it be despairing of a future to which God invites us. Good friends, this is not 1860, it is 1880. Let us press forward, following the pillar of cloud and of fire always. With health and peace, with friends and homes, with civil liberty and social order, with national prosperity and domestic comfort, with bountiful harvests—with all these blessings, and good hope of heaven through Jesus Christ our Lord, let us all lift up our voices in the glad psalm of praise and thanksgiving: "Oh praise the Lord, all ye nations: praise him, all ye people. For his merciful kindness is great toward us: and the truth of the Lord endureth forever. Praise ye the Lord" [Ps. 117:1-2].

EDITOR JAMES BUCKLEY EXPRESSES PUBLICLY THE NEED FOR METHODIST HOSPITALS

Source: James M. Buckley, "Methodism and Charitable Institutions," Christian Advocate *(New York) (27 January 1881): 49-50.*

The time has come when the Methodist Episcopal Church should turn her attention to providing charitable foundations. She is to-day, so far as we can learn, without a hospital, a bed in a hospital, a dispensary, an industrial school, or, except in Mission fields, an orphan asylum under her control. We have heard that an orphan asylum had recently been provided for in Baltimore, but have not fully learned the facts. Our Church has, indeed, a very few homes for the aged and the indigent. They are well-managed, and abundantly useful. Yet more apply than can be admitted. We are far behind the other leading Protestant Churches in respect of charitable institutions.

We do not for one moment believe that this is the outcome of unfriendly conviction. It is the outcome of preoccupation. But now that we have supplied ourselves with schools, colleges, theological seminaries; Missionary, Church Extension, and Freedmen's Aid Societies, is it not time that somewhere we built a hospital or an asylum?

We need only to look about us to see how little we have done and how much others have done. The Protestant Episcopal Church has St. Luke's Hospital in New York and St. John's in Brooklyn as part of her Church charity foundation. The Presbyterian Hospital is one of the noblest in the land. The Jews have Mt. Sinai, a well-managed and well furnished hospital. Other charities have been provided by these Churches. A member of our Missionary Committee from the West, taken sick among strangers, was cared for in St. Luke's until he died. An eminent Methodist layman, once Mayor of New York, was carried there to die. Since the foundation of St. Luke's it has treated 883 Methodists. The Presbyterian Hospital during the last year has cared for thirty-four Methodist patients. Even the Jewish hospital has opened its doors to our stricken ones. But nowhere in this metropolis, and nowhere else, so far as we have been able to learn, can a Methodist find congenial Church surroundings in a hospital. A Brooklyn Methodist was once taken to the Homeopathic Hospital in Brooklyn, and, though undenominational, it was then administered by a Protestant Episcopal sisterhood.

It is not enough to say that we contribute money and social aid to the unde-nominational institutions. So we do, but these are few in number, unless those supported by taxation be included. The city institutions are poor places for Methodists. The abominable spoils system has largely put such under the care of Roman Catholics. It is distasteful, to say the least, for a Protestant to endure such associations. The Romanist sisterhoods undoubtedly alleviate much suffering, but they never forget to thrust their Catholicism before their patients.

The genial story of the late Rev. Dr. Muhlenberg illustrates the embarrassment of our clergy and laity. It seems to have been a rule of St. Luke's that no religious services but Episcopalian should be conducted there. A terrified nurse once ran to the Doctor, saying, "Doctor, Doctor, a Methodist preacher is praying with one of the patients." "Stop him, stop him," said he, "before his prayer reaches heaven."

While it is true in England charitable foundations have been so multiplied as to be a nuisance, creating the evils they were meant to cure, we are far yet from such a danger. We shall be for a long time to come. Such pauperism as England knows is the result of centuries of overcrowding and of unjust land tenure. We need not be deterred by fears from this source. We are losing power while we fail to attend to these good works. As a Missionary Church our means and strength have thus far been given to the spread of the Gospel. The institutions for which we plead are commonly the outcome of the older denominations and of a settled condition of society. But we have more than a century behind us. We are here to stay. In numbers we have gained the first rank among Protestant denominations. We have accumulated ninety millions of Church property. We have rebuilt our churches. We have established societies for the West and South. Let us now, without neglecting others, erect some monuments to charity at home.

While we neglect these, we leave ourselves without the most striking evidences of our good-will to all men. Our churches are for the well. The wretched, sick, and poverty stricken do not come to them. If they could get there, most are poorly prepared to appreciate the offices of a purely spiritual salvation. But when such see a hospital, a home for incurables, or an asylum, it is something they can understand. The Master glorified good deeds done to the body in his name. And just as the individual Christian must in good works follow his Lord, so the Church that does not provide the visible monuments of her charity will be believed to be without a full comprehension of Christianity.

We are doing wrong while we neglect this work. These institutions afford opportunity for the full round of Christian work. We have godly women among us who would find in them their true career; we have organizers and executants ready to manage them; we have physicians as learned and skillful as any; we have pastors of piety and tact. Why, then, should we allow these forces of adaptation to go to waste, or to be diverted into less useful channels? Such institutions have their own evangelizing and edifying power. They are the churches of the sick, of childhood, of the infirm. The victories of faith leap into light from the darkened chamber of the sick. Christ grants his gracious presence to loneliness and infirmity. And where these are accumulated by the care and generosity of the Church, he is preached more touchingly than in the speech of the strong. We have built churches for ourselves and our families. Would it not be well for us soon to build something for all mankind? Shall Romanism seem to be truer to the benevolent side of the gospel than we are?

Bishop Simpson Touts Family Ties at World Gathering

Source: Matthew Simpson, "Sermon at Opening Service," Proceedings of the Oecumenical Methodist Conference Held in City Road Chapel, London, September, 1881 (Cincinnati: Walden & Stowe; New York: Phillips & Hunt, 1882), 1, 16-18.

OECUMENICAL METHODIST CONFERENCE

First Day, Wednesday, September 7th

The First session of the Oecumenical Methodist Conference was held in the City Road Wesleyan Chapel, London, on Wednesday, the 7th September, 1881. The Chapel was densely crowded with delegates and ministers.

The opening service in the morning was conducted by the Rev. George Osborn, D.D., President of the British Wesleyan Conference.

The sermon was preached by the Rev. Matthew Simpson, D.D., LL.D. of Philadelphia, Senior Bishop of the Methodist Episcopal Church of America, from the text:

"The words that I speak unto you, they are spirit, and they are life."—John 6:63

. . . .

There are those who disparage Methodism, because it has had divisions, and they predict its early disintegration. For the same reason Christianity itself might be disparaged. The learned and eloquent Bossuet wrote a work against Protestantism on account of its variations—showing its weakness; but, nevertheless, in the last century, its progress has been more rapid than ever before. I am not sure that these divisions are an unmixed evil. They seem to me to have compensation also. With the different tastes and habits of men, I fancy that, through churches somewhat differently organised and with different usages, more minds may be won for Christ. Certainly we may be provoked even to love and good works. It seems also to me that as God has showed us physical life in almost every possible form, He means that we shall understand that Christian life may exist and flourish in different organizations and usages. He would show us that there is no sacredness in mere ecclesiasticism. Organisation has its value, and every member of each church should be true to his association; yet the organization is only the temple in which the life dwells. The organisation is of man. The life is of Christ. Were there but one organisation with certain usages that prospered, we should think its forms and usages were in themselves sacred, we should grow narrow and bigoted. Our church would be *the* Church, and all others would be schismatics. But when we see life in other churches, we learn that the God of the Jew is the God of the Gentile also. We recognise a brother beloved in every member of the family, and praise God for the infinitude of His grace. Quite possibly, also, in these separate organizations, a little more flexibility may be gained, and, while holding fast to the Great Head of the Church, and contending earnestly for the faith once delivered to the saints, we may learn from each other something that may help us in conquering the world for Christ.

As to the divisions in the Methodist family, there is little to mar the family likeness. For, first, there has been among the Wesleyan ranks no division as to doctrines. The clear statements in Mr. Wesley's sermons, and the doctrinal character of the hymns constantly sung, have aided in keeping us one. All over the world Methodist theology is an unit. Nor, secondly, is there any radical difference in usages. The class-meeting, the prayer-meeting, the love-feast, the watch-night, though more or less strictly observed, are known everywhere in Methodism. So far as the membership is concerned, there is scarcely a single difference. Even in the Connexional bonds there is general likeness. The itinerant ministry, and the quarterly and annual conferences, exist in almost every branch. In the manner of legislation, and in the mode of effecting ministerial changes, there are some differences; but the points of agreement are so numerous as compared with the differences that we are emphatically one. We have no divisions as to vestments, and candles, and genuflections. We have no High Church, or Low Church, or Broad Church.

Differ as we may, there is something in all of us which the world recognises. Does a minister preach with unusual fervour, does he in all his duties exhibit unusual zeal? Does not the world say, He preaches like a Methodist? Does a congregation meet, and sing, and pray and rejoice? Does not the world say, They are like Methodists? This Conference evinces a yearning for closer union, for more fraternal feeling. It is in the spirit of Mr. Wesley, who sought a closer union among all Christians. His societies were at first independent. When, by the formation of a Conference they were united, he greatly rejoiced. Not only so, but wrote in 1764, "I have long desired that there might be an open, avowed union between all who preach those fundamental truths—original sin, and justification by faith, producing inward and outward holiness; but all my endeavours have been hitherto ineffectual. God's time has not fully come" [*Journal*, 16 March 1764]. Again he wrote, "I do not desire a union of opinion among them. They might agree or disagree touching absolute decrees on the one hand, and perfection on the other. Not a union in expression. These may still speak of imputed righteousness, and those of the merits of Christ. Not a union with regard to outward order. Some may remain still quite regular, some quite irregular, and some partly regular and partly irregular" [*Journal*, 19 April 1764]. Again he wrote, "I ask but one thing, 'Is thy heart right as my heart is with thine?' If it be so, give me thy hand" [*The Character of a Methodist, 1742*].

His great heart was a hundred years in advance of the Christian world. Recently we have seen a Pan-Anglican Congress [Lambeth Conference, 1877], a Pan Presbyterian Council [World Alliance of Reformed Churches, 1877], and now a Methodist Oecumenical Conference. Do not these foreshadow an Oecumenical Protestant Conference, when Mr. Wesley's hope shall be realised, and the world shall see that evangelical Christians are one in heart and one in effect? Certain I am that there will be an Oecumenical Conference, if not on earth, at least in heaven, when the good and the wise of all ages and of all churches shall meet at the Redeemer's throne. The nearer we rise toward the spirit of that heavenly union, the closer we come together here.

CREEK CHIEF SAMUEL CHECOTE
PENS AUTOBIOGRAPHICAL LETTER

Source: Samuel Checote, "Letter from Chief Checote,"
Our Brother in Red *1/10 (June 1883): 2.*

MR. EDITOR:—In compliance with a request at our last Annual Conference, by Dr. Kelley, I undertake to give some notes of my life and labors as an Indian Missionary. I was born in the year 1819 on Chattahooche River, Ala. At that time my parents had no knowledge of the *good word.* They seemed to know there was a Supreme Ruler of the universe; that Christ came upon earth; but seemed ignorant of his mission. I was sent to the Methodist boarding-school, near Fort Mitchell, in the fall of 1828. My parents immigrated to this Territory [Oklahoma] in 1829, and they brought me with them. In a few years after our arrival, missionaries came among us; of the number was the Rev. John Harrell. Those missionaries occupied their spare time in teaching day-schools, at which I attended. I was then impressed with the talks and actions of those good men, and frequently had a desire to unite myself with the Church before I did, but no one gave me encouragement to do so. At the baptisms of children I have lingered with desire of being baptized, but postponed from time to time for the want of encouragement. In 1835 the Creeks in Council passed a resolution ordering all the missionaries out of the country. After this, the members of the Church remaining in the country grew cold in the cause, and the people forgot how to pray. This state of affairs continued for quite a number of years, when the Indians began to congregate and sing the old songs of Zion, and to revive the spiritual feelings once enjoyed while the missionaries were among them. They invited missionaries to come among them again, and in response to the invitation, Revs. Thomas Bertalf, Walter Collins, and James Essex, returned and renewed their labors. My father was then about 70 years of age, who then united himself with the Methodist Episcopal Church, and was baptized. My mother died years before this, but had embraced religion and died in the triumph of a living faith. The Creeks in Council, again in 1844, made a law prohibiting any of its citizens from preaching, under penalty of fifty lashes on the bare back for each violation. The Indians regarded preaching as belonging to white folks alone. Many persons were severely whipped under this law, and many fled from their homes in

411

order to escape the clutches of the officers, and I was one of that number. I appeared before General Roley McIntosh, who was at that time chief of the Upper Creeks, and complained of the persecution, and requested he would stop it, and he did so. I was admitted into the Indian Mission Conference in 1852. I was located by the Conference in 1861. I was re-admitted a short time after the close of the [Civil] war. In consequence of poor health and feeble condition, I have been placed on the superannuated [retired] list for the past two years. My constant desire has been to labor earnestly wherever I might be—in the itinerancy or local ranks.

I am glad to say that my people have learned to love the glad tidings of salvation, and that we as a people have emerged from the dark clouds that once overshadowed our intellectual and spiritual horizon, and that religion is no more regarded as an enemy to the Indians, but esteemed as their best friend. Since the adoption of our Constitutional Government, which was in 1867, and when I had the honor of being inaugurated principal Chief, the sessions of both branches of the National Council have been opened and closed each day with a prayer by a chaplain.

I think the cause of Christ is still prospering among us notwithstanding the hindrances occasioned by our domestic troubles. I pray that the gospel may run and be glorified, and that salvation may come to all.

Samuel Checote

Okmulgee, I. T. [Indian Territory], June 1, 1883.

WCTU HEAD FRANCES WILLARD ADDRESSES WOMEN ON TRANSFORMING SELF, FAMILY, CHURCH, AND SOCIETY

Source: Frances E. Willard, Woman and Temperance; or, The Work and Workers of The Womans Christian Temperance Union *(Hartford: Park Publishing Co., 1883), 42-47. Excerpts. Italics added.*

The W.C.T.U. stands as the exponent, not alone of that return to physical sanity which will follow the downfall of the drink habit, but the reign of a religion of the body, which for the first time in history shall correlate with Christ's wholesome, practical, yet blessedly spiritual religion of the soul. "The kingdom of heaven is within you" [Luke 17:21]—shall have a new meaning to the clear-eyed, steady-limbed Christians of the future, from whose brain and blood the taint of alcohol and nicotine has been eliminated by ages of pure habits and noble heredity. . . .

The women of this land have never had before such training as is furnished by the topical studies of our society, in the laws by which childhood shall set out upon its endless journey with a priceless heritage of powers laid up in store by the tender, sacred foresight of those by whom the young immortal's being was invoked. The laws of health were never studied by so many mothers, or with such immediate results for good on their own lives and those of their children. The deformed waist and foot of the average fashionable American never seemed so hideous and wicked, nor the cumbrous dress of the period so unendurable as now, when from studying one "poison habit," our minds, by the inevitable laws of thought, reach out to wider researches and more varied deductions than we had dreamed at first. The economies of co-operative house-keeping never looked so attractive or so feasible as since the homemakers have learned something about the priceless worth of time and money for the purposes of a Christ-like benevolence. The value of a trained intellect never had such significance as since we have learned what an incalculable saving of words there is in a direct style, what value in the power of classification of fact, what boundless resources for illustrating and enforcing truth come as the sequel of a well-stored memory and a cultivated imagination. The puerility [simple-mindedness] of mere talk for the sake of talk, the unworthiness of "idle words," and vacuous, purposeless gossip, the waste of long and aimless letter-writing, never looked as egregious [absurd] as to the [WCTU] workers who find every day too short for the glorious and gracious deeds which lie waiting for them on every hand.

But to help forward the coming of Christ into all departments of life, is, in its last analysis, the purpose and aim of the W.C.T.U. For we believe this correlation of New Testament religion with philanthropy, and of the Church with civilization, is the perpetual miracle which furnishes the only sufficient antidote to current skepticism. Higher toward the zenith climbs the Sun of Righteousness, making circle after circle of human endeavor and achievement warm and radiant with the healing of its beams. *First of all, in our Gospel temperance work, this heavenly light penetrated the gloom of the individual tempted heart* (the smallest circle, in which all others are involved), illumined its darkness, melted its hardness, made it a sweet and sunny place—a temple filled with the Holy Ghost.

Having thus come to the heart of the drinking man in the plenitude of his redeeming power, Christ entered *the next wider circle in which two human hearts unite to form a home,* and here, by the revelation of her place in His kingdom, He lifted to an equal level with her husband the gentle companion who had supposed herself happy in being the favorite vassal of her liege lord. "There is neither male nor female in Christ Jesus" [Galatians 3:28]; this was the "open sesame," a declaration utterly opposed to all custom and tradition. But so steadily the light has shone, and so kindly has it made the heart of man, that without strife of tongues or edict of sovereigns, it is coming now to pass that in proportion as any home is really Christian, the husband and wife are peers in dignity and power. There are no homes on earth where woman is "revered, beloved," and individualized in character and work so thoroughly as the fifty thousand in America where "her children arise up and call her blessed, her husband also, and he praiseth her" [Proverbs 31:28] because of her part in the work of our W.C.T.U.

Beyond this sweet and sacred circle where two hearts grow to be one, where the mystery of birth and the hallowed face of child and mother work their perpetual charm, comes the outer-court of home, *that third great circle which we call society.* Surely and steadily the light of Christ is coming there, through the loving temperance Pentecost, to replace the empty phrase of punctilio [petty formality] by earnest words of cheer and inspiration; to banish the unhealthful tyranny of fashion by enthroning wholesome taste and common sense; to drive out questionable amusements and introduce innocent and delightful pastimes; to exorcise the evil spirit of gossip and domesticate helpful and tolerant speech; nay, more, to banish from the social board those false emblems of hospitality and good will—intoxicating drinks.

Sweep a wider circle still, and behold in that ecclesiastical invention called "denominationalism," Christ coming by the union of His handmaids in work for Him; coming to put away the form outward and visible that He may shed abroad the grace inward and spiritual; to close the theological disquisition of the learned pundit, and open the Bible of the humble saint; to draw away men's thoughts from theories of right living and center them upon right living itself; to usher in the priesthood of the people, by pressing upon the conscience of each believer the individual commission, "Go, disciple all nations" [Matthew 28:19], and emphasizing the individual promise, "Lo, I am with thee always" [Matthew 28:20].

But the modern temperance movement, born of Christ's Gospel and cradled at His altars, is rapidly filing *one more circle of influence, wide as the widest zone of earthly weal or woe, and that is government.* . . . "Thy kingdom come, thy will be done *on earth.*" Christ shall reign—not visible, but invisibly; not in form, but in fact; nor in substance, but in essence, and the day draws nigh! Then surely the traffic in intoxicating liquors as a drink will no longer be protected by the statute book, the lawyer's plea, the affirmation of the witness, and decision of the judge. And since the government is after all a circle that includes all hearts, all homes, all churches, all societies, does it not seem as if intelligent loyalty to Christ the King would cause each heart that loves Him to feel in duty bound to use all the power it could gather to itself in helping choose the framers of those more righteous laws? But let it be remembered that for every Christian man who has a voice in making and enforcing laws, there are at least two Christian women who have no voice at all. Hence, under such circumstances as now exist, His militant army must ever be powerless to win those legislative battles, which, more than any others, affect the happiness of aggregate humanity. But the light gleams already along the sunny hilltops of the nineteenth century of grace. Upon those who in largest numbers love Him who has filled their hearts with peace and their homes with blessing, slowly dawns the consciousness that they may—nay, better still, *they ought* to—ask for power to help forward the coming of their Lord in government—to throw the safeguard of their prohibition ballots around those who have left the shelter of their arms only to be entrapped by the saloons that bad men legalize and set along the streets.

"But some doubted" [Matthew 28:17].

This was in our earlier National Conventions. Almost none disputed the value of the added weapon in woman's hand—indeed, all deemed it "sure to come." It was only the old, old question of expediency; of "frightening away our sisters among the more conservative." But later on we asked these questions: Has the policy of silence caused a great rallying to our camp from the ranks of the conservative? Do you know an instance in which it has augmented your working force? Are not all the women upon whose help we can confidently count, favorable to *the "Do Everything Policy,"* as the only one broad enough to meet our hydra-headed foe? Have not the men of the liquor traffic said in platform, resolution, and secret circular, "The ballot in woman's hand will be the death-knell of our trade?"

And so to-day, while each State *is free to adopt or disavow* the ballot as a home protection weapon, and although the white-winged fleet of the W.C.T.U. in a score of States crowds all sail for constitutional prohibition, to be followed up by "Home Protection," still though "the silver sails are all out in the West," every ship in the gleaming line is all the same a Gospel ship—*an "old ship Zion—Hallelujah!"*

415

MEA IV:
1884–1939

MORRIS CRAWFORD NOTES CHANGING DUTIES OF DISTRICT SUPERINTENDENTS

Source: Morris D'C. Crawford, "Changes in the Duties of the Presiding Eldership," Christian Advocate (New York) (12 February 1885): 4. Italics in original.

Address by the Rev. M. D'C. Crawford, D.D., at a Conference of Presiding Elders, in New York City, Dec. 8, 1884, and published at the request of the Conference.

I am requested to discuss the *"Changes in the Duties of the Presiding Eldership, and the Causes Thereof."* That great changes have taken place in these duties—changes so marked as to give a new aspect to the office—must be apparent. It seems to me equally clear that all these changes have been caused by changes in the condition of the Church. No change has been made in the status of the office, or in its relation to the economy of Methodism, from the beginning until now. The section entitled *"Presiding Elders and Their Duty,"* was first framed and put in the Discipline in 1792. . . .

But, notwithstanding the unshaken stability of the Presiding Eldership, great changes have taken place in its duties.

Relatively, the quarterly meeting has become unimportant, and, in its old-time grandeur, an impossibility. . . .

To break up all the congregations on that territory now, for a whole Sabbath, to attend some general gathering, would be absurd, if not criminal.

Do not understand me to say that the Quarterly Meeting has lost its value. On the contrary, it is indispensable. The presiding elder's visits, however, are not now, as formerly, chiefly to preach and conduct other religious services, but much more to *"oversee the spiritual and temporal business"* of the various charges of his district. This means vastly more than in former days.

When Bishop Asbury, in 1788, gave Freeborn Garrettson the Hudson River Valley for a district, with a dozen pious young men for preachers, among whom he divided the territory, this pioneer presiding elder traveled up one side of the river and down the other, meeting and encouraging all the preachers in turn, and, by his ministrations, making every-where a profound impression. But

certainly *supervision* was among the least of his duties, because there was very little to supervise. Now how changed. We have everywhere large property interests,
which the presiding elder is directed to promote by every means in his power. To
see that the churches and parsonages are held by proper tenure, are well insured,
and kept in repair, and freed from debt. To encourage generous provision for the
support of the preachers. To urge liberality toward our great charities, missions,
Church Extension, Conference claimants, Freedmen's Aid, education. To visit
and foster Sunday-schools, and urge the formation of lyceums and reading circles, and all feasible methods for securing the religious training of our children
and young people. He is never to lose sight of the evangelistic work of the
Church, every-where, and on all suitable occasions exhorting preachers and people to seek directly the salvation of souls. There are many incidental duties.
Frequently some pastor on his district will fail in health, when satisfactory provision must be made for the church[,] and the welfare of the pastor tenderly cared
for. There are always embarrassed churches to be relieved, and discouraged
workers to be helped. . . .

A most important class of duties, always connected with the office, has never
appeared in the Discipline. I allude to the information and advice given to the
Bishop at Conference respecting the appointments. As the Church grows this information and advice becomes more and more nearly indispensable. How else will you
provide for them? You may properly rate a Bishop's discernment of character very
high. He becomes an expert. . . . So men continually busied with men, as our
Bishops are, come to estimate the whole man by some one word or act. But it is
impossible for them to know the majority of the churches or a majority of the
preachers, since they never can visit the one or be brought face to face with the
other.

Now, who can suggest, in the whole range of human administration, a more delicate or difficult work than making the appointments of an Annual Conference? To
deal judicially fair with the preachers, and not wrong the churches—to assign every
preacher to a congenial field where he will be at his best and accomplish the most,
and to give every church an acceptable and successful pastor—this is the ideal, but,
alas, it is hopeless. When you have done your utmost you will be dissatisfied with
your own decision. You will often see hardship and disappointment inevitable to
noble, sensitive men and their families. But to approach the ideal, to be in any
sense fit for his place, a presiding elder surely should be a man of high character,
sound judgment, and incapable of yielding to partialities or prejudices. His office
is disgraced when it is used to help his friends or to disparage those who are
unfriendly to him.

He needs to bring to his work all the power God has given him. He is a leader of
preachers and of churches. He cannot escape responsibility if the spiritual and
temporal interests of his district are not advanced. In this Centennial year of our
Church but one watchword will save us from dishonor—*Speak unto the children of
Israel, that they go forward [Ex. 14:15]*. We have received from our fathers, in our
great denominational interests, a sacred trust which we are to study and guard and

administer with intelligence and zeal. It will not answer to attempt to do over again the things they have done. We cannot bring back or repeat the past. The Church life of to-day must be distinctive of to-day. We must meet and grapple with the living problems of the present. But we shall triumph. God has not forsaken us. To him be all the glory.

Henry Appenzeller begins mission in Korea

Source: Henry G. Appenzeller, "Report of the Korean Mission,"
Annual Report of the Missionary Society, 1885, Methodist Episcopal Church
(New York: The Society, 1886), 235-37.

We left Nagasaki [Japan] March 31 [1885] for Korea, stopped at two small islands on the way, and arrived at Fusan, an open port on the south-eastern coast of the country on the morning of April 2. . . .

At nine o'clock we went ashore, called on Mr. W. N. Lovatt, the collector of the port, and soon after started for a walk of three miles to Pousan (Fusan), the old Korean village. . . . We left Fusan the next day for Chimulpo. The day was cold, rainy, disagreeable. This kind of weather continued the rest of the voyage, so that the speed was slow and the sea-sickness long and severe. We came round the southern extremity of the peninsula, up the western coast, entered the mouth of the Han River at noon Sunday the 5th [of April], and at three P.M. dropped anchor at this port. . . .

Mrs. Appenzeller first stepped from the sampan upon the bare rocks. Where to go? What to do? were questions that needed immediate attention, as it was beginning to rain. There are no hotels here kept by Americans or Europeans; but hearing of a Japanese one, I motioned to a coolie to carry our baggage and off we started. The rooms at the hotel are comfortably large, but might be warmer. When we sat down to the table it was to eat foreign food, well prepared, and palatable.

Politically, the country is still unsettled [China and Japan vie for dominance]. There are disturbing elements at work at the capital, and until they are rooted out, and the weak disordered government made strong, we may expect little progress and much discord in the "Land of the Morning Sun."

We came here on Easter. May He who on that day burst asunder the bars of death, break the bands that bind this people, and bring them to the light and liberty of God's children!

Source: Henry G. Appenzeller, "Report of the Korea Mission,"
Annual Report of the Missionary Society for 1886,
Methodist Episcopal Church (New York: The Society, 1887), 266-70.

In presenting our second annual report of this mission we desire first of all to render thanks unto a kind Providence that has watched over us and permitted us to labor without interruption another year. It has been a year of constant anxiety, of much prayer; a year that marked the successful opening of our work here. For this God be praised. We are the only persons in Seoul that are entirely dependent upon our own resources; we are not under the wing of the government, but single-handed and alone we do the Lord's work. In May last . . . there was considerable talk of removing foreigners from Seoul, but all save our mission were in some way working for, or connected with, the government, which would have made an excuse for them to remain in the city.

Last year we had time only to buy homes for ourselves, and fit them up for winter. At the beginning of this year we began to enlarge our borders east, south and north. We could not "go west," as our property joins the city wall. The Woman's Foreign Missionary Society is to be congratulated on the most admirable selection Mrs. Scranton made for their work. The hospital grounds to the east of and adjoining Dr. Scranton's lots are large and well adapted for the purpose, while the school grounds immediately in front of H. G. Appenzeller's house and south of it are in every way suited for the work. We now own about 5 acres of ground in Seoul, situated in that part of the city sure to be the home of the foreigners who may come after us.

The enthusiasm for the study of English has always been great among the Koreans. A little knowledge of the new tongue was and still is a stepping stone to something higher. Ask a Korean, "Why do you wish to study English?" and his almost invariable answer will be "To get rank." As a sort of skirmish battle our mission school was opened June 8th and continued in session until July 2, during which time 6 were enrolled. Soon one had the proverbial "business in the country," another one found June a bad month for hard work on a new language and left, while a third one had a death in his family and could not attend. The school was reopened Sept. 1, 1886, with 1 in attendance. The lack in actual attendance was made up in part by those who said they would come. We have now, Oct. 6, 20 on the roll, with an actual attendance of 18. New students apply for admission almost every day. We have every reason to believe the school will be crowded, at least in our present quarters.

The present social and political condition of Korea is such that it is the unanimous judgment of all the missionaries here not to attempt to open evangelistic work. We do not go about in the mourner's garb of the natives as do the Jesuits, but are open and frank in all our dealings with the Koreans. In this way we are fast gaining their confidence. We believe in a few years, having established ourselves and mastered the language, the seed now sown in a quiet way will bear an abundant harvest. Medical and educational work are very acceptable, and great good can be done in these lines.

Our catechism is translated and published in the Korean language. We are translating other books and tracts, seeing in this way the introduction of Christian literature. . . .

Woman's Foreign Missionary Society—It is a cause for sincere gratitude to God that the W.F.M.S. entered Korea when we did. We are breaking the fallow ground together; we are sowing the seed broadcast at the same time, and at the harvest time we will rejoice together. From the time that Mrs. Scranton came to Korea not a moment was lost in laying broad plans for reaching the women of this dark land. Property was purchased last fall, work on the building commenced last February, just about the time the unpleasant news, that no extra appropriation for the home was made, reached us. It drove us to our knees: every cent was counted twice to see how far it would reach, and the urgency of the case was restated to the friends at home. The prayers and petitions were not in vain. Mrs. Blackstone's liberal gift of $3,000, an additional gift of over $700 from the New York branch, came just at the right time, and ere this report will reach you Mrs. Scranton will be in her home, which for beauty of location there is not any more desirable in the city. The building is 88 feet long and 80 feet wide, so arranged to make a comfortable home for the teachers, and also a home to the women who may come to it for instruction.

The women of Korea can be reached. This is no longer an experiment, but a fact. The strong walls of isolation have been sapped, and while there are still very many and serious difficulties in our way, God has vouchsafed his blessing unto us, and permits us to report that Mrs. Scranton had for several months under her instruction a married woman of high rank. This lady left, finally, when compelled to do so by sickness. Three little girls are now taught in this home, and others are coming soon.

More workers are needed at once, and will of course come and bear their part in this glorious work of saving souls. What this society has accomplished in other lands she will do in the Hermit Nation.

Annual Medical Report. Our medical work began with the arrival of Dr. Scranton in Korea. From May 22 to June 24, 1885 this work was with Dr. Allen of the Presbyterian Board in the Korean government hospital. At that place a daily average between 40 and 70 patients were treated.

Our medical year, entirely under our own auspices, began Sept. 10, 1885. Until June 15 of this year our dispensary conveniences were very imperfect. Work was carried on in Dr. Scranton's home. In that place 522 patients were seen and treated. Since that date until Sept. 10, the close of 12 months' work, 320 patients have been treated at our dispensary, making a total of 842 patients for the whole year.

Our receipts for this year from sale of medicine have not been large. It has amounted to only $34.83. During the cholera epidemic just passed, no charge was made for medicine: first, because the epidemic chiefly raged among the very poorest class, and, second, because we thought only of haste in getting the needful treatment to the patient.

It is thought that with a fuller knowledge of our circumstances some of our receipts will be larger somewhat, as soon as we get into our perfected plans for work.

It has been chiefly among the poorest classes that we have done our work, often even among outcasts. The latter have to rely on us for full support during treatment, if the complaints are sufficiently severe to make them give up all work.

Quite a good many of the better classes also have been treated at the dispensary, and seen at their homes. It is proposed soon to regulate the prices so that the wealthier shall bear more of the burden of expense in favor of the poorer, who shall then have less to pay, accordingly, and often nothing at all. . . .

We have already helped hundreds, but there are thousands more. As I intimated, we desire as soon as we have another physician to go to the patients who lie in the open air, outcasts without friends and without hope, the helpless ones who will die from neglect and exposure, where if these obstacles did not exist, the disease might not prove sufficiently powerful to overcome them.

FREDERICK MASTERS ENVISIONS EXPANDING MINISTRY TO JAPANESE AMERICANS IN CALIFORNIA

Source: Frederick J. Masters, "Our Asian Work in California—II," California Christian Advocate (9 June 1886): 1.

Our work amongst the 600 Japanese in this city is somewhat different to the Chinese. They [the Japanese] come here to learn; for the most part, with a view to improving their condition in their own country, where a knowledge of English is a *sine qua non* for any official post. They belong to a nation that is fast breaking away from the superstitions and barbarisms of the past, and is rushing with breakneck speed to overtake the more powerful and energetic nations of the civilized world. . . . These young men come to us, some already Christianized, some favorable to Christianity, others in a chaos of speculation, imbued with agnostic teachings and disposed to treat Christianity as a system of exploded myths, soon to take its place among the dead and dying superstitions of the past. In the majority of instances they come to us with receptive minds and hearts, believing this country to be the depository of everything great and wise, and are prepared to make any sacrifice and fill the most menial occupations, in order to obtain that wisdom which they believe to be of such advantage to themselves and their country. With no hostile bias or deep prejudices to be eradicated, as in the case of the Chinese, the Japanese are disposed to accept whatever we give them. Taught to believe in our institutions, and to think the American as near social and political perfection as possible, it will not be surprising if some of these our admirers should be found accepting our heresies as well as our orthodoxies, and imitating our vices as well as our virtues.

There are three Japanese associations in San Francisco. Our M.E. Gospel Society numbers over 100, the Presbyterian 60, and the Science, or Herbert Spencer Society, where all Christian teaching is excluded, numbers only 20. Our Society is, therefore, the most flourishing, and since its establishment eight years ago, 62 Japanese have been baptized, and nineteen admitted by church letter. Some of these young men are members of Methodist Universities and Seminaries; some are studying in the public schools, while others take advantage of our night schools to learn the rudiments of the English tongue. With those immediately under our influence there is not much difficulty in finding men willing to profess Christianity;

the difficulty is in getting them to remain on probation long enough to test the strength of their faith and the reality of their conversion. With strong emotions they easily enthuse, and their convictions are carried by storm. In too many instances this is followed by a reaction; the ordinary exercises cease to interest; they seem to pine for something new, and their faith vacillates amidst the ebb and flow of conflicting influences, good and bad. . . . A democratic spirit also asserts itself in an impatience of the restraints of rules, and a claim to have a voice in the direction of church affairs, "the same as American men." While this liberalizing tendency on the part of a few volatile spirits causes us some solicitude, we are able to gather comfort from the steady faith, integrity of life, and unshaken loyalty of a large number of our Japanese members. The older and more experienced members are the life and stay of the church, and have walked with even footsteps from the day of their conversion until now. Had this mission done no other work than to mold the characters of men like these—of [Sennosuke] Ogata, for instance, who is now an ordained missionary of our church in Japan, and of half a dozen whose names I might mention whose lives "adorn the doctrine of God our Saviour in all things" [Titus 2:10]—this mission would not have been in vain.

MARY CLARKE NIND AND FRANCES WILLARD
COMMENT ON ELECTION TO AND DISMISSAL BY
GENERAL CONFERENCE, 1888

Sources: Mary Clarke Nind and Her Work, *by her Children (Chicago: Woman's Foreign Missionary Society, 1906), 47; Frances E. Willard,* Glimpses of Fifty Years *(Chicago: Woman's Temperance Publication Association, 1889), 615-21.*

Mary Clarke Nind

[General Conference, MEC] New York City

Wednesday, May 2, [1888]. Bishops' address and report on eligibility of women all against us, but if the Lord be for us, what matters?

Friday, May 4. Another day of sharp debate, but no conclusions reached. Saturday, May 5. Still another day.

Monday, May 7. Today we were ejected from our seats by a majority of 37 clerical and 2 lay votes, and the great debate is over, to come up again in 1892. All is serene in my soul.

Frances E. Willard

In October, 1887, Anna Gordon and I were at Binghamton [New York], attending the W.C.T.U. Convention of New York State. It was a grand occasion, so many delegates being present that the large church was filled with them. We were entertained in the home of Mrs. Mather, granddaughter of Jonathan Edwards, and while sitting at the breakfast table in her pleasant home, I opened a telegram there handed to me, and read these words:

CHICAGO

I suppose you know that the Rock River Conference has chosen you one of its lay delegates to the General Conference.

S. A. KEAN.

The tears sprang to my eyes, and turning to my dignified hostess I said: "You can hardly imagine how much this means to me. The dear old Rock River Conference of which my brother was once a member, and many of whose ministers I have known from girlhood, selects me as one of its two lay delegates, and my father's business partner of twenty years ago kindly telegraphs the pleasant news. Why should I not think well of men when they can do things so magnanimous? Every one who voted for me would have given his eye teeth to have gone in my stead, yet they set to work and sent me, just out of brotherly good-will."

Much more after this sort I poured out, in my gratitude and gladness, to the quiet old lady, whose face lighted up as she "rejoiced in my joy."

No one had ever named to me the possibility of such an honor, save that Miss Phebe and Mrs. Frank Elliott (daughter and daughter-in-law of Rev. Dr. Charles Elliott, former editor of the *Central Christian Advocate*, but now deceased) had sent me a letter stating that they thought women should go to the General Conference, as they had for years helped to elect those who did go as lay delegates, and had themselves been chosen alternates, and their names placed without question on General Conference lists. I had always thought that no fair-minded person could have a doubt of their inherent right to go, since women constitute at least two thirds of the church membership, bear more than one half its burdens, and have patiently conceded to the brethren, during all generations, its emoluments and honors.

No more was known to me until, on returning West, I heard that certain lawyers of the contrary part (*i. e.*, well-known opponents of woman's larger recognition in these modern days) had said that I would never be allowed to take my seat. But my friends declared, what I fully believed, that the Discipline was so explicit, that "the wayfaring man, though a fool," could not fail to find its meaning friendly.

. . . . I went to New York a few days before the great Conference was to begin its quadrennial session as the Supreme Court of our church, representing over two millions of Methodists. By this time, Dr. Buckley had taken his position against the admission of women, the tintinnabulation of tongues had set in, and the pent-up pendulosity of pens had fairly burst forth.

I arrived in New York on the Friday previous to the Conference, and wishing to know just what was the best course for me to pursue, I went over to the Opera House where the Conference was to hold its session and inquired for General Fisk, finding him already conferring with grave dignitaries of the church and busy with his duties as chairman of the Committee of Arrangements. He went with Mrs. Carse and me into the Opera House and we took our seats on the platform with the great yawning auditorium before us, empty and dark. He told me there was going to be a vigorous fight, but he thought the women would get in. I asked his advice about sitting with my delegation, assuring him that I would on no account take a wrong attitude toward the controversy. He replied, "Your moral right, there is none to dispute, and if you are ruled out it will be on a pure technicality and not upon the merits of the case. This being true, I advise you to be on hand bright and early the morning that the Conference opens, and if you like, I shall be glad to escort you along the aisle to your place with your Rock River brethren." But there had come to me that morning a disquieting telegram from home; my dear mother had not been well for two or three weeks, but I had received repeated notes in her usual hand and as I knew her cheery spirit and great desire that I should be a member of the Conference, I had gone on with my engagements, knowing that she was in the very best of care, and believing that I should be able to enter on my novel duties. However, on receiving the morning telegram that mother was not very well and Anna Gordon would perhaps better go to her, I telegraphed at once, "Would it not be better for me to go?" That this made it almost a foregone conclusion that I should return to my home, I knew, for my faithful secretaries there would hardly take the risk of telling me not to come when I had so plainly expressed the thought and purpose of doing so. Therefore, I was prepared for the response that soon arrived, "Do not be anxious, but come." And so on Saturday night I took the limited express, for the first time in my life deliberately setting out on a Sabbath day's journey. . . .

My kindest of neighbors in the "annex," as we call the cottage that my sister built joining our own, were at the depot in Chicago. Helen L. Hood, that staunch white ribboner of Illinois, reached out her strong hand to me before I left the platform of the car, and said, "Your mother is better." I think no words were ever sweeter of all that I have heard. Now followed a month in which I exchanged the busy and constantly varied activities of a temperance reformer for the sacred quiet of my mother's sick-room. I had never seen her so ill, but she was, as always, entirely self-possessed. We had a council of physicians and she went through the diagnosis with even smiling cheerfulness, saying, "I think I shall get well, but I am not at all afraid to die." Little by little she crept up again under the skillful care of that noble woman, Dr. Mary McCrillis, who by day and night was with us in our trouble.

Anna Gordon arrived in New York the day I left, and remained, at my request, until the great question was decided, sending me constant bulletins from the Opera House box where General Fisk, with his customary thoughtfulness, had assigned her a seat. Nothing could exceed my surprise when I learned that our good bench of Bishops had prejudged the entire case in their opening address. Only the cold type of the Associated Press dispatch, giving their language, could have made me believe this possible. Anna Gordon pictured the scene dramatically, catching on the wing many of the bright turns and arguments of the debaters, and seeming full of expectation that the women would carry the day. She wrote that there was unrivaled commotion, that our side felt confident, that friends were urgent for my return and strongly counseled it, but without saying anything to my mother, who is so self-sacrificing that I knew she would tell me, "By all means go back, my child," I fully determined that I would have nothing to do with the controversy, directly or indirectly, and so in great quietness of spirit awaited the result. When the morning *Inter Ocean* was thrown on the steps, I would refrain for some time from going after it, and mother asked no questions. But when I read that the lay delegates gave a majority against the admission of women, and remembered that the vote of women, as they well knew, at the time of the debate on the eligibility of the laity to the General Conference, had forced open its doors to the laymen who now deliberately voted to exclude women, I had no more spirit in me. Once more it was a case of "Thou, too, Brutus!" That the Bishops should have "left us lamenting," grieved me, but when the lay delegates did the same, I said in my heart, "Once more the action of my fellow mortals weans me from love of life, and by so doing they have doubtless helped me more than their generosity of action could possibly have done." However, I lost no sleep and wasted no tears over the curious transaction, and I confidently predict that we five women, whose election was thus disavowed, will have more enviable places in history than any who opposed us on those memorable days. Of them it will be written, while doubtless they did not so intend, that they committed an injustice: of us, only that in silence we endured it.

The champions of equality made a splendid record, of which they will be prouder with each added year. They are forerunners of that grander, because more equitable, polity that shall yet glorify our Methodism when in her law, as in Christ's gospel, there shall be "Neither male nor female."

DEACONESS CONFERENCE SETS RULES FOR DEACONESS HOMES

Source: Notes Concerning Management of Deaconess Home (*New York: Methodist Book Concern, 1889*), 1-4. Excerpts.

BY ACTION OF GENERAL CONFERENCE [1888]

The duties of the Deaconesses are to minister to the poor, visit the sick, pray with the dying, care for the orphans, seek the wandering, comfort the sorrowing, save the sinning, and, relinquishing wholly all other pursuits devote themselves, in a general way, to such forms of Christian labor as may be suited to their abilities.

No vow shall be exacted from any Deaconess, and any one of their number shall be at liberty to relinquish her position as a Deaconess at any time.

When working singly, each Deaconess shall be under the direction of the pastor of the Church with which she is connected. When associated together in a home, all members of the home shall be subordinate to and directed by the superintendent placed in charge.

BY ACTION OF DEACONESS CONFERENCE [1889]

Admittance and Support

Approved applicants may be admitted as members of the Home on one of the following conditions:

a. That they pay their board and expenses.

b. That they pay their expenses only.

c. That they pay neither their board nor expenses.

Members and candidates under the last condition shall be entitled to comfortable maintenance and clothing during their connection with the Home, in conformity with its regulations.

No salaries shall be paid, but the work of the Deaconesses shall be on the basis of self-sacrifice "for Jesus' sake."

Any Deaconess becoming disabled while in active service, or worn out by age, shall be entitled to a comfortable support by the Home during her life or while so disabled, unless otherwise provided for.

None shall solicit money unless duly authorized.

All donations and money received where service is rendered shall be paid into the treasury of the Home.

We recommend that the Deaconesses not in Homes be supported by the churches with which they labor, and as far as possible in harmony with the spirit in which this work has been carried on.

Costume

We recommend that a uniform and distinctive dress be worn by all Methodist Episcopal Deaconesses.

That the color of the uniform dress be black.

That the gown be made without drapery, with plaited or gathered skirt, with round waist or basque, and bishop sleeves with a cuff.

That linen collar and cuffs or plain flat ruching be worn.

That the hair be worn plain.

That no jewelry be worn except a pin or a brooch for the collar.

That the outside garment be a long peasant cloak.

That a black bonnet of the prescribed shape with white ties be worn.

That the working dress of the Nurse Deaconess be of blue and white striped seersucker, and the ordinary nurse's cap and apron.

That the dress for summer wear be of black challie, made in the adopted style.

Matriculation

That Deaconesses be asked to sign the following on entering Homes, "We, the undersigned, members of the_____Deaconess Home, promise to try to observe the rules of the Home, and to abide by the decisions of the Superintendent."

LOCAL MANAGEMENT

Deaconesses will receive their allotment of work direct from the Superintendent or Committee on fields of labor, and will not take up other work than that which is regularly assigned to them.

All gifts received by Deaconesses on account of service rendered, or from acquaintances made during service, will be reported at once to the Superintendent. No gifts of general value will be received personally; but will be gratefully accepted for the Home.

The nurse's ward costume will be provided at the close of the period of probation; and the street costume, at the time license is given, except in special cases when it may be provided earlier. Deaconesses are expected to adopt the costume as soon as provided, and to wear it exclusively. Members leaving the Home will please return street uniform, cloak and bonnet, to the Home. But reasonable provision will be made that ladies shall be comfortably apparelled as they leave.

The true Deaconess will at all times subordinate social interests to her work; and outside the society furnished by her co-workers in the Home and found among those she serves, such interests will be reduced to a minimum. Friends must be invited to meals only after consultation with the Superintendent; and no regular and exclusive calls must be received. . . .

Members of the Home are expected to be present and prompt at meals, except when duties assigned make exceptions absolutely necessary. In such cases, the Superintendent will willingly grant excuses.

Deaconesses will cheerfully assume such share of the house-work of the Home as may be assigned them by the Superintendent or Matron. Such duties rarely occupy more than one hour daily, usually much less. . . .

Lights will be extinguished at 10:30 P.M., or as soon afterward as possible, in case a deaconess is delayed on duty. . . .

Woman's Caucus Crusades for/Church Editor Buckley Crusades Against the Admission of Women to General Conference

Source: "An Open Letter to Methodist Women," Christian Advocate *(New York)* 65/25 *(19 June 1890): 392. Italics in original.*

Dear Sisters: As Methodist women, we have a special cause for gratitude to God for the freedom and opportunity that are accorded to us. A woman [Susanna Wesley] was the founder of our Church; another [Hannah More] originated the Sunday-school idea, suggesting it to Robert Raikes; and yet another founded Methodism in America [Barbara Heck]. The saintly women who gathered about the Wesleys have a noble succession in our own day in the brave, thoughtful host who have launched and carried loyally and well our two great Missionary Societies. The Woman's Christian Temperance Union, that most potent temperance organization, has been led by Methodist women from the hour of its birth at Chautauqua.

Our General Conference, not unmindful of these facts, has accepted us to be stewards, class-leaders, and Sunday-school superintendents, has admitted us to the Quarterly and Lay Electoral Conferences, thus giving us a voice in matters of finance and local church control, and allowing us to vote in the beginning of their career, upon those who may become our pastors and general superintendents. Recognizing the fact that we are now two-thirds of the Church, and that we have heavy moneyed interests to be legislated upon, not only as financial supporters of the Church, but as managers of two of its large Missionary Societies as well as of its training-school and deaconess work, the Church is planning for our more formal admission to its law-making department.

Let us consider prayerfully the responsibility involved in these trusts. Let us take the places that have been given us in Quarterly and Lay Electoral Conferences that we may continue to perform all our Church duties. Let those of us who are class-leaders and stewards study the work of the noble men and women who have filled those offices, and, with God's help, bring increased strength to our mother, the Church. Let those who are Sunday-school superintendents give generously to that work their time and thought and prayer, so that we may co-operate with our pastors and please the great Head of the Church. Since we expect to be represented by our sex in the General Conference, let us make ourselves familiar with the history and polity of our Church. Above all, let us seek humbly and earnestly the baptism of the Holy Spirit, that we may safely accept the responsibilities that are being placed upon us by our God and the Church.

[Signatures of fifty women follow.]

Source: James M. Buckley, "Because They Are Women," Christian Advocate *(New York) 65/41 (9 October 1890): 659-60. Excerpts.*

All objections to the admission of women into the General Conference come at last to this—that they are *women* and not men. Not because they are inferior in intellect or piety, does any one object; nor allege that those likely to be elected are inferior to the average of men in knowledge or general adaptive facility; nor that there are none equal in intelligence and piety to the best of men, but because they are women, intrusted by God with a form of mental and spiritual influence, and a corresponding work different from that of man.

That each sex is endowed with qualities fitting its members for a peculiar kind of influence and work, and to introduce women into the General Conference, or any corresponding position in the State, would embarrass the work of such bodies, and exert an unfavorable influence upon women, interfering greatly with the performance of their own work, which, if not performed by them, will not be done at all, are the grounds of doubt and opposition.

Women should not be given legislative functions, because they are preoccupied with work of equal importance to that of legislation, and when they do that work properly and confine themselves to it they exert a greater influence for good, even over legislation and its results, than they could if members of legislative bodies. . . .

To state it in yet another way: the results of legislation—with men legislating and women *outside* of the General Conference living as they may and should—will be better for the Church than for women to be *inside*, and their general temper and work modified to agree with their eligibility and service as members.

What kind of an assembly is the General Conference of the Methodist Episcopal Church? It is a very large body, with more members than the Legislature of any State, and a third more than the House of Representatives of the United States. The accumulated law making and changing of four years for a Church of two million members must be done in a month. Among so many, with a limited time for speaking, the demand for the floor is great; and it is not uncommon to see forty or fifty shouting for the ear of the chairman, and gesticulating wildly to catch his eye. To secure the floor peculiar knowledge of parliamentary law, strained attention, the most rapid physical movements, and the most piercing voice—unless the member be fortunately situated—are necessary. Most women would be utterly lost in such contests. The diffident, after a first failure, would relinquish the effort. Only the vociferous and unabashed could hope to succeed. To give the floor to women by courtesy when they appeared as members would be in violation of the principles upon which their admission is urged. For all special courtesy to women at its last analysis grows out of a recognition of a kind of influence from them and a kind of dependence on their part which will be swept away when they are placed on the same plane with men in the arena.

The admirable manner in which they conduct their own meetings will delude only the thoughtless observer; there are no men there struggling for the floor. Since *masculine* mental and moral qualities cannot be eradicated, to give women any opportunity in the General Conference, a plan must be devised to *feminize* the body.

The very qualities that fit woman for wife and mother unfit her for such a fray. She, even according to JOHN STUART MILL, lives in the sphere of sentiment and affection. Men may debate in apparent rage and tremendous vehemence of manner, and five minutes after it is over—whether in the Courts or in ecclesiastical bodies—they can usually resume their former relations. The intensity of woman's feelings makes such a thing impossible with her; and if a generation were trained to be able to do these things, it would consist of women whom men in general would look upon as admirable but unlovable prodigies. . . .

To the religious training given by mothers in the formative period of life must be attributed, more than to any other cause, the conversion of their children. What the pastor receives credit for is often the resurrection under the stimulus of his preaching of the influence of the mother through the sentiments that she implanted. In the early days of Methodism, and until a recent period, her thoughts were upon the conversion and religious growth of her children and husband; and many a non-church-going son and husband, without a word of preaching, has been won by the chaste conversation of wife and mother. They never intermingled the discussion of Church government, officers, and offices with their exhortations to give the heart to GOD. *To introduce the competitive ecclesiastical spirit into the homes of Methodism, so that the ardent temperament, quick perceptions, intense personal affections and attachments of women* should be enlisted, must greatly weaken what has been the stronger arm of the Church's moral power. There is already too much of this in local church contentions, likes, dislikes, and change of pastors, Sunday-school superintendents, etc. . . .

Those [women] who know how to exercise that [moral] power, and are content with it, need no ruling authority conferred upon them by law. They are queens, whether single or married, wherever they are, according to their natural gifts and spiritual graces.

Those who do not know how to use that power, *or are not content with it,* can add only an *imitation* masculine element to the General Conference, which will misrepresent rather than represent God's true woman.

Source: "An Appeal [to the Clergy]," Christian Advocate (New York) 66/8 (19 February 1891), 117. Excerpts.

AN APPEAL

Dear Brethren in the Ministry of the Methodist Episcopal Church: The aggregate vote of the laity on the eligibility of women to the General Conference is decidedly in favor of the measure. The vote thus far reported is 216,960 for to 132,949 against, a majority of 84,011 in the affirmative. Not all of even the most active and intelligent members of the Church voted. But the voters belong almost universally to this class; and the vote, therefore, represents the most devoted and progressive of our laity. The subject was thoroughly and ably discussed in our papers. Some of the most earnest members of the Church have feared that the proposed movement is contrary to the ordinances of GOD. Had our members generally shared this conviction, the measure would have been defeated overwhelmingly. If to any the vote seems small in proportion to our membership, its very lightness shows conclusively that the body of our Church does not for a moment hold that the eligibility of the sisters to the General Conference is a violation of the principles of the Bible, any more than was the admission of the lay brothers to that council. A similar fear was indulged formerly in regard to permitting women to speak in religious meetings. But the blessing of the Lord has rested upon Protestant Christianity and upon Methodism in unsealing the lips of woman. We are equally confident that His blessing will abide upon our Church in admitting her to higher responsibilities and in summoning her to greater devotion. Surely it is no more than just that two-thirds of the laity, who are always invited by their brethren to join them in toil and in gifts for the upbuilding of the our Church, should also be at least eligible to share with their brothers in planning for the work which all must perform together. We therefore appeal to our brothers in the ministry to ratify the expressed wish of the laity, and thus make our mother Church even more dear to her daughters than she has ever been before.

[Signatures of 115 women follow, including]

Mary L. Dickinson (Gen. Sec. King's Daughters)
Mary Sparkes Wheeler (Pres. [Philadelphia Branch] W.F.M.S.)
Frances E. Willard (Pres. W.C.T.U.)
Mrs. R. S. Rust (Cor. Sec. W.H.M.S.)
Jenny Fowler Willing (V. Pres. W.H.M.S.)
Lucy Rider Meyer, M.D. (Prin. [Missionary Training School, Chicago])
Mary E. Griffith (Gen. Org. W.H.M.S.)
Charlotte O'Neal (Cor. Sec. [Pacific Branch] W.F.M.S.)

CONNECTICUT PASTOR FRANK MASON NORTH
EXPRESSES CONFIDENCE THAT
SOCIALISM CAN BE CHRISTIANIZED

*Source: Frank Mason North, "Socialism and the Christian Church,"
Zion's Herald (January 14, 21, 28 and February 4, 1891):
9, 17, 24, and 34. Excerpts. Emphasis in the original.*

Second Paper

THE CHRISTIAN CHURCH AND SOCIALISM

It is only at this sunset hour of the nineteenth century that we have evidences of a genuine appreciation of this movement [Socialism] to declare "things secular" as "things sacred." Christian thought has deepened and widened until now the seers—it is not the whole church—understand three facts. 1. That *every* phase of human life is a concern of the church. . . . . 2. That this well-being is not a demand upon individuals alone, but upon the church as the formal expression and instrument of the Spirit of Christ. 3. That the problems are not those of Christian *charity* chiefly, but those of human *justice*. . . . . A sterner arbiter between wealth and poverty, between labor and capital, between the masses and the classes, is at last recognized as presiding at the assize where human wretchedness seeks redress for its wrongs, and the church is beginning to acknowledge the jurisdiction of this court.

Of this **reversal of the tendency to ignore the second great commandment** we have many signs. Doubtless a central force is in the principles and practices of [British Anglican] Frederick Denison Maurice, who with his friends dared to seek the Christian solution of problems which philanthropy failed to settle and statesmanship was reluctant to consider. . . .

Such are some of the indications that the Christian church is consciously adjusting itself to the new relations of social need. What now of our own Methodist Church? It inherited from its founder a mission to the poor and the oppressed. Methodism was a social as well as a spiritual reformation. That quaint document we call the General Rules is **packed with the seed principles of a new social order.** The recruits of the early Methodist ministry were largely from the working classes. Negro laborers and German artisans with scores of thousands of other wage-earners make a large minority, if not a majority of its membership. Its wealth is chiefly in the hands of those who have themselves been privates in the ranks of labor. Its career has been evangelistic; its spirit is humanitarian. If any organized body in the world today is prepared by its genius, experience and contacts to study social and industrial problems and apply the Gospel to their solution, it would seem to be the Methodist Episcopal Church. . . . . [Yet] its colleges present few advantages for adequate study of the science of society. As far as can be learned, not one of its theological schools, where are trained the men whose very first hand-to-hand encounter with the world of their work will be with other men who hunger and toil and curse a social order which often denies them manhood's first right, gives any specific attention to the living problems of sociology. . . . Methodism awaits thought[ful] leadership on these themes. The Episcopal Address to the last General Conference [1888] contained a paragraph upon the labor question. To what committee was it referred? Who thought the subject sufficiently vital to have place in the discussions of the church's representatives? To which official paper of the church are we to direct thoughtful inquirers for some systematic, comprehensive and sympathetic consideration of the urgent questions of social economics? On the contrary Methodism tolerates and approves a system of church management which practically excludes the poor, deepens the lines drawn by the caste-spirit of the world, withholds the millions which would unlock the secret of dealing with the "down-town" populations, and looks with suspicion upon men who assert that the "kingdom" for which Christ taught us to pray, will certainly not come until we help Him answer the other prayer which to millions of our fellow-men seems so necessary and so vain: "Give us this day our daily bread."

To those who rejoice in the splendid testimony of the Methodist church against slavery and intemperance and ignorance, there must come an ardent hope, a genuine confidence, that its best thought and noblest enterprise may be consecrated to the reconstruction of the corporate wrong, the relief of the artificial inequalities, the rebuke of the selfish injustice by which, through no defect of their own and contrary to the purpose of their Maker, human souls are trodden beneath the feet of the advancing armies of a civilization men call Christian.

In a word Methodism has long been conscious of its mission to regenerate souls. Let it now realize also that God calls it to regenerate society.

Third Paper

THE CHRISTIANITY OF SOCIALISM

It is not an accident that the watchwords of Socialism and of the Gospel are the same. **Equality.** "Of a truth I perceive that God is no respecter of persons, but in every nation he that feareth Him and worketh righteousness is accepted with Him" [Acts 10:34-35]. **Liberty.** "Stand fast, therefore, in the liberty wherewith Christ hath made you free" [Galatians 5:1]. "If the Son shall make you free, ye shall be free indeed" [John 8:36]. **Fraternity.** "Therefore, all things whatsoever ye would that men should do to you, do ye even so to them, for this is the Law and the Prophets" [Matthew 7:12]. . . .

Let us test this general statement in a few particulars. **The common brotherhood of man** is at once the Gospel of Christianity and the gospel of socialism. The ideal of the former is certainly immeasurably superior, yet neither has with complete success worked the principle into actual life. . . . **The law of mutual help** is a further striking illustration of the general fact. The student of social phenomena has no more powerful force to reckon with than that which in all the civilized world is drawing or forcing men together for the attainment of common ends. That we have here a principle fundamental in the whole structure of the Christian life needs no demonstration, "Look not every man upon his own things, but every man also on the things of others" [Philippians 2:4], is not a maxim, but an element of the Gospel. . . .

Is there Christianity in the proposed **substitution of industrial cooperation for competition?** All forms of socialism, from the Christian to the anarchistic, aim at this change in the present industrial system. Its intrinsic evils are at last being treated not as the faults, but as the wrongs, of its victims. . . .

Is, then, this whole mighty movement anti-Christian? Is it even un-Christian? Is it not in essential harmony with the teachings of Christ? . . .

Such a coincidence between the Socialist attack upon the unequal distribution of wealth with all its brood of wrongs and the testimony of the Word of God adds one more to the illustrations of the general statement that the ends for which Socialism is striving are essentially those which are central in the "promise and potency" of the Gospel. The contention is not that all Socialism is Christian. There is a Socialism that is as subversive of the Sermon on the Mount as it is of the Decalogue. Nor do we find wisdom, justice and mercy in all the diversified schemes by which theoretical and practical reformers seek social perfection. And even should true Socialism attain its highest ideal, it would not be Christianity—since the one deals with the humanity of one world, the other with the humanity of two. Yet, none the less, within its limitations Socialism is not the foe, but the brother, of Christianity.

Fourth Paper

THE SOCIALISM OF CHRISTIANITY

If the contention be admitted that touching this present world the essential aims of Socialism and Christianity are identical, what are **the practical methods** by which the church can assume and retain its true place as the leader in social reform?

At once it is urged that the Gospel has to do with the individual. The mass is reached only through the unit. . . . For the almost angry admonition that we sometimes hear to "let the church keep to its work of saving souls from sin" cannot blind us to the fact that . . . the moral convictions which the Gospel creates must become crystallized in customs and laws and institutions in order to construct the new and higher plane for the betterment of that very individual life for whose blessing the Christ came into the world. It is no part of the principle of the leaven that the meal shall ever go unbaked. Ideas must harden into facts. Principles must put on form. Liberty creates institutions. Justice becomes courts of law. Charity is organized into hospitals, and the Gospel must govern life. It is not true that we are to be content with the fact that the ideals of a perfect social order are in the Gospel. It is only a part of the truth to declare that those ideals are to be reached not by edict, but by a power working within. The past shows that wherever this inworking power has achieved anything in the advance toward the ideal, the Gospel has acted not only upon the hearts of men, but upon the social order which expresses and controls their relationships. . . .

Only when the church acts from the conviction that Christianity relates itself to the life both of the individual and of the community, can its true mission be accomplished. It must cure its fevered patient and at the same time drain the marsh where lurk the germs of disease.

Certain specifications under this twofold form of the church's influence may be briefly stated:

1. It can hasten the better time by **more urgent application of Christ's teachings** to personal, domestic, commercial and political life. . . . The fiction of a dual conscience, of which one part acts in the business world and the other in ordinary life, has wide sway among men of affairs. . . .

It certainly should be within the province of the Christian church to teach, exemplify, and enforce the true principles of commercial and political morality. The dealings between men, and their public acts, whether they relate to money or values, either in wages or exchanges, or to services rendered, should be by the church tested not in terms of popular but of Christian morality. . . .

This, then, first, is the church bound to do—to apply its own ethics to life. This could conciliate master and man, destroy domestic slavery, i.e., the slavery of domestics, declare the bargain-counter a shame, put an end to extortion, abate extravagance, prevent the misuse of funds and credit, overthrow the tyranny of power, dignify labor, and establish in the world of action true ideals and honest methods. Let Christians live Christianity; let the second great commandment have the right of way, and Socialism will find its occupation in part gone: for its problems will be nearing solution. . . .

2. But if the church is to help solve social problems, by enforcing the individual application of Christian ethics to life, she must **herself illustrate the same principles.** The alienation of the wage-earners from the church is not a fiction. . . . . It is in part due to the usurpation of the Lord's house and the distribution of its privileges upon the basis of commercial and class distinctions. The church is thought to be on the side of wealth and capital and leisure. . . . The Gospel stands for brotherhood, simplicity, humility, helpfulness, self-sacrifice. The church belies it when it encourages caste, extravagance, pride, exclusiveness, selfishness. Let the Spirit of Christ dictate the policy of our churches, and His method become that of His peo-

ple, and the genuine brotherliness of Christians will show Socialism the substance of which its fraternity is but a shadow.

3. Thus the salvation of Christianity will ask for far better individual living, and for truer illustration of the teachings of Christ in the theory and practice of the church itself. These at least all may agree to urge. But there is one other range of influence. Shall the church aim directly at securing the welfare of humanity, not by transformation of character alone, but by **betterment of conditions?** Do we mean by entering politics? No assuredly. By secularizing the church? Never. But we do mean that the whole force of Christian thought and action should be turned upon the world's wrongs and miseries, that it is the church's duty to make social ethics a prime study in our colleges and seminaries; to treat sympathetically all honest effort for reform; to agitate against the overcrowding of the poor, the false methods of business, the public crime of monopoly, the injustice of the competitive system, the cruelty of child labor; to plead for the community control of what concerns the community as such, for the reorganization of labor on some cooperative basis, for the radical change of our treatment of criminals, for the reduction of the hardship of toil, for the abolition of pauperism, and the prohibition of the liquor crime. . . . There will be disagreement as to methods . . . , but the church—in its pulpit, through its press, in its legislative discussions, and in its guidance of the thought and action of the individuals who compose it—must accept the challenge thrown down to it by the spirit of this age and become the antagonist of all evils, the protector of all the unfortunate, and the avenger of all the wronged. . . .

All this Christ came to accomplish. Most of this Socialism is seeking to do. Upon the church the age lays a two-fold demand—that it *prove the truth of its faith* and *apply its morals to life*. Many are busy about the former; the latter is the responsibility of the whole church. If Christians shall only realize their opportunity, the twentieth century must shake with the tread of the allied hosts as they cross, with "the swing of conquest," its wide threshold.

Epworth League initiates new members

Source: Joseph F. Berry and Charles H. Gabriel, eds., Epworth Songs for Use in the Epworth League, The Junior League, The Sunday-school, and in Social Services (*New York: Hunt & Eaton, 1893*), 4-5. Excerpts.

RECEPTION OF MEMBERS

[*With the Cabinet and Candidates in proper position, the President shall say:*]

Dear Friends,—You are about to become members of a vast army of young people, known as the Epworth League, with Chapters in every part of the world. This organization is designed for the religious, intellectual, and social upbuilding of our young people. Wherever you may go, you will be very apt to find Epworthians, and this will secure for you the companionship of young Christians who will at once become interested in your social and religious welfare. The First Vice-President will give you our motto, and Scripture references illustrating its meaning.

First Vice-President. The motto of the Epworth League is, "LOOK UP; LIFT UP." You will find it on our badge, which I now present you.

"My voice shalt thou hear in the morning, O Lord; in the morning will I direct my prayer unto thee, and will look up."

"Two are better than one; because they have a good reward for their labor. For if they fall, the one will lift up his fellow."

President. Our Second Vice-President will now instruct you with reference to the League idea.

Second Vice-President. The League idea is based upon the law of Christian fellowship, which is a most potent factor in helping us to become what God designed us to be. Spiritually, intellectually, and socially, the associations of the Epworth League are delightful and helpful. The young people of our Church are brought into closer relation with each other, and in their zeal to look up and lift up, social distinctions are forgotten, selfish ambitions are lost, heart beats with heart, pulse throbs with pulse, and all because our faith, aims and service are one.

Third Vice-President. The colors of the Epworth League consist of a narrow white ribbon, through the center of which, from end to end, runs a red silken thread. The signification is beautiful. The white ribbon symbolizes the desire of every

Epworthian to become pure in heart, in thought, in life, earnestly striving for

> "A heart in every thought renewed,
>   And full of love divine;
> Perfect and right and pure and good—
>   A copy, Lord, of thine."

The red silken thread is emblematical of the "blood of Jesus Christ, his Son," which "cleanseth from all sin."

Fourth Vice-President. I place in your hands our Constitution. In it you will find the Epworth wheel—a diagram representing the workings of the League. At the center of the organization stand the President, pastor, and Junior League Superintendent. Surrounding them are four Vice-Presidents, a Secretary, and a Treasurer. These constitute the Cabinet. There are six departments of work; namely, those of Spiritual Work, Mercy and Help, Literary Work, Social Life, Correspondence, and Finance. Through the work planned in these various departments we seek the symmetrical development of Christian character. With their practical workings you will become more familiar as you give them your personal attention, which we trust you will do.

[*In case the Chapter has adopted the pledge, the President shall address the candidates for admission, and say:*]

We understand that you desire to become active members of our Chapter?

Answer. I do.

President. That we may mutually understand and help each other, will you answer "I will" to each of the following questions:

Will you earnestly seek for yourself, and do what you can to help others attain, the highest New Testament standard of experience and life?

Will you abstain from all those forms of worldly amusement forbidden by the Discipline of the Methodist Episcopal Church?

Will you attend, as far as possible, the religious meetings of the Chapter and Church, and take some part in the same?

[*Whether the Chapter has adopted the pledge or not, the President shall close the service as follows:*]

President. In the name of our Chapter and of all true Epworthians, I extend to you the right hand of fellowship, and welcome you to membership in this great army of young soldiers. I take pleasure in assigning you to the Department of . . . and I trust our fellowship will be mutually profitable and a blessing to God's Church.

[*Following this service a ten-minute reception may be held.*]

RECOGNITION OF OFFICERS

If convenient, the Recognition Service should be held on Sunday evening, and the whole congregation invited to be present and participate.

The Secretary may read the names of the newly-elected officers, and they will respond by coming forward to the altar.

The Secretary should then read the action of the Quarterly Conference approving the President elect.

Lucy Rider Meyer describes
Deaconesses and their work

Source: Lucy Rider Meyer, "Deaconesses and Their Work,"
Woman in Missions, Papers and Addresses. Presented at The
Woman's Congress of Missions October 2-4, 1893, *compiled by E. M. Wherry*
(New York: American Tract Society, 1894), 182-98. Excerpts.

Deaconesses are trained, unsalaried and costumed women, providentially free—sometimes most sadly free—from the responsibilities that occupy the time of most women, banding themselves together to aid and supplement other agencies in carrying the gospel in all practical, helpful ways to those who have it not. They differ from Bible women in that they *must* be trained. Bible women, and indeed all other missionaries, *may* be trained, but deaconesses *must* be. They are costumed, and unsalaried, and they usually live in communities called Homes. In addition to this, the deaconess in all denominations usually has formal churchly recognition and authorization. She is, in a special sense—as was Phoebe, whom Paul called a *"diakonos"* and whom our revisers have done the tardy justice of calling a *deaconess* in the margin—a servant of the church. . . .

Deaconesses wear a costume: for instant recognition, for economy, for accessibility to the poor. We concede there is something of artificiality in our conventional—not conventual—dress. We willingly admit that in a natural and normal state of society each member should have the privilege of individuality in dress, the same as in her words. But the organic whole of society—for social science has just discovered what Christ taught 2,000 years ago, that society is a unit, every member of which is bound to every other member by a thousand indissoluble ties—is not, at present, in a normal state. The segregation of classes, which is so marked a characteristic of even American society, is not normal. The outbreaking moral diseases of some of the poor, the effeminacy and self-seeking of some of the rich, are not normal conditions. A wise physician charged with the care of a well person needs to do nothing but advise a simple and natural life; called to the bedside of the sick, we find him pursuing a totally different course: making use of artificial means—of the plaster cast, or the penetrating knife. So, in dealing with the open wounds and sores of the social body of a great city, we are justified in adopting some peculiarities in our work. The only criterion by which we can be judged is, Do they help us in helping our patients? We do not deny that it does involve some little self-denial to don our serge bonnets. We feel that we too, as well as you, ladies, have a right to retain our individuality in dress, to array ourselves in bright colors and soft textures; but the most sacred right a human being can have, after all, is *the right to give up* her rights, if by so doing a greater good will come to humanity. We wear our uniform for our work's sake. We are not in ordinary family and social life; we are providentially free from the duties and responsibilities—blessed though they are—that bind most women to their homes and their friends, so that we can devote ourselves to this work as others cannot. And because of certain manifest advantages we wear the costume, relinquishing the bright colors and bright textures to those whose vocation in life is so different, and to the oft-quoted flowers and birds and sunset clouds, in whom, however, let me say in passing, there abides no moral quality, and in whose gorgeous array there is not involved the needless expenditure of money which in the present abnormal state of our social body is so certainly and constantly convertible into terms of redeemed souls. Moreover, we have a conviction, based on experience, that our women are safer wearing the costume. You know very well there are sections of many large cities where it is not safe for a well-dressed person to be seen alone after nightfall. Our deaconesses, especially the nurses, are actually called into these localities, not only by day, but by night. We have never yet prohibited them from going alone into any part of the city in any of the twenty-four hours of the day. They are necessarily associated with all kinds of women, they perform their labor of love in all kinds of houses; they would not be safe from physical harm or social suspicion had they not some distinguishing characteristic in their garb. This is, indeed, the one great reason why we wear the costume, but there are other excellent reasons: it is economical; it prevents hurts and grievances in the Home, where some are and will be clothing themselves out of an income which renders them independent while others are dependent upon garments furnished by the Home; it gives an *esprit de corps* to our workers. What the blue coat of the United States soldier is to him the white ties and serge bonnets are to us.

But notice further. Deaconesses are volunteers, and this simple fact at once places our work on a plane which raises it above whole classes of motives appealing to ordinary workers. Our women come when they will—provided they will submit themselves to the requirements of training, etc.—they go when they please. That is, theoretically they "go"—actually they stay. The work has been established in our church now more than six years, and it numbers more than three hundred women, and one of the great surprises in connection with it has been that, while some have resigned on account of health, so few have left. Some have gone home to care for dependent parents, four have been married in our parlors or chapels, but most of them stay by the work. We ask but one question of importance, of women desiring to become deaconesses, and that is, "Do you believe God has called you to the work?" And if God calls them they will stay. I used to fear that money inducements would affect our workers, especially our nurses; but, though offers of salaried positions have frequently been made them, very rarely has there been a response, even when the position has been associated with other philanthropic work. Our women use money mostly to give it away, and the longer they remain with us the more fully does the power of money as a motive seem to vanish from their lives.

Chicago pastor William Carwardine supports workers in the Pullman strike

Source: William Carwardine, "The Pullman Strike," The Pullman Strike (Chicago: Charles H. Kerr & Co., 1894), 11-14.

The Pullman strike is the greatest and most far-reaching of any strike on record in this country. It is the most unique strike ever known. When we take into account the intelligence of the employees, always the boast of the Pullman Company; the wide-spread advertisement of the town as a "model town," established as a solution of the industrial problem upon the basis of "mutual recognition;" it is no wonder that the world was amazed, when, under such apparently favorable conditions, in the midst of a season of great financial depression, the employees laid down their tools, and, on the 11th of May, walked out of the great shops to face an unequal and apparently hopeless conflict.

After seven weeks of patient waiting, the American Railway Union, having espoused the cause of the Pullman employees, declares a boycott on the Pullman Palace Cars. This action is repulsed by the Railroad Managers' Association. The conflict is transferred at once to the arena of public commerce; organized labor and organized capital are pitted against each other; stagnation of all business interests results; the highways of trade are blocked; the great unoffending public is the innocent sufferer, riots ensue, the military are ordered out, the foundations of government are threatened; the strong arm of the law is put forth, the public demand for peace is heard, and the crisis reached.

Now the public mind reverts to the original cause. What made these intelligent employees at Pullman strike? Were they rash and inconsiderate, or were they driven to their course by certain conditions over which they had no control, and which justified them in their action?

These and a hundred other questions are coming to me by every mail from all parts of our country. Ten days after the employees struck, I delivered a sermon from my pulpit, which created profound interest in Pullman and Chicago, and which has since been copied broadcast in newspapers all over the United States. Owing to this fact, I am accosted on all sides for information concerning the true condition of things in this model town.

For two years I have been the pastor of the Pullman M. E. Church, and closely related to the moral and social life of the town. During that time I have been a silent spectator of the life and character of the town. I have studied carefully and with much interest the Pullman system. I have had abundant opportunity to observe the town from the standpoint of a student of the industrial problem.

I wish to be fair and impartial. I have seen many things to admire as well as to condemn. My sympathies have gone out to the striking employees. Never did men have a cause more just—never did corporation with equal pretenses grind men more unmercifully. I contend that I have a right to publicly criticise a public man or a public institution, so long as I do not depart from the path of truth or make false imputations, willfully knowing them to be such. No one has deplored this strike more than myself. I wish that it might have been averted. But so long as the employees saw fit to take this action I believe that it is the duty of all concerned to look the issue squarely in the face, without equivocation or evasion, consider the matter in its true light, and endeavor to bring about a settlement of the difficulty as speedily as possible.

I make no apology as a clergyman for discussing this theme. As ministers of the gospel we have a right to occasionally turn from the beaten path of biblical truth and consider these great questions of social, moral and economic interest. He who denies the right of the clergy to discuss these matters of great public concern has either been brought up under a government totally foreign to the free atmosphere of American institutions, or else he has failed utterly to comprehend the spirit of the age in which he lives.

Sometimes we preachers are told to mind our own business and "preach the gospel." All right; I have preached the gospel of Christ, and souls have been redeemed to a better life under the preaching of the gospel. I contend now that in the discussing of this theme I am preaching the gospel of applied Christianity—applied to humanity—the gospel of mutual co-operation, of the "brotherhood of humanity." The relation existing between a man's body and his soul are such that you can make very little headway appealing to the soul of a thoroughly live and healthy man if he be starving for food. Christ not only preached to the multitude, but he gave them to eat. And I verily believe that if he came to Chicago to-day, as indicated by the erratic yet noble [William T.] Stead, he would apply the whip of cords to the backs of some of us preachers for not performing our full share of duty to "his poor." . . .

We as a nation are dividing ourselves, like ancient Rome, into two classes, the rich and the poor, the oppressor and the oppressed. And on the side of the oppressor there is power and protection, class legislation and military support. Should this policy continue for a generation or two, there can be no doubt at all that working men who in times of war and invasion are the protectors of our liberties and homes, would refuse to take up arms in their defense. We are following in the tracks of ancient Rome, instead of learning useful lessons from their failures and defeats. No country can prosper, no government long perpetuate itself and its institutions, which does not administer judgment and justice alike to all of its people. . . .

ARCHITECT GEORGE KRAMER FAVORS "AUDITORIUM/AKRON PLAN" CHURCHES

Source: George W. Kramer, The What How and Why of Church Building (New York: The Author, 1897), 49-59. Excerpts. Italics in original.

The Ideal Church should minister to the whole man: spirit, mind and body; should preach, teach, heal and reach the spirit through the body and mind. To accomplish this the church must break from the conventional traces and introduce new methods. Let innovation follow innovation. . . . The interior [of the building] therefore must first be planned and arranged to meet these various requirements, and then the exterior designed to consistently give expression to and explain the interior and indicate the character of the edifice, with a force and grace of outline in proper proportions and harmony. How often is the opposite course pursued and utility and convenience sacrificed to secure a handsome, attractive exterior! . . .

In the Ideal Church an ideal auditorium is essential, in which the ministers should be able to see each member of the congregation, and of such shape that the audience is as compact as possible, and, so to speak, within the angle of vision. The speaker should be located as to be within the closest personal sympathy with those he would instruct and lead. As the oblong, rectangular auditorium and straight pews do not secure this result, we must ascertain what will.

Instinct is often a safe guide where even reason fails. Observe how an audience will shape itself about a speaker in the open air where each instinctively endeavors to secure the best position; how the hill-side or natural amphitheatre is selected; how they form concentric circles to the front and sides. . . . Is there any valid reason why the modern type of Church should not be based on the Concert Hall or Opera House? . . . Should not our church be as comfortable and attractive as buildings devoted to secular uses?

The auditorium should therefore be provided with seating semi-circular in arrangement, or may be pulled out to the elliptic. On the center of the one side facing the seats should be a platform for the speaker; the seats should rise as they recede from the platform and will form concentric curves, every one facing the pulpit squarely. For access and egress there must be a commodious passage, entirely around the pews next to the outer wall, with inner radiating aisles dividing the seats into convenient lengths. The proper height of platform, the incline of the floor as well as the intersection of levels with incline, must be determined by rules governing the laws of acoustics and sight. Necessarily the floor will assume the form of a half bowl, hence called "bowled floor," with a certain distance from the pulpit and the space back of seats level. . . .

Essentially a part of the [worship] service which must be provided for is the music, generally consisting of organ and choir. . . . Whatever method may be adopted, provision must be made for it, as the music is essentially a part of the service, or should be, and its location and source should be near the pulpit, whether back of it, above it, or at one side.

The various parts of the service should be in sympathy and in communication during the devotional exercises. The congregation enjoy the service and are benefitted thereby in direct proportion as they can hear and see the same to advantage. . . . . Hence . . . the seats should squarely face all exercises of the speaker or choir. . . . The platform should be large enough to accommodate all speakers on special occasions, and of such height and location as to bring the speaker in the very midst of his audience. If symmetry is desired, the organ should be located back of the speaker either central or divided, and a musical chorus should be arranged in terraces a little above and back of the pulpit platform. Should this symmetrical arrangement not be considered essential, a very advantageous arrangement is to locate the choir at one side and the organ at the other. . . . The *form* of the building should accommodate itself to this development with proper provision in the way of exits, entrances, vestibules and corridors.

The proportions of room should be such that the most remote portions should not be greater than the width of the main body of the church facing the speaker, and the nearer the main body can be contained within a sector of ninety degrees the more advantageous will be the arrangement. Unless the church is built for pageants avoid the broad center aisle—the best location for seats. A source of annoyance to any sensitive speaker is to have the audience divided by a broad, vacant avenue, compelling him to look two ways or address the divided halves alternately. To secure proper proportions and especially in larger churches, there will be an apparent waste of space in height, in proportion to that occupied; hence by properly constituted galleries much additional seating capacity may be secured without increasing the dimensions of the building, thus placing the audience in layers. . . . Having thus demonstrated what the ideal Auditorium should be, let us consider that next in importance, the Sunday School.

In the various denominations, with few if any exceptions, the Sunday School is now recognized as an integral part of the Church organization. . . . For the requirements of this service, a specially constructed and arranged building is necessary. The Sunday School, being a modern institution, there are no examples or traditions to govern, but we must plan and arrange the buildings as all buildings should be; especially adapted to the requirements of the service for which it is intended.

The Sunday School must be broken up into certain general divisions and some of these again subdivided into classes. These must be separated and isolated as much as possible for class exercises. This change occurring two or three times in a single session should be effected quietly and quickly. To move the whole school would result in confusion. We therefore arrange the building to secure this change by other methods. The arrangement of plan best adapted has been found to be that of a central rotunda or auditorium, approximately of a semicircular form, with added width equal to about one-forth the radius. Thus in a theoretical room with thirty feet radius the length will be sixty feet and the width about thirty feet, one side being semi-circular. Adjoining the curve of the wall or periphery are small alcoves or class rooms, about ten in number. A second story of these alcoves is located directly over, the dimensions of these alcoves being regulated by the size of the classes, and of height as low as possible to avoid high stairs and bring the school nearer together. Above the upper rooms light for the central rotunda may be secured by clerestory windows or skylight. The alcoves are separated by radiating partitions; omitting partitions and combining two or more rooms will accommodate larger classes, especially on the angles. The larger rooms obtained at angles are generally fitted for the Primary [classes]. Entrance vestibules are secured in the portion added to the semicircle at either side, in which are stairways to the second tier of class rooms, access to which is obtained by a balcony with a low open front. . . .

The medium separating these small rooms from the central one is mainly by doors, folding back against the side portions; sometimes the rolling partition is employed, either vertical or horizontal, and sometimes doors operating vertically as sash, also by doors folding on themselves like a fire screen, and in some cases portiere curtains. Folding doors are the most convenient for ingress and egress; also in that glass panels may be used for light and through which the superintendent and class may be visible to each other. . . . When the doors or openings are closed, each alcove becomes a private class-room, and when open the whole becomes one large auditorium with a wide gallery encircling the outer wall. The change can be effected from one large public assembly to a score or more of classrooms in a moment and without confusion.

The central part should be occupied by those who receive general instruction, generally subdivided into numerous classes, occupying chairs grouped around tables. In the opening and closing exercises the small groups face the superintendent who occupies a platform located on the centre of the straight side. Thus during the opening and closing exercises every member is in direct sight and hearing of the single speaker, while during the class exercises they are transformed into a collection of small companies entirely independent of one another, the relative proportions of and arrangement varying according to the organization of the School. . . .

In this peculiar arrangement the beauty that flows from utility is easily developed. The most matter-of-fact simplicity of construction will give an effective interior. The principle can be adapted to smaller or larger buildings than indicated with equal advantage. . . .

A third department of the church will probably be the chapel or lecture room for smaller meetings of the church, in connection with what may be called church parlors. . . . Ample provision must be made for the various church societies, as Christian Endeavor, Epworth League, King's Sons, King's Daughters, etc., etc. There should also be provided Reading Rooms, which should be open every evening in connection with the library.

A cozy convenient study should be provided for the pastor, as well as an office for the various Boards in which should be constructed a fire-proof vault for church papers, etc. . . .

When possible a room or department for physical exercise [i.e. gymnasium] is a valuable adjunct which may also serve as a drill room for the Boy's Brigade or Cadet Corps. This room or the lecture room or parlors, if properly located, may also serve as a social-room in which tables may be placed, in connection with which will be required a kitchen with range, sink, hot and cold water, cupboards and all modern conveniences; also a general store room for surplus seats, tables, banners, decorations, Christmas fixings, etc. etc.

Thus the possible uses of the modern church edifice are practically only limited by the accommodations which can or may be provided. . . .

Missions executive Adna Leonard applauds new mission fields gained by victory in Spanish-American War

Source: Adna B. Leonard, "Prospective Mission Fields,"
Gospel in All Lands 19/8 (August 1898): 363-64.

Startling and momentous events are transpiring in these closing days of the nineteenth century. The kingdom of Spain and the republic of the United States are at war. Spain is the foremost representative of political tyranny and religious intolerance among the civilized nations of the world. For centuries she has done her utmost to block the progress of Christian civilization. Possessed at one time of vast territories, including the principal parts of two continents on this side of the Atlantic, she has, by pursuing a course of tyranny and intolerance at war with the progress of civilization, lost her prestige among the nations, her credit in the world's money markets, and is now on the verge of utter collapse. Had Spain pursued an enlightened policy in politics and religion toward her subjects she might now rank with Great Britain, rather than with decaying nations such as China and Turkey.

In the place of fostering intelligence among her subjects, she has kept the masses in dense ignorance and under the influence of blind superstition. In a population of eighteen millions in the kingdom of Spain all except two millions are illiterates. Of the two millions who can read and write only four hundred thousand have anything to do with the government, except to pay the enormous taxes that are levied and to go into the ranks as common soldiers in time of war.

The republic of the United States stands among the nations of the world the foremost representative of political liberty and religious toleration. Here schools are provided for all, and even compulsory education is widely enforced, while the right to freedom of worship is absolutely unchallenged.

Spain and the United States represent respectively mediëvalism and modern progress. The two policies have been brought face to face in Cuba, and it is not surprising that war should be the result. Spain must be permitted to go on with her policy of tyranny and intolerance, even to the annihilation of the native Cubans, or the United States must intervene.

We blamed England for allowing the unspeakable Turk to murder the

Armenians, but a greater criminal, the Spaniard, by fire, sword, and starvation, was desolating, within hailing distance of our Southern borders, one of the finest islands of all the seas—the gem of the Antilles. Miss Clara Barton is reported to have said, after seeing both: "Armenia was a comedy, but Cuba is a tragedy."

There can be but one outcome of the conflict. Spain must retire from all governmental authority on this side of the Atlantic, and Cuba and Porto Rico must be free. Having broken the yoke of the oppressor, the United States will see to it that these islands shall have a stable government of their own, or, what is not unlikely, become integral parts by their own choice, as in the case of the Hawaiian Islands, of the country that has made them free.

Meanwhile an overruling Providence has thrust us out to the "uttermost parts of the earth," there also to break the power of Spanish despotism. When Admiral Dewey was ordered to proceed with his fleet of war-ships to the other side of the globe, he is reported to have said to a friend that he would greatly prefer to remain at home, as he anticipated war with Spain, and he would like to be here to have a hand in it. He did not know what an important part he was to play in the strife which was fast coming on. When war was declared Admiral Dewey was in the harbor at Hongkong, which belongs to Great Britain. By the neutrality laws in force he must quit British waters. Where would he go? He was worse off than Noah's dove when first it was thrust out of the ark, for though the dove found "no rest for the sole of her foot," she could and did return into the ark. The admiral, thrust out of the harbor of Hongkong, must conquer a place for the sole of his foot and a harbor in which to anchor his ships. Six hundred miles to the southeast, at Manila, was a harbor belonging to Spain, and toward that harbor he steered his course. Seven days later he entered that harbor and destroyed the Spanish fleet, without the loss of a ship or even of a sailor, and found himself in the possession of a harbor all his own.

Since that time the Ladrone Islands have been taken. Sampson's fleet has annihilated the Spanish squadron under Admiral Cervera, just outside the harbor of Santiago de Cuba, and while these words are being written our army and navy are bombarding Santiago, with the certainty of its surrender or reduction. Six months ago whoever should have prophesied such results in so brief a time would have been regarded as a fanatic, if not indeed insane.

These marvelous events are now history, but no mortal ken can foretell their far-reaching influences. But we do know that great opportunities are suddenly open before the Christian Church for advancing among long-oppressed peoples the kingdom of God. The Philippines, on the other side of the world, and Cuba and Porto Rico, on this side, are by the naval and military prowess of a Christian government suddenly thrown open for evangelistic operations. The Christian Church must follow the army and occupy the territory conquered by the war power of the nation.

In this forward movement the Methodist Episcopal Church must and will do its part. This new call to duty comes at a time when our Missionary Society is emerging from an embarrassment it has experienced for several years, by reason of a debt incurred during the period of financial depression through which the nation has for more than a half decade been passing.

The first and most pressing obligation upon us is to wipe out the remaining debt, which before this paper is in print will probably have fallen below $30,000. Until the debt is paid no advance can be made, but with that burden removed the way will be clear. At least forty people are needed who will give $500 each to provide for the last dollar of debt. O, stewards of the Lord's money, will you not heed his call? The national Congress a few weeks ago wisely placed $50,000,000 in the hands of our President, to be used at his discretion for war purposes, and since that time other millions have been voted for like uses, and taxing laws have been enacted to secure the money for their payment. The Church cannot vote appropriations, and then by law levy taxes for their payment. It can only make known its pressing needs and appeal to the Christian conscience and the sense of Christian obligation and self-sacrifice for the money needed. Was there ever a time when the providential call to enlarged liberality was more distinct and emphatic? Can it be true that that call falls upon deaf ears? Must the Lord's treasury remain unreplenished and his army stand unshod and unarmed, while by the clash of fleets and the thunder of battle his voice commands an advance? Not only must the debt be wiped out, but there must be an enlarged and constantly enlarging income for missionary purposes if our Church is to keep step with the other great division of the Lord's army.

When our General Missionary Committee shall meet, on the 9th day of next November, not only should the debt be paid, but there should be added to our regular missionary income the sum of at least $200,000. Ten cents extra from each of two million of our nearly three millions of members would make this additional sum. But this is a time when wealthy Methodists should do something unusual. Let some one contribute the sum of $10,000 with which to open a new mission in the Philippines. Here is a great opportunity. Who will embrace it?

Black deaconess Anna Hall reports on her ministry in Atlanta

Source: Anna E. Hall, "An Interesting Letter from Our First Colored Deaconess," Woman's Home Missions *20/2 (February 1903): 37.*

South Atlanta, GA., December 18, 1902.

DEAR FRIENDS: It is now a little more than a year since I began my work here, and varied indeed have been my experiences. During the winter the cry of the poor is constantly heard. With money furnished from various sources I have been able to relieve many. Into many poor homes where there was illness I have gone with simple remedies which have proved of great use. In one home I found an aged lady suffering from the grip [influenza]. I called a physician, but as he was unable to come at the time I purchased a package of boneset and went back, made a tea, gave the old lady a hot bath, and the next morning we did not need the doctor. She was soon able to be about again.

As I have charge of our sewing class, and am thus brought into contact with the children, the pastor decided that I would do well with the Sunday school, so I was elected superintendent. During the year, through house-to-house visitation and in other ways, I have been able to bring two hundred and twelve children and young people into the Sunday school, many of whom I had to supply with clothing from our poor closet. Our teachers are some of the best young people of the State. One lady principal and a half dozen teachers in our public schools, and others, who are graduates largely from Clark University, are among our teachers. In addition to the Sunday school I am superintendent of the Junior League, and have the Junior class meeting of the church. Nine of the Juniors have been converted and joined the church. One little girl who was converted in our meeting was from a Baptist home. I knew her people would rather have her go with them, although they consented to let her attend our church. I talked with her about it, and advised her to go with her family, but she said, "Why, then you won't love me any longer, and won't pray for me?" When I assured her that I would and promised to see her baptized, she felt differently, and indeed she was very happy about it. In one of our small churches where I go on Monday afternoons ten of the children have decided to follow Christ and have joined the church.

Last summer while we were out on a picnic with the sewing school children they wandered up a hill where they found a lonely log cabin. One half of it had fallen down. An old lady came to the door who was extremely ragged and dirty. The children called me, and I went up to see her. They brought her water from the spring, and we talked with her, finding that she lived with a son who imagined that he was taking care of his mother by furnishing her a shelter and giving her a little food and cool spring water. The children sang for her, and there out in the open air I read the fourteenth chapter of John and we prayed. O how she shouted and praised the Lord for sending the angels (the children) to sing for her, and some one to read and pray with her! The children brought her a part of their lunch, and she had a picnic too.

The next morning I took one of our girls and went over to clean up the cabin, which was in a frightful condition. We made a bonfire and burned the worst of the rags and straw, cleaned the cabin thoroughly with boiling water containing a strong disinfectant, and then a mattress was furnished from Thayer Home, and a decent bed was made for her on an old bedstead which had been thoroughly cleansed. Miss Mitchell sent some clothing for the old lady, and she really seemed like another person. When we left the cabin that day we prayed together again, and she was happy and full of hope. A little later she became ill, and I was much with her to do what I could, but one night when the son came she was almost gone. The wood gave out, there was no light, and he fell asleep to awake the next morning to find his mother cold in death. A neat coffin was purchased, and with the help of some women we placed her in it, and then a few of us with the son gathered in that lonely place and with the assistance of our prison chaplain conducted a simple funeral service and laid away the remains of this poor old woman to await the sounding of the trumpet.

I am constantly receiving calls to talk to the people about my work as a deaconess or to organize auxiliaries of the W.H.M.S. Miss Mitchell, who has charge of the deaconess work in the South, seizes these opportunities to give me change and rest, and sends me forth to answer such calls. I am just now at home from visiting the Alabama Conference. A Conference society was organized, and several auxiliaries. The people seem very willing to help our work in the South. The work in Georgia needs the assistance of friends everywhere. We need material for our Sunday school, and also for our cooking classes, and better facilities and clothing for the poor, especially for the children.

For the love of Christ and in his name,

ANNA E. HALL

NEW YORK EAST CONFERENCE TRIES BOSTON UNIVERSITY SEMINARY PROFESSOR BORDEN PARKER BOWNE FOR HERESY

Source: George Elliott, editor, "The Orthodoxy of Bowne," Methodist Review *(New York) 105/3 (May 1922): 403-409.*

[Professor Bowne:]

MR. CHAIRMAN: It hardly seems worth while to take up your time. You know very well that these biblical questions have been burning questions of late years. There has been a great deal of uncertainty in popular thought, especially among educated people, graduates from our high schools and colleges, and those who have been familiar with the literature there, and when I wrote this book, or these books rather, I meant to meet difficulties which are in the minds of those persons. Philosophy is not everybody's fad, and so biblical discussion is not everybody's fad; and this is so in the religious use of the Bible and biblical questions. There is many an old saint whose reading is "The Lord is my Shepherd, I shall not want," and there is a religious use and a great use of the Bible by a great majority of the people. But then there are these other questions which belong to scholarship and which, in the long run, are very important. In the confused condition of things it has seemed to me very desirable to reach some point of view which would serve as a kind of *modus vivendi*, and so I have raised the question, What is the central thing in Revelation? and I have said it is the revelation of God. It tells us what God is, what he means, what his relation to us is, what is his purpose concerning us, what he is going to do, and what the meaning of life is. Now I consider we get through Revelation certain ideas which I call the "Christian Revelation," the essential thing, and I believed it was important to fix our thought upon these central things in order that we might have the great value of Revelation. For, really when we take the book from many a point of view, and look around for specific treatises in speculative theology, it does not seem that we have much of value, and when you look upon it as a Revelation of God we see the significance of it. We as Christians are living in the light and power of certain great Christian conceptions which are here, have been here, are believed here, and will be here as long as the world endures. . . . If we hold these central ideas we are Christians. I think you will admit that I affirm nothing here. I affirm nothing as to the composition of the Pentateuch or the Second Isaiah. A great many scholars at least agree concerning the Pentateuchal question; that we find something originally written by Moses, but also redactions and additions. Let that turn out as it may, they still have the Christian idea. Or "The Second Isaiah." They still have the Christian idea. Now these are questions for expert scholars. I do not claim the ability to decide them, and I know very well that many cannot; they are questions for expert scholars, and will be decided by expert scholarship, and nothing can be settled by hue and cry. Those must be settled by scholars, and we must be perfectly assured that, in the long run, the truth will make its way—*truth will make its way*. In the meantime, we fall back on the great essential ideas of God, what he is, what he means, and we live on those ideas, and we rule our lives by them. It is a *modus vivendi* which I conceived, and to secure such, I wrote the book [*The Christian Revelation*].

Now concerning page 65: "However we insist on the presence of mythical and unhistorical matter in the Bible, it has not prevented God's highest revelation of himself. . . . All we can insist upon is, that the record, the legend, the myth, if there be such, shall not obscure the purpose of the whole, the Revelation of God."

My thought is that the revelation of God is the great central thing. There are persons who say it is a myth and unhistorical matter; and I say, well, suppose that is so? nevertheless, it does not obscure the great thing, the great revelation of God; the important ideas concerning God, what he is, what he means, these come to us along the lines of revelations in the Scriptures.

Dr. Buckley: The complainant in this matter has mutilated the passage and withheld from the church and the committee a very remarkable passage which runs in the other direction. I will read from the book and request the committee to compare what I read with what is presented in the charges: "However we insist on the presence of mythical and unhistorical matter in the Bible, it has not prevented God's highest revelation of himself. This is the treasure which the vessel of Scripture, however earthen, demonstrably contains. What the Christian thinker should maintain is the divine presence and guidance in the rational movement as a whole. He need not concern himself about details whether for better or for worse." What that was omitted in the affirmative proposition concerning nature or revelation I do not know, but that was omitted.

Professor Bowne: Now with regard to the remarks on pages 79 and 80. I think that there is no question that the Jews spoke of the supernatural in a way that showed that God was the agent in all things, and they referred things to God without reference to a secondary, intermediate causation. . . .

Now, with regard to this other passage: "When we come to the distinctively miraculous, to that which breaks with the natural order and reveals the presence of a supernatural power, we may still look for some of the familiar natural continuities. Miracles which break with all law would be nothing intelligible." While we believe in a good deal that is supernatural without affirming that it is miraculous, we believe in the divine presence in our lives, but we do not mean by that that we have angels or anything of that kind coming and directing us. But we believe that our times are in God's hands. And so our lives go on, and we still believe we are in

God's hands. There would be a supernatural guidance without anything miraculous grating with the laws of life and psychology. I believe that all the processes of nature are supernatural. They obey the divine will and are carried on with the ever-living will in which we live, and move, and have our being. I do not think everything is miraculous. On the contrary, there are other ways of doing things.

But, suppose we come now to the distinctly miraculous. How think of it? It would be no more divine than the outgoings of the world; no more dependent upon God than the sparrow which does not fall without the Father. What is the meaning? Why, it would be necessary to attract sense-bound minds who would otherwise be immersed so that they might know God as theirs.

A. C. Eggleston: Do you believe that?

Professor Bowne: I am a crass supernaturalist.

Dr. Buckley: Speak of the Resurrection of Christ.

. . . .

Professor Bowne: I believe in the Resurrection of Christ. I believe in it.

A. C. Eggleston: You say: "With this view you can dispense with everything else." What does that "everything else" convey? Is it a general feeling that whatever was said—

Professor Bowne: Of course the language must be applied to the subject under discussion. If we are able to hold the Christian view concerning God and man; and if we are Christians and have that, we are Christians. We can let everything else go that need be. It must apply to a great many persons. Many are not sure of this or that. But I say if you can hold on to God and Christ and to the view of the relation of God to us, with the Christian view of what God is, and the meaning of life and destiny, leave out other things.

A. W. Byrt: Let other things go.

Professor Bowne: It is unessential for Christianity. I do not hold that in order to be a Christian one must believe that the ax swam.

. . . .

Dr. Kidder: In the passage referred to, pages 41 and 42, as a quotation you say: "This conception of a dictated book has always ruled popular theological thought, and for manifold reasons. The notion of a revelation through history, through the moral life of a community, through the insight of godly men, is comparatively difficult and uncertain." Do you give these two as the only interpretation of inspiration of God's revelation to man as recorded in the Scriptures or out of the Scriptures? Do you mean that the revelation through history, through the moral life of the community, comparatively uncertain though it be, is the better revelation or the more accurate revelation of God?

Professor Bowne: I think that is the way revelation has been made. Revelation has been made in that way, and that the Bible has not come through such dictation. There may be passages, here and there, where it says, "The Word of the Lord came to me."

Dr. Kidder: Then the conception of a dictated book you rule out?

Professor Bowne. I lay that aside.

Dr. Kidder. Then we have no other alternative except this, "through the moral life of a community, through the insight of godly men." If that is the only other alternative, does your conception of the Bible mean that God is still making a progressive revelation of himself with equal authority by which he made it through Isaiah, Paul, and John? You say there is a middle ground that is not defined. In other words, . . . does God still reveal himself to us in precisely the same manner as he did to Isaiah and Paul? Or did those men have the inspiration of the Holy Spirit of God revealing himself to them, so that they spake with authoritative utterance?

Professor Bowne. It would depend altogether upon the contents of the revelation and the cogency with which they appealed to Christian thought. As a matter of fact the Christian Church has agreed that we have received a revelation through those men which outranks the revelation in any other way. If anyone should start up with a revelation that was distinctly contradictory to the revelations which came through those men, we should think this new revelation was a mistake. At the same time it is also perfectly clear that the subjects which they had, have been brought out in their meaning in the light and life of the church, as the Spirit was promised to lead us into Truth. The early Christian Church accepted the germ, had no such clear ideas as we have. I say nothing at all about it, but there is a question whether Saint Paul himself had as clear a conception of what was meant as we have now. We cannot separate the authority of the Bible from the authority of the church and the authority of the Christian Conference [consciousness?] that would set up one as independent of the other. This question of authority is something which can never be settled except in practise. To attempt to discuss authority in an abstract way, and get it drawn out in logical formulæ, always ends in confusion. Precisely the same thing you have in the general question of certainty. How do I know that I am saved? The next thing is to plunge into the very depth of uncertainty. I fall back upon the use of our faculties, and reach such certainty as experience gives. And so with regard to the Bible and religious certainty in general. There is a great blunder that the churches largely make. First, we have churches resting on the authority of the church. It is a perfectly easy thing to explode. Then we have the Protestant Church with the authority of the Bible, and it is perfectly easy to take that abstract thought and make it uncertain. We have the authority of the church and the Bible, the authority of the religious community, all the work of God, including great conflicts, vital functions, but there is no possibility of separation. I do not believe, for instance, that any church would long consent to accept statements in the Bible which were agreed upon as distinctly contradictory to reason and conscience. On the other hand, I do not believe that reason and conscience would very long support themselves without the use of the Bible. I do not think that either one of them would support themselves without the Christian community in which the Christian life were going on.

. . . .

A. C. Eggleston. Where do you make a difference or distinction between the "insight of godly men" and "man's invention"?

Professor Bowne: Insight is one thing, and invention is another. . . . Revelation leads to insight.

A. C. Eggleston: How did Moses come upon that wonderful characterization of God, "long-suffering, full of compassion, and that will not acquit the guilty." Did he get that from his insight?

Professor Bowne: God gave him the insight. That is the way I should put it. I suppose he had the insight that God was there.

A. C. Eggleston: I suppose that too. But now about this "inerrancy of the Bible." "And thus it appears how barren and practically irrelevant is the abstract question as to the inerrancy of the Bible" (page 57). How does that come in there? "The doctrine is of no practical interest."

Professor Bowne: Well, it is not. Let me talk about that for the moment. I am speaking of the "absolute inerrancy of the Bible," the technical inerrancy, such absoluteness of statement as forbids the notion of mistake. . . . For instance, the inscription on the Cross in several forms; there is a high probability that one was not exactly so. Then you have thousands of different readings in the manuscripts, and it is plain that there cannot be absolute equal inspiration in everything. The great thing is to obtain its general trustworthiness. One says, "If you admit inerrancy at all, how can you be sure of anything?" I say, that is an abstract question which does not admit of answer and which doesn't need any.

Dr. Buckley: I would ask, Dr. Bowne, whether you believe that the revelations in the Bible have come with abiding power and definiteness in the world's thought and life, only along the line of God's revelation of himself and God's providence.

Professor Bowne: All this I steadfastly believe.

Dr. Buckley: I am asking whether he believes certain things here; I would like to find out whether he believes these things. Do you believe that when you compare Christianity with outlying religions we feel its measure of superiority?

Professor Bowne: All this I steadfastly believe.

Dr. Buckley: When we compare it with the revelation of nature, etc.

Professor Bowne: All this I steadfastly believe.

TYPOGRAPHICAL UNION APPEALS TO CLERGY ON BEHALF OF EMPLOYEES OF PUBLISHING HOUSE; MEMBERS PETITION GENERAL CONFERENCE FAVORING ITS UNIONIZATION

Source: Broadside printed by Typographical Union No. 6. Methodist Episcopal Church. General Conference Papers, 1908. United Methodist Archives, Madison, N.J.

A Macedonian Appeal to the Methodist Clergy.

Jan. 10. 1906.

Reverend and Dear Sir:

The officers of the Typographical Union No. 6 regret the break that has come between the members of our Union and the Methodist Book Concern and have done all they could to avert it. Notwithstanding the attempt of the Typothetae to befog the issue and mislead the public, there is only one question involved in this strike—the eight-hour day. On that question, believing that "thrice is he armed that hath his quarrel just," we are supremely confident that we shall win.

Out of 316 employers in this city who employed only Union men up to Jan. 1, 282 have shown that they are in accordance with the progressive and enlightened spirit of the times by granting the eight-hour day.

We fully expected that when this crisis came, the Methodist Book Concern, as an exponent of the Golden Rule and in accordance with the best traditions of the great Church which it represented, would be one of our heartiest and most earnest coadjutors in helping to better the condition and lighten the burden of the large army of workers throughout the country who are "cabin'd, cribb'd, and confined" in an occupation notoriously unhealthy. But the "business management" of the Methodist Book Concern has decreed otherwise. From the commercial greed of that management we now appeal to the Clergy of the great Church whose name is the most valuable asset the Book Concern controls. If the Clergymen of the Methodist Church will meet us in a frank, man-to-man talk, learn the story of the great patience and forbearance we have displayed during the two years the negotiations for the shorter workday have been under way, also meet and talk with the employés [*sic*] of the Methodist Book Concern who are now on the street, out of

465

work in the middle of winter, we are confident that the beloved memory of the mighty John Wesley, whose work among the working people of England is still the brightest and the most highly treasured jewel in the crown of the Methodist Church, will exert an influence so potent and compelling as to make the cold-blooded greed of the grasping "business management" give way to a more humane treatment of its employés and pay the same wages and grant the same hours as, for instance, the printers who print The Churchman and much other work for the Episcopal Church, Messrs. Sherwood & Co.; and emulate the New York Presbytery, whose representative, the Rev. John B. Devins, made the proud boast to the Central Federated Union at its meeting last Sunday, that "the New York Presbytery, although anxious to help men out of work, never have sent a man to seek work in a place where there was a strike."

We don't believe the Clergy of the Methodist Church are against us in our efforts to shorten the hours of labor in an admittedly unhealthy, consumptive-breeding occupation. We do believe that when they know the "true inwardness" of this strike they will range themselves manfully on our side and compel their "business management" to act more in accordance with the Golden Rule and the enlightened spirit of the twentieth century.

We therefore invite the Clergy of the Methodist Church to meet us and the striking employés of the Methodist Book Concern next Thursday, Jan. 18, at Webster Hall, East 11th St., between 3d and 4th avs., at 4 P.M. We urge all to come and learn our story from ourselves, and those who cannot come to communicate with us by letter. We hope there will be a large attendance of the Clergy to meet the striking workmen of the Methodist Book Concern. The meeting will be confined to representatives of the Book Concern solely.

Respectfully and fraternally yours,

The Officers of Typographical Union No. 6
and
The Chapel of the Methodist Book Concern

Source: Printed petition. Methodist Episcopal Church. General Conference Papers, 1908. United Methodist Archives, Madison, N.J.

Petition to General Conference 1908

To the General Conference of the Methodist Episcopal Church, in session at Baltimore, Md.:

We, the undersigned members of the Methodist Episcopal Church, respectfully present for your consideration the following statement in relation to the conditions existing in the printing plants of the Methodist Book Concern and the effect of such conditions upon us:

As you are undoubtedly aware, the conditions of employment in the Methodist Book Concern since the inauguration of the eight-hour movement by the International Typographical Union have caused much dissatisfaction in the ranks of members of the Methodist Episcopal Church who are also affiliated with the Typographical Union and other labor organizations, and it is in sincere hope that the causes which have led to this dissatisfaction may be removed, and the former harmonious relations between the Methodist Book Concern and the Union restored, that we address this communication to you.

In August, 1904, the International Typographical Union adopted a set of resolutions looking to the inauguration of the eight-hour day for their members on January 1, 1906. After numerous attempts on the part of the Union, both before and after August, 1904, to persuade the United Typothetae (an employing printers association) to enter into negotiations with the Union on the eight hour proposition, which attempts only resulted in the Typothetae declaring that it was "unalterably opposed" to the eight-hour day and would fight its introduction to the last extremity, members of the Union were compelled to cease working for all employers who refused to grant the eight-hour day. The Methodist Book Concern, which at that time was a member of the Typothetae, allied itself with that organization in opposition to the eight-hour movement, and the members of the Union employed by the Methodist Book Concern were compelled to quit their employment.

This unfortunate severance of the friendly relations that had previously existed between the Methodist Book Concern and the Union resulted in placing the signers of this petition in an embarrassing position. We could not help sympathizing with our brothers in the Union who lost their situations on account of the uncompromising attitude of their employers. On the other hand, we found it extremely difficult to reconcile the action of the agents of the Methodist Book Concern with the principles upon which the Methodist Episcopal Church is founded. Great numbers of our associates and fellow-workers in the labor world sharply criticized the action and attitude of the Methodist Book Concern, and even the Methodist Episcopal Church itself was placed in the unfortunate position of allying itself with the forces which opposed the introduction of the eight-hour day. To such an extent did this feeling prevail that many members of the Methodist Episcopal Church have ceased to take the active interest in church work which they took before the Methodist Book Concern opposed the introduction of the eight-hour day. The work of the Church among members of the various Unions has been seriously handicapped and the unfortunate tendency of many labor men to hold aloof from the Church and its activities has been aggravated.

As a result of the general criticism of the policy of the agents of the Methodist Book Concern in fighting the shorter workday movement, the eight-hour day was established in the printing plant of the Methodist Book Concern in Chicago in November, 1906, fourteen months after the proposition had been originally refused. Notwithstanding this fact, it is a melancholy truth that the members of the

Union which inaugurated the eight-hour day are prevented under existing conditions from securing employment in the Methodist Book Concern.

In presenting this matter to you for your consideration, we do so with the urgent request that the Conference take such steps as it deems proper to restore the harmonious relations that formerly existed between the Methodist Book Concern and the Union, to the end that many of your petitioners, as well as former members of the Church, may be enabled to engage in church work with the same zeal and consistency as before the inauguration of the eight-hour day.

Name	Address	Church of which signer is a member
J. T. Huffman	Goldfield [Nevada]	1st M. E. Chicago
J. A. Wilson	Goldfield?	Plymouth Ave. M. E., Buffalo
[+10 other	Signatures]	

When this sheet is filled add blank paper for additional names.

President Theodore Roosevelt addresses General Conference on social reform

Source: *"President Roosevelt's Address,"* Methodist Episcopal Church, Daily Christian Advocate *16/12 (19 May 1908): 5.*

Bishop Cranston, I want to thank you personally for that introduction. I value it more than I can express. I do. I feel akin to you. I would be glad to address you at any time, in any place. But I am doubly glad to address you here; and I most earnestly wish you well in your purpose to plant here a great American University—a university that shall fulfill the dream of the greatest and first American President, George Washington.

And let me say a special word of thanks to those brethren who sang that hymn that I happen to be fondest of. I sing very badly, but I joined with you in all three verses—

"Ein feste burg ist unser Gott."

And now, friends, it is indeed a pleasure to be with you today and to bid you welcome on behalf of the nation, here in the capital of the nation. I am glad to meet here good Methodists from so many lands. The Methodist Church plays a great part in many lands: and yet I think I can say that in none other has it played so great and peculiar a part as here in the United States. Its history is indissolubly interwoven with the history of our country for the six score years since the constitutional convention made us really a nation. Methodism in America entered on its period of rapid growth just about the time of Washington's first presidency. Its essential democracy, its fiery and restless energy of spirit, and the wide play that it gave to individual initiative, all tended to make it peculiarly congenial to a hardy and virile folk, democratic to the core, prizing individual independence above all earthly possessions, and engaged in the rough and stern work of conquering a continent. Methodism spread even among the old communities and the long-settled districts of the Atlantic tide water; but its phenomenal growth was from these regions westward. The whole country is under a debt of gratitude to the Methodist circuit riders, the Methodist pioneer preachers, whose movement westward kept pace with the movement of the frontier, who shared all the hardships in the life of the frontiersman, while at the same time ministering to that frontiersman's spiritual needs, and seeing that his pressing material cares and the hard and grinding poverty of his life did not wholly extinguish the divine fire within his soul. Such was your work in the past; and your work in the present is as great, and even greater; for the need and opportunity for service widen as the field of national interest widens. It is not true in this country that the poor have grown poorer. It is not true. (Cries, "No! No!") And the judgment that we speak of will come on those who tell too much untruth. Sometimes I feel a little like a Methodist lay preacher myself. But it is true that in many sections, and particularly in our large cities, the rich have grown so very much richer as to widen the gulf between the man of very large means and the man who makes each day's livelihood by that day's work; and those who with sincerity, and efficiency, and deep conviction, band together for mutual help, as you are banded—not only for one to reach down and help another, but for each to extend his hand in help to, and to take the hand extended to him in help by his brother. Those of you who do that are those who can do most to keep the gulf from becoming too wide. Join with a man in doing something of common interest to both of you, and you find there's not going to be, even, any gulf between him and you. Is not that common sense? Exactly! Exactly!

True religion, through church organizations, through philanthropic organizations, in all the field of kindred endeavor, can manifest itself as effectively in the crowded and complex life of today as ever it did in the pioneer yesterdays; and the souls of men need the light now, and strive blindly toward it, as they needed it, and strove toward it in the vanished past. Glory in the past! But treat it as an incentive to do well in the present. Do not confine yourselves to being so proud of it that you forget to do similar work today. It is your task to do the work of the Lord on the farm and in the mine, in the counting room and the factory, in the car shops and beside the blasting furnaces, just as it was the task of your spiritual forebears to wrestle for the souls of the men and women who dwelt on the stump-dotted clearings in the wilderness.

No nation in the world has more right than ours to look with proud confidence toward the future. Nowhere else has the experiment of democratic government, of government by the people and for the people, of government based on the principle of treating each man on his innate worth as a man, been tried on so vast a scale as with us: and on the whole the experiment has been more successful than anywhere else. Moreover, on the whole (when I say this I think you will acquit me of having made any attempt to minimize the evils of the present day. But, on the whole) I think it can be said we have grown better and not worse; for if there is much evil, good also greatly abounds, and if wrong grows, so in even greater measure grows the stern sense of right before which wrong must eventually yield. It would be both unmanly and unwarranted to become faint-hearted or despairing about the nation's future. And the Methodist Church would not be the Methodist Church if it either were unmanly or grew faint hearted! Clear-eyed and far-sighted men who are both brave of heart and cool of head, while not for a moment refusing to see and acknowledge the many evils around us, must yet also feel a confident assurance that in the struggle we shall win and not lose, that the century that has just opened will see great triumph for our people.

But the surest way to achieve this triumph is, while never losing hope and belief in our progress, yet at the same time to refuse to blind ourselves to what is evil in the complex play of the many forces, working through, and with, and against one another, in the upbuilding of our social structure. There is more of good than evil; but there is plenty of evil, and it behooves us to war against it. There is much that tends toward evil as well as much that tends toward good; and the true patriot is that man who, without losing faith in the good, does his best to combat the evil, to stamp it out where that is possible, and if that is not possible, at least to minimize the harm it does. Prosperity such as ours, necessary though it be as the material basis of national greatness, inevitably tends to undue exaltation of the merely material side of the national character; and we must largely rely on the efforts of such men and women as those I am addressing to build up the spiritual life without which the material life amounts in the end to nothing.

I do not want to be misunderstood. I do not want to seem to be guilty of cant. The material success is a good thing. Don't ever let me be misunderstood as saying to a man or the nation to disregard material success. You want your son to be able to pull his own weight—not to have to be helped by somebody else to keep himself and his wife and his children, and I hope he will have plenty of them. (Laughter and applause).

You want him to be able to care for himself and for those close to him and dependent upon him. But you do not want him to be content with only taking care of his body. Let him take care of his body; but remember that it amounts to nothing if he does not take care of his soul. And as it is with the man, so it is with the nation.

As generation succeeds generation the problems change in their external shape; old needs vanish, and new needs arise; but it remains as true as ever that in the last analysis national greatness, national happiness, national success, depend upon the character of the individual man and individual woman. Nothing can supply the place of that individual character. We need good laws; we need to have these laws honestly and fearlessly administered; we need wealth; we need science and art and all the kindred activities that spring from the clever brain and the deft hand. But most of all we need the essential qualities that in their sum make up the good man and the good woman; most of all we need that fine and healthy family life the lack of which makes any seeming material prosperity but a glittering sham.

If the average man is brave and hard-working and clean-living—he has got to be that; he has got to be brave; the timid good man is not worth much. He has got to have common sense. He has got to be willing to work hard, and to be clean of life and thought. If he is that type of man; if the average woman has the qualities which make a good wife and good mother, if each of them alike has self-respect, and if each realizes that the greatest thing in life is the chance to do service; if that is true of the average man and woman, we need not bother about the future of the nation. It is secure. But, men and women, we can not stand up for what is good in manhood and womanhood without condemning what is evil.

We do not want to be too hard upon the sinner. But we do not want to spare the sin; and sometimes; as an incident to that, you must condemn the one guilty of the sin. We must condemn the man who is either brutal and vicious or weak and cowardly; the man who fails to do his duty by the public, who is a bad neighbor, an idler—let not the idler lay the unction to his soul that he has not harmed anybody. If he does not benefit anybody he cumbers the ground. We must condemn the man who fails to do his duty by the public, who is a bad neighbor, an idler, an inconsiderate and selfish husband, a neglectful father.

Just one word to the man whose goodness is confined to affairs outside his own house. Let him remember that by being selfish, inconsiderate, exacting in his own home, he may be able to inflict considerably more misery than he can ever offset outside. So much for the man. I am better fitted to preach to him than to the woman. But the woman likewise is to be condemned who, whether from cowardice or coldness, from selfish love of ease or from lack of all true womanly quality, refuses to do aright her great and all-essential duties of wifehood and motherhood. We admire a good man; but we admire a good woman still more.

I believe in the future of this nation, because I think the average man is a pretty good fellow. But I think his wife is a still better fellow. But in the case of war she is not; I am not going to say that she is. All honor to the man who does his full duty in peace; and honor evermore to the man who does his full duty in war—as the Methodists did in the civil war. (Applause.) But there is one person whom I put above the soldier, and that is the mother who has done her full duty. For every man worthy the name must recognize that the birth pangs make all men the debtors of all women. No human being has quite the title to respect that the mother has who does her full duty. It is owing to her that the nation can go on—that it grows and not decays; so that in quality and in quantity the citizenship of the nation shall increase and not decrease. The measure of our belief in and respect for the good man and the good woman must be the measure of our condemnation of the man and the woman—of either man or woman—who, whether from viciousness or selfishness or from vapid folly, fails to do each his or her duty in his or her special sphere. Courage, unselfishness, common sense, devotion to high ideals, a proper care for the things of the spirit—which does not in the least mean that there shall not also be a proper care for the things of the body—these are what we most need to see in our people.

It is not genius, brilliancy, keenness of intellect, that we most need in our people. We most need the common, everyday, humdrum qualities which make up the ordinary good man and good woman. These are the qualities that make up the right type of family life; and these are the qualities that by precept and by example you here—you Methodist men and women whom I am addressing—are bound to do all in your power to make the typical qualities of American citizenship. (Great applause).

The President: I just wish I could stay longer with you, but I have another engagement—I have been leading a quite busy life recently—and I am a little late for it now. It has been a very real pleasure to meet you here today. I am not at all sure that I have helped you, but you have helped me. (Great applause.)

BELLE HARRIS BENNETT ADVOCATES LAY RIGHTS FOR WOMEN IN MECS

Source: Methodist Episcopal Church, South,
Daily Christian Advocate *16/15 (20 May 1910): 117-18.*

Miss Bennett spoke as follows [to the General Conference]: Brethren, I am not unmindful of the very great courtesy you are doing me in giving me the time to speak before you here, and I believe I can convince some of you at least, that what we have asked from you in this amendment is neither unwomanly nor unreasonable.

The women who ask this of you are the same women who sit beside you in the pew every Sunday morning. They are the same women that kneel beside you at the altar to take of the body and blood of Jesus Christ. They are the same women that go out into the hard places, the lanes and by-ways of towns and cities; the very same women. I never heard one of you say that a deaconess by doing that work can become unwomanly. I never heard one of you say that these women who go out into the dark, hard places of the foreign field, who work beside the most degraded in the heathen lands, and the home lands, have become unwomanly because of the work they have done.

I stand here this morning to say that the great Church of God that you represent today needs the womanhood of the Church in the councils of the Church. Four years ago, this great body, assembled at Birmingham, helped to pass the law concerning the Woman's Home Missionary Society, which, last year, raised $264,000, a restrictive law saying that these women should not without the consent and approval of the General Board of Missions take more than $5,000 of money which they raised for buying property, etc. Men! if one woman had been on this floor, and had risen to protest against that, or to explain to you that which was hard to understand, or if there had been one woman to whom you had looked to explain this provision, you would not have done it. If there had been a woman at that time in your General Board, and could have counciled with your Missionary Committee at that time, who could have taken some control of the work in the foreign land, you would not have done that thing. It was not that you meant to do that unkind thing. At that time you passed a law that the missionary women should have two years of training in a training school, and two years of testing, before such one went out to the field, and should look to your General Board for supervision and instruction. You need us in the council of the Church.

Objection has been made that so few women want this thing. May I ask you, my brethren, when any great forward movement of the world ever went forward with a majority vote. Always in the beginning of great events, or in great movements, the beginning must be with a few. This I say to you today. It is not a few who believe that the fullness of time has come. A great part of every household of men and women are feeling that our sisters should sit on terms of equality in the Conference of the Church. . . .

I believe the minority report says that we do not want to put on our women this great additional work. Today I look around this house, and I see women here from all parts of the world, from far off Seattle, from San Francisco, from everywhere. Are not these the mothers of the land, the very mothers that you say cannot leave their duties at home. I wonder if there are any babies at home today whose mothers are here, who will not accept these additional burdens. . . .

I speak not for the women who sit in their parlors, with carpeted floors and curtained windows, with the tenderness of love of brethren and friends and little children around them. I do not speak in their behalf. . . .

Today in Dallas, Texas, as for the last twelve years, we have had a little, though unworthy home, where the poor unfortunate girls of that section have been gathered in, and mothered. It is for the three hundred thousand such girls in the State of Texas alone, those poor fallen girls,—I stand in the councils of Church to speak for them.

And I stand here to speak for the seven millions of wage-earning women who are in this land today.

My brothers and friends, Mr. George Stuart said to me some years ago, in speaking of these women: "I would put them all back into their homes, and let them have the comfort of their homes."

Gentlemen, if you had been in some of the homes where we have been! I stood in one of the great packing houses of Kansas City, and saw all those women; I have been in the cotton mills of all these various sections, and seen these women with their little children who had no other way of earning their living, earning their daily food, and we have these mothers whom I saw going back to their wretched homes, where they were huddled, three, five, yes, fifteen, in rooms only fifteen feet square, and I say is God pushing them out of their homes, and has the Church taken no step to protect these women by going down into the great cities and giving them sanitary homes. I do not plead for those to whom you give love and affection, and kindness, but I do ask you to let us into the councils of your Church, and bring before you the need of these women down in the hard places. Why should we not sit beside you in the Boards of Education? Seventy years ago there were less than a hundred women who taught school. Seventy years ago they had no part in higher education. Today seven-tenths of the Sunday School teachers are women, and yet you say you don't think your women ought to sit on the Boards of Education. . . .

I can point out to you women in your Church who have the Doctorate conferred on them, and you cannot tell me of a woman in this whole country who has had a degree conferred upon her by a second rate university, or bought for her by money, but it is a reward of merit when a woman becomes a Doctor of Philosophy. And I give you my word that they have plenty of equipment. They are well equipped I believe to sit with you. If I could have been on the boards of education Kentucky Wesleyan would have had a better equipment. And it is true in every college today, if the women could have been on Conference Education Boards.

Why not sit beside the men in your Sunday School Board. You know that seven-tenths of the teachers in your Sunday School are women, and why should we not help to frame the policy of your Sunday Schools.

As I look over your arena here today, I could see that the sentiment back of you all of these years is such that you would say, "This is hardly a place for a woman." But in the Conference the question is not one of the loudest voice, but it is the question of the speaker on the stand. Don't you think women could be seen as well as men if she had on a white dress, and a blue ribbon and flowers?

Now my brethren, I believe that our voices are just about as good as most of yours. I have strained my ears as I sat back there, and it is just occasionally that a man could be heard at the rear of this hall, and I believe our voices could penetrate as far as the men's do sometimes.

My brethren, this is not a matter of reason with you. You do not protest against this with your reason. It is a matter of prejudice, it is a matter of sentiment. You are burning incense to an ancestral tablet. Methodism has been doing a great deal of that.

But there are so many things I would like to say in behalf of those who stand for this. I know that there have been plenty of silly women, of gossiping women, and plenty of idle women. But you may remember what the old Yorkshireman said in Adam Bede, I believe, "God Almighty made them to match the men." I have seen many women that I thought had met more than his match.

According to the ruling of the Church, to which I listened eagerly, this matter cannot come under four years. If you put this measure on its passage, and let it go down to the Annual Conference, it must come back, and it will be eight years before some women might possibly sit in this General Conference. I do not believe you would object if there was a little corner of women over there, and I think that, if such a woman as Miss Laura Haygood sat in this body, and some question as to the foreign field came up, you would be glad to hear her. There are not a great many of our women who would sit in your Annual Conferences or General Conferences, but our contention is this, I repeat it again, you need the women in the councils of the Church,—the Church needs it, the world's evangelization needs it, and we believe that the fullness of time has come for this thing. I hope you will put this measure on its passage. If you do not, we are to have four years of education. You must have that because there are plenty of men, as well as women, who need to be educated on it. Put this act on its passage, and it will come back to another General Conference to be ratified, and even then there would not be many of you here in the Conference. A great many of us will be gone home to God. We have not done this work in our own strength. We have gone to our boarding houses to ask God to guide us. Week after week we have said we thank Thee, O Lord, that I stand here today, after seventeen years of work guided by the same commission that brought me into the Church, and the Master has said "go." Bishop Hendrix said look at the men on this platform—one here from Asia, another from China, another from Korea represented on this platform, and I said a woman is not considered worthy to stand on this platform.

Not yet can the women sit on the platform of the Church of Christ with her brothers. After twenty centuries we stand knocking at the door of the Church of God, saying yet, "My brothers, brothers, won't you take us in?" God made man and woman co-ordinate. Without the co-ordination of man and woman there is no reproduction of life, no perfect government of the home. Let the father die, and the mother and the little children all along through the years miss that government. They miss in the home what makes the perfect home. Let the mother die, and again the government of that home is broken. The Church is the house of God and the mother of God's people. You need the perfect government of the man and woman in the Church. Put this measure on its passage, and let it go down to the conferences and come back to you; and eight years from now perhaps there will be one or two women in the General Conference. I thank you again, my brethren.

BLACK LEADERS DEMAND BLACK BISHOPS

Source: Robert E. Jones, "Representation of Our Colored Membership in the Episcopacy—The Why and How," Southwestern Christian Advocate *(New Orleans) 41/11 (14 March 1912): 1, 8-9. Excerpts; italics and capitals in original.*

The appeal of the colored membership in the Methodist Episcopal Church for recognition in the Episcopacy is purely an impersonal one. It is not promoted in the interest of any man or any particular group of men; it is a spontaneous and consistent appeal on the part of 325,000 loyal members and their many thousand more of adherents and sympathizers. It is an appeal based upon the needs of the situation; the need being interpreted by the people who are in the very crux of the situation. Two things our white friends should always do: first, lend themselves to every movement in the interest of fair play for the colored man; and, secondly, they should be willing and eager to place every Negro at the vantage point where he can fight the battles of his own people. To dub this contention as a political scheme is unworthy of the loyalty of our 325,000 members, and is taking an undue advantage of a people who are struggling for an existence under a great handicap in the midst, and a part, of the greatest civilization the world has ever seen.

We take it for granted that the sentiment in favor of the Negro separating from the Church, among our white membership, is not very formidable; among our own membership it is practically *nil.* As a matter of fact, the Methodist Episcopal Church, from the beginning welcomed Negroes within its fold, and John Wesley himself preached to the "Africans and Americans" in Georgia with equal satisfaction. It would be a *repudiation* of the work of John Wesley, of his conception of the breadth of the Kingdom and his effort to save all men, as it would be likewise a repudiation of the fathers who sought to carry forward the work of Wesley, in his name and in his spirit to all men, to set the Negro membership apart. . . .

We take it that we are a part of the Church because of the spirit that brought the Church into existence, and secondly, we assume that the Church is the Church of Jesus Christ and cannot recognize caste and race discrimination. On the other hand, if we should want to go out, it would be the imperative Christian duty of the Church, in the name of our common Master, and on the basis of the New Testament idea, not to assist us in going, but to stand up and prohibit us from going, and at least, make a protest in the name of our common Lord and His universal Kingdom.

With the foregoing as a basis, may we not state briefly some reasons why a Negro should be elected to the episcopacy?

I. The Church has led us to expect it. If the utterances of the General Conferences of 1872, 1876, 1880, 1892, 1896 and 1900 specifically on the Negro Bishop question, has not given us a hope that a Negro Bishop ultimately would be elected, then the Church is guilty of insincerity which is fearful to contemplate.

II. The Church has heard the appeal of our constituents in foreign lands—namely, South America, Europe, China, India and Africa. In response to the petition of these people (foreigners) we have granted them ten Bishops. . . . On the direct proposition of numbers, has not our time come for at least one Bishop for our American Negro work? Are not we worth as much to the Church, which is largely American, as those who are not familiar with, and who care little for, American institutions? In other words, is not a Negro American worth as much from a patriotic standpoint as a Chinaman?

III. Our work is a distinct work, with problems and situations and difficulties and emergencies as distinct and as emphatic as any foreign field.

IV. More and more the country and the Christian churches are realizing that to most effectively meet the issues in the race problem it must be done by specialization. General superintending fails to meet the issues in the case. It must be a superintendency that, by consecration and training and self-surrender and specialization goes in to save this mass of Negroes to the American Republic and to God.

V. The next fifteen years will determine the status of the Negro for the next two hundred years. Shall the radicalism and oppression and tyranny of men like Vardaman, Tillman, Dixon, and other men of their kind succeed or, shall we give back an emphatic reply to that propaganda which seems at present to be so popular. Is the Negro to be a man among men, or is he to be reduced to peonage in the Church and State?

VI. The step taken in the election of Negro Bishops would not be nearly as hazardous, so radical and so far-reaching as the step taken by Abraham Lincoln in the emancipation of slaves. There were all sort of prophecies of dire disasters when Lincoln made the heroic step, but the prophecies failed and the North and the South alike recognize Lincoln as a great emancipator and the emancipation of the slaves as absolutely just.

We are now approaching the semi-centennial of our emancipation. Fifty years is long enough to wait for another step forward. We want the election of a Negro Bishop as a fitting tribute to our past record and of our struggle upward during these fifty years, and as a semi-centennial offering on the part of the Methodist Episcopal Church, and as a word of God-bless-you, and commendation for the long struggle that is yet before us.

[VII. Missing in original.]

VIII. We are unevenly matched in holding our membership, with thirty Negro Bishops of other denominations travelling continuously up and down and through the South. Say what you will, it is a terrific struggle to hold the young people from our schools when we are loudest in our acclaim of the standard of man among men, when these Negroes, fresh from these schools do not see our men brought into recognition as men are in other churches. . . . Have we not grown in fifty years men who can be trusted with large responsibility, under the direction of the church?

IX. There are conditions in the South, which we deprecate, and which cannot be changed all in a moment, that make it embarrassing for our Bishops to administer our work in many sections, and, at times, furnish no little embarrassment to ourselves.

X. Leadership has been made for our people variously and often. The most influential Negro to-day holds his commission for large service through the endorsements that he has received at the hands of the white people in the South as well as in the North. This is no reflection on him. It is a tribute to what he has been able to accomplish, being absolutely true at all times to the interests of his people, and with the confidence of the others that make him a potential factor in the entire race situation. What is the opportunity of the Methodist Episcopal church in this regard?

XI. The Government of the United States, in the face of all that is being said, has been advancing Negroes to positions of prominence, of trust and of responsibility in many instances with a large number of white men under them. The justice of the promotion, and at the same time the intelligence and the common sense and gentlemanly bearing of these Negroes have met the approbation, certainly not in every quarter, but by an overwhelming majority in this country, so that, the political party which has advanced the Negro is kept in power. If it were a hazardous undertaking to recognize Negroes, no man would scent it quicker than the politician.

XII. There are 6,000,000 unchurched Negroes in this country. The increase of the Negro population in the State of Mississippi alone, during the last ten years, was 100,000. The best way to reach them is to reach them through their own men. If we want to go really into the business of the salvation of this great number of people, the Church needs a more vital connection with them from the episcopacy down.

XIII. The Christian church of America and of the world must ultimately turn itself in a more aggressive way to the evangelization of Africa. Christianity never gets a foot-hold among the natives except through missionaries who are indigenous to that people. All things else being equal, black lips for black ears are decidedly preferable. We have within our 325,000 membership, the best plant-bed in America for growing of missionaries who shall throw themselves into the situation in Africa, and bring glory and achievement and honor to the great Methodist Episcopal Church. Are we going to build a world-program that will include Africa? If so we ought to get at it.

XIV. Whenever a Negro in the Church has been trusted with the large responsibility of leading our people to self-support, there has been a marked advance and in every instance—namely: in the Freedmens Aid Society, in the Board of Foreign

Missions and Home Missions, and the Board of Sunday Schools. The election of a Negro to the episcopacy would give to the work in the South a leadership that would make for self-support in a more rapid and certain way than in any other way.

HOW IT MAY BE DONE

By the way of preface, let it be stated that nothing we have said or that may be said later on in this article or at any other time is to reflect on the Bishops of the Methodist Episcopal Church. We take it that they, as well as ourselves, appreciate the problems of our Southern work. In no part of the Church are our Bishops more uniformly accepted, and the office and the man more generally honored than among the colored Conferences of the Methodist Episcopal Church.

Again, there is no attempt to minimize our episcopacy and there is no desire to change it, nor is there any attempt to do away with it. . . . The episcopacy should remain as it is. What we are contending for is a different *method of administration.* And this could apply to any other part of the Church, as well as our own. . . .

At the close of the [Civil] War we had white pastors for colored congregations, and white District Superintendents for colored districts. In the evolution of things the white pastor was succeeded by the Negro pastor and the white District Superintendent by the Negro District Superintendent. There is absolutely no risk in carrying the evolution a step further and completing the itinerancy among our people by electing a Negro to the general superintendency. . . . THERE IS NO CONTENTION FOR A NEGRO TO PRESIDE OVER WHITE CONFERENCES. WE WANT A NEGRO BISHOP FOR NEGRO CONFERENCES. . . .

Briefly, then, in conclusion, there are three points upon which we may hang our contention of the election of a Negro to the episcopacy.

FIRST. The need in the interest of efficiency.

SECOND. Not a change of the constitution or a doing away with episcopacy, but simply a change of the *method* of administration.

THIRD. The Unwritten Law, under which we are now already operating [i.e., black pastors, superintendents and bishops shall be restricted to black churches and black conferences].

If a colored man were elected to the episcopacy, there would be enough work to keep him busy, and, in addition thereto, it would require, as it does now, a large part of the time of several other bishops. The field is large enough with problems of sufficient intensity and variety to keep several Bishops busy.

This is given in no sense as the *ex cathedra* statement of the question, but it expresses the conviction that is shared by a large majority of our people.

Bishops call for a new financial system

Source: "Episcopal Address," Methodist Episcopal Church,
Journal of the General Conference (1912), 198-202.

Nor dare we longer ignore the cost of multiform administration. No Church has had more loyal support than our own from its men of means, but they themselves will agree that the Church can not consistently depend upon a few rich men, either for local or connectional support. God put far away the day when poor people shall feel that they can not afford to be Methodists, and when spiritually-minded Methodists shall conclude that, the prayer service being entirely left to them, they are to be excused from further part in the affairs that concern the entire membership.

Here we confront a large question. It is plain from recurring debts that our Home and Foreign Missionary work must be placed upon a more stable footing than is guaranteed by existing plans. Persuaded that we have already reached a crisis in the working of our financial methods, and that the Church is being retarded spiritually, its growth hindered and congregations depleted by the ever multiplying public appeals for money, we felt warranted in instituting an inquiry to determine the reliability of this conviction. The result reveals even more than was anticipated. From more than two thousand pastors and district superintendents, representing seventeen Conferences, and all territorial conditions between the two oceans, we have gathered the following specific judgment as to our present methods:

The questions sent out were as follows:

1. "To what extent have you found the multiplicity of collections and special appeals a hindrance to the growth or religious zeal of the Church?"

2. "Can you state the number of public or systematic appeals to your people during the past year outside of our general benevolent collections and of your local budget?"

3. "If the number be irksome to the people, have you any suggestion as to a practical method of relief without risk to the causes that may be maintained?"

The answers to these questions will be available for the use of any committees who may care to examine them. From a careful analysis and summary of these replies, prepared at our request by the skillful secretary of the Laymen's Missionary Movement, we present a few suggestive figures and facts. (Not all the replies dealt distinctly and separately with all the questions as presented, hence the figures given do not cover the entire number received.)

Question 1 was answered by 1,639 pastors and 271 district superintendents; 1,475 out of the 1,910 declared the multiplicity of collections and special appeals to be a hindrance to the growth of the religious zeal of the Church; 410 believed that people are kept from the Church by this cause; almost 400 explained that they have been compelled to adopt the omnibus plan of collections. The answer to the second question showed also the regular benevolences of the Church do not represent half the number of appeals presented to the average congregation. Aggregating the figures given, it appears that in less than 25 congregations 224 various causes outside of regular benevolences and Sunday school collections had demanded access to the generosity of the people, indicating that the regular calls are only about half the number of public appeals.

We regret that the time allotted for this Address will not permit a résumé of the intelligent and convincing statements offered in these replies from representative district superintendents and leading pastors. Taken together, they alone would afford abundant explanation of certain deplorable conditions which are being mistakenly attributed to other causes. On circuits visited semi-monthly by the pastor there is a collection for almost every service, leaving the local congregation little opportunity to care for itself—one reason why the rural Church is waning. That means peril to the city Church. Hundreds of the larger congregations have been absolutely forced into the budget system. When pastors are compelled to give more time to working out money problems than to preparing sermons, it is plain that spiritual interests must suffer.

Let it be remembered that these answers represent not cities alone, but whole Conferences and wide areas in the East, Central West, and West—our base of supplies. Nor are they the outcry of an unwilling people nor an indifferent ministry. The pastors and people who carry the burdens of our great connectional operations have been wonderfully patient and nobly responsive.

Not one district superintendent or pastor intimates, nor do we believe that our connectional work has ever called for too much money, but the answers must indubitably show that many thousands of people who love the Church and would profit by her ministry remain away from public service rather than be subjected to the embarrassment of incessant appeals to which they are not able to respond, and that thousands of pastors are seriously hindered in their ministrations by the same cause.

If it be said that systematic giving by all the people would at once solve the problem of our Church benevolences and relieve the overtaxed, it may be instantly answered that system in asking is absolutely essential to systematic giving. When the asking is haphazard and the response dependent upon the emphasis of the hour, the giving will be impulsive and irregular. As now made, no appeal can reach the entire membership. Hence the faithful minority is unduly taxed.

First, we must devise a more systematic method for financing our connectional benevolences. Next, the hundreds of reform and charitable organizations, many of which seem to be little more than bureaus of employment for their promoters, should be forced to consolidate their work. Very few of them as now conducted are of sufficient importance to claim a hearing before a congregation assembled for worship. Indisputable facts make it plain that our congregations must be protected against promiscuous appeals.

For our own work we need, first of all, an equable basis of apportionment. This can be secured only by co-ordination of all the factors that indicate the relative ability of Conferences and Churches.

It is well known that Official Boards are guided largely by local interests as they conceive them. Acting on the theory that apportionments for benevolences are figured on the *per capita* basis, they prune the membership tree in season and out of season until the roots are in danger of being devitalized. Our actual growth during the closing quadrennium was hardly less than 650,000. It is a fair estimate that more than 400,000 members disappeared from the rolls under this interpretation of a defective method of apportionment.

It can hardly be doubted that in some instances the estimate for the pastor's support is fixed at a smaller sum than should be provided in order to lessen *pro rata* assessments. Thus pastoral support, as well as the membership roll, must be kept down in order to protect partially civilized communities against encroachment by the needs of the heathen world or the cry of our frontiers for help. And it is even said that a few Official Boards have gone so far as to discourage the admission of children into the Church in order to keep down the roll of membership.

We submit that in the presence of a formidable political-ecclesiastical organization, which carries its rapidly increasing cradle roll through life, if not beyond the grave, and claims and secures political influence largely on its supposed numerical strength, transmuted into votes, Methodism can not afford to wantonly waste its actual increase and misrepresent its real potentiality under the operation of a haphazard plan—we will not say system—of conducting its benevolent operations, which are really the expression of its abounding spirituality.

Having recently established a more equitable method of apportioning the sums required for our general work, we need next a more systematic method of securing the amounts asked. What member applying his tithe can now forecast the demands of the twelve months ahead and plan an equitable distribution of his gifts? As for the wealthier class of willing givers, when once known they find no rest from special appeals. It becomes an expensive tax upon the business hours of a busy man even to give the hearing necessary to an intelligent and conscientious decision, however well disposed he may be in spirit.

To educate the Church in the principles of Christian Stewardship and systematic giving is a tremendous task, but it must be undertaken. And the first step toward it is to find a rational, Scriptural, systematic basis for asking. As the head of a family anticipates and provides for the incoming year, as a business man estimates the capital required for his contemplated improvements as well as for conducting present enterprises, so should the Church forecast her needs and consolidate her estimates for all connectional demands—not by the uncertain process of five or six boards and committees sitting apart and acting independently, if not competitively, but by a competent connectional board or commission—in which or before which all interests may be represented—and with final authority to fix the aggregate budget and properly apportion the total amount among the Conferences, to be by Annual Conference Commissioners apportioned to districts and charges after the approved method. This consolidated apportionment, covering all needs of the benevolent work of the Church, with a safe percentage for shrinkage and emergencies, should be ready at the meeting of every Annual Conference and go immediately to the local Churches to become a part of the entire financial asking for the year, and to be collected by the weekly or monthly duplex envelope along with the regular expenses of the charge. All connectional special appeals, having first been authorized by the commission on finance, should take their chances with the general budget or in private subscription.

Advantages:
1. Economy in administration. The United States Government conducts its business under one central executive management and through one treasury.
2. Protection for public congregations against numerous Sunday subscriptions and appeals from the pulpit.
3. Protection for the pastor in his regular ministrations.
4. Less of distracting incident and more of reverence in public worship.
5. Better opportunity for spiritual appeal to the unsaved in regular services.
6. The transformation of the Annual Conference from financial to spiritual functions.

7. Training to the habit of systematic giving will become imperative. Christian stewardship will be emphasized. Every pastor will be compelled to explain, instruct, and exhort when the annual budget is presented. Nor is there anything in this method to prevent occasional special addresses carrying inspiration and illumination concerning every cause. On the contrary, the general boards uniting in the common interest could afford an educational organ and program of high grade, and thus banish competitive appeals. The district superintendent would have an inspirational errand for every visitation. The treasuries would save interest money by the regularity and stability of their income. A steady breeze is better than a storm followed by a dead calm, with unpleasant memories and doleful anticipations of frequent repetition. Best of all, such giving would be on Scriptural principles, and hence a truer gauge of spiritual progress.

What the ordinary envelope has done for ministerial support the duplex envelope may do for the entire financial budget. So the proposition is not revolutionary. Indeed, many of our progressive Churches are using the plan. It can not be at once legislated into all Churches, but it will commend itself to every business man in our boards, and speedily find acceptance.

In answer to Question 4, namely, "Have we too many organizations, general or local? Is the Church being hindered in the spiritual life or individual efficiency of its members by over-organization?"—the pastors, by almost three to one, and the district superintendents, by nearly two to one, express an affirmative judgment. This seems to be a final argument for the simplification of our working methods.

Agency executive Clarence Wilson leads Church to campaign for prohibition

Source: Clarence T. Wilson, "Report of the General Secretary to the Board of Temperance, Prohibition and Public Morals, December 9, 1916," The Voice of the Board of Temperance, Prohibition and Public Morals of the Methodist Episcopal Church 3/12 *(December 1916), Supplement, 3-5.*

A New Era Dawns

When we came to the general conference of May 1916, there was no cause more popular than the prohibition cause; and no organization met with more universal appreciation than the Temperance Society. It is significant that there was not a single adverse vote against any plan of ours, either in the open general conference or in the committee on temperance, at either the Saratoga [1916] or the Minneapolis [1912] general conferences, and when our needs were considered both in committee and in the general body, a unanimous vote ordered our apportionment doubled to $100,000 annually. Our name was broadened to The Board of Temperance, Prohibition and Public Morals. Our constitution was re-written, giving us at every point of our work equal authority and standing with every other board of the church; and after a careful discussion and consideration of more than a week it was almost unanimously agreed that as the West and South had been nearly won, we were needed in the East to aid the forces in this difficult field, and that among various voices that are heard in official lobbies at Washington, our church must be heard in the presentation of all questions of public morals upon which Methodism takes a stand. Already the action has been more than vindicated; and our strategic and providential location in Topeka for four years will be more than matched by the wisdom of our coming to Washington for such a time as this.

Immediately upon the adjournment of the general conference we came to the Capitol City [Washington, D.C.], accepted the offer of the International Reform Bureau to occupy their building at a nominal cost until such time as we were able to arrange for the erection in this city of a permanent home for our Board, which will be needed here to watch legislation and the cross-currents influencing administration as long as there is a nation. Other organizations have powerful lobbies here to promote their own interests, why should not Methodism maintain one to promote the welfare of the people and the honor of the Flag?

What the Work of the Board Is

Let me outline for your imagination some of the departments of our work: There are 18,000 Methodist preachers who meet at the annual conferences. Our board has for six years taken upon itself to place an anniversary or mass meeting in the interests of the prohibition movement at all of these conferences. The year we began this work there were seven anniversaries for temperance held at the conferences. In 1914, 1915 and 1916 there has not been a conference held, with two exceptions, that did not provide in its program for the temperance cause.

We found one greatly neglected class to be our Negro population of ten millions, with not a supported worker among them to promote total abstinence or prohibition. We have for about four years maintained the only salaried man giving his time to this work. We have an ever-widening opportunity to serve the cause and the nation by teaching to our negroes the danger of using habit-forming drugs, patronizing saloons, or tying up with the liquor traffic in politics. . . .

Foreign-Speaking People Must Be Reached

A wide-open door for our board to enter is the work among the foreign-speaking class of the United States. There is a constant call at our office for literature in various tongues and for speakers who can address these foreign-speaking peoples. We shall have fewer hyphenated Americans when they have assimilated the moral ideals of this country, and this never can be while they are environed by the saloon and debauched by beer. We should have this department of our work supervised by the best equipped man we can secure between these oceans. He could translate or have translated into various tongues our *Clipsheet* articles and wedge them into the various foreign language newspapers of the United States; he could devise means of circulating books and leaflets in these tongues; he could procure deaconesses in Methodist garb, working and speaking in the language of the immigrant, and enlist tens of thousands of them in the ranks of the total abstainers and advocates of prohibition. And when a fight is on such as is now raging in Chicago, he could go to the foreign-speaking sections of the city and through the churches, the press, the semi-political clubs; he could help to swing the foreign vote to the prohibition columns, and every man knows that until that is accomplished our cities cannot be carried. . . .

The Extension Department

We have an Extension Department. Through this we have conducted educational work in co-operation with Sunday School conventions, Epworth League Institutes, Camp Meetings, and have secured the co-operation of many who were not ordinarily gathered into our fold. . . . [We have prepared] Temperance Day programs with recitations, responsive readings and songs, total abstinence pledge cards, and buttons for the members of the temperance bands.

The Research Department

The Research Department has been for three and a half years conducted by Deets Pickett. . . . He has edited our *Clipsheet,* going out to thousands of editors every week. He has edited our *Voice,* going to 20,000 ministers every month. He has edited both volumes of our *Cyclopedia* and sent out 27,000 [copies]. He has answered 1,200 letters per year, giving dictated answers on every conceivable phase of the problem and showing an amazing amount of accurate information. He has sent to our own speakers the latest known facts that ought to be given to the public. . . .

Plans for Congressional Work

For some time the Board has been working energetically to arouse sentiment in favor of laws which would wipe out the liquor mail order business. The liquor industry has openly said that by the use of mails and the express they could simply make prohibition result in a change in the method of liquor distribution. Laws prohibiting the use of the mails for advertising and solicitation of sales for liquor would head them off. . . . We have planned to aid in bringing this feeling to a head by sending out some 45,000 personal letters [to legislators, newspaper editors, and pastors]. . . .

The Department of Campaigns

We have come to the department of campaigns, to which I have devoted considerable strength. On June 1st we found we had promised help to every state that had a fight on. . . . When these plans had been made, we undertook to fulfill our promises to the various Dry Federations, Anti-Saloon Leagues, State W.C.T.U. Committees, and other organizations that had asked our co-operation in state fights. We shipped all our literature, post or express paid, to these various workers. It consisted of more than a hundred thousand big red posters, twelve in number, . . . so printed and illustrated so as to catch the eye and the thought. We had a couple of millions of leaflets and these all went to the states where the fight was fiercest. We purchased all the books that we could secure and donated about seven hundred to the various workers connected with the campaigns in these states. We raised and handed over sums of money for two or three of the states. But the most urgent call for help came in requests to lead automobile campaign tours, similar to the one of two and four years ago in Oregon and Washington, for which our Board purchased a "Reo Six" [automobile], equipped it with men, literature and posters in which 460 meetings were held, or more meetings than all the other agencies combined in the state of Oregon. It is usually spoken of as "The tour that put Oregon dry." . . .

COMMISSIONERS DEBATE STATUS OF BLACKS IN PROPOSED UNITED CHURCH

Source: Joint Commission on Unification, Proceedings of the Joint Commission on Unification *(New York: Methodist Book Concern; Nashville, Publishing House of the MEC, South, 1918–1920) 2 (1920), 100-103, 128-31, 136-41, 162-75. Excerpts.*

REPORT OF THE COMMITTEE ON THE STATUS OF THE NEGRO IN THE REORGANIZED CHURCH.

The Committee on the Negro met at the close of the meeting of the Joint Commission in Traverse City, Mich., July 3, 1917, and appointed a subcommittee of two members from each Commission. The subcommittee made the following preferential and alternative reports. The committee herewith presents these two reports as submitted to it to the Joint Commission, without recommendation.

REPORT OF SUBCOMMITTEE.

Your committee have found it impossible to present their conclusions as to what should be the status of the negro membership in the reorganized and unified Church without stating the same in form which relates this subject to questions already reported upon or to be reported upon by coordinate committees and tentatively adopted by the Joint Commission. We present as our preferential report the following, which places the negro membership in a Sub-Regional Jurisdiction of the kind and powers herein indicated:

Associate Regional Conferences.

Section I. There shall be the following Associate Regional Jurisdictions, each having its own Associate Regional Conference:

(1) The Afro-American, which shall embrace within its jurisdiction all Annual Conferences, Mission Conferences, and Missions composed of persons of African descent in the United States and in the Continent of Africa.

(2) The Latin-American, which shall embrace within its jurisdiction all Annual Conferences, Mission Conferences, and Missions in Latin-American countries, including Porto Rico, Cuba, Mexico, Central America, and South America.

(3) The European, which shall embrace within its jurisdiction all Annual Conferences, Mission Conferences, and Missions in the countries of Europe, Northern Africa, and the Madeira Islands.

(4) The Eastern Asiatic, which shall embrace within its jurisdiction all the Annual Conferences, Mission Conferences, and Missions in China, Korea, Philippine Islands, and Malaysia.

(5) The Southern Asiatic, which shall embrace within its jurisdiction all the Annual Conferences, Mission Conferences, and Missions in India and Burma. . . .

ALTERNATIVE REPORT.

We present as an alternative report the following, which places the negro in an Associate General Conference:

1. Create an Associate General Conference which shall comprise within its jurisdiction the negro membership of the Church in the United States and Africa, and which shall have complete legislative, judicial, and executive powers in the ecclesiastical government of said negro membership in harmony with and subject to the Constitution of the unified Church. Said Associate General Conference shall have the power to elect the bishops, constitute the boards, and elect their general administrative officers, for the said negro Conferences and membership.

2. Create a Judicial Council for and out of the said negro membership, whose duties and prerogatives shall be the same or similar to those of the other membership and jurisdictions of the unified Church, represented by the General Conference.

3. Create a Constitutional Council, to which shall be referred all and only questions as relate to and affect the Constitution of the unified Church and which demand consideration and determination. Said Constitutional Council shall be constituted of representatives of each of the Jurisdictions in proportion to the Church membership represented by the respective General Conferences.

4. Provide for the representation of each jurisdiction in the connectional administrative boards in proportion to the Church membership and interests involved. . . .

Dr. Downey [David G. Downey, New York City, MEC minister]: I suppose somebody has to begin the afternoon session, and possibly I might as well say what is in my heart to say now as at any other time. . . .

Now, as to the immediate question which is before us: The negroes in the Methodist Church have a certain position. They are in the Church. Quite naturally our preference is that they be continued in the relation in which they now are. We do not see any very good reason for a change. It ought, however, to be clearly in mind as to just what the *status quo* is and what it implies. It does not imply social equality. This is not a matter that is at all before us. Social equality is something that takes care of itself. It is really hardly a matter to be considered by thoughtful men who are handling Church matters. Again, the *status quo* does not mean mixed Churches or mixed Conferences. Of course, there will be sporadic instances in which there may be a few negro members in some Churches of the South as well as of the North. . . . It is not a question of mixed Churches, it is not a question of social equality, it is not a question of mixed races. These things are not at all in our thought. They are not in the mind or conscience of the M. E. Church. It simply means ecclesiastical equality. That is all. Now, it has been said here and said, I believe, with a good deal of truth, that the color line is already drawn in the M. E. Church. This is unquestionably true. We have colored Churches, we have colored Conferences, and we have colored ministers in our Annual Conferences, ministering only and always to colored congregations. But we do not need to be misled by this. This is largely just the same color line that you have here. But there is no color line in the M. E. Church on the manhood rights of the negro in the Church. That is the point—that is the main point in our Church. He has all the rights of a minister. He has his judicial rights—his legislative rights, his right to appointment, his right to appeal, and everything of that sort. It is not a color line on the question of his manhood rights and his manhood standing, and I do not think the M. E. Church would be willing to write into the Constitution of the reorganized Church anything that would be a discrimination upon the manhood rights of any man in the reorganized Church. There is no discrimination against the rights of the negro in the Constitution of the United States. There is no discrimination on his manhood rights, I take it, in the various States. I do not believe that you would expect that we should write into the Constitution of the reorganized Church of Jesus Christ what is not written into the constitutions of the States and the Nation. . . .

[*H. H. White, Alexandria, Louisiana, MECS lay*]: . . . . I believe that our position may be condensed into the following statement:

The South and our grand division of the Methodist Church believe:

(a) That the color line must be drawn firmly and unflinchingly, in State, Church, and society, without any deviation whatever; and no matter what the virtues, abilities, or accomplishments of individuals may be, there must be absolute separation of social relations. If the color line is disregarded in relations so intimate as those necessitated by the equal status theory, demanded, as I understand it by the strongest negro members of the Methodist Church, North, it will be impossible long to continue the fixed status of separation in affairs governmental, civic, and social.

(b) We further believe that in this matter the South is but fighting the preliminary battle of the North, and is but now further advanced along the path which the North has already entered and will unfalteringly follow. . . .

We further believe that the leaders of Southern thought and policy should keep step in Church and in State; and it is but well-known history to state that for forty years the South struggled, with an eagerness surpassing that of war, to throw off and to keep off the burden and the shadow of negro influence in political affairs; and only now are the labors of the men who led in that struggle being crowned with a moderate degree of success. It was only yesterday that constitutional provisions, such as the understanding clause in Mississippi and the grandfather clause in Louisiana, took the place of harsher and more dangerous means of correcting the evils turned loose upon the South by the adoption of the fourteenth and fifteenth amendments.

But why has the South demanded and endured the storm and stress of reconstruction? We answer that it was to attain and maintain Caucasian supremacy, unadulterated and untainted in political and civic affairs. *GROSS*

But can the South, or what we fondly consider its leading Church, admit negroes on the plane of perfect equality in its religious councils and lawmaking or interpreting bodies, while it denies, or helps to deny, correlative rights and privileges in those so much less intimate relations of official and legislative life?

There is no use to blink the question: Until we are ready to admit that we and our fathers have perpetrated and assisted to perpetrate civil wrong in the reestablishment of purely Caucasian government in the South, we cannot permit the admission of any tincture into the pure Caucasian control of our ecclesiastical council and Conferences or courts. . . . *Ugh*

I take the liberty of trying to draw some general conclusions from the foregoing statements, which, while they have been presented in the form of conclusions, could in my opinion be supported by sound argument. Among those conclusions are these:

1. That the Southern Church will not be willing to go into any arrangement by virtue of which the colored delegates sit either in a General Conference or Supreme Court, and take part in their deliberations, on any basis whatever. *and getting worse*

2. That the colored ministry and congregations of the Northern Methodist Church would resent very determinedly and even bitterly any proposition to assign them any sort of a minimum or modified representation in the General Conference. They are demanding, as I understand, full, absolute, and unqualified equality as members of the Church with all other members. This view on their part has been recently expressed very forcibly by Dr. [Robert E.] Jones, who is on this committee which is meeting here, and who edits the leading *Advocate* for the colored Methodists in the Southwest, published at New Orleans.

3. The Southern Methodist Church would not feel justified in going into a union which would take care of, say, three hundred and fifty thousand colored members, now belonging to the Northern Church, but would not fully and adequately take care of or provide for the other, say, million and a half or two million negro Methodists belonging to other organizations, as the African Methodist, C.M.E., and others.

4. The only way in which a union of the Northern and Southern Churches can be brought about will be by the immediate or gradual elimination of the negro membership and in good faith attempt on the part of both Churches, North and South, to cause all negro Methodists to unite in one great body, which should be brought, in so far as may be, under the tutorship, and which would receive the encouragement of the white Church. . . . *asshole*

I belong to the class of white men who believe that the relations of the races should be governed, and are occasioned, by race difference rather than by matters of artificial caste. I champion negro education and the safeguarding of the rights of the negroes both as to property and person, but I have not been able to persuade myself that they ought to have been admitted into partnership in the political government of the country, or that it would be wise to give them such position in the Church as we feel we must withhold from them in the realm of politics.

R. E. Blackwell [Ashland, Virginia, MECS lay]: I feel that we are discussing a subject that is the most momentous that has ever been discussed by any Church assembly on this continent. It is a question that concerns not merely the Northern and Southern Churches: the whole Christian world is looking at us to-day. When it was announced that I was on this Commission, I got letters from men of various denominations expressing the hope that we would show Protestantism how to get together. It is not a question therefore, that concerns us alone. If we refuse to unite because of an almost negligible number of negroes in the General Conference, I believe it will go down in ecclesiastical history as "the great refusal." The most pathetic spectacle in history is the negro. He was brought here against his will. We Southern people have profited by him. I stand here as one who has profited by him. As far back as the records of two Virginia counties go, my ancestors were slave owners. I was helped in getting my education with money that was mine through my mother's slaves. I owe him a debt. I have not paid it. Many of my fellow Southerners have not paid the debt they owe the negro. We Southern Methodists were paying it at one time. I think we wanted to pay it. My heart beats with noble emotion when I think of what Bishop Capers did for the negroes. I think we are all proud of it. I am not proud of anything my Church has done for the negroes since they were set up for themselves. . . .

[margin, handwritten: wow – powerful witness]

We have hardly more concern about the negroes of the Colored M. E. Church than we have about Presbyterians or Episcopalians. Our people did not intend that it should be so, but it came as the result of putting the negroes off to themselves. But, as has been said here to-day, we are getting a new conscience on the subject of the negro. The young men who are to be leaders of the country are studying this problem at all Southern universities. Every State University in the South has a fund at its disposal to be expended on the study of this problem; and men of our own Methodist institutions have said to me that the relation between the negroes and the white people in the unified Church must be made closer than the relation that exists between us and the colored M. E. Church. . . .

Robert E. Jones [New Orleans, MEC minister, one of two African-American members]: When I spoke to you at Baltimore, I uttered the conviction that as one man I would do everything I could for the consummation of the union of these two great Churches. I am of that opinion to-day, but I speak this morning with just a little misgiving and some personal embarrassment. I do not like to be the occasion of all this.

E. C. Reeves [Johnson City, Tennessee, MECS lay]: You cannot help it.

Robert E. Jones: If anybody knows my intense feeling, if he knows something of my inner life, if he knows something of the policy of aloofness I have pursued, he will understand that personally I would rather be elsewhere. I am in favor of the union of these two Churches. I am absolutely sure it ought to come. . . . I do not know that I say with others that it ought to come to-day; God grant it may. I do not believe that if it does not come to-day it is not coming. I do not believe that you can stop it. I do not believe we ought to take that position at all. I think as Commissioners we are here custodians of an idea, that it is not necessarily our task to frame a plan that will pass. I rather think it is our task to frame a plan that will meet our own judgment and that will be a working ideal for the Church. But be that as it may, that is absolutely on the side. I had a great experience yesterday. As a negro, yesterday was a revelation to me and a real joy. I enjoyed Judge White's speech, really I did. There is no camouflage in that at all. I did not agree with all he said—of course, I did not—but I enjoyed the speech. I enjoyed its frankness. I think when men can come together in the beautiful spirit in which we talked yesterday there is hope for the future. . . .

God knows that for twenty-one years in New Orleans I have been doing everything that I knew how to do that there might be peace and good will. I have preached to my people over and over again that it made no difference what a man should do to me or what a race of men should do to me, I should hate no man. . . .

Bishop [Edwin] Mouzon [MECS] said yesterday that every man should have a chance. That is all I want. I do not want anything else but simply a man's chance. I want a square deal and fair play, and I want the cards dealt fairly so that I can have a man's chance in the game of life. Now, you will indulge me, I am sure, just a minute. It is so easy for a man to trump up a position at a time like this. That you may quite understand me this morning, let me read where I stand on this matter, and this speech was delivered at Evanston and recorded a year or so ago when I had no thought of ever being on a Commission such as this:

Now I state in a sentence the program: The largest possible contact of the negro with the white man with the largest possible independence of the negro. Both sides of the proposition are for the good of the negro, contact for inspiration and for ideals, independence for growth and for development. The weak grow by doing. A man ought not to do for another what the other man can do for himself. A man ought not to permit another to do for him that which he can do for himself. The day is passing when the white man is to work over the negro. Maybe the day is waning when the white man is to work among us, but the day is at sunrise when the white man is to work through the negro for the uplift of millions, and this latter program for stimulating the ideals of civilization can be carried forward just as effectively and even more effectively than by former methods. . . .

There is no servile blood in me. If I thought I had one drop of it, I would open my veins and let it out. I hope, however, that every drop is thoroughly saturated with the humility of Jesus Christ. And in this spirit I try to live a humble, devout, God-fearing man. I do not know how much I have done, but I have tried to do my level best every day of my life to develop among my people a love for our section, for its industries, for our neighbors, and for all that would make for peace and happiness. . . .

Maybe you ask the question, Why don't you people withdraw from the Church? Do you stay here for office? God forbid. I do not want any office, men. Principle is above preferment with me, and whatever office I have to-day was not given to me by my people. It was given to me by the vote of an assembly eight-ninths of which was white, and can be taken away tomorrow as easily as it was given. You know it and I know it. Is it for money? There are men in the Church who have made generous offers to us in the way of money if we go out. They have said, "If you will go out, you can have your property." Why, we would be the richest negro Church in the world. Is it money? I don't want any price put on my head, my heart, or my convictions, whether it be ten dollars or ten million dollars. I want to be somewhere that I will be above money, above place, and above preferment. I have already answered the question as to social equality, that it is not for social equality. "Then why do you cause all this confusion; why do you remain?" I am asked. First, I believe it promotes the best interests of my people. I think it is best for my people to be somewhere close to a large Church with great ideals. I have been able to do things for my people, I have been able to say things in correction of their lives and to give to them ideals that I never could have done if I did not have a strong organization behind me standing for those ideals. Then, you will excuse me: to give you a concrete example, I stood before a Conference the other day and lambasted those negro preachers about not paying a debt, and I did it straight from the shoulder— and I have to have the suffrage of those men. But I did not care for that. I was standing by the principles of my Church. Second, I stay in the Methodist Episcopal Church because I believe it is a Church founded on a New Testament basis and American democracy. I believe it is New Testament teaching for the Church to take into it all people and I do not believe I should run at the first fire of a gun. Third, Bishop Mouzon said the other day that he loves his Church as he does his life. Well, I love my Church, I honestly do, with all my heart. I was born in it and was brought up in it. My grandfather was brought up in it and it has done much for me. But I love it beyond what it has done for me. I actually love my Church beyond and above all other Churches. Then I stay in my Church, the Methodist Episcopal Church, because I believe a large part of my Church desires me to stay; and whenever the time comes when any large part of the people in the Methodist Episcopal Church does not want me in its communion, whether it is for convenience or organic union or otherwise, I shall not stay in that Church. If I believed to-day that I were unacceptable to any considerable number of the members of the Methodist Episcopal Church, I would step down and out. Self-respect would work automatically. I believe in my Church because it has made it better for the South. . . .

Now, there are just two or three other things I want to say. Much has been said about the negro Church coming under; and so, to pursue some of the methods used by you and your friends, I thought I would get in touch with some of these negro bishops to find out if it were actually true that they were looking forward to us to bring them all together. So on Saturday night before I left home, I dictated a letter to all the negro bishops and I inclosed the proposition of the Rev. Dr. Blake and of that *Zion's Herald* up there in Boston, and I said: "Tell me frankly if it is true—maybe I don't quite understand—if it is true that you men are now going to come under the Black proposition." And I will read two or three of the letters.

[Here followed extensive quotations from eight letters, all saying "not interested."]. . . .

Now, what do we want? You will be interested in that. First of all, we do not want any caste written in the Constitution. That is fundamental. We do not do that in Louisiana, and we do not do it in the nation, and we should not do it in the Church. Second, we do not want any offensive name in whatever arrangement you make. We want to be "Samuel" and not "Sambo." We want some sort of dignified name to whatever arrangement you may make. And it is fundamental that we should ask for representation in the General Conference. We will agree to the formation of our membership from one end of the country to the other in a centralized Conference. The Supreme Court of the United States has wiped out the Segregation Ordinances, and it was a unanimous court that did it and there were Southern men on the Supreme Court bench. Segregation in temporal affairs has been wiped out; and the only segregation that ought to obtain is segregation by the choice of the people, and there is a good deal of that. We don't have any trouble over that in Louisiana—we don't have any trouble in New Orleans. We will agree to show you our spirit. I don't think it is fair and I don't think it is democratic, but we will agree on a basis of non-self-support. Mark you, Dr. Goucher, the Church, the white Church, did not give the negro $500,000 a year.

John F. Goucher [Baltimore, MEC minister]: I would like it if it would.

Robert E. Jones: We negroes are a part of the Church that does that. Now, as to our representation in the General Conference, Wisconsin has eight delegates, with 28,000 members. The South Carolina Conference has eight delegates and 55,000—There are no small Conferences that have a membership between 900 and 1,000 among us—these are white Conferences; the smallest Conference we have is 5,000. But be that as it may, we are just as dead in earnest as you are. We will agree to a largely reduced representation in the General Conference. By the way, before the war three-fifths of an ignorant, helpless negro down on the plantation in the South was the basis of representation in Congress. A negro was three-fifths of a man. Five thousand counted for three thousand then. And in this new day I am at least four-fifths of a man, but to show that I am square I will agree to a reduced representation in the General Conference; I will not agree to elimination. I want the right of the initiative and referendum. I want to do just as I do in Louisiana: vote on constitutional questions. I do. . . . The question of the bishops does not concern us. We will agree to our bishops having jurisdiction within our territory—that is, that by some process they shall be limited to our people, so that there will not be any fear that any of our bishops shall ever preside over a white Conference.

Bishop [Frederick D.] Leete [MEC]: What is the concession you are making on that?

R. E. Jones: I said we will agree to a reduced proportionate representation in the General Conference, and we will agree that our bishops shall be limited to our jurisdictions. I think that is all. O brothers, let us not think the task is hopeless. Don't make us prevent reunion. Don't put upon me and upon my people any more burdens than we have, don't make us the scapegoat—we cannot stand it. Don't let us go out and have it said that these two Churches did not unite because the negro was not willing to do his share. We are. We don't want to stand in your way. Appreciate how we are situated, and God give us grace and wisdom to reach a final conclusion.

Book Agents Force Editor of German Methodist Newspaper to Comply with Government Censorship

Source: "Important Statement by the Publishing Agents," Der Christliche Apologete *(18 January 1918). The lead editorial and only English language item in the issue. Also* Northwestern Christian Advocate *(30 January 1918): 122.*

The Methodist Episcopal Church in the United States is unequivocally against the Central Powers of Europe and whole-heartedly with the United States and her Allies in the present war for freedom, democracy, and humanity.

The officers and members of the Church desire to put the total force of the Church behind the Government now, as in all our previous wars. We cannot be dumb, nor sound a doubtful or uncertain note.

Since the United States declared war with Germany, the Publishing Agents have felt that the policy of the editor of *Der Christliche Apologete* was not in full harmony with the spirit of the Church and the country.

The attention of the editor has been called to this condition without the desired result in a change of editorial policy. Under the law, the Publishing Agents are responsible to the Government for the utterances of a paper which has the use of the mail service, and circulates among the people of the United States and other countries.

The Agents distinctly and sincerely regret that the *Apologete* has not been out-spoken in its support of the United States and our Allies—Great Britain, France, Italy, and the other nations, and in its opposition to the war spirit, the war conduct, the broken treaties and the unspeakable atrocities of Germany and the other Central Powers; that it has not rung clear for the victory of the Allied nations over the Prussianized autocracy that has broken the peace and threatened to destroy the liberty of the world.

There can be but one attitude consistent with the American and Methodist spirit. In what it has said as a whole, in what it has refrained from saying, in the spirit and atmosphere it has created, the *Apologete* has not contributed, as it should in our judgment, either to the best interests of the Germans themselves, or to the cause of the United States and her Allies.

The Agents have therefore felt obliged to make such arrangement for the editorial conduct of *Der Christliche Apologete* as will relieve it of all the criticism of its patriotism. Henceforth it will sound a clear note for the utter defeat of Germany, and its despotic military system and rulers, together with the other Central Powers, and for the complete victory of the United States and France and Italy and Great Britain, and the other nations joined with them. There shall be no half-hearted or divided allegiance.

The Publishers firmly believe this to be the best for our German Methodists themselves. We can understand the affection of the German-born for the Germany of which they dream, but neither we nor they can have two countries. We have but one, the United States, and to that we are committed heart and soul. And, in the name of our Master and our common country, we ask and expect our German brethren to accept the new arrangements with heartiness, and to unite with us to make the honored and historic old *Apologete* a new advocate of democracy and humanity against tyranny, despotism, and military autocracy.

In order that all these conditions shall be fully met, we have arranged for the appointment of an associate editor for the *Apologete*, who shall have entire charge of all matter appearing touching the war in editorial, history, or comment, relieving the present editors from that department of the paper. The name of this associate editor will be announced soon.

In reaching the above conclusions, we are under obligations to the Local Committee at Cincinnati, and three of our bishops, who were with us at the meeting and who have greatly aided us by their advice and counsel.

H. C. JENNINGS,
EDWIN R. GRAHAM,
JOHN H. RACE,
Publishing Agents.

We, the undersigned, the editor and assistant editor, heartily subscribe to the above as a correct statement of the situation occupied by *Der Christliche Apologete* in the past, and agree to abide by the policy as here set forth by the terms which are to govern *Der Christliche Apologete* in the future.

ALBERT J. NAST, Editor,
FRANK T. ENDERIS, Assistant
Editor.

METHODIST FEDERATION FOR SOCIAL SERVICE EXECUTIVE HARRY WARD PRESSES CHURCH TO ENGAGE SOCIAL ORDER

Source: Harry F. Ward, *"Social Service and the Church,"* Centenary Celebration of American Methodist Missions, Columbus, Ohio, June 20–July 13, 1919, *Souvenir Book (Cincinnati: Methodist Book Concern, 1919), 25.*

The Spirit which gave Methodism birth was a spirit of service. Wesley's philanthropy at Oxford began with his sympathy for prisoners. Under his leadership a reading club became a center for brotherly services to the unfortunate; releasing prisoners held for debt, helping the poor with money and medicine, maintaining children at school and providing winter clothing for them. These and other demands came with such power and conviction to the little group that the very walls of their club were stripped of its pictures to meet the needs revealed.

From the day of the famous club to the end of his life Wesley's days were filled with practical service to the needy of every description. Furnishing employment, mapping out the city of London into districts with volunteer visitors appointed for each to look after the poor and sick, establishing a lending society, creating dispensaries, founding schools and orphanages, even publishing the classics in cheap editions, these were some of the activities in which that restless doer of good works engaged.

The followers of Wesley never lost altogether the initial impulse toward practical service given by their leader. In these later days the spirit of service to every individual need is once again stirring the church with new life; and from that idea of service to the individual, the local churches are beginning to reach out into the field of community service, until now the ideal of service to the whole community is fairly well established as the direction in which the church is moving.

But the past few years have revealed a far larger task than had appeared on the horizon of Wesley's day, or upon the day of any generation until the present one. That task is the regeneration of the social order itself. For its accomplishment, there is no lack of guiding principles, either in the early tradition of the church, or in its later ideals. What remains now to be done, is to make full and complete use of those principles in the construction of a Christian order of society.

A three-fold challenge comes to the church today as it stands, with immense resources, power and influence, before this call to a new application of its ideals.

First, is the church to be content merely to carry forward on a larger scale than ever before the services which it has already established? Or will it seek also the creation of a society in which many of those services will be forever unnecessary?

Again, will it use its power and influence merely in an attempt to coerce the opposing forces on the industrial field into "right relations" with one another, or will it give itself also to the utmost to build that kind of a social order in which there shall be no opposing camps, but only cooperation in a common task?

Finally, will it be content to teach the necessity of good material conditions for all? Or will it challenge as well the righteousness of a system of society which perpetuates power and profits for one group and wages and work for the other, to the spiritual destruction of the wielders of power and the physical and moral degradation of those over whom the power is held?

If the church would today meet the challenge of the times, it must bear its full share of the task of breaking new paths to the goal of economic brotherhood. Only so can it fulfill its ministry to a world weary of strife over material possessions, and hungering for the spiritual joy which comes only with the opportunity of working together in fellowship at a common task for the good of all men.

WESTERN JOURNALIST DISCERNS ROLE OF METHODIST PASTORS IN KOREAN INDEPENDENCE MOVEMENT

Source: Nathaniel Peffer, "Korea's Rebellion: The Part Played by Christians,"
Scribner's Magazine 67/5 (May 1920), 518-20.

On my first day in Korea I went to the old Methodist church here in Seoul [Chong Dong MEC, Seoul] where the annual conference was in session [November 6-11, 1919]. There, I was told, I could find Korean Christians and foreign missionary workers from every province in the country, and thus get at once a national picture of existing conditions. Squat, of dark-red brick and with a cube of a tower over its entrance, it is the conventional church of any small Middle Western American town—a stone's throw from the former imperial palace, now empty of concubines and singing-girls, eunuchs and yang ban [old gentry], pomp and intriguery; and on all sides the thatched roofs and mud walls of the Korean houses and the half-Eastern half-Western houses nondescript of the new Japanese wishes. It is fantastic or incongruous as you wish, but also typical of the "new" Korea—of the new East, in fact.

The church auditorium was a similar mixture of times and manners and civilizations. There was a sprinkling of foreigners, a yet larger sprinkling of Koreans in ill-fitting Western clothes . . . and the others all in the flowing white native garments and the small inverted flower-pot hats of transparent bamboo thread, the distinguishing mark of their people. On the proscenium were an American bishop [Herbert Welch], a Korean secretary, and an American minister as interpreter, who spoke the two languages with equal fluency.

It seemed a tame enough gathering and I wondered what it could tell me of revolutions. Then a Korean pastor arose to speak. The old resident who was escorting me whispered that he was one of the men involved in the independence movement in March and that he had just been released from prison. I showed my surprise and expressed a desire to meet him. A converted Korean, now a minister of the gospel, who has been in prison as a political agitator, ought at least to give me an interesting view, I said. My companion laughed.

"In this room," he said, "there are sixty Koreans, all [Methodist] pastors or evangelists. About forty of them have been in prison. There are some twenty-five more who ought to be here who are still in prison serving out their sentences."

It is a representative picture of Korea, a good introduction to the nature of its uprising. Surely no man can say a revolt so expressed is the work of "professional agitators." To this at least no man can cry the familiar "Bolshevik." It is simpler than that. It is a purely political movement; a struggle for liberty as we knew that word and such struggles a hundred years ago.

KANSAS LAYWOMAN MADELINE SOUTHARD
LAUNCHES RENEWED EFFORT ON BEHALF
OF THE ORDINATION OF WOMEN

Source: A letter to delegates attending 1920 General Conference, Des Moines. From M. Madeline Southard, Lay Delegate from Southwest Kansas Conference, 5 May 1920. Methodist Episcopal Church, General Conference Papers, 1920. United Methodist Archives, Madison, N.J.

GENERAL CONFERENCE, DES MOINES.
MAY 5, 1920.

Dear fellow Delegate:—

During these busy days I hesitate to intrude upon your time. I do wish however to invite your attention to a Memorial coming from several Annual Conferences. A copy of it is here enclosed.

Possibly you have not given much thought to this particular question, so I am enclosing two pamphlets, one written by Frances E. Willard, the other a reprint of an article of mine in the November-December number of the *Methodist Review* ["Women and the Ministry," *Methodist Review* (New York) 102/6 (November/December 1919): 918-23].

In behalf of those interested in this great question I thank you for giving careful attention to these enclosures.

Very truly yours,

M. Madeline Southard
[Lay] Delegate Southwest Kansas Conference

Enclosures

A MEMORIAL

Inasmuch as equality of opportunity is being rapidly granted to women in educational, political, economic and professional life; and

Inasmuch as the Church in the service it now asks women to render, practically repudiates every argument hitherto urged against woman's ministry; and

Inasmuch as the woman's missionary societies have amply demonstrated the administrative ability of women, while the service of women in most difficult fields both at home and abroad has clearly revealed their courage, consecration and adaptability; and

Inasmuch as women are now hampered by the restrictions of the Church in their service for the Kingdom of Christ; in the foreign field women may expound the Word and lead souls to Christ, but they are not authorized to receive their converts into the Church nor administer to them the sacraments; in some instances they must send fifty or a hundred miles to get a man to attend to these matters, perhaps a native preacher whom they themselves have taught—and similar conditions prevail in the home field; and

Inasmuch as many Churches now ordain women, and the two most conservative, the Episcopal and the Presbyterian, have now commissions appointed to go into this whole matter in their respective denominations; and

Inasmuch as the Church can safeguard herself from undesirable women by making her own requirements; and

Inasmuch as the lack of a modern policy in the Church's attitude toward women is driving to humanitarian and other fields some of her most highly gifted and best trained women who would prefer to engage in definitely religious work; and

Inasmuch as there is not now in either home or foreign fields a sufficient number of ministers to break the Bread of Life to the people who are asking for it;

Therefore we, the undersigned, respectfully memorialize the General Conference assembled in Des Moines, Iowa, in May 1920, to carefully consider the whole matter of the status of woman in the Methodist Episcopal Church, to take such action as shall secure for women that equality of opportunity in the church that is rapidly coming to her in other fields, and that shall make it regular for properly trained women to be appointed to preach when the interests of the Kingdom demand it.

African American bishop Robert Jones
Promotes interracial cooperation

Source: Robert E. Jones, "Co-operation Between White and Colored Churches," in Cooperation in Southern Communities: Suggested Activities for County and City Interracial Committees, *T. J. Woofter, Jr. and Isaac Fisher, eds. (Atlanta: Commission on Inter-Racial Cooperation, 1921), 30-31.*

If the churches cannot function in the inter-racial program we cannot hope for the movement to succeed. Everything in the church life is conducive to inter-racial co-operation. Within the church there should be a minimum of suspicion and mistrust and a maximum of good will and mutual helpfulness. And if white and black alike regard Jesus Christ as the active leader of the church, and His teachings as the basis of our Christian life, then we shall have little or no difficulty in inter-racial co-operation, for in Christ is neither Greek nor Jew nor Gentile nor bond nor free. There are recognized at once the great difficulties that face us in inter-racial co-operation, even with so logical and so sympathetical an approach as that of the Christian church. The church is a divine institution, but its agencies on earth are human and it is only fair to admit that with humanity as it is, that we must not expect the Church to do everything at once. There are a great many things it can do and unless it does these things, it is recreant of its trust and disloyal to the great head of the church.

Wherein may the white and colored churches co-operate?

First—White and colored preachers in every community in the South should meet at least once a month for the discussion of community, educational and religious activities. Some will think this is impossible, but it is quite practical and has been in vogue in a number of communities; notably in Chattanooga, Tennessee, where the chairman of the preachers' meeting, composed of both races, is a white man and the secretary a colored man. These preachers meet without the slightest embarrassment to themselves, to their members, or to the community. On the other hand, their meeting together in this way promotes confidence, trust and good will.

Second—Each local inter-racial committee ought to have a sub-committee on inter-racial co-operation between the churches. The members of this committee ought to be outstanding men of both races, not less than three and perhaps not more than five, but they should be the best men; wise, discreet, tactful, but courageous.

Third—For the present, white ministers should fill the pulpits of Negro churches as often as possible and they should preach a pure gospel without seeking to give the Negroes patronizing advice. Nothing is more objectionable to Negroes than to have some white preacher fill a pulpit and build his entire sermon on the "black mammy" romance. However sympathetic this may be, it always puts the Negro audience in bad humor. This is not the intention of the white preacher, but the fact remains as stated. It is not practical, except in very rare cases, for an exchange of pulpits between white and Negro preachers in the South, although Negro ministers have been known to fill white pulpits in the South with great acceptability. If it is possible, this should be done, and, where the message is of a high order and in the right spirit, it will go a long way toward the promotion of inter-racial co-operation. But for the present, this pulpit exchange will be one-sided. But as a compensation:

Fourth—Negro choirs and quartettes and soloists could be asked to sing in the white churches of the South. This may seem a little radical at first, but when it is thought over, it would not be at all strange. Where this has been tried, it has proved very popular. The Fisk University quartette sang in the First Presbyterian Church in New Orleans and in the Jewish Synagogue, and instead of striking a discordant note, it was a great hit. It never fails to work, especially when the Negro folklore songs are sung with the beauty and pathos characteristic of Negro choirs and quartettes.

Fifth—Community Sunday schools should be developed in the needy sections of the cities and in the rural sections for that matter, and consecrated white men and women invited to teach in these Sunday Schools. Here is a need that we have neglected, and it has all the prestige that one wants when it is known that Stonewall Jackson taught a Negro Sunday School.

Sixth—In Lake Charles [Louisiana] recently, I learned of an outstanding Southern woman in that community, the wife of a preacher of the Methodist Episcopal Church, South, who was the leader of a Negro Woman's Community Club, developing play-ground and other social activities. Here is another field for inter-racial co-operation between the churches.

Pastor Cooke and Bishop Mouzon exchange letters on the Ku Klux Klan in Texas

Source: Letters Between Harold Cooke and Bishop Mouzon Regarding the Ku Klux Klan, November 1922. Dallas: Mouzon Collection, Bridwell Library, Southern Methodist University.

Harold G. Cooke
Tulsa, Okla.
[November 20?, 1922]

My Dear Bishop Mouzon—

Your letter, and answer to my telegram received. Both because I love you, and because I feel I should give you an explanation to my wire, I am writing you. Your letter, while appreciated deeply, disturbed me exceedingly. I am sure I can say a few things to you in confidence. The criticism which you mentioned, and which I was distinctly aware of, I felt to be grosely [*sic*] unjust. I have long recognized the dangerous tendencies of the Klan. I also know it to be composed of the choice men of the land. I also know that the things about it that you and I do not approve of are not part of the organization itself, but are <u>due to the exceedingly disturbed condition of society itself, especially on the part of our best citizens who see the most precious things in our civilization crumbling at their feet</u>, and men in public office, in the control of well organized vicious groups, utterly untrue to their trusts and oaths. The reason for this rapidly growing organization is fear and alarm, lest this whole country should be swept into the control of those who despise law, have a contempt for Christianity, and propose to destroy the fundamental tenants [tenets] of our government. In their method of operation they may be wrong, in their hearts they are sincere. I know this to be true,—some of your Bishops are members, all but two of the Presiding Elders in this state were, at least 75% of our preachers, and dozens of our Churches have their entire official boards, or the large majority, within the organization. I know this to be true, I am sure you will not betray this confidence. I also know it to be a fact that the vast majority of them [Klan] are masons, and most of the 33rd degree masons in the country are. The majority of the state legislatures of Texas and Oklahoma, many members of the Congress of the United States, and that a small majority of our general conference that met in Hot

Klan & Masons

Springs, Ark. last May, was. I do not tell you this to justify the organization, nor myself, but to show you the injustice of myself having been made the butt of criticism coming from those in this city who I have been opposed to because of their corrupt hold in the political affairs of Tulsa. At the present time every public officer in Tulsa and Tulsa County are Klansmen, and never before was Tulsa one half so decent.

The insistant propeganda [*sic*] conducted by the World against me, has been founded on lies. The story of the wedding in the woods was a fabrication and a lie. The story of me having been driven from Tulsa this Summer when I went to Chicago is as you know, a lie. The infamous attempts to destroy the reputation of Richard Lloyd Jones, and E. S. Hutchinson, whom I had the courage, (and lack of wisdom) to publicly defend was based on the most contemptable [*sic*] falsehoods, fabricated by the Tulsa world, whom you know as well as myself. For which I know I have suffered criticism, and knew I would at the time, yet would never have had my own self respect if I had failed to do what I did. This is the price that a man pays for doing what he thinks to be right. Having said this, let me now say, I have not served on a committee in the Klan for more than a year. That I never was the leader of the organization in Tulsa, as was repeatedly printed in the world, am not an officer, and have not been in a meeting in Tulsa for more than six months.

However, I love the Church of Jesus Christ better than I love my life, and am willing to sacrifice anything that threatens to diminish or destroy my usefulness in the Church, and further let me say, I have always looked upon you as my safest councelor [*sic*] and truest friend.

I wired you because I felt that my marked demotion was inevitable, and as I felt that way I prefered [*sic*] at least that it should be at the hands of one in whom I had confidence. However Bishop Moore came to see the situation as it was, and appointed me to Epworth, Oklahoma City, where there is a great opportunity, and tremendous building program, and as he said to me the most difficult work in the state of Oklahoma.

I do not attempt to defend myself in my mistakes. I know I have not always acted wisely, but as the Lord is my Judge, I have been sincere. I confidently believe, in spite of the Tulsa World, the flesh, and the Devil, I have more friends in Tulsa today than I have ever had, and probably as many as any other man in the city.

Finis.

My three babies have all been confined to their bed the past week with Dyptheria [*sic*], but after the antitoxine treatment are nearly recovered.

With love to yourself, and best wishes to your family,

Harold Cooke.

The above information is in Masonic Confidence.

November 22, 1922.

Rev. Harold G. Cooke
Epworth Methodist Church,
Oklahoma City, Okla.

My dear Harold:

I am sorry indeed to know that your babies have been sick with diphtheria. I sincerely trust that they have made a perfect recovery before this time.

I think Bishop Moore has given you an opportunity in Oklahoma City commensurate with your abilities. I expect to see something happen at Epworth now.

I am sure that you are greatly in error touching some things you have to say about membership in the Ku Klux Klan. I happen to know that some unprincipled men connected with it have put out many false reports as to certain men of light and leading having membership in it. I do not doubt that in Oklahoma and Texas some of our very best men have been mislead and for the very reasons you indicated but the whole thing strikes at the very foundations of our government and the sooner our good men who have gotten into it get out of it the better it will be for them and for all concerned.

Fraternally yours,

EDM:PC
[Edwin D. Mouzon]

GENERAL CONFERENCE PROMOTES WORLD PEACE

Source: Methodist Episcopal Church, "Springfield Declaration on World Peace,"
Journal of the General Conference *(1924), 721-22.*

WORLD PEACE

Millions of our fellow men have died heroically in "a war to end war." What they undertook must be finished by methods of peace. War is not inevitable. It is the supreme enemy of mankind. Its futility is beyond question. Its continuance is the suicide of civilization. We are determined to outlaw the whole war system.

The patriotism of the Methodist Episcopal Church has never been challenged. Neither our motives nor our loyalty must be impugned when we insist on the fulfillment of pledges made to the dead and assert our Christian ideals for the living. Governments which ignore the Christian conscience of men in time of peace cannot justly claim the lives of men in times of war. Secret diplomacy and political partisanship must not draw men into the dilemma of deciding between support of country and loyalty to Christ.

The world is now open to a crusade for peace. War-weary nations everywhere are eagerly waiting. America should lead the way. The nation and the Church can do now what they may never, never be able to do again.

We set ourselves to create the will to peace. We recommend that a prayer for peace be prepared and used at every communion service. Through its educational program, our Church must do its full share to mold the present youth of all races into a peace-loving generation. We shall launch an aggressive campaign to teach the nature, causes and consequences of war. The glorification of war must end.

We set ourselves to create the conditions for peace. Selfish nationalism, economic imperialism and militarism must cease. We demand the establishment of the principle that conscription of wealth and labor must be the counterpart of any future conscription of human life. As great odium must be put upon the war profiteer as is put upon the slacker. The protection of special privileges secured by investors in foreign lands has too often imperiled the peace of nations. This source of danger must be prevented. The rights of the smallest nation must be held as sacred as those of the strongest. We hold the cause of peace dearer than party allegiance and we shall tolerate no dilatory or evasive attitudes on the part of those who represent us.

We set ourselves to create organization for peace. Grateful to our government for leadership in the movement toward reduction of armaments and the promotion of tribunals for international arbitration, we insist upon a still more decided and aggressive policy in these directions. We urge the President of the United States to summon another Conference of the nations for the more drastic reduction of armaments. We likewise urge upon the Senate the immediate entrance of the United States into the Permanent Court of International Justice. The participation of the United States in a League of Nations will receive our active aid. We call upon all our people to support for public office men pledged to secure these ends. The ballot and other direct processes of democracy must now be employed in securing a warless world.

World Christianity is enlisting in the campaign for peace. We seek alliance with all the forces which make for the principles here advocated. We therefore propose that our Church now assume its full share of responsibility by appointing at this General Conference a commission of twenty-five members, composed of five bishops, ten ministers, and ten laymen authorized and instructed to invite the religious forces of the world to unite in a conference to consider the best plans and methods for making the impact of a world-wide religious sentiment against the evils we deplore.

The principles of brotherhood are plainly challenged. The progress of the kingdom of Jesus Christ is clearly at stake. The issues are so momentous, the opportunity for leadership is so great, that we here and now call upon all people to avoid divisive and fruitless discussions and unite their energies in this great movement for a war-free world. To this sublime end we dedicate ourselves, and for its accomplishment we invoke the blessing of Almighty God.

Adopted, May 24, 1924.

GEORGIA HARKNESS SUPPORTS ORDAINED MINISTRY AS A VOCATION FOR WOMEN

Source: Georgia E. Harkness, "The Ministry as a Vocation for Women," Christian Advocate (New York) (10 April 1924): 454-55.

It is generally recognized that church work is a useful avocation for women. Since the church began our religious leaders have borne witness to the assistance rendered by the faithful Lydias and Dorcases of their flocks. If perchance the Ladies' Aiders sometimes get quarrelsome and require some smoothing of ruffled feathers, they more than atone for their misdeeds when they vote a new coat of paint for the Sunday-school room or a new parlor rug for the parsonage. And what would the Sunday school or the prayer meeting amount to without the women? Well, there probably would not be any.

But while nobody questions the value of the volunteer service rendered by women to the Church, there are many who still seem to consider that a special dispensation has been granted to men to fill most of the paid positions within the Church. They are willing enough, to be sure, that a woman should be a missionary or a deaconess or a church secretary. But for a woman to preach—impossible!

NOT MANY ARE CALLED

Now lest some ministerial brother be alarmed for fear a feminine aspirant may be seeking to usurp his legitimate place, let me say at the outset that I do not think many women at present are likely to attempt to enter the ministry. The wall of prejudice is too strong for any except the most courageous. A few remarkably gifted women such as Maude Royden have been able to make a place for themselves in the ministry, but the Church which would not choose a mediocre man in preference to a superior woman is one among a thousand.

I do not maintain that this prejudice can be attributed exclusively to the ministers themselves, for most of them are more broad-minded than their congregations. There is, however, a deep seated relic of medievalism in the attitude of the Church at large which the clergy has not done all it might to eradicate. Such is the shortage of ministers that in many denominations almost any man of good moral character and religious convictions can get a pulpit. But when men are permitted to preach whose education does not extend beyond the eighth grade, and women college trained and sometimes theologically trained are denied the privilege, something is wrong.

Margaret Slattery tells of an experience wherein she was requested to address a large church audience, not from the pulpit, but from a little oak table down by the register, because, as the church officials told her, "no woman's foot has ever stood in this pulpit." It was only when she firmly gave them the option of permitting her to speak from the pulpit or cancelling the engagement that they reluctantly capitulated. This may be an extreme case, but the fact that it can occur at all in this enlightened age affords food for thought.

One does not need to be an ultra-feminist to recognize that such a state of affairs ought not to exist. The church has a task on its hand big enough to demand the consecrated talent of both sexes, and many of us believe that it is neither wise nor Christian deliberately to reject the assistance which trained women would gladly render in its ministry if given an opportunity. When it is announced that in our largest Protestant denomination twenty-seven per cent of its ministry have had less than a full-high-school education and that in this same denomination there has been a net loss of 613 ministers during the past four years, one wonders if it is not time to bring about a change in established traditions.

WHY WOMEN ARE EXCLUDED

In these days of many investigations, would it not be well to investigate the causes of the exclusion of women from the ministry? The reasons generally given are as follows: (1) that according to Scripture women must "keep silent in the churches," (2) that the ministry would take woman out of her natural sphere, (3) that she is by nature unfitted for success in such work, (4) that she would not be apt to make it a permanent occupation, (5) that increased competition would tend to interfere with the tenure or salaries of men, (6) that the Church would lose in public esteem by the general admission of women to its ministry.

The first argument can be disposed of without much controversy. One does not have to be a very profound Biblical scholar to recognize the difference between our modern social regime and conditions in wicked, conservative Corinth in the days of Paul, when Christian women must walk warily lest they be confused with the brazen women of the street. A prudent bit of advice to the Corinthian women of the first century ought scarcely to be made a stumbling block to progress in the twentieth. The prayer meeting and the Epworth League and the Sunday school would have a sorry time of it if we were to take Paul's words literally as a permanent injunction!

The second objection has more supporters, for from time immemorial we have heard that "woman's sphere is the home." Undoubtedly it is true that for the majority of women the care of the home is the first duty, and we are not advocating that the preacher's wife exchange places with the preacher (though we may have known cases where such an arrangement would not be disadvantageous!). But in spite of the fact that the "woman's sphere" argument has been urged against every movement for the political and professional advancement of women, an increasing number of intelligent people have come to recognize that woman has also a legitimate sphere outside the home. It is not our purpose here to enter into a discussion of the whole feminist controversy; but if it is granted that woman has a rightful place in business and professional life, there is no more reason why she should be excluded from the ministry than from medicine. Practically every avenue of leadership today is open to woman save in the Church, and there she must content herself either with rendering volunteer service or working in a subordinate capacity.

TRY AND SEE

To those who fear that we women would not make a success in the ministry, we reply, "Try us and see." Is there anyone who really believes that a woman with proper training cannot preach as good a sermon as a man? Our voices to be sure may not carry so far, but there are few churches where this would be a serious obstacle and we are not likely very soon to get a chance to preach in those churches. And as for what our voices say, we invite you in all modesty to compare the sermons of the average woman preacher with that of the average man—take the best of each, or the poorest of each, or use any standard you wish so long as it is impartial—and examine the result. We are not afraid to submit to such a comparison. Are you?

But of course preaching is not the only work a minister has to do. A minister must be a pastor, an executive, an educator, a financier—a host of other things. But is there any one of these capacities in which women have not proved their ability? If women are strong enough in physique, intellect and personality to pursue successfully every other profession, why not the ministry? We are not claiming for women any sexual superiority, but it seems a matter of plain common sense that equality of ability ought to bring with it equality of opportunity.

The argument that the ministry ought to be a life job and that a woman might relinquish it to marry after a few years is a more tenable objection. But suppose she should! Does this nullify the value of her work in the years before her marriage? And does it interfere with the continuance of her work during the second leisure of middle life after her children have grown to maturity? Furthermore, while most women with professional interests regret the necessity of having to choose between a husband and a career while a man can have both, there are many capable women who in full sincerity decide they can render more service to the world by remaining unmarried; and if the Church does not offer an opportunity to invest their talents, some other and perhaps less worthy agency will.

COMPETITION

The argument that women might supplant men in the ministry or lower their salaries is not very often publicly advanced by the clergy themselves. However, in the eyes of many people who argue from the general conditions of woman's participation in industry, this seems an important factor. They seem to anticipate a greater influx of women at whose advance the present occupants of the pulpit must courteously rise and withdraw to give the ladies their pulpit chairs. There is about as much soundness in this argument as in that of the anti-suffragists who feared that if women were given the vote, Congress would be overrun with them and a woman might (*horrible dictu!*) be seated in the Presidential chair! Women will find a place in the ministry only so fast as their ability and training win them a legitimate place, and the demand for ministers is such that if any man is crowded out in the process, it will be because he is unfit for survival.

To those who say that the standing of the Church in the eyes of the public would be lowered if women were admitted to its ministry, we reply that if it would, then it is time for public opinion to be remodeled. Does anyone think any the less of the medical profession because women may enter it on an equal footing with men? The public expects and desires men to do its preaching—simply because men always have. The Church is probably our most conservative institution. There are many within its fold who, perhaps unconsciously, adopt as the guiding motto of their lives, "Not so, Lord, for I never have——." It is obvious that if the church is going to keep abreast of the times and meet the spiritual challenge of the new age it must relinquish some of its conservatism; and whatever our theological convictions may be, it might not be a bad idea to introduce some "modernism" into our conceptions of the function of women in the work of the Church.

ORDINATION DESIRABLE

Some denominations, to be sure, are willing to ordain women, and it is easy to say that if women want to preach they should enter those denominations. But the issue does not lie wholly in ordination. Not many more women are preaching in those denominations where ordination is possible than in those where it is denied. The crux of the matter, to put it baldly, is that women cannot enter a field where they are not welcome. Ordination is desirable, I believe, to put the stamp of the Church's approval upon the admission of women to its ministry. But what is needed even more is a general recognition by pulpit and pew of the legitimate place of trained women in this field. Women will never find a welcome in the ministry until the press and our present religious leadership have remolded public sentiment. Ordination is a step in this direction, but it is a step—not the final goal.

I am not blind to the fact that some other religious vocations are open to women. In fact, I am in another myself. Every year I have the privilege of directing a good many young women who are thinking seriously of religious or social work as a vocation. But I never advise any of them to prepare for the ministry, though I consider it the highest religious calling. Under present conditions it would be folly for them to think of it, for they might take three years of theological training beyond their college work, only to find themselves superseded by men with high-school training or less. If there are men enough in the ministry to do the work and do it well, we are willing to let them. But are there? We wonder if the advancement of the Kingdom is not more important than the maintenance of an ancient prejudice.

Elmira College, Elmira, NY.

WINIFRED CHAPPELL CHAMPIONS "WOMEN OF PASSAIC" IN LADIES GARMENT WORKER'S STRIKE

Source: Winifred Chappell, "Women of Passaic,"
Christian Century 43/18 (6 May 1926): 582-83.

Every observer of the present strike in Passaic and the neighboring textile towns notices and comments on the women. Not the girls who flutter in and out of strike headquarters, busily helping with the distribution of relief funds, or bantering with the young men strikers—like other girls the world around. These would admit probably that they are "getting a kick" out of the situation. . . .

PEASANT TYPES

But what of the women—mothers of children—some of them leading kiddies by the hand or even trundling baby carriages in the picket line; middle-aged women; elderly women? They are of the European peasant type; many of them must within the decade have changed their old country life for the textile mills of New Jersey. So obviously they are not the sort who would be class-conscious. Yet so very obviously they are becoming class-conscious. Their faces attract one in the strike meetings, more than the faces of the girls who flutter in and out of the halls, or the young men who stand on the side lines; more even than the faces of the middle-aged men, peasants also from the fields of Europe, husbands of the women.

No word escapes these listening women. One of the speakers is asking a question and answering it. "When the bosses wanted to cut your wages, did they talk it over with you? No, they put up a sign saying that wages would be reduced." Peasant woman looks at neighbor peasant woman nodding vigorously, and receives a vigorous nod in return. "Why yes, that is the way it was," the nods say. . . .

There is something of religious atmosphere in the meetings. It reminds a Methodist observer of a revival meeting. An elderly man with saintly face is pleading with the strikers to join the new union. "If there is a single person in this house who is not a member of the union, let him not go to sleep tonight until he has taken out membership." . . .

THE PART OF THE CHURCH

It is when the meetings become most intense that one becomes most aware of the women. Someone reports that a striker was viciously beaten by the police and died from the blows—the sort of rumor that gains easy credence in the tense strike atmosphere. Through the woman part of the audience ripples the tch! tch! tch! with which women through the ages have expressed sympathetic horror. A speaker ventures to turn his criticism on the Catholic church. "Over in Garfield the halls have been closed. Someone asked the priest for the church house and he refused. He, a priest, sided with the bosses. Why should he side with the bosses? The priest belongs with the oppressed people. If priests refuse the church houses, use them anyway. Who pays to support the church? You do." It is an audacious thing to say. How will these peasant women, the very backbone of the church, respond? They waver a minute. They seek support in each other's eyes and in the eyes of the men. Their old religious emotions are struggling with their new emotions of group solidarity, of class consciousness. But the young men on the side lines are leading with the hand-clapping; presently the women join the applause.

So is it with their Americanism. America, they must have been taught, is the land of the free. Their communist leaders, but no less the speakers from outside—socialists, trade union folks, students from theological seminaries, preachers, are helping them to see that when the constitutional rights of freedom of assembly, including picketing, collide with intrenched business interests, the former, as Walter Rauschenbusch once put it, "go down with sickening regularity." The speakers, though, would talk against the tide as far as the women are concerned but for the fact that those women have seen in action fire-hose and tear bombs and police clubs; that they have seen terrorized neighbors fleeing—have themselves joined in the flight—as officers on motorcycles have ridden into the picket lines.

THEY STICK!

When, in 1920, the Consumers League investigators interviewed one hundred night-working women of Passaic, picked after the manner of statistical sampling, they reported: "Take almost any house in the non-resident section, knock at almost any door, and you will find a weary, tousled woman, half-dressed, doing her housework, or trying to snatch an hour or two of sleep after her long night of work in the mill." Much water has gone under the bridge that spans the stream of American industrial life in these six years. But the women of Passaic and the other textile towns still work at night, and by day care for babies and get meals and wash and mend clothes, snatching sleep as they can. But it is not chiefly pity that one feels as one looks into their faces. Chiefly one feels admiration. For when their families needed much more than their men's wages provided, they themselves went into the mills—and they chose night work instead of day work, because their families needed them by day. And they have not been done to death by this cruel experience of double work. They have sufficient spunk left so that when in January a ten per cent cut of wages already unendurably small was announced, they walked out of the mills with their men and their young folk. For three months now they have been living on meagre strike funds. And their spirits are still undaunted. Go back to work? Not a bit of it. Not till everybody goes. "Me no scab," they say. "Solidarity forever" is the new battle-cry not only of the vigorous and spirited youth but of the working women of Passaic.

CHURCH ARCHITECTURE EXECUTIVE ELBERT CONOVER FAVORS GOTHIC CHURCHES

Source: Elbert M. Conover, Building the House of God (New York: Methodist Book Concern, 1928), 69-73, 100-111. Excerpts. Italics in original.

CHAPTER VI. THE PROBLEM OF MODERN CHURCH BUILDING

We now face the problem of leadership in church building of a type worthy of the present generation, which commands resources undreamed of in the thirteenth century. Can we equal those builders of the past in abandon and devotion to a great cause? Some American churches frankly broke with the churchly order of the past and set up in this country as independent denominations but failed to give to the people the full ministry properly expected of a church. Too often men have come to look upon the house of God as just another civic structure that might in design and expression be little different from the town hall, theater, library, schoolhouse, or bank. Wise leadership in a church-building enterprise must insist that just as there are fundamental truths in our holy faith, so there are certain facts essential of maintenance in Christian architecture; otherwise it is as incongruous for its purposes as the Koran in a Christian pulpit. While local conditions and the materials of construction widely differ, there are motives and features that should mark the house of God regardless of its location. There is a language of architecture in which either truth or falsehood will be expressed.

Some Essential Elements That Must Obtain
in a Worthy Church Architecure

Church architecture should express religious truth. The language of architecture may not consciously be understood but its influence is potent. When this influence is negative, there is a real loss to the community. Particularly should the church be careful of her architecture—it speaks directly to the feelings. It is the duty of the church builder to understand this language, absorb its vocabulary, and through it proclaim such a message as cannot otherwise be expressed. We are coming more generally to realize the influence of buildings. . . . The churches of a denomination that invests millions of dollars in church buildings ought to realize what a power for good, evil or indifference such an expenditure may become. The inappropriateness of pagan forms of architecture in connection with the Christian Church should be quite evident. Quite likely all people are strongly influenced by their architectural environment even if they are not able to analyze its effect. Doubtless the architecture with which the almost illiterate Roman Catholics in isolated parts of the world are familiar has had a most effective influence upon their lives, and we may venture the assumption that conditions of irreverence of which some folks anxiously complain have been induced by the conglomerate or sterile architecture that has prevailed in our churches. To-day there is a tendency to give tone and meaning to the structure used for the activities of commerce and industry. The community is beginning to question the right of an industry sordidly to devastate the possible beauty of a locality by the erection of ugly buildings. How much more should be expected of a church!

The church building should express aspiration. In the upward trend of all the parts of the [Gothic] building is seen the influence of a faith that finds its climax in the heavenlies. Crude and stubby towers ended abruptly before reaching the height of the roof ridge, fail to lead one's mind far upward.... The square library type of building does not aspire at all. It may be a ... safe storage place for books and relics, or works of art, but does not attempt to point upward. The architecture that came out of pagan thought and worship [classical revival] cannot express the Christian hope....

Christian architecture should express a spiritual faith. It should witness a faith that sustains the people during an earthly existence. It must express more than a cold utility. Some plans would indicate that the people who propose to use the church have not an idea in the world disassociated from their commercial pursuits. A church building enterprise is a venture of faith. It should speak of the faith and sacrifice that make the house of worship and Christian service possible.

It should inspire worship. A Christian church building should promote worship. The architect should be clearly informed as to the program of public and private worship, so that proper facilities may be provided for these services. Especially should the interior of a church stimulate a devout frame of mind. A sanctuary fashioned after a concert hall cannot produce the warmth of heart that will lead to the thought, "This is none other than the house of God." Windows that do not glare, decorations that are refined in tone, uplifting lines of structure with something that reminds of God go far toward producing the realization of God's presence. Nothing should intrude between the prayerful state of the soul and the thought of God....

Modern church building calls for a leadership definitely and intelligently devoted to this noble endeavor. Aside from its practical considerations, Christian architecture may be the very highest expression in the realm of art. How much, then, depends upon those who are called to this work! To build the house of God and make it a place where people can realize the Divine Presence, where little children will be instructed in the Way, the Truth, and the Life, and where Christian fellowship and service will evidence the presence of the Divine Spirit in human living, is a work of art in the supreme sense....

CHAPTER X. BUILDING FOR WORSHIP

In divine worship, the human personality enters into its most sublime experience. If the service appointed for worship does not make the Divine Presence appreciable and does not inspire or comfort or create humility of mind, it fails of its purpose. . . .

The Nave. The nave should be at least twice as long as it is wide; the height at least equal to the width. In this manner of planning the maximum number of worshippers is seated in front of the aisles straight. A sloping floor in a church is of no real advantage. If the height of the pulpit is increased a few *inches,* this will compensate for any advantage of pitching the floor a corresponding number of feet. . . .

There has been a regrettable tendency in America to build our churches of too great width. If there is no clerestory, the walls must be carried up to a greater height, risking a barnlike appearance; if the ceiling is too low, the room appears squatty. Another fault has been to have the sanctuary too large. The growing opinion is that it should be of such size that it will be well filled on normal occasions. . . . It is unwise to allow the needs of an occasional convention to determine the size of the church auditorium. . . .

The Chancel. The chancel is the separated place in front of the church in the apse—if there be one—in which are the minister, the choir and the equipment required for conducting the services of worship and preaching. . . . In most of the so-called non-liturgical churches there is a very marked increase in the use of the open chancel arrangement. In brief, this open or churchly chancel arrangement calls for a point of focus or highlight for the entire sanctuary. This is provided by giving the communion table a central position. . . . At one side of the chancel is the lectern, devoted to the ministry of reading the scriptures and at the opposite side the pulpit, which gives the ministry of preaching a separate, distinct, and permanent setting. The baptismal font, a constant symbol of entrance into the Christian fellowship is just within the railing or in some permanent and dignified position. . . .

Provision for the Holy Communion. Give to the table of the Lord the position of honor due it, with nothing but the communion rail between it and the people. To place the communion table in a narrow passage, or to overshadow it by a so-called pulpit-desk, is to detract from the high significance of the service and all that it represents in the life of the Christian Church. . . .

BISHOP RYANG DESCRIBES THE FORMATION AND UNIQUE FEATURES OF THE AUTONOMOUS KOREAN METHODIST CHURCH

Source: J. S. Ryang, "How Two Methodisms Unite," Missionary Voice 21/10 (October 1931): 13-15, 50. Excerpts.

UNDER THE AUTHORITY OF THE GENERAL CONFERENCES, *the Korea Annual Conference of the Methodist Episcopal Church and the Korea Annual Conference of the Methodist Episcopal Church, South, have united and organized into the Korean Methodist Church, which is an autonomous church.*

There are several features which make the Korean Methodist Church unique among Methodisms of the world:

Its Relationship. The Korean Methodist Church is an autonomous church, but it retains an organic or vital relationship to the Mother Churches in America. By an agreement with the Commissioners from America, a provision has been made in the Constitution of the Churches, which reads as follows:

> The General Conference of the Korean Methodist Church may send a representative or representatives to the General Conference of the Methodist Episcopal Church and to the General Conference of the Methodist Episcopal Church, South, to give information and to render assistance on legislation relating to the Korean Methodist Church and to world brotherhood.
>
> The General Conference of the Methodist Episcopal Church and the General Conference of the Methodist Episcopal Church, South, may each send a representative or representatives to the General Conference of the Korean Methodist Church to give information and to render assistance on legislation relating to the Korean Methodist Church and to render assistance on legislation relating to their respective Churches and to world brotherhood.
>
> The representatives of the General Conference of the Methodist Episcopal Church and the Methodist Episcopal Church, South, shall be given full membership in the General Conference of the Korean Methodist Church.

As a connecting link, a Central Council has been provided. . . .

1. Ex-officio, the General Superintendent of the Korean Methodist Church, and the Bishops of the Methodist Episcopal Church and of the Methodist Episcopal Church, South, officially appointed to Korea.
2. Sixteen members from the Korean Methodist Church, including ministers, laymen, and lay women, to be elected as the General Conference of said Church may direct.
3. Sixteen missionaries, eight of the Methodist Episcopal Church, South, four men and four women, and eight of the Methodist Episcopal Church, four from the Board of Foreign Missions and four from the Woman's Foreign Mission Society, to be elected as the Bishops officially assigned to Korea and the missionaries may determine.

The functions of the Central Council have been defined, and they are concerning the work that relates to the Korean Methodist Church, the missionaries, the mission institutions, and the Mission Boards in America. . . .

Services of Missionaries. The services of the missionaries from the Mother Churches have been solicited by and enlisted in the Korean Methodist Church. They shall enjoy all the privileges in an Annual Conference of the Korean Methodist Church exactly the same as the Korean preachers. . . .

Its Superintendency. In order to supervise the whole Church, the General Conference is authorized by the Constitution to elect a General Superintendent from among the ministers for a term of four years. He is empowered to perform almost all the duties of a bishop, but he is not a bishop in the ordinary sense of the term. His duties are clearly defined, and in a real sense he is the servant of the Church. He is eligible to be reelected for a second term, but not for a third.

Its Ordination. The Korean Methodist Church has renovated the method of ordaining its preachers. The offices of Deacon and Elder have been abolished, and the preacher who has been on trial in an Annual Conference for four years (instead of two years as formerly) and prepared to meet all other requirements may be ordained as a minister only once. No ordination for local preachers has been provided.

Its Democracy. Formerly all the officers of a local church were nominated by the preacher in charge. But in the Korean Methodist Church all the officers of a local church, before they are elected at the Charge (Quarterly) Conference, have to be nominated by ballot at the Church Conference, which is composed of all baptized members of that church.

Its Recognition of Equality of Sexes. The Korean Methodist Church has abolished all the discriminating features between sexes, so any woman who meets the requirements may be licensed to preach, ordained as a minister, and received into an Annual Conference as any man. It has been based on the New Testament teaching, "There is no male or female in Jesus Christ." A special legislation has been enacted by the first General Conference, which reads as follows: "The missionaries of the Methodist Episcopal Church and of the Methodist Episcopal Church, South, who have been appointed to the Church work in Korea for eight years or more may be received into an Annual Conference as full members by two-thirds majority vote of the Conference." Another clause reads as follows: "Those missionaries who shall be received into the Annual Conference under the special rule shall be ordained as ministers by two-thirds majority vote of the Conference; provided, however, this clause shall be effective only through 1932." By the advantage of this special legislation, about a dozen or more women missionaries may be ordained at the coming Annual Conference which is to be held in Songdo from June 10 and also at the Annual Conference of 1932.

Its Creed. The General Rules and the Articles of Religion have been included in the Historical Statement, and the First General Conference has adopted a Doctrinal Statement which can easily be understood by believers and which has omitted nothing essential. It is regarded as unique, and it reads as follows:

1. The fundamental principles of Christianity have been set forth at various times and in various form in the historic creeds of the Church and have been interpreted by Mr. Wesley in the *Articles of Religion* and in his *Sermons* and *Notes on the New Testament.* This evangelical faith is our heritage and our glorious possession.

2. Upon those persons who desire to unite with us as members, we impose no doctrinal test. Our main requirement is loyalty to Jesus Christ and a purpose to follow him. With us, as with Mr. Wesley in the earliest General Rules of the United Societies, the conditions of membership are moral and spiritual rather than theological. We sanction the fullest liberty of belief for the individual Christian, so long as his character and his works approve themselves as consistent with true godliness.

3. It is fitting, however, that we should state the chief doctrines which are most surely believed among us.

(1) *We believe* in the one God, Maker and Ruler of all things, Father of all men; the source of goodness and beauty, all truth and love.

(2) *We believe* in Jesus Christ, God manifest in the flesh, our Teacher, Example, and Redeemer, the Saviour of the world.

(3) *We believe* in the Holy Spirit, God present with us for guidance, for comfort, and for strength.

(4) *We believe* in the forgiveness of sins, in the life of love and prayer, and in grace equal to every need.

(5) *We believe* in the Word of God contained in the Old and New Testaments as the sufficient rule of faith and of practice.

(6) *We believe* in the Church as the fellowship for worship and for the service of all who are united to the living Lord.

(7) *We believe* in the Kingdom of God as the Divine rule in human society; and in the brotherhood of man under the Fatherhood of God.

(8) *We believe* in the final triumph of righteousness, and in the life everlasting. Amen.

To the extension of this gospel of life and freedom and joy and power to all people and to all realms of thought and action, our Church is consecrated.

General Board. In order to save overhead expenses, only one General Board of the Church has been provided. This Board has been authorized to do all the evangelization, including missions; education, including Sunday school and Epworth League work; social service, including rural work, with four Departments—namely, Department of Evangelization, Department of Education, Department of Social Service, and Department of Finance.

Its Task. The main purpose of the unification and organization of an autonomous church is twofold: To have one united Methodism in Korea and to make the Church more efficient in meeting the needs. The Survey and Census show that the area and population of Korea are 85,000 square miles, and 21,000,000, respectively, in round figures. The Methodist work has covered about 27,000 square miles, the population of which is about 5,800,000, whose souls the Methodism in Korea has pledged to save in the agreement between the different Missions working in Korea. This requires an enormous number of workers and different kinds of institutions. Considering the man and economic powers of the Korean Methodist Church today, the task seems to be an impossible one from a human standpoint, in spite of the tremendous help from the Mother Churches, both in men and money. But our resources are unseen. We believe that as long as our God is in heaven, our Mother Churches are interested in us, and we ourselves are consecrated to the cause, there will be enough strength and power to bring the whole population to the feet of Jesus Christ! May we not ask the members and friends in the Mother Churches to pray for the success of the Church in Korea?

Charles Tindley preaches to Philadelphia's black community

Source: Charles A. Tindley, Book of Sermons (Philadelphia: Charles A. Tindley, 1932), 16-21. Excerpts.

Text—*Behold, I have refined thee, but not with silver; I have chosen thee in the furnace of affliction.*—Isaiah 48:10.

My friends:—We are to study God's dealings with His people in a light which seems incompatible with what we know of His love and Fatherly feelings. What could present a more tormenting picture than a furnace? What could indicate more wrath and ill-will than punishment by such cruel means? All this, to our senses, would at once contradict every notion and thought of the love of God toward his creatures, if the interpretation of our text did not, in the light of heaven, show the smiles of a loving Father behind this awful looking providence. This whole sinful world has become one great big furnace heated more than seven times hotter than needful. From its flames, few, if any escape. Let us notice:

1.—*God Is Not the Author and Maker of This Furnace.*
If you will read His plans for the happiness of mankind, in the creation, you will see that all ideas of afflictions and hurt were eliminated. The eye was furnished with a feast of beauty, whether it turned upward, earthward, to the right or to the left; blue skies, green grass, pretty colors, pretty shapes and beauty everywhere were made for the pleasure of the eye. For the ear, one perpetual concert of music was arranged. The Cosmos Oratoria was selected by the greatest musician that ever handled a baton. The millions of voices, from thunder to the sigh of a blade of grass, have been tuned and pitched to a degree of harmony impossible to any save the Almighty God. For the dietetic taste, the Creator prepared every necessity. The flavor and nutrition of fruits and vegetables bespeak a knowledge of the taste of creatures for whom these are given for food. There was absent in everything conditions calculated to make trouble. In mankind nothing but love; in the fields, no briers, thorns or thistles; no enmity between the human race and the serpent, and, I am inclined to the thought that there was no bad feeling in any creature toward

another; no cursed ground for man's sake, and, as I believe, no disease to make sick and kill. I have nothing to do with trying to explain what the final disposition of man was going to be had not sin entered the world. This only is mine to consider; God, in imposing the penalty of transgression, said, "From dust thou art and unto dust shalt thou return." You say this was not a penalty for sin, but a condition that was, and would be, without sin. I ask then, what was the penalty for sin? Eh? Ah, my friends, I am of the opinion that physical death came because of sin. There seems no good reason for the Creator to make mention of returning to dust in connection with other penalties of sin, if this was not one of them. No, if this world is a great big furnace, whose flames torture and consume the lives of mankind, it is because sin has changed the world from a paradise to a place of suffering and death. In the greatest of these sufferings, in the hottest of the fires of this furnace, God chooses those whom He would call for special work. Perhaps it is for the following reasons, namely in order that we may be properly shaped. There is everywhere in the Bible the thought that our afflictions are made to serve in preparing us for a higher state. "These light afflictions, which are but for a moment, worketh out for us a far more exceeding and eternal weight of glory" [2 Corinthians 4:17]. This is the opinion of St. Paul: "Before I was afflicted I went astray." This is what David said: "Has afflictions ever changed you?" My father carried some old iron to the blacksmith shop to have some links made for his ox-chain. I noticed how the old blacksmith put the bits of rusty ill-shaped iron in the fire and began to blow up the fire with a sort of bellows. When the iron was red hot he took it out and began to put it in shape. It was softened by the heat. I think that is the idea in this text. God would have us take back His shape as when He breathed His spirit in the first human being. "As you have borne the image of the earthly ye shall also bear the image of the heavenly," says the Bible. You know poor lost and wasted human nature is all out of shape. It has become hard and unyielding. It will take sorrows to soften it; it will take trials to shape it. Notice—

2.—These Trials of Afflictions Come in Order That We May Be Tested.
Not that God would find us out, but that we may find out ourselves. He knows us now, but we do not know ourselves. You know how given to overestimating we are, when it comes to counting on ourselves. We overestimate our goodness. Have you not known those who thought they were almost good enough? Just in proportion as one can depend upon his own goodness, will he fail to depend upon the goodness of another. That poor fellow that came to Jesus with an array of virtues saw no lack in his moral equipage. When Jesus pointed out just one thing he went away feeling worse than when he came. Have you not surprised yourself before now by doing some things that you thought you were too good to do? Those who do not trust their all to the goodness of God will be surprised in the last day to find that all of their goodness has been rated as filthy rags.

We are tried also in order that we may not overestimate our strength. I should know my limitations. I should know my own weakness. How else could I trust God for His strength, than to despair of my own, as insufficient? "When I know my weakness, when, according to my judgment, I am weak, then am I strong," says the Bible. Why? Because I will take a hold on the Almighty strength. When I get that Almighty strength, then will I be strong. "I can do all things," said Saint Paul. How did he know that? Because his strength had been tried and he had, by the trial, found out how much he really had. He added, "through Christ which strengthened me." He could trace the source of his strength, and knew it was from God. Was he far out of the way in his reckoning? No. He could do as much as the strength he made use of could do. It could do all things; so could any one who used it. God gives me His strength and wishes me to prove it so that I may be able to trust it. He allows heavy burdens to fall upon it, saying all the while, "I will not suffer more to come upon you than I will make you able to bear." When I look back through the years and see what great weights the might of God has stood, and what great deeds the strength of God has done, I am assured that all the burdens that can come upon me will not be—cannot be—too great for my strength, if God is mine. These trials come also to test our faith. What a mighty testing is going on in this world all the time! When I came in on the train the other day some men were seen going from car wheel to car wheel testing the wheels. The company could not trust the car out again until the wheels had been tested. Could I expect to be put on the track that is to reach from earth to Glory without having every wheel tested? These train men were using hammers and nails; God may use trials. I used to hear my 'phone ring almost every morning about the same time. When I would go to answer a voice would say, "testing wires, thank you." This, I took it, was to prevent any serious hitch in the messages of that day. There should be a great deal of communication over the lines between me and my Creator. Should not the lines be tested? I may have to use them hastily some unexpected moment, and would not want a hitch. Some heavy trial may come when I am not aware. I may want to get the ear of God in the night when all are still and silent. I would rather have the wires tested. I would rather know that they are all right. I welcome the testing. No untried faith can stand the new trials of each day. No untried faith can give the proper assurance in the time of great trouble. If the faith has been able to bear up under all of the trials of life, if it has stood all the strains and jerks and pulls that are caused by the awful and sudden jolts of this world, you may be able to trust it in the strong and swift currents of the Jordan of Death. In this will be the severest test our faith shall ever come to. We shall need all the strength that faith has; we shall need to be sure of that strength. It will take no weak rope of faith to keep the soul true and straight in the swellings of Jordan. I would rather have my faith well tested now so that in that awful hour I can trust and not be afraid. Notice—

3.—*These Afflictions Come That We May Be Purified*
It will take rare and choice souls to enter heaven. We must be like Christ in our thoughts and in our lives, in order to enter Heaven. We must have love like the love of God. His love went out for his enemies. I have thought of the scene of the Crucifixion. There Jesus was nailed hands and feet, His brow bleeding from the thorns that had been pushed through the flesh. . . . Have you read His prayer upon

that occasion for the men who had treated Him so shamefully? It was this: "Father, forgive them; they know not what they do." My friends, we have got to get that kind of love before we can get through the golden gates of Heaven. I do not mean merely saying so, but we must mean it from the bottom of our hearts. We must forgive others, and nothing but the love of God can do that. I do not know what it will take to bring me to this high point of perfection. It may require all the trials that I have had and that I am still to have to bring me there. If so, I welcome this morning, all the persecutions, unkindnesses, hard sayings and whatever God allows to come upon me. I welcome the hottest fire of trials if it is needed for my purification.

O, the things that we have in our lives that can never go in heaven are more numerous than we are apt to think. They must all be taken out before we leave this world. God's way to get them out may be the way of the furnace. He says, through the notes of an old song, "The flames shall not hurt thee, I only design thy dross to consume and thy gold to refine." In England some time ago, so the story goes, a man whose business it had been for years to superintend the refining of silver, sat looking through a small hole through which he could see the silver in the refining oven. He kept his eye on the silver and his hand upon a little wheel with which he could regulate the temperature of the furnace. He would turn the little wheel a bit to the right—now to the left—then to the right again—keeping his eye all the while on the silver. Some of the workmen shouted to him to turn off the heat, saying the silver would be ruined. To all shouts and sayings he gave no heed. He had been trusted for years by the king and had never spoiled the stuff. He knew what he was doing. Suddenly his face lighted up, he turned the wheel quickly, the heat was off. Do you know what happened? The old refiner saw the image of his face in the silver. That was all he wanted. I think God is watching my soul with His hand upon the powers that control all the trials that can come to me. I have shouted to Him more times than one, asking Him to turn off the heat. He did not. I know now why. He is waiting to see His image upon my soul. As soon as I am "Like Him" He is going to give the wheel of providence a quick turn and the heat will be off. When I reach heaven and stand by His side redeemed forever, He will say to me, "I have redeemed thee, but not with silver; I have chosen thee in the furnace of affliction."

METHODIST DELEGATE ARLO AYRES BROWN
SUPPORTS FINDINGS OF ECUMENICAL
LAYMEN'S FOREIGN MISSIONS INQUIRY

Source: Arlo Ayres Brown, "The Laymen's Foreign Missions Inquiry," Christian Advocate (New York) (8 December 1932): 1318-19. Excerpts.

No commission ever started out with a more overwhelming sense of the immensity of its task than the Appraisal Commission of the Laymen's Foreign Missions Inquiry. We knew that we were trying to solve some problems that might be insoluble, problems as complicated as human life itself. We had no illusions about our ability or about our difficulties. To understand the religious movements in the country of one's birth would be difficult enough; to understand such movements in the Far East after a visit of a few months was almost unthinkable, no matter how much our previous study and experience might help us.

Methods of the inquiry. But the laymen who sent us out also appreciated these difficulties. To make the project successful, they gave us definite questions to answer. They first sent out Fact Finders with these questions to India, China and Japan. When these groups of investigators . . . returned, we received their printed reports. . . . Our party at its full strength numbered approximately thirty-five. . . . Each commissioner had definite assignments. Committees were set up for The Church, Higher Education, Elementary and Secondary Education, Women's Work, Medicine, Agriculture, Industry, Christian Literature, and General Administrative Problems. Most of the commissioners served on two committees. The writer was asked to study the Church and also higher education. . . . While the writer was the only Methodist on the commission, he found other commissioners exceedingly well informed about Methodism, and sympathetic to its work.

Results Summarized. What were the results of our inquiry? These should be read carefully in the forthcoming volume in which the commissioners have given their recommendations. However, a brief summary from the writer's personal standpoint may be useful.

Should the [overseas] missionary project go on? Our answer to this question was unanimously in the affirmative, but with significant recommendations as to how it should go on. We received many criticisms of missionary effort with much useful advice, but there was practically no dissent from nationals when we asked: "Would you like to have missionary work continued or discontinued?" They all want our educational work and our medical work. They all want the cultural contacts with great Christian personalities from the Western world. Hence, even though they might hate to see the Christian constitution grow very rapidly, they want the missionary "of the right sort" to live and work with them.

Perhaps the place where the commission would differ most emphatically from some missionaries and their supporters at home is in the following particular: Some told us, "If we only had money enough, everything would be all right"—or words to that effect. Our feeling is distinctly against such a position. The missionaries do need more money, and most of them would do a great deal of good with more. But the problem is not so simple as such a statement would indicate. Indigenous, self-supporting churches in these lands will never be produced by the present program, no matter how much money is poured in. Nor will educational institutions or hospitals of distinctive excellence be developed under present policies.

Our commission is not criticizing the great pioneers for meeting their problems as they did. We are asking rather for a revival of the pioneering spirit and of the pioneer's resourcefulness to meet the new opportunities. We do not claim originality for any of our suggestions. They came to us principally from the forward looking leaders, Christian and non-Christian, whom we met in the Far East.

Wanted—a New Approach. Briefly our appraisal asks for a new approach to the problems of the Far East, for the development of missionary personnel along somewhat different lines, for a new plan of co-operation at the home base, and for churches in these lands which are truly indigenous. One other important recommendation—hospitals and schools must be good hospitals and good schools, not second-rate institutions with evangelism as their first objective. . . .

But someone will ask, "What is there so new about these recommendations? Are not the boards at home and the workers—missionaries and nationals—moving in this direction?" The answer is, yes and no. Forward-looking leaders are doing so, but many others are not, and the resulting progress is not satisfactory. More than once we were told by intellectual non-Christians, "Your missionaries do not know their own religion, much less ours. How then can they help us?" The plea most often made was for "missionaries who understand us, our language, our culture, our ways of thinking and doing. The missionary has much which we need, but too often he lives in a 'little bit of America.' He is so busy with his institutions and his other work that we never see him." . . . Of the high character of the missionary and of his desire to serve there was practically no adverse criticism. But of his breadth of view, his range of cultural interests, and his ability in special fields, we heard frequent criticism. Nor did we lay all of the blame for this at the door of the missionary, for it was clear that very often indeed the fault was with the sending agencies. . . .

The Christian Nationals. The report urges very strongly that the development of churches, the local church societies, and the larger denominational or union organizations, should be chiefly in the hands not of missionaries nor of the sending boards, but of the Christian nationals themselves. A few missionaries with unusual tact and with the ability to enjoy the role of counselor rather than that of a chief executive, will render great service; but as Americans we have no right to impose our forms of worship or of Church government or our doctrines upon these people. They will eagerly learn from us, but they are now competent not only to help themselves, but also to teach us many things about the meaning of Christ to an individual and to a nation. Radical measures to stop pauperizing Christian nationals must be taken, not indiscriminately, but with great care and with equal firmness. American Christians should continue to invest heavily in promoting the Christian movement in the Far East, but times have changed since yesterday, and very great wisdom must be used if the churches abroad are to be aided in such a way as to stimulate them to do their utmost for themselves.

United Administration. One of the most significant recommendations of the commission was its proposed plan for unifying the administration of the foreign service enterprise at the home base. We do not suggest the organic unity of all the denominations studied, either at home or abroad. We do, however, believe that more united effort is prerequisite to great success in the future. The nationals in India, China, and Japan, if given the proper encouragement from the boards at home, will work out some form of effective Church unity in their countries. . . .

No one believes that the appraisal commission has said the last word on any subject. . . . They have made what to them is an honest appraisal, and have pointed out what they think are ways in which the missionary endeavor may meet one of the greatest opportunities which ever confronted any generation of Christians. Speaking personally, may I say that we ask for careful study of just what we have said, and then that the suggestions be heeded or else that some other group work out better plans for the ongoing of the Christian movement in the Far East.

review bf continuing

EDWIN LEWIS LAMENTS "THE FATAL APOSTASY OF THE MODERN CHURCH"

Source: Edwin Lewis, "The Fatal Apostasy of the Modern Church,"
Religion in Life 2/4 (Autumn 1933): 483-92. *Excerpts.*

Modern theological liberalism undoubtedly rendered the church an important service. It helped to break the strangle-hold of terms and phrases which had become in all too many cases merely empty shibboleths. It re-established, after the fashion of the thirteenth century, the rights of the intellect in the evaluation of the things of the spirit. It garnered for the use of the church the rich harvest of scholarship in many fields—biblical, historical, sociological, psychological. It served notice to a world too often skeptical that a man could believe in Jesus and at the same time be fully aware of all the amazing kaleidoscopic changes occurring in contemporary life. For such a service we cannot but be grateful. Nevertheless, all is not well with us. Liberalism has not brought us to the Promised Land. We may have gained a battle, but the campaign is still on, and there is more than a suspicion that the gain made at one point involved a serious loss elsewhere. We yielded positions whose strategic significance is becoming more and more manifest. We so stressed the Bible as coming to us in "the words of men" that the sense in which it is also "the word of God" has become increasingly vague. We so freely allowed the influence of contemporary forces in the development of doctrine as to have endangered the continuity of that living core of truth and reality for which contemporary forces were but the *milieu.* We exposed all the delicate nuances of spiritual experience to the cold dispassionate gaze of psychology, until it has become a question whether psychology of religion is not in danger of destroying the very thing it lives by. And in particular we were so determined to recover for the church "the human Jesus" that we lost sight of the fact that the church is the creation of "the divine Christ," or at least of faith in Christ as divine. Have we sown the wind, and is the whirlwind now upon us? . . .

THE ORIGINAL CHRISTIAN MESSAGE

The Christian "facts" are not to be limited to what fell between Bethlehem and Calvary. What was then said and done was but part of a larger whole—of a movement taking place within the very being of God. Men believed that this was implied in the indubitable historical and experiential facts. They therefore wrought out the idea of "preexistence" as applied to their Lord, identified him as the permanently active occasion of that life of fellowship in which the church as they knew it was constituted, and from this were led on step by step to formulate finally the doctrine of the Trinity. It is easy enough to complain that this was to transform "the simple Gospel" into a *Weltanschauung*, yet we have no evidence that the so-called simple Gospel was ever preached, even at the beginning, apart from at least some of the elements of this philosophy. Not that unlettered apostles suddenly found themselves possessed of a full-blown philosophy that answered all questions in the world and out of it. But they were making affirmations of such an astounding character as that inevitably before long took to themselves coherence, and the original Christocentric religion became a Christocentric philosophy.

As to this, the New Testament is the evidence, and the New Testament reflects the life and faith of the primitive church. Here we read of a God who had an eternal purpose respecting mankind, a purpose that had to do specifically with delivering men from the power of sin and bringing them to holiness. We read that such a deliverance could not be an arbitrary act upon the part of God, since in all that he does he must be true to the demand of his own holy nature. We read that God himself was so constituted that he could enter in the most intimate and personal way into the stream of human life both to experience all its limitations and struggles and to establish within the stream the principle of its purification, and that the point of this entry was the man Jesus, who would never have existed at all but for the eternal purpose of God. We read that the ensuing intimacy of relationship between the Eternal God and this human life was such that the experience of the man thereupon became the experience of God—which makes it actually true to say that the Infinite knows finitude, that the All-Holy knows moral trial, that the Creator knows creatureliness, that the Deathless knows death. We read that therefore something has "happened" to God which makes his relation to men different from what it would have been had this not "happened." And we read that henceforth in speaking of God men may speak of him as One who was in Christ reconciling the world unto himself: therefore the Christian God is God suffused with all the qualities men saw in Jesus, and a God so suffused and transformed is also that divine Christ who is the very source and center of the life of the redeemed.

What then is the object of Christian faith? Not a man who once lived and died, but a Contemporary Reality, a God whose awful holiness is "covered" by one who is both our representative and his, so that it is "our flesh that we see in the Godhead," that "flesh" which was historically Jesus of Nazareth but is eternally the divine Christ whose disclosure and apprehension Jesus lived and died to make possible. I do not deny for a single moment that this overwhelming conception lent itself to all sorts of crudities of expression, impossible analogies, and gross materialisms. But he is blind indeed who cannot see what the New Testament is trying to say. Though language were not adequate to the thought, we can see what the thought aimed to be. It was that thought that created and sustained the church, and the church languishes to-day because it has substituted that thought with one of lesser power as it is of lesser truth.

THE REPUDIATION OF CHRISTIANITY

Many reasons are alleged for the modern turning away from Christianity as thus understood. Not one of these reasons can touch its intrinsic credibility. A philosophical view that precludes it is quite possible. A philosophical view that allows for it is equally possible. Why is the first view so generally accepted? Because Christianity, with the view of things it necessarily calls for, makes such a terrific onslaught upon human pride. We would fain be self-sufficient, and this means that we are not. We would fain be the masters of our fate and the captains of our souls, and this says that our fate is in another's hands and that our souls are not our own but have been bought with a price. We do not like Christianity, not because it is intrinsically incredible but because it is so vastly humiliating. We do not *want* it to be true that "the Son of Man came to give himself a ransom for many," and so we find "critical" reasons for doubting that the words were ever spoken—as though by proving that Jesus did not say them we should prove that they were not true! We do not *want* it to be true that "the Word became flesh and dwelt among us": therefore we get rid of one of the most profound, heart-searching, and revolutionary truths ever uttered—the truth which must always be the touchstone of any proposed Christology—by the simple device of labeling it "Platonism." We do not *want* it to be true that "through one act of righteousness the free gift came unto all men to justification of life": this being so, we ask by what right Paul "distorted" the simple Gospel of brotherhood and service and good will by introducing into it misleading analogies from temple and law-court.

No; we do not like Christianity. We do not like its cosmic audacity. We do not like its moral pessimism. We do not like the way it smashes the beautiful orderliness of our metaphysical systems. We do not like its uncompromising insistence on the possibility of our being damned souls, whose only hope is in the sovereign grace of God—a God who voluntarily endured self-immolation as the cost of his own gra-ciousness. We be *men*—men whose prerogative it is to stand before God, face him without a tremor, and *demand*; not slaves whose duty it is to kneel before him with covered face, humbly and reverently and gratefully to *accept*. Away with this doc-trine of grace! Away with this whole mythology of Incarnation! Away with this out-worn notion of Atonement! Make way for emancipated man!

THE PLIGHT OF THE CHURCH

But in this pride lies our shame, our weakness, and our defeat. What has it done for us? What has it done for the church—at least for evangelical Protestantism? How far have we gotten with our various substitutes? Look over our churches: they are full of people who, brought up on these substitutes, are strangers to those deeper experiences without which there had been no New Testament and no Church of Christ. Thousands of clergymen will go into their pulpits next Sunday morning, but not as prophets. There will be no burning fire shut up in their bones, by reason of which they cannot forbear to speak. Those who come to listen will not be brought face to face with eternal verities. Hungry sheep will look up, but will not be fed. Men harassed with a thousand problems and seeking not inexpert advice on how to solve them but the sense of another world in whose light they can see this one and find strength to cope with it and remold it nearer to the heart's desire, will go away as impotent as they came for anything the preacher has to say. Grievous is the hurt of the daughter of God's people, and slight is the proffered healing. They go to Gilead, and there is no balm. They go to the fountain of waters, and they find there a broken cistern. They cry for bread, and behold a stone.

And to a large extent, this plight of the church is traceable to a weakening of its dogmatic basis. Whether the phrase, "humanitarian Christology," is defensible or not is a question. Unless Christ is conceived as one who "stands on the divine side of causality in effecting redemption," it is difficult to see why we need a doctrine of him at all. If Jesus is not specifically related to God's eternal purpose to enter sacrificially the stream of our humanity, to the end that he might thereby change its direction and set it flowing toward himself, then we no more need a doctrine of Jesus than we need a doctrine of Jeremiah or a doctrine of Paul. There is no permanent resting-place between *some form* of the Logos Christology and a "humanitarian Christology" (allowing the phrase) which in effect surrenders the whole idea of direct divine sacrificial saving activity. And what we mean theologically by a Logos Christology we mean practically by a Christ-centered religion rather than a "religion of Jesus." If the emulation of "the religion of Jesus" were presented as the possible end of a Christ-centered faith, that would be different. What we are actually doing, however, is supposing that unregenerate men can be "like Jesus"! Even a casual acquaintance with great sections of modern Protestantism makes it evident that it has departed very widely from the Christocentric emphasis. We must recover that emphasis, or perish. . . .

It is not that men cannot live "the good life" without faith in the divine Christ. It is not that there cannot be a profound appreciation of the character of Jesus without it. But Christianity does not consist simply in the good life and in moral appreciation and endeavor. It *is* this, of course. . . .

But it means an "experience" as well—an experience falling within that "unleaguerable fortress" of the innermost soul "whose keys are at the cincture hung of God," and which is something one can better know for oneself than describe to another. And this experience, whence comes it? It comes of *belief*. If we are going to psychologize religion, well and good; but by what imaginable psychological process can there be "spiritual experience" completely independent of all intellectual assent? It were absurd to say that Christianity is *only* credal; to say that it is in no sense credal would be equally false. And to say that "it does not matter what one believes" so long as one "lives the good life" and "has a religious experience" reveals rather an amazing *naiveté* than any profound insight into the life-movement.

But what *does* the modern church believe? The church is becoming creedless as rapidly as the innovators can have their way. The "Confession of Faith"—what is happening to it? Or what about the "new" confessions that one sees and hears—suitable enough, one imagines, for, say, a fraternal order. And as for the Apostles' Creed—"our people will not say it any more": the Virgin Birth and the resurrection of the body, have elected the easy way of believing in nothing at all—certainly not in "the Holy Catholic Church." So we are going to allow them to be satisfied with "The Social Creed of the Churches," quite forgetful of the fact that unless the church has a "religious" creed besides a "social" creed the church as such will cease to exist long before it has had time to make its "social" creed effective in the life of the world. "But the social creed is religious." Yes; but has its religion proved dynamic enough, impelling enough, to maintain itself at the high point—the Himalayanly high point—necessary to make its creed effective? The church has set itself to do more at the very time that it is lessening its power to do anything.

"WHAT MUST WE DO TO BE SAVED?"

The church, especially the American evangelical churches, must re-enthrone Christ, the divine Christ, in the life and thought of the people, or cease to exist. Not that the church merely as an institution is the necessary desideratum. But the church in the high New Testament sense of "the body of Christ"—this *must* be saved for the sake of the world. Here is the world's one redeeming force because here is the world's one redeeming message—if the message be *complete*. It is that completeness whose lack is the secret of our impotence. Can we recover it? Nay rather, do we here highly resolve that we will recover it? Let us be done with compromise, and let us affirm—affirm magnificently, affirm audaciously. Let us affirm God—his unchanging love for men, his unchanging hatred of sin, his sacrificial presence in all the life and work of Jesus. Let us affirm Christ—Christ as the meaning of God, Christ as what God *is* in virtue of that mysterious "kenosis" by which he made himself one with a human life, and at the same time that he was doing the utmost he could do for men endured the worst—a Cross—that men could do against him. Let us affirm the Spirit—the divine concern to bring to bear upon the hearts and consciences of men the impact of what God in Christ has done and is forever doing on their behalf, to the end that they may be moved to repentance, to that faith which ensures forgiveness, to that love which brings moral empowerment, and to that surrender of the will which makes God's purposes their purposes. Let us affirm the church—the community of the redeemed, those who in all their life seek the regnancy of the spirit of Jesus, carrying on and extending the mystery of the Incarnation against that day when God, the Christ-God, shall be all and in all. Let us affirm the Kingdom—the Christianizing of life everywhere, children with straight backs and happy faces, women released from drudgery and set free for creative living, industry conducted for the good of all, war and kindred evils done away, racial antipathies lost in a universal brotherhood, the rich heritage of culture made available to the last man. O there is no limit to the affirmations, and better still, no limit to the dynamic needful to make them effective, once we grasp the profound structural coherence of Christianity, the wide sweep of its thought, the absoluteness of its demands, the revolutionary results of its consistent application. "That in all things he, who is the image of the invisible God, might have the pre-eminence" [Colossians 1:15, 18].

MISSIONS EXECUTIVE MARK DAWBER PROPOSES NEW DIRECTIONS IN NATIVE AMERICAN MINISTRIES

Source: Mark A. Dawber, "After One Hundred Years,"
Christian Advocate (New York) (20 August 1934): 727.

One hundred years ago the first organized mission to the Indians of the Northwest was inaugurated. The experiences and thrilling exploits of this early mission are being recognized this year in a Jason Lee Centennial.

After one hundred years of missions and the so-called advantages of our American civilization, the Indian remains a neglected group, this in spite of the millions that have been spent upon him both by church and state, for it is true also that more has been spent per capita both by church and state than upon any other group.

The trouble lies in the fact that we have done so much for him and so little with him. The next step lies in helping the Indian do something for himself. This means that the nation will do more in the direction of self-government, or training the Indian to take charge of his own affairs and in opening up more of the jobs now held by the white men with comfortable salaries, so that the Indian may aspire to some status of leadership in government among his own people and in the nation at large. There ought to be some way in which the Indian can be represented directly in Congress.

The church must also make more progress in developing the Indian for religious leadership. Wherever this has obtained—and there are a few instances on record—there we find the best work is being done. Too long we have taken the attitude that the white man alone is able to lead the Indian. The American Indian will be Christianized by the Indian himself. There is great need for some service that would enable the Indian missionaries and workers to get together to discuss their common problems, to exchange experiences, and to help each other to do better work.

The Indian is more naturally religious than the white man. The fact that he is an outdoors man, a forest man, living his life in an ordered world with divine oversight, explains in large part the mystical sense of life that is characteristic of Indians everywhere. He feels that he is part of a universe that is ruled by a Great Spirit to whom he is personally related. The Indian lives closer to the deep springs of life in which he is conscious of an eternal purpose. His life has ever been influenced by this intuitive sense of religion. When he arose in the morning he turned his face to the East to greet the sun and to worship the Great Spirit that gave the day. He smoked his pipe ceremonially as a token of thanksgiving to Him who sent all the good gifts of life. When he danced, he danced religiously to express his feelings in rhythm to the Spirit of all movement.

I feel that, somehow, we have failed to capitalize on these crude but natural expressions of religion that are inherent in Indian life. Indian missions of the future must find some way to interpret Christianity in terms of some of the religious methods and ceremonies that are already accepted by Indians.

The future has much in store for the Indian. I believe the Government will correct the mistakes and abuses that have taken place in dealing with him in the past. Let the church also face the future with equal frankness and a desire to correct her mistakes and to discover those means whereby we might give to the Indian a more satisfying religious life and a greater opportunity to share in the common experiences of Christianity.

call to correct mistakes

JESSIE DANIEL AMES DECRIES LYNCHING AS "THE SHAME OF A CHRISTIAN PEOPLE"

Source: Jessie Daniel Ames, Commission on Interracial Co-operation, "The Shame of a Christian People," World Outlook 24/2 (February 1934): 57, 68.

Again our country faces the world ashamed and humiliated. It has seen our men and boys turned into savage mobs, snarling, burning, torturing human beings to death; armed groups of men, sometimes disguised in white robes, attacking individual citizens and riddling their bodies with bullets, or tying them and flogging them to death. So degrading, brutal, and cowardly have been the lynchings of this past year that it is hard to understand how these crimes could be supposed to have grown from the seeds of chivalry. From the Atlantic to the Pacific, in aristocratic old Maryland, in opulent and boastful California, in midwest Missouri, under the shadow of an hundred-year-old Southern State University, in small towns and rural communities in eight Southern states, these outbreaks of mobs and gang murder have appeared. And why?

The courts will not punish criminals? The mob must execute because of the breakdown of law? So we have been told in the press and by high officials of our country. Lynchers have read these papers and heard these words of justification of their acts. They have seen themselves pictured in movie reels. They have added a new halo to their old one of chivalry, and this last one is more insidious in its dangers to our government than the first one. They are now patriots as well as gentlemen defending the people against organized crime and rebuking judicial laxness of the courts.

But who compose the courts? Who elect the officials intrusted with the enforcement of these laws? Do the people think for a moment that the courts are controlled by persons imposed upon the community from the outside? Do the people believe that the officers are strangers in our counties sent in to obstruct our will? Some of us still hold that the courts are our creatures made up of citizens of our own choosing. We are not deceived into believing that officers who live in our communities and seek our suffrage are not sensitive to the wishes of those who elect them. When Governor Rolph congratulated his citizen lynchers on their burst of misguided patriotism, his act of commission in congratulating them for their

540

lawlessness was no worse than our acts of omission in failing to punish our own citizen lynchers and the officers who fail to bring them to the bar of justice. The Governor acted openly and debasingly; we, as private citizens, have been silent and cowardly.

The *Williamson County Sun* says: "All a mob can do is kill; death is all that can be meted out; then why soil our hands with blood either by act or commendation? The mob spirit is a dangerous element; the mob today might be the victim of a mob tomorrow. No man can commend mob rule without injury to himself, and we care not what alleged excuse he may offer."

When lynchings occur, the people have failed, not the courts. We will continue this supine policy, childishly laying the blame for our failure on something else until the Federal Government is compelled to come in and make us law-abiding through force. When this happens we will have declared to the world that the American people are incapable of local self-government, just children who have been playing with fire and have been burned. We are facing the crossroads. We will either turn into the road of adult Christian manhood or womanhood, a strong people able to govern ourselves, or we will choose the road leading to a state of dependent helplessness that demands a benevolent despot to feed us, clothe us, and punish us because our individual moral fiber is gone.

Four spectacular lynchings in the country have brought to full flower the claim that lynchings result from the loss of confidence in our courts which amounts to saying that we have lost confidence in ourselves. The whole country has read these claims, and the press has confirmed them. Public opinion has furnished a poisonous alibi for more lynchings. Besides these four lynchings there were as many as twenty-four others this past year. About these the public has heard little or nothing. If all the victims of mob executions in 1933 had been found guilty of the alleged charges lodged against them, and had been sentenced by the courts, it would be illuminating to consider the full penalty that could have been inflicted upon them. *Nine would have been given death; five would have been sent to prison, and one other possibly; seven would have been fined; five would have been arrested. Under mob law, they all received death.* Have the courts broken down, or have the people broken down?

The Executive Committee of the Council of Women of the Southern Methodist Church are still sure in spite of the distressing situation that there is latent in the body of their membership sufficient courage and determination to put a stop to lynching. At its fall meeting it passed a recommendation based upon the activities of the auxiliaries of the two Mississippi Conferences. Unaware of the importance of the project they were working out, the women of this state were doing the simple and obvious thing—giving information of conditions to every society in their state. They had shown themselves willing to face the most devastating facts if in so doing they could clear the way for the restoration of the principles of self-government and for the vindication of their claims to be a Christian state.

The plan is simple. At the first zone meeting of the year 1934, or as early in the calendar year as possible, *present* the purposes of the movement to educate against lynching, outlining the goals which must be reached before the work is done.

Request each auxiliary in every zone to devote at least one entire program to the study of lynchings in all its aspects; its destructive influence on our government; its tremendous handicap in the spread of the principles of Jesus Christ; its degrading and debasing effect upon all persons involved; its justification as a protection to Southern womanhood; its latest justification on the grounds that the courts have failed; a recognition that though other sections lynch, *the heavy responsibility for wiping out this crime rests with the Southern people* or the Federal Government.

When they have completed this study, the women of the Methodist Church are asked *to find out* the public opinion which controls their own community; *to inform* the officials how the people who elect them to office expect them to act to prevent a lynching; to *broadcast* through the country and the state by means of resolutions, talks before organized groups of men and women, the facts as they see them in regard to lynching; finally, *to make public the position to which they as members of a mighty church and citizens of a mighty nation are committed.*

If all the auxiliaries in Southern Methodism carry out this program, lynchings will stop.

plan of women of church

National Council of Methodist Youth petition Board of Education to approve a Nationwide Student Demonstration against War; Board Denies Request

Source: Proceedings of the Board of Education of the Methodist Episcopal Church *(Chicago: Board of Education, 1936), 35-37, 64-65. Used by permission of the General Board of Higher Education and Ministry of The United Methodist Church. Excerpts.*

Proceedings of the Annual Meeting of the Board of Education of the Methodist Episcopal Church, January 29-30, 1936, Methodist Book Concern Building, Chicago, IL.

Afternoon Session, January 29, 1936
Bishop Edgar Blake, presiding

Bishop Blake called the meeting to order at 2:00 o'clock. The session opened with the singing of the hymns, "Am I a Soldier of the Cross?" and "Art Thou Weary, Art Thou Troubled?"

Hayes Beall, the President of the National Council of Methodist Youth, presented a request from that organization, as follows:

A Proposal for Peace Action

Shall the National Council of Methodist Youth sponsor the National Student Strike Against War?

. . . . Under the tutelage of parents, teachers and ministers, we of the younger generation have developed an intense interest in the cause of peace. Likewise we dread and fear war. What is more, we have come to realize that it is we and not our elders who will be conscripted to kill and be killed in the event of another war, or to suffer in prison if our Christian consciences prevent our participation in war. The outlook we have is the product of your teaching and preaching. . . .

When the National Council met in executive session at Garrett Biblical Institute [Evanston, Illinois] in September 1935, the question of our relation to the 1936 Student Strike Against War was the subject of prolonged discussion. Many who were there had participated [in the first National Strike Against War] last April [1934] and so were qualified to speak about it more realistically than others could or can. The following is the resolution adopted by the National Council outlining the conditions upon which it would sponsor the Strike Against War this spring:

NCMY Resolution on April 1936 Demonstration Against War

We move that the following resolution be adopted and that a committee of five, not less than three of whom are students, be appointed to carry this resolution to the [1936] annual meeting of the Board of Education, asking their approval. This committee shall report the action taken by the Board of Education to the Executive Committee of the National Council of Methodist Youth for decisive action.

We recommend that the National Council of Methodist Youth take part in some kind of a student demonstration against war next April, 1936, on the following basis:

1. That it be a nation-wide student demonstration against war.
   A. 1917 saw the entire social system swept by the all-consuming flame of war frenzy. We feel that students and faculty who desire to see peace must unite students and faculty to the end that the schools of America will not become an instrument of the war machine. This must be done around a clear-cut statement such as is embodied in the Oxford Pledge in England which reads: "That this House will in no circumstances fight for 'King and Country.' " The effectiveness of this pledge can only be accomplished in a time of crisis through the cessation of activity, a refusal to co-operate with the government in its promotion of the war. The student demonstration is an attempt to build a mindset and to strengthen the inner resources of youth against the eventuality of war. Our slogan is: "Stop the Next War."
   B. Last year the demonstration against war was known as the Student Strike Against War. A strike against war, at the beginning of hostilities, would paralyze activities and prevent their continuation. Toward this end the student demonstration is aimed. We would make this student demonstration a "fire drill" or "dress rehearsal" for a general strike against war should a war crisis arise. The student demonstration is intended to emphasize its relation to the general strike against war which is an effective non-violent means of halting the mass destruction of human personality. The student demonstration invites the co-operation of all school authorities who will accept either one of two positions. (1) Agreement with our statement of objective. (2) Agreement of our right to maintain and act upon our statement of objective. The national student committee for this demonstration will invite the co-operation of the American Federation of Teachers, the National Education Association, Association of American College Presidents, and others. The national student committee against war shall make no major decisions without a unanimous vote on the part of the entire committee.

2. We participate in this nation-wide demonstration on the condition that the Christian principle of non-violent non-co-operation against war shall dominate its conduct and we reserve the right to withdraw our participation if this principle is not accepted by the participating groups.

We request the Christian Youth Council of North America to participate in this demonstration.

We recommend that a committee of five be selected from the National Council of Methodist Youth to appear before the present National Committee on the Student Strike Against War to present the position of the National Council of Methodist Youth herein stated. In the event that our participation in 1936 is impossible, we recommend that the local constituent groups in the National Council of Methodist Youth take definite action with reference to their own participation on the merits of their local situations.

In the event of participation we respectfully request the World Peace Commission of the Methodist Episcopal Church to give us financial assistance. . . .

Evening Session, January 30, 1936
Bishop Edgar Blake, presiding

The Board was called to order in open session at eight o'clock, with Bishop Blake presiding.

John H. Race [Senior Publishing Agent, New York City] led in the singing of "The World's Astir, the Clouds of Storm Have Melted into Light."

President [Tully C.] Knoles [University of the Pacific, Stockton, California] led in prayer.

Earl E. Harper [President, Evansville College, Evansville, Indiana] presented the report of the committee appointed to reformulate the reply to the representatives of the National Council of Methodist Youth on the proposed peace action. On motion, the statement was adopted as follows:

Reply of the Board of Education

The Board of Education of the Methodist Episcopal Church received and welcomed representatives of the National Council of Methodist Youth, and records its appreciation of the information they brought.

The members of the Board have deep sympathy with the desire of youth everywhere to maintain the United States of America in peace with the world and to promote the cause of world peace by any and all intelligent, effective and legitimate means.

The Board, however, in its representative capacity, cannot approve a policy of refusal to cooperate with the government of the United States in the event of war, and it cannot look with favor upon any method or means of agitating for peace which involves rebellion against lawful authority on any American college or university campus.

The Board of Education does encourage, and through its staff, will assist any earnest and well-ordered effort on the part of Methodist youth to promote the cause of peace and to make manifest their hatred of war. . . .

Delegates debate Plan of Union at MEC General Conference

Source: *Methodist Episcopal Church*, The Daily Christian Advocate (5 May 1936): 86-90. *Excerpts. Headings omitted.*

Bishop Edwin H. Hughes, presiding.

L. O. Hartman (Clergy, New England): We are in a very critical hour. It is possible to unite and pile up a great total of millions of members and yet lose our spiritual power.

Fellow delegates, I cannot bring myself to endorse unification at the price of the Negro. In recent months, moreover, this conviction has deepened with the discovery that very many of the rank and file of our Negro brethren, both ministers and laymen, are looking with sad disapproval upon the plan here under consideration, though it should be said in fairness that not a few of their leaders endorse it. I have also heard inklings that ultimately our Negro friends will go out from us if the plan is finally adopted by the three churches. I hope not. I trust they will not under any circumstances leave their old home. They need us; but in an even deeper sense of the word, we need them.

Just one hundred years ago the General Conference, meeting at Cincinnati in one of its sessions, rebuked with a stinging resolution its two delegates from New Hampshire for advocating the abolition of human slavery at a meeting held the previous evening. God grant that this General Conference, as it faces another and later phase of the Negro question, may make no mistake.

I intend to vote against this report but with no abatement of love and respect in my heart for those who differ from me on this most important issue. . . .

Ernest F. Tittle (Rock River): I may truthfully say that never in my life have I wanted so much as now to support an organizational plan before the church in which it has been my privilege to serve for more than a quarter of a century. Bishop William F. McDowell, utterly sincere in his belief that this plan if adopted would create a church which the living Christ may use as perhaps he may use no other now in existence; I just as sincere, however, in my belief that this plan which does, I think, undeniedly make a concession to race prejudice, would, if adopted, present a church which the Christ could not use without considerable embarrassment. . . . All our other jurisdictions are geographic. This is racial. If that is not a concession to race prejudice, what is it?

To be sure, by segregating Negroes in a Negro Conference we give them political opportunities which they would not possess as minority groups within our white conferences; but we take away from them the experience of Christian brotherhood which, in my judgment, is far more important than is political opportunity.

I am very much afraid of the effect of this plan, if adopted, upon the younger people of our churches—black and white—who are to constitute the church of tomorrow. . . .

I am fearful, also, of its effect upon the thinking of colored peoples in mission lands and indeed, the world around. In India today are sixty million outcasts looking for a spiritual home in which they may enjoy the elementary human right—to live as men, as sons of God. If this plan is adopted, will that large group look sympathetically in our direction?

For every other feature of the plan I am prepared to vote. I wish it were not necessary to vote "yea" or "nay." If we could make this one reservation I would be voting with all my mind and all my heart. As it is, my belief is that we should wait another quadrennium, if necessary two quadrenniums, when I fully believe we can have union without compromise; and in that case we will have a church which the living Christ can use, I profoundly believe as he may use no other now in existence.

Lynn Harold Hough (Clergy, New York East): . . . I think the time has come when it is necessary for us to speak very frankly. The Utopian, sir, who substitutes an undisciplined and uncritical idealism for a cool and clear analysis of the practical elements of a situation has been for centuries, without desiring or meaning to do so, the greatest foe of the on-going of the Kingdom of God. It is, sir, when, we ask what in a particular situation we cannot have; instead of being content to take a step, with the other steps to be taken when the proper time comes. It is precisely by doing that that century after century the really on-going movement of the Kingdom of God has been made practically impossible.

Let us look at this situation. What, sir, would give all of us the right? No, I would say, what would impose upon us the responsibility of voting against this plan if in any way this committee had given a report which closed the door, fastening us in such a situation that no forward movement was possible, saying to men of particular color—not the color of some of us—in all the future, by this structural plan we are adopting, you must stay at the point of the adoption of this plan? Had that been so, I would have been making a speech, provided I had gotten the floor, against the adoption of the report.

What have we done? In every way we have left the future free to follow the guidance of the spirit of the living God just as rapidly as with wholesome majority we can go. It is true now that a vote against this report is a vote of want of confidence in the members of this United Church which is to be.

That is the thing we ought all to remember. I want to say this, too, that, after all, the success of this plan is not going to depend upon any formula. It will depend upon the men and women who belong to the church; and if our preliminary attitude is that we are afraid to trust them, what a curiously cynical attitude that is.

I want to remind you and the members of the Conference that this report does go as far as the Methodist Episcopal Church has gone in seventy years, when it has regarded itself as the particular guide and philosopher and friend of those who are in our thought this morning. To say that we will not adopt the report, unless it goes farther than we have cared to go—when we ourselves possessed a majority at every point to say that—is to ask something incredible of those who are anxious to meet us, and go forward with us. . . .

David D. Jones (Clergy, North Carolina): I realize the situation in which I am when all of the heavy artillery, the finest munitions in the world, are aimed at a little nation, and one ragged Ethiopian runs out and pulls a pop gun; but I am here because I cannot do otherwise, God help me. I am here because my brethren bid me speak, not that I chose to speak. In our meeting last night, there were forty-four Negroes. Thirty-three of them put up their hands and wrote their names and said to me, "Protest in a mild, but manly, way against this Plan of Unification."

Why do we protest? In the first place, there has been a good bit of specious argument about this Plan. Everyone knows the Plan is segregation, and segregation in the ugliest way, because it is couched in such pious terms. My friends, what does segregation do for a people? It sets them aside, it labels them, it says that they are not fit to be treated as other people are treated. My friends, you have that privilege of saying that to us, but surely you will expect us to be men enough not to say it ourselves. This Plan turns its back on the historic attitude of the Methodist Episcopal Church. All through the years we have had inter-racial fellowship. Some people are good enough to say that the Negroes have made more progress than any other race so situated. I say to you if we have made progress it has been in a measure due to the kind of fellowship and the kind of leadership we have had. Do you ask us today to turn our backs on those men who have come and labored with us? Do you ask us to turn our backs on Hartzell, on Mary Haven Thirkield, on people who have come and given their lives to us? We cannot do it. . . .

In conclusion, you may adopt this plan. We are powerless to prevent it, absolutely powerless. All we can do is to appeal to time. That is all we can do: appeal to time; but maybe in the years that are to come we can paraphrase Edwin Markham's poem, the poem of Brotherhood, and say

> Ye drew a circle to shut me out,
> Heretic, rebel, a thing to flout,
> But love and we had the wit to win,
> We drew a circle which took you in.

Matthew S. Davage (Clergy, Louisiana): I am for it.

The proposed Plan of Unification is not something that was ruthlessly thrust upon us. Two of the ablest men of our group (one a bishop, the other the president of a theological seminary), men of mature judgment, of skill in leadership and of exceptional experience in ecclesiastical statesmanship, helped to formulate this Plan, and the whole commission unanimously concurred in it before it was submitted to the church.

Granted that it is not a perfect instrument—and that it does not wholly satisfy the desires of any single group—in making our decisions this day we are not called upon to agree that the thing proposed is perfect, but to decide whether or not this endeavor to bridge the gap between this ultimate ideal and the immediately possible real is a step in the direction of the attainment of the ultimate goal of one fold and one Shepherd.

I have no word of censure for those who disagree. I know their fears and their anguish of heart. Because of inadequate information and lack of faith they fancy themselves mourners at the grave of a dead ideal; but, watchmen of the night who look carefully toward the past through westward windows and mourn the deepness of the shadows marking the departure of a dying day, turn you about and face with me toward the east, and you will discover that already the dawn heralding the beginning of a new and better day has appeared, a day of enlarged opportunity and of increased responsibility.

> Ye fearful saints, fresh courage take;
> The clouds ye so much dread
> Are big with mercy, and shall break
> In blessings on your head.

After all of these years the Methodist Episcopal Church has been our unfailing friend, she has never failed us, and I do not believe she will fail us now.

May I say—and I may be pardoned to humbly follow the example of the Episcopal Address in the momentous General Conference of 1936—concerning the proposed Plan of Unification future historians will find this question: "Are the rights of the Negro members of the Methodist Episcopal Church adequately protected and completely and constitutionally guaranteed?" The answer is: "Indeed they are."

Paradoxical as it may seem, the very thing which more than anything else guarantees this right is the very thing which is the occasion of our fears and the object of our bitterness and attacks, namely, the Jurisdictional Conference. This guarantees as a minority group we shall always have proportionate representation at the General Conference, that we shall have fair representation on the boards, that we shall have bishops—and they will be bishops of our own choosing. We shall not lose anything, but we shall gain much.

Bishop Hughes: . . . .

I think I will recognize the only lady who happens, so far as the Chair can see, to be appealing for the floor; Dr. Mary McLeod Bethune, of South Florida.

Dr. Mary McLeod Bethune (Lay, South Florida): I approach this stand with great sacredness, and with a very heavy responsibility resting upon my heart and my shoulders. When I was elected as a lay delegate to this General Conference from the South Florida Conference, I realized the responsibility that rested upon me as a delegate, not only to this General Conference throughout the world but to the Negro race at large. I am very happy to announce that I believe that I have been wonderfully created. I have no superiority complex or inferiority complex. I believe very firmly and fully in the spirit of the Fatherhood of God and the brotherhood of man. I am very happy to hail the day when there seemingly shall be no North, no East, no South, no West. All of us together in this great, wonderful, beautiful world, our God's world, working together, aspiring, building, carrying out as nearly as we can the spirit of the Great Leader, the Master, who came as an example for us all.

I wish that every woman in this audience and every man in this audience could turn black just for a season and come up against some of the problems that we have confronted for these years. I think possibly there might be a little sensitiveness in your hearts that you do not have today to see a sign here and there, "Negroes; white folks sit here. You can't sit there." We feel that it is an indictment upon our growth. For seventy years you have been developing us, and it seems to me that while we are all so anxious for this united church to do a greater and more efficient job for God and humanity, it seems to me that the progress that the Negro race has made in their cultural development, in their contribution to the great Christian Church, is being penalized now when we are to be set aside for whatever reason you may have in your minds. I have not been able to make my mind see it clearly enough to be willing to have the history of this General Conference written, and the Negro youths of fifty or a hundred years from today read and find that Mary McLeod Bethune acquiesced to anything that looked like segregation to black people.

Therefore, my friends, in appreciation for the confidence that the youth of America, Negro youth and white youth, have in us, and for the efforts we are putting forth all over the world to bring peoples together in a larger brotherhood and a greater understanding, in my simple opinion it seems to me that the great church—because if we are going to get through it is only going to be through the church and those higher realms of justice and fellowship and understanding—and if today in this great momentous task of setting up this new program it seems necessary to the great Methodist Episcopal Church that has advocated for all of these years this marvelous fellowship and open door for Negro people to set up a special program for Negro people at this stage of development, I am very sorry that I shall not be able to give my vote to the united effort that we all so much desire. What would Jesus do? Answer for yourselves.

METHODIST WOMEN IN THE SOUTH OPPOSE SEGREGATED PLAN OF UNION

Source: Woman's Missionary Council of the Methodist Episcopal Church, South, 27th Annual Report (1936-37), 140-41. Excerpts. Italics added.

Committee on Interracial Co-operation
Study Group on Unification and Race Relations

At the meeting of the Executive Committee of the Woman's Missionary Council in November 1935, plans were made for a number of studies of matters considered important for our work. Since some of us had been troubled about the racial aspect of the proposed plan for the unification of Methodism, your Interracial Committee was asked to make a study of that aspect of the plan and to report their findings to the Executive Committee. When the report was presented last November, the Executive Committee requested that the Interracial Committee continue their studies, reporting to the Council.

The plan proposes to unite into one church the entire membership of the Methodist Episcopal Church, the Methodist Episcopal Church, South and the Methodist Protestant Church in the United States of America and abroad. Provision is made for one General Conference, for Annual Conferences as the fundamental bodies of the church, and for another type of conference new to Methodism, to be composed of a number of annual conferences contiguous to each other, intermediate in its scope between General Conference and the annual conferences. These conferences are called *Central* in the foreign fields; in the United States they are called *Jurisdictional* conferences. Five of them are geographically described: the Northeastern; the Southeastern . . .; the North Central; the South-Central; and the Western. The sixth jurisdictional conference is called the *Central [Jurisdictional] Conference* and is composed of the Negro Annual Conferences of the Methodist Episcopal Church as now constituted, extending over the United States, except in New England and in twelve of the states of the West. In New England and in these western states Negro churches will remain in the Annual Conferences composed chiefly of white members within whose geographical boundaries they are situated. The great bulk of the Negro membership will fall in the Central Conference which includes all the southern and southwestern states, and the large cities of the East and Middle West. . . .

The racial aspect of Methodist unification has been widely discussed in the church press and in Negro newspapers and journals. Several outstanding church papers have criticized it severely as unchristian, unbrotherly, and insulting to the Negro. The Negro press has been for the most part bitterly opposed to the plan, although here and there Negro writers have defended it as offering the Negro larger autonomy than he has heretofore had in the Methodist Episcopal Church, and as involving no greater segregation than has been practiced for decades, and that through the expressed choice of the Negro membership. Some defend it as the only basis in which the Northern and Southern churches can be united, the Negro's status in the Methodist Episcopal Church being sacrificed in order to bring about an important and long-overdue union of the two.

Your committee agrees that the plan is less than ideal; that it leaves much to be desired if the Methodist Church is fully to represent the Kingdom of God on earth. For Methodist Churches in the same city to be related to each other only through a General Conference that meets once in four years, seems consistent neither with Methodist connectionalism nor with Jesus' concern that "they all may be one." And yet is that not what we have had in Methodism, both North and South, for a generation or more? And is it not preferable to a nation-wide church with only white members? Is it not preferable to a church in which a Negro minority is included, but with little if any opportunity for developing a leadership of its own and church program suited to its needs and interests?

Your committee believes that certain provisions of the plan represent an advance in interracial respect and co-operation. The plan provides the same autonomy, including the election of bishops, for the Central Conferences as it does for the other Jurisdictional Conferences. In the General Conference, the Negro Jurisdictional Conference, the Negro delegates and the Negro bishops will have equal representation and equal participation with white conferences, white delegates, and white bishops. *The inadequacy of the plan lies in its failure to provide for co-operation between white and colored Methodists in annual and jurisdictional Conferences and in local communities.* We think we may safely say that the Commission on Unification did not make provision in the plan for more direct relationship between white and Negro Annual Conferences and white and Negro local churches because our churches as a whole are not yet ready for such co-operation. These being the facts, we may perhaps agree that the commission has done the best it could under the circumstances.

There remains the question what can we do to set in motion forces that will build up a desire for co-operation between white and colored Methodist churches in our own communities? We think we have already found the answer in our increasing fellowship with the Colored Methodist Episcopal Church. It was about ten years ago that we began working together as missionary women in Leadership Schools for colored women. Many of us, through participation in these schools, have grown in our knowledge and experience of God and have found joy in a broader and *women already working together* (handwritten marginal note)

more satisfying Christian fellowship than we had ever known before. This year we are finally merging our Leadership schools for colored women with the training schools of the C.M.E. Church, their Board of Religious Education carrying the final responsibility for the schools with the officers of our Conference Missionary Societies and the conference secretaries of the Board of Christian Education of our church participating in the planning of the schools, in their financing, in the recruiting of students, and, where it is desired, in teaching and administration. Is not this a good road for us all to travel? Can we not extend this type of co-operation to the Negro groups of the M.E. Church within the bounds of our annual conferences?

We are not suggesting a procedure identical to this, but we are suggesting that we become aware of the Negro congregations in our midst, especially of the M.E. connection, and that we seek to find ways of co-operating with them in the good work of the Kingdom. Let us seek to know their leaders in the missionary societies and let us ask our pastors to go with us in this adventure in Christian understanding. As we find work that we can best do together, let us undertake it together. Let us sometimes worship with one another. Those of us who have had such worship experiences will testify that they have brought us new visions of God and of his love for all men. Is not this the practical way to do our part toward building a great church in which men of all races and nations may find fellowship, in which we may all learn to build together the Kingdom of God?

We as women know the value of having an organization of our own in which we may do things our own way, with our own leaders, meeting at times that are convenient for us. There is room in the world for organization by age groups, by sex, by occupations, by special interests, by races, by geographical areas, for the pursuit of special objectives. But the Church of God must include all such groups, excluding none and discriminating against none, but uniting all and relating each to all for the sake of the Kingdom.

We rejoice that Methodism around the world includes men of so many races and nations and we pray that it may be used of God to further international justice and good will. We rejoice also that Methodism in America has in many instances and in many communities stood for interracial justice and good will when it required Christian insight and Christian courage to do so. We believe that we have a great opportunity to help to solve the race problem in America in a Christian way through strengthening the church ties between white and colored Methodists. We believe that such a Methodist connectionalism transcending race and nation and economic class will be better able to create in us the mind which was in Christ Jesus, who taught us of one God who is the Father of all and in whom we are all brothers one of another.

Louise Young, *Chairman*;
Mrs. R. P. Neblett, *Secretary*

MEA V:
1940–67

SUPERINTENDENT OF CITY WORK
CHANNING RICHARDSON PROPOSES SUBURBAN
CHURCH DEVELOPMENT

Source: Channing A. Richardson, "The Challenge of the City's Change," World
Outlook *1/6 (February 1941): 111, 129. Excerpts.*

An item of profound interest to all persons who are related to urban church
work has been the releasing of information concerning the [1940] federal decen-
nial census of religious bodies. . . . Advance releases give many significant facts to
which the leaders of church life in our cities will do well to give attention. . . . [An]
item which has had much prominence . . . is the statement that city populations are
declining: that people are moving away from the cities. Usually there is no attempt
to indicate to what section they are moving.

In the list of 92 cities of 100,000 inhabitants or more, there are 27 which show a
decline in population. Among these are Philadelphia, Cleveland, St. Louis,
Pittsburgh, San Francisco, Rochester [New York], Toledo, Akron and Youngstown
[Ohio], Kansas City [Kansas], Camden [New Jersey], Cambridge [Massachusetts],
South Bend [Indiana], and Duluth [Minnesota]. . . .

I have taken occasion to study most of these cities and I find that while the enu-
meration shows a decline within the city limits, the metropolitan area in every case
shows a striking growth. New houses for single families are being built by whole sub-
divisions at a time. I have found in many cities that blocks of fifty to two hundred
houses are being erected on attractive sites. These divisions are given full public util-
ities service, including bus lines. Government subsidies in building loans, reported to
be as high as 90 percent or more of the cost of the building, with long term repay-
ments, make it possible for families to occupy new houses at no more cost than cheap
rent. Coupled with this is the increasing use of private automobiles for transporta-
tion, plus increasing taxation on all property within the limits of the city and comparatively little taxation outside the limits. The destination of the city dweller is not
far to seek. He has moved to a new house, being bought, perhaps, on a long term
loan from the government at a cost no greater than his former monthly rental.

The city movement is to the periphery, and is not a desertion of the city. The city
is still the place of employment, of trade, and of recreation. Sleeping quarters are
merely moved out a little further.

I have gone into this somewhat fuller because, as I see it, this is the next serious problem before the urban church. Unless definite steps are taken at once to occupy and serve these new sections two things will happen: numberless communities will be rearing young families in which both parents and children receive little or no religious ministry, and our churches will find in fifteen or twenty years that the natural growth of their congregations has stopped. There ought to be definite plans put forth in all cities to the end that steadily, year by year, one or more of these fields not now occupied by any evangelical denomination should be entered with an adequate Christian service. There are scores of such situations needing aid on the basis of opportunity and with prospects of self-supporting congregations within two to four years.

This, it seems to me, is the most urgent need in our planning for the city field across America today. The past decade will surely be known as the decade of struggles with overwhelming church debts. It has been a decade of great sacrifice, but unless we at once capture these new suburban fields with a definite and adequate Christian ministry, Methodism will lose opportunities which will not come again. The next decade ought to be one of capturing new communities for Christ.

Woman's Division protests Japanese relocation

Source: Journal of the Third Annual Meeting of the Woman's Division of Christian Service of the Board of Missions and Church Extension of The Methodist Church, Cleveland, Ohio, November 29–December 4, 1942, 37-38.

Resolution Concerning Japanese. Presented by Miss Miriam Ristine and adopted, as follows:

We deplore the circumstances that have eventuated in the evacuation from their homes on the West Coast of 110,000 Japanese-Americans, aliens and citizens alike—and their removal first to temporary assembly centers and now to more permanent relocation projects.

We desire to express our heartfelt sympathy to our [Methodist] pastors and members and to all the evacuees in the hardships this experience has brought them. We realize that many have suffered great financial losses, and all have undergone much inconvenience. The plans of years have been wrecked and the education of the children and young people interrupted.

It is a cause of reassurance that the authorities have carried out this measure with consideration and kindliness. The evacuees, too, have co-operated with admirable courage and loyalty. Christian pastors have been and are the leaders in seeking to bring forth from these painful experiences many fruitful results, and in sustaining the morale of the entire group. We are proud of their splendid spirit and service.

We desire to reiterate our confidence in the loyalty of our citizens who stem from Japanese ancestry. Hundreds of young men, many of them sons of our own pastors and members, are serving in the United States Army. Japanese-American soldiers are now giving their lives at Guadalcanal, New Guinea, and North Africa.

With much appreciation we would commend our Caucasian churches for their splendid expression of Christian love in self-sacrificing services rendered the evacuees during their days of greatest need.

We note with hopefulness the present policy of the War Relocation Authority in promoting as wide as possible a dispersal of the evacuees through individual resettlement in normal American communities. We view this as a challenge to our people and would prayerfully commend it to them, bespeaking for selected and accredited individuals or families a friendly welcome and such aid as they may need.

We desire to continue to assist the young people who are being and will be released from camps to pursue their education in our colleges and universities. They need our friendship and practical help.

As a long-time objective we would pledge our Board and summon our entire church to unceasing efforts in the Christianizing of attitudes toward racial minorities among us, and not least toward those of Oriental extraction. We hope for the repeal of the Oriental Exclusion Act, for the full protection of civil rights, and the natural return to free American life of all persons now affected by emergency war measures. We must work for the renewal [removal] of all traces of racial discrimination in the treatment of our fellow Americans.

The assignment of missionaries, returned from Japan, to "Reconciliation Ministry" in this country has proven farsighted strategy. We rejoice in the remarkable work they have accomplished and heartily recommend their continuance in this vastly important field.

These returned missionaries have brought untold spiritual and practical reinforcement to the Japanese Provisional Annual Conference, as it faced exceedingly difficult and perplexing problems. They have also been builders of good will and understanding in a multitude of Caucasian groups.

We note with profound appreciation the remarkably able service of Dr. Frank Herron Smith, not only to our own work, but to the work of all the Protestant churches. As chairman of the Protestant Commission for Japanese Service, he has helped to unify all Protestant activities. At the same time he has been a valuable liaison officer between the church and the government.

The unity of this Board of Missions and Church Extension has been strikingly revealed in the hearty co-operation of all its divisions and departments in this overwhelming task for which there were no guiding precedents.

We feel the particular urgency of this entire undertaking in view of its direct relation not only to the unity of American life, but also to the future of the World Mission, and of that new and better order in which, under God's Providence, we are to have our part.

Adjourned with prayer to meet at 5:00 P.M., Friday, December 4.

JANET METZGER ATTENDS FIRST NATIONAL CONVOCATION OF METHODIST YOUTH FELLOWSHIP

Source: Janet Metzger, "Five Days: A Personal Story of the National Methodist Youth Convocation," Highroad 1/15 (December 1942): 12-15.

September 1, 1942

This opening day of the Convocation was a busy twenty-four hours—twelve hundred Methodist youth were lined up the length of a city block, standing, leaning, and reclining on baggage as they waited to register. From Maine to Florida, from the Atlantic to the Pacific, they have come! And, girls, the majority of the delegates are boys!

Our first meeting as one large body of Methodist youth had a magnificent start. From the time of the dramatic worship program to the powerful address by Bishop Kern, we were stirred with a new vision of our task!

With such a dynamic beginning, individuals topped off the day with hearty greetings to friends from all over the country. Music drifted over the campus as groups met for community singing and folk games.

We retired to our beautiful dorms with hearts, souls, and minds filled to overflowing. I believe in every heart there must be a prayer of thanksgiving for the opportunities that are open to Christian youth.

September 2, 1942

. . . .

Nothing develops friendship more quickly and thoroughly than working with others on special committees. We had splendid proof of that when about ten committees were named and set to work. The special committees were appointed to work out specific items on the agenda, and present reports for adoption. This eliminates lengthy debates by the larger body in session, and saves a great deal of precious time. Every member of the National Conference of the Methodist Youth Fellowship present was placed on a committee, and each member will share personally in the work that is to be done. Each member will, thereby, have an opportunity to inject his ideas and personality into the group thinking.

A special feature of the day was a Fiesta which was conducted as a sing-talk fest in a very informal group. Countries represented in the Fiesta were India, China, Peru, Korea, Brazil, Mexico, Cuba, Porto Rico, Malaya, and Japan. Most of the representatives were natives of these countries and wore typical costumes. . . .

Our local church hosts shared their resources most generously tonight when we were privileged to hear the group of Wesley Players conduct the worship service. It was beautifully done as the players dramatized the thing that is happening to young people all over the world: sweethearts are being separated by calls to [military] service, and young women, as well as young men, have adjustments to make. It was pointed out that some young women are completely broken by such an experience but that others, through prayer and clear thinking, hold fast to the way of Christian service.

Dr. [Albert] Outler's address tonight was certainly timely because both conscientious objectors and conscientious soldiers are present at the Convocation. For the living of these days, when much is being said about both of these positions, we need a better understanding of the principles of defenders of each position to fully appreciate the contributions and sacrifice all are making to society.

September 3, 1942

. . . .

I can't get over the enthusiastic response that always comes from united Methodist youth. During the afternoon session of the National Conference of the Methodist Youth Fellowship, specific youth action projects were accepted and adopted that call for real sacrifices. Of course, the proof will come when the projects become realities. The earnest hope of the boards and agencies, through [which] the promotion will come, is that we young people attending the Convocation will be strong enough in our leadership to act as hypodermics in the arms of Methodist youth in local communities. Time and time again this desire on our part for creative services has been expressed and fallen short of the "do," but I am convinced that there is real activating sincerity here.

Debates arose on the conference floor which were so lively that even the least-interested person could not help becoming involved. At every opportunity there have been meetings for the purpose of understanding more fully the work in C.P.S. Camps [Civilian Public Service Camps for conscientious objectors], learning how to start F.O.R. [Fellowship of Reconciliation] groups, and thinking through various issues in pacifism. Dr. Charles Boss and other faculty members are making excellent contributions.

At the evening session, when Dr. Walter Van Kirk addressed the group on the topic of "The World of Tomorrow," twelve hundred Methodist youth gave him the greatest response yet accorded a speaker. Challenges and amens to Dr. Van Kirk's philosophy were made with such rapidity that three and four young people at a time were calling for recognition from the chairman, and the group was reluctant to stop even when time was called.

At the conclusion of the question period, a telegram of greeting from a Japanese internment camp was read and received immediate recognition in the form of a motion for a special offering to be sent to this center. The offering will be taken some time during the remaining period of the Convocation, and is to be used for recreational equipment and other needs. . . .

September 4, 1942

Our day would not be off to the right start were it not for the personal meditation period each morning. Our devotional guide sheet, *motive*, is of tremendous help and will be especially fine to keep for future references.

Dean Faulkner's morning devotions stir our thinking, and, because they come from deep religious experiences of his own, have been especially meaningful. This part of our day is truly a challenge to personal development.

The Youth Symposium today was of tremendous value. The six avenues of youth service, which were explained in ten-minute periods, gave us a much broader conception of what many of our young people are doing. These workers in the areas of Cooperatives, Race Relations, Summer Service Projects, Men in the Armed Services, Men in Civilian Public Service, and Missions enlightened me considerably on many details that I have often overlooked. . . .

Tonight the entire Convocation again enjoyed a picnic dinner. Groups of us who had worked together in various projects reserved spots on the athletic field where we ate together and exchanged experiences. There were the groups who had been caravaning together, the Lisle Fellowship group, many state groups, and even a National Council meeting.

Dr. James Chubb, in his straight-to-the-point manner, gave an address tonight that struck right at the heart of every listener. He strongly emphasized the extreme importance of moral and spiritual self-discipline for Christian youth.

September 5, 1942

All week we have had a special Convocation *Highroad* as our daily program guide, a special *Workshop* for our notebook, a *motive* for daily devotions, and *Classmate in Oxford* for our Convocation newspaper. So the periodicals have been well represented.

Today's business session of the Convocation was really attended by alert members. The meeting began rather quietly, developed into heated debate, but ended in good spirit. . . .

The closing address by Dr. Harold Case was truly a fitting end to a significant Convocation. His address was also a perfect background for the Communion Service as he dramatically closed with the thought that in spite of complications and opposition, there is still work that can be done.

A unique and beautiful Communion Service, in which all twelve hundred Methodists were served, officially closed the National Convocation of the Methodist Youth Fellowship.

As I look back over the five days I have spent in Oxford, I know that I, for one, have been inspired to really get under our load of responsibility and truly lift.

Janet Metzger

President Franklin Roosevelt commends the Methodists for undertaking the "Crusade for a New World Order"

Source: Franklin D. Roosevelt, Letter to editor Elmer T. Clark, World Outlook 34/1 (January 1944): 6.

The White House
Washington
August 30, 1943

Dear Dr. Clark:

I have learned with great interest of "The Crusade for a New World Order" which will be conducted under the leadership of the Bishops of the Methodist Church.

We can now say with confidence that the New Order of our enemies will never be a reality. As the United Nations press on to final victory, that grandiose plan to enslave the peoples of the world becomes more and more a mere historical curiosity. The day will surely arrive when our children shall study that design for bondage in their school books and thank God for life and for enduring peace in a free world.

That free world we are striving now to build. It cannot be built by military victories alone. It cannot be built by selfish indifference to the welfare of other peoples. We are in truth members one of another, and the fortune, good or ill, of one is, in the long run, the fortune of all. It certainly can be built if we have faith in our fellow man and in our fellow nations, a faith exemplified by planning and working in common for common goals.

Very sincerely yours,
Franklin D. Roosevelt

Rev. Dr. Elmer T. Clark,
Editorial Secretary,
Board of Missions and Church Extension
    of the Methodist Church,
150 Fifth Avenue,
New York, N.Y.

BISHOPS STAMM AND CLIPPINGER CELEBRATE THE NEWLY FORMED EVANGELICAL UNITED BRETHREN CHURCH

Source: The Year Book of the Evangelical United Brethren Church *(1947), 26-29. Excerpts.*

Union Is Consummated
Bishop John S. Stamm
[formerly of the Evangelical Church]

On Saturday morning, November 16, 1946, in the city of Johnstown, Pa., the negotiations between the Church of the United Brethren in Christ and the Evangelical Church, issued in the consummation of the union of these two churches into The Evangelical United Brethren Church. This means that there is one denomination less, but also, that there is an added witness to Christian unity expressed in this union.

At the very beginning of these negotiations it was agreed that, if there is to be a union, it must be effected in terms of the Kingdom of God. This union was not an organizational necessity. Both churches were numerically and financially stronger, better organized, and more effective than ever before in their history. Both felt, however, that in their union they could bear a more effective witness, and render a larger service than they could do in their separate existence. This conviction led them to make a new commitment of themselves and their resources to Christ in the interest of the Kingdom of God. In this spirit the union was negotiated, consummated, and will be carried forward.

This union is more than a declaration of union. It is a spiritual triumph. Those who shared in the [uniting] General Conference bear witness to the marvelous spirit of unity in union.

It is a complete union. All conferences are included. All congregations are co-operating. It may take a little while until all catch the full rhythm of step but all are in the marching line. The Boards and agencies are now in the process of unification. Beginning with January 1, 1947, a unified program will be carried forward. The consummation of this union makes it possible for us to say, "We are not divided, all one body we."

The Evangelical United Brethren Church Looks Forward
Bishop Arthur R. Clippinger
[formerly of the United Brethren Church]

The membership of this New Church has been looking forward to this day of union for twelve years. The union is a reality today so far as organization is concerned, but ties of Christian love and fellowship must bind together these legal steps so as to make a perfect union. We will continue to look forward to higher plains of Christian experience and more fertile fields of service.

It would be rather surprising if some good folks did not hark back and speak of the good old times before the days of union. That we may expect. But the leadership of the Evangelical United Brethren Church must map out a challenging program that will catch the imagination of every spiritually-minded member. There will be just as many bright days in the future as there have been in the past and the glory of increased strength will give inspiration to every worker. The uniting churches supplement each other in many a local field and thus strengthen the forces already present. There are many things that can be done more efficiently in a united program than can be done separately. . . .

The whole program of the New Church must go forward together. The exchange of new ideas and the inspiration of additional workers will surely make for advancement. There is a determined effort on the part of all our leaders to make this union count for God and righteousness. The program will be large and very complex, but with prayer and a united front all along the line, victory will attend our efforts.

GEORGIA HARKNESS INSTRUCTS LAITY ON THE BASICS OF THE CHRISTIAN FAITH

Source: Georgia Harkness, Understanding the Christian Faith *(New York: Abingdon-Cokesbury Press, 1947), 9-13, 16-23, 93-103. Excerpts.*

[T]he libraries and the newsstands are full of popular expositions of science. The "story" of philosophy and the "outlines" of history, literature, music, and art are available in most small-town libraries. Profound political issues are treated simply, not always polemically, in many books and magazines. There is no corresponding presentation of theology.

Is this because laymen are not interested in theology? There are doubtless many who think they are not. But if one listens carefully to any informal discussion of life and its problems—whether in church, club, dormitory, barracks, or living room—one is certain to hear theological issues raised before the discussion gets very far. Why is there all this misery in the world? Why do good people have to suffer when they don't deserve it? Does it do any good to pray? If there is a God, why didn't he prevent the war? Was it right to use the atomic bomb to stop it? What are we coming to? Is the end of the world coming soon? Do you expect to go to heaven when you die? Anyway, what is in heaven? Where is it, if it isn't up in the sky? Will sinners burn in hell? With all this hell on earth, isn't Christianity a beautiful but impractical ideal? What is the difference between a Christian and any other decent person? What does it mean to be saved by Christ? Was Jesus divine in any way that we are not? Can you believe everything in the Bible? What are you going to do when religion and science conflict? Does the Church have any real message? Start in almost any way, and the conversation comes around to these and other theological questions.

"Theology" means "the study of God." It is a systematic attempt to understand what God is and does, how he is related to the world and to ourselves. It views life from the standpoint of Christian faith and attempts to say what a Christian may believe about such questions as those raised in the last paragraph. There is, of course, no answer that is acceptable at every point to all Christians. God has not run his truth, or our minds, into a single mold. Yet there is a great body of common Christian convictions, and it is with these that we shall be mainly concerned in this book.

Theology is basic to religion, for while it is not the whole of religion, an emotional experience has no firm rootage without it. There can be no Christian faith without belief in something. If one believes the wrong things, his entire life can be distorted, for the world is so made that a firm structure of personal living can rest only on true foundations. And if one does not know what to believe among many conflicting possibilities, one may be left permanently unsettled and unnourished—like Buridan's ass that starved to death between two equally attractive bales of hay. . . .

Lack of clear understanding of the Christian faith stands in the way of an effective attack on the evils of our society. Laymen make the greater part of the political, economic, and social decisions on which human destinies depend. There are enough Christian laymen in the world to establish "peace on earth, good will among men" if laymen understood the Christian gospel and acted upon it. Knowledge alone will not guarantee right action, but lack of understanding can scatter and weaken Christian action until it fails to be very different from that of the secular world. This is illustrated by the lack of any clear principle on which lay opinions are held regarding such vital matters as the control of atomic energy, treatment of vanquished enemies, peacetime conscription, the settlement of labor disputes, the right of the Negro to fair conditions of employment. The more fully one understands the Christian gospel, the less his mind is prey to the newspaper, the radio, and the conversation he hears around him.

Everywhere are persons—some who are Christians, others interested inquirers—who would seriously like to know what a Christian may believe about God, and Christ, and prayer, and sin, and suffering, and salvation, and death, and destiny. It is for these that this book is written. Let no one suppose that it will give all the answers, or do one's thinking for him! Its purpose is to set forth the basic Christian convictions for the *lay*, not for the *lame*, mind. . . .

CHAPTER I
THE MEANING OF FAITH

. . . .

1. *What faith is not*

. . . .

2. *What faith is*

Faith, then, does not mean belief without any basis, or intellectual assent to certain ideas, or a leap from solid footing into a chasm of mystery. But what does it mean?

It means, first, *positive trust* in somebody or something, the willingness to commend one's life to another's keeping or to act on some conviction believed to be true. The familiar definition, "Faith is *assurance* of things hoped for, a *conviction* of things not seen," brings out this meaning. Go through all the biblical statements quoted above, and there is not one of them that does not emphasize this active, positive aspect, both in the exercise of faith and in its fruits. . . . Life could not go on fruitfully without a large-scale exercise of faith in our everyday social relations.

Transfer this principle to our relation to God, and what do we find? The basic atheism is not intellectual rejection of belief in God's existence. If one cares enough to question about God, there is far more hope for him than if he is indifferent. . . . The basic atheism is unwillingness to commit our lives to God's keeping, callousness to God's demands, the ordering of life as if God did not exist. This is the "sin of unbelief," a lack of faith so widespread in our time that society has been honeycombed by it and engulfed in world-wide destruction. To have faith in God is not merely to assert that God exists (which few people dispute) but to do the much harder thing of putting our trust in God and his way as the basis for individual and social living.

This suggests a second meaning, that of *courageous adventure*. Indeed courage is presupposed in faith as trust and commitment, for while there are some things to which to commit ourselves without incurring risk, this is not true of many things of importance. To get married, or choose a vocation, or give oneself to a cause is to act on faith—not blindly, but with full awareness that difficulties as well as delights are in store. We must count the cost and be willing to pay it before we can go ahead. . . .

But what does it mean to be "saved by faith"? Part of it is man's trusting and obedient response to God, of which we have been speaking. But before we can respond, God must have acted. So a third meaning of faith appears.

Saving faith means *saving help*—an experience in which one feels that light and strength and the joy of victory over temptation flow into his life from God. Submitting one's life in confident assurance to God, obedient as far as one is able but still unable to master himself, one feels lifted by a power not his own. A sensitive Christian never ceases to wonder at the mystery and marvel of inflowing power that comes, all undeserved, from God's gracious love. . . .

Faith then means confident trust, courageous adventure, and an inflowing of God-given power. But has it nothing to do with truth? It has a great deal. This leads us to a fourth meaning, which we might call *illumined belief.*

It is faith that enables us to have eyes to see and ears to hear. It is faith as "insight" that quickens the mind to truer "sight." As one learns the truth about science only when his eyes are opened by an eagerness that drives him to learn, as one really sees great art or listens to great music only when his soul is sensitive to it, as one finds depths of richness in a friend only through an outgoingness of spirit that opens new channels, so one learns the truth about God only when he "stands in faith." One may get a detached sort of knowledge, which is true enough as far as it goes, by a weighing of arguments and canvassing of evidence as to the existence and nature of God. One does not really get to Christian faith until he lets God capture his spirit. Then, with no setting aside of the mind and its faculties but with a wiser use of them, we can move upward toward truth, outward toward victory over the world, inward toward the faith that makes us whole.

This gives a clue to the relations of faith to reason, which are not so contradictory as they are sometimes assumed to be. Faith does not mean something that must overrule reason; nor does it mean something that must give way before reason. Faith and reason ought not to be kept in watertight compartments, as if one might overflow and put out the other's fire. Rather, they are to be regarded as two necessary and closely related approaches to life. The intellectual processes give us much valuable knowledge for which no amount of faith is a substitute; yet as vision and active commitment, faith is essential to all of life including the search for truth. . . .

Faith is the union of trusting confidence and courageous action with response to God's leading, and of all these with the insight that lights the way toward truth. It is this combination that makes Christian faith such a powerful force. Our world, far from having outgrown it, desperately needs more. Faith is not all there is of religion, but without it we shall have neither saving hope nor conquering love. . . .

CHAPTER VII
WHAT IS MAN?

. . . .

The reason why it is not easy to say clearly just what man is, is the fact that when one begins to describe one aspect of man's nature, another apparently contradictory but equally real aspect presents itself. Then unless both sides are included, the description becomes not only fragmentary but false. The Christian understanding of man can best be stated in four of these paradoxes:

1. Man is both nature and spirit.
2. Man is both free and bound.
3. Man is both child of God and sinner.
4. Man is both transient and eternal.

. . . .

4. *Man as sinner*

But not only is it necessary to preserve a sense of man's dignity as God's child; it is equally, and perhaps even more, necessary to see all men including ourselves as sinners. What, then, do we mean by sin? . . .

In the first place, any act or attitude that is sinful runs counter to the nature of God and the righteous will of God. This is the truth that lies in the often distorted doctrine of human depravity. When we measure even our best acts and aspirations by the standard of God's holy will as revealed in Christ, we all have sinned and come short of the glory of God. The eclipse of the concept of sin during the brief ascendancy of humanistic liberalism was a direct outgrowth of our failure to take seriously God's holiness and the rigor of his moral demands. When man becomes the measure of all things, we talk of "cultural lags" and "antisocial behavior." When God is restored to his rightful place of primacy in human thought, sin, our ancient enemy, again is seen to be our ever-present and most malignant foe.

In the second place, any sin, whether of overt act or inner attitude, presupposes freedom to do or to be otherwise. To the extent that a person really does what he must do or is what he must be, *and cannot help himself,* to that extent he is victim and not sinner. As nobody is wholly free, so nobody is wholly depraved. But the other side of this comforting truth is that one rarely, if ever, is wholly helpless and therefore free from guilt. In almost every situation there is freedom enough left to do better than one does. Certainly if we view life, not as separate incidents, but as a whole, nobody ever reaches the upper limits of his freedom. In those large areas of choice which God has given us but within which we do not choose according to his will, we sin and stand under his righteous judgment.

In the third place, sin presupposes a knowledge of good and evil adequate to form a basis of choice. . . .

And in the fourth place, sin, according to the Christian frame of thought, involves at the same time relation to our neighbor and to God. As the Christian requirement of love links love of God and love of neighbor in a twofold Great Commandment from which neither element can be dropped, so sin against neighbor through lack of human love is sin against God. The distinctive character of Jesus' ethics lie in the fact that for him religion and morals were all of one piece. To do the will of his Father and to serve those in need were for him not two requirements but one, a supremely costly but supremely joyous adventure in self-giving love.

When these four requirements are put together, at least the outlines of the meaning of sin become clear. There is a sinful state of pride and rebellion against God. . . . There are sinful attitudes and acts. . . .

There are also what are usually called social sins, such as racial prejudice, economic injustice, tyranny, persecution, and war. . . . Actually no clear distinction can be drawn between individual and social sins, for every sin proceeds from the attitude of an individual, and every sin in its consequences affects somebody else besides the sinner.

All sin roots in self-love, in preferring to have our own way when we ought to love God and our neighbor. . . .

There is born in all of us, not "original sin" as a hereditary corruption passed on from Adam's guilt, but a biological tendency to self-centeredness. This is as natural and unsinful in little children as is the impulse to eat or sleep or cry from discomfort. It is a useful endowment, not only for self-preservation, but for the growth of personality through the relating of all experience to the self. But such self-centeredness, though very necessary, is very dangerous, and in adult life easily passes over into willful selfishness. If uncurbed, it becomes the self-love which is the root of all other sins and of most of our unhappiness.

The forms such self-love takes, in the ordinary events of living, are manifold. It shows itself in desire to have our own way regardless of the wishes or rights or needs of others; in the narrowing of interests to what immediately touches us; in thirst for personal recognition, compliments, and applause; in eagerness in conversation or action always to occupy the center of the stage; in jealousy of others who secure recognition or privileges or goods we want; in self-pity; in peevishness and petty complaint when things do not go as we would have them. These are, at best, unlovely traits when we see them in others. As indications that we love ourselves more than we love our neighbor or our Lord, they are evidences of sin so life strangling that God alone can give release.

SEMINARY DEAN WALTER MUELDER PROTESTS HIGH'S "PINK FRINGE" MAGAZINE ARTICLE

Source: Walter G. Muelder, "Mr. Stanley High's Fringe of Conscience,"
Zion's Herald 128/7 (15 February 1950): 147-48. Excerpts.

Mr. Stanley High has done responsible churchmanship and Protestantism a real disservice in his current article in *Reader's Digest* called "Methodism's Pink Fringe." Years of experience have taught him to cut skillful figures of insinuation and distortion of truth on the ice of misrepresentation without passing the fringe of libel and falling into the open water of character assassination.

Two groups in the world today are trying to destroy the vital center of responsible Christianity—the extreme right and their hirelings and the totalitarian left. Both would destroy the independent Christian conscience on social questions and both would liquidate civil, academic and religious liberties. Both hate the vital, crucial and creative forces of social democracy more than they hate each other. Both appeal to mass hysteria to destroy freedom of thought and action by concerned groups of denominational and ecumenical churchmen. The Communist Party smears the vital center of Christian social democracy by the tar of "fascist reaction." The reactionary right smears the same group with the rouge of "pink fringe." It would use the stronger word "Communist" except that that is now a libelous term. Neither the extreme right nor the extreme left is hindered from its course by a strict statement of the truth, but especially not by a statement of the whole truth.

Let me be more specific:

1) Mr. High begins his article by a quotation from the masthead of the *Social Questions Bulletin*. He fails to state the whole masthead which gives the portion he quoted its proper setting and perspective. What he deliberately neglects to quote is that the Methodist Federation for Social Action is a "membership organization which seeks to deepen within the church the sense of social obligation; [to provide an] opportunity to study, from the Christian viewpoint, social problems and their solutions; and to promote social action in the spirit of Jesus." In other words he omits the *principle* and the *spirit* of the whole enterprise, the kingdom of God as the major premise and the spirit of Jesus as the motive of the method. Both the

extreme right and the extreme left are careless about first principles and methods to achieve their ends.

2) The handling of Mr. McMichael's Christmas message illustrates the same distortion by Mr. High. "The Christmas Story, the story of Mary . . ." refers, of course, in the right context, to the *Magnificat* and Mr. McMichael's words must be read as a modern paraphrase of that. Bible loving Christians will recall Luke 1:45-56 and find no complacency about the social order there.

3) Mr. High nowhere in his article quotes a single resolution or official action taken by the Methodist Federation for Social Action. All his material is made up of fragments of articles and speeches—none of them the formal action of the Federation. For the historical deposit of Federation work through 40 years, along with the growing social conscience of The Methodist Church as a whole, see The Social Creed and miscellaneous social resolutions in *The Discipline* [1948].

4) The article tries to give the impression that the Federation is in reality, if not in name, a "humanitarian facade" for promoting the cause of the Soviet Union. As a matter of fact the MFSA has an official policy *not* to affiliate with Communist Front organizations. As a matter of fact, also, the Federation is *not* so affiliated. There are many causes in the field of social welfare and justice on which similar stands are taken by Catholics, Jews, and Protestants, Republicans, Democrats, Socialists and Communists. Journalism which insinuates "guilt by association" in however remote a relation is undermining the moral foundations of the Bill of Rights.

Mr. High's methods are not new. When he was in the employ of the Roosevelt government, he prepared and distributed a lengthy document designed to commend the principles and program of the "New Deal" to church leaders. He did this by showing how parallel the Social Creed (originated by the church he now attacks) was to the platform and program of the Democratic Party. In other words, he has used his journalism to commend the Democrats to the church by showing how much they were like the Federation and bodies with similar views. Now he uses his journalistic position to tie the same principles of social Christianity to the Soviet Union.

Anyone who knows the history of the MFSA knows that it is older than the Russian Revolution and totally independent of it. Let us pray that it will bear an ecumenical prophetic witness down through the years when the present unhappy totalitarian and imperialist-militarist era has been ended. . . .

8) Finally, a word in response to Mr. High's personal attack on me. My own position has been stated in many places: *Zion's Herald, Motive, Religion in Life, Economic Justice* (the source of the quotation Mr. High uses fragmentarily), *Christendom, Fellowship, The Personalist*, etc. As an active member of such non-communist organizations as the Fellowship of Reconciliation, the Civil Liberties Union of Massachusetts, the Religion and Labor Foundation, and the Workers Defense League, I am not surprised that Mr. High's mountain of prejudice labored and brought forth only a mouse.

BLACK CONFERENCE PETITIONS GENERAL CONFERENCE TO ESTABLISH POLICY AND PRACTICE OF RACIAL INCLUSIVENESS

Source: Charles F. Golden, "Memorial Presented to the Lexington Annual Conference," Lexington Conference Journal (1951), 54-55.

Hartzell Methodist Church, Chicago, IL, May 23-27, 1951, for consideration of Memorial to General Conference 1952 on Racial Inclusiveness:

WHEREAS we believe the continuing practice of segregation on the basis of race and color to be denial of religious liberty and an anachronistic limitation of free movement among the children of God, and

WHEREAS in keeping with the spirit of the Christian Gospel, we look to the elimination of racial discrimination within The Methodist Church in this generation, and

WHEREAS, we believe the continued growth of The Methodist Church among Negroes to be basically dependent upon its adoption of a racially inclusive policy at all organizational levels, and

WHEREAS, we believe the Inter-Agency Committee on Social Issues, because of the composition of its membership, and the nature of its several functions and duties, to be too limited in available time, resourcefulness, and interest to make adequate study leading toward the program of integration which the times demand—

BE IT RESOLVED that the Lexington Annual Conference, now in session at Hartzell Methodist Church, Chicago, memorialize the General Conference of The Methodist Church, 1952—

1. To make provision for a racially inclusive policy at all organizational levels in The Methodist Church where such policy is not in violation of civil laws.

2. To establish a special Study Commission, with adequate representation of the racial groups in The Methodist Church in the United States, to discover the most expeditious and sound ways and methods of establishing racial inclusiveness in The Methodist Church at all levels and in all geographical areas, [and].

To provide adequate financial resources for such meetings, research and surveys, and professional assistance which the study may require.

BE IT RESOLVED that this Study Commission shall make annual progress reports to the Council of Bishops who shall make provision for the publishing of such parts of these reports which in their judgment shall serve to prepare the general church membership for intelligent action of the Study Commission's Quadrennial report to be made to each General Conference, and

BE IT FURTHER RESOLVED that this Study Commission or its successor shall be in force until its mission shall have been accomplished.

signed
Charles F. Golden

WOMAN'S DIVISION ISSUES CHARTER OF RACIAL POLICIES

Source: Methodist Church (U.S.) Board of Missions and Church Extension, Woman's Division of Christian Service, Journal of the 12th Annual Meeting, Buck Hill Falls, Pa., January 8-12, 1952 *(New York: Woman's Division, 1952)*, 47-48.

from women

CHARTER ON HUMAN RIGHTS

We Believe

1. We believe that God is the father of all people of all races and we are His children in one family.

2. We believe that the personality of every human being is sacred.

3. We believe that opportunities for fellowship and service, for personal growth, and for freedom in every aspect of life are inherent rights of every individual.

4. We believe that the visible church of Jesus Christ must demonstrate these principles within its own organization and program.

5. We believe that the Woman's Division as an agency of The Methodist Church must build, in every area it may touch, a fellowship and social order without racial barriers.

6. We believe that progress may be advanced by declaring emphatically those policies on which the Woman's Division is determined to move in order to come nearer the ideal.

POLICIES

1. Persons to fill positions within the official body or staff of the Woman's Division of Christian Service shall be selected on the basis of qualifications without regard for race.

The committee on Nominations of the Woman's Division shall consider all openings for service in the Division or staff on this principle, giving due consideration to circumstances which will offer opportunity for fruitful and happy service.

2. The institutions and projects of the Division are instruments by which we may translate the Christian ideals and attitudes of this charter into action.

a. We will employ all missionaries, deaconesses and other workers, regardless of racial or national background, on the basis of qualifications, and the promise they show for effective work in the field to which they will be sent.

b. The facilities and opportunities offered by our projects and institutions shall be open to all people without discrimination because of racial or national background.

c. Where law prohibits or custom prevents the immediate achievement of these objectives, workers and local boards are charged with the responsibility of creating a public opinion which may result in changing such laws and customs.

3. All promotional plans of the Woman's Division must take into account the various racial groups within its organization pattern and related to its program emphases.

4. Special guidance toward the integration of all groups into the life and work of the church shall be given to the auxiliary societies of the Woman's Division.

5. Summer Schools of Missions and Christian Service of both Jurisdictions and Conferences are urged to seek increasingly to establish a working relationship across racial lines in planning and carrying out all phases of the programs, taking into account geographical accessibility of groups involved.

6. Summer school subsidies provided for or by any Jurisdiction or Conference should be available when requested for use at the school most accessible to the person receiving the subsidy.

7. Workshops, seminars, and institutes should be set up on a geographical basis with full opportunity for initial participation by all racial groups in the making and execution of the plans.

8. Local Societies and Guilds should give increased emphasis to the working together of all racial groups and study and action that affect the life of the church and community.

9. All Jurisdiction and Conference societies are urged to work for the enactment of policies at all Methodist Assembly grounds that will enable the full participation of any racial group in any phase of the assembly program.

10. The Woman's Division has consistently observed its established policy for holding its meetings in places where all racial groups can have access to all facilities without discrimination in any form. To further extend this policy Jurisdiction and Conference Societies are urged to work for its implementation as a basic step toward building a Christian fellowship within the organization and toward an impact on the community as a whole.

The Woman's Division of Christian Service calls with new urgency on the Jurisdiction and Conference Woman's Societies of Christian Service to study the principles and policies stated in this charter, looking toward early ratification by each Jurisdiction and Conference. Such a ratification will constitute a commitment to work for the speedy implementation of those principles and policies within the bounds of a respective Jurisdiction or Conference.

BISHOP OXNAM PUBLICLY PROTESTS
McCARTHY COMMITTEE CHARGES

Source: U.S. Congressional House Committee on Un-American Activities: Testimony of Bishop G. Bromley Oxnam, July 21-22, 1953. (See also "Bishop Oxnam Committee Hearing: Complete Text of 10-hour Session Before the House Committee on Un-American Activities," U.S. News & World Report [7 August 1953]: 40-43.) Excerpts.

Bishop Oxnam: My name is G. Bromley Oxnam.

Mr. Kunzig: And your address, please.

Bishop Oxnam: 100 Maryland Avenue, Northeast, Washington, D.C.

Mr. Kunzig: I see that you are accompanied by counsel. Will counsel please state his name and address for the record?

Mr. Parlin: My name is Charles C. Parlin. My address and office is 20 Exchange Place, New York City. I am a member of the New York bar.

Rep. Velde: Mr. Counsel, may I interrupt just a moment? It has been the usual custom of the committee to ask the witness whether or not he objects to being photographed and being televised and also to have their pictures taken by the newsreel, and I believe that you have already stated that you are willing to have your pictures taken.

Bishop Oxnam: I have no objection, Mr. Chairman. . . .

Mr. Kunzig: Mr. Parlin, it is my understanding that you have received copies of the rules of procedure of this committee and that you fully understand the rules and the position of counsel in this congressional hearing. Am I correct, sir?

Mr. Parlin: I have received the rules, and I think I understand them.

Mr. Kunzig: I believe at this time, sir, Bishop Oxnam has a prepared written statement to read.

Rep. Velde: Yes, and I would ask the members of the committee to please not interfere with the Bishop's reading, and wait until after the Bishop has finished with his statement to question him, if you have any questions concerning it.

Bishop Oxnam: Thank you, Mr. Chairman and members of the committee. I have requested opportunity to appear voluntarily before this committee, in public session, to secure redress for the damage done me by the release of information in the files of this committee. I deeply appreciate the grant of this privilege. Such releases, made at various times for a period of nearly seven years, have contained material, much of which is irrelevant and immaterial, some of which is false and some of which is true, but all prepared in a way capable of creating the impression that I have been and am sympathetic to Communism, and therefore subversive.

These files, so released, have been used by private agencies as evidence of Communist sympathies. A member of this committee apparently drew that conclusion. Speaking of the work of this committee, upon the floor of the [U.S.] House of Representatives itself, he said: "Bishop Bromley Oxnam has been to the Communist front what Man-O-War was to thoroughbred horse-racing, and no one except the good Bishop pays much attention to his fulminations these days. Having served God on Sunday and the Communist front for the balance of the week over such a long period of time, it is no great wonder that the Bishop sees an investigating committee in every vestry. If reprinting Bishop Oxnam's record of aid and comfort to the Communist front would serve any useful purpose, I would ask permission to insert it here, but suffice it to say that the record is available to any member who cares to request it from the committee."

If a member of the committee can be so misled by this material, it is no wonder that uninformed citizens are similarly misled.

When I declare, "I believe in God, the Father, Almighty," I affirm the theistic faith and strike at the fundamental fallacy of communism, which is atheism. I thereby reaffirm the basic conviction upon which this Republic rests, namely, that all men are created by the Eternal in His image, beings of infinite worth, members of one family, brothers. We are endowed by the Creator with certain inalienable rights. The State does not confer them; it merely confirms them. They belong to man because he is a son of God. When I say "I believe in God," I am also saying that moral law is written into the nature of the things. There are moral absolutes. Marxism, by definition, rules out moral absolutes. Because I believe the will of God is revealed in the Gospel of Christ, I hold that all historically conditioned political, economic, social and ecclesiastical systems must be judged by the Gospel, not identified with it. This is to say, I reject communism, first, because of its atheism.

When I declare, "I believe in Jesus Christ, His only Son our Lord," I am affirming the faith in a spiritual view of life. By so doing, I repudiate the philosophy of materialism upon which communism is based and thereby undermine it. I reject the theory of social development that assumes social institutions and even morality are determined by the prevailing mode of production. When I accept the law of love taught by Christ and revealed in His person, I must, of necessity, oppose to the death a theory that justifies dictatorship, with its annihilation of freedom. I am not an economist, but have studied sufficiently to be convinced that there are basic fallacies in Marxian economics. Believing as I do that personality is a supreme good and that personality flowers in freedom, I stand for the free man in the free society, seeking the truth that frees. I hold that the free man must discover concrete measures through which the ideals of religion may be translated into the realities of world law and order, economic justice, and racial brotherhood.

As a result of long study and of prayer, I am by conviction pledged to the free way of life and opposed to all forms of totalitarianism, left or right, and to all tendencies toward such practices at home or abroad. Consequently I have been actively opposed to Communism all my life. I have never been a member of the Communist Party. My opposition to Communism is a matter of public record in books, numerous articles, addresses, and sermons, and in resolutions I have drafted or sponsored in which powerful religious agencies have been put on record as opposed to Communism. It is evidenced likewise in a life of service and the sponsorship of measures designed to make the free society impregnable to Communist attack.

Loyalty to my family, my church, and my country are fundamental to me; and when any man or any committee questions that loyalty, I doubt that I would be worthy of the name American if I took it lying down.

First, this committee has followed a practice of releasing unverified and unevaluated material designated as "information" to citizens, organizations and Members of Congress. It accepts no responsibility for the accuracy of the newspaper clippings recorded and so released; and insists that the material does not represent an opinion or a conclusion of the committee. This material, officially released on official letterheads and signed by an official clerk, carried no disclaimer, in my case, and the recipient understandably assumed it did represent a conclusion. I am here formally to request that this file be cleaned up, that the Committee frankly admit its inaccuracies and misrepresentations, and that this matter be brought to a close.

It is alleged that the committee has files on a million individuals, many of whom are among the most respected, patriotic, and devoted citizens of this nation. This is not the proper place to raise question as to the propriety of maintaining such vast files at public expense, but it is the proper place, in my case, to request that the practice of releasing unverified and unevaluated material, for which the committee accepts no responsibility, cease. It can be shown that these reports are the result of inexcusable incompetence or of slanted selection—the result being the same in either case—namely, to question loyalty, to pillory, or to intimidate, to damage reputation, and to turn attention from the Communist conspirator who pursues his nefarious work in the shadows while a patriotic citizen is disgraced in public. The preparation and publication of these files puts into the hands of irresponsible individuals and agencies a wicked tool. It gives rise to a new and vicious expression of Ku-Kluxism, in which an innocent person may be beaten by unknown assailants, who are cloaked in anonymity and at times immunity, and whose whips are cleverly constructed lists of so-called subversive organizations, and whose floggings appear all too often to be sadistic in spirit rather than patriotic in purpose.

I had planned at this point to set forth specifications of what I believe is false. The rules of this committee gives me but fifteen minutes for this statement. The specifications cannot be listed in fifteen minutes. Therefore, I must respectfully request the committee members, or its counsel to question me concerning some of the material released by the committee, namely:

First, a release dated July 3, 1946 in which it is alleged I sponsored The League against War and Fascism, and in which it is suggested by implication that I would substitute dialectical materialism for religious freedom.

Second, a release dated September 4, 1946 in which it is alleged that I am "referred to as a collectivist bishop," that I presided at a meeting addressed "by one B. Gebert, President of the Polish Section of the International Workers Order," that I have been "associated with several groups in which Langston Hughes has also held membership."

Third, a release dated September 13, 1950 in which quoting the *Daily Worker* as authority, I am alleged to have been invited by the Government of Yugoslavia to tour that country, in which I am alleged to have written an article for Stalin for a [Methodist youth] magazine called *Classmate*.

Fourth, releases of different dates alleging I have delivered an address to the prisoners of the Indiana State Reformatory, February 10, 1930.

Fifth, a letter from Mr. Frank S. Tavenner, Jr. dated March 21, 1953, relative to covering letters alleged to accompany releases.

Sixth, a release sent out by the chairman of this committee [Senator Joseph McCarthy] dated March 31, 1953.

Seventh, letters from two members of this committee, one dated March 9, 1953, and the other alleging the committee did not release this material, dated March 13, 1953.

If I may be asked questions concerning these items, I will leave it to any fair-minded man whether I have been misrepresented. In this connection I would like to file with the committee a bibliography, covering my personal position relative to Communism.

Second, when I had the honor of debating this issue with the Honorable Donald L. Jackson, a member of this committee, he said, "The committee in its work, accumulates all pertinent information relative to any given individual, whose name is listed in the files. That is the only way by which one can determine the philosophical bent of any given individual."

Can the philosophy of an individual be determined by a scissors and paste process of cutting out clippings that damn? Why did the individual who clipped derogatory statements concerning me fail to clip such announcements as the following: My appointment by the Joint Chiefs of Staff to visit the Mediterranean Theater and the European Theater of Operations during the war [World War II]; or my appointment by Secretary Forrestal as a member of the Secretary of the Navy's Civilian Advisory Committee; or the announcement that the Navy had awarded me the highly prized Certificate of Appreciation for services during the War; or that I had been invited to be the guest of Archbishop Damaskinos, then Regent of Greece, and that the King of Greece had awarded me the Order of the Phoenix; or that I had represented the American churches at the enthronement of the Archbishop of Canterbury; or that I had been appointed by the President as a member of the President's Commission on Higher Education; or that I was chairman of the Commission approved by the President to study postwar religious conditions in Germany? This might be called pertinent information. I have held the highest offices it is in the power of fellow-churchmen to confer upon me, such as the president of the Federal Council of the Churches of Christ in America. I am one of the presidents of the World Council of Churches, perhaps the highest honor that can come to a clergyman. I hold positions of responsibility in the church I love and seek to serve, among them secretary of the Council of Bishops.

We cannot beat down the Communist menace by bearing false witness against fellow Americans. The Communist wants a divided America, an America whose citizens are suspicious of each other, an America without trust, an America open to infiltration. I believe this committee will wish to end a practice that plays into Communist hands.

Third, Congress is considering proposals for the reform of investigating committee procedures. It may, at first, seem drastic to propose that the so-called "public files" be closed out, but is there any need of any file other than the investigative files as they have been recently described? Could not all material that is of value in the public files be included in the investigative files? If, for purposes of education or exposure, the committee decides that public statements must be made, is there any reason why a careful statement that will stand scrutiny cannot be made by studying the material in the investigative files? The committee informs us that it does not vouch for the accuracy of the public files, that everything in those files is available to the public elsewhere. Why, then, should public money be spent in maintaining such public files? Would it not be well for the committee to appoint a subcommittee to investigate its own files and those who compile them, and to secure answers to questions such as the following: How much duplication is there in the public and investigative files of this committee and the files of the FBI? Is the FBI better equipped to get the facts on real subversives? Why was appendix IX withdrawn from the public and why is it under lock and key in the Library of Congress? Was it because of inexcusable inaccuracies and vicious slanting of material? How much of it is still the core of the public files? If there is a real misunderstanding, would it not be well to ascertain who is misinforming whom and why?

I respectfully ask the committee to order that my file be corrected so as to tell the truth, if that is all that can be done; that it publicly announce its mistakes in my case; but better, that the public files be closed out, and the releases of unverified material described herein be discontinued. When Mr. Jackson discovered that he had misunderstood the chairman of this committee with reference to an announcement concerning possible investigation of churchmen, he in the manly, the American, the Christian way apologized on the floor of the House. It takes a big man to admit a fault. I respectfully request Mr. Jackson to apologize on the floor of the House [of Representatives] for his unprecedented and untrue statements made there concerning me. I will be the first to shake hands with him and to call the incident closed.

I conclude. I believe the churches have done and are doing far more to destroy the Communist threat to faith and to freedom than all investigating committees put together. I think the chairman of this committee, after a friendly interview, concurred publicly in that statement when I made it in his presence. This committee might well have the co-operation of millions of citizens who belong to the churches if it would cease practices that many of us believe to be un-American and would turn itself to the real task and the real threat. But those citizens will never co-operate in practices that jeopardize the rights of free men won after a thousand years' struggle for political and religious freedom. They will co-operate effectively with agencies everywhere that honestly seek to build the free society where free men may worship God according to the dictates of their own conscience, and serve their fellow men in accordance with Christ's law of love.

Editor of black church paper, Prince Taylor, and Council of Bishops assess landmark Supreme Court decision on school desegregation

Source: Prince Taylor, "Editorial[s]," Central Christian Advocate (June 1 and June 15, 1954): 247, 273-74.

The Decision Against Segregation
[June 1, 1954]

The decision of the Supreme Court outlawing segregation in public schools has just been announced. In a latter issue, we shall comment in further detail, but we hasten now to say that it is one of the most historic since the Emancipation Proclamation. And we are convinced that the people of this nation will accept it as the only decision that a Supreme Court in a democracy could make. The fact that the decision was unanimous further attests to the court's recognition of the equality of man under the Constitution of this nation.

But the decision in itself does not mean the end of segregation; it simply destroys the legal barriers and the real task has just begun. The Supreme Court will hear proposals this fall as to how and when segregation in the schools will end. This procedure will require the sympathetic understanding and cooperation of all the citizens of this country.

There will be politicians, of course, who will excite the fears of people in order to promote their political ambitions. This is to be expected. But there are multitudes of sincere and well-meaning citizens who will work toward desegregation, not only of the public schools but in our total American life. And they are these individuals who are the "salt of the earth." They form a significant nucleus for the development of a truly democratic America. What is needed now is the creation of a climate of understanding in which the problem can be handled in a constructive way.

At this point the Church has inescapable responsibility. It is natural that persons who have lived under a segregated system for so many years would be at least apprehensive to give it up. Even many persons who accept the decision intellectually will find emotional blocks as they face the actual situation. But they can find the new venture a rewarding experience for all the children of the nation, and thus, greater education in human relations will result.

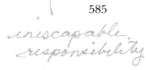

The Decision and Parental Responsibility
[June 15, 1954]

Now that the Supreme Court has declared segregation in the public schools unconstitutional, it becomes the responsibility of every parent to prepare the children to function constructively in a desegregated society. Looking at the issue from one angle, the children are better prepared than many parents. They do not have the hardened fears and prejudices which their parents possess. And they learn many of these prejudices from their parents. Nevertheless, parents are responsible for guidance.

We frequently hear it said that if we would just leave the children alone they would work the problem out satisfactorily. This is perhaps only a half-truth at best. At its worst it is a denial of the fundamental function of parents to guide the growth of children into the development of wholesome and mature living. And a child left alone is a neglected child, blindly stumbling along in a trial-and-error fashion in an effort to discover his place and purpose in the world.

Children need guidance, help and example, and if they do not get it from their parents, they are likely to be miserably handicapped. We cannot afford to leave them alone when destiny-making decisions are at stake. On the other hand, we cannot afford to misguide them or to be a partner in creating among them unwholesome thinking. They need our encouragement and co-operation in facing the issues of life creatively.

As we have pointed out previously, it is one thing to give intellectual assent to a given proposition, and another to deal with it in a practical situation. And in working out the problem in practical situations, many children of both races will need a lot of help. It will be a new experience for them and they will have to overcome the initial barriers which a segregated society has set up. The only differences in children racially are those differences which the culture has imposed upon them. Consequently, the same cultural opportunities provided in an atmosphere of good will and understanding will be an added advantage for all the children. Parents have a real responsibility in helping their children become emotionally prepared for this new experience.

It is important to realize that the Supreme Court decision is not a victory for Negroes and a defeat for the white South. Any person who looks at it from that angle fails to get a grasp of the issues involved. Rather it is a victory for the American people. It is more than that. It is victory for democracy around the world. For persons who are acquainted with the world scene declare that the decision has done much to lift the morale of nations whose confidence in us has been shaken due to our racial practices. Its implications are as broad as the world itself, and as parents, we have responsibility in helping to create a climate of understanding in which the experiment can successfully work.

In this endeavor, Negro and white parents will need to develop a spirit of amity across racial lines. They will need, also, to teach their children the dignity and worth of every person and his God-given right to equality before the law of the land.

Parents should teach their children the cardinal principles of Christianity and democracy in reference to the rights of every individual as a fellow human being. This will do much to allay the fears and hatreds which might otherwise breed among them.

In this respect, the church should lay increasing emphasis on its program of family life. This is an issue which families can do much to advance, and this is a duty which parents cannot afford to neglect.

Some Implications of the Decision
[June 15, 1954]

The implications of the Supreme Court decision outlawing segregation in the public schools are far wider than they appear on the surface. When one realizes that the decision was unanimous among judges who usually differ in political philosophy and points of view, he gets a deeper appreciation of the impact of the issue.

There was no hesitation nor vague generalities in the decision. It stated simply, clearly and categorically that segregation in the public schools is unconstitutional. The court declared that the equal protection clause of the Fourteenth amendment is violated by a segregated school system in states; and the due process clause of the Fifth amendment is violated by a similar school system in the District of Columbia. The court left no grounds for the further argument upon the technicalities of the specific amendments by declaring that segregation in the public schools is out of harmony with the spirit of the Constitution. Thus the nine judges said: "In approaching this problem, we cannot turn the clock back to 1868 when the amendment was adopted nor even to 1896 when *Plessy vs. Ferguson* was written (the case that established the 'separate but equal' doctrine), but will meet the direct issue here present.

"We conclude," said the Court, "that in the field of public education the doctrine of separate but equal has no place."

The decision implies a new concept of law as it relates to human beings. The court re-stated the historic principles of equality under the law in relationship to the democratic demands of today.

It implies a new national direction in race relations. The Constitution no longer serves as a protecting agency for segregated education. The court observed that public school segregation is "not reasonably related to any proper government objective," and "education is the most important function of both state and national government," providing of such education on nonsegregated basis means new opportunities for better education for all the people.

The implementation of the decision implies higher levels of functioning students and teachers alike. We do not follow the school of thought which holds that Negro teachers will lose their jobs in a desegregated school system. Among many of the Negro teachers, there are some of the best teaching potentialities in this nation. And the school systems of the various communities could ill afford to be robbed of the services of these people. This is especially true in view of the national shortage of public school teachers.

protection for black teachers

587

But it is well to face the fact that in this new venture in public school education, only people who can measure up to normal educational standards will be able to command job security. This will be a disadvantage only to those who refuse to grow.

Both legal and educational experts agree that it will take several years to completely put the new system into operation. And Negro teachers should take advantage of this time for self-improvement and additional qualifications. The implications are endless and one needs only observe future development to see them unfold.

this is not right

COUNCIL OF BISHOPS APPLAUDS DESEGREGATION DECISION DESPITE SEJ QUALMS

Source: Minutes of the Council of Bishops of the Methodist Church, *Chicago, (November 1954)*, 390-91. *United Methodist Archives, Madison, N.J.*

The Council resumed consideration of the Message [on the School Desegregation Decision] which had been read at the Fellowship Dinner last evening but consideration of which had been postponed at the request of the College of Bishops of the Southeastern Jurisdiction.

The Bishops of the Southeastern Jurisdiction requested that the following statement be inserted in the record at this point:

> We, Bishops of the Southeastern Jurisdiction, have examined with care the proposed statement concerning the recent decision of the Supreme Court relative to segregation in the public schools submitted to the Council for its consideration. We accept the Court's decision as being in harmony with the pronouncements of The Methodist Church, and in our respective [Episcopal] Areas we are seeking to lead our people to a Christian attitude and an orderly adjustment to the changes that are involved.
>
> *tensions in context*
>
> We, however, call the attention of the Council to the fact that vast numbers of the people among whom we labor have not made such adjustments, and we minister in a region where acute tensions are developing. The Court in its decision recognized the healing effect of time. This principle is equally applicable to the Church. We are attempting to be shepherds of all our people and we are convinced that any statement from the Council at this time will result in no great gain and will make our task more difficult. We therefore respectfully request that you, our colleagues, refrain from making any further statement at this time.

The Council voted to consider these items seriatim.

Item 1 [the Message on Desegregation] was read and Bishop Kennedy moved its adoption. After a lengthy discussion in which a number of the members of the Council participated, the Council, at the request of the College of Bishops of the Southeastern Jurisdiction, recessed.

When called to order, Bishop Hammaker led in prayer.

Consideration of Item 1 was resumed, and it was adopted after deleting the words "gladly" and "unqualified." The Item, as adopted, read as follows:

> The historic Decision of the Supreme Court abolishing segregation in the public school system is in keeping with the attitude of The Methodist Church. In our official pronouncements, including the Social Creed and the Episcopal Address adopted by the 1952 General Conference, our position has been clearly stated. The Supreme Court itself recognized that such a ruling brought with it difficulties of enforcement, and thereby made provision for sufficient time to implement its Decision. The declaration of the Decision was made in the magnificent home of the Supreme Court in Washington, DC, but the ultimate success of the ruling will be determined in the hearts of the people of the nation. Thus the Church is furnished with an unequaled opportunity to provide leadership during this period in support of the principles involved in the action of the Court. We accept this responsibility, for one of the foundation stones of our faith is the belief that all men are brothers, equal in the sight of God. In that faith, we declare our support of the ruling of the Supreme Court.

The following Bishops of the Southeastern Jurisdiction reserved the right to say to their constituents respectively that they expressed to the Council their opinion that it would be better that no statement be made at this time: John Branscomb, Marvin A. Franklin, Paul N. Garber, Costen J. Harrell, Arthur J. Moore, Clare Purcell, Roy H. Short, William T. Watkins.

EUB CHURCH WOMEN DEPLORE SEGREGATION

Source: "Resolution of the Assembly of the Division of Home Missions,"
World Evangel 75/3 (March 1956): 84.

Resolution on Segregation

This Assembly of the Division of Home Missions [meeting in Buck Hill Falls, Pa., December 11-14, 1955] desires to record its unanimous judgement that the problem of racial segregation is one of the paramount issues now facing our churches and our society. The unanimous decisions of the Supreme Court of the United States declaring varying types of segregation by law unconstitutional express in legal form the ethical principles which national and international church bodies have set forth as demanded by the Gospel over a period of years, particularly since 1946.

We deplore official and unofficial efforts and movements to circumvent the clear intent of these decisions of the highest court and to penalize persons of all races who are endeavoring to move towards a racially inclusive church and society.

We warmly endorse the actions of the General Board (of the National Council of Churches) taken at Omaha on December 1, [1955] and pledge our individual support and the support of the Division of Home Missions for the program of financial assistance and counselling in behalf of political refugees in our nation and for plans being developed for augmenting leadership in areas of racial tension.

We join with the whole church in acknowledging our sins of commission and omission in this regard and seek divine grace and power to do those things which our Lord commands us to do.

Maud Keister Jensen Remembers Honor of Being First Woman Granted Full Clergy Rights

Source: Maud Keister Jensen. United Methodist Women's Oral History Project. Interviewer: Naomi Kooker. Transcriber: Karen Heetderks Strong. Finished transcript with editions by Maud Keister Jensen and Carolyn De Swarte Gifford. Women's History Project. General Commission on Archives and History, The United Methodist Church. Madison, N.J. 1984.

Kooker: Well, on May 25th in 1952 you received your elder's orders.

Jensen: Yes. I was here, and the four years had passed so that I could get my elder's orders. A member of Conference could get his elder's orders after two years. But if one wasn't assigned regularly by the Conference, it took four years. And since I was assigned by the Board, and not a member of a Conference (because no woman could be a member of Conference at that time), I'd had to wait the four years. So in 1952, between speaking and studying at Drew and so on, I received my elder's orders. It was the proper time; there was no question, no problem at all. And it was to me a great moment. I asked three very good friends, elders, to put their hands on my head: one who had given me my first license to preach, one minister in whose house I had lived while I was a student at Bucknell, and another who had been a good friend of my mother (quite an elderly man, they had been friends in *their* youth). So there were those three men in addition to the bishops who normally put their hands on the heads. I was horrified when the hands began to be placed on my head, because nobody had warned me that hands are heavy. And a number of men's hands with the men leaning over, putting weight on them—and at the time when I should have been thinking only the most spiritual thoughts, I was thinking, "Will my neck break? Can I hold it up?" But I did, and then the rest of it meant a great deal to me. So I, of course, had been presented to the Conference at that time. I was sorry my husband wasn't there to put his hand on my head, but I was very glad for the occasion and for what it meant. Usually, when a man got elder's orders, he was taken into the Conference. Of course, with deacon's orders he is often taken in on probation, and then with elder's orders taken into full membership. They have to be presented to Conference, but of course I was presented to Conference for the ordinations just the same, even though I wasn't a member of the Conference as such. It was called a local ordination. The ordination was the same, everything was the same except that a woman was *not* a Conference member. . . .

Now to return to the subject of ordinations. Kris was with me when I was

local ordination?

ordained deacon, and that added to the happiness of the occasion. But he was still in North Korea when I was ordained elder, and I regretted not having his hand laid on my head. I needed and desired both ordinations, as any minister would, but particularly for my work in Korea. There is satisfaction in fulfillment of a lifetime ambition. This did not concern women's rights, however, nor give me a feeling of having won a battle of this kind. It was simply the achievement of a normally desirable end. But of course it did not mark equality of the sexes in the church, and I was well aware of the struggle others were making to gain this result, with strong leadership by Dr. Georgia Harkness. Our annual conferences, to be sure, were attended by lay and clergy, and women were represented in the laity more and more as time went on. But *clergy* membership was limited to men. Finally in May, 1956, the General Conference passed the enabling act that permitted fully ordained and prepared women to belong to annual conferences on the same basis as men, and I was immediately accepted by the Central Pennsylvania Conference (in which I had been ordained) as soon as it met—right after the General Conference. So on May 18, 1956, 1 had the honor of becoming the first woman in our American Methodism to receive full clergy rights; that is, to become a member of an annual conference with voting rights and the right to regular appointment by the bishop. The rules were slightly bent perhaps, in my case, by Bishop Oxnam (who presided at the Conference sessions), as a candidate is supposed to appear before the Conference in person. Since I had already fulfilled the presentations when receiving the ordinations, at the time the male members usually were taken into Conference, the personal appearance had been fulfilled in that way. I had earlier sent a complete set of answers in writing to the questions always asked of candidates for admission to the Conference, so that was also cared for. And since my ordination was recognized fully by the *Korean* Methodist Church (which did admit women after 1930 when it became independent), and I was a full member there, Bishop Oxnam felt all requirements had been met, and I was admitted without further question. As I was in Korea with my husband at the time, I learned of my acceptance through an article in the military paper, *The Stars and Stripes*, before hearing through church channels. This was interesting, and also seemed a bit humorous to us—to learn through the military. But the *meaning* was never funny, but deeply appreciated. I had to be grateful for the personal honor, and it seemed only right that at long last the equality of men and women in the ministry should be recognized in this way. At first only a few women followed, but gradually more and more females opted for freedom to become ministers for Christ, until today almost half of the incoming students in seminaries may be women—older women, divorced women, women who have experience that can be invaluable in leading a church. The whole attitude of the church has changed in many ways—accepting divorce, and divorced women and men, in this high office. Age is no longer a barrier. Women no longer feel out of place in the ministry, though there are certainly still sections of the United States where conservative Christians are not too willing to accept a woman as a pastor. My own experience on the mission field was not affected in this way, but I do know that women here *have* suffered rejection in some cases.

MISSISSIPPI PASTORS SPEAK OUT
AGAINST RACIAL DISCRIMINATION

Source: "Born of Conviction," Mississippi Methodist Advocate
(2 January 1963): 2. Emphasis in the original.

Confronted with the grave crises precipitated by racial discord within our state in recent months, and the genuine dilemma facing persons of Christian conscience, we are compelled to voice publicly our convictions. Indeed, as Christian ministers and as native Mississippians, sharing the anguish of all our people, we have a particular obligation to speak. Thus understanding our mutual involvement in these issues, we bind ourselves together in this expression of our Christian commitment. We speak only for ourselves, though mindful that many others share these affirmations.

Born of the deep conviction of our souls as to what is morally right, we have been driven to seek the foundations of such convictions in the expressed witness of our Church. We, therefore, at the outset of the new year affirm the following:

I. The Church is the instrument of God's purpose. This is His church. It is ours only as stewards under His Lordship. Effective practice of this stewardship for the minister clearly requires freedom of the pulpit. It demands for every man an atmosphere for responsible belief and free expression.

II. We affirm our faith in the official position of The Methodist Church on race as set forth in paragraph 2026 of the 1960 Methodist Discipline: "Our Lord Jesus Christ teaches that all men are brothers. He permits no discrimination because of race, color or creed. 'In Christ Jesus you are all sons of God, through faith . . .' (Galatians 3:26)."

The position of The Methodist Church, long held and frequently declared is an amplification of our Lord's teaching: "We believe that God is Father of all people and races, that Jesus Christ is His Son, that all men are brothers, and that man is of infinite worth as a child of God." (The Social Creed, paragraph 2020)

III. We affirm our belief that our public school system is the most effective means of providing common education for all our children. We hold that it is an institution essential to the preservation and development of our true democracy. The Methodist Church is officially committed to the system of public school education and we concur. We are unalterably opposed to the closing of public schools on any level or to the diversion of tax funds to the support of private or sectarian schools.

IV. In these conflicting times, the issues of race and Communism are frequently confused. Let there be no mistake. We affirm an unflinching opposition to Communism. We publicly concur in the Methodist Council of Bishops statement of November 16, 1952, which declares:

> The basic commitment of a Methodist minister is to Jesus Christ as Lord and Savior. This sets him in permanent opposition to communism. He cannot be a Christian and a communist. In obedience to his Lord and in support of the prayer "Thy kingdom come, Thy will be done on earth as it is in heaven," he champions justice, mercy, freedom, brotherhood and peace. He defends the underprivileged, oppressed, and forsaken. He challenges the status quo, calling for repentance and change wherever the behavior of men falls short of the standards of Jesus Christ.

We believe that this is our task and calling as Christian ministers. FINDING AUTHORITY IN THE OFFICIAL POSITION OF OUR CHURCH, AND BELIEVING IT TO BE IN HARMONY WITH SCRIPTURE AND GOOD CHRISTIAN CONSCIENCE, WE PUBLICLY DECLARE OURSELVES IN THESE MATTERS, AND AGREE TO STAND TOGETHER IN SUPPORT OF THESE PRINCIPLES.

[Signatures of 28 pastors follow.]

LIBERIA CONFERENCE REQUESTS AUTONOMY FROM AMERICAN CHURCH

Source: Liberia Annual Conference. Memorial to the 1964 General Conference of The Methodist Church, February 27, 1963, in Papers of the Consultation on the Structure of Methodism Overseas [COSMOS]. United Methodist Archives, Madison, N.J.

At the time when our Bishop, Prince Albert Taylor, Jr., was assigned as the Episcopal head of the Monrovia Area, the challenge was great, the problems greater and the difficulties multiplied themselves; but the assignee was thoroughly able, experienced and equal to the responsibilities. With such given [quantities] and facts Bishop Taylor unrelentingly set about to determine his great goals for the work and gradually but progressively over the last seven years the problems yielded to the superb leadership of our Bishop, and the interest and cooperation from the Methodist Liberian leaders and the Liberian Annual Conference. If the laity and ministerial sections of the Liberian Annual Conference have developed amazing confidence to pursue the challenges of expanded Christianity and education in Liberia, and are responding by realistic achievements, it is due in a large measure to the practical objectivity and the exemplary leadership which Bishop Taylor has awakened and demonstrated.

But in recognition and appreciation of the fact that the Monrovia Area was the first overseas African field that the American Methodist Foreign Board undertook to operate and assist, and that such activity and assistance now covers a period of over 100 years, and during all those years Liberia was and still is an independent and sovereign nation governed by its own nationals;

And in view of the fact that many other African colonial dependencies have within the last few years achieved national independence and sovereign status, and already many of the Christian churches in these independent nations have their Christian churches represented, led and directed by their own African nationals as Bishops;

Moreover, because of the fact that unlike the dependent status of the churches of the Liberia Annual Conference as it was for a long time in the past, each church of our Conference now assumes its own financial responsibilities and not only pays its own pastors but in addition contributes substantially to the overall projects of the Conference;

And in realization of the fact that not only are Liberian Methodists imbued with a new and contagious sense of responsibility to raise and sustain themselves by their own effort, in the wake of the expanding economy of the nation and the fastly advancing status of its people and their standard of living over the past 19 years;

The Liberal Annual Conference is profoundly cognizant and aware of the Christian and missionary sacrifices and services of the Methodist Foreign Mission Board of America through the men and women who toiled over the years in different sections of Liberia to propagate Christianity and to increase educational opportunities in Liberia. We recollect with insuperable pride and gratitude to the days of the late Melville B. Cox, to the establishment and maintenance of the College of West Africa in Monrovia, the Gbarnga Mission in Gbarnga, the Ganta Mission in Ganta and the several missionary outposts in Grand Cess, Sasstown, Cape Palmas and other parts, as well as the Boys Dormitory and the Hostel for Girls in Monrovia, which have been made possible through the financial gifts and contributions of the Foreign Board and Christian-hearted men and women of America. These installations and the services of the missionary men and women from overseas who man them, in spite of any changed status of the Liberia Methodist Church, we desire to be continued in the true Christian spirit, with the Methodist Church in America and toward which we pledge our moral and financial assistance not unlike what has been forthcoming from Liberian Methodists in the past.

We, the undersigned members of the Committee representing the Laity of the Liberia Annual Conference of the Methodist Church in Liberia, respectfully beg to be granted permission to present the following memorial for consideration and adoption by the session of the Liberia Annual Conference sitting in Lower Buchanan, Grand Bassa County, Liberia, for submission to, and consideration by, the General Conference of the Methodist Church sitting during 1964 in the United States of America, as follows:

1. That although our present Bishop, Prince A. Taylor, Jr., as mentioned herein supra, has laboured satisfactorily in promoting the work of Methodism in this jurisdiction, yet the national pride and self respect of the laity and clergy of The Methodist Church in Liberia, and the universal upsurge of nationalism on the continent of Africa impels and compels the Methodist Church in Liberia to ask for a Bishop of Liberian nationality, but would prefer to maintain its connection with the American Church with a Liberian consecrated as Bishop of the Liberia Annual Conference, the Liberian Church becoming responsible for the salary and other financial and material obligations for a Bishop.

2. That should it not be practicable for some arrangements to be made whereby the desire of the Liberian Church specifically mentioned in Count one of this memorial could be granted, then the Liberian church hereby requests and prays to become an autonomous church.

Finally, we should like to emphasize and clarify our motives for this change beyond doubts and suspicion. We are still and shall always be Methodists by faith, doctrine, practice and kinship, like the Methodists of Korea, Mexico and other

mission institutions

places, whose churches are headed by their own Bishops. In our opinion, emergencies and necessity impose responsibility and stimulate change, action and progress. And under such realities, we must "sink or swim, live or die, survive or perish."

NOTE: The above memorial was unanimously adopted by the Liberia Annual Conference, February 27, 1963. While it mentions the possibility of a Liberian Bishop being elected under the present framework, they now understand that that is not practical. What they are really requesting is an autonomous church. It is the same request the conference made last year, in somewhat different language.

CHARLES KEYSOR SPEAKS UP FOR "ORTHODOXY," LAUNCHES GOOD NEWS MOVEMENT

Source: Charles W. Keysor, "Methodism's Silent Minority," Christian Advocate 10/14 (14 July 1966): 9-10. Excerpts.

Within The Methodist Church in the United States is a silent minority group. It is not represented in the higher councils of the church. Its members seem to have little influence in Nashville, Evanston, or on Riverside Drive. Its concepts are often abhorrent to Methodist officialdom at annual conference and national levels.

I speak of those Methodists who are variously called "evangelicals" or "conservatives" or "fundamentalists." A more accurate description is "orthodox," for these brethren hold a traditional understanding of the Christian faith.

Orthodox Methodists come in theologically assorted shapes, sizes, and colors. But, unfortunately, the richness and subtlety of orthodox thought are often overlooked and/or misunderstood. There lurks in many a Methodist mind a deep intolerance toward the silent minority who are orthodox. This is something of a paradox, because this unbrotherly spirit abounds at a time when Methodism is talking much about ecumenicity—which means openness toward those whose beliefs and traditions may differ. . . .

Webster's Dictionary tells us that orthodox means "conforming to the Christian faith as formulated in the church creeds and confessions." These are Catholic, Lutheran, Reformed, and Anabaptist, which means that orthodoxy is the ultimate in ecumenicity.

But what *is* orthodoxy? . . .

We who are orthodox believe that the Christian faith is comprehensively declared in Holy Scripture and is succinctly summarized in the Apostles' Creed. Here, we feel, is faith's essence, doctrinally speaking.

Orthodoxy in America has developed a theological epicenter known as the "five fundamentals." These are by no means the whole of orthodox doctrine, as many people mistakenly suppose. Instead, these five points constitute a common ground for all who are truly orthodox. But beyond this common ground lies an enormous area of Christian truth where orthodox Christians disagree vigorously. Some of

598

these areas are in definition of original sin and its mode of transmission, the nature and mission of the church, and the relationship of justification to sanctification.

Despite the broadness of orthodoxy's doctrinal scope, one must examine the five fundamentals in order to understand orthodoxy's point of view.

(1) *Inspiration of Scripture.* Orthodoxy believes with a passion that the whole Bible is God's eternal, unfailing truth. Some portions of this truth are more important than others (Isaiah 53 towers above Esther, for example), but everything in the Scriptures has sacred significance. A thing is not true because it happens to be included in the Bible; we believe it is in the Bible because the thing itself is true. Orthodoxy believes that God has expressed scriptural truth through human personality, by the agency of God's Holy Spirit. Perverted orthodoxy limits inspiration to the King James Version, as though God had somehow lowered it from heaven on a string back in 1611. Another unfortunate mutation of orthodox doctrine is the idea of mechanical dictation: that human beings were nothing more than stenographers, recording mechanically every jot and tittle that was dictated from above.

True orthodoxy shuns these mistaken views of inspiration. Instead, historic orthodoxy regards inspiration of Scripture as a dynamic, continuing activity of the Holy Spirit:

First—God's Spirit inspired the original authors, causing them to perceive and record God's truth in their own God-given literary styles. (Hence the difference between James and Ezekiel.)

Second—Acting through translators, redactors, and canonizing bodies, the Spirit has preserved Scripture from significant error during the long and torturous process of transmission, right down to the present moment.

Third—The Spirit enables believers to get God's intended meaning from Scripture. To properly understand Scripture without the Spirit's illuminating inspiration is no more possible than for an airplane to fly without wings and engine! This is why pure orthodoxy considers invalid any hermeneutic which disregards or minimizes the Spirit's threefold work of dynamic inspiration.

(2) *The virgin birth of Christ.* We believe that our Lord was, literally, "conceived by the Holy Spirit, born of the virgin Mary." This must be true, or it would not have been written and transmitted in Holy Scripture. Naïve? If so, we who are orthodox accept the label—along with such naïve men of faith as the authors of Matthew and Luke, St. Augustine, Martin Luther, John Calvin, and our own John Wesley.

We do not believe in Jesus because of the unusual circumstances surrounding his entry into the world via Incarnation. On the contrary, our experience of Christ's lordship teaches us empirically what Scripture tells—that the entire realm of nature is subject to his sovereign authority. Therefore, Christ is not subject to known limitations of "natural law." He is, in fact, the source of "natural law." Order and unity and coherence for the entire cosmos center in Christ. Believing this about him, we logically believe that our Lord could be virgin born—just as the Bible reports.

(3) *The substitutionary Atonement of Christ.* What happened on Calvary is a mystery which can never be adequately explained by theories and/or analogies. Scripture seems to justify several explanations of the Atonement. . . .

Orthodoxy believes that the main channel of Atonement truth lies in the area of substitution: that somehow Christ on the cross paid the price of transgression which a righteous and holy God properly requires. We do recognize certain validity in "moral influence" and other such theories. But orthodoxy believes it is more correct to say that our Lord, "for a world of lost sinners was slain."

(4) *The physical Resurrection of Christ.* We think that Christianity is a hoax unless Christ rose bodily from the grave—as the Scriptures report. We do not believe that the Bible would make such a central emphasis on His being raised from death bodily if this were not true. Frankly, we are tired of ingenious theories which charge the Resurrection up to the wishful thinking of primitive Christians. More convincing to us is the Spirit of our risen Lord, bearing witness with our spirits that "He lives!"

(5) *The return of Christ.* Orthodox Christians hold various views of the Parousia's place in the order of last things. But all truly orthodox believers agree that Jesus Christ will return physically to "judge the (living) and the dead." We do not regard the Great Assize passage (Matthew 25:31-46) as parabolic teaching; instead, we believe it is a literal foretelling of the future judgment which Christ will execute when he comes again.

Perverted orthodoxy has made an illusory religion out of millennial speculation. This clearly ignores Jesus' teaching that the time of His appearing is known only to the mind of God. Jesus did not intend for His disciples to dawdle with date setting. We are not to waste time peering into the sky waiting for a homecoming Hero to solve the world's problems!

Instead we are to let our Christian light shine in a dark world. Our calling is to be redeeming the time, for the days are evil. This precludes two extremes: (1) setting dates for His return; (2) pointing negatively to the fact that early Christian expectations have not been fulfilled according to man's time scale. To both, orthodoxy says, "Be ready! But as you wait in confidence, be a Christ to your neighbor."

Orthodoxy clings with joy to the "blessed hope" of Christ's physical return. This expectation strengthens us for the living of these days. One of the most pronounced characteristics about authentic orthodoxy is its vibrant sense of eschatological expectancy. This is God's gift to those who cling to the "blessed hope" as we live in the eschatological twilight zone, between promise and fulfillment. . . .

Orthodoxy seems destined to remain as Methodism's silent minority. Here lies the challenge: We who are orthodox must become the *un*-silent minority! Orthodoxy must shed its "poor cousin" inferiority complex and enter forthrightly into the current theological debate. We who are orthodox must boldly declare our understanding of Christian truth, as God has given these convictions to us. We must speak in love and with prophetic fearlessness, and we must be prepared to suffer because we are a minority.

But regardless of the consequences, we must be heard in Nashville, in Evanston, and on Riverside Drive. Most of all, we must be heard in thousands of pulpits, for the people called Methodist will not cease to hunger for the good news of Jesus Christ, incarnate, crucified, risen, and coming again.

We must not speak as right-wing fanatics, intending to subvert the "establishment" and remake it in our own orthodox image. Instead, we must speak to our Christian brothers as Christian brothers, trusting that God will direct and prosper our witness to the truth as we see it in Christ Jesus our Lord.

EUB BISHOP WASHBURN ANSWERS QUESTIONS ON CHURCH UNION WITH THE METHODISTS

Sources: Paul Washburn, "Questions on Church Union," Church and Home 36/1-2 (January 15 and February 1, 1966): 14-17; 9-12. Excerpts.

Question—*Just how did this discussion of union get started within the present generation? Who took the initiative—Methodists or EUB's? What was the basic motivation?*

Answer—The current attempt to unite the Methodist Church and the Evangelical United Brethren Church began in 1957 at two quite dissimilar places. Grass-roots persons in Illinois and Kansas prepared petitions which were submitted to the General Conference of 1958 asking that this attempt be undertaken. Leader persons of the two churches, attending the assembly of the National Council of Churches at St. Louis, talked about investigating the possibility of such a union. Deeper and more important, however, than these wellsprings was the growing awareness that while the church is one church under the Lordship of Christ it looks very divided to the world to which it seeks to minister.

Question—*Up to the present moment, what appear to stand forth as the principal reasons (briefly and pointedly stated but not argued) for continuing to pursue this proposal of union?*

Answer—Principal reasons for pursuing the proposed union are of two types: (1) reasons based on biblically and theologically oriented convictions and (2) reasons based on obedience to our church's government and character. Some reasons of the first type are: (1) Jesus Christ is now the one Lord of all. (2) His body, the church, is one body now. (3) He can comprehend and command diversities of servanthood in his one body, but his body is wounded by divisions between the members of his body. (4) We want to do what we can to heal that broken body.

Based on obedience to our church way of life some reasons are: (1) The Evangelical United Brethren Church, acting through its General Conference, instructed its Commission on Church Union to prepare a plan of union if possible. The commission is trying to be obedient. (2) Facts discovered in the process of negotiation indicated that these churches can be one new church. The joint commissions in obedience are following the facts to logical conclusions. (3) Attitudes of some members and some ministers, in both churches exposed under the pressure of this venture, reveal extensive need for a renewed emphasis upon the kind of holiness proposed by John Wesley. It is, therefore, by reason of obedience to the holiness we profess that we pursue this union. (4) The church exists to continue Christ's ministry to the church and to the world. In more than 100 communities in America, Methodist and Evangelical United Brethren congregations (and congregations are the basic agents of ministry) have united to exercise a better stewardship of ministry. Our commission acts in obedience to this fact. . . .

Question—*Just how is this movement toward organic union related to the very general slogan of "renewal" and how will union specifically and in detail contribute toward more "spiritual" church life:*

Answer—Both the words "renewal" and "spiritual" are words which have different meanings for different people. Many have said "Union, yes, if it will renew the church," but we know we can not expect a committee of nineteen members (Commission on Church Union) to renew the church by writing a *Discipline*. We know the renewal of our congregations waits for all of us as members of the congregations to meet the divinely appointed conditions of such renewal. We know, also, that nineteen members out of 750,000 cannot make the church "spiritual." This responsibility belongs to all of us.

We can be confident that our Lord desires his church to be "renewed" and "spiritual." We can also be confident that this union can contribute to both of these ends if we will allow it to be a genuine gathering of Methodists and Evangelical United Brethren about Christ in repentance, trust, obedience, worship and mission.

Question—*We have been told that the result of this union will be a "new church." Precisely just what will be new? Would we not really be "joining" the Methodist Church? Would it not be more ethically sound to admit this?*

Answer—The union promises a new church because: (1) It will provide forms for mission to individuals, congregations, and conferences heretofore unavailable. (2) The plan declares that Christ has given his ministry to all Christians. As laymen realize this they will have new definitions of themselves and new duties to perform. (3) It will bring to such union Christians who have not been united in worship and witness previously. Possibilities for fellowship and cooperation in mission will be new at many levels because relationships of persons will be different. It will be a different dialogical situation. (4) It will force all who take the union seriously into an extensive study of the history of a new church hitherto unpossessed and unknown. (5) It will require that responsible members study and use new patterns of congregational and denominational life.

Question—*In the light of "grass-roots" lack of success in the 1946 union of Evangelicals and United Brethren, and unfulfilled promises (reduced costs, more efficiency, numerical growth, deepened spirituality) together with questionable accretions (growth in personnel and administrative offices, vast sums spent for promotional gimmicks, continuing local rivalries between congregations that should have merged, even annual conferences actually voting against conference merger)—is not this Methodist proposal premature?*

Answer—I did not understand that search for "success" was the motivation for our 1946 union. Even if "success" were the motive, I doubt that "reduced costs," "efficiency" and "numerical growth" are the symbols of "success" as the church of Jesus Christ spells "success." If the 1946 union was a failure (and I do not think it was) ought we not try another one in order to do better the next time? What the true church seeks is not success but opportunities to serve under Christ's Lordship and that to the point of extensive sacrifice. . . .

Question—*What are now the prospects for a completely integrated (racially) church in the union—in jurisdictions? in conferences? in congregations?*

Answer—In three of the five geographical jurisdictions of the Methodist Church integration is a fact at jurisdictional and conference levels, and to a great extent at the congregational level. In the other two jurisdictions there is readiness to experience integration at the jurisdictional level. It now appears that God by his Holy Spirit has some more convicting to do if total integration is to come. In terms of eliminating structures of segregation this is a Methodist problem, but in terms of the eliminating of actual segregation it may be even more so an Evangelical United Brethren problem. We are still very segregated. . . .

Question—*What are the principal theological and liturgical differences to be resolved? And what are the proposals thereto?*

Answer—Methodist Articles of Religion were adopted in 1784. The revised Evangelical United Brethren Confession of Faith was adopted in 1962. Both are included in the plan. The Joint Commissions on Union will propose, if union comes, that a theological commission be appointed to study and recommend what should be done about the two statements. However this kind of activity holds little promise for the united church. Promise for a church theologically united is in the measure of testimony to faith experience which United Methodists will share with each other and with the world in effective mission confrontations.

Liturgical materials are the scripture lessons, the hymns, and the rituals. I perceive that the lessons are from the same source. Sixty-seven per cent of the hymns in our hymnal are in the new Methodist hymnal. The rituals are very much alike. The Plan of Union authorizes both hymnals for use in the united church. . . .

Question—*How will the two ministries be completely integrated: in terms of ordinations? in terms of educational requirements? in terms of salary standards in the conference? What is to become of the Methodist practice of "approved supply pastors" licensed, perhaps also ordained, but not voting members of the annual conference?*

Answer—The united church will unite the ministers of the two former churches, guaranteeing to each minister privileges and standing like unto those held in his former church. A new pattern of ministry will be introduced at the time of union but it will not be retroactive. It will be open to women. It will probably have one ordained order, that of elder.

Question—*What elements in the current EUB structure, program and emphases (different from theirs at present) are Methodists actually accepting in the basis of union proposed? What will happen to our program council, for instance? Will jurisdictional structure of the Methodist Church remain?*

Answer—It is not a question of what Methodists are accepting in order to console Evangelical United Brethren. It is a question of what will be best for a church of 11 million members united in Christ and committed to mission. Some features which have been and may be finally accepted from us as best for the united church are: (1) The Council on Local Church Program; (2) The Bureau on Long Range Planning; (3) Cooperation in United Campus Christian Fellowship as well as Methodist Student Movement; (4) One order of ministry; (5) Our people, our ministries, and our ministers. The jurisdictional structure will remain to guarantee some balance of representation for geographical areas of the church. . . .

Question—What is the answer to those who express fears that, ultimately if not immediately (ratio of 13 to 1 or more) the EUB element in a united church will be outvoted and absorbed?

Answer—The Plan of Union indicates that members of the boards and general agencies of the united church will be 13 per cent former Evangelical United Brethren and 87 per cent former Methodists. From the beginning of the united church Evangelical United Brethren will be outvoted; 13 per cent of a board cannot determine any decision by voting. However, this does not mean that they will be absorbed. A vital Christian cannot be absorbed, nor can a vital Christian congregation.

Question—What is the prospect for a clear and positive "temperance" position in the united Church, along lines that are traditionally Methodist, Evangelical, and United Brethren?

Answer—The Social Creed of the Methodist Church and the Moral Standards of the Evangelical United Brethren church will become official documents of the new church. What they say about temperance will be the official position of the United Methodist Church.

Question—Just what finally is to be the recommended name? And what is the reasoning behind this choice?

Answer—The Joint Commissions will recommend the name the United Methodist Church for the following reasons: There will be eleven former churches within it. The name can be used legally in all countries where our two churches now minister. It has in it at least some evidence of each of the uniting churches. It will reflect adjustability on the part of both of the uniting churches. . . .

Question—If this union with the Methodist Church should be consummated, what is the prospect of actual identification with the larger union movement—of six or more denominations, the Blake-Pike proposal?

Answer—At the present time both the Methodist Church and the Evangelical United Brethren Church participate as fully as any other churches in the Consultation on Church Union. This participation in personnel, study-paper preparation, financial support and consultation is total and will continue as long as our two General Conferences or the United Church's General Conference request its continuance.

Question—How would this church union affect the retirement status and financial benefits of EUB ministers?

Answer—The chapter on "The Ministry" guarantees to every minister of both churches the same rights, privileges and obligations guaranteed to him by his present church. The chapter on "The Board of Pensions" guarantees that no minister will receive less pension in the new church than he would have received were he to have continued in his present relationship. He may receive much more.

Question—*What in current thinking is to be the ultimate use or disuse of such present church centers as Dayton, Nashville, Evanston, Harrisburg, New York and Cincinnati?*

Answer—Agreements have not yet been reached about the future use of the many fine buildings which house the general agencies of our two churches. All buildings will be needed to house the church's agencies. . . .

Question—*What are the plans, or perhaps only the unwritten intents, in the Plan of Union as far as local situations are concerned—for the uniting of congregations where this appears desirable?*

Answer—Methodist and Evangelical United Brethren congregations in all areas of the church will desire to study how they may most effectively continue Christ's ministry through the United Methodist Church in their own communities. If they find that they will be better able to minister as united congregations, they will themselves decide to unite. If they find that they may best continue as they are, they may decide that. . . .

EDITOR OF CAMPUS MINISTRY MAGAZINE, B. J. STILES, CHALLENGES THE CONSCIENCE OF AMERICA ON THE WAR IN VIETNAM

Source: B. J. Stiles, "Vietnam: Challenge to the Conscience of America," Motive *27/8 (May 1967): 6-7. Used by permission of the General Board of Higher Education and Ministry of The United Methodist Church. Excerpts.*

Why *are* we in Vietnam? The query lies at the center of our public debates, almost regardless of the announced topic, and it lingers in our private ruminations. We look for new meaning in old arguments, we grasp for new arguments, we persistently piece together some defensible synthesis between domino theories and withdrawal urges. But to no avail.

Confronted by complexity and immersed in tension resulting from patriotic vs. humanistic impulses, we tend to slouch into silent passivity. There's always that reassuring, universal abdication: "Don't worry. Our leaders know best."

For more than a year, a cartoon released in 1966 by the Los Angeles Times Syndicate has been taped to my office door. It shows two well dressed, shaven students holding signs. One reads, "Get out of Vietnam." The other reads, "Stay in Vietnam." A third sign, held by the proverbial little old lady in tennis shoes, reads, "I honestly don't know."

Originally, the cartoon seemed justifiably humorous. But as the months have passed and thousands of lives have been lost and even more thousands of bodies mutilated, diseased, hungered, and refugeed, the cartoon has become macabre. This doesn't mean that I have personally received some momentous revelation which offers a politically viable answer along any of the lines advocated in any one of the three placards in the cartoon.

Rather, the sheer intransigence of these cartoon figures on my wall has become a glaring symbol of the forces at work in the war itself. What distance toward peace and settlement have the deaths and destruction of these past months brought us?

This cartoon, plus the experience and conversations resulting from three months in Europe last summer, provide the incentive and part of the rationale for this issue of *Motive* [May 1967].

An American cannot appear anywhere outside our country without repeatedly facing the question, "What is America doing in Vietnam?" But nowhere did this question become more pointed—and difficult—for me than when I was in Germany.

Friends and strangers hounded me with discussions of the Vietnam predicament. German Christians—both East and West—drew parallels between what they faced as *Christians* in relationship to their national destiny and what American Christians now face relative to our own national destiny. By reporting that they raised parallels, I do not mean or imply that they or I assumed that these two situations are exactly synonymous. Of course not. But there are some analogies, and the consequences on world affairs seem to have some significant similarities.

These Germans and I struggled with the observation that the national objectives of one body can achieve such strength and proportions as to enable that nation in its corporate actions to deny, violate, and finally liquidate the dreams, values, and bodies of any who stand—or are accused of standing—in the way of those declared objectives.

Some of my friends were blunt and dogmatic. "Oradour and Lidice are today towns in Vietnam!" Others were sympathetically reflective, in a most unsettling way. "Yes, we remember our own indecision in 1936-37." A journalist recalled; "We well remember what it is like not to know the truth."

The conversations and the diverse points of view flowed into a provocative and pertinent question: "What do Germans have to say to and about Americans regarding the war in Vietnam?"

And so this issue [of *Motive*] resulted.

We have intentionally published statements which vary, and occasionally even contradict. Christians and non-Christians alike differ frequently in how they view the world. But these differences in observation do not negate the underlying unity of concern which runs throughout this issue. Without exception, our German friends are saying: our present military tactics are inhuman, our current political strategies are generally unsuccessful in the eyes of both our friends and our enemies, and our continual declarations of peace seeking are unconvincing in their words and tone and are inconsistent with our actions in their timing and scope. . . .

We conclude our publishing year with a lamentation: In the name of God, *this* war, in *this* place, at *this* time, against *this* people, must stop.

To fail to apply our most diligent political, human, rational efforts toward that end is a travesty against civilization.

To meekly (no matter how sincerely) plead with the little old lady, "I honestly don't know," is to abdicate our human sanity and our Christian heritage.

MEA VI: 1968–98

BLACK CHURCH LEADERS REJECT TOKENISM AND FORM BLACK METHODISTS FOR CHURCH RENEWAL

Source: James M. Lawson, Jr. "Black Churchmen Seek Methodist Renewal,"
Christian Advocate 12/5 (7 March 1968): 24.

In the last days of 1967, a call went out across The Methodist Church inviting more than 1,000 Negro Methodists to a national conference in Cincinnati. An ad hoc committee of well over 100 included bishops, pastors, laymen, staff members of annual conferences and general boards, students, and young people. The call said in part:

"Together we shall look at the 'new' situation before us in The Methodist Church; explore new strategies for helping The United Methodist Church to be a 'new' God-happening. . . ."

On February 6, [1968] for the first time in the history of American Methodism, Negro Methodists from coast to coast gathered. They came from all levels of the church's life and ministry—some 300 strong. They came deeply loyal to our Methodist heritage, wanting to renew the church, and determined that being together was crucial for this period in church history.

Dr. Earnest A. Smith, former president of Rust College, summoned the delegates to hammer out a relevant philosophy of righteousness, for "righteousness is a power for operation." Seventeen work groups met for 13 hours discussing these topics: The Negro in The Methodist Church—Where Are We?; Black Power in The Methodist Church; Black Churchmen and Black Revolution; General Conference Legislation and Strategy, The Local Church and New Forms of Ministry; and Beyond General Conference and What?

James Farmer, former Methodist, founder of CORE and a former National Director of CORE, spoke to a public meeting. He was invited because he left the church over the question of segregation. Stokely Carmichael, likewise a product of Methodism, participated in a number of work group sessions. The charismatic "Black Power" advocate perceptively illustrated the need for serious dialogue between churchmen and those who think they are militant. For most persons this was a first encounter with Mr. Carmichael. Some exclaimed, "I've been misled. You are a different person from the picture I've received in the press."

Work group discussions and proposals went to a Findings Committee where their reports were lifted, sifted, and discussed. Then the Findings Committee produced a document for the further study and use of the delegates and as a word from the conference to Methodism.

Let it be understood that the conference was and is a word of repentance for Negro Methodists. We said at Cincinnati that for too long we have played the game of being church-men in The Methodist Church; participated in the politics of seeking prestige and position without sacrifice and obedience; that, like our white brethren, we wore masks where too frequently we said what we thought others wanted to hear.

A major concern was the mission of Negro congregations in our cities. Many insisted that structurally and financially local churches are not organized to minister to their neighborhoods or to the inner city. For example, Negro congregations have a per family income approximately one half the income of white congregations. Yet these congregations, often located in the ghetto, pay World Service and conference benevolences which for the most part do not serve specific projects among the poor. The denomination's urban work budgets are embarrassingly low. If the Negro congregation pays its Methodist assessments, chances are it does not then have money for day care centers, for poverty programs, and other efforts to make the city more human.

Another concern of the conference centered around Dallas and the Uniting Conference. The suspicion is that we Methodists are playing a "mickey-mouse" game and that after Dallas the deadening game of racism will go on in less visible ways. Apparently very little creative dialogue among the races is going on in Methodism anywhere in the country. The explosive urban situation has not become the foremost mission of the church. We play with the Consultation on Church Union trusting that nothing will happen, rather than uniting with other denominations at the point of urban ministry or Christian social concerns. We "take in" the EUBs but pretend that Negro Methodist denominations do not exist.

Cincinnati asks [the Uniting Conference in] Dallas to authorize genuine urban priorities and to get the Methodist household in order. A thorn in the mind of many Negro Methodists is the failure of the Methodist Publishing House to reflect the stated policies of The Methodist Church, including the hiring of minorities at every level of its operation. Cincinnati also is asking the Uniting Conference to insist that the publishing house adopt Project Equality. The delegates at Cincinnati urge Methodists who want serious Christian change and a "new" church to meet together in Dallas and insist that the Uniting Conference be a renewing and reforming council.

Delegates agreed to return home and continue or begin experiments in ministry. A flood of ideas were suggested: Apportionments must be evaluated. Should a black congregation give monies to Methodist institutions which discriminate in employment or service? We need a great variety of programs to train laity and clergy for transforming service in the ghettos. Local churches can unite their ministries and resources. Even schools of mission require new curricula which relate to ghetto problems and encourage black identity. The local congregation must move from normative churchmanship to radical Christian obedience to change the cities.

Let me summarize the conference another way. The Methodist Church has never listened to responsible Negro leadership. In 1939 Negro Methodists rejected segregation. Yet union dictated the creation of the Central Jurisdiction. From that time on Negroes agitated for the integrated church. Only Central Jurisdiction leaders made the effort to study, discuss, and define "The Inclusive Church" and how racism could be ended at all levels of the church. Their counsel and advice were summarily refused. Since 1964 mergers in Methodism have not been grounded in Christian encounter, grass-root faith, and programming or courageous leadership. Today most white Methodists still suspect that the Gospel of Jesus Christ and racial myths are consonant.

Cincinnati was necessary in order to say to our church that we reject tokenism. We refuse to tolerate a cheap, meaningless fellowship not rooted in Christian acceptance, dialogue, and mission. We will settle for nothing less than a church where the love of Christ rules and where a man is a man not by race, or blood, but by the will and power of God.

From the very beginning of the meeting it was obvious that the delegates wanted to stay together—that is, they felt the need for a continuing organization that would express their concerns in the months to come. So we established an organization called Black Methodists for Church Renewal.

Plainly this is a different day. Our hope is that Black Methodists for Church Renewal will soon be out of business. For years we have hungered not only for the end of the Central Jurisdiction but for the end of segregation in all its forms—explicit or implicit. Perhaps now we can so move in obedience to God's demand that we be one in life and ministry and work and structure—as well as in word. If Cincinnati somehow enables us to see this need and to commit ourselves with courage to His task, then the conference may prove to be the most exciting and historical event in American Methodism.

Professor Albert Outler details "unfinished business" in sermon to Uniting Conference

Source: Albert C. Outler, "Uniting Conference Sermon," United Methodist Church, Journal of the General Conference (1968), 2: 995-1003. *Excerpts.*

Tuesday Morning, April 23, 1968
"Visions and Dreams"

Fathers and Brethren and Sisters in Christ:

Here we are this morning, gathered together from over the world and from all sorts and conditions of men—to celebrate a birthday, *our* birthday as The United Methodist Church. In just a few moments now, we shall join in a ceremony symbolizing our new covenant of unity and mutual growth together. The aura of every newborn thing is an aura of hope. And so it is with us today. We stand here on a threshold. A new horizon looms ahead.

In some ears, it may sound fantastic to relate *this* day to the first Pentecost recorded in Acts 2—what with no rushing mighty wind, no tongues of fire, no glossolalia, and so forth. But actually, the lasting meaning of *that* Pentecost was its opening the way for others to follow after.

And while the day of Pentecost was getting on, they [the disciples] were all together with one accord in one place. . . . And they were filled with the Holy Spirit . . . and began to speak . . . as the Spirit gave them the power of utterance . . . about the great deeds of God. . . .

This is, of course, an abridgement of the longer text, with the marvels omitted and also those two bits of local color that still intrigue me: the one where Peter denies that the disciples are drunk because it was too early in the morning (about the same time of day as *now!*); and that other one about the 3,000 new members added in one day. What a frustration it must have been for Peter to have all that happen, with no board to report it to!

Clearly, though, that *first* Pentecost was less significant for what happened *then* than for what came after. Pentecost *was the day when the real work of the church began,* when the Christian people accepted the agenda of their unfinished business in the

614

world and began to get on with it! Those first Christians were not very well furnished in terms of ecclesiastical apparatus. Their organization was shaky, their polity and discipline sketchy. Their theologians were in typical disagreement, and their most prominent "lay leaders" were Ananias and Sapphira!

Even so *that* Pentecost was ever thereafter memorable as the Church's *birthday,* as the day when Joel's prophecy was fulfilled—when the Holy Spirit would come and abide as God's governing presence in the midst of his People—and this memory remained, even when the rushing mighty wind subsided to homiletical zephyrs, when glossolalia was relegated to the margins of Christian experience, when the tongues of fire gave way to controversy and conflict. Pentecost is rightly remembered as the day when the Christian church was launched on its career *in* history, *for* the world. In every age, her performance has been scandalously short of her visions and dreams—and her plain imperatives. And yet also in every age since the first Pentecost, it is the Christian church that has marked off the crucial difference between man's best hope and his genuine despair.

I know as well as anyone that this analogy between that first birthday and this one of ours does not apply four-square. Our new church does not represent a radical break with our several past histories, nor is there a comparable intention toward a radically new future. Even so, the analogy between the first Pentecost and this one could be edifying to us, too. This is the day when *the real work of the UMC begins.* It is a day when doors are opened that heretofore were closed, when new possibilities of reformation and renewal are literally "at hand."

The essence of the event is self-evident: it is the accomplished fact of The United Methodist Church. Where once, scarcely a generation ago, there were five churches, now there is one. Where once our differences kept us apart—with different languages and folkways—now they are overcome or at least contained within a larger circle of committed fellowship. We have been Christian brethren, after a fashion, for the better part of two centuries—but *separated* brethren. Now our memberships and ministers have been mingled without compromise or indignity; our separate traditions have been sublated and made one.

Obviously, no part of our venture in unity is really *finished* as yet! Our joy in *this* union ought to be tempered by our remembrance, in love, of those others of our Christian brethren, whom we acknowledge as such, and yet from whom we are still separated. Moreover, the various practical, domestic problems posed by our agenda in this Conference loom large and exigent. It will *not* be a debonair fort-night; few of us are likely to be content with the outcome. And yet, here we are and this is our birthday. Here we turn a new page in modern church history—and just as smugness is excluded from our celebration, so also is cynicism.

Let us then ask ourselves what this fact of a new church makes possible. What will it take to turn this beginning into the reality of its promise and of our hopes? We can offer our ungrudging gratitude and honor to all those whose toil and tears, faith and fortitude have led us to this hour—so long as we are all clear that none of their laurels (and certainly none of ours) is for *resting on.* We have much to be grateful for, nothing to be complacent about. Our joy this day is foretaste: foretaste of a future that can be even more creative than we have yet dared to ask or think.

This means that, as we turn from ceremony of beginnings to the tasks that follow, our foremost need is for a vivid sense of the church we have been called to be. By what norms shall we seek to transform our covenant into genuine *koinonia?* By what principles are we willing to be guided in the agonies of growth that lie ahead? To what heavenly vision are we prepared to be obedient in the difficult days and years that even the blithest optimist can foresee?

One thing is for sure: what has served till now as our *status quo ante* will simply not suffice for the upcoming future. For all its great merits—for all its saints and heroes—the standing order is now too nearly preoccupied with self-maintenance and survival. The world is in furious and agonizing turmoil, incomprehensible and unmanageable. The church is in radical crisis, and in the throes of a profound demoralization, at every level: of faith and order, life and work. In such times, business as usual simply will not get our business done. Our own past golden age (the 19th century)—the heyday of pietism in a preurbanized society—has faded. Frontiersmen for tomorrow must be as dynamically adaptive to the *new* "new world" as our forefathers were in theirs.

There is, of course, a bit of glibness here—for the brute fact is that we have no clearly visible alternative to the *status quo* ready to hand, available merely for our choice and application. For all their advertisements, none of the new experiments of celebration of our own brave new world can honestly be hailed as the shape of things to come. Nor is it the case that any of our sister churches have had vouchsafed to them, the blueprints for Zion's Ark, space-age model—though some (notably the Roman Catholics) have recently exposed themselves to more massive and more fruitful self-examination than we.

For freedom we have been set free, from the outdated past—but it begins to look as if we have been condemned *to* freedom as well: condemned to come up with something better than protests and complaints and self-righteous criticism of others; we are condemned to *responsible* prophecy, reform and renewal—or else to the fatal consequences of destructive discontent. If, in this new church of ours, we are to avoid "the dinosaur-syndrome" (with its zeal for furnishing later ages an abundance of fossils) or its opposite, "the Elijah complex" (with its self-pitying, self-righteousness about our minority status), we *must* find our way forward in conscious concern for the continuum of the Christian tradition and history in which we stand with our forefathers: always aware of God's habit of linking the past and the future by means of the hopeful acts of men in decisive *present* moments—like *this one!* We must learn to discipline our imaginations and inventions, not by our own constrictive biases, but by God's open-hearted mandates for his people, by patterns that will serve our *common* life in the Body of Christ. . . .

It may seem to some a mite unseasonable to suggest that the UMC needs to take conscious, urgent thought of being or becoming "truly reformed," *just now!* We *are* a Church re-formed: what with our new plan [of union] and our newer report and with ten more days to pull and haul away at their discussion, amendment, and adoption. Surely *this* is enough for the present moment. Well, ye-s-s—in a way—but that's partly my point. This plan and the report in the form in which they will stand when we adjourn will doubtless be the very best we can do, under *all* the circumstances, etc., etc. But for how long will *that* be good *enough*? The answer: not much beyond the results being printed in the new *Discipline*. Wherefore, *now* is the time, as at that first Pentecost, for young men to see visions and for old men to dream dreams—visions and dreams that ask more of the Methodist people than we have ever asked before, visions and dreams that offer a richer, fuller life for all God's People, visions and dreams that see this "new" Church *renewed* yet again and again, not only "in the Spirit" but in her structures, functions, folkways.

This is not a proposal, not even indirectly, for any special reform—yours or mine or anybody else's. It is, however, an open advocacy of the *idea* of reform and of "the Protestant principle" of *semper reformanda*. When more of us get accustomed to the notion that this new church of ours *can* be remade for yet more effective mission, for still more authentic democracy and local initiative, for still more efficient, adventurous leadership—and that all this *can* be done and *should* be done forthwith!—then the pooled wisdom of our fellowship will surely be enabled to prove that rational, responsible change is a far more faithful pattern of obedience to Christ than the most devoted immobilism can ever be.

This, then, is our birthday—a day to celebrate, a day to remember, a day for high hopes and renewed commitments. This is a day when the eyes of the whole Christian community are focused on us and especially those of our Methodist brethren in Britain who are with us here in spirit. This *is* the day that the Lord has made. Let us *really* rejoice and be glad in it—glad for the new chance God now gives us to be a *church united in order to be uniting, a church repentant in order to be a church redemptive, a church cruciform in order to manifest God's triumphant agony for mankind,*

> Till sons of men shall learn *his* love
> And follow where *his* feet have trod
> Till, glorious from the heavens above,
> Shall, come the city of our God!

[Frank Mason North, "Where Cross the Crowded Ways of Life," v. 6, *The Methodist Hymnal* 1966, no. 204.]

Let us pray:

O God, of unchangeable power and eternal light, look favorably on thy whole church, that wonderful and sacred mystery; and, by the tranquil operation of thy perpetual providence, carry out the work of man's salvation; and let the whole world feel and see that things which were cast down are being raised up, that those things which had grown old are being made new, and that all things are returning to perfection, through him from whom they took their origin, even Jesus Christ our Lord. Amen.

MISSION EXECUTIVE TRACEY JONES
LOOKS TO THE FUTURE

Source: Tracey K. Jones, Jr., "A Look to the Future,"
World Outlook 29/8 (April 1969): 190.

The shape of the Christian Mission for the 70's, blurred as some outlines are, is still sufficiently clear to risk a few predictions.

First, the mood will, I believe, be affirmative. We are moving out of a period of negativism. To see the space ship Earth, as did the Apollo 8 crew, bright and shining in the blackness of cold space, cannot help giving a new importance to the deep questions of man's destiny. For Christians to miss this new situation of world-wide expectancy would be to miss one of the great missionary opportunities in man's history. We are not at the end of the Christian Mission but the beginning of a new lease on life.

Second, the language of Missionary Theology will change. For the past hundred years we have talked about Jesus as Saviour. This assumed there was a literal hell, equated the conversion experience of the adolescent as the prototype for all men, separated the "lost" from the "saved," and accentuated man's weakness. In the years ahead Missionary Theology will, I believe, talk about Jesus Christ as Lord over all men. Such a theology does not focus so much on man's weakness as on his sense of responsibility for himself and his neighbor. It assumes the unity of mankind and probes the meaning of how all men are to become a new humanity in Jesus Christ. It sees the test of discipleship to Christ in terms of adult decisions dealing with complex and ambiguous issues. It stresses both the individual and social aspects of the experience of salvation and redemption.

Third, the arena of missionary activity will be the public sector. To liberate men from hunger, war, fear and human degradation; to confront political and social power groups that take advantage of the weak; and to cooperate with government in the private sector in serving mankind will be more and more the order of missionary priorities. Christian churches have a critical role to play. They can interpret, in the light of Christ, the issues that men face when they confront injustice and need. They can exhort and inspire governments and the private sector to responsible action in meeting these needs. Furthermore, the churches can provide "models" as to what can be done. What we have seen in recent months in meeting the famine crisis in Biafra, the attempt to deal with the difficulties in the American cities is illustrative of what the churches can do.

Fourth, the test will be competence. Good intentions, important as they are, will not be enough. The task of redeeming men from themselves and their environment will require the specialist skills not only of the clergy but planners, TV communicators, community developers, politicians, teachers, doctors and many others. Whether it be locating new church sites, or assessing the Christian involvement in city programs or dealing with national policy, or opening hospitals and schools, there can be no substitute for specialized competence.

Fifth, the channel will be ecumenical. It is questionable whether the old denominational wine skins can hold the new wine. The ecumenical trends that are emerging, I believe, will be two.

First of all, the conciliar movements such as the National Council of Churches, the World Council of Churches, and the regional ecumenical councils in Asia, Africa, Latin America, Europe and North America will be more and more the channels for Christian healing, teaching and preaching. At the same time, with the Roman Catholic church and the Orthodox churches more and more involved in these conciliar movements, there is no question but that they will go through a radical change.

Along with the conciliar movement, a second ecumenical trend is to be seen in church union. I believe this movement toward church union in the different countries of the world will gain momentum. In the United States, nine (9) denominations (including The United Methodist Church) are today in these church union negotiations. By 1980, we will probably have to make a choice. My own surmise is that church union movements are the wave of the future.

It is important to remember that these parallel ecumenical movements—the conciliar and church union ecumenicity—can be effective only as each relates to a much broader ecumenism which calls for closer working relationships with all other religious communities and secular agencies.

Sixth, satisfaction will come through participation. The giving of money and formulation of resolutions will not be enough. Men and women, to get satisfaction out of the Christian Mission, will have to be involved themselves. They will not be sure at all times just what they should do. They will have to live with ambiguous and complex choices. However, as they are willing to do so, they will find themselves caught up in exciting and demanding missionary concerns. They will feel under tremendous necessity for personal growth and a deeper awareness of the biblical and devotional roots of life in Christ. They will also see the need for closer personal ties across racial and cultural lines. They will need silence, more leisure and deeper devotional life. Through it all they should be able to see the possibilities as well as the excitement of growing into a deeper mature mind of Jesus Christ.

HISPANIC CAUCUS APPEALS TO GENERAL CONFERENCE

Source: "Proceedings of the General Conference of The United Methodist Church,"
Daily Christian Advocate 2/4 (23 April 1970): 147.

Tuesday evening session, April 21, 1970
Bishop James Thomas presiding

Leo L. Baker (North Texas): As a matter of special privilege, Mr. Chairman, I would seek the minor change in the Agenda to allow the Reverend Elias Galvan to speak for a few brief moments on MARCHA.

Bishop Thomas: All right. . . .

Is the person here to speak? Oh yes. Excuse me, will you take microphone 1 please? Excuse me, I'm not seeing too well; is it a statement that you would like to deliver from the platform?

Mr. Elias Galvan [clergy visitor, Southern California Conference]: I would like to do so, sir.

Bishop Thomas: All right, sir. Fine.

Mr. Galvan: In the first place I would like to express our appreciation to the General Conference for giving us the opportunity to present before you the following statement. However, before I do this, I'd like to present to you the steering committee of MARCHA. . . . Our statement is short. We're only asking for five minutes. We will not take any more time. We know that you are a busy Conference. . . .

Before I begin reading this statement that was prepared by MARCHA, I'd like to remind this Conference that we do not only want your applause and your congratulations, we want your action. The action of this General Conference. Now the report:

We Methodists Associated Representing the Cause of Hispanic Americans, known as MARCHA, have come to this General Conference to proclaim the impending death of the United Methodist ministry among Spanish-Americans. This, despite the fact that there are 11 million Spanish-Americans in the United States, and increasing at the rate that will see 22 million by the year 2000. If the present needs of the Spanish-Americans in the United States are not met with a new sense of urgency, our ministry will be obliterated. We are churchmen who speak a different language and feel a profound passion for our people. Yet, we are bound with you in the total ministry of Christ to all people. We come to ask for your help, but we are not begging. We are appealing to your sense of mission which we trust is still alive in The United Methodist Church for the Spanish-Americans.

We, therefore, request that (1) this General Conference accept the ministry to the Spanish-Americans as a top priority, recognizing the needs that are affecting this ministry, such as leadership development, economic development, salaries, scholarships, pensions, lack of employed staff at the General Board levels, lack of proper facilities, and lack of proper representation in decision-making places that affect the ministries to the Spanish-Americans; (2) that this General Conference instruct the General Boards and Agencies to appropriate funds, staff, and other available resources for all programs that affect this ministry as they are requested by the representatives of Spanish-American Methodist groups; (3) that this Conference instruct the General Program Council to employ a Spanish-American executive as an Associate General Secretary with the responsibilities to the Spanish-American ministries.

Respectfully submitted, MARCHA. (Applause)

Bishop Thomas: Thank you very much.

Josafat Curti [clergy visitor, Rocky Mountain Conference]: . . . The ones that can say "Viva" please stand up. "Viva La MARCHA!" (VIVA!)

Spanish-American ministry needs

Student movement magazine "comes out" in favor of gay and lesbian rights

Source: Roy Eddey and Michael Ferri, "Editorial:
Approaching Lavender," Motive 32/2 (1972): 2. Used by permission of the General
Board of Higher Education and Ministry of The United Methodist Church.

This issue is for you and us, Gay men, knowing that in our strength we are proud and glad to be Gay, to be able to love other men, both emotionally and sexually, and knowing that this is beautiful even though our anti-Lesbian/anti-Faggot society denies our existence by dismissing us as "sick," and "misfits." We know we exist. We are *gay* and we are proud. *Motive*, even with its long history and affiliation with the United Methodist Church, has *come out!*

And gay people have brought it out. Virtually every aspect of both the Lesbian/Feminist and the Gay men's issues have been produced by and for Gay people. Lesbians and gay men have written all the articles and poetry in our respective issues, have created the art work, and done all of the editing and technical layout and production; a lesbian collective has printed both issues. As Gay men, we see this issue as a beginning in our struggle to explain how we feel about gayness. We hope it will reach you at some point in your life and say that you as a Gay man are not alone.

We have tried to bring together in this issue a collection of articles that reflect part of our personal history and future direction as Gay men. We have included come-out experiences, examples of specific society oppression, gay poetry, and finally some analysis and suggestions for the eventual direction of our liberation movement. We have included the come-out experiences because we want to show the commonality of feelings—fear, guilt, aloneness, isolation—that Gay men have had when they begin to react physically and emotionally to other men. We feel that these negative feelings arise not from honest, innate experiences but from a societal value system based on a straight phobia of homosexuality. This fear of homosexuality permeates all American cultural institutions: young people growing up in nuclear families, attending schools and churches, being exposed to medical and therapeutic models. All are inundated with anti-homosexual male-supremacist values. From our efforts to *understand* these experiences, we have begun to see the true source of our oppression. And from that understanding, we can move toward a truly *Gay* analysis that will enable us to successfully fight for our freedom.

*Source: Joan E. Biren, Rita Mae Brown, Charlotte Bunch, and Coletta Reid,
"Editorial: Motive Comes Out!" Motive 32/1 (1972): 1.*

Women are moving. We are moving out of passivity, out of the closets; we are moving toward control of our own lives, and the overthrow of male supremacy. The aim of this magazine is to express this motion and to move you by sharing the ideas, experiences, and feelings of many lesbians. Today, lesbian/feminist politics, are taking shape. Our analysis is crystallizing and we are starting on the path to effective action. Some of the women contributing to this magazine were "happy" heterosexual housewives not long ago. Some were homosexuals in hiding, either from their "friends" or from their own self-hate. Starting from these different places, we have all become lesbian-feminists. Lesbian feminism is the ideology that unites us. It is the way of thinking that enables us to understand our past and chart our future. Only if we understand how and why we have been oppressed can we successfully fight for our freedom.

You are part of that past and in the belief that you will want to shape that future, we have put together a magazine of lesbian-feminist writing, art, and poetry. Some of the work here is reprinted, but most was created especially for this issue.

Motive, a monthly magazine published by the United Methodist Church for over twenty years, is no more. This is its final issue. Throughout *Motive*'s history, radical dissension within limits was tolerated with a few slaps on the wrist, but the church fathers really squirmed when the special issue on women appeared in March-April 1969. In the aftermath of the controversy over the women's issue, the church began to reduce its support of *Motive* and *Motive* decided it could no longer function under the church. *Motive* could not survive without church money, so the staff and editorial boards decided to close up shop, using the remaining resources of the magazine to put out one final *gay* issue. The Furies, a collective of twelve lesbians in Washington, D.C., which included a member of the old *Motive* editorial board, assumed editorial responsibility for the lesbian issue. Within the collective, four of us took major responsibility for this project, but everyone has contributed to it.

We are not professional publishers or editors. We are political lesbians who wanted to create a magazine that would communicate our ideas to you. It was exciting to have the resources of our own magazine. We were determined from start to finish lesbians would do it all. A publication produced with men could not proclaim the strength and promote the independence in the way we hoped to.

In the process of putting this issue together we built bonds with lesbians around the country who sent in articles, graphics, and poetry in response to our requests. In order for lesbians to complete the entire production, we gained many new skills. Lesbians from several cities produced the design and layout. The Sojourner Truth Press in Atlanta printed the whole issue. Where things were needed, we did them ourselves. Lesbians who could never write articles before wrote. Lesbians who never typeset before learned composing. Women who never published a magazine before did it.

We are proud that this issue was put out by women. Gay men have also produced their issue of *Motive*. Although originally scheduled as one gay issue, we made a political decision to do separate women's and men's issues. At this time, we are separatists, who do not work with men, straight or gay, because men are not working to end male supremacy. Sexism oppresses men, especially gay men, by suppressing the "female" in them, and amputating their self-development. But all men still receive concrete benefits, privileges, and power from that system. Male supremacy subordinates women in every way. Ending gay oppression will not automatically end woman oppression. Only a complete destruction of the whole male supremacist system can free women. When men renounce the power and privilege they gain through the domination and subordination of women and join the struggle to end all male supremacy, they will be allies of the strong and independent lesbian-feminist movement we are building. Those men, straight or gay, who cling to male power and privilege continue to oppress us and stand in the way of a women's revolution.

We hope you will read the magazine, pass it on, talk about it with women you know and women you are getting to know; keep in touch with us and join the struggle.

GENERAL CONFERENCE LAMENTS TRAGEDY OF VIETNAM WAR

Source: The United Methodist Church, Book of Resolutions *(Nashville: United Methodist Publishing House, 1972), 19-21.*

In 1968 the General Conference of The United Methodist Church emphasized "that the first allegiance of Christians is to God, under whose judgment of the policies and actions of all nations must pass. The Church as an institution, while existing within particular nations and cultures, must constantly stress the universal values which must find expression in national policies in our day, if mankind is to survive.

"This responsibility of the Church leads us to express a growing concern over the cause and consequences of United States foreign policy, especially in Southeast Asia. The rising toll of casualties among all involved, military and civilian, in the Vietnamese war, and the continued diversion of resources from the heightened crisis in American cities confine and compound the tragic situation." (1968 General Conference Statement on Vietnam)

In 1972 the war in Indochina continues with undiminished intensity, even though there are fewer U.S. casualties, increased troop withdrawal, and lower draft calls.

Nevertheless, in the four years since the General Conference Statement was issued, what was then an urgent priority concern has become an intolerable monstrosity. The United States Armed Forces since then invaded Cambodia, widened the war into Laos, unleased millions of tons of bombs over the entire area (estimate: 6.4 million tons in all of Indochina—Cornell University Study) leaving more than 20 million craters in those lands, defoliating one-eighth of the acreage in South Vietnam, destroying food crops and millions of acres of valuable forest.

While it is difficult to obtain exact facts, it has been estimated that more than 450,000 Asian civilians have been killed, more than 1,000,000 wounded, and up to 10,000,000 people have become refugees. More than 790,000 Asian military personnel have been killed and countless have been wounded.

More than 55,000 American military personnel have been killed, more than 350,000 have been wounded, and large numbers maimed for life, while thousands more have been caught in patterns of boredom, discontent, prostitution, and drug addiction.

The cost of the war has denied resources desperately needed to solve high priority domestic problems and to act responsibly in aiding developing nations.

We who are American delegates to the 1972 General Conference of The United Methodist Church are therefore moved to confess our own continuing complicity in the violence and death. We have sinned against our brothers and sisters, against the earth and our Creator. We have paid our taxes without protest; we have closed our eyes to the horror of our deeds; we have driven families from their homes into endless lines tracking across the pockmarked earth.

We are exposed for caring more for the lives of Americans than Asians, and for blocking from our minds the horror of our continuing bombing.

Further, our own sons and daughters, veterans of Vietnam, others in prison and refugees from their homeland—who first sensed the magnitude of our immorality in Indochina—bear on their bodies and in their souls the wounds and scars of this hell.

God grant that we may say "yes" to this judgment upon us and our nation and that the Indochinese, and we, might be delivered out of this anguish.

We further call upon the leadership of the United States to confess that what we have done in Indochina has been a crime against humanity, and to take the following responsible steps to bring U.S. involvement in this war to a swift conclusion:

1. We call upon the President of the United States to cease immediately all bombing in Indochina.

2. We plead with the governmental leaders of Hanoi and the United States to agree immediately for the release of all prisoners of war at the earliest specified date, no later than Dec. 31, 1972.

3. We call upon the President of the United States to proceed with the withdrawal of all United States military forces from Vietnam, no later than Dec. 31, 1972.

4. We call upon the Congress of the United States to cease providing any funds for the support of military activities in the war in Southeast Asia, no later than Dec. 31, 1972.

5. Cease all efforts to control the results of the political settlement, leaving such political determination in the hands of the Vietnamese.

6. Declare our national intention to pay for reparations to victims of the war under United Nations auspices.

7. This resolution and the Bishops' Call for Peace shall be taken directly to Washington, D.C. by a committee of bishops, and every effort be made to present it directly to President Nixon.

SEMINARY PROFESSOR JAMES WHITE INTRODUCES REVISED RITE FOR HOLY COMMUNION

Source: James F. White, "The Sacrament of the Lord's Supper: The New Alternate Rite," Christian Advocate 16/16 (14 September 1972): 13-14.

For the second time in eight years, the Commission on Worship of The United Methodist Church has published a new communion service for use throughout the church. Why has a new service appeared so soon, especially since some congregations have barely become acquainted with the 1964 service in the *Book of Worship* and *The Methodist Hymnal*?

It is because the eight years between the 1964 and the 1972 General Conferences span some of the most rapid changes in Christian worship since the Reformation in the 1500s. The most obvious changes, this time, have been in the Roman Catholic Church. The middle ages in Catholic worship lasted until December, 1963 when the *Constitution on the Sacred Liturgy* was promulgated, almost at the exact time that the final text of our 1964 *Book of Worship* was finished.

Changes in Catholic worship have given tremendous impetus to change in Protestant worship patterns. Many pastors have taken their youth groups to mass, and the young people have come back wondering out loud why the Catholics should be having all the fun.

More important forces, though, resulted from the sociological upheavals in American society in the 1960s. We saw a gradual acceptance of cultural pluralism with a toleration of parallel moralities, generation gaps, and contrasting life-styles. This made it seem slightly absurd that religious worship should be an exception to the rest of life. Why should it remain solely in the language, mentalities, and surroundings that seemed most natural to the minority in our country (though not our churches) which was over 30, white, and well-educated?

Our Commission on Worship responded to this new situation by appointing a Committee on Alternate Rituals, chaired by Professor H. Grady Hardin of Perkins School of Theology. The first effort of this committee was presented to the church with the publication in April, 1972 of *The Sacrament of the Lord's Supper: An Alternate Text, 1972.* . . . The 1972 General Conference opened with this service.

It should be clear that the new alternate rite *does not replace* that in the present

Hymnal. It is proposed as an alternate to it and as a guide to those who are experimenting with the Lord's Supper. In this latter sense, it can serve as a model, presenting the theological and liturgical essentials of the sacrament. Used in this way, the service should help induce more responsible experimentation rather than inhibit it.

From the start the committee was determined that this rite, in company with those other denominations have produced in recent years, should be in contemporary English. But determining what that was was far from simple. Eventually a rather middle-of-the-road language style was adopted.

On the other hand the new rite purposefully avoids the balanced cadences and parallelisms of Cranmerian prose. Behind such poetic prose lies a concept of an orderly universe which modern man does not share. Cranmer wrote only a century and a half after Chaucer and more than four centuries distant from our day. His prose was only slightly ahead of its time (if at all) and avoided such colloquialisms as the "-e(s)" endings for third person singular verbs which have since become standard. If anyone calls our language "undistinguished," we will take it as a compliment (just as Cranmer might have) and anyone calling it "poetic" will offend us.

Perhaps as important to modern man as the actual language in a printed service is the appearance of the page. Graphic art gives a first impression and perhaps a more lasting one even than the printed language. In this case, we have made limited progress: the rubrics appear in red, probably for the first time in an official liturgical publication for United Methodists, and the texts set in "sense" lines mark a major improvement.

The committee took seriously the United Methodist commitment to ecumenism. This appears most obviously in the use of texts produced by the International Consultation on English Texts (ICET). The "Holy, holy, holy Lord" is the ICET text and the same is true of "Lift up your hearts" and the Lord's Prayer (with some changes). These texts were produced by an international body of Catholic and Protestant scholars and are in use throughout the English-speaking world. One good feature of this is that musical settings produced by different churches, such as those commissioned by the InterLutheran Commission on Worship, may be used by all churches.

But the ecumenical theme runs much deeper than the identity of key portions. From 1784 to 1964, Methodist communion services were simply revisions within the basic pattern that the Anglican prayer books had developed from 1549 to 1662. Though Cranmer's genius is unquestioned, the Anglican tradition is only one portion of Christendom.

Now at last we have broken the habit of simply revising within the Anglican-Methodist pattern and opted for one that reflects the breadth of modern Christianity and the depth of classical practice. Our sources range from the third-century liturgy of Hippolytus to the new Presbyterian, Episcopal, United Church of Canada, and Roman Catholic services of the 1970s.

The most important single accomplishment of the new alternate rite is its preference for the emerging ecumenical consensus as to the essentials of the Lord's

Supper rather than the tradition of a single denomination. It is hard to believe that any future United Methodist services will give up the riches of the whole Christian tradition to return to those of a single segment of it. Our newest service, in a real sense, is also our oldest. It recovers elements of the classical Christian tradition of giving thanks that were obscured in the Middle Ages or became victims of controversy during the Reformation.

A number of suggestions as to the use of the service appear in the sheet of rubrics intended for the minister's use. The committee decided to restrict the rubrics printed in the service to an absolute minimum in order not to confuse people and to permit maximum flexibility. Even indications of when to stand and when to sit are largely missing and may cause some awkwardness. But this decision was consistent with the committee's insistence that congregations will need to adapt the service to their own circumstances.

The minister and worship committee will need to bring more creativity and imagination to all aspects of the service than previously. For example, service music was printed in the *Hymnal*, but it is left to the discretion of each congregation in the new rite. There are places for at least five hymns, if desired, plus those sung while the people receive communion. Appropriate communion hymns are suggested from the *Hymnal*. (The practice of having people sing while waiting to receive communion seems preferable to the table dismissals that have lengthened the service so much and done more than any single item to make communion Sunday unpopular in Methodism.) For the closing hymn, the use of a variety of doxological stanzas is encouraged.

In addition to music, the new rite gives opportunity to accent the sign value of various communal acts. Many congregations will need to have the meaning of "the peace" explained to them, and Matthew 5:23-24 is not a bad place to start. The offering of the bread and wine from and by the congregation or the breaking of the loaf of bread are sign-acts that we have neglected in the past but which may communicate well to a generation accustomed to television.

Other word options abound. The number of lessons and the psalms or musical elements between them will depend on the time and place. Various creeds, including the new ICET texts of the Apostles' or the Nicene creeds, may be used. Three quite different approaches to the prayers for others are suggested: spontaneous prayers from the congregation, extempore prayer by the minister, or from the text provided. The form of the peace and the act of offering are left open for a variety of options.

The great prayer of thanksgiving follows the classic Christian pattern of giving thanks yet allows variety. The prayer follows the pattern of anaphoras of the great Eastern liturgies, emphasizing the works of the Old Covenant before the great Old Testament acclamations of the *Sanctus* (Isa. 6:3) and *Benedictus* (Ps. 118:26). However on special occasions proper prefaces can be substituted for the words indented. On great festivals of the Christian year, weddings, and ordinations, appropriate thanks may be given.

The recital of works of the New Covenant commences after the *Benedictus* and points much more in an eschatological direction than we have been accustomed. The second acclamation of the people can also vary. The prayer continues with *anamnesis*, oblation, and the invocation of the Holy Spirit. The concluding doxology (and many other parts of the great prayer) comes from our oldest communion liturgy, the third-century rite of Hippolytus.

No rubric specifies how the bread and wine are given to the congregation. The method best suited to the particular people present will have to be determined in every case. The sacrament concludes with a rather strong indication of the continuity of worship into service.

The new alternate rite is intended to be used as an entire service, not as an appendage to a preaching service. Some pastors have begun using it when communion is not celebrated, moving from the offertory to a final hymn and benediction.

The committee hopes that the alternate rite will be helpful in increasing congregational participation. Considerable teaching will be necessary before some possibilities, such as spontaneous prayers, become understood and appreciated. And the theology of the rite, perhaps the most important and the most neglected part of any communion service, will certainly need to be taught. In some congregations this might take the form of a demonstration service in which the place of a sermon is taken by brief words of explanation and interpretation of the service.

Certainly the new alternate rite will demand more work on the part of the minister and congregation, but the Committee on Alternate Rituals hopes that it will serve our churches well in this time of liturgical ferment and change.

THELMA STEVENS CHRONICLES FORMATION OF THE UNITED METHODIST WOMEN'S CAUCUS

Source: Thelma Stevens, "Old Roots and New Flowering for UM Women's Caucus," Christian Advocate 16/17 (28 September 1972): 7-8. Excerpts.

The year 1972 finds a great many women . . . tired of waiting to be full, equal, and responsible participants in the total life of the church. Small tokens and symbols of power are not enough in the Church of Jesus Christ! Of course the United Methodist Women's Caucus had to be born and named. Its roots are a century old, but oppression, visible and invisible, intentional and unintentional, has dwarfed both tree and branches. The objectives today are much the same but clothed in new faith and hope in a day when justice and personhood are the overarching hope of peoples everywhere, including the majority group—women.

The majority of the women who met initially in 1971 in Evanston, Ill., to caucus together as United Methodist women were young (some under 30). But there were others too—some of whom were a bit tattered after decades of effort, sometimes fruitful but too often fruitless. But hope ran high among those assembled; it was a coming together for mutual support and sharing concerns.

In the words of one of the caucus members, scarcely out of her teens, a small measure of concern and motivation comes clear:

"It is significant to me that enough women were motivated to group around the issue of their own relationship to the church—our church! In our first meeting that weekend in 1971 following Thanksgiving, we shared our experiences as women within the church. Our shared frustrations and anticipations became the basis on which we began to build our group. Our style was flexible, open, ready to accept the emerging agenda! We shared leadership tasks and responsibilities. We set our priorities as two-fold: (1) to influence legislative policy at General Conference in '72 and (2) to seek to "humanize" the structures and process of decision-making in our church.

"When our second meeting convened in March, 1972, in Nashville, we were ready to make specific our priorities in a task-oriented setting with a more broadly representative working group which included blacks, Hispanic-Americans, and others."

At this Nashville meeting, as the group looked toward the task at General Conference, the majority felt that a coordinator and steering committee were essential if plans and strategies were to be effective in realizing objectives. Carleen Waller of Nashville, an experienced and effective political strategist and committed churchwoman, was asked to guide the caucus through the General Conference.

Priorities that developed in Nashville evolved around two primary points. The first concern was for petitions to General Conference. These petitions were concerned with such matters as:

1) a call for new mandates to recruit women for the ministry;

2) new opportunities in the ministry including assignments of ordained persons to ministries that may be of a part-time nature;

3) a demand for fair and equal opportunity for ethnic minorities and women in the church;

4) a call for courses in seminaries that take account of historical roles of women and their contribution to the development of Christian theology;

5) a call for the creation by annual conferences of task forces to study, promote, and implement plans for specialized ministries;

6) a call for more adequate scholarship funds for ethnic minorities in seminaries with a recruitment goal of 25 percent from ethnic groups by 1976;

7) a full concurrence with the Planned Parenthood principles and programs as embodied in the petition sent by the Women's Division to General Conference.

The second and major priority was a proposal to General Conference for the establishment of a Commission on the Status and Role of Women in the total life of the church. The women envisioned this commission having as its primary mandate the establishment of guidelines for the implementation of the goals and objectives set forth by the Study Commission on Women.

As the caucus came into being and developed its plans and strategies, the base of its greatest support was and continues to be lodged in the Women's Division of the Board of Mission. Both division members and staff were concerned participants from the beginning and fully supportive of the caucus plans.

It is important to remember that it was the Women's Division in 1968 that called for a study commission whose report is referred to above. Any "competition" between the Women's Division and the caucus was and is a pure figment of the imagination of "wishful blockers" of women's empowerment in the life of The United Methodist Church.

Any assessment of the General Conference's response to the requests of the caucus must of necessity be made through "the eyes of the beholder" and rooted in the hopes and concerns of the "accessor." Within these fallible limitations, therefore, the following points seems to be a fair judgment.

First there was evident both a subtle and overt antagonism toward the caucus and its agenda even among a few of the women delegates. Such antagonism represented in many instances a failure to understand history as well as a lack of knowledge of what a real caucus is. Bishop Roy Nichols has provided a valid helpful interpretation of what a caucus should be and do.

"A caucus is a legitimate expression and we have always had them in The United Methodist Church. A brother was disturbed the other day and berating the fact that we had caucus groups. We've always had them! The function of a caucus is to crystallize its judgments, to promote the influence of its thinking; if it wins the support of the body it seeks to influence, then it's an effective caucus."

Second, there seemed to be a well-planned strategy to limit real discussion of the purpose of the Commission on Women by confusing the conference with parliamentary restrictions along with the unclear presentation by the chairmen of the two responsible committees. The reports for the conference from the two committees were basically different in three major aspects, yet the two chairmen represented the reports as basically the same! This seemed a strange judgment from men of such great competence.

Women who sought to get the floor to clarify the confusion were unable to do so. The results left many both inside and outside the delegated body disturbed. One distinguished woman delegate said later: "Do you know what sustained me? I kept thinking, if they don't let me speak and if they go back to other things, I'm going to organize a revolt and ask every woman in General Conference to march out."

Third, in general, despite planned restrictions, some of which were essential with time pressures, more women spoke out on the conference floor than in any General Conference held during the past 32 years. Women chaired three of the legislative committees.

Fourth, because of the limited sphere of operation set by the Women's Caucus, it did not surface at most places where it had vital concern. It was felt that the real priority was an adequate mandate for a Commission on Women. Even so the issues of abortion, homosexuality, funding minority development programs, black colleges, the Viet Nam War, South Africa, amnesty, and many other deep concerns were of great importance to the caucus group.

The loosely structured caucus has both long-range and immediate tasks before it. At times as priorities are set, the caucus may need more carefully structured plans of operation for their successful achievement. This should never be a liability when the democratic process is safe-guarded. The extent to which the future task is accomplished will depend upon the unity of purpose and the commitment of caucus participants, as well as the understanding of the task and the strategies needed for achievement.

Since Atlanta we have a Commission on [the Status and Role of] Women authorized within the official structure of the church itself to serve as an "advocate" for full equality of women in the total church. Our women's caucus, as a caucus, has no "official" relationship to the commission, even though it was in large measure the result of caucus effort.

The caucus may need to keep clear certain perspectives as it seeks to make its relevant witness: (1) Some of the most prophetic ideas and plans for the renewal of the church over the years have come from outside the official structures. Their effectiveness has depended upon the extent to which the official structures *heard* the voices! (2) The validity and power of the new and relevant factors of change must be felt within the institutional life of the church if the church is to move forward and understand its task. This means a caucus voice must be everlastingly at it—and unafraid. (3) The church is forever in need of voices from somewhere that demand a worthy witness.

The United Methodist Women's Caucus is only one of many caucuses within the church's life concerned to effect change and achieve justice, but the goals of the Women's Caucus will be more difficult to realize because they have roots in biblical history, church history, secular history—not just for 400 years but for thousands of years. The Women's Caucus includes among its participants the women from various ethnic minorities who face "double jeopardy" in surmounting the wall of discrimination. The newly authorized commission will have this issue in its drawer of top priorities.

The time is ripe for women to emerge as fully empowered human beings in The United Methodist Church, responsible participants in its total life. Such empowerment demands a commitment to seek those qualities of Christian life that will save us all from the bigotry and self-centered motivation that hampers our Christian witness—and keeps the church from being God's people responding worthily in his name.

BLACK WOMEN IN TRIPLE JEOPARDY, ASSERTS THERESSA HOOVER

Source: Theressa Hoover, "Black Women and the Churches: Triple Jeopardy,"
Response 5/5 (May 1973): 17-21.

To be woman, black and active in religious institutions in the American scene is to labor under triple jeopardy. There is little or no mention of black women in accounts of any black church or black theology. In the *Ebony* special issue on "The Negro Woman" (August 1960) she is treated in every way except in the area of religion. Two 1972 books give a bit more dimension to the strength and courage of black women now and in the past. They are: *The Making of Black Revolutionaries*, by James Forman, and *Black Women in White America*, by Gerda Lerner.

Any thinking person cannot help but wonder why so little has been written, since women are by far the largest supporting groups in our religious institutions, and in the black church, are the very backbone. One might conclude that where something is written about women in general in religious institutions, black women are included. This, too, is not a true picture for even in predominantly white denominations, the black woman is in black local congregations.

During the period 1948 to 1958 I traveled 11 months out of each year, in and out of every major United States city, in countless small towns, and on the back roads. Needless to say hospitality for me in those days was always arranged for in the home of some black Methodist family. During those 10 years of travel I discovered that black women were truly the glue that held the churches together. The women worked, yet found time to be the Sunday school teachers, sing in the choir, and support the church's program in every way. They were domestics of the community or teachers in black schools.

In most of these communities the blacks were either Methodist or Baptist, or "someone had been tampering with their religion." Methodists were a mixture. Some belonged to a primarily white denomination even though they found local expression in black congregations. Others belonged to one of the three primarily black Methodist denominations—African Methodist Episcopal, African Methodist Episcopal Zion, or Christian Methodist Episcopal. All, however, were related to a connectional system. The Baptists tended to belong to a fellowship of Baptists, but each local church was autonomous. In both Baptist and Methodist churches the women were the "backbone," the "glue." They were present at the mid-week prayer services, the Monday afternoon women's missionary meeting, and the Sunday morning, afternoon and evening preaching services. There has been no great distinction between men and women holding office or sharing in decision-making in local black churches.

In the 1950's women in the various Methodist groups began to discover one another. While there had been a sharing of programs and other resources in many local communities, there had been no real coming together nationally. Women of the basically white Methodist Church had a joint committee with women of the basically black Christian Methodist Episcopal Church. Coming together in the World Federation of Methodist Women, they extended the fellowship to include women of the African Methodist Episcopal and the African Methodist Episcopal Zion churches.

Each of the four Methodist women's groups has a history of mission work—in this country and overseas. They have supported their own programs even as they aided the mission outreach of the denomination of which they were a part. The regular mission channels of the denominations were controlled by the clergy to the point of women's deliberate exclusion. To give expression to women's felt needs the women's missionary society was organized as a parallel or auxiliary group. That felt need, and that exclusion from main church channels, still exists. Today these groups are strong numerically and financially.

Relationship with Other Church Women

In the late 1960's the religious institutions in America toward which the Black Manifesto was directed were in disarray. Once legally achieved, integration was found wanting in quality and in practice. For the liberal white integrationists, the apparent move toward separatism, signaled by the Black Power movement and culminating in the Manifesto of 1969, was mindblowing to say the least. To some, separatism represented a threat or a cop-out.

Not long after the Black Manifesto was made public, I was called by the executive director of Church Women United to a conference to discuss what impact this move would have on black women in that organization. My counsel to her then, later borne out, was that it would produce no "break-off" though it might well call forth some soul-searching as to the seriousness with which women honor our differences and pool our resources and resourcefulness on behalf of all.

Nevertheless, to test my counsel, Church Women United called a small consultation of black church women in September 1969 at Wainwright House, Rye, N.Y. to consider their role and expectations in the aftermath of the Black Manifesto. The group concluded that church women—black and white—must function under the limitations of religious thought and practice. There was no purpose to be served by further splintering ourselves along the lines of race.

We talked about the role women can play in the total life of the Church, about areas the Church has not yet given evidence of serving, about the gap between mainline black church women and their younger black sisters. Most of us represented the former category. We were the ones who attended the colleges set up by the churches to educate the recently freed slaves and had gone on to become teachers in them or staff in their national headquarters. We had little experience with overt assignment of women to second-class posts in churches, largely because we were so vitally needed if churches were even to exist. We were the ones who had been taught and had accepted a role on behalf of "our people" even if it meant foregoing a personal life exemplified in husband and children. We were the ones who, if married at all, had married "beneath us"—meaning that we had married men with less education who did manual labor. (Note the influence of white society's value system.) This was not true for the young black woman of the late 1960's.

These are some remarks heard at that weekend consultation:

"The young blacks' mistake is in not making enough of their American experience. We will never be Africans. In slavery only the strong and those with a will to live survived—those with spiritual resiliency."

"Black people once thought education was the answer; they found it wasn't. Now they think economics is the answer; we'll find it won't be either. We have to find something else—we have to deal with the attitude of people on the top in order to solve this. As church women and as black women, how can we do this?"

"To accomplish a specific goal, an organized minority can bring about change. It is not necessary to have great numbers."

"Women must be accepted as persons. The black man wants to assert today his so-called masculinity, but it is really *personhood*—for both sexes."

"So far as young women versus men are concerned, let the men have their power and status; we organize the women's caucus; when the men are ready for our help, they will have to bargain for it."

Ethnic Caucuses in White Churches

Ethnic caucuses in white denominations sprang up in the aftermath of the civil rights struggle. The soil had been prepared for their advent. It took an act of national significance to release the simmering disenchantment of minority groups with their place in white denominations. What is interesting is the role and status of women within the ethnic caucuses.

Not unlike the role of women in the civil rights struggle of the 60's, women in the caucuses have been assigned (and have accepted) a supportive role. Most of the decision makers have been men, primarily clergymen.

It might help to look closely at the "life and growth of caucuses" in a major, mainline denomination whose membership is a replica of the nation at large. Let's take The United Methodist Church (which has 54 percent women members) as a case study.

1. At the 1966 Special Session of General Conference of The Methodist Church, with the Evangelical United Brethren Conference in session across the hall, there

was only one visible caucus, Methodists for Church Renewal. This caucus cut across race and sex lines, though the dominant group consisted of white male clergy.

2. At the regular Methodist General Conference in 1968 (with the EUB Church holding a simultaneous Special Session), a second caucus was present, Black Methodists for Church Renewal (BMCR). At this session the union of the two denominations was consummated and, with it, the official end of the Methodist all-Negro Central Jurisdiction.

In February 1968, just two months prior to General Conference, over 200 black Methodists had gathered in Cincinnati, Ohio. They came from the far west and east where structural segregation included only the local church; from the middle west (Illinois to Colorado, Missouri to Kentucky) where conferences had already been merged with their white counterparts; and from the southwest and southeast where no noticeable changes was in the offing. While it was church renewal that brought them together, it was their blackness which made the gathering imperative.

Black clergymen were by far the majority of those attending, but a real effort was made to get lay men and women. Both were there. Strategically, many of them would be voting delegates in the upcoming General Conference. The national board of directors elected before the conference closed totaled 44, with nine women, a number not commensurate with black women's presence or support in black churches—but done without recourse to pressure by women.

One directive to the board of directors says something about the group's awareness of the black woman. They were directed to "employ an assistant director which shall be a woman, *if* the executive director is a man." There was not the assumption which is so often true, that the director *would be* a man. Instead it was an assurance that the leadership of the staff would reflect the talents of both male and female.

Black women and men, lay and clergy, were visible at the luncheons, after-hours caucuses and the "on-floor" debate at the General Conference. As a result our denomination created and funded a Commission on Religion and Race. When the Commission was organized and staffed, however, there were no guarantees for participation of women, and the Commission cannot be applauded for their involvement. In fact, it is fair to say that women have been generally disregarded in its life and work. So the struggle must go on.

3. At the 1970 Special General Conference, still another caucus, youthful United Methodists [National Youth Ministry Organization (NYMO)], secured the right to self-determination.

4. At the 1972 General Conference the youth caucus was the only caucus that included women in the warp and woof of its proceedings and decision-making. BMCR, barely visible and still masculine and clergy, saw the rise of a women's caucus in its own ranks before it got the message that "coalition around common interests" was not only desirable but imperative.

The newest caucus—the women's caucus—was a great new fact. Black women were among its members and took active roles. Representatives of the BMCR women's caucus were a bridge so that BMCR, the Women's Caucus, and the Youth-Young Adult Caucus formed a working coalition to achieve common goals. As a

women not represented in # 's that reflect black reality

result a Commission on the Status and Role of Women was created and funded though not to the desired degree. The Commission has organized with a black woman as its chairperson. The effort brought together still another interesting phenomenon—the joint effort of young, unorganized women with the older, organized women's group in the denomination.

At the 1969 Assembly of the National Council of Churches, it was noted that "In 1950 when the NCC was organized only five out of 82 members of the General Board were women (6 percent). Twenty-four churches out of 29 (82 percent) had no women in their delegation. Nineteen years later (1969), 11 out of approximately 200 members of the General Board are women (9.5 percent). Out of a total of 786 official delegates to the General Assembly, 95 are women (12 percent). There are still 13 of the 33 member denominations which have no women in their delegations."

The present General Board of the NCC has about seven black women, two from black denominations and five from predominantly white churches.

Judith Hole and Ellen Levine in *Rebirth of Feminism* (Quadrangle Books, New York City, 1971) include a chapter on The Church. They say: "Feminist activities within the Christian community most often fall into three categories: (1) challenging the theological view of women; (2) challenging the religious laws and/or customs which bar women from ordinations; (3) demanding that the professional status and salaries of women in the church be upgraded."

These categories may apply to the total feminist movement in the churches, but do not yet reflect the view of many black women. First, the economic necessity of the black woman's efforts on behalf of the church has not pressured her to the point of accepting the prevailing theological view of women. When she gets a little release from other pressures, she will look beyond her local church and realize that such theological views and practices are operative both in her exclusion from doctrinal decision-making and in her absence from national representation.

Second, in the predominantly black churches women are not excluded from ordination by law, though they may be in practice. Third, most of the black denominations are not financially capable of maintaining even a minimal professional staff (outside the clerical hierarchy). Where there is staff, women already know the necessity of insisting on comparable salaries.

Strengthened by Faith

The black church woman must come to the point of challenging both her sisters in other denominations and the clergy-male hierarchy in her own. In many ways she has been the most oppressed and the least vocal. She has given the most, and in my judgment, gotten the least. She has shown tremendous faithfulness to the spirit of her church. Her foresight, ingenuity, and "stick-to-it-ive-ness" have kept many black churches open, many black preachers fed, many parsonages livable.

She has borne her children in less that desirable conditions, managed her household often in the absence of a husband. She has gathered unto herself the children of the community . . . she has washed them, combed their hair, fed them and told them Bible stories . . . in short, she has been their missionary, their substitute mother, their teacher. Many leaders of the present-day black church owe their commitment to the early influence of just such a black woman.

In James Forman's book, referred to earlier, there is a chapter on "Strong Black Women." Forman speaks of the heart that women bring to the black church, indeed to the entire religious community, in references to women in the Albany, Ga. protest of the 1960's:

"The strength of the women overwhelmed me. Here they were in jail, but their spirits seemed to rise each minute. They were yelling at the jailer, cursing, singing, ready to fight if someone came to their cell to mistreat them. Images of other strong black women resisting slavery and servitude flooded my mind. I thought of Georgia Mae Turner and Lucretia Collins and the young girls in the cell block next to me now as the modern-day Harriet Tubmans, Sojourner Truths, and all those proud black women who did not allow slavery to break their spirits. . . . As I thought about the women protesting their arrest, I knew that the black liberation movement would escalate, for too many young people were involved. Most of the women in the cells were very young, one of them only 14."

With such a heritage of strength and faith, black women in the churches today must continue strong in character and in faith. They must reach other sisters and brothers with a sense of the commonality of their struggles on behalf of black people and, ultimately, all humanity. They must continue to work within the "walls" of the church, challenging theological pacesetters and church bureaucrats; they also must continue to push outward the church "walls" so it may truly serve the black community. They must be ever aware of their infinite worth, their godliness in the midst of creatureliness, and their having been freed from the triple barriers of *race*, *sex* and *church* into a community of believers.

Bishop Muzorewa Cites Missionary Mistakes Made in Africa

Source: Abel Muzorewa, "Bishop Muzorewa Cites Missionary 'Mistakes' Made in Africa by West," United Methodist Reporter (7 February 1975): 1.

Those from other lands who first brought the Gospel to this continent genuinely and sincerely believed that Jesus Christ should be known to Africans. Though they made blunders in their effort, they did preach about Christ, build schools and clinics, began carpentry and agricultural programs so that people could truly have an abundant life. Over 90 percent of the national leaders in Africa south of the Sahara owe a great debt to the church for their education and training. . . .

1) Missionaries regarded many African customs as evil and forbade their use. Innocent tribal dances, the use of instruments like drums, and time-honored marriage and funeral customs were banned.

2) Missionaries believed Africans did not know anything about God. Yet our fathers worshipped God who was known to them by different names. . . . Admittedly, the missionary's main contribution to our religious vocabulary was the name of Jesus Christ.

3) A devastating and far-reaching blunder was that missionaries tended to make the newly converted into their own image. One example was having converts at Baptism adopt foreign names as opposed to African names, which have a definite meaning.

4) The fourth mistake was the practice of paternalism, which was usually mistaken for racism by many people. I do not believe that missionaries who were brought up in democratic countries were that racialistic, but I believe they were paternalistic. "Father knows best" was their problem. Even to this day the most retarding factor against the growth of the church is this very attitude.

Today we see people who are very peculiar in that they do things which are neither truly European nor African, hence we have Christians who worship, preach, conduct services and sing in European style. Big, well organized choirs as well as small ones will sing great English songs to congregations that are 95 percent Shona and Ndebele. Even those who understand English many times cannot understand what the choir is singing about. . . .

African Christians in many instances behave like adolescents rather than standing on their own feet. And even Africans who are heads of their denominations are often still subject to direction from the Mother Church in Europe or America. Such leaders find themselves with back-seat drivers who are trying to keep a hand on the wheel.

Along with accepting the Gospel, we [African Christians] have often adopted some of the weaknesses of the western Church, as the practice of separating life into compartments of religion, economics, politics. Thus the church is not part and parcel of life. Further, Christian fellowship in Africa, as it is elsewhere, is too narrowly limited to one's own denomination, keeping us still separated at the Table of Our Lord who prayed that we might be one.

THOMAS ROUGHFACE SPEAKS FOR NATIVE AMERICANS AT GENERAL CONFERENCE

Source: "Proceedings of the General Conference of The United Methodist Church,"
Daily Christian Advocate (8 May 1976): 957-58. Excerpts.

Friday Evening Session, May 7, 1976
Bishop Dwight E. Loder, presiding

G. Ross Freeman (clergy delegate, South Georgia Conference): Thank you very much, Bishop Loder. I refer you now to page 477, Calendar Item 527. This is the recommendation for a quadrennial study committee on Native-American Ministries. We had 100 percent of those voting in favor of this. It calls for the creation of a Quadrennial Study Committee with about 21 voting members. It calls for a staff to be composed of three Native Americans. It calls for the committee to report its recommendations to the General Conference in 1980. It will be under the guidance of and direction of the GCOM and the committee moves concurrence.

Bishop Loder: What was the vote [in the Legislative Committee on Council on Ministries], please?

Freeman: The vote was 69 for; none against; 8 abstaining.

. . . .

Bishop Loder: All right, ready to vote? As many as will approve, yes—over here to the right. Question? Microphone 4.

Reta Barto (lay delegate, Eastern Pennsylvania Conference): Tom Roughface told us that a subcommittee—meeting the other day—[said] that they [Native Americans] were sick and tired of study. May I ask who initiated this study?

Freeman: I believe that it came from them. I'm not going to—

Bishop Loder: All right, are you ready to vote? Brother Roughface—the gentleman here to my left. Microphone 1.

Thomas Roughface, Sr. (non-voting clergy delegate, Oklahoma Indian Missionary Conference): Mr. Chairman, obviously I am speaking for the Native American Studies Commission for the quadrennium. Throughout our history we have been one of the most studied species. At one time even considered an endangered species. Volumes have been written about us. Many, many conclusions drawn in our regard.

Now, we call upon General Conference to give us the right to set up the machinery by which we will be able to effectively conduct our own study. We believe we have the structure and the dynamic leadership within the ranks of Native Americans to do just such a study, and deal with the real issues now confronting Native Americans. And I want to say to General Conference, in 1966 I attended a first what was labeled a Consultation on Indian Work held at Riverside Drive, New York City. Then the Board of Missions, representatives of all Indian work of the former Methodist Church were invited and present. There were many in attendance. However, I was the only Native American. For obvious reasons I felt as though I was the Lone Ranger. (Laughter and prolonged applause)

That was 10 years ago. Time and determination has made a big difference. Native Americans are now visible and attempting to find their place in our Church community, and have demonstrated they are quite capable of giving leadership in our crucial times. I appeal to your support for our study committee. Thank you. (Applause)

Hispanic Women Want No Melting Pot

Source: Celsa Garrastegui, *"No Melting Pot Wanted by Hispanic Women,"* Response 10/2 (February 1978): 21-23, 36.

1978

The Melting Pot Myth

The Hispanic woman in the Church and in society suffers a triple oppression: that of being a woman, that of being Hispanic and that of being a woman within the Hispanic group.

Within the social context of the United States, the entire Hispanic group—men and women—are an example of one pluralism inside another. We are a diverse, heterogeneous group composed of people who have in common, first a language, Spanish, then a long history of oppression and violation of our human rights inside this country.

Though the idea of the melting pot still permeates the thought of a society that does not want to hear the claims of its ethnic minorities, the persistent struggles of the blacks, Chicanos, Native Americans and others demonstrate that the concept is only a myth in the imagination of the Anglo majority. Part of the dictionary definition of the word *melt* is "to be changed from a solid to a liquid state, usually by heat, to disappear by being dispersed of dissipated, as clouds to vanish, to blend, to lose distinct form." But the history of the ethnic minority groups could well be summed up as the survival—not the disappearance—of the right *to be* and to be different.

The situation of Hispanic women cannot be understood apart from this context. Because they belong to an oppressed minority and participate in its struggle for identity and justice, they know first hand what it means not to be counted. Besides struggling with the powerlessness of all women of this country in the total system, they are discriminated against because of being Hispanic and they are oppressed also by the Hispanic male.

In Puerto Rico, whenever a baby girl is born, the father is teased as having a *chancleta*—a slipper. She is raised to be dependent and to let the men make the important decisions. Hispanic culture generally has tended to place women in a

Hispanic male domination over women [handwritten margin note]

non-affirmative, non-participative role. The female image has been idealized and patterned after the Virgin Mary's suffering and sacrifice, as presented by the traditional [Catholic] Church. Women are expected to step aside in order to let the men be active in the representation of the group. Although women participate in the struggle for the liberation of the whole group, and work as hard as men whenever they are able to be in the labor force, it is the men who get the glory, and a woman is expected to rejoice by herself in silence.

Hispanic women in the Church continue the same passive roles: being active in the women's group, preparing food for church activities, washing communion glasses. The Hispanic woman is a sustainer of the work, a follower. There is more awareness now of the problems of women, but little progress has been made toward acquiring the means for developing their potentialities.

Church Reflects Society

The United Methodist Church is a reflection of our society at large. Its theology and structure come entirely out of the experience of its Anglo constituency, the majority culture of the United States. The special character of the Hispanic group, like those of other minority groups, tends to get lost because it has to function in an organization created by the dominant Anglo culture. The organization, so much larger than the individual groups, has already formed its patterns and the prerequisite for participation is that the minority group conform to them.

Despite this undeniable truth, there is a growing emphasis on action by the different ethnic minority groups within the United Methodist Church. During the last quadrennium several minority consultations have taken place. Documents were published emphasizing the presence of the ethnic minorities and demanding that their needs be filled out of their own experience. Minorities asked that they participate on the basis of equality, that they stop being used as objects of mission and that their identity be respected. The time is gone when the Anglo majority can think, judge and interpret for ethnic minorities.

While it is not true to say that nothing has been accomplished, there is still a long way to go, for the church does not escape the previously mentioned societal forces in which it exists and operates.

Concerns Within the Church

When we come to the situation of Hispanic women, specifically, in the United Methodist Church structure, there are even more glaring omissions. There is a general lack of participation of Hispanic women at local, district, conference and national levels. Even though there has been an effort to employ more Hispanics on our national churchboards and agencies, you can still count the number of persons working in executive positions on the fingers of one hand. The same can be said for directors of the boards. If you look at the organizational charts of the general agencies of the United Methodist Church, you will find the names of only five

Hispanic women directors, four of them in the Board of Global Ministries and one in the Commission on Religion and Race.

There are some special concerns and needs that Hispanic women have within our church. Let us look at some of them.

We want the right to maintain our cultural heritage: language, customs, ways of doing things. Here the language issue is important. Spanish is not going to disappear. It was spoken before the pilgrims came to New England. There are around fifteen million Spanish-speaking persons today in the United States. Why close our eyes to a reality that is part of the country and of the church? As a part of this need we must have materials in Spanish at all levels, not only translations but resources written by Hispanics out of the Hispanic experience.

Through the United Methodist Women Spanish Program Resources Book, we are beginning to cultivate some of the talents Hispanic women have. We should be able to have other things published as well.

The right to be involved in policy making at all levels, and to be counted as equals is greatly desired.

We need more educational opportunities. We must develop grass roots education out of the Hispanic experience, including opportunities for training and development at local, conference and national levels. We need continuing education on women's issues not only for women, but also for the whole church. We need more opportunities in higher education.

Hispanic women need to be organized at a national level. This will help break the isolation that we experience. Seminars could be fostered to deal with problems and serve as a link among all Hispanic women in the church. We need a publication in Spanish, edited by Hispanic women, perhaps a circular. It would communicate, for example, what women in California are doing, so that women in New York would know. There would be a sharing of problems, opportunities and educational issues. It would help provide mutual support.

We have a need to share with other ethnic groups to foster a better knowledge of one another in equality. We need to cooperate with non-United Methodist groups. We need communication with women in Latin America and the Caribbean through seminars, working with materials produced in these regions. We need to understand better the economic and political policies of the United States toward them as well as their own situations.

We need a study of the history of Hispanic women in the United States, their contribution, struggles, their historical presence inside the church and society. We need to promote a better understanding of Hispanic groups in the United Methodist Church. Their uniqueness as Hispanics must be recognized and understood.

Quadrennial Priority Fallacy

In 1976 the General Conference responded to the claims of the ethnic minority churches by establishing a quadrennial priority in order to strengthen them. This is a very important step toward reconciliation, but the way it has been worked out continues these churches in the role of being objects of mission and not as being part of the national church. When you are an object you are something that is being watched from outside, and you have the feeling of being tested. This continues to nurture the "good old paternalistic feeling" in the church. With much concern people ask what will happen after 1980. It is naive to think that the needs and problems will disappear.

Since the church is just an organization inside the entire cultural, political and economic system of the United States, and the evils alive in our society, such as class consciousness and racism, are also in the church, the church should keep a continuous critical watch over itself in order to move ahead, despite them. It should move toward a future of being really inclusive, opening its doors to ethnic minorities as equals in the midst of difference.

Hispanic caucus issues "Vision for Century III"

Source: Metodistas Asociados Representando la Causa de los Hispano-Americanos (MARCHA), The Hispanic Vision for Century III (San Antonio: MARCHA, 1985). Excerpts.

The Vision

Hispanic Americans within the United Methodist Church are growing. They are growing in numbers. They are growing in Christian faith and discipleship. As both church and nation move well into their third centuries, Hispanic American United Methodists are growing in influence and in responsibility for the sometimes difficult, sometimes exhilarating mission of Jesus Christ.

Populations of the so-called "developing nations" are increasing at a far greater rate than those of the "developed nations" of the northern hemisphere. As their numbers increase, so does their influence on the world scene, and in the churches of many lands.

In the United States the proportion of the population that is non-white continues to increase, and the role of ethnic minority peoples continues to broaden. Though still marginalized in many ways, the people of color are bringing ever more effective influence to bear on both society and church. Hispanic Americans have been in the vanguard of this movement, bringing to it a rich heritage of spiritual depth and suffering.

In at least three respects, today's United Methodist Church in the United States brings to mind the primitive Christian church described in the Book of Acts:

- We have been a vigorous church, experiencing phenomenal development from the time of our founding by John Wesley. Our church has exhibited a contagious vitality springing from an enduring spiritual source.
- We have been a church that, though ethnically diverse, has been largely controlled by a single ethnic group. As the Jerusalem church was composed primarily of Jews, so the United Methodist Church comprises mostly white Anglo-Saxons. In both cases, the majority group has had the major influence.
- We are a church of people on the move. In the early church people were moving out of Jerusalem and Judea to such places as Samaria, Caesarea, Damascus,

Antioch, Cyprus and beyond. Today we are experiencing masses of people arriving in the United States from Cambodia, Vietnam, the Philippines, Cuba, Haiti, Chile, El Salvador, Nicaragua, and Mexico, to name but a few nations. Like the first and second century immigrants, these are people seeking relief from oppressive economic and political situations.

Through the ministry of Paul, the early Christian church grew from a Jerusalem-centered church, of primarily Jews, to the major spiritual power of the Roman world, involving Gentiles of many racial and cultural groups, as well as Jews. Can we learn from Paul's vision and experience? Can we too respond to the Spirit's leading, employing the varied gifts of a diverse church to become again "the people of God," revitalized and resanctified for Christ's imperative mission, the transformation of this world?

The early churches moved from being small "in-groups" of Jews to accepting the "out-groups" of Gentiles—who then finally all became the whole Body of Christ, neither Jew nor Greek, slave nor free, male nor female (Gal. 3:28, Revised Standard Version). So in our time, the "unacceptables" are accepted, and in this movement of the Spirit we all discern that we are truly accepted by the Lord. But more than that: we find that we are all—majority and minority, old residents and new immigrants—"rich in faith and heirs of the kingdom . . ." (James 2:5, RSV).

In 1984 the United Methodist Church elected its first Hispanic bishop, its first Japanese-American bishop, and its first black woman bishop—Elias G. Galvan, Roy I. Sano and Leontine T. C. Kelly. Is this not a sign of the future into which we are called?

Thus the vision that enlivens Hispanic United Methodists in the early years of our church's third century is one of continued growth as responsible participants in Christ's contemporary mission, wherein our special gifts are recognized, accepted, and used to the glory of God and the service of humankind. It is with high hope and deep commitment to this challenge, this opportunity, that the National Hispanic United Methodist Caucus (MARCHA) offers this program—for itself, for all Hispanic United Methodists, for our whole denomination.

The recommendations that follow are addressed primarily to the annual conferences and general agencies of the United Methodist Church. They have been developed and honed through an extensive process of consultation guided by MARCHA. Input has been received from (1) key Hispanic laypersons and clergy from various parts of the United States and Puerto Rico, (2) Hispanic staff of general agencies, (3) the National United Methodist Hispanic Staff Forum, (4) the directors of MARCHA at their December 1984 meeting, and (5) the delegates to the annual convocation of MARCHA immediately following. . . .

Continuing Issues

Although the goal of the Missional Priority of the United Methodist Church over the last two quadrennia has been to develop and strengthen the ethnic minority local church, this goal has not been broadly reached in the Hispanic church. Most

Hispanic congregations, especially those outside the Rio Grande and Puerto Rico Annual Conferences, still face such problems as these:

- *Isolation:* Hispanic congregations are separated from one another and from our United Methodist structures. Often Hispanic involvement in district and annual conference program is minimal, due in part to the lack of sensitivity by leaders at these levels.

- *Lay leadership training:* Further development and strengthening of the Hispanic church demands committed and trained lay leadership. Yet annual conferences have not always provided the needed training and enlistment. In many cases where training has been offered, it has not taken into consideration the special needs of the Hispanic situation.

- *Clergy recruitment and deployment:* Very little has been done to enlist, train, and deploy new Hispanic clergy leadership. Some programs undertaken have lacked clear direction and strategy. In many cases, the result has been poor leadership, and therefore, poor congregational development.

- *Clergy itinerancy:* In many conferences, *itinerancy* has become an empty word, for the numbers of Hispanic congregations are so small. Limited itinerancy takes its toll in the morale and work of Hispanic clergy, and congregations suffer further.

- *Clergy education:* The problem of clergy enlistment is aggravated by the indifference of many of our United Methodist seminaries to Hispanic ministries. In both seminary education and continuing education, the curricula fail to address the needs of Hispanic pastors, and financial aid is inadequate.

- *Annual Conference commitment:* The commitment of our conferences to Hispanic congregations has varied. The needed support has often been only lukewarm—and in some cases paternalistic, encouraging dependency. Some conferences have practiced forms of institutional racism—such as giving leadership to Hispanics who are known to be subservient, who do not have at heart the real interests of Hispanic people and congregations.

- *Social ministries:* The need grows for special ministries in urban areas where Hispanics are concentrated, and to undocumented persons and political exiles.

Although here and there commendable progress has been made in strengthening Hispanic clergy, lay leaders, and congregations, the agenda before the church is still long, still complex, still urgent.

Seven Objectives for 1985–88

During the last several years MARCHA has focused its effort on three areas of ministry with Hispanics in the United States: (1) congregational development, (2) clergy and lay leadership recruitment and training, and (3) human rights. In developing the Missional Priority for the current quadrennium, the Inter-Ethnic Strategy Development Group outlined seven objectives:

A. Witness
B. Discipleship
C. Liturgy
D. Outreach
E. Leadership
F. Structures
G. Facilities

The MARCHA directors and the Hispanic team were intimately involved in developing and presenting these goals, and the MARCHA goals from previous years are seen as concomitant with these seven.

Thus the adoption by the 1984 General Conference of the current Missional Priority, "Developing and Strengthening the Ethnic Minority Local Church for Witness and Mission," mandates attention by the whole denomination to the seven goal areas listed above. And they provide the framework for presenting the following needed Hispanic ministries, hereby recommended by MARCHA, to the entire church.

HYMNAL REVISION COMMITTEE PROMISES POLITICALLY CORRECT HYMNAL

Source: Carlton R. Young, "Sing an Old Faith in a New Day: Responses to the Language Guidelines," Circuit Rider 10/1 (January 1986): 6-7.

[Language] guidelines unanimously adopted by the 25-member Hymnal Revision Committee were developed over a six-month period of study and testing by a special subcommittee of laypersons, hymnologists, language experts, pastors, and college and seminary teachers. As the group turned to the church for opinions and help in defining the issues, they soon discovered a controversy with much heat and little light, a controversy stemming at least in part from four sources:

1. The role of women in the church has changed, particularly in the increasing number of women clergy as pastors-in-charge.
2. Successful changes in liturgical language (in a nonliturgical church, such as Methodism) are not easily transferable into the vast repertoire of traditional hymns composed in the language base of the *Book of Common Prayer*, 1549, and the King James version of the Bible, 1611—a language base employed by most if not all English hymn writers and translators from the 17th century until the middle of this century.
3. Language and verbal communication skills have been neglected in seminary education with a related decline, since the 1950s, in the requirements for seminary graduates to have courses in hymnody, worship and preaching.
4. Not by definition but by practice, the hymnal constitutes the prayer book of corporate and private piety, prayer, and praise for large numbers of United Methodists. The hymnal in effect represents the ethos received from the past, celebrated in the present and transmitted to future generations. Many fear that substantive changes in the hymnal will have the effect of discontinuity of tradition.

In their work, the subcommittee has faithfully attempted to review opinions and insights from the sizable bibliography on the language of hymns which has developed both in Great Britain and in the United States since the 1960s. The presence of Professor Emeritus S. Paul Schilling of Boston University on the subcommittee has proved very helpful, particularly in the use of his important recent book, *The Faith We Sing*. In addition, the subcommittee has studied the problem and solutions contained in recent hymnals, including the *Lutheran Book of Worship*, 1978, and the Episcopal hymnal, which is to be published in late 1985. The guidelines address only issues prompted by the words of hymns that are written in traditional language, that is, most of those found in the present *Book of Hymns*. The guidelines do not address problems that might occur in the language of the hymns written since the publication of the *Book of Hymns*, 1966.

The guidelines do address four important considerations:

1. Hymns ought to be examined by some more objective criteria than "familiarity" and "popular use." Thus, the Wesleyan quadrilateral and the Social Principles are instruments which constitute, in part, a measuring stick for the adequacy of hymn texts, yet allow for sufficient flexibility to express the diversity of our church in matters of theology as well as controversial social issues.
2. The guidelines firmly address the subject of how we address one another and talk about each other in the assembly. All that is involved is the exchange of former words of exclusivity, i.e., *men*, for commonly accepted modern words of inclusivity, i.e., *ones* or *all*.
3. The forms and descriptions of God will be left for the most part as they have been transmitted to us from the richness of our evangelical and catholic hymnological repertoire.
4. The guidelines instruct the subcommittees to examine texts carefully for the scourge of racial discrimination or discrimination implied or directed to a class or condition of people.

In every regard, it should be repeated over and over that the integrity of the poets' original works, not the substitution of the committee's poetry for that of the initial poet, is at the heart of the guidelines. These guidelines should allow the traditional hymns of the church to be changed only where such change does not constitute a serious alteration of the poet's work. The option with the committee is, of course, either to delete whole stanzas or the whole hymn in instances where change means substantial alteration of the poet's original intent.

These are, in the opinion of the committee, guidelines which the committee can apply with full sensitivity and flexibility as they prepare the church's book of prayer and praise.

Bishops Issue Pastoral Letter on the Nuclear Crisis and a Just Peace

Source: Council of Bishops of The United Methodist Church, "A Pastoral Letter to All United Methodists," United Methodist Reporter (9 May 1986): 2.

A PASTORAL LETTER TO ALL UNITED METHODISTS

In Defense of Creation: The Nuclear Crisis and a Just Peace

From your brothers and sisters in Christ Jesus, the Council of Bishops, to all those people called United Methodist in every land; Grace to you and peace in the name of our Lord Jesus Christ.

With hearts and minds open to Christ, who is our peace;

In obedience to His call to be peacemakers;

And in response to the biblical vision of a wholistic peace, **shalom**, revealed in Scripture to be God's will and purpose for all of creation:

We, the bishops of The United Methodist Church, have been moved by the spirit of Jesus to send you a message which we have titled "In Defense of Creation: The Nuclear Crisis and a Just Peace," a message we believe to be of utmost urgency in our time.

This message has been prepared over a span of two years during which time we have earnestly sought to hear the Word of God through the scriptures. At the same time we have prayerfully and penitently reflected on the continuing build-up of nuclear arsenals by some of the nations. We have become increasingly aware of the devastation that such weapons can inflict on planet Earth. We have watched and agonized over the increase in hostile rhetoric and hate among nations. We have seen the threat of a nuclear confrontation increasing in our world. We have been motivated by our own sense of Christian responsibility and stewardship for the world God created.

This brief pastoral letter is an introduction to a substantial Foundation Document which we have produced as the major portion of our message to the church. In our Foundation Document we have attempted to state with clarity the biblical witness for our concerns and our conclusions about the issues we are addressing. We have set forth a theology for peace with justice in our time which

655

reflects our understanding of the mind and will of Jesus Christ. This theology for a just peace reflects also our understanding of those insights of both pacifism and just war theory which speak with relevance to the issues of the present nuclear crisis.

We write in defense of Creation. We do so because the Creation itself is under attack. Air and water, trees and fruits, birds and fish and cattle, all children and youth, women and men live under the darkening shadows of a threatening nuclear winter. We call the United Methodist Church to more faithful witness and action in the face of this worsening nuclear crisis. It is a crisis that threatens to assault not only the whole human family but planet Earth itself, even while the arms race itself cruelly destroys millions of lives in conventional wars, repressive violence, and massive poverty.

Therefore, we say a clear and unconditioned NO to nuclear war and to any use of nuclear weapons. We conclude that nuclear deterrence is a position which cannot receive the church's blessing. We state our complete lack of confidence in proposed "defenses" against nuclear attack and are convinced that the enormous cost of developing such defenses is one more witness to the obvious fact that the arms race is a social justice issue, not only a war and peace issue.

Our document sets forth a number of policies for a just peace including such disarmament proposals as a comprehensive test ban, a multilateral and mutually verifiable nuclear weapons freeze and the ultimate dismantling of all such weapons, and bans on all space weapons. However, the nuclear crisis is not primarily a matter of technology; it is a crisis of human community. We encourage independent U.S. and Soviet initiatives to foster a political climate conducive to negotiations. We urge a renewed commitment to building the institutional foundations of common security, economic justice, human rights, and environmental conservation. And we make appeal for peace research, studies, and training at all levels of education.

This message which we are sending to United Methodist people is not meant to be a consensus opinion of our church or a policy statement of our denomination on the nuclear crisis and the pursuit of peace. It is given from the bishops to the church as a pastoral and a prophetic word. It is pastoral in that we as bishops will seek to lead the church in study, prayer and action related to this issue and this theme, using this document as a basic resource and guide. It is prophetic in that this document is our response to the Word of God. It faithfully states our understanding of that Word to our world at this moment in history.

Our message is the result of many months of prayerful study, research and reflection. It is not given to the church with any feeling that it should be the final word on this issue or with the hope that it will silence all contrary opinion, but rather, we are sending this statement to the church seeking the fullest and fairest possible discussion of our understandings and convictions, together with a honest consideration of different and critical opinions.

Peacemaking is ultimately a spiritual issue. It is a sacred calling of Jesus. All dimensions of church life offer openings for peacemaking: family life, Christian education, the ministry of the laity, pastoral ministry in every respect, political witness, and the great fact of the church as a worldwide company of disciples which transcends all nations, governments, and ideologies.

Now, therefore, we ask you, our sisters and brothers, to join with us in a new covenant of peacemaking; to use the Bible together with our Council's Foundation Document as basic resources for earnest and steadfast study of the issues of justice and peace. We call upon each local pastor and lay leader to give leadership in a local church study of the issues surrounding the nuclear threat. We ask you all to open again your hearts, as we open our hearts, to receive God's gracious gift of peace; to become with us evangelists of **shalom**, making the ways of Jesus the model of discipleship, embracing all neighbors near and far, all friends and enemies, and becoming defenders of God's good creation; and to pray without ceasing for peace in our time.

Now we draw this pastoral letter to a close with prayers for all of you and for all the nations and peoples of the Earth.

We humbly pray that God will accept and use our lives and resources which we dedicate again to a ministry of peace.

May the love of God, the peace of Christ, and the power of the Holy Spirit be among you, everywhere and always, so that you may be a blessing to all creation and to all the children of God, making peace and remembering the poor, choosing life and coming to life eternal, in God's own good time.

Amen.

NATIVE AMERICAN CAUCUS ISSUES VISION DOCUMENT

Source: Native American International Caucus, The Sacred Circle of Life: A Native American Vision (*Norwalk, California: Native American International Caucus*, 1988), *1-12. Excerpts.*

Theological Statement. The theology of Native Americans within The United Methodist Church has been born out of pain: the pain of oppression; the pain of knowing that missionary efforts at "Christianizing the Indian" actually meant "civilizing the heathen"; the pain of powerlessness. Yet, even pain signifies life and provides for growth. Therefore, theology for the Native American is alive and open to wrestling with understandings of God, His creation, and Others that are constantly being brought into proper focus.

To grasp an understanding of how God is understood by Native Americans, one must examine the dynamics of relationships between God (the creator), His creation, Others and the individual (the Me). Native American theology can best be understood graphically, in what can be best described as **The Sacred Circle of Life**.

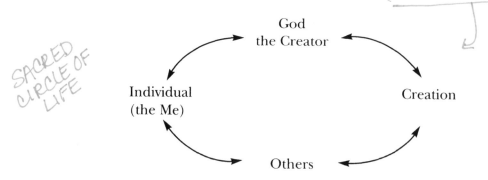

When these linked relationships are in balance, or in harmony, there is shalom, wholeness, salvation. **The Sacred Circle of Life** contains, when not distorted, the basic elements in God's plan for humankind.

The United Methodist Church, in applying this to the task of proclaiming the Gospel and making disciples . . . , must affirm the spiritual values of Native

Americans. Accepting the spiritual values of Native Americans will become a stabilizing force that can bring the Native Americans and the world into balance, and holds our families together. In this scheme, there is an understanding of universal relatedness of all God's creation that can be learned and shared by all.

The church's role in affirming the tribal identity of Native Americans, and giving affirmation to their cultural and spiritual values, will provide the arena where new concepts may occur. For example, new concepts of land stewardship and new forms of worship become possible. The integration of Christian and Native American traditional spiritual teachings can bring excitement, healing and renewed efforts for self-determination to a people frustrated by the lack of sensitivity to them as people and to their culture.

The affirmation of cultural values will enable the forming of ministries and leadership development programs that are compatible with traditional Native American leadership styles. The affirming of Native American spiritual and cultural values will begin to move us as a church toward the creation of a Sacred Circle of Life.

FUTURES: RELIGHTING THE FIRE

A Second Look. The United Methodist Church in America had been in existence for about 35 years before it became formally involved in missions among Native Americans. That was in the year 1820. Now 168 years later, this generation of Native Americans within The United Methodist Church must review the fruits of those labors and seek an honest balance of judgment in the good and bad which must find expression in our time. The intent of such a critique would be to recommend to the Native American people and the whole church what trails must be taken to prepare the way for Christ to visit his scattered people in the tribal lands, the countryside, and the cities.

The Native American International Caucus has spent considerable time discussing these matters and the fruit of those discussions is contained in this comprehensive document.

The purpose of this section is to state the future context within which the ministry must take place. . . .

Perceiving the Mission: Vision of a Task Completed A review of dialogue material shows that three basic questions are being confronted: (A) What do we want to happen between 1988 and the year 2000? (B) When do we want it to happen? (C) Who do we want to do it? Basically what is wanted is for *Christianity to be expanded among Native American people.* But, that expansion as well as all future work must be genuine and not superficial. It is superficial when it is imposed within an absolute cultural vehicle that is foreign to the recipient culture. The cultural implications of contemporary American Christianity must be neutralized. That is, **cultural conversion as an imperative in Christian evangelism must be eliminated.**

Leadership is greatly needed. It is a special kind of leadership that is now desired. Appropriately trained indigenous leaders are needed to assist in the expansion. One or more of the United Methodist schools of theology will help lay the

[handwritten margin note: seminary not helpful for Nat. Am.]

groundwork for developing an appropriate Christian ideology compatible with the United Methodist heritage and Native American spirituality. Seminary education is desired, but present day seminary training is not helpful or appropriate for Native American clergy going into Native American churches or ministries. . . .

The Church must give more than sympathetic attention to issues affecting the quality of life of Native American people. Primary among many issues is the land base of Native American tribes. Protection of the existing land base of each respective tribe and the consolidation as well as the expansion of the land base are desired. The church should review its land holdings on or adjacent to tribal reservations and turn over any land that is no longer used for mission purposes to the tribes without compensation.

[handwritten margin note: turn over land]

The Task of Envisioning the Future. . . . The effort of Native American leaders in the church will be to guide the church in its relationships to Native American people throughout the remainder of this 20th century. The church will be asked to be more sensitive to the humanity of native peoples. . . .

The church must also avoid participating in any event designed to compromise the humanity of Native people in the Americas with special regard to the free expression of traditional views and the exercise of traditional freedoms of religion and culture.

Most important for a vision of things to come is that Native Americans should be [a] people united in a common goal and purpose—the betterment of life for all Native American people and a working reconciliation among all people in the whole church.

COMMUNICATIONS. Inasmuch as Native Americans are the most oppressed group within our society, and inasmuch as their isolation contributes to many negative factors within their community as a whole, the Native American International Caucus has set *better communications* as one of its primary goals. . . .

CONGREGATIONAL DEVELOPMENT. By the year 2000, to double the number of Native American churches and/or ministries within The United Methodist Church. . . .

Request the General Conference to mandate that the establishment of Native American Church growth/revitalization within The United Methodist Church be given high priority.

ISSUES. Native Americans are encountering more issues today than they have ever encountered before. Such issues as Native land claims, fishing and hunting rights, jurisdictional disputes, self-sufficiency, and those problems that the rest of society deals with: alcohol and drug abuse, suicide, nuclear war, changing family systems, etc.

With these ever-changing and continuing problems, we have an urgent need to improve our communication skills across the church so that accurate information can be shared and a support network be formed. . . .

LEADERSHIP DEVELOPMENT. In Mark's Gospel (Mark 1:16-20) Jesus called the disciples and they followed. Jesus continues to call today! However, one of the indictments against The United Methodist Church has been its failure to develop and train Native American "community leaders" who are sensitive to the cultural, sociological, political, and economic needs within the Native American community. **The future of the United Methodist Native American ministries is dependent upon developing indigenous leadership**—indigenous leaders who are sensitive to the expressed needs of "grassroots" Native Americans. . . .

CONCLUSION. Congregational development, Leadership Development, Communications, Issues, and Future Development for Native American ministries for 1988 and beyond can be implemented only with the combined efforts of the Native people and friends within The United Methodist Church.

The church is strengthened when tensions based on misunderstandings and neglect are released and when mutual love and respect are present. The United Methodist Church has rich traditions and spiritual values which we as Native Americans wish to share. And likewise, we want to share those rich spiritual qualities inherent in the traditions of our forefathers and the present generation. We are mutually blessed.

The Christian faith and the Native American "traditional" beliefs walk a parallel path. The "Good" has been part of our culture since the time of Creation. In Christ's name, we pray for the continued support of the church for Native American ministries and we pray for a great blessing for the whole church.

BISHOPS ISSUE PASTORAL STATEMENT ON MINISTRY TO UNDOCUMENTED PERSONS

Source: Council of Bishops of The United Methodist Church, On Undocumented Migration: To Love the Sojourner: A Statement of Concern to United Methodists in the United States of America (Cincinnati: Service Center, General Board of Global Ministries, 1988).

Love the sojourner . . . for you were sojourners in the land of Egypt.

—*Deuteronomy 10:19*

We, the bishops of The United Methodist Church, moved by our concern for the plight of undocumented immigrants sojourning in the United States, urgently invite you to share with us in the effort to love the sojourner.

Anxious parents, hungry and frightened children, tortured and abused peasants, students, workers looking for opportunity, all have left the land of their birth in the hope that they might satisfy the desire for life that moves all human beings. Many immigrants come to us voluntarily as a result of the difficult decision to leave home in quest of better circumstances; others, like the Haitian and Central American refugees, who are forced out of their homeland by persecution and the terrible dislocation of armed conflict, come involuntarily. These people arrive among us not only with their need, but also bearing gifts of energy, resourcefulness and fundamental hope that may contribute to the renewal of the society and the church. Above all, these strangers bear to us the Christ. These are they of whom Jesus spoke when he said, "I was a stranger (sojourner) and you welcomed me" (Matt. 25:35).

God comes in the form of the sojourner, the vulnerable person who lacks the benefit of status and protection in an alien land. In the flesh of Jesus of Nazareth God chose to sojourn in a particular way for the sake of all humankind. In Jesus the sojourning God broke the power of sin, death, and injustice, and restored the possibility of authentic community in which love and justice reign, and peace prevails.

The sojourning God cares especially for sojourning peoples and invites all who would know the fullness of life to share in caring for such people. We in the Christian community experience that invitation in very particular ways. Our ancestors in the faith from the time of Abraham and Sarah have been sojourners. Indeed, the faithfulness of Abraham and Sarah in abandoning their home in response to God's call and in trust of a seemingly impossible promise is presented by the Apostle Paul as the model of authentic Christian faith (Rom. 4:18-25). Isaac, Jacob, Joseph, Moses, Miriam, Joshua, Deborah, Ruth, Mary, Paul, to name but a few, are our sojourning ancestors in the faith. By God's grace the Christian church is made part of this great pilgrimage toward fulfillment. It is rightly called the pilgrim people of God.

As God's pilgrim people the church inherits the unique vocation of being that community through whom the peoples of the earth shall be blessed. The church models in its own life God's intention for all humankind. We reaffirm our conviction that:

> The church of Jesus Christ, in the power and unity of the Holy Spirit, is called to serve as an alternative community to an alienated and fractured world—a loving and peaceable international company of disciples transcending all governments, races and ideologies; reaching out to all "enemies"—and ministering to all the victims of poverty and oppression. (*In Defense of Creation: Foundation Document,* 19, 9.37)

As a world church that lives in the United States of America as well as other countries, we acknowledge our common journey with the United States in the effort to form a just society.

In the spirit of the covenant that binds us all as Christians and under the divine mandate received through the history of that covenant in the Scriptures and enacted in our own tradition and practice, we seek to address the injustice and hardship inflicted upon sojourners and, indeed, upon United States citizens, by the United States Immigration Reform and Control Act of 1986. It appears that the United States Immigration Reform and Control Act of 1986 offers hope for some persons and renders life much more difficult for the vast majority of immigrant peoples in the United States. These circumstances cry out for attention from the church and from Christian individuals.

The legalization program that helped legitimize the Act obscured the repressiveness of the law. While a minority of undocumented persons are enabled to regularize their status in the United States, most immigrants will never experience legalization. Even those who have been fortunate enough to get through the unnecessarily difficult first step of the program still face another round of arbitrary requirements and confusing procedures.

Benefit for the few has been achieved at the expense of the many who are pressed even deeper into the twilight existence of the undocumented person who is so easily exploited, used when convenient and expedient, but then cast aside as an obsolete tool or a spent resource. Every provision of the Act, including the one for legalization, dehumanizes the sojourner. When the sojourner is welcomed, it is because of economic or political expediency. As the Special Agricultural Workers, the Replenishment Agricultural Workers and the H-2A provisions make abundantly clear, sojourners are welcome to the extent that they may be productive instruments in an economic enterprise that robs work of its capacity to humanize and to express the creativity of the human spirit.

Our concern for the family, for the well-being of children, the equality of women and men, go for naught before this Act. We rejoice with those for whom the law does bring relief and the opportunity for citizenship and pledge them our full support in the pursuit of that goal. But the inadequacies of the Immigration Reform and Control Act of 1986 call for an entirely new look at our immigration policies.

Acknowledging our particular role among the pilgrim people of God, we invite all those whose hearts are as ours to join hands with us in declaring our uncompromising intention to welcome the sojourners in our midst and to walk with them toward our mutual fulfillment as human beings. We pledge ourselves to know them, their circumstances and needs; to love them, to embrace them and their struggle; to bid them welcome to our communities, religious and civil, for as long as is necessary, or as they should decide to remain. We commit ourselves to walk humbly with God toward that realm where justice is done because tender love dwells in the hearts of women and men.

As servants of God, and in the company of the prophets of Israel, we dare to challenge our own values, institutions, and practices as a sign and means of transformation of the total sociopolitical and economic environment, so as to create a world community in which none is in want because all share the earth's resources for the common good.

Genuine hospitality for the sojourner requires not only a welcoming embrace, but also the effort to address the conditions that uprooted them from native soil. God's pilgrim people in the United States are called to recognize and repent their participation in systems that result in injustice and contribute to the circumstances that lead people to undertake the risk of sojourning. Fully to love the sojourners, acting justly on their behalf, challenges the ultimate commitments and fundamental values of the sociopolitical and economic systems of which we are all a part. The church cannot easily extricate itself from those unjust systems and wash its hands of the problems. The United Methodist Church can act justly within the systems by challenging them through the management of its considerable resources, and through advocacy of foreign and domestic policies that value human welfare above a narrow concept of national security. In concert with other Christian communities, transformation of these systems can begin. The pilgrimage to human fulfillment for some cannot be fueled at the expense of any human being. If anyone is diminished as a person of dignity and worth, all persons are diminished.

Genuine hospitality ultimately receives the most precious gift the sojourner brings to the host: fulfillment in actualizing the capacity to love as God loves. In their quest for abundant life, the sojourners bring to those who will receive it no other gift than the Christ.

As United Methodist bishops we urge that you read prayerfully and with openness to the prompting of the Spirit, the document that is fundamental to this appeal: *To Love the Sojourner: A United Methodist Response to the United States Immigration Reform and Control Act of 1986.* Let the document provoke your thinking and your response to the sojourners among us. Join with us in the effort to correct the injustices that may be perpetuated by the United States Immigration

Reform and Control Act of 1986. Above all else, let us pray that we may be enabled by God's grace to love the sojourner by acting justly, loving tenderly, and walking humbly with God.

United Methodist Council of Bishops
April 20, 1988
Kansas City, Missouri

Conservatives Issue Right-to-Life Declaration on Abortion

Source: "The Durham Declaration: To United Methodists on Our Church and Abortion," in The Church and Abortion: In Search of New Ground for Response *(Nashville: Abingdon Press, 1993), 11-15. End notes omitted.*

1990

INTRODUCTION

United Methodists, abortion is testing our church. Abortion is testing our church today as deeply as slavery tested our church in the nineteenth century. Abortion is stirring up great confusion and exposing deep conflicts in our community of faith. This condition continues, in part, because The United Methodist Church has not addressed the problem of abortion theologically. Our church has been content to debate abortion with the merely political terms that American society has made available. This is an insufficient response to an historic test.

The time has come to call The United Methodist Church to a scriptural, theological, and pastoral approach to abortion. This we will attempt to do. As United Methodists addressing United Methodists on abortion, we hereby declare our beliefs, confess our sins, and pledge ourselves to a new life together.

DECLARING OUR BELIEFS: OUR BODIES, CHRIST'S BODY, AND CHILDREN

Contemporary culture insists that we own our bodies and that we have a right to do with them whatever we want. However, we United Methodist Christians declare that this is false.

We believe that we are not our own (I Cor. 6:19). We do not own our selves or our bodies. God owns us. "It is he that made us, and we are his" (Ps. 100:3). Furthermore, it is God who "bought [us] with a price" (I Cor. 6:20) with the life of Jesus sacrificed on the Cross. And it is God who sanctifies us to be "temple[s] of the Holy Spirit" (I Cor. 6:19).

We believe that, through faith in Christ and baptism into His Body, God has made us "members of Christ" (I Cor. 6:15). That is, we are incorporated into the Body of Christ, the Church. "So we, though many, are one body in Christ, and individually members one of another" (Rom. 12:5). Partaking of the Bread and the

Cup, we as members of the Body of Christ demonstrate that we are not accountable merely to ourselves. We are accountable to God and to one another. That means we care and provide for one another as brothers and sisters.

We believe that caring and providing for one another includes welcoming children into the family of the Church. As members of the Body of Christ, we know that children—those who are hidden in the womb and those who are held by the hand, those who are labeled "unwanted" and those who are called "wanted"—are gifts from God. In this we follow the example of our Lord, who, during His earthly ministry and in the face of opposition, welcomed children to His side (Matt. 19:13-15). And we conform to the example of the early church, which, though living in the midst of a pagan empire that casually practiced abortion and abandoned children (usually to slavery, prostitution, or death), helped to provide refuge for unwanted little ones and their needy parents.

We believe that God welcomes us through the outstretched arms of His Son on the Cross: "The arms of love that compass me/Would all mankind embrace" (Charles Wesley, "Jesus! the Name High Over All"). Because this God has welcomed us into the Church, we can likewise welcome the little ones.

CONFESSING OUR SINS: OUR REBELLION, COMPROMISE, AND FEAR

We confess that we have rebelled against God. We have rejected the light of Christ and turned to the darkness of the world. We have denied—by thought, word, and deed—that we belong to God.

We confess that we have often compromised the Gospel by submitting to the seductions of society. We have exchanged the message of salvation in Jesus Christ for a false message about human potential. We have capitulated to extreme self-involvement and self-interest. Neglecting the call to discipleship, we have treated matters related to marriage, sex, and children as if they were merely lifestyle questions. We have lived as if the church is simply another voluntary association of autonomous individuals. We have lived as if the church is not the Body of Christ in which we "bear one another's burdens" (Gal. 6:2). We have lived as if we are our own, not God's.

We confess that, as a part of the People of God, we have not honestly confronted the problem of abortion. Fearing division, we have removed abortion from the concerns of our church's mission. Thereby our church has reduced the abortion problem to private choice and to just another issue for partisan politics. Therefore, in our churches we have selectively applied the truths of God's ownership of us and God's gift of children. We have neglected our sister who is in a difficult pregnancy and offered her no alternatives to abortion. Rarely have we offered, through our ministries, the forgiving love of Christ to the woman who has aborted. Nor have we hospitably welcomed the so-called "unwanted child" into our churches and families. Nor have we challenged or worked to alter the mindset and social realities that sustain our abortion-conducive culture.

PLEDGING OURSELVES TO A NEW LIFE TOGETHER: OUR PROMISES

1. We pledge, with God's help, to become a church that unapologetically proclaims the message of salvation in Jesus Christ to a world that is usually apathetic and sometimes antagonistic.

2. We pledge, with God's help, to practice and to teach a sexual ethic that adorns the Gospel. Christian discipleship includes, though is not limited to, the ordering of God's gift of sexuality. Sexual discipline requires, at minimum, "fidelity in marriage and celibacy in singleness." According to Biblical teaching, sexual relations outside the boundaries of "fidelity in marriage and celibacy in singleness" (*Book of Discipline*, 1988, Par. 404.4e) are manifestations of sin that call for repentance and reconciliation. This ordering is a part of the excellent way of Christian discipleship. It stands over against the jungle of modern sexuality, which is most evident in our society's inability to hold men sexually accountable.

Biblically based sexual discipline should be directly and consistently advocated—by our church's bishops, district superintendents, clergy, parents, church schools, publishing programs, colleges and universities, hospitals, children's homes, boards, and agencies—among United Methodist children, youth, and adults. In addition, the church should teach the responsibilities for men and women that accompany sex. The church should strongly condemn sexual promiscuity.

3. We pledge, with God's help, to teach our churches that the unborn child is created in the image of God and is one for whom the Son of God died. This child is God's child. This child is part of God's world. So the life of this child is not ours to take. Therefore, it is sin to take this child's life for reasons whether of birth control, gender selection, convenience, or avoidance of embarrassment.

4. We pledge, as people of a community whose sins are forgiven by God, to offer the hope of God's mercy and forgiveness to the woman who has obtained an elective abortion. God's forgiveness and healing are also to be offered to those who have assisted a woman in aborting and now repent.

5. We pledge, with God's help, to become a church that hospitably provides safe refuge for the so-called "unwanted child" and mother. We will joyfully welcome and generously support—with prayer, friendship, and material resources—both child and mother. This support includes strong encouragement for the biological father to be a father, in deed, to his child.

6. We pledge, with God's help, to honor the woman who has, under difficult circumstances, carried her child to term.

7. We pledge, with God's help, to call our church's boards and agencies to end their support of pro-choice political advocacy and also to develop ministries that support women in difficult pregnancies.

8. We pledge, with God's help, to encourage United Methodist-related hospitals to adopt medical ethics guidelines which are protective of the unborn child and mother.

9. We pledge, with God's help, to consider how our church should best apply dis-

cipline to her members who reap profits, small and large, from the advocacy and performance of elective abortion.

CONCLUSION

In a society that is so obsessed with material success and pleasure that it wantonly destroys over 1.5 million of its unborn children every year, we United Methodists hear the words of our Lord, "Let the children come to me, and do not hinder them" (Matt. 19:14). We heed these words of Jesus by ordering our life together so that we can joyfully receive the children.

To accomplish this task, to meet the massive test that abortion now poses to The United Methodist Church, we rely only upon Christ until His Kingdom comes. It is Christ who promises, "My grace is sufficient for you, for my power is made perfect in weakness" (II Cor. 12:9). He, above all else, is to be trusted.

Study committee splits on homosexuality issue

Source: United Methodist Church, "Report on the Study of Homosexuality," Daily Christian Advocate (1992), 1:276-77. Excerpts.

Things the Church Can Responsibly Teach

In order to bring the results of our study into sharper focus, it may help to summarize our conclusions about some of the specific points we believe the church can responsibly teach on the subject of homosexuality.

- Homosexuality is best considered in the context of a more general Christian understanding of human sexuality.
- Human sexuality is God's good gift. Our fundamental attitude toward this gift should be more one of gratitude than of apprehension.
- In the expression of our sexuality—as in the expression of all aspects of our existence—we are invited by God's grace to a life of love and self-discipline. Sexual expression is most profoundly human when it takes place in the context of a caring and committed relationship where each partner can be an expression of God's grace for the other.
- There are substantial numbers of persons of homosexual orientation within the church whose gifts and graces manifest the work of the Spirit among us.
- The specific causes of homosexual orientation remain unclear, although various scientific theories about this contribute to our overall understanding.
- It is a responsible expression of Christian ethics to advocate for those things which minimize the spread of sexually transmitted diseases and to support work towards adequate health care and research in these areas.
- The basic human rights of gay and lesbian persons should be protected by the church, and the general stigmatizing of such persons is inappropriate in a church which understands all its members to be sinners who live by the power of God's grace.
- In the church's own dialogue on this as well as other controversial issues, persons of conflicting viewpoint should respect one another, recognizing that before the mystery of God, our knowledge and insight remain partial and imperfect.

Things the Church Cannot Responsibly Teach

In the course of its study, the Committee has noted that advocates of various sides of the debate sometimes use arguments that ultimately cannot be supported. It may be helpful to review some of these:

- The church cannot teach that the Bible is indifferent to homosexual acts. Although there are only a few passages where such are in view, in every one of those passages a negative judgment about homosexual practice is either stated or presumed.
- The church cannot teach that all biblical references and allusions to sexual practices are binding today *just* because they are in the Bible. Specific references and allusions must be examined in light of the basic biblical witness and their respective socio-cultural contexts.
- The church cannot teach that certain sexual behaviors are morally acceptable just because they are practiced by substantial numbers of people, nor just because it corresponds to their subjective inclinations. Not all expressions of sexuality can be affirmed by the church as moral or life enhancing. The basis of moral judgments among Christians is deeper than statistical headcounts or subjective feelings—even though statistical studies and subjective reports can be an important part of the process of forming moral judgments. This applies to both heterosexual and homosexual practices.
- The church cannot teach that gay and lesbian persons are generally dysfunctional or characteristically preoccupied with sex—some are and some are not, just like their heterosexual counterparts.
- The church cannot teach that gay and lesbian persons are prone to seduce or corrupt others—some are and some are not, again, just like their heterosexual counterparts.
- The church cannot teach that the same percentage of every society is gay or lesbian. That is not borne out in the limited reputable cross-cultural studies. It does appear that homosexual relations exist in some form in all cultures studied.
- The church cannot teach that sexual orientation is fixed before birth, nor can it teach that it is fixed only after birth. The scientific evidence is insufficient to allow a judgment either way, particularly considering the diverse types of both heterosexuality and homosexuality.
- The church cannot teach that sexual orientation, either heterosexual or homosexual, is deliberately chosen. It is clear that substantial numbers of persons have experienced their sexual orientation from early childhood.
- The church cannot teach that there is a single theory of homosexual orientation or behavior—or, for that matter, of heterosexual orientation or behavior. No one theory is sufficiently supported by empirical evidence to be taught as generally accepted truth.
- The church cannot affirm any sexual practice, heterosexual or homosexual, that is exploitative, casual, or physically threatening.

WOMEN CHURCH LEADERS ISSUE REPLY TO "RE-IMAGINING" CONFERENCE CRITICS

Source: "A Time of Hope—A Time of Threat" [a statement in response to public attacks on the leadership, theology, and funding of the international, ecumenical Re-Imagining Conference held in Minneapolis, November 1993]. New York City. 22 February 1994. United Methodist Archives, Madison, New Jersey.

1994

A TIME OF HOPE—A TIME OF THREAT

This is a time of hope. The partnership of women and men in the United Methodist Church is growing—in the Council of Bishops, in Annual Conferences, in local congregations, and in theological schools. Christian community and sharing of leadership are broadening across racial and ethnic lines. Globally, the voices of women are being heard, and cooperation among Christian women increases denominationally and ecumenically. In theological books, sermons, and liturgies, women are singing a new song.

But this is also a time of threat. Hostility toward outspoken, creative, and courageous women of faith is not new, but it is now more sharply focused. Public attacks on the leadership, theology and funding of a recent conference call us to speak out. We are convinced that people are frightened by fresh theological insights and by challenges to narrow orthodoxy are attempting to discredit and malign women. Constructive dialogue is welcome, but irrational and distorted attacks increase an environment of violence against women.

For years the United Methodist Church has been divided by controversy over the leadership of women, reproductive rights, inclusive language, and homosexuality. As women have addressed these issues, the clash of theological perspectives has intensified. At the heart of the conflict are diverse images of God, the meaning of a multi-racial, multi-cultural church, ecumenical commitment, equal participation of women, and the dynamics of control and power. What is at stake is who will name these issues, how the issues will be described, and who will set the agenda for the future of the church.

We are clear that the verbal attacks on the Re-Imagining Conference in Minneapolis (November, 1993) are not isolated. While some naysayers have rushed to judgment on the basis of hearsay, others appear to be part of an ongoing design to split and weaken the United Methodist Church:

- Criticizing the Women's Division and undermining the effectiveness of local units of United Methodist Women are affronts to over a century of faithful witness and missionary service.
- Refusing to acknowledge the positive relationship between sexuality and spirituality, present in both Christian tradition and contemporary theological writings, deprives the church of a rich and essential wholeness.
- Accusing feminist, womanist, and other women theologians, as well as our theological schools, of departing from historic Christian faith is an attempt to constrict the work of the Holy Spirit.
- Engaging in verbal violence against lesbians reveals the homophobia in the church and denigrates the rich contributions that homosexual persons have made to the church through the centuries.
- Creating a climate of witch-hunting, name-calling, and fear destroys Christian community and erodes the church's capacity to proclaim the gospel of Jesus Christ.

We have to ask how it is that so much time, energy, and money can be put into these invectives instead of into mission and ministry.

The use of the term, "heresy," in our time, may be a way of refusing to hear the voices of those who have been marginalized in the life of the church. Today creative theological minds explore a whole range of issues, including the biblical meaning of God's Wisdom, Sophia, (like God's Word, Logos). Similarly, in light of social experience, such as slavery and female sexual abuse, understandings of sacrifice, atonement, and martyrdom are being reexamined.

The scriptural promise of the Holy Spirit creates the space and the inspiration for new faith experience and fresh theological insights of every era. We stand strongly in the United Methodist tradition which honors theological diversity and encourages openness to emerging theological initiatives. We believe that God needs no defense, and that God's children of all backgrounds are called to be true to their own experiences and to articulate their faith, faithfully.

Today's "reformation" holds the potential for life-giving renewal in the United Methodist Church and in the hearts and lives of women and men alike. We, the undersigned women, loyal and committed to the United Methodist Church, call on all sisters and brothers to join us in celebrating and living into this movement of the Holy Spirit.

22 February 1994, New York City

Beryl Ingram-Ward	Patricia J. Patterson	J. Ann Craig
Susan Murch Morrison	Ruth M. Harris	Jeanne Audrey Powers
Heather Murray-Elkins	Peggy L. Halsey	Barbara B. Troxell

CONSERVATIVES CALL FORTH "CONFESSING MOVEMENT"

Source: The Confessing Movement Within The United Methodist Church, "An Invitation to the Church" [adopted by an ad hoc coalition of "traditionalist" United Methodists meeting in Atlanta, Georgia, April 6, 1994], Web site http://www.confessingumc.org.

AN INVITATION TO THE CHURCH

I.

The United Methodist Church is at a crossroads. We face either the peril of abandoning the Christian faith, thereby becoming unfaithful disciples of Jesus Christ, or embracing the promise of becoming God's instrument in a new awakening of vital Christianity. The causes of the crisis are complex and multiple. However, we believe that the central reason is our abandonment of the truth of the gospel of Jesus Christ as revealed in Scripture and asserted in the classic Christian tradition and historic ecumenical creeds. Specifically we have equivocated regarding the person of Jesus Christ and his atoning work as the unique Savior of the world. We have been distracted by false gospels. We have compromised in our mission to declare the true gospel to all people and spread scriptural holiness. For the sake of the kingdom of God, it is now time for action.

II.

The renewal, reform, and healing of our church can come only through the life-giving power of the Holy Spirit. We cannot yet see clearly how God will lead us along this path. However, with John Wesley we affirm the apostolic faith of the universal Church and the Wesleyan distinctives which give form to our faith as articulated in the doctrinal standards of our own church (viz., the *Articles* and *Confession of Faith, Wesley's Standard Sermons* and *Explanatory Notes*). These constitute the essential, unchangeable truths of our tradition. We gladly own this anew for ourselves and seek to reclaim it for our whole church.

III.

Under God's judgment and by God's grace we covenant to participate in the Spirit's reconstruction of the church, which has been built upon the foundation of the faith once for all delivered to the saints. We covenant to engage in a revitalized mission which expresses our historic concern for social holiness and fidelity to the fulfillment of the Great Commission. To all United Methodists—regardless of race or gender—who desire to contend for this faith, we extend an invitation to join us in this endeavor.

In order to enact the Discipline's call to "doctrinal reinvigoration," and to avoid schism and prevent mass exodus, we intend to form a Confessing Movement within the United Methodist Church. By this we mean people and congregations who exalt the Lordship of Jesus Christ alone, and adhere to doctrinal standards of our church.

We call upon all pastors, lay persons, and congregations to join with us in this Confessing Movement, and to challenge and equip their people as agents of God's kingdom.

We look to the Council of Bishops for doctrinal oversight according to paragraph 514.2 "to guard, transmit, teach and proclaim, corporately and individually, the apostolic faith as it is expressed in Scripture and Tradition, and, as they are led and endowed by the Spirit, to interpret that faith evangelically and prophetically." In particular, we ask the bishops to affirm their own teaching authority and to declare our church's commitment to Jesus Christ as the only Lord and Savior of the world.

We call upon the seminaries of our church to transmit the historic Christian faith. We call upon the boards and agencies of the church to fulfill their primary role of being servants of the local church.

IV.

The crisis we discern extends beyond our denomination. We witness similar strains and struggles among our sisters and brothers in all the churches of the West. Because we are baptized into the one universal Church, and because the problems we face will best be resolved by utilizing the gifts God gives to the whole community of faith, we rejoice in the stirrings for renewal that we see among other communions. We commit ourselves to praying with them for the coming of the kingdom in our midst.

KOREAN AMERICAN CAUCUS FAVORS FORMATION OF SEPARATE KOREAN MISSIONARY CONFERENCE

Source: National Association of Korean-American United Methodist Churches. "An Open Letter to the Delegates to 1996 General Conference Regarding Korean American Missionary Conference." Petition No. 21731. United Methodist Archives, Madison, N.J.

[April 1996]
Dear General Conference Delegates:

We are writing this letter to you in the hope that it will help you better understand the petition and respond to it prayerfully during the legislative sessions. By now you are aware of the petition to create Korean American missionary conferences for the next two decades for more effective evangelism and mission. You are also aware of the fact that the National Program Division of the General Board of Global Ministries voted not to recommend the petition that its own committee, the National Committee on Korean American Ministries, drafted after eight years of study and formulation; such an absurd turn of the event forced the National Association of Korean American United Methodist Churches (the Korean Caucus) to petition directly to the General Conference.

For the last two decades, Korean Americans within United Methodism demonstrated remarkable growth and vitality, and that without systematic support from the denomination. The fact that such a growth has come to a plateau signals that we have reached that limit of the current denominational structure to meet the needs of Korean American community. Therefore, the fact that we need a national strategy and structure for more intentional and effective mission and ministry for and with Korean American United Methodists, by now, should be obvious to all who care. It should also be clear to anyone who is serious about the church-in-mission that the direction of such strategy should also be in line with the same principles that allowed one of the most phenomenal success stories in mission history in Korea, namely John L. Nevius's principles of self-propagation, self-supporting and self-governing. Such an empowerment of one of the most vital sectors within the United Methodist Church will surely contribute to the strengthening of the entire denomination.

The critical question remains as to how we would devise strategies and the structure to carry out our mission objectives. Korean American community has been working with the leadership of the denomination to work out the details. The denominational leaders said that missionary conference with specific sunset date would be the best structure, and then advised the Korean American community that because missionary conference belongs to the Jurisdictional structure according to the current *Book of Discipline*, we need to propose three missionary conferences in three Jurisdictions where most Korean American communities currently reside, even though that was against our best wishes because that would structurally fracture the community and not cover the entire Korean American United Methodist church community. The rationale was that it would be easier to convince the General Conference to support the proposal if we do not have to amend the *Book of Discipline*. Now the same agency that has advised the Korean American community in this effort for the last eight years, and also has actually drafted the petition, that is virtually identical to what you now have in your hand, has rejected the proposal without alternative plans. This profoundly shakes the ground of trust and faith on the part of the Korean American United Methodists regarding the commitment of their own denomination vis-a-vis the missional needs of Korean Americans. Some even question the need to stay with the United Methodist Church. In our last effort to remain as faithful United Methodists, we are petitioning directly to the General Conference.

One important change we hope to make to the petition in your hand is to propose one Korean American missionary conference as we originally wanted, rather than three. We decided that we have to propose a structure that will work more effectively, even if that means amending the *Book of Discipline*. We will attempt through the legislative process to add a paragraph to the Discipline and amend the petition in such a way that we can create one Korean American (Missionary) Conference with a specific sunset date. This will help even more the newly created missionary conference be self-supportive financially as well as administratively.

There are several related issues that we like to inform you. First, the language issue has been the major point of difficulties regarding Korean American pastors' full and meaningful participation in the life of annual conferences because of their limited English ability and the lack of effort and hospitality on the part of geographical annual conferences to accommodate their needs and utilize their gifts and graces. The Korean American Missionary Conference with bi-lingual administration will help all Korean American United Methodists to participate fully in the life of their annual conference. This will also bring about the generational unity among Korean Americans on the same issue of language.

Second, there are over 50 mission congregations (among 94 mission congregations that have been developed by five jurisdictional Korean American Missions) that need an annual conference home, but are having a difficult time joining an annual conference due to the cultural and political walls (as well as lingual) set up by annual conferences. A Korean American Missionary Conference is an answer to absorb them and strengthen them to be fully chartered congregations actively contributing to the missional efforts of the denomination. It is important to note that six of these as well as several other previously chartered UM congregations have left our United Methodist connection, and joined the Overseas Missionary Conference of the Korean Methodist Church, which incidentally has developed 160 congregations in the United States since 1992 due to their open arm policy. The United Methodist Church needs to make decision as to whether it is committed to Korean American ministries, and has to act very quickly.

Third, this petition is receiving a strong support from the absolute majority of the entire Korean American communities. It is true that the women clergy group raised a strong reservation about the gender inclusiveness given the cultural history, yet not to the point of exacerbating the opposition that the National Program Division and United Methodist media played it out. Unwittingly or perhaps wittingly, our mission board played the time honored oppressive tactic of divide and rule. The drafting committee from its inception has been inclusive of gender, generation, geographical distribution, the size of congregation and variety of appointment settings. Thanks to the effort to listen to all the constituents as far as possible, the petition went through many revisions, to the point where one Transgeneration pastor commented that "this is the most inclusive and finest document ever produced by the Korean American United Methodists," without denying the fact that we still have a long way to go in complete inclusiveness. Contrary to common perception, not all women clergy opposed the petition, and not all male clergy supported it, either. Furthermore, not all (male and female) pastors serving Korean American congregations supported it, while not all pastors, male and female, serving non-Korean congregations opposed it. In our most recent survey, 71% of Korean American churches are in favor of forming a missionary conference, 13% in opposition, and 16% are undecided, including "do not understand." Such an agreement for any proposal is rare in our entire denomination.

The United Methodist Church prides itself in the diversity of views on almost everything; we cover the entire spectrum. Complete agreement is not characteristic of our church. Nonetheless, we find ways to live and work together under the grace of our Lord Jesus Christ. We wonder whether the denomination is willing to grant that virtue to all its entirety inclusive of gender—not, yet. It is by structurally giving women the voice and vote that their collective will influences the annual conferences and the entire denomination, and never simply because of the good will of the liberated male within the church; that's how we are slowly on the way to better gender inclusiveness. Once all Korean American churches and clergy members are in a missionary conference, women in alliance with Transgeneration can form a formidable block vote that will dictate the direction of the functioning of the missionary conference. This new structure actually gives more political power to women and Transgeneration than now, when they are only a tiny minority in the dispersed geographical annual conferences.

Fourth, the Korean American Missionary Conference, once formed, is a UMC structure accountable to the *Book of Discipline* and the traditions of the church. It is not a separate church outside of UMC. It will continue to receive supervision from the general church and the presiding bishop, who will be assigned by the Council of Bishops. One important theological and missiological question we need to raise is this. When we look at many national strategies for ethnic minorities, they come with enormous price tags. Yet, the general church is eager to bless them. When Korean Americans propose a self-supporting possibility once given a chance to self-govern, the general church is hostile. What does that mean? The Church would rather give money, but never allow the actual empowerment? If so, then let us be honest and admit that UMC is still a colonialist church, and is not willing to repent, and stop pretending and playing institutional games. We often wonder what God would think of the United Methodist Church.

The most important question at hand is our missional mandate to spread the "Scriptural Holiness" throughout the land. We, the current Korean American United Methodists, believe that we are called to do our part by focusing on the people we know how to reach, namely Korean Americans. We believe that we have reached the limit of growth possibility with the current structural arrangement. We believe that the creation of the missionary conference allows all the resources of Korean American United Methodists to be channeled more effectively to carry out this missional mandate. We also believe that given the rhythms of immigrant life and the current history, *kairos* is upon us to act swiftly lest we miss very important God-given opportunity. This is also a "pilot" project for the entire UMC to see if an annual conference can run without current institutional burdens.

The Spirit of God that has been working mightily among the people of Korean descent in this country will continue to work through them—with or without UMC. The United Methodist Church in turn has a choice whether to work with this Spirit or not. The decision of this General Conference will set the course for the future, and all of the delegates and the UMC will have to answer to the future and finally to our God in Jesus Christ. We pray that you will take time to pray, listen and discern the yearnings of the Spirit of God, and prayerfully respond to our petition.

Peace and Love in Our Lord Jesus Christ.
Gary Hyunsuk Lee, Acting President
Seung Woo Lee, Executive Secretary
The National Association of Korean American United Methodist Churches

First Lady Hillary Clinton confesses indebtedness to Methodism

Source: "Address by Hillary Rodham Clinton," Daily Christian
Advocate 3/10 (25 April 1996), part 2, 655-58.

I have to confess to you that I have not been this nervous, with 150 bishops, someone told me, behind me, since I read my confirmation essay on "What Jesus Means to Me" in my home church. (*laughter and applause*) And I got through that all right. I hope I am able to convey to you my great sense of honor and pleasure at being here.

This quadrennial General Conference is important to all of us who are Methodists. And Methodism has been important to me for as long as I can remember. My father came from a long line of Methodists who had immigrated from England and Wales. And they took their church very seriously. And when my brothers and I were born, despite the fact we were then living in Chicago, my parents took us back to the Court Street Methodist Church in Scranton, Pa., to be christened in front of my grandfather and other relatives. We recently took back my nephew to go through the same experience at that church.

My parents belonged to a very large and active congregation in Park Ridge, Ill., the First United Methodist Church. It was the center not only for Sunday morning worship, but Sunday evening youth groups, and often during the week, for other activities. My mother taught Sunday school, and my brothers and I were there as often as the church doors opened, sometimes, although my mother later confessed that one of the reasons she taught Sunday school was to keep an eye on my brothers, so that they actually showed up and stayed after they were dropped off.

The church was a critical part of my growing up. And in preparing for this event, I almost couldn't even list all the ways it influenced me, and helped me develop as a person, not only on my own faith journey, but with a sense of obligations to others.

It taught me practical lessons as well; for example, how to recover from the embarrassment of passing out in an over-heated sanctuary when I was playing an angel during the Christmas pageant. [*laughter*] That particular lesson has stood me in good stead on many occasions in my adult life.

But most importantly, I learned from the ministers there, and the lay leaders there, the men and women such as yourselves, who ran the church life, about the connection between my personal faith and the obligations I faced as a Christian, both to other individuals and to society.

I am particularly indebted to the many people who taught Sunday School and Vacation Bible School. I can remember the lessons there, sometimes more vividly than what I have read or seen just last week. How many times did I sing the song, "Jesus Loves the Little Children of the World—red and yellow, black and white, they are precious in his sight." Those words have stayed with me more personally and longer than many earnest lectures on race relations. And to this day, I find myself wondering how anyone who ever sang them could be prejudiced against any group. [*applause*]

When I graduated into Methodist Youth Fellowship, I was fortunate to have a youth minister who arranged for us, living in our very comfortable, middle-class, all-White suburb of Chicago, opportunities to go into the inner city; to have exchanges with church groups of Black and Hispanic youngsters; to baby-sit for the children of migrant workers who, for those of you who did not grow up around Chicago in the 1950s and can only imagine flying into O'Hare where everything looks developed, might find it hard to believe how many farm workers we would have. And our church took some responsibility for helping. We visited the residents of nursing homes. We would go to public events that would feature speeches by people we'd barely heard of like Dr. Martin Luther King, Jr. We discussed what our faith meant in the world; and I am so grateful for those lessons and those opportunities.

I am equally grateful that my daughter has had the same, both at her church in Little Rock, and now at her church in Washington. Her Sunday School teachers there have helped her and her peers explore and express ideas and fears. One time just this past year, Bill and I went to a meeting of the teen-age Sunday School group where the teen-agers talked about what bugged them about their relationships with their parents. And it helped to have another child say what your own child didn't want to say to you directly. It was one of the many experiences that we have had because of the loving and faithful adults who care for young people in the Methodist Church. [*applause*]

And I hope that one of the lessons that we all take from our own experience, and one of the messages that comes forth from this conference, is that despite all the headlines and the problems that we face in helping our children and young people, we have so many wonderful young people. [*applause*] And just a few days ago, I received a letter from a young man who is a delegate here from Arkansas. You are going to think that between the bishop and me, we are promoting Arkansas. He wrote to me about all the good things that were happening in his church and conference, and he said to me, "Our church and our world must know that youth are not just involved in gangs, drugs, and violence; they are also involved in youth programs, missions, and the life of our church."

And I hope that each of us, and certainly from my background with the debt I owe to so many who helped me, understand that in today's world, churches are among the few places in society where young people can let down their guard, let off steam, and be part of a fellowship that offers them the opportunity for religious and spiritual expression and acts of humanity. And if we look at the positive side of what we can offer to young people, then we know that at the center of that experience is our faith and our mission as Methodists and as Christians.

That faith has certainly meant a great deal to me over the years. But I know that today, here at this conference and throughout the world, we are faced with many new challenges and opportunities that test and try us; that ask us how we will put into action what we believe. We know we need to strengthen the spiritual and moral context of our lives. And we know that we need a new sense of caring about one another in which every segment of society, every institution, fulfills its responsibility to the larger community, and particularly to families and children.

Here, in the United States, and certainly in the other countries represented here, we see too many children and people who remain on the margins of society. We see children who are unloved, unfed, unhealthy, and unschooled. We see women and people of color who are marginalized because they are denied the opportunities they deserve to become full participants in society. Those are the continuing challenges; and yet, we now know much more about what we can do together to meet those challenges. Despite the problems of poverty, and illiteracy and violence, there are solutions being born, being born in churches and communities, throughout the world.

The bishop mentioned a book that I have written, *It Takes A Village*, which really does, for me, express my fundamental belief that we all have an obligation to reach out to assist each other; and that we all should be willing to work toward solutions to our problems. It is easy to complain about the problems we face. It is harder but far more rewarding to roll up our sleeves and work together to solve them. [*applause*]

I was heartened, therefore, when I read a text of this year's episcopal address, to see that the Council of Bishops has renewed its call to make the welfare of children a top priority. And I commend the council for adopting the Episcopal Initiative on Children and Poverty, which will amplify the discussion of this very important issue world-wide. Children need us. They are not rugged individualists. They depend, first and foremost, on their parents who bare the primary responsibility for their upbringing.

And, yet, as a mother, I know that my daughter's life has been influenced and affected by countless other people, some of whom I know; many, many others I will never meet. Think of it: the police who patrol our streets to keep our children safe; the government officials who monitor the quality of air and water and food; the business leaders who employ parents and make decisions about what kind of income and benefits they will receive; the executives who produce the programs that our children see on television.

As adults we have to start thinking and believing that there isn't really any such thing as someone else's child. [*applause*] My child, your child, all children everywhere must live and make their ways in society. And now, in the increasingly shrinking world we live in, in the larger *globe* as well.

For that reason, we cannot permit discussions of children and families to be subverted by political or ideological debate. There are strong feelings about what should or should not be done, but there are also, I believe, strong areas of agreement where people should get beyond their disagreements to work together. There should be no disagreement about the fact that the family structure is in trouble; not only here, but in many parts of the world. There should be no debate that children need the nurturing and care that a stable family can provide. And there should be no debate about a common sense truth that children are the result of both the values of their parents and the values of the societies in which they live.

And so, if we look honestly at the problems we have, as the Episcopal Initiative is doing, then we should be asking ourselves, "What areas of common agreement do we have that can lead us as individuals, as a church, as community and society to work together on behalf of our children?" We know the biblical admonitions about caring for each other. We know so well what Jesus said to his disciples in Mark, holding a small child in his arms, "that whoever welcomes one such child in my name, welcomes me, and whoever welcomes me, welcomes not me, but the one who sends me." If we could only keep that in mind, and see in every child's face that faithful hopefulness. Take the image we have of Jesus—I can remember so clearly walking up the stairs so many times to my Sunday School class and seeing that picture that is in so many Methodist Churches of Jesus as the Shepherd—taking that face and transposing it onto the face of every child we see. Then we would ask ourselves, "Would I turn that child away from the health care that child needs? Would I say, that there is no help for that child because, look who he is, or look who her parents are?" No, we would take a deep breath in the face of disappointment in our efforts to help, and we would continue to try.

For me, the Social Principles of the Methodist Church have been as much a description of our history as a prod for my future actions. We can find direction if we look to the church's call to strengthen families and renew our schools, and encourage policies that enable each child to have a chance to fulfill his or her God-given potential.

Now, it is not easy to do that. I don't think it ever has been. I believe if one looks back, not only into the Bible but certainly since then, and reads the stories of John and Charles Wesley, and looks to other church leaders in the last century, we know that acting on our faith is never easy. And it is often a test of our own resolve as much as anything else. I think of the stories that I heard, even as a child, of John Wesley preaching to people who did not want to hear him. There was that one memorable story of where they were throwing whiskey bottles at him. And I think to myself, how many of us, myself included, would even go into places now where we were likely to be the object of thrown whiskey bottles? Not many of us. And in part what we have to confront is our own willingness to take the blessings we have and take them into a world that is complex, often turns away, and may even be hostile.

But just look at the tradition we come from. We continue in this church to answer John Wesley's call to provide for the educational, health, and spiritual needs of children. We can be proud that our church has been a leader in the fight to improve the quality of education, promote parental responsibility, curb smoking among young people, expand comprehensive health care, strengthen marriages, and help people of all kinds of backgrounds. I'm heartened by the work I see being done in the Communities of Shalom Initiative, where individual churches and churches in union are looking to transform just four city blocks in some instances. But taking that responsibility on, being there one-on-one with people unlike ourselves, often letting people hear the message of the gospel as well as the example of our works, will do more to change lives than any program that could be passed by any legislative body. [*applause*]

As I look at this great gathering, I see reflected here John Wesley's words that "the world is my parish." And if that be the case, then I am optimistic. Despite the headlines of the moment, and all of the difficulties we know lurk outside in this city we are in today, and every other one, I am optimistic because I see spiritual growth and action, based on that, beginning to manifest itself in so many different ways. In my book I wrote a little chapter called "Children Are Born Believers" because I feel so strongly that we owe our children a chance for them to have a spiritual life; for them to be part of a church. And it is not only something we do for them; we do it for ourselves, and we know that in ways we might not even predict, consequences can be positive.

A recent survey of young people and drug use found that children and youth who had regular religious involvement and attendance in a church or synagogue were far less likely to engage in self-destructive behavior like drug use. So we do it because we believe. And we do it because we trust that it will lead our young people to a better life for themselves.

Just this past month, I attended the funeral of a young man who epitomized the Methodist spirit of compassion and charity. He was the grandson, the son, and the nephew of Methodist ministers. His name was Adam Darling. He attended Foundry Church in Washington, as my husband and daughter and I do. And he had accompanied Commerce Secretary Ron Brown on his trip to Bosnia and was among the men and women who died on the side of that mountain in Croatia. He was only 29 years old. But in the four years the President and I had known him, we had seen a young man who not only blossomed professionally, but was committed to rebuilding cities, rebuilding communities, living in one of the toughest neighborhoods in Washington, getting to know his neighbors, babysitting for their children when he had time, hitting a ball with them in the street. Because he understood from the way he was raised that fame and success were fleeting. But a commitment to the spirit, involvement in the work of his church, would give him satisfaction and build a legacy that others, themselves, could take advantage of. I raise his name because when one contrasts what his short young life meant, and what he was attempting to rebuild, it gives me a great deal of energy and optimism about what all young people can do if they are given a chance.

I know that we have disagreements in society. We even have disagreements in the church. I think one of the reasons that I'm a Methodist is because I think disagreements are part of life. I think [*applause*] it's part of how we grow together. And I think all of us know that despite our disagreements, as the *Book of Discipline* puts it, we are engaged in a task to articulate our vision in a way that will draw us together as a people in mission. In the name of Jesus Christ, we are called to work within our diversity, while exercising patience and forbearance with one another. Such patience stems neither from indifference toward truth nor from an indulgent tolerance of error, but from an awareness that we know only in part, and that none of us is able to search the mysteries of God except by the spirit of God. That call to humility, and forbearance, and patience is not only important for the work of the church within the church, but it's critical to our work outside. It calls us to try, time and again, to reach into the lives of those who are left out. And it also prods us to look for ways we can work together to help our children.

If we were able, even within our own church in every congregation represented here, to help every mother and father be the best parent that parent could be, we would have done a wonderful piece of work. [*applause*] If we were able to persuade every parent that it's important to talk to a baby, to be affirmative toward a child, to wrap that child in the love, attention and discipline every child needs, then by the time those children reached our schools we would be able to persuade our teachers to look at every child and see hope, and see possibility. And we could renew and reform our schools so that they involved—even welcomed—parents, threw open their doors to the community, and were determined to leave no child behind.

We would also ask those in the business community to think about the decisions they make in terms not only of their primary responsibility to their bottom line, but also to the communities that they serve and work in. To ask how they, too, could be [*applause*] part of strengthening families. [*applause*]

Even simple things, like giving time off to parents to go to parent-teacher conferences in schools, would send a wonderful signal about what is important. [*applause*]

And if we were able to persuade everyone who has any control of what appears on our televisions and what we hear on our radios, to think about their own children (would they want their own children to see and hear what comes into our homes on a daily basis, or would they rather not?) [*applause*] and therefore change what they produce. [*applause*]

And we would ask all of us who are members of churches, and synagogues and mosques, we would ask all of us to set an example of love and respect. We would ask all of us, in whatever form it appears in our holy writings, to follow what we call "the Golden Rule." We would ask all of us to act on the outside of church the way we try to act inside, [*applause*] and throw open the doors [*applause*] of our churches, and welcome in those who John Wesley sought out. And open those doors after school, on weekends, especially in some of our tougher neighborhoods, so that children have places that are safe to go.

There is so much we can do in meeting these challenges; and so many opportunities for us, as Methodists, to grasp and be part of fulfilling.

I am grateful for my Methodist upbringing. I am grateful for this church. I watch with great interest and appreciation those of you who struggle to make the decisions that will govern us for the next four years. And I appreciate that you are grappling with the hard issues; being willing to debate and discuss what needs to be done. And I would hope that many of us, not only members of this church, but all people of faith, would say we have so much in common that we can do, and summon our energy on behalf, first and foremost, of our children.

If we were to do that, I know we would see changes before our very eyes; and that the church you serve, and that has served us, would continue to grow because it was serving the world, living out the gospel, and being a servant for those who need to hear that message.

With that in mind, I thank you for keeping alive the Methodist traditions and teachings; for helping to awaken and strengthen the spirit and faith of men, women, and children; and for helping all of us to have courage in the face of change; to be willing to struggle forward doing what we can individually; and to make common cause with others who believe that we are called, both for personal salvation, but also for the work we must do in this world. Thank you very, very much. [*applause*]

NEBRASKA PASTOR JIMMY CREECH DEFENDS "HOLY UNIONS" OF SAME-SEX COUPLES

Source: Jimmy Creech, "Response to the Judicial Complaint, presented to the Committee on Investigation, Nebraska Conference, January 26, 1998." United Methodist Archives, Madison, N.J. Excerpt.

Introduction

On September 16, 1997, a judicial complaint was filed against me, alleging that I am in "disobedience to the Order and Discipline of The United Methodist Church" because I "performed a 'covenanting ceremony' that celebrated a homosexual union between two women," based upon Paragraph 65c of the Social Principles and Article IV, Paragraph 15.6, of *The Book of Discipline.*

On January 23, 1998, the Committee on Investigation of the Nebraska Annual Conference referred the complaint to a church trial to be prosecuted as a chargeable offense. I welcome the trial as an opportunity to both make my case and to challenge the unjust position of The United Methodist Church regarding lesbians and gay men. It is my hope that when the final verdict has been determined, the Social Principles will be affirmed as "advisory and persuasive" and that there will be greater openness, acceptance, and justice for gay men and lesbians in The United Methodist Church.

I contend that I have not acted in disobedience to the Order and Discipline of The United Methodist Church, but, after "prayerful, studied dialogue of faith and practice," have acted in a way consistent with the gospel of Jesus Christ and with my calling as a pastor in The United Methodist Church. It is my intention in this response to describe what led to this discernment.

The Covenant Ceremony

[Rev. Creech described how two women "spoke vows of love and fidelity to each other" in the presence of their family and friends in the sanctuary of First United Methodist Church, Omaha, on September 14, 1997.]

In short, it was a very moving, intimate, simple, beautiful and holy occasion, a true celebration of love and lifelong commitment these two people have for one another in the context of their faith, and in the presence of God, their families and friends.

I was honored and privileged to be a part of this occasion. It was an occasion of worship that all United Methodists and people of faith should celebrate.

[Aware of strong feeling against "practicing" lesbians and gay men, Creech conducted the service over the objections of Bishop Joel Martinez.]

It is my belief that the position taken by The United Methodist Church regarding same-sex unions, as well as that regarding "the practice" of homosexuality, is wrong, unjust, discriminatory and inconsistent with the spirit of Christ and our Wesleyan and Methodist traditions. As a pastor, I could not in good conscience say "no" to the invitation. To do so would be to give my assent to this unjust position of the Church and, consequently, to give it power. This would be a failure on my part to be true to my calling as a minister of the gospel and a loyal United Methodist. To say "no" would be tantamount to forfeiting my calling as a pastor.

yes!

In addition, while I respect the opinion of Bishop Martinez, I believe his instruction to me not to celebrate the covenant ceremony was based upon his interpretation of the Social Principles as Church Law, an interpretation I believe to be insupportable and erroneous. Consequently, I did not believe his instruction to be compelling. . . .

Background

no word for homosexuality

Since that day, I have talked with and studied the works of biblical scholars, ethicists, psychologists, historians and social scientists in regard to issues related to sexual orientation, specifically same-sex orientation. I have learned that there was no understanding of sexual orientation in the culture and time when Scripture was written. There was not even a word for "homosexuality" or "homosexual" in Hebrew, Greek and Aramaic, the original languages of Scripture. . . .

There are Biblical references that condemn same-sex sexual behavior, but they are all within contexts related to violence, idolatry, promiscuity, and exploitation. Careful reading within the historical setting reveals that it is the violence, idolatry, promiscuity, and exploitation that is condemned, not the same-sex sexual behavior. The same condemnation is given to opposite-sex sexual behavior that is violent, idolatrous, promiscuous, and exploitative. Although it must be observed that there is much less tolerance for violence against and exploitation of men and boys in the Bible than there is violence against and exploitation of women by men in the Bible. This relative intolerance has to do with patriarchy, not anti-homosexual bias.

[Several pages of evidence from the early church, background from the social sciences and evidence from personal stories follow.]

As a pastor, these stories, along with the studied investigation, have made it impossible for me to give assent and support to the prevailing condemnatory attitudes of our culture, including those embodied by policy, doctrine and practice within the Christian Church in general, and The United Methodist Church in particular. I cannot perpetuate the sin of heterosexism in the church through my pastoral office.

[Several pages of pastoral reflections on heterosexism and racism, scriptural reflections on celebrating a covenant ceremony, tradition and the social principles, and faith into practice, follow.]

Conclusion

I believe I acted faithfully as a witness to the grace of Jesus Christ. While my action was in conflict with the prohibition of same-sex unions within the Social Principles, it was consistent with Our Theological Task (Paragraph 63, section 30: "As United Methodists, we are called to identify the needs both of individuals and of society and to address those needs out of the resources of Christian faith in a way that is clear, convincing, and effective. . . . Conferences speak and act for United Methodists in their official decisions at appropriate levels. *Our conciliar and representative forms of decision-making do not release United Methodists as individuals from the responsibility to develop sound theological judgment.* . . . [T]heological reflection is energized by our incarnational involvement in the daily life of the Church and the world, as we participate in God's liberating and saving action. . . . We seek an authentic Christian response to these realities (perils, injustices, misuse of resources, secularism) that the healing and redeeming work of God might be present in our words and deeds. *Too often, theology is used to support practices that are unjust.* We look for answers that are in harmony with the gospel and do not claim exemption from critical assessment" (emphasis added [by Creech]).

I acted out of loyalty to The United Methodist Church. I am devoted to it. . . . Had I not this love for The United Methodist Church, it would have been easy and convenient to leave when I began to understand its sin. My hope is, by being faithful to the liberating gospel of Jesus Christ, I can serve The United Methodist Church by calling it to turn away from the sin of heterosexism and to faithfulness.

While a charge has been brought against me, I believe that in this case it is The United Methodist Church that is being placed on trial. Does the Church really want to judge me wrong for praying God's blessing upon Mary and Martha in their commitment to each other? Would such a judgment bear witness to the love of God in Jesus Christ for all the world to see?

[handwritten margin note: consistent w/theological task]

BISHOPS ISSUE PASTORAL STATEMENT ON "HOLY UNIONS" AND HOMOSEXUALITY

Source: The Council of Bishops of The United Methodist Church.
United Methodist News Service (30 April 1998).
Web site http://www.umc.org/umns/98/may/269t.htm. Notes deleted.

A PASTORAL STATEMENT FROM THE COUNCIL OF BISHOPS

Dear Sisters and Brothers in Christ:

Grace to you and peace from God our Father and the Lord Jesus Christ! We greet you in the name of Jesus Christ who has broken down all dividing walls of hostility and made us one with Christ, one with each other, and one in ministry to the world.

Your bishops recognize and hear the pain within our church surrounding the recent church trial in the Nebraska Conference and the responses to the verdict. We acknowledge the concerns regarding the United Methodist Church's stand on issues, particularly homosexuality and homosexual unions, and the church's ability to maintain discipline, order, and unity.

While recognizing the importance of these issues, we challenge the church to remain focused on the mission of God and our unity in Christ and to set its priorities accordingly. Issues within the church must not be allowed to distract us from the missional needs of the world and our call to make disciples of Jesus Christ. In keeping with the New Testament and our Wesleyan tradition, we affirm that the church's authority and unity are inextricably bound to our sharing in Christ's ministry with and presence among those whom Jesus called "the least of these" (Matthew 25:45).

Although the church trial in the Nebraska Conference heightened concern among many regarding our denomination's position on homosexuality and homosexual unions, the church's position as defined in *The Book of Discipline* remains unchanged. *The Book of Discipline* states: "Homosexual persons no less than heterosexual persons are individuals of sacred worth. All persons need the ministry and guidance of the church in their struggles for human fulfillment, as well as the spiritual and emotional care of a fellowship that enables reconciling relationships with God, with others, and with self. Although we do not condone the practice of homosexuality and consider the practice incompatible with Christian teaching, we affirm that God's grace is available to all. We commit ourselves to be in ministry for and with all persons." Further, the Discipline states, "Ceremonies that celebrate homosexual unions shall not be conducted by our ministers and shall not be conducted in our churches." Furthermore, *The Book of Discipline* states, ". . . self-avowed practicing homosexuals are not to be accepted as candidates, ordained as ministers, or appointed to serve in The United Methodist Church."

We continue the commitment we made in our consecration as bishops "to guard the faith, to seek unity, and to exercise the discipline of the whole church; and to supervise and support the Church's life, work, and mission throughout the world." In covenant with one another, we are committed to uphold the General Conference's action on the theological, ethical, and polity matters defined in *The Book of Discipline*, including the statements on homosexuality and all specified issues contained in the Social Principles including the prohibition of ceremonies celebrating homosexual unions by our ministers and in our churches. At the same time we also affirm our pastoral responsibility to all peoples including those who feel excluded from the church. We call upon the whole church to deal with these matters with faithfulness rooted in the love of Christ, as revealed in Holy Scripture. We believe with John Wesley, "It is the nature of love to unite us together . . ." and "To separate ourselves from a body of living Christians with whom we were before united is a grievous breach of the law of love."

Issues currently creating concern and pain within the church call for renewed commitment to our doctrinal foundations as contained in the *Articles of Religion*, the Confession of Faith and *Wesley's Sermons and Notes*. We call all United Methodists to the fulfillment of the teaching office of the church and to ground the church's actions more deeply in the foundational doctrines and theological task as set forth in *The Book of Discipline*. Moreover, as an exercise of our teaching office, the Council of Bishops commits itself to engage in further prayerful study and dialogue and to develop a teaching paper as a means of identifying critical doctrinal and ecclesial foundations for addressing current and other issues. We solicit your prayers and support as together we seek to anchor the church more firmly in our biblical and theological foundations.

We acknowledge the desire to resolve current conflicts around issues of homosexuality. We have prayerfully considered the appeal to resolve legislatively the tensions through a called session of the General Conference. In anticipation of deliberations by the Judicial Council and the need for continued discernment and Christian conferencing on these matters, the calling of a special session does not seem wise at this time. Further, as we respond to the crises in the world, especially among children and the impoverished and those who desperately need the gospel, a special called session might further distract us from our central mission.

As a sign and instrument of Christ's coming reign over creation, the church lives with the tension between Christ's final victory and the present reality of sin. We do not, however, live with despair or impatience. With confidence, we as bishops continue our individual and corporate commitment to proclaim, defend, and live the doctrines, order, and mission of the church. The decisive victory has already been won in Jesus Christ. Therefore, we confront tension, conflict, and unresolved issues with patience, hope, and love. We know that in Jesus Christ "all the fullness of God was pleased to dwell, and through him God was pleased to reconcile to himself all things, whether on earth or in heaven, by making peace through the blood of the cross" (Colossians 1:20).

"Peace be to the whole community, and love with faith, from God the Father and the Lord Jesus Christ" (Ephesians 6:23).

JUDICIAL COUNCIL DETERMINES DISCIPLINARY PROHIBITION AGAINST HOMOSEXUAL UNIONS ENFORCEABLE

*Source: Judicial Council of The United Methodist Church. "Decision No. 833,"
8 August 1998. United Methodist News Service (11 August 1998). Web site
http://www.umc.org/umns/98/aug/471t.htm.*

DECISION NO. 833

IN RE: Request from the College of Bishops of the South Central Jurisdiction for a Declaratory Decision on Whether the Language "Ceremonies That Celebrate Homosexual Unions Shall Not Be Conducted by Our Ministers and Shall Not Be Conducted in Our Churches" in ¶65 of the 1996 Discipline Constitutes a Chargeable Offense under ¶2624.

IN RE: Request from the Illinois Great Rivers Annual Conference for a Declaratory Decision on Whether the Social Principles Are to Be Understood as Law for United Methodists and the Relationship Between the Social Principles and Chargeable Offense.

IN RE: Request from the North Alabama Annual Conference for a Declaratory Decision That All Homosexual Union Services Are Illegal under ¶15 of the 1996 Discipline.

IN RE: Request from the Nebraska Annual Conference for a Declaratory Decision on Whether the Performance of a Ceremony Celebrating a Homosexual Union or a Same-Sex Covenanting Ceremony by a United Methodist Pastor in a United Methodist Church Is a Violation of the Discipline And, Therefore, a Chargeable Offense under ¶2624 of the 1996 Discipline.

DIGEST

The prohibitive statement in ¶65.C of the *1996 Discipline:* "Ceremonies that celebrate homosexual unions shall not be conducted by our ministers and shall not be conducted in our churches," has the effect of church law, notwithstanding its placement in ¶65.C and, therefore, governs the conduct of the ministerial office. Conduct in violation of this prohibition renders a pastor liable to a charge of disobedience to the Order and Discipline of The United Methodist Church under ¶ 2624 of the *Discipline.*

STATEMENT OF FACTS

The College of Bishops of the South Central Jurisdiction of The United Methodist Church pursuant to the provisions of ¶2616 of the *1996 Discipline* has petitioned the Judicial Council for a declaratory decision upon the following question:

Does the language:

> Ceremonies that celebrate homosexual unions *shall not* be conducted by our ministers and shall not be conducted in our churches. (emphasis supplied)
>
> in ¶65.C) of the *Discipline* govern the conduct of the ministerial office in The United Methodist Church and does violation thereof constitute a chargeable offense pursuant to the provisions of subparagraph "1." of ¶2624. of the *Discipline?*

The Illinois Great Rivers Annual Conference has petitioned the Judicial Council for a declaratory decision on the following two questions:

> THEREFORE BE IT RESOLVED that the Illinois Great Rivers Annual conference request the Judicial Council issue a declaratory decision whether or not the Social Principles (¶¶64-70 of the *1996 The Book of Discipline of The United Methodist Church*) are to be understood as law for United Methodists; and

> BE IT FURTHER RESOLVED that the Illinois Great Rivers Annual Conference request a second decision as whether the Social Principles, as currently written can be properly used to establish grounds for the chargeable offense for clergy of "disobedience to the order and discipline of The United Methodist Church." (¶2624)

The North Alabama Conference requests a declaratory decision "that all homosexual union services are illegal under ¶15, page 25 of *The Book of Discipline*."

The Nebraska Conference of The United Methodist Church, meeting at its annual session, petitioned the Judicial Council to make a Declaratory Decision on the following question of law:

> Is the performance of a ceremony celebrating a homosexual union or a same-sex covenanting ceremony by a United Methodist pastor in a United Methodist Church a violation of the *Discipline* of the United Methodist Church and therefore a chargeable offense under ¶2624 of the 1996 *Discipline?*

At a hearing in Dallas, Texas, on August 7, 1998, oral presentations were made by Bishop Dan E. Solomon and Bishop Bruce P. Blake, representing the South Central Jurisdiction College of Bishops. Also appearing were Michael McClellan, Douglas Williamson, and Jimmy Creech.

Jurisdiction

The Judicial Council has jurisdiction under ¶2616 of the *1996 Discipline.*

Analysis and Rationale

The council has received more than thirty briefs representing many views of the questions involved. The council is quite aware of the very sensitive and volatile nature of the issues. For these reasons, it must be stated, as has been stated in other decisions, that the Judicial Council is not a legislative body. The council's role, power, authority and scope are defined in the *Discipline* of The United Methodist Church, which includes, but is not limited to the Constitution. Briefly, under ¶ 2616 the role of the council in declaratory decisions, is to determine ". . . the constitutionality, meaning, application, or effect of the *Discipline* or any portion thereof or of any act or legislation of a General Conference; . . ." The council further recognizes that for more than twenty-five years the issue of homosexuality has been debated and discussed in The United Methodist Church, and that the discussion and debate will continue long after this decision is rendered.

Having so stated the above, Docket Nos. I, IV and V basically address the same questions and are to be considered in the council's determination of the meaning, application, or effect of the legislation involved and will be considered together. Docket No. III involves the same principles of law, but is much broader in its scope and will be addressed separately in this decision.

The Judicial Council takes jurisdiction for the narrow purpose in this decision of dealing with the requests for declaratory decisions surrounding only the amendment by the 1996 General Conference to ¶65.C.

The General Conference under the Constitution has the following specific power and authority as stated therein:

> ¶15. The General Conference shall have full legislative power over all matters distinctively connectional, and in the exercise of this power shall have authority as follows: . . .
> 2. To define and fix the powers and duties of elders, deacons . . .

In accordance with these powers and authority the General Conference adopted the amendment to ¶65.C. A review of the legislative history of the addition of the sentence: "Ceremonies that celebrate homosexual unions shall not be conducted by our ministers and shall not be conducted in our churches," reflects the legislative intent of the 1996 General Conference.

The prohibition against United Methodist ministers conducting ceremonies that celebrate homosexual unions was enacted by the 1996 General Conference. The legislation came before the Conference on a petition presented by the Administrative Council of Grace United Methodist Church, Newport, Kentucky. The petition was assigned to the Church and Society Legislative Committee and was assigned number 22493-CS-71-D. It was submitted as follows:

Add new text to ¶71.C of the *1992 Book of Discipline*. "Ceremonies that celebrate homosexual unions shall not be conducted by our ministers and shall not be conducted in our churches."

The Legislative Committee brought Petition number 22493 to the Thursday evening, April 27, 1996, Plenary Session of the General Conference as Calendar Item No. 2402. (*Daily Christian Advocate*, Vol. III, p. 583, April 25, 1996) The chair of the committee presented it in its original form. The subcommittee chair also presented the item and commented "One of the questions that we had was whether we should have received this petition or whether it should have gone to the Board of Ordained Ministries. But we acted on this petition and the vote, 29 to 25, felt that ceremonies should not be conducted by ministers in our churches" (*Daily Christian Advocate*, Vol. III, p. 778, April 27, 1996).

After placing the petition before the body, there was debate and a motion was made to refer the petition to the "Board of Ordained Ministry-Board of Higher Education in Ministry." Debate on the motion to refer ensued. The debate centered upon the nature of the Social Principles and whether the legislation was appropriate for the Social Principles. The motion to refer the petition was defeated (*Daily Christian Advocate*, Vol. III, p. 779, April 27, 1996).

The vote to approve Calendar Item No. 2402 was taken and the General Conference approved it on a vote of 553 for and 321 against (*Daily Christian Advocate*, Vol. III, p. 780, April 27, 1996).

The 1996 General Conference dealt with other issues on homosexuality during the April 25 evening session. After the vote approving Calendar Item No. 2402 prohibiting homosexual unions, the Conference turned to Petition No. 22408 titled "Creation of Commitment Ceremonies for Same Sex Couples within The United Methodist Church." The Legislative Committee recommended nonconcurrence with this petition and the General Conference voted 628 to 190 in support of the committee. A similar petition was also defeated by a vote of 655 to 203 (*Daily Christian Advocate*, Vol. III, p. 788 ff., April 27, 1996).

The next items presented to the General Conference on homosexuality during this session were from the General/Judicial Administration Legislative Committee. These petitions were on the subject of Chargeable Offenses for Pastors. The chair of the Subcommittee on Judicial Matters in the General/Judicial Administrative Committee presented three petitions that asked "the General Conference to amend 2623.1 of the *Book of Discipline* by adding to the list of chargeable offenses for pastors [those] who participate in leadership of same-sex covenant services uniting gay and lesbian persons." The committee voted nonconcurrence, with 44 for, 23 against and 3 abstaining. The vote of nonconcurrence, the chair explained, was based especially on the fact that the committee did not feel that it should vote to add items "to the *Book of Discipline* that appear to be self-evident or already and adequately cared for under other paragraphs within the *Book of Discipline*." With respect to adding to the list of chargeable offenses, participation in leadership of a same-sex covenant service uniting gay or lesbian persons, the chair said nonconcurrence was voted because the committee "felt there is more than adequate paragraphs within the *Book of Discipline,* including actions . . . taken today on the new 71.C [now ¶65.C], . . . but specifically in ¶2623.1e, which declares 'Disobedience to the Order of the *Discipline* of The United Methodist Church' as a chargeable offense, adequately and effectively covers this particular petition . . ." The General Conference supported the Committee's recommendation of nonconcurrence with a vote of 730. The record does not reflect the vote against nonconcurrence (*Daily Christian Advocate,* Vol. III, p. 783, April 27, 1996).

In rendering this decision the Judicial Council must decide whether ¶65.C is law and whether ¶65.C governs the conduct of the ministerial office. Under ¶15, the General Conference has the authority to speak on connectional matters, and, when this authority results in a legislative enactment stated in mandatory language, it is the law of the church, notwithstanding its placement in the *Discipline.*

The second question raised is: Does the last sentence of ¶65.C of the *1996 Discipline:* "Ceremonies that celebrate homosexual unions shall not be conducted by our ministers and shall not be conducted in our churches," govern the conduct of the ministerial office in The United Methodist Church and does violation thereof constitute a chargeable offense pursuant to the provisions of ¶2624 of the *Discipline?* Par. 304 states that persons to be ordained in The United Methodist Church are to ". . . Be accountable to The United Methodist Church, accept its *Discipline* and authority, accept the supervision of those appointed to this ministry, and be prepared to live in the covenant of its ordained ministers."

The deliberations of the General Conference are indicative that the Legislative Committees and the delegates to General Conference were enacting legislation that would be binding as the law of the Church.

The prohibitive statement governs the function of all clergy members of The United Methodist Church. The amendment language is descriptive of expected functions of a clergy member, who has accepted a covenant relationship to uphold the "Order and Discipline of The United Methodist Church." Failure to do so is a disciplinary violation, and therefore, subjects a pastor to the process of formal complaint, including Fair Process as defined in the *Discipline.*

The General Conference, as the legislative body of the Church, has the constitutional authority to define and fix the powers and duties of the ministers of the Church. Pursuant to its constitutional authority, the 1996 General Conference was endowed with authority to enact legislation that fixes the parameters of United Methodist ministers' power to conduct ceremonies celebrating homosexual unions. The General Conference has said that United Methodist ministers shall not conduct such ceremonies. The added language of ¶65.C is a proper exercise of the General Conference's authority.

Decision 694 holds that the General Conference is the body that has prerogative power over matters distinctively connectional. In Decision 694, the council was asked to decide whether an Annual Conference had the authority to establish or alter the official rites and rituals of the Church. The case came before the Judicial Council as a result of the action of the Minnesota Conference in approving a resolution which gave reconciling congregations the right to offer services of blessings and celebration of committed relationships of couples of same gender, and the action of the Troy Conference in approving a resolution permitting ministers to participate in covenant services. The Judicial Council held that the Annual Conference had no authority to establish or alter the official rites and rituals of the Church. That authority was lodged in the General Conference by the Constitution of The United Methodist Church. The council went on to declare that "it is the responsibility of pastors in charge to perform their duties in compliance with the *Discipline* and be obedient to the Order and Discipline of the Church." This Decision clearly states that the legislative enactments of the General Conference regarding the duties and powers of ministers are binding on ministers in the connection and their conduct must conform to those provisions.

The *Discipline* states that "disobedience to the Order and Discipline of The United Methodist Church" constitutes a chargeable offense, rendering a pastor liable to a charge of disobedience to the Order and Discipline of the Church.

The Judicial Council reaffirms Fair Process (¶2623) and Decisions 557, 723, and 724, in any action leading to a complaint and charge.

As to Docket No. III, the request from the Illinois Great Rivers Annual Conference for a declaratory decision on whether the Social Principles are to be understood as law for United Methodists and the relationship between the Social Principles and chargeable offense, the council is unable to render a definitive decision on all of the specific provisions of the paragraphs under the section designated as Social Principles without a reference to a specific paragraph. This is especially true when the request includes relating these matters to chargeable offenses.

Decision

The prohibitive statement in ¶65.C of the *1996 Discipline*: "Ceremonies that celebrate homosexual unions shall not be conducted by our ministers and shall not be conducted in our churches," has the effect of church law, notwithstanding its placement in ¶65.C and, therefore, governs the conduct of the ministerial office. Conduct in violation of this prohibition renders a pastor liable to a charge of disobedience to the Order and Discipline of The United Methodist Church under ¶2624 of the *Discipline*.

August 8, 1998

DIVERSITY DIALOGUE TEAM DEVELOPS RECOMMENDATIONS FOR THE UNITY OF THE CHURCH

Source: In Search of Unity: A Conversation with Recommendations for the Unity of The United Methodist Church. *New York: General Commission on Christian Unity and Interreligious Concerns, 1998. Excerpts.*

DIALOGUE ON THEOLOGICAL DIVERSITY WITHIN THE UNITED METHODIST CHURCH, NASHVILLE, NOVEMBER 20-21, 1997; DALLAS, FEBRUARY 19-20, 1998

I. Preamble

The unity of the church is a gift of the Triune God through the working of the Holy Spirit. As such this gift is a great treasure which is intrinsically worthwhile. It also brings great benefits, not least its role to make Christ more manifest in the world (John 17). In giving us unity the Holy Spirit works in our hearts to create a disposition to seek unity. Thus we find ourselves with a common desire to be united together in truth, love, and justice, with a common affection and concern for one another, and with a steady resolve to work through those things which divide us and create dissension in our midst. These dispositions are gifts of the Holy Spirit in our midst, which we cherish and celebrate.

The gift of unity fosters our celebration of the diversity which the Holy Spirit brings into the fellowship of the church. There are differences of calling, varieties of gifts, and distinct orders of ministry. There are also differences of race, gender, temperament, opinion, and modes of thinking and operating. These contribute to the richness and manifold bounty of the people of God. They spur our creativity and praise; they challenge us to deeper reflection, action, and commitment; they are vitally important in our mission and work in the world. We cherish the diversity that belongs together in the one body of Christ.

Not only is unity a gift given to us, it is also a calling and a challenge. We yearn for the time when we are truly one in Christ so that the whole world may believe. We confess our brokenness. We often mistake uniformity for unity, and we confuse indiscriminate, theological pluralism with the diversity of the Spirit's gifts. The unity we seek is not only to be united in name and body; it is a unity of community, of communion with one another, worshiping and proclaiming the same Jesus Christ who frees and unites us.

Pausing to think through the challenge of maintaining our unity does not prevent us from celebrating the valuable ministries that are currently being carried out by our church. There are a myriad of ministries which give us great joy. We believe that unity fuels these ministries with greater energy and zeal; disunity puts them at risk and draws away vital resources, commitment, and dynamism. We trust that God's presence through the Holy Spirit will guide us as we examine our unity and disunity.

II. Unity Gained and Sustained

The Holy Spirit works in, with, and through human actions and institutions to create and sustain unity in the body. It is through worship and the sacraments that we have most consistently experienced the Spirit's unity. We believe that as a people we have been guided over the years in the ordering of the church's institutional structures and decision-making. Fallible and abused as any human endeavors are, they have been means whereby the Holy Spirit has held us together and has kept us accountable to the task and challenge of unity in one body.

how unity is created

We have identified a host of factors, which have created and sustained unity across the years. These range all the way from our love for the church, through our system of itinerancy, and our faith in God, to our complex means of meeting in conference, our commitment to evangelism, our Wesleyan and Evangelical United Brethren heritage and our pledge to seek justice, particularly as it relates to racism, sexism, and the environment. We pray that the Holy Spirit will continue to work through these means, just as we pray that the Holy Spirit will use our deliberations to be of service to the church as a whole.

III. Unity Challenged

strain on unity

There are many ways in which the unity of our church has come under strain over the years. Some of the factors at work are easy to identify; some are not. Some are relatively isolated and independent; others are deeply intertwined in complex and even enigmatic ways. It is useful to distinguish between three kinds of challenges to unity: 1) Some challenges are those that we associate with the human condition (the fall from original righteousness); 2) Other challenges extend from disagreements that harm the quality of our existence in a variety of ways; and 3) Yet other challenges run so deep as to harbor the danger of explicit disunity or schism.

A. Challenges Stemming from the Fall from Original Righteousness

The most basic challenge stems from how far we have fallen from an original righteousness that was a gift from God. Continually we are inclined to do that which distances us from God and from each other. Scripture continually calls us to accountability for the way we live and act towards one another. We need to repent continually and patiently strive to implement the vision our Savior has given to us.

We can identify some of the failings we seek to correct:

- our impatience with one another;
- our tendency to believe rumor and innuendo;
- our lack of love;
- our lack of trust in God and each other;
- our ignorance of each other's trials and tribulations;
- our lack of humility concerning our own knowledge and wisdom;
- our adoption of strategies to further our particular concerns and causes in the church as a whole.

B. Challenges to the Quality of our Existence Together

There are other challenges to unity which affect the quality of our existence in disturbing ways. The list includes:

- our inability to agree on how to relate our commitment to justice and to God's sovereign purposes for creation to the task of making disciples.
- a lack of agreement on the boundaries of assent and dissent;
- a lack of trust in the general agencies of the church;
- the politicization of our commitments, resulting in stereotyping, misunderstanding, the attribution of unworthy motives to those who do not share our judgments, and the manipulation of the courts and processes of church life to serve partisan ends;
- a sense of alienation among various sectors of the church, both "conservative" and "liberal."

C. Challenges that Harbor the Danger of Explicit Disunity or Schism

There is no easy or fully agreed way to describe those factors which threaten explicit disunity or schism. Some think that naming them either helps bring them into existence or magnifies them. Others are convinced that we face a formidable set of problems which must be named and described as best we can. For them failure to name and describe is not just a failure of nerve; it may be an unacknowledged or deliberately concealed strategy for excluding the voice of a significant number of people. Clearly we enter troubled waters at this juncture.

We believe that we may experience substantive disagreement around a variety of theological issues: the nature of Trinitarian faith; the meaning of incarnation; and our views of the saving work of Christ, to name a few. All these arise out of differing understandings of scriptural authority and revelation. However, in this document, we have turned to the practice of homosexuality as illustrative of our divergence because it is the one most visible presenting issues in United Methodism today.

Some see the ordination of practicing homosexuals and the adoption of same sex union ceremonies akin to marriage as consistent with or commanded by the Christian faith. Others see these practices as inconsistent with the Christian faith; they involve a breach of Christian conscience and a failure to provide appropriate ministry in an area marked by sensitive pastoral challenges.

1. Different Understandings of the Authority of Scripture and Divine Revelation

These moral and theological commitments about sexuality, like many issues that divide us, are linked to deeper convictions about the warrant for Christian moral behavior. They involve the issue of the authority of scripture and divine revelation.

Those who see no barrier to full admission of homosexuals who are morally responsible and committed Christians to the church's orders and rites believe this to be consistent with Christian teaching, or required by the love and compassion expressed by Christ in the Bible. Some believe that this is what the Word of God, or God's definitive revelation, or what scripture supports. The precious words and actions of our Lord and Savior compel them to support these practices.

Others believe themselves to be the recipients of new and expanded revelation from God that is beyond the canon of scripture; or, they believe that the scriptures properly understood in the light of reason and experience permit homosexual practices under some circumstances.

Those who oppose the admission of homosexuals to the Church's orders and rites believe that such a proposed practice is inconsistent with Christian teaching. They believe themselves to be either explicitly or implicitly forbidden by scripture or by the teaching of our Lord Jesus Christ as reliably witnessed in scripture to accept this practice. From their point of view, to accept or condone these practices would be to undermine the authority of scripture and of Christ. It would be to reject the healing authority or the Word of God, or of God's definitive revelation, or of scripture in the church.

The aforementioned convictions about divine revelation and scripture are set in the context of beliefs about the boundaries of the church in our day.

2. Disagreement Over the Boundaries of the Church

The consensus of the Committee is that the boundaries of what is acceptable opinion within the United Methodist Church may vary depending on the issue, historical context, conviction, and the person. However, in the case of the issue of homosexuality before the church in our time, we believe the following distinction is helpful. It is one approach in describing the complexity of our differences.

There are those who in conscience can accept the continuation of divergent points of view within the church structure and those who in conscience cannot. Within each of these groups—compatibilists and incompatibilists—we can identify people representing perspectives which are both "more liberal" and "more conservative." In the following we will try to articulate different points of view within this delineation.

Compatibilists are convinced that the diversity of points of view can remain together within the denomination. Incompatibilists are convinced that the divergent points of view as they understand them are in such conflict that they cannot be sustained within the same denomination.

Compatibilists believe that both sides on the issues of the morality of homosexual behavior and the nature and status of divine revelation, can be held together within the same denomination. Such unity will be no easy achievement. It will require great skill, humility, and patience. In principle it can be achieved and in so far as it exists, bears witness to the diversity of the body of Christ. Compatibilists believe the church can and should live with its disagreements. . . .

Incompatibilists do not believe that these divergent judgments can be housed indefinitely within the same denomination. They believe that the church is faced with a difficult choice many will want to avoid but which cannot ultimately be ignored. The difference with the compatibilists goes beyond the issues of sexual morality and authority. In part, the difference is ecclesiological; it concerns the nature of the church as the body of Christ. At stake is a crisis of conscience about the very identity and continuity of the church. It is a question of ecclesiological integrity. Incompatibilists with completely different points of view regarding the morality of homosexual practice join together in believing that the continuation of the position opposing their own will lead to the further erosion of loyalty to the church, to the possible departure of many faithful members, and, ultimately, to the internal fracturing of the denomination. They realize that this is not always easy to grasp on the part of those who do not share their conviction; yet, unless it is acknowledged, a matter of the highest consequence is ignored.

Many incompatibilists believe that there is a limit to the amount of cognitive dissonance any group can endure on the issues of sexual morality and the nature and status of divine revelation. In this instance, the limit is breached. It is best that this judgment be openly acknowledged and worked through carefully. It is precisely in so far as this judgment is openly acknowledged that the depth of the problem of unity is uncovered and that due fairness is given to all sides of the discussion.

In addition, many incompatibilists, both liberal and conservative, believe that failure to face up to the issues constantly inhibits the freedom to practice ministry in ways which are fully consonant with their moral, theological, and pastoral convictions. This inhibition arises either because of opposition to their particular ministries or because they do not want to undermine the church's unity. . . .

IV. Sustaining Unity and Avoiding Schism

The challenges facing the church in the preservation of unity are daunting. Our judgments, of course, are fallible; but we would not have given ourselves so thoroughly to our conversations if we felt that nothing of substance was at stake.

Foremost in the preservation of unity is the love of Jesus Christ and the active presence of the Holy Spirit in our hearts and in the life of the church as a whole. To this end we urge persistent prayer, fasting, rigorous thought, and compassion through Christ-like dialogue. This is not a pious comment but a lasting judgment derived from our conviction that it is God who holds us together in the church and not we ourselves. We depend upon grace from beginning to end, in this, as in every other venture of Christian service and pilgrimage. We hold, moreover, that with grace there comes truth, love and justice, each of which is essential for unity. Further, we believe that the quest for unity will be greatly enhanced by the practice of faith, hope, and love.

We come to the task of unity with treasures brought with us from our own history as a church. We recommend the reading of the writings of John Wesley as they relate to the topic of unity. We have found the following sermons especially pertinent: On Schism, A Caution Against Bigotry, Catholic Spirit. We recommend also the exploration of the history of our tradition, as of the wider Christian tradition, for help in understanding and resolving the complex issues related to unity. We further recommend a thoughtful reading of the history of racial ethnics and women in the United Methodist Church and its predecessor bodies, including the tragic Methodist schism over slavery.

Receiving and creating the unity that Christ wills for us will always be a task. Yet there are differences in the kind of challenges we face which we should observe as best we can. As already noted, there are some factors which are always with us because we are human, others which inhibit the quality of our life together in a significant way, and others which seriously threaten to undermine unity itself. We deem it especially important to focus upon actions that can be taken to preserve unity.

Proposed Action Steps

1. Since our reflection indicates diverse differences that have deep theological bases, we recommend that the Council of Bishops immediately create a Committee on Theological Dialogue. The proposal was adopted at the 1996 General Conference. [Text in the original as an appendix.] The committee would include theologians, bishops, clergy and laity.

The purpose of the committee would be to assist the Council of Bishops in finding ways of fostering doctrinal reflection and theological dialogue at all levels of The United Methodist Church, thereby helping the Church recover and update our distinctive doctrinal heritage—catholic, evangelical, and reformed—and thereby enabling doctrinal reinvigoration for the sake of authentic renewal, fruitful evangelism, and ecumenical dialogue.

We urge implementation of the proposal during the current quadrennium with funding requests by the Council of Bishops to the General Council on Finance and Administration and/or the General Council on Ministries. We recommend that the General Commission on Christian Unity and Interreligious Concerns staff be available to assist the Committee on Theological Dialogue and to assist the Council of Bishops in disseminating the work of the committee.

2. Since our reflection indicates diverse differences that have deep theological bases, we request that the Council of Bishops prepare a teaching paper on the authority of scripture and the authority of divine revelation which:

   a. reflects, but is not confined to, our historic Wesleyan understanding;

   b. focuses on the implications of scripture and revelation for discussions of unity/disunity in The United Methodist Church;

   c. would be available for study throughout the church.

3. We request that the Commission on General Conference provide a time for open discussion in a non-legislative session of the teaching paper from the Council of Bishops.

4. We request that the Board of Higher Education and Ministry and the Editorial Board of the *Quarterly Review* publish articles on the significance of the Trinitarian and Incarnational faith as contained in the classical creeds.

   a. for the unity of the church, for understanding the classical faith of the church today.

   b. for understanding the classical faith of the church today.

5. In order to model for the church our journey toward unity, we (a.) urge the Council of Bishops to conduct their own dialogue around the document coming out of this dialogue, "In Search of Unity," and that (b.) subsequent to this, they and the District Superintendents provide a forum for dialogue around "In Search of Unity" through the Annual Conference and at the local church level.

6. We recommend "Guidelines for Civility in The United Methodist Church"

   a. Respect the personhood of others, while engaging their ideas.

   b. Carefully represent the views of those with whom we are in disagreement.

   c. Be careful in defining terms, avoiding needless use of inflammatory words.

   d. Be careful in the use of generalizations; where appropriate offer specific evidence.

   e. Seek to understand the experiences out of which others have arrived at their views. Hear the stories of others, as we share our own.

   f. Exercise care that expressions of personal offense at the differing opinion of others not be used as means of inhibiting dialogue.

   g. Be a patient listener before formulating responses.

   h. Be open to change in your own position and patient with the process of change in the thinking and behavior of others.

   i. Make use of facilitators and mediators where communication can be served by it.

   j. Always remember that people are defined, ultimately, by their relationship with God—not by the flaws we discover or think we discover in their views and actions.

7. We further recommend that a copy of "In Search of Unity" be sent to the Connectional Process Team for serious consideration as an important component to be included in their restructuring discussions.

8. We recommend that the General Commission on Christian Unity and Interreligious Concerns be responsible for ensuring that the recommendations

from the Dialogue of November 1997–February 1998, contained in "In Search of Unity," be brought to the attention of The United Methodist Church and its appropriate bodies.

V. Conclusion

As we conclude our dialogue, it is very evident that it is only a beginning. Our document is imperfect. It reflects the start of an open and honest conversation. This conversation must be continued. Given the reality in our church of compatibilists and incompatibilists on both liberal and conservative sides, we pray for the Holy Spirit's leadership in the opening of doors and in the emergence of models whereby we can live as one family in the same house. Therefore, we call upon the Council of Bishops to prayerfully provide leadership in pursuing dialogue and in providing such models.

What we have offered here is a set of considered judgments concerning the unity of The United Methodist Church. We do not presume to be right. The only requests we make are that our motives to serve the church be taken seriously and that our deliberations be given the weight that truth and love require. We have had serious conversations together. We have done our best to seek God's will, to be faithful to our convictions, and to be fair to everyone. We offer this report to the church as a whole, bearing testimony to what we have found, and trusting the Holy Spirit to use our work together for the good of all. We commend to the church the words of John Wesley, who declared that "happy" was the person "that attains the character of a peacemaker in the church of God." In his sermon "On Schism" of March 30, 1786, he urged:

> Why should not you labour after this? Be not content not to stir up strife, but do all that in you lies to prevent or quench the very first spark of it. Indeed it is far easier to prevent the flame from breaking out than to quench it afterwards. However, be not afraid to attempt even this: the God of peace is on your side. [John Wesley, *Works* (Bicentennial edition), *Sermons* 3:58-69, 69]

AFRICAN AMERICAN

1769	Boardman describes North American Methodism's biracial character
1771	Pilmore writes about black class meetings
1784c	Hosier rides circuits with Coke and Asbury
1785a	First Discipline deplores slavery
1788	Bruce reports large numbers of black converts in Virginia
1792b	Allen leads blacks out of St. George's Church, Philadelphia
1800	General Conference issues pastoral letter on slavery
1810a	Coker dialogues with slave master
1811a	Jarena Lee hears call to preach
1815	Stewart begins mission to Wyandott Indians in Ohio
1816	Coker celebrates liberation of Bethel Church, Philadelphia
1821a	Black Methodist preachers in New York City seek ordination and organization
1832a	Black members petition for appointment of black pastors
1832b	Bascom promotes colonization
1833	Capers publishes special catechism for use in slave missions
1834	Abolitionist clergy urge immediate emancipation
1836	South Carolina conference upholds slavery
1842b	Abolitionist clergy issue public letter of withdrawal
1844a	General Conference considers resolutions on slave-holding Bishop Andrew
1844b	General Conference debates slavery and episcopacy
1844c	General Conference adopts "Plan of Separation"
1856	Professor Smith defends slavery
1867a	Editor Haven pleads against "caste"
1870c	Former slave members request permission to organize separate church

ARCHITECTURE

ASIAN AMERICAN

DOCTRINE

ECUMENISM

EDUCATION

EPISCOPACY

EVANGELICAL UNITED BRETHREN

POLITY